S0-AEA-092

Criminal Justice

Criminal Justice

Jay S. Albanese

Virginia Commonwealth University

To [illegible]

Here's all you need to know about criminal justice — and the family managed — to survive in the process!

Happy

Jay [illegible]

Allyn and Bacon

BOSTON LONDON TORONTO SYDNEY TOKYO SINGAPORE

Editor-in-Chief, Social Sciences: Karen Hanson
Editorial Assistant: Heather Ahlstrom
Senior Editorial-Production Administrator: Joe Sweeney
Editorial-Production Service: Colophon
Composition Buyer: Linda Cox
Manufacturing Buyer: Megan Cochran
Cover Administrator: Linda Knowles
Text Designer: Design Associates, Inc.
Photo Researcher: Helane Prottas
Text Composition: Omegatype Typography, Inc.

160 Gould Street
Needham Heights, MA 02494
www.abacon.com

Library of Congress Cataloging-in-Publication Data
Albanese, Jay S.
Criminal justice / Jay S. Albanese.
p. cm.
Includes bibliographical references and index.
ISBN 0-205-19354-4 (alk. paper)
1. Crime–United States. 2. Crime–Government policy–United States. 3. Criminal justice, Administration of–United States. I. Title.
HV6789.A366 1998
364.973–dc21

98-50830
CIP

Printed in the United States of America
10 9 8 7 6 5 4 3 2 1 VHP 00 99 98

Photo Credits:

p. 3, Liaison International/Sandra Baker; p. 5, Liaison International/Hulton Getty; p. 9, Liaison International/Bill Pugliano; p. 10, The Image Works/Bob Daemmrich; p. 15, The Image Works/Bob Daemmrich; p. 16, Impact Visuals/Rick Reinhard; p. 23, The Picture Cube/James Lemass; p. 27, The Image Works/Bob Daemmrich; p. 35, AP/David Kohl;

Photo credits continued on page 584 which constitutes a continuation of the copyright page.

For my father,

Samuel S. Albanese

and in memory of my mother,

Doris Mather Albanese

Contents

Preface

Due to the serious and personal nature of crime and justice, people think viscerally and often emotionally about particular incidents. Therefore, facts are needed to determine whether these incidents are typical or unusual. It is only in this way that we can properly gauge our fear, decide precautionary measures to be taken, and determine whether or not we should support various new laws or policies being proposed.

Criminal Justice provides these facts by examining the nature of crime and the criminal justice system to reveal significant history, facts, and trends, and systematically traces them from the past to the present and into the future. The term *Criminal justice* refers to the operation and management of police, courts, and corrections agencies. The decision to punish certain behaviors as crimes, the arrest decision, charging decision, jury decision, and sentencing decision are a few of the far-reaching decisions made many times each day in criminal justice. Striking a balance among public safety, concern for victims, and the protection of the accused is fundamental and is reflected throughout this book.

For many years, surveys have reported that the fear of crime is steadily increasing, especially among the poor and disenfranchised who often lack the ability to change the nature and condition of their communities. There is evidence that this fear reduces the mobility of citizens, reduces their social interactions (through increased fear of strangers), hurts the commercial sector (especially nighttime shopping), and generally affects the quality of life by which we judge our leaders, our communities, and our country.

This fear is intensified when reports of new crimes, new criminals, police problems, plea-bargaining, overcrowded courts, and ineffective prisons leave the individual citizen with the feeling that little effort is being made to improve existing conditions and that life is becoming more dangerous. One consequence of such feelings is the declining participation in the political process, as witnessed by the continuing drop in the percentage of eligible citizens who vote. People also react unexpectedly, and sometimes violently, to additional stresses placed on them exemplified by the increased instances of workplace violence and road rage.

In the pages that follow, the issues of crime and justice that affect us all are clearly presented. It is hoped that readers, through greater understanding of these problems which have such far-reaching personal and social consequences, will be better able to participate in informed strategies for their amelioration.

Organization of the Book

Perhaps the most useful aspect of this book is that it is written like a book rather than an encyclopedia. The chapters read as a narrative rather than an encyclopedia of facts too numerous for readers to learn, prioritize, or connect together. Emphasis is placed on fitting together concepts and the criminal justice system rather than cramming as many facts as possible onto each page. This is extremely important for students taking what might be their first course in criminal justice. This book is written so students are able to read with understanding and not be lost in an avalanche of facts and figures that serve to confuse rather than inform.

The topics are arranged logically beginning with a comparison of the fear of crime with other dangerous life events. This is followed in Chapter 2 with a discussion of the borderland of criminal behavior including the history of the vices and how we have come to define behavior as criminal. The nature, definition, and extent of crime and trends over time are presented in Chapter 3, permitting an objective look at the extent of crime and violence in America. In Chapter 4 the causes of crime are examined with a summary of the history of thinking about this fundamental subject. A unique section on ethical explanations of crime highlights this chapter. Chapter 5 explains the scope of the criminal law in how we define crime in precise terms, determine liability, and excuse conduct under certain circumstances. Chapter 6 provides an overview of criminal procedure, showing in exact terms how an individual case proceeds from arrest through disposition.

In Chapters 7, 8, and 9 address the history and organization of police, together with how their discretion is exercised and the legal limits on police conduct. As the gatekeepers of the criminal justice system, an understanding of police is central to the study of criminal justice. Chapter 10 explains how courts are organized in the United States and how they operate in practice. Chapter 11 offers an interesting discussion of prosecutors and their role in criminal justice. A unique section is included on the role of independent counsel in prosecuting crimes by federal officials.

Chapter 12 is devoted exclusively to understanding the defense of criminal cases. This chapter is the only one of its kind in introductory criminal justice textbooks. It addresses the important issue of the competing interests between seeking the truth versus winning criminal cases. Chapter 13 presents the history and philosophy of sentencing and recent innovations in the sentencing of offenders. Chapter 14 discusses prisons and their role and purpose in dealing with offenders, including trends in prison populations.

Chapter 15 introduces the reader to the concepts of authentic versus restorative justice and how alternatives to prison often can serve the dual purposes of deterrence and rehabilitation. Recent cases where offenders are "shamed" or embarrassed are assessed in this chapter. Chapter 16 illustrates the crimes, including smuggling and terrorism, that are increasingly occurring across borders and what the prospects are for an international system of justice.

Chapter 17 offers a unique look at the sophisticated crimes, including white collar crime, computer crime, and organized crime. The similarities among these crimes are presented as well as a typology to understand them more clearly. Chapter 18 presents the history, current status, and future directions in juvenile justice. How we deal with juveniles today will have a dramatic impact on criminal justice and on society in general in the years to come.

Features of the Book

There are numerous important features that distinguish this book. Each feature adds to the book's usefulness as a source of information and as a tool for teaching and learning.

1. Two *Critical Thinking Exercises* are included in each chapter. These exercises describe an interesting issue, relate some facts, history, and research about it, and then ask the reader two or three questions that query them to *think* about alternatives, rather than merely to *recall* facts. The critical thinking exercises force readers to think about issues of concern and come up with thoughtful responses, rather than rehearsed answers. Examples of critical thinking topics included in the book are hate crimes, overcriminalization, homicide, pit bulls, Theodore Kaczynski and legal insanity, justice on the Carolina frontier, responding to spouse abuse, unannounced entry by police, sex offender castration, registering sex offenders, terrorists on the Internet, and abolishing the age of majority.
2. In each chapter, a *Contemporary Issue* is featured that highlights a current issue that provides a jumping-off point for discussion of current events in the news, projects, or further reading. Examples include obscenity, drug-abusing women offenders, serial murders, campus law enforcement, race and the death penalty, private prisons and liability, the rebirth of youth gangs, and avoiding cyber-theft.
3. Each chapter highlights an issue that is bound to become more significant in the future. Following each *Future Issue,* readers are asked a question that requires an original response, one based on reflection. Examples of these features include school violence by children, crib death or infanticide, why we buy guns, television crime dramas and homicide, blame and believability in rape cases, preventing subway crime, pursuit driving, and prosecuting false statements.
4. Each chapter has at least one feature titled *Media and Criminal Justice* that summarizes a film that deals with criminal justice issues. Each media feature is followed by a question that requires the student to respond thoughtfully. Featured films included in media features are *A Clockwork Orange, Primal Fear, Star Chamber, Dead Man Walking, Falling Down, The People v. Larry Flynt,* and *New Jersey Drive*.
5. This is the only book of its kind that features a separate chapter on *criminal defense.* This chapter presents information on the legal and ethical issues that face defense attorneys today. The issues of the scope of the right to

counsel and whether an attorney should defend a guilty person are addressed in this chapter.

6. This is the only book of its kind with a separate chapter on *sophisticated crimes*. The chapter addresses the growth of white collar, organized, and computer crimes thereby expanding the scope of criminal justice books from traditional street crimes. As technology advances, the economy changes, and the population ages, these crimes will continue to grow in number and severity.
7. A major section on *restorative and authentic justice* takes a close look at new alternative sentences by placing them in context so that students may understand how the aims of restorative and authentic justice compare to more traditional notions of justice.

Supplemental Materials

Criminal Justice is accompanied by an expansive package of supplementary materials to facilitate teaching and learning. These materials include:

INSTRUCTOR'S MANUAL Each chapter of this valuable teaching tool includes a chapter outline, annotated lecture outline, summary, learning objectives, key terms, class discussion questions, essay questions, projects, and guest speaker suggestions. And to assist your transition from another text, the Instructor's Manual also contains conversion notes from other popular Introductory Criminal Justice texts.

COMPUTERIZED INSTRUCTOR'S MANUAL The Instructor's Manual is also available on disk for both Mac and IBM (Windows).

TEST BANK More than 1,500 test questions are contained in this test preparation aid. There are approximately 40 multiple choice, 30 true-false, 15 fill-in, and 5 essay questions for each chapter of the text.

ALLYN AND BACON TEST MANAGER—COMPUTERIZED TEST BANK The Test Manager contains all of the questions from the Test Bank, plus you may customize it with your own questions. Test Manager produces a variety of statistics that allow you to analyze the performance of test questions students, an individual class or section, and assessment types such as homework and online tests.

PRACTICE TESTS Consisting of approximately 15 questions per chapter, these self-tests help students gain mastery of the material covered in the text, above and beyond their reading in the text and the study guide.

POWERPOINT This PowerPoint presentation provides approximately 500 graphic and text images, in addition to links to the Internet, enabling you to create complete multimedia presentations in the classroom. The presentation is available on disk for IBM users, and online at www.abacon.com/albanese for Mac users. PowerPoint software is not required to use this program; a PowerPoint viewer is included to access the images. Each chapter of the text has its own corresponding PowerPoint module.

TRANSPARENCIES Available online at www.abacon.com/albanese, these transparencies are another way to enhance your classroom presentation. This transparency set contains approximately 100 pieces, including all figures, charts and tables from the book, plus additional art from outside sources.

STUDY GUIDE PLUS This Study Guide provides learning objectives, key terms, self-tests, and glossaries. Students who need special language assistance will find a glossary for potentially confusing idioms and colloquialisms.

COMPUTERIZED STUDY GUIDES This valuable resource includes comprehensive chapter outlines, and comprehensive question sets consisting of multiple choice, true/false, and short-answer questions for each chapter. Questions are presented randomly and missed questions are presented more frequently. The questions are designed to cover all the material in the chapter, and serve to reinforce each other—knowing the answer to one question can assist the student in correctly answering other questions. Also included are flashcards that allow the student to view the term and give the correct definition or use it jeopardy style and view the definition while responding with the correct term. A performance appraisal shows students how they did by question type or topic. The Computerized Study Guide is available in two versions: single user for individual student use or multi user, designed to be installed in a learning resource center or computer labs, either on individual machines or network servers.

ALLYN AND BACON INTERACTIVE VIDEO—PRIME TIME CRIME This custom video covers a variety of major topics of interest to Criminology and Criminal Justice. The video segments are great to launch lectures, spark classroom discussion, and encourage critical thinking. The accompanying video user's guide provides detailed descriptions of each video segment, specific tie-ins to the text, and suggested discussion questions and projects. Prime Time Crime is organized as follows: Predatory Crimes; Domestic Violence; Organizational Crime; Corporate Crime; State Crime; and Crimes Against Humanity.

ALLYN AND BACON INTERACTIVE VIDEO FOR ALBANESE This custom video covers a variety of topics in the field of Criminal Justice, which are linked tightly with the text. The up-to-the-minute video segments are great to launch lectures, spark classroom discussion, and encourage critical thinking. The accompanying video user's guide provides detailed descriptions of each video segment, specific tie-ins to the text, and suggested discussion questions and projects.

THE BLOCKBUSTER APPROACH: A GUIDE TO TEACHING SOCIOLOGY WITH VIDEO This manual provides extensive lists, with descriptions, of hundreds of commercially available videos, and shows how they can be incorporated in the classroom. The videos are organized by topic and presented in an order common to most introductory textbooks.

ALLYN AND BACON QUICK GUIDE TO THE INTERNET FOR CRIMINAL JUSTICE, 1999 This handy reference guide contains a relevant discussion of Internet basics written for students in a language to which they can relate. It includes criminal justice Internet activities; a section on critical evaluation of Internet sources; proper electronic documentation guidelines for both MLA and APA styles; and a multitude of criminal justice-specific URLs.

CAREERS IN CRIMINAL JUSTICE This supplement goes beyond the academic career path of the criminal justice major and explores careers in criminology and criminal justice, showing how people entered the field, and how a degree in criminal justice can be a preparation for careers in a wide variety of areas.

A&B VIDEO LIBRARY Qualified adopters may select from a wide variety of high quality videos from such sources as Films for the Humanities and Sciences, and Annenberg/CPB.

WEBSITE An extensive website has been developed for this text at www.abacon.com/albanese. Features of the online study guide portion of the website include learning objectives; practice tests (interactive multiple choice, true-false, fill-in and essay questions); web destinations; exploring the Internet; chapter chats, etc. There are numerous non-text specific criminal justice resources included on this exciting site!

INTERACTIVE EDITION The Criminal Justice Interactive Edition combines the complete textbook with the latest in multimedia, taking your students beyond the traditional learning experience. The Interactive Edition CD-ROM contains the complete book in full color as well as more than 500 contextually placed media links. All of the media links take students to additional content that directly relates to key concepts in the text. There are video and audio clips, activities, practice tests, and links to websites, including the online study guide specific to this text. Because the Interactive Edition CD-ROM allows students to walk through a variety of media, it accommodates a wide variety of individual learning styles.

Acknowledgments

This book is much more than a collection of several hundred thousand words. It took a significant portion of my life to gather the personal and social experience that resulted in this book. It began while a senior undergraduate at Niagara University when my sociology professor, Nicholas Caggiano, mentioned in class that Rutgers University was opening a new School of Criminal Justice. I applied and was admitted. It was the only graduate school to which I applied. To this day, I do not believe I would have heard about the Rutgers' program if I had cut that class.

After finishing my Master's degree at Rutgers and entering the work force as a criminal justice planner, I considered attending law school. An emergency appendectomy the night before the law school admission test sidetracked those plans. Instead, I received a call from Rutgers a few weeks later, inviting me to apply to their newly established doctoral program at the School of Criminal Justice.

I entered the Ph.D. program that Fall. I am indebted to Rutgers for starting the School of Criminal Justice when it did and also for supporting my studies with assistantships and fellowships during my time there. I finished the Ph.D. in 1981, having obtained a variety of work experiences in the process. These experiences included research, consulting work, and a great deal of teaching. The opportunity to teach enabled me to discover I enjoyed it, and that I improved with each class I taught.

I returned to Niagara University in Fall, 1981 and taught there for 15 years. During that time I had the opportunity to revise the undergraduate curriculum in criminal justice, write the curriculum for a Masters program, and at one time or another teach most of the courses there. I have gained more knowledge through teaching than through any other activity because good teaching requires preparation. The lack of many good books in the field, especially during the early years of my career, forced me to look to primary sources. This instilled an appreciation of the history and philosophy that underlies the field of criminal justice which is reflected in this book. Teaching is a very important profession, and I am gratified to have the opportunity to do it for a living. I thank my students for providing the forum to do so.

I began this manuscript while serving as president of the Academy of Criminal Justice Sciences and moved to my current position as chair of the Department of Criminal Justice at Virginia Commonwealth University in 1996. These undertakings slowed my progress on the book somewhat, but the delays added to the book's interest in light of a series of major events in criminal justice that have occurred recently including major acts of domestic terrorism, the acceleration in media coverage of criminals trials, and significant growth in international and sophisticated crimes.

The reviewers who made many helpful suggestions on early drafts of this book's manuscript include Nola Allen, University of South Alabama; Jennifer M. Balboni, Northeastern University; John K. Cochran, University of South Florida; Richard H. DeLung, Wayland Baptist University; David Friedrichs, University of Scranton; Herbert C. Friese, Burlington County College; Dennis Hoffman, University of Nebraska; Terrance W. Hoffman, Nassau Community College; Katherine Jamieson, University of North Carolina; William E. Kelly, Auburn University; JoAnne M. Lecci, Nassau Community College; Larry Rostintoski, Trident Technical College; Carl Russell, Scottsdale Community College; Jo Ann M. Scott, Ohio Northern University; Donald H. Smith, Old Dominion University; Gregory B. Talley, Broome Community College; and Angela D. West, Indiana State University. Their comments undoubtedly improved the quality of the final book.

My editors deserve recognition for their help in seeing this project through to publication. Karen Hanson, editor-in-chief, thought the idea for this book was a good one and I thank her for her tactful yet persistent attention to details and deadlines. In a similar way, Carolyn Smith's editorial assistance was invaluable. Susan Brown and Heather Ahlstrom provided cheerful assistance in the book's production and marketing, and the many field representatives I have met impressed me with their knowledge of both publishing and the field of criminal justice.

Like most families, mine is active and involved. I thank mine for helping me keep my work on this book in context, while they wondered if it would ever end.

Character-building exploits such as coaching a soccer team of 7- and 8-year-olds, teaching forensic science to middle school students, and managing a little league team provided me with wonderful experiences of the possibilities for constructive behavior by day, while I wrote about the often dark side of life at night. Without all these experiences, this book would have been quite different and probably not as good.

About the Author

JAY S. ALBANESE is Professor and Chair of the Department of Criminal Justice at Virginia Commonwealth University. He received the M.A. and Ph.D. from Rutgers University, where he was the first Ph.D. recipient from the Rutgers School of Criminal Justice. At Virginia Commonwealth University, Dr. Albanese directs a 500 student undergraduate program in criminal justice, and Master's programs in forensic science and criminal justice with a total enrollment of more than 100 students. The graduate program is one of the seven largest in the nation.

Dr. Albanese served as Interim Research Director at the Training and Research Institute of the National White Collar Crime Center during 1998–1999. In this capacity, he has developed a 3-year research plan for the Institute and directed their research projects.

Dr. Albanese is author of seven books, including *Organized Crime in America* (Anderson, 3rd edition, 1996), and *White Collar Crime in America* (Prentice Hall, 1995). He is editor of the book *Contemporary Issues in Organized Crime* (Willow Tree Press, 1995).

Jay Albanese was recipient of the *Excellence in Teaching Award* from the Sears Foundation, and is listed in *Who's Who in America, Who's Who in American Law, Who's Who in Education,* and *Who's Who among America's Teachers.* He is a past president of both the Academy of Criminal Justice Sciences and the Northeastern Association of Criminal Justice Sciences.

Criminal Justice

chapter one

Concern about Crime and Violence

It is better to know some of the questions than all of the answers.

JAMES THURBER
(1894–1961)

CHAPTER OUTLINE

There is disagreement on many of the central problems of criminal justice:

- Is crime caused by social injustices or is it the result of bad individual decisions?
- Do we need more laws to control crime or fewer laws enforced more effectively?
- Is greater police power needed to control crime or are expanded police powers a threat to the public?
- Will longer prison sentences reduce crime or produce repeated crimes by those released?
- Is the death penalty necessary to achieve justice or is it barbaric?
- Are prison chain gangs an effective deterrent to offenders or are they merely degrading and humiliating?

So it goes for virtually ever issue of criminal justice, and in few fields is there as much confusion. Everyone has his or her favorite "solution" to the

problem of crime. One result of this confusion is the continual reinvention of the flat tire, that is, repeated experimentation with unworkable "solutions" to the problems of crime and violence. The typical student or citizen rarely encounters the basic facts about the impact of criminal justice policies. As a result, when citizens vote for candidates for public office, participate in public hearings, or otherwise express their views, they do not have access to all the information they need to make an informed judgment. This book is designed to provide important information about crime and justice in a concise but understandable manner. The latest information and research are utilized, and their implications for informed criminal justice policies are presented.

Most assessments of the costs of crime use monetary estimates. However, the true cost of crime lies in its impact on individuals. For more than thirty years surveys have reported that fear of crime is increasing steadily, especially among the poor and disenfranchised, who often lack the ability to change the nature and condition of their communities. There is also much evidence that fear, whether it be self-imposed or based on reality, has effects beyond the psychological ones. It reduces citizens' mobility, affects their social interactions (through increased fear of strangers), hurts the commercial sector (especially at night), and affects the overall quality of life, a standard by which we judge our leaders, our communities, and our country.

Fear is intensified when constant reports of new crimes, police cutbacks, widespread plea-bargaining, and lenient sentencing of offenders leave citizens with the feeling that no effort is being made to improve existing conditions, reduce their fear of crime, or improve the quality of life for law-abiding individuals. Such feelings can have dangerous consequences. Citizens may stop participating in the political process, or they may react in unanticipated, sometimes violent ways to additional stresses placed on them.

In the pages that follow, the issues of crime, violence, and justice that affect us all are presented. It is hoped that through greater understanding of these issues, individual citizens will be better able to participate in developing policies to address them effectively.

Concern about Crime in the United States

Since the 1960s, public concern about crime has risen dramatically, and crime and "law and order" have become national political issues. The 1964 Presidential election campaign saw Republican Senator Barry Goldwater criticize the Kennedy–Johnson administration for its failure to deal with "crime in the streets."[1] Although Goldwater lost the election, President Lyndon Johnson recognized the public's sensitivity to the issue of "lawlessness." On July 23, 1965, Johnson signed an executive order establishing the President's Commission on Law Enforcement and Administration of Justice to "deepen our understanding of the causes of crime and how society should respond to the challenge of the present levels of crime."

criminology
The study of the causes of crime and the treatment of offenders.

criminal justice
The management of the criminal justice system, including the study of police, courts, and corrections in addition to criminology.

In addition to the public interest in law and order aroused by Goldwater, other events during this period undoubtedly influenced Johnson's decision to form the Commission. In 1963, an informant, Joseph Valachi, testified in televised Senate

contemporary issues

Criminology versus Criminal Justice

Historically, there has been some confusion between the terms *criminology* and *criminal justice*. **Criminology** is the older term. It refers to the study of the causes of crime and the treatment of offenders. Its contemporary roots can be found in the application of the scientific method to police work, pioneered by August Vollmer in the early 1900s, and his development of the first police crime laboratory. As an academic field, criminology was a specialization within the field of sociology. In some programs it is still taught from the sociology department, but the enormous body of research and theory developed over the course of the twentieth century has resulted in the establishment of a separate curriculum in many schools.

This separate curriculum has come to be called **criminal justice** in most colleges and universities. This term refers to the management of the criminal justice system and includes the study of police, courts, and corrections in addition to criminology. Therefore, criminology as the study of the causes of crime and treatment of offenders has become part of the larger field of criminal justice, which includes the study of the criminal justice process.

This view of criminal justice as a process can be traced to the 1967 report of the President's Commission on Law Enforcement and Administration of Justice. The Commission's recommendations were supported by the Law Enforcement Assistance Administration, which provided funds for higher education for criminal justice professionals during the 1960s and 1970s. It was during this period that the first academic programs in higher education in criminal justice emerged, corresponding to the growing recognition of crime and justice as social and legal processes that require examination of their causes, enforcement, adjudication, and correction, rather than as individual events that do not necessitate systematic study.

hearings that there existed a nationwide criminal conspiracy called the Cosa Nostra, which was responsible for most of the illegal gambling, loansharking, and narcotics trade in the United States. In November 1963, President Kennedy was assassinated and the governor of Texas seriously wounded while riding in a motorcade in Dallas. Two days later the suspected assailant, Lee Harvey Oswald, was murdered before he could be brought to trial. In June 1964, the U.S. Supreme Court held in the case of *Escobedo v. Illinois* that crime suspects have the right to legal counsel during certain types of police interrogations. In 1966, the Court held that suspects in custody have the right to an attorney and to remain silent during questioning. These decisions led to widespread belief that the police were being "handcuffed" and could not carry out their duties effectively under such restrictions. All of these events, many of which occurred in the space of little more than two years, help explain the public's responsiveness to Goldwater's "lawlessness" theme and Johnson's willingness to act on the issue.

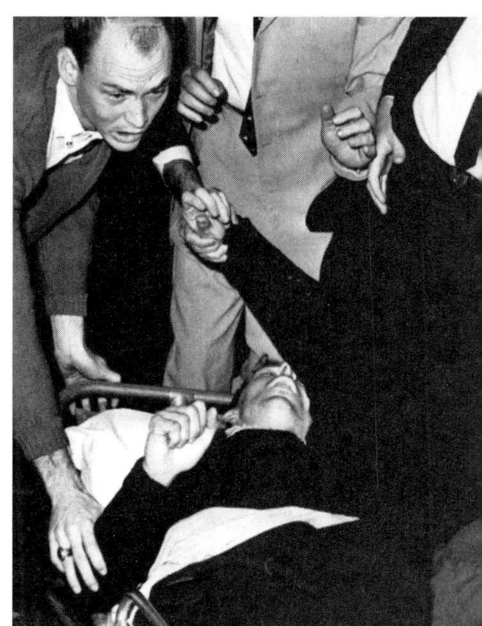

Lee Harvey Oswald, the assassin of President John F. Kennedy, after he was fatally shot by Jack Ruby in Dallas, Texas in 1963.

The Commission was the first in a long line of national commissions formed to study various aspects of the crime problem. Table 1.1 presents a chronology of these investigations. Each of these commissions was formed in response to a specific issue or event for which there was no easy answer. The Commission on Civil Disorders investigated the causes and response to urban riots and civil rights and anti–Vietnam War demonstrations. The other commissions investigated other major problems of crime and justice, including violence, assassinations, obscenity, pornography, drugs, political corruption, misconduct by the Federal Bureau of Investigation (FBI) and Central Intelligence Agency (CIA), and organized crime. A seemingly endless series of political scandals, such as the

TABLE 1.1

National Commissions, 1967–1987

1967	President's Commission on Law Enforcement and Administration of Justice
1968	National Advisory Commission on Civil Disorders
1969	National Advisory Commission on the Causes and Prevention of Violence
1970	President's Commission on Campus Unrest
1970	National Commission on Obscenity and Pornography
1972	U.S. Commission on Marijuana and Drug Abuse
1973	National Advisory Commission on Criminal Justice Standards and Goals
1974	U.S. Senate Watergate Report
1975	President's Commission on CIA Activities within the United States
1976	U.S. Senate Select Committee Report on Intelligence Activities
1979	U.S. House of Representatives Final Assassination Report
1982	President's Task Force on Victims of Crime
1986	Attorney General's Commission on Pornography
1987	President's Commission on Organized Crime

Iran–Contra affair and the savings and loan scandal, as well as hate crimes, serial and mass murders, acts of domestic terrorism, family violence, and so on, have occurred in recent decades. The underlying message the public receives from such events is that crime and lawlessness are rampant and that American society is being destroyed from within.

Crime Victimization versus Other Life Events

When one compares the actual risk of being victimized by crime to the risk of experiencing other negative events, crime does not appear so rampant. For example, each year approximately 242 of every 1,000 adults in the United States are hurt in accidents—almost a 1 in 4 chance of injury in any given year. The odds of being struck by lightning are 1 in 9,100, those of dying from heart disease are almost 4 in 1,000, and those of dying from cancer are 2 in 1,000, all far higher than the risk of being victimized by crime. The top twelve causes of death in the United States are presented in Table 1.2.

TABLE 1.2

Odds of Occurrence of Death

CAUSES OF DEATH	ODDS OF OCCURRENCE (PER 100,000 POPULATION)
1. Heart disease	288
2. Cancer	206
3. Stroke	58
4. Lung disease	39
5. Pneumonia and flu	32
6. Diabetes mellitus	21
7. Motor vehicle accidents	16
8. All other accidents	15
9. Suicide	14
10. Liver disease	10.4
11. Homicide	10
12. Kidney disease	8

SOURCE: U.S. Bureau of the Census, *Statistical Abstract of the United States: 1996*, 116th ed. (Washington, D.C.: U.S. Government Printing Office, 1996).

Table 1.2 shows that health problems and accidents are far more common causes of death than criminal homicide. A person is 29 times more likely to die of a heart attack than to die as a homicide victim. Likewise, a person is twenty times more likely to die from cancer and six times more likely to succumb to a stroke than he or she is to die from homicide. In fact, an individual is almost twice as likely to die in a car accident than to die from homicide and nearly four times more likely to die in some kind of accident than he or she is to be a homicide victim. When one views homicide in context, therefore, it is clear that other risks, especially poor health and accidents, pose a much greater threat to life.

The same is true for nonlethal injuries. As Table 1.3 illustrates, the odds of injury from accidents at home or on the road are higher than the odds of most forms of criminal victimization. One is eight times more likely to be injured in an accident than to be hurt in a violent crime, and more than three times more likely to be injured in an accident than to have something stolen from one's person. It is also apparent that being a victim of theft is more than twice as likely as being a victim of criminal violence (72 versus 31 per 1,000). Why then are people not more afraid of accidents and health problems than they are of crime?

Part of the answer is found when one examines statistical trends in the causes of death. Perhaps our fear is related to the *direction* (up or down) in rates of certain causes of death rather than to the odds themselves. Table 1.4 presents trends in the most common causes of death in the United States over three decades.

It can be seen from Table 1.4 that the rankings of the various causes of death have shifted only slightly since 1960. The largest jump has been in deaths from lung disease, the number ten cause of death in 1960 and the number four cause today. When calculated in deaths per 1,000 population, this represents an increase of 352 percent. The second largest increase in risk of death is from homicide, which rose by 277 percent between 1960 and 1990. This increase is eight times higher than the increase in cancer deaths, which went up by 36 percent over the same period. Clearly, the risk of homicide has increased dramatically since 1960 and may account for some of the public's fear of crime.

This risk is amplified when one realizes the relative lack of control that an individual has over homicide compared with other leading causes of death. Decreases in rates of death from heart disease, strokes, pneumonia and flu, and liver disease are due to changes in the lifestyle, exercise habits, and diet of U.S. citizens over the last 30 years. Through research findings and public education regarding the links between personal habits and bad health, many Americans have gained increased awareness and adopted healthier lifestyles. The same is true for accidental deaths. Seat belt laws, child bicycle helmets and car seats, airbags, and greater regulation of dangerous devices have done much to reduce the rate of deaths caused by accidents. The point here is that each of us can exert a certain amount of influence over the causes of bad health and accidents by changing our

TABLE 1.3

Odds of Experiencing Nonlethal Injury

CAUSES OF NONLETHAL INJURY	ODDS OF OCCURRENCE (PER 1,000 ADULTS PER YR)
1. All accidents	242
2. Accidents at home	79
3. Personal theft	72
4. Accidents at work	58
5. Violent crime	31
6. Motor vehicle accident	17
7. Injury from fire	0.1

SOURCE: Marianne W. Zawitz, ed., *Report to the Nation on Crime and Justice*, 2nd ed. (Washington, D.C.: U.S. Bureau of Justice Statistics, 1988).

TABLE 1.4

How the Odds of Death Have Changed since 1960

CAUSES OF DEATH IN 1990	1980 RANK	1970 RANK	1960 RANK	CHANGE 1960–1990 (%)
1. Heart disease	1	1	1	−28
2. Cancer	2	2	2	+36
3. Stroke	3	3	3	−46
4. Lung disease	4	9	10	+352
5. Pneumonia and flu	5	4	4	−14
6. Diabetes mellitus	8	7	7	+15
7. Motor vehicle accidents	6	5	5	−12
8. All other accidents	7	6	6	−41
9. Suicide	10	10	9	+17
10. Liver disease	9	8	8	−8
11. Homicide	11	11	12	+277
12. Kidney disease	12	12	11	+9

SOURCE: U.S. National Center for Health Statistics, *Vital Statistics of the United States*. (Washington, D.C.: Public Health Service, published annually).

behavior. In contrast, homicide is thrust on us by others. It is also sudden and violent, distinguishing it from most other causes of death. Fear of homicide, therefore, is justified to some extent by the significant increase in its occurrence over the last 30 years and the comparative lack of control over its occurrence.

Effects of Fear of Crime

Psychological Impact

As was noted earlier, public concern about crime can be traced to events that occurred in the 1960s. This concern grew when the FBI reported that the number of crimes of violence (i.e., homicide, rape, robbery, and aggravated assault) rose 156 percent from 1960 to 1970. From 1971 to 1980, the number of violent crimes reported to police rose an additional 60 percent, and from 1981 to 1990 it increased another 34 percent.[2] In 1964, a Gallup Poll asked, "What do you think is the most important problem facing this country today?" Forty-six percent of respondents cited international problems (mostly relating to the Cold War), 35 percent cited racial problems, and 6 percent or fewer cited the high cost of living, unemployment, or too much government control.[3] Given the series of events mentioned earlier, it is surprising that crime was not among the most frequently cited problems. This was to change over the next three decades. When asked the same question in 1993, a representative sample of the U.S. population ranked the country's most pressing problems as health care (28 percent), the economy (26 percent), crime (16 percent), and poverty and education (6 percent each). The end of the Cold War and the uncertainty of the national economy appear to have shifted public concern from international relations and domestic race relations to health care, the economy, and crime.

Table 1.5 traces changes in public perceptions of crime over the last thirty years. It reveals that a marked increase in the level of fear took place during the 1960s that has since leveled off. Approximately 43 percent of Americans are afraid to walk at night in areas near where they live, a proportion that has remained virtually unchanged for more than two decades. Therefore, the level of fear of crime among the public has been high for more than two decades. Other surveys of public attitudes provide further evidence of widespread fear of crime. A Life Quality Index poll conducted by the Gordon Black Corporation found that feeling safe from crime is more important to citizens than job satisfaction, financial security, marriage, and even health.[4] In 1993, a *USA Today*/CNN/Gallup poll found crime to be a greater concern than even the economy.[5]

TABLE 1.5

Levels of Fear of Crime: "Is there an area near where you live (within a mile) where you would be afraid to walk alone at night?"

YEAR QUESTION ASKED	PROPORTION AFRAID (%)
1993	43
1990	40
1983	45
1977	45
1972	42
1967	31
1965	34

SOURCE: George H. Gallup, *The Gallup Poll: Public Opinion, 1993* (Wilmington, DE: Scholarly Resources, 1994), p. 204.

Behavioral Effects

The consequences of a high level of fear include much more than the psychological impact it may have. A survey undertaken by the Metropolitan Washington, D.C., Council of Governments more than two decades ago reflects concerns that continue today: "Sixty-five percent of the city's largely white suburban residents visit the downtown area less than once a month, and 15 percent come downtown less than once a year." The chief reason given was fear of crime. The Task Force on the Assessment of Crime and Its Impact to the President's Crime Commission also considered the consequences of fear:

> **The fear [of crime] leads many people to give up activities they would normally undertake, particularly when it may involve going out on the street or into parks or other public places at night. The costs of this fear are not only economic, though a burdensome price may be paid by many poor people in high crime rate areas who feel compelled to purchase protective locks, bars, alarms, who reject an attractive night job because of fear of traversing the streets or who pay the expense of taxi transportation under the same circumstances. In the long run more damaging than costs are the loss of opportunities for pleasure and cultural enrichment, the reduction of the level of sociability and mutual trust, and perhaps even more important, the possibility that people will come to lose faith in the trustworthiness and stability of the social and moral order of the society.[6]**

Neighborhood watch groups have formed in response to high levels of fear about crime in local communities. Surveys have found that fear of crime remains one of the most serious concerns of the general public.

Beyond these economic, attitudinal, and quality of life consequences, *fear changes behavior* as well. It can turn otherwise law-abiding citizens into outlaws. Robert Lejeune and Nicholas Alex discovered this in interviews with two mugging victims.

> **After my second mugging I told the sergeant: "I got mugged twice and I got my apartment robbed twice. And I said, that officer came up and asked me questions like I was the one doing the robbery, but I'm going to get something to protect myself." So he laughed and said, "Don't be too drastic and get a gun." I said, "No, I'm not going to get a gun, but I'm going to get me a knife." So he said, "Get two." If there ain't nobody around and if I get the advantage of him, I would plant the other knife on him. [This respondent bought both a knife and a .22 caliber pistol.]**
>
> **Since then I've been more alert in carrying a little gas gun. I was given two by a private detective. And I've talked since with a . . . lawyer friend of mine in Harlem that I've known for many years. He encouraged me to use it. I said, "It's illegal." "Of course, but don't hesitate to use it," he said. "And your story should be. . . ." Now this man is a man whom I respect highly—a highly moral man in many ways. "Of course you use it and if the police say anything about it, or find it, say they used it on you first. And that's your story: you took it away from them. And you stick to it."[7]**

When many people are thinking and acting in anticipation of being victimized, life in society becomes fraught with peril. As Lejeune and Alex observe, "In his own protection the victim may become a 'criminal,' just as in his own protection the victim becomes adept at evasion and deception. In order to survive, the victim may become as ruthless as the victimizer. Under such prevalent conditions of anomie, the barrier separating the victim and the victimizer tends to break down."[8]

Perhaps the definitive example of what high levels of fear can produce is the case of Bernhard Goetz. In 1984, Goetz, a 37-year-old white man, was riding on a New York City subway train when one of four boisterous black youths said to him, "How are ya?" Two of them approached Goetz, and one asked him for five dollars. Goetz asked him what he wanted, and he repeated, "Give me five dol-

Fear about crime contributes to more gun purchases for self-protection. Sometimes these guns are used aggressively, rather than in self-defense, due to the fear of being victimized.

lars." Goetz proceeded to shoot at the youths five times, emptying his .38 revolver. He wounded each of the youths, paralyzing one of them.[9] The Goetz case illustrates what can happen when a citizen experiences high levels of fear over a prolonged period. Citizens arm themselves (sometimes illegally), focus on events that feed their fears, and sometimes act violently, convinced that they are acting in self-defense. Goetz was found guilty only of criminal possession of a weapon (his revolver), but it is clear that his actions pushed the rules of self-defense to their limit. (See Chapter 5 for a discussion of the limits of self-defense.) Since the Goetz case, a number of states have passed laws making it easier for homeowners and battered spouses to employ force in self-defense, although the new rules apply to very few situations.[10]

The changes in behavior provoked by fear of victimization are not confined to individuals. Businesses also may alter their policies. For example, in an effort to prevent carjacking, in which criminals force their way into occupied vehicles, commandeering the car and sometimes robbing, assaulting, or killing the driver,[11] car rental companies have removed their corporate logos and license plates from rental cars in order to make it harder for car thieves and robbers to identify tourists.[12] Some are warning their customers *not* to stop when bumped from behind or when told that something is wrong with their car. Similarly, after a series of thefts and violent crimes occurred in South Florida in the wake of Hurricane Andrew,[13] the level of fear and concern about crime led several Miami hotels to block local television news from TV sets in guest rooms to shield them from "body-bag journalism."[14] Fear of crime is not limited to Florida, however. In 1994, New York City Mayor Rudolph Giuliani announced a crackdown on "quality of life" crimes that "affect the daily lives of millions of New Yorkers."[15]

Even places that are usually considered safe, such as the workplace and the home, have been the scenes of serious violence in recent years. More than 40 people were killed in post office shootings throughout the United States in the last decade.[16] In fact, the U.S. Department of Labor reported that more than 1,000 workplace homicides occurred during 1992 alone,[17] and nearly one million individuals are victims of violent crimes while at work each year.[18] Homes do not appear to be any safer. In 1995, Susan Smith was tried for murder in the killing of her two children in North Carolina. In Chicago a mother was sentenced to 55 years in prison for forcing her 11-year-old daughter to have sex with a man in exchange for money. A man critically burned his girlfriend's 10-year-old son in an effort to find out who had taken twenty dollars in food stamps. A Wisconsin high school teacher was convicted for hiring three students to kill her estranged husband. In Rochester, New York, four young teenagers were charged with spraying nail polish remover on an eight-year-old boy and setting him on fire.[19] These are just some of the hundreds of shocking, bizarre, and violent crimes that have occurred throughout the United States in recent years.

It does not take many such events to produce such high levels of fear and behavioral changes. This is especially true when the response of the criminal justice response is considered unsatisfactory. Government agencies often aggravate the situation by responding in ways that add to the public's fear and frustration. In 1994, for instance, the FBI reported that for the first time, a person is more likely to be killed by a stranger than by a family member or friend. The FBI's report stated that "every American now has a realistic chance" of being murdered.[20]

Media and Criminal Justice

FALLING DOWN

Americans list crime as their number one concern, convinced that crime is on an upsurge and threatening their quality of life and safety. But is our concern about crime and violence accurate? Do Americans embrace stereotypes about who the typical criminal is? Does our fear of crime create a world or distrust, suspicion, and frustration that actually impacts the crime rate?

The idea that crime and violence in America is a normal, even cyclical, phenomenon in our culture was graphically depicted in the 1993 film *Falling Down.* The film's main character William (Michael Douglas) is a patriotic, hardworking engineer for the defense industry. He believes in the American dream, having spent his life following the rules, fitting society's "norms," shrugging off the everyday "injustices" of life in Los Angeles. His devotion to his profession, or perhaps his declining patience for a crumbling society, is indicated by his personalized license plate that reads: D-FENS.

In *Falling Down,* William "D-FENS" represents the common citizen who is fed up with the disrespectful, irresponsible, and downright *criminal* behavior of the people and government around him. He dedicates himself to his job for twenty years, only to be laid off in his prime. He tries to make his marriage work, but his wife divorces him and uses his temperamental outbursts as a means to keep him from seeing his daughter. He sits in a traffic jam in sweltering heat every day, but the construction work is never completed.

And then one day he snaps.

William "D-FENS" goes on a violent rampage, a virtual crime spree, that a viewer might consider both criminal and heroic. Tired of sitting in a stagnant traffic, "D-FENS" simply abandons his car in the middle of the highway and takes off on foot. Territorial street thugs who refuse to let him rest on "their" turf are met with a swinging baseball bat. A Korean grocer who refuses to give him change for the phone without making a purchase is given a xenophobic lecture on foreign aid, and subsequently has his store trashed by "D-FENS." A right-wing militia member dealing illegal arms out of his military surplus store finds himself stabbed with his own hunting knife when he accuses "D-FENS" of being just like him. A drug gang crashes their car in a failed drive-by shooting; "D-FENS" picks up their satchel of assault weapons and later uses a bazooka to blow up a stretch of road that has been under construction for years. A seven-year-old child shows "D-FENS" how to operate the rocket-launcher, explaining that he had "seen it on TV."

It is no surprise that *Falling Down* has been categorized by reviewers as an "action movie," "drama," and "black comedy." Indeed, the violence depicted by both the clear-cut criminals and the vigilante superhero "D-FENS" has been used as the basis for both criticizing and praising the movie's cultural message. The theme of *Falling Down* transcends the main character's crime spree; homeless people sit near a playground, a peaceful protester is arrested by police, and an Order of Protection for the former wife of "D-FENS" is regarded as useless. Are these serious crimes, minor injustices, or simple realities of life in America?

Film critic Roger Ebert likened *Falling Down* to films such as *Joe* and *Deathwish,* but these older movies offered an exaggerated depiction of clearly justified revenge. Ebert noted: "If this film had been made 10 or 20 years ago, it might have been an audience-pleaser in which we cheered as the white hero shot up druggies, or got vengeance on rapists. [The director and screenwriter] have not made a revenge movie, and the film isn't constructed to inspire cheers when Douglas pulls the trigger. Maybe it will play that way for some audiences, but more thoughtful viewers are likely to pick up on Douglas's anomie—his soulsickness that has turned to madness, his bafflement at becoming obsolete and irrelevant."[A]

In *Falling Down,* the patriotic, hardworking, law-abiding citizen *is* depicted as obsolete and irrelevant. The criminals appear to be winning, and no one seems to notice or care. Why does the Korean grocer have a job, and not "D-FENS"? Why is the hamburger at the fast-food restaurant nothing like the one in the glossy advertising photographs? Why can't the police catch "D-FENS" with their massive manhunt as he continues his crime spree across an entire city?

The utter hopelessness and powerlessness of the common citizen are the basis for the character's "falling down," but the inference is that crime begets crime. American society is depicted as having become desensitized to violence and immune from responsibility. The irony of *Falling Down* is that it is both inspired by, and imitates, the horrific stories that appear on our nightly news. As disgruntled employees respond to the pink slip with mass murder at their former place of employment, spree killers evade police despite leaving taunting and obvious clues, and "road rage" becomes a frightening reality of driving, *Falling Down* presents a society in which crime is not only common, but is normal.

MEDIA AND CRIMINAL JUSTICE QUESTION

Compare William's behavior in *Falling Down* with that of Bernhard Goetz and the related incidents cited in this chapter. How are they similar and different?

NOTE

[A]Roger Ebert, *Chicago Sun Times,* February 26, 1993.

A high level of fear can make criminals out of victims, as the Bernhard Goetz case illustrates. More "law-abiding" people own and carry guns illegally in order to protect themselves. A Texas man formed an organization called Dead Serious that offered members $5,000 for legally killing a criminal who attacked them at home.[21] A relatively crime-free Chicago suburb has placed security checkpoints on the streets entering the area.[22] Unlike the situation in other fear-ridden communities, the police department, rather than a private security agency, is staffing the checkpoints, stopping cars, and making inquiries. This arrangement raises questions about how police should be employed and the extent to which citizens are trading their privacy to quell their fear of crime.

Is Crime Normal?

The prevalence of crime in societies throughout the world raises the question of whether crime is actually a "normal" part of modern life. More than a century ago, the French sociologist Emile Durkheim made the following observation:

> **Crime is present not only in the majority of societies of one particular species but in all societies of all types. There is no society that is not confronted with the problem of criminality. Its form changes; the acts thus characterized are not the same everywhere, but, everywhere and always, there have been men who behaved in such a way as to draw upon themselves penal repression.[23]**

Writing in 1895, Durkheim made the point that there has yet to be a society without crime of some type. In this sense, crime is "normal" inasmuch as every society has it and it would be abnormal to expect no crime.

Nevertheless, crime is not a desirable phenomenon. Although we cannot expect a society to have no deviance whatsoever, there is considerable variation in the rates of crime in different societies. As a result, it is not unrealistic to seek significant reductions in crime rates, at least for certain types of crimes.[24] Related to this issue is the fact that there is evidence that concern about crime may be a cyclical phenomenon. The President's Crime Commission identified several historical periods in which concern about crime was at high levels:

> **A hundred years ago contemporary accounts of San Francisco told of extensive areas where "no decent man was in safety to walk the street after dark; while at all hours, both day and night, his property was jeopardized by incendiarism and burglary." Teenage gangs gave rise to the word "hoodlum"; while in one central New York City area, near Broadway, the police entered "only in pairs, and never unarmed." . . . And in 1910 one author declared that "crime especially in its more violent forms, and among the young, is increasing steadily and is threatening to bankrupt the Nation."[25]**

The fact that concern about crime and violence may be cyclical does not mean that its causes and its level remain the same. The nature and extent of crime differ widely from one time and place to another. The next two chapters examine the nature and extent of crime and violence in the United States and how they have changed over the years.

The Criminal Justice Response

The criminal justice response to crime and violence has not met the demand for justice and public safety. In 1993, for example, budget cuts forced district attorneys' offices in California to lay off prosecutors; as a result, in some counties misdemeanors were not prosecuted. Store owners, home owners, commuters, and others responded to this situation by arming themselves.[26] Throughout many parts of the nation, the perception that the government is not adequately protecting public safety has contributed to the arming of the citizenry. As noted earlier, when this occurs, more people take the law into their own hands, and instances of wrongful shooting, vigilante activity, and lawlessness among otherwise law-abiding citizens increase. In Baton Rouge, for example, a home owner shot and killed a 16-year-old Japanese student wearing a white tuxedo when the student mistakenly came to his house while looking for a Halloween party. The home owner, who shot out of fear (the student did not understand the command "Freeze!"), was acquitted of manslaughter, but he was required to pay the boy's family $653,000 in civil damages for negligence in causing his death.[27]

sudden infant death syndrome (SIDS)
Infants die from prolonged sleep apnea in which breathing stops for fifteen seconds or more.

FUTURE ISSUES

Crib Death or Infanticide?

One reason for high levels of fear of crime is that what was formerly considered accidental is now sometimes considered criminal. Motor vehicle accidents are now investigated to determine whether they are "alcohol-related." Gunshot accidents are investigated to see whether improper supervision of minors or illegal handguns are factors. **Sudden infant death syndrome (SIDS)** is increasingly seen as a form of criminal homicide (infanticide), and investigations are carried out to determine culpability. This shift in perception has occurred over the last two decades as authorities have become increasingly reluctant to accept these incidents as accidents.

More than 3,000 infant deaths each year are listed as resulting from sudden infant death syndrome. SIDS is said to be caused by prolonged sleep apnea, in which breathing stops for fifteen seconds or more. Recent studies have shown that at least some SIDS deaths are the result of foul play. In England, a video camera in hospital rooms uncovered thirty-nine instances of mothers trying to smother their babies after they had been admitted for interrupted breathing. Other studies suggest that SIDS is overdiagnosed, noting that SIDS cases fell 30 percent between 1992 and 1995 after pediatricians began recommending that babies sleep on their backs rather than on their stomachs.[A]

Videotaping is being done increasingly often in sleep apnea clinics, but no one knows for sure what goes on at home. SIDS support groups fear that families who suffer the loss of a baby will be placed under suspicion of murder, furthering aggravating their loss.[B] The growing skepticism about SIDS thus is a double-edged sword. The facts of each case must be made known if intelligent judgments are to be made on this issue.

FUTURES QUESTION

How would you propose to reduce the incidence of infanticide that is misdiagnosed as SIDS?

NOTES

[A]Richard Firstman and Jamie Talan, *The Death of Innocents* (New York: Bantam, 1997).

[B]Sharon Begley, "The Nursery's Littlest Victims," *Newsweek* (November 22, 1997), pp. 72–3.

Fear of crime also enhances fear of strangers and promotes stereotypes and scapegoats. Attacks against Japanese, Canadian, German, and other tourists, immigrants, and residents in recent years offer evidence of this problem.[28] This situation contributes to a self-fulfilling prophecy in which criminal incidents lead to fear, which then leads to more criminal incidents when people react incautiously to perceived threats to their well-being brought about by fear.

Reported incidents of crimes committed by those released on bail or on parole provoke further public apprehension, even though these events are rare. In a similar way, acquittals of suspects in high-profile cases and inflammatory statements by criminal justice officials, noted earlier, feed public fear of crime. Widespread use of inflammatory terminology, such as "epidemic," "war," and "battle," in referring to crime causes it to be viewed in the same context as disease and war. This contributes to high levels of fear that give rise to the undesirable behaviors described earlier. Chapter 3 examines trends in the *actual* chances of being victimized by crime and sheds light on whether such high levels of fear of crime are justified or exaggerated.

Education and Professionalism

Growing public concern about crime, combined with an unsatisfactory response from the criminal justice system, causes one to question the prospects for the future. However, a closer look at changes in the field of criminal justice provides reasons for optimism. These changes include better education and training and a more sensitive public response by criminal justice professionals.

Seventy years ago the U.S. National Commission on Law Observance and Enforcement, headed by Attorney General George Wickersham, found the criminal justice system to be uneducated, undertrained, and ineffective. The Wickersham Commission, as it came to be called, found that only 10 percent of police officers were high school graduates, that police departments were often controlled by politicians, and that police brutality and use of the "third degree" (i.e., torture in interrogating suspects) were common.[29] Through the efforts of experts such as August Vollmer and O. W. Wilson, the criminal justice system began to become more professional in its outlook and activities. Police departments began to appoint and promote officers on the basis of merit rather than political connections. Basic training in police and corrections was developed. High school education became a minimum requirement for all criminal justice professions.

In 1967, the President's Commission on Law Enforcement and Administration of Justice recommended that police departments take "immediate steps" to require individuals in supervisory and executive positions to have a degree from a four-year college.[30] In 1973, the National Advisory Commission on Criminal Justice Standards and Goals recommended that police officers be required to have a Bachelor's degree by 1982.[31] These national commissions also recommended additional preservice training, mandatory in-service training, improved salaries, and merit-based selection processes for judges, prosecutors, and corrections officers. Professional associations such as the International Association of Chiefs of Police and the American Correctional Association have published guidelines that incorporate many of these recommendations in an effort to advance professionalism in the field.

National Commissions have recommended that all police become college-educated. Thus far, this has taken place primarily at the federal level, although progress is being made in a number of state and local law enforcement agencies.

Not all of these recommendations have been implemented, but the trend is clear. Virtually all federal law enforcement posts now require at least a Bachelor's degree; a growing number of police, court, and corrections administrators have Master's or law degrees. Training has improved, and the quality of justice administered by the system is considerably better than it was during the Wickersham investigation of the 1920s. Some of these recommendations gained urgency over the years through court mandates and legislation, and some improvements emerged from the recognized need for greater professionalism in order to respond more effectively to the problem of crime.

As the President's Commission observed in 1967, recognition of the interdependent nature of the criminal justice system is necessary for improvements to occur. The three main parts of the criminal justice system—police, courts, and corrections—have their own hierarchies and tasks to perform, but to be effective they must rely on each other.

> **The courts must deal, and can only deal, with those whom the police arrest; the business of corrections is with those delivered to it by the courts. How successfully corrections reforms convicts determines whether they will once again become police business and influences the sentences judges pass; police activities are subject to court scrutiny and are often determined by court decisions. And so reforming or reorganizing any part or procedure of the system changes other parts or procedures.[32]**

Increased professionalism is necessary in all the agencies of the criminal justice system because the performance of one agency has a direct impact on the performance of others. The criminal justice process is not "a hodgepodge of random actions." Instead, it is a "continuum—an orderly progression of events" that are interdependent. Therefore, a study of the criminal justice system must begin by examining it as a whole.[33]

In recent years there has been growing concern about the nature of the education received by individuals working in the criminal justice system. Variations among college-level programs, together with the development of the new academic field of criminal justice, raised questions about the purpose and quality of education for members of the criminal justice professions. This led to the formation of the Joint Commission on Criminology and Criminal Justice Education and Standards, which published a book-length examination of standards for higher education programs in the field in 1981.[34] In 1995, the Northeastern Association of Criminal Justice Sciences developed a model educational curriculum and minimum standards for faculty, students, and administration for criminology and criminal justice programs.[35] National minimum standards for higher education programs were drafted in 1997 by the Academy of Criminal Justice Sciences, the largest association of criminologists and criminal justice educators in North America. Clearly, in the decades since the 1920s there has been growing interest in professionalizing the response to crime.

Critical Thinking EXERCISE

The Causes of Fear

Fear of crime has insidious effects on both community solidarity and economic investment. It also promotes public cynicism and xenophobia. Victimization surveys have found levels of fear to be high even among citizens living in low-crime areas. Therefore, it is important to recognize that the causes of fear pose a problem distinct from that posed by the causes of crime.

Studies of the causes of fear of crime have found that perceived risk of victimization is the single most important variable in explaining high levels of fear.[A] The more a person believes that he or she is likely to be the victim of a crime, the more fearful he or she is. Interviews with samples of the U.S. population have found perceived risk of victimization and fear of crime to be higher among women and younger people. Significant racial differences have also been found.

The fear of crime is not restricted to high-crime areas. Even people from low-crime areas have been found to have high levels of fear, resulting in cynicism, fear of strangers, and unwillingness to use mass transportation.

Several studies have found that whites who believe that they are in a racial minority in their neighborhood are more likely to be fearful than blacks who believe that they are in a racial minority in their area.[B] This level of fear holds true regardless of the *actual* racial composition of the neighborhood. Therefore, fear of crime varies significantly both within neighborhoods and among residents of different kinds of neighborhoods.

Critical Thinking Questions

1. Why do you believe that fear of crime is unrelated to actual risk of victimization but strongly related to perceived risk of victimization?
2. How do you account for higher levels of fear among women and younger people?
3. How might you explain the higher levels of fear among whites than among blacks who perceive themselves to be a minority in their neighborhood?

Notes

[A]Randy L. LaGrange, Kenneth F. Ferraro, and Michael Supancic, "Perceived Risk and Fear of Crime: Role of Social and Physical Incivilities," *Journal of Research in Crime & Delinquency,* vol. 29 (1992), pp. 311–34; Pamela W. Roundtree and Kenneth C. Land, "Perceived Risk Versus Fear of Crime: Empirical Evidence of Conceptually Distinct Reactions in Survey Data," *Social Forces,* vol. 74 (1996), pp. 1353–76.

[B]Ted Chiricos, Michael Hogan, and Marc Gertz, "Racial Composition of Neighborhood and Fear of Crime," *Criminology,* vol. 35 (1997), pp. 107–31; Wesley G. Skogan, "Crime and the Racial Fears of White Americans," *The Annals of the American Academy of Political and Social Science,* vol. 539 (1995), pp. 59–71.

Critical Thinking EXERCISE

Real versus Apparent Hate Crimes in a Time of Fear

In 1990, the federal government enacted a law that called for the counting of hate crimes, or criminal acts motivated by racial, religious, or sexual bias. There were 4,755 reported incidents of hate crimes in the United States in 1991. This number increased 25 percent over the next three years. More than 70 percent of these incidents were racial or ethnic in nature, and a majority of these involved antiblack motives. Nearly 18 percent of all reported incidents were religious in nature (mostly anti-Jewish), and 12 percent were directed against homosexuals.[A] It is likely that these figures undercount the true extent of hate crimes, because of the difficulty of determining the true motives of offenders in many cases.[B] Simple greed or personal advantage is difficult to distinguish from "hate-related" motives without obvious clues left by the offender. Even when these clues are found, however, hate may not be the true motive.

hate crimes Criminal acts motivated by racial, religious, or sexual bias.

The public fear and outrage engendered by hate crimes have been seized on by unscrupulous individuals to "fake" hate crimes in a way that benefits them. In 1995, a woman in Fargo, North Dakota, reported that she had been assaulted, that a swastika had been carved into her stomach, and that her family's restaurant had been burned down. It was later discovered that she

had staged the entire episode. In 1996, a mechanic and his son in Miami vandalized a school with anti-Semitic slogans. The pair hoped to profit from doing the anticipated repair work. In Jonesboro, Georgia, the home of an interracial couple was burned and swastikas were painted on the fence. The couple was charged with 23 counts of fraud for allegedly staging a series of events like this one. A black minister in Iowa claimed that his Mercedes-Benz had been spray-painted with racial slurs. An investigation revealed that he had sought repainting estimates before the alleged spray-painting incident.[C]

There are no statistics on faked hate crimes, but their incidence makes it difficult to distinguish true victims from those who are simply seeking money and attention. High levels of public fear about crime in general help create an environment in which staged incidents are easily believed.

Critical Thinking Questions

1. **Why do you believe the public is ready to believe that alleged hate crimes have been committed before an investigation is conducted?**
2. **If faked hate crimes proliferate, what impact are they likely to have on the public and on true crime victims?**

Notes

[A]Federal Bureau of Investigation, *Hate Crime Statistics* (Washington, D.C.: U.S. Government Printing Office, 1996).

[B]James Morsch, "The Problem of Motive in Hate Crimes: The Argument Against Presumption of Racial Motivation," *Journal of Criminal Law and Criminology,* vol. 82 (1991), pp. 659–89.

[C]Art Levine, "The Strange Case of Faked Hate Crimes," *U.S. News & World Report* (November 3, 1997), p. 30.

Summary

CONCERN ABOUT CRIME IN THE UNITED STATES

- Public concern about crime has risen dramatically since the 1960s.
- Beginning in 1967, a series of national commissions have investigated various aspects of the crime problem.

CRIME VICTIMIZATION VERSUS OTHER LIFE EVENTS

- Health problems and accidents are far more common causes of death than criminal homicide.
- Fear of death due to homicide is related to the increase in the risk of homicide since 1960 as well as to the relative lack of control that an individual has over homicide compared with other leading causes of death.

EFFECTS OF FEAR OF CRIME

- Polls have found that citizens place feeling safe from crime ahead of job satisfaction, financial security, marriage, and health.
- Fear of crime leads many people to give up activities they would normally undertake, especially those that involve going to public places at night.
- High levels of fear can turn otherwise law-abiding citizens into outlaws.
- Businesses and governments may also modify their actions in response to high levels of fear of crime.

IS CRIME NORMAL?

- Crime of some type is present in all societies, but its nature and extent differ from one time and place to another.

THE CRIMINAL JUSTICE RESPONSE

- The criminal justice response to crime and violence has not met the demand for justice and public safety.
- In recent decades efforts have been made to improve the education and training of members of the criminal justice professions.

Key Terms

criminology	hate crimes
criminal justice	sudden infant death syndrome (SIDS)

Questions for Review and Discussion

1. What are some of the events that led to an increase in public concern about crime in the 1960s?
2. Compared to the risk of dying in an accident, how great is the risk of being a homicide victim?
3. Is there any justification for the public's increased fear of violent crime?
4. What are some psychological and behavioral effects of fear of crime?
5. In what sense can crime be considered "normal"?
6. What changes are occurring in the criminal justice system in response to growing public concern about crime?
7. Why is it important to recognize the interdependent nature of the criminal justice system?

Notes

[1]James O. Finckenauer, "Crime as a National Political Issue: 1964–76, From Law and Order to Domestic Tranquility," *Crime & Delinquency,* vol. 24 (January 1978).

[2]U.S. Department of Justice, *Crime in the United States* (Washington, D.C.: U.S. Government Printing Office, published annually).

[3]George H. Gallup, *The Gallup Polls: Public Opinion, 1935–1971,* vol. III (New York: Random House, 1972), p. 2108.

[4]Marilyn Adams, "Life Quality Survey Finds Safety Top Concern," *USA Today* (March 13, 1995); Sam Meddis and Jack Kelley, "Crime Drops, But Fear on Rise," *USA Today* (April 8, 1995).

[5]Bruce Frankel, "'Our Problem' Cuts Across All Groups," *USA Today* (October 28, 1993), p. 1.

[6]President's Commission on Law Enforcement and Administration of Justice, *Task Force Report: Crime and Its Impact—An Assessment* (Washington, D.C.: U.S. Government Printing Office, 1967), p. 94.

[7]Robert Lejeune and Nicholas Alex, "On Being Mugged: The Event and Its Aftermath," *Urban Life and Culture,* vol. 2 (October 1973), pp. 282–3.

[8]Ibid.

[9]George P. Fletcher, *A Crime of Self-Defense: Bernhard Goetz and the Law on Trial* (New York: The Free Press, 1988).

[10]William Wilbanks, *The Make My Day Law: Colorado's Experiment in Home Protection* (Lanham, MD: University Press of America, 1990).

[11]Deborah Sharp, "Car-jacking Trial Opens in Florida," *USA Today* (February 24, 1993), p. 3; "Life Sentence Given in Brutal Car-jacking," *USA Today* (August 19, 1993), p. 3.

[12]"Florida's Inroads to Rental Car Safety," *USA Today* (June 21, 1993), p. 5D.

[13]Deborah Sharp, "In South Florida, Raising the Roof and the Crime Rate," *USA Today* (February 15, 1993), p. 3.

[14]Deborah Sharp, "In Miami Hotels, Checkout Time for TV News of Violence," *USA Today* (June 6, 1994), p. 8.

[15]Bruce Frankel and Maria Puente, "New York Tackling 'Quality of Life' Crimes," *USA Today* (July 7, 1994), p. 3.

[16]Jonathan T. Lovitt, "California Postal Worker Held in Boss' Slaying," *USA Today* (July 10, 1995), p. 3; Carrie Dowling and Bruce Frankel, "Former Postal Worker Held in New Jersey Shootings," *USA Today* (March 23, 1995), p. 5; "Postal Feud Ends in Fatal Shootings," *Richmond Times-Dispatch* (December 20, 1997), p. 3.

[17]Carol J. Castaneda and Kevin Johnson, "Employers on Guard for Violence," *USA Today* (April 5, 1995), p. 3.

[18]Ronet Bachman, *Violence and Theft in the Workplace* (Washington, D.C.: Bureau of Justice Statistics, 1994).

[19]"Murder for Hire," *USA Today* (May 22, 1995), p. 3; "Boy Burned," *USA Today* (March 27, 1995), p. 3; "Mom Sentenced," *USA Today* (October 25, 1993), p. 3; "Four Teens Charged After 8-Year-Old is Set on Fire," *The Buffalo News* (March 21, 1995), p. 14.

[20]Federal Bureau of Investigation, *Uniform Crime Reports—1993* (Washington, D.C.: U.S. Government Printing Office, 1994); Robert Davis and Sam Vincent Meddis, "Random Killings Hit a High," *USA Today* (December 5, 1994), p. 1.

[21]Mark Potok, "A Deadly Serious Call to Arms," *USA Today* (February 17, 1995), p. 3.

[22]Kevin V. Johnson, "Chicago Suburb a Fortress Against Crime," *USA Today* (July 5, 1995), p. 3.

[23]Emile Durkheim, *The Rules of Sociological Method* (originally published in 1895) (New York: The Free Press, 1964), pp. 65–6.

[24]Freda Adler, *Nations Not Obsessed with Crime* (Littleton, CO: Fred B. Rothman, 1983); Jay S. Albanese, "Moving Towards Utopia: Elements of a Crime-Free Society," *Justice, Privacy, and Crime Control* (Lanham, MD: University Press of America, 1984), pp. 46–56.

[25]*Task Force Report: Crime and Its Impact—An Assessment,* p. 19.

[26]Richard Price, "Crime May Pay Thanks to California Budget Crisis," *USA Today* (May 10, 1993), p. 3.

[27]Steve Marshall, "$653,000 Awarded in Killing of Japanese Teen," *USA Today* (September 6, 1994), p. 1.

[28]Richard Price and Jonathan T. Lovitt, "Murder of Two Students Stuns Japan," *USA Today* (March 29, 1994), p. 1; Jeff Leen and Don Van Natta, Jr., "Canada Fears Escalating Crime While Miami Can Barely Keep Up," *The Buffalo News* (September 11, 1994), p. 12.

[29]National Commission on Law Observance and Enforcement, *Report on Lawlessness in Law Enforcement* (Washington, D.C.: U.S. Government Printing Office, 1931).

[30]President's Commission on Law Enforcement and Administration of Justice, *The Challenge of Crime in a Free Society* (New York: Avon, 1968), p. 280.

[31]National Advisory Commission on Criminal Justice Standards and Goals, *A National Strategy to Reduce Crime* (New York: Avon, 1975), p. 311.

[32]President's Commission, *The Challenge of Crime in a Free Society,* p. 71.

[33]Ibid.

[34]Joint Commission on Criminology and Criminal Justice Education, *Quest for Quality* (Chicago: University Publications, 1981).

[35]Northeastern Association of Criminal Justice Sciences, *Minimum Standards for Criminal Justice Education* (Niagara University, NY: Northeastern Association of Criminal Justice Sciences, 1995).

For Further Reading

Steven R. Donziger, ed., *The Real War on Crime: The Report of the National Criminal Justice Commission* (New York: Harperperennial Library, 1996).

Robert Jerin and Laura Moriarty, *Victims of Crime* (Chicago: Nelson-Hall, 1998).

Harold J. Rothwax, *Guilty: The Collapse of Criminal Justice* (New York: Warner Books, 1997).

Anne Strick, *Injustice for All* (New York: Barricade Books, 1996).

chapter two

The Nature of Crime

The intention makes the crime.

ARISTOTLE
(384–322 B.C.)

Suppose that you are frustrated with all the rules and regulations in American society. You purchase an uninhabited island somewhere in the Pacific and decide to start your own country. Living by yourself would be lonely, so you invite some of your friends, who in turn invite some of their friends, to join you. It does not take long before you find that there is little on which you and your new fellow residents agree. For example, some members of the new society may want to have several wives or husbands simultaneously. Others may want to grow marijuana and smoke it all day long. If you believe that monogamous relationships are fundamental to stable families and child rearing, you have to establish strong rules prohibiting bigamy. Likewise, people who smoke marijuana all day are not likely to be productive members of your new society, which needs farmers, builders, and artisans. Therefore, you choose to limit or prohibit marijuana smoking.

CHAPTER OUTLINE

DO NOT
STEAK TIPS KIELBASA
HOT DOGS CHICKEN SODA
KIELBASA
HOT DOGS CHICKEN
FRESH

As your society becomes larger, the diversity of opinions about almost everything will multiply. You will need rules prohibiting the settling of disputes by means of fistfights; otherwise the society will effectively be controlled by bullies. You will need rules to guarantee sharing, or proper exchange, of goods that are grown and manufactured in your new country to ensure that people do not victimize one another through greed or malice. As you can see, the number of rules is likely to increase rapidly as your society grows and becomes more complex. (It is estimated that the introduction of automobiles into American society had the effect of doubling the number of laws owing to the need to properly control the manufacture, ownership, and operation of vehicles.) To prevent confusion, you will have to codify your society's rules into specific categories so that individual citizens know which behaviors are permitted and which ones are not.

Aspects of Crime

As the scenario just presented illustrates, the development of a criminal code, or rules that prohibit certain forms of conduct, occurs naturally in a society. As a society becomes larger and more complex, rules are required to ensure that the citizens do not victimize or exploit one another. This is one of the reasons why crime rates are generally lower in small towns than in cities where most people are strangers to one another. People feel more responsible for others when they have a sense of attachment to their community.[1] It is difficult to achieve such a sense of attachment when one lives as a stranger without ties to one's community. To illustrate: If you were to sit in a room with five people and make a list of *everything* you agreed on, the list would probably be quite long. If you attempted the same thing in a room with one hundred people, the list of agreed-upon issues would shrink considerably. If you placed more than 200 million people in a single country, there would be little consensus, making it necessary to establish rules to regulate conduct.

Added to this problem is the growing complexity of modern societies. To give just one example, the invention and popularity of automobiles made transportation much easier, but they also led to manufacturing flaws, dangerous operation, registration requirements, repair frauds, storage (parking) problems, misuse by untrained operators, and theft. In recent years the invention and popularity of the personal computer created the need for rules to reduce the same set of problems.[2]

Crime is a natural phenomenon because people have different levels of attachment, motivation, and virtue. All societies have some level of deviant behavior that is disruptive of the social order. If people are to live in groups (i.e., society) successfully, rules are required to make sure they can live together peacefully with a high degree of order. Of course, there will always be some people who do not obey the rules. The rules therefore must carry penalties to serve both as a warning and as an enforcement mechanism. Rules that prohibit certain forms of conduct so as to maintain social order identify a set of behaviors termed **crimes,** which form the basis of the **criminal law.** Violations of the criminal law are considered crimes against society because they break rules designed for the common good. That is to say, the rules elevate the good of the community over the desires

crime
Conduct that threatens the social order as defined by legislatures.

criminal law
The legal definitions of all crimes taken together.

of any given individual. Without such a system, anarchy would prevail as individuals competed to fulfill their own wants and needs without regard to those of others.

Thinking versus Acting

All of us have occasionally wished that something bad would happen to another person. You may have cursed out the driver of an automobile you believe cut you off; you may have wished your employer or professor would become ill; you may have said nasty things about a former lover. When do such thoughts or statements become crimes?

As a general rule, crimes prohibit only acts or omissions of acts. Therefore, it is a crime to strike or steal from someone without a compelling justification (legal excuses are discussed in Chapter 12). Omissions that constitute crimes are rare; they include forms of inaction such as *failure to stop* for a stop sign or *failure to file* your income tax return.

There is a middle ground where the line between thinking and acting becomes thin. What if you *think* evil thoughts about someone but do nothing else? Fortunately, that is not a crime (otherwise we would all be in jail). It is also impossible for law enforcement officials to know what a person is really thinking, although they may *infer* thoughts from evidence provided by polygraphs, surveillance, and other methods. But what if you want to punch your boss in the face, and take a swing at him, but miss? What if you want to kill someone, go out and buy a gun, but take no further action? The history of American criminal law is filled with cases like these, in which the distinction between thought and action is at issue. These cases have helped refine our definitions of crimes and the allowable defenses for questionable actions.

The precise behaviors needed (beyond thought) for actions to be considered crimes are explained in Chapter 3 with reference to the more serious violent and property crimes. The elements of conspiracy, or the planning of a criminal act, are detailed in Chapter 16. Suffice it to say here that the criminal law punishes *actions,* not *thoughts.* This is because it is impossible to know with accuracy a person's thoughts, and thoughts alone do not pose a threat to social control (which is the purpose of the criminal law). Only actions can pose a threat to society. Therefore, the criminal law is concerned only with actions.

The Political Nature of Crime

The history of American criminal law is a history of change. Some acts that were once against the law later became lawful (e.g., profanity, sale of alcoholic beverages during Prohibition). Other acts that were once lawful later became illegal (e.g., possession of slaves, sale of alcoholic beverages after Prohibition). Are such changes random, depending only on the whims of legislators? Or do they reflect true changes in public views of certain acts? Moreover, are there "fundamental" crimes that do not change over time?

As a society grows larger, it becomes less and less feasible for all citizens to participate in the daily operation of government. In a representative government, the people elect representatives to direct governmental affairs on their behalf.

These governmental affairs include the creation and punishment of crimes. It has been argued that some crimes are "created" or selectively enforced by government without the consent of the public in order to protect the government from perceived threats to its existence. During times of war, conflict, or civil unrest, the government has sometimes used its legislative and enforcement powers to persecute alleged enemies rather than seek justice.

In 1920, for example, Nicola Sacco and Bartolomeo Vanzetti were arrested and charged with a Massachusetts robbery during which two people were killed. Sacco and Vanzetti had been anarchists in Italy in the period immediately following World War I. In the United States at the time there was widespread paranoia about sedition, or inciting the overthrow of the government. That paranoia had led to the passage of the Espionage Act, which outlawed sedition in 1918. This act was a thinly veiled effort to suppress speech and actions that were not considered supportive of existing U.S. policy.[3] Sacco and Vanzetti were convicted of espionage on the basis of the robbery attempt and their earlier activities in Italy. They were sentenced to death on the basis of questionable evidence of espionage.[4]

During the post–World War II era, there were similar instances in which the government overzealously identified crimes and criminals, resulting in several miscarriages of justice. In 1949, the infamous "Tokyo Rose" was convicted of treason for broadcasting propaganda to American troops in the Pacific. She was sentenced to ten years in prison, again on the basis of dubious evidence.[5] During the 1950s, the era of McCarthyism, many reputations were destroyed through false charges of communist association by U.S. Senator Joseph McCarthy.[6] In 1951, this hysteria resulted in the trial of Julius and Ethel Rosenberg for allegedly giving U.S. nuclear secrets to the Soviet Union. The Rosenbergs were convicted of espionage—on debatable evidence—and sentenced to death. Historian Lawrence Friedman comments on these events as follows:

> **The debate over their guilt or innocence goes on—perhaps it will never end—but the punishment, in retrospect, seems grossly disproportionate to what the Rosenbergs did, if they did anything, or to the harm their actions may have caused. Judge and jury were in the grip of Cold War hysteria; and to a great extent, so too was the population at large. They were victim, too, of the American search for scapegoats.[7]**

The Vietnam War produced a similar outcry against perceived anti-American sentiment, with aggressive prosecutions of draft dodgers and antiwar protestors.[8]

In recent years the "political" nature of crime has focused less on perceived foreign threats and more on internal problems. This is undoubtedly due to the demise of the Soviet Union, the reunification of Germany, and the movement toward democratic forms of government in Eastern Europe. The "criminalization" or "decriminalization" of certain behaviors, and the public's reaction to them, continue to make the application of the law controversial. Thus, when four Los Angeles police officers were acquitted in the beating of black motorist Rodney King, a riot erupted that lasted several days. When Timothy McVeigh was charged in the bombing of the federal office building in Oklahoma City in 1995, many believed that antigovernment militias were unfairly investigated and treated as suspects. In the Rodney King case, the *failure* of the government to treat questionable

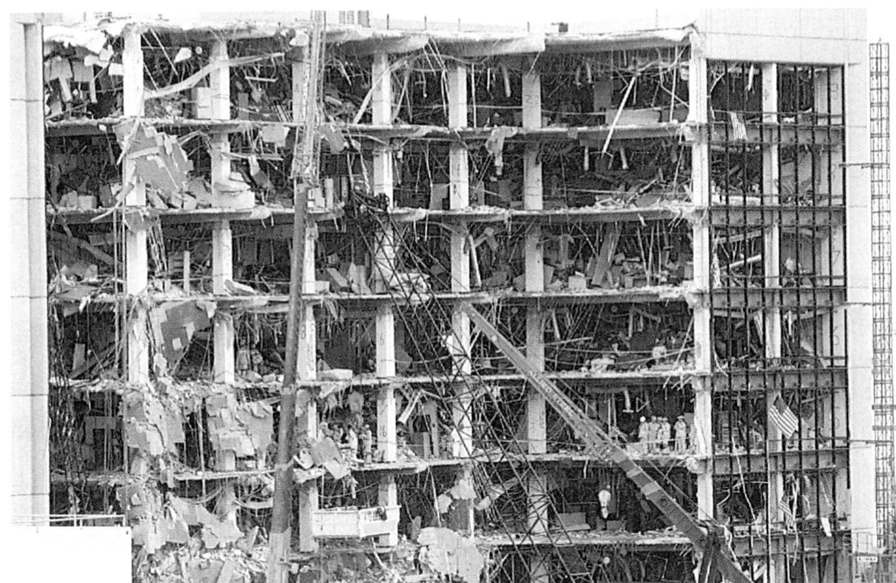

Timothy McVeigh was charged in the bombing of the federal office building in Oklahoma City in 1995. During the investigation, some people believed that antigovernment groups were unfairly treated as suspects, resulting in questions about how to properly apply the law in practice.

police behavior as criminal caused public outcry. In the Oklahoma City case, it was the government's *action* to criminalize the activities of groups opposed to the government that caused division among the public. These debates have not been completely resolved, and the public is likely to remain divided and wary of the role of government in creating and administering the law.

Crime as Social History

It is apparent that perceptions of crime and what constitutes criminal conduct change over time. These changes are far from random, however. They emerge from the public and political concerns that characterize different historical periods. Definitions of crime can therefore be viewed as a form of social and political history.

The social history of crime is most clearly illustrated when one examines its failures to capture public sentiment. For example, in 1920 the Eighteenth Amendment to the U.S. Constitution went into effect, banning the manufacture, transportation, or sale of alcoholic beverages to any person of any age. This policy, Prohibition, was enforced by the Volstead Act, passed by Congress in the same year. One can imagine what would happen if such a law was in effect today. Prohibition failed to address the demand for liquor, and it is not surprising that millions of people manufactured, sold, and bought alcoholic beverages in violation of the law. In 1933, the Eighteenth Amendment was repealed by the Twenty-first Amendment, which permits the sale of alcoholic beverages under the regulated system that exists today.

What caused the outright prohibition of such a desired commodity? For a brief period in American history, the temperance movement's intolerance of *all* liquor consumption garnered enough political support to bring about the enactment of Prohibition and the Volstead Act.[9] As the history of Prohibition illustrates, laws passed without widespread public support are ultimately changed. Therefore, control of the political process results in only temporary changes; it is necessary to have true public support for laws to be effective.

Although it may be said that Prohibition did in fact reduce liquor consumption in the United States, there are no reliable estimates of the true extent of the illegal manufacture and sale of alcoholic beverages during this period.[10] The criminalization of a desired product may change when, where, and how one consumes it, but it usually does not affect *whether* one consumes it. That decision is an individual one that has nothing to do with the law. Instead, it involves personal views, religious beliefs, family influences, and health concerns. The law is remarkably ineffective when it comes to so-called victimless crimes in which "offender" and "victim" are the same individual.

Though laws without public support are sometimes passed (and invariably changed or never enforced), such temporary attempts to mold social history, rather than react to it, can exact a high price. Thousands of people were arrested and convicted during Prohibition. In 1924 alone, more than 22,000 cases related to liquor were pending in the federal courts.[11] When it became apparent during the late 1920s that Prohibition was not working, the government did what governments often do when a "crime" problem appears out of control. It increased the penalties for violation (through the Jones Act). The result was additional thousands of arrests for liquor law violations.

An even more pernicious result of such an unpopular law was the creation of a black market for liquor. Studies have found that Prohibition was responsible for the creation of organized criminal syndicates, some of which still exist today. The influence of Al Capone and Johnny Torrio in Chicago and the beginnings of the Cosa Nostra in New York can be traced to Prohibition.[12] In addition, a great deal of public corruption in Chicago, New York, and other cities was rooted in Prohibition.

The Prohibition experience has been paralleled in many ways by the ebb and flow of laws against gambling, drugs, and prostitution—the other consensual crimes in which the line between offender and victim is not clear or does not exist at all. These "vices" have alternatively been defined as crimes, highly regulated behaviors, or mere leisure activities. The contemporary debate over the role of the law in the "war on drugs" (discussed later in the chapter) has many similarities to what occurred during the 1920s, when alcohol was the drug of choice.

The lessons of history are rarely so clear. Crimes are properly the reflection of a society's views of right and wrong at a certain point in history. Attempts to shape this history without public support are ultimately undone and have significant and disturbing long-term costs for the society in which they occur.

Mala in Se versus Mala Prohibita

If crime is a function of a particular time and place in history, is the notion of crime a subjective one? Or are some behaviors objectively and inherently criminal, regardless of when and where they occur? It appears that they are.

Although the criminal law had its origins among the ancient Greeks and Romans, the primary source of American criminal law is England's common law. Under common law, crimes were seen as being of two types. Acts were considered either as evil as themselves (**mala in se**) or as simply prohibited by law

mala in se
Acts evil in themselves.

mala prohibita
Acts prohibited by law that are not necessarily evil in themselves.

(**mala prohibita**). Mala in se offenses include serious crimes of assault and theft, such as murder, rape, robbery, larceny, and burglary. Mala prohibita offenses are the result of legislative decisions to prohibit certain undesirable behaviors, such as alcohol use, drunkenness, drug use, and gambling.

The number of mala in se offenses has remained fairly constant over the centuries. That is, acts that are identified as evil nearly always involve crimes against persons or property. In fact, crimes of assault (murder, rape, robbery) and theft (burglary and larceny) are illegal in societies of all types. This universality of certain serious crimes demonstrates that crime is neither entirely a subjective phenomenon nor arbitrarily created by particular nations during particular historical periods. From the earliest years of recorded history, basic acts of assault and theft have been criminalized in most of their forms.

The reasons for this uniformity are fascinating. If the law against murder were abolished tomorrow, it is unlikely that the murder rate would increase. This is because a strong moral force exists independently of the law. The law against murder merely reinforces a strongly held community sentiment. The same is true of *all* crimes of assault. It is doubtful that assault would become common if the criminal laws against it did not exist. The same is true for crimes of theft, although thefts are perceived as less serious than assaults (which is probably why they are more common). Clearly, then, there exist crimes that transcend the boundaries of time and place.

It is sometimes argued that *no* acts are inherently criminal. This argument is based on the idea that the precise definitions of murder differ among societies over time. For example, abortion is considered murder in Ireland but is not so defined in most other nations. Revenge killings also were permitted in some societies in earlier times.[13] All that changes, however, is the *breadth* of the circumstances under which the act is permissible. Thus, as government became more competent and better able to protect citizens, the need for revenge killings disappeared. There is now consensus in society that the government's criminal justice system is able to determine justice more objectively and safely than any revenge killing. Likewise, scientific knowledge regarding when human life begins in the womb (made possible through technological advances) has complicated the abortion debate, as has the need to balance the competing interests of the mother and child in light of society's long-term interests. Thus, while the cases of abortion and revenge killings may *modify* the scope of the definition of murder, they do not cause it to appear or disappear from the criminal law.

On the other hand, the number of mala prohibita offenses has grown dramatically in the United States. These offenses can be grouped into three general categories: crimes without victims, political offenses, and regulatory offenses. Crimes without victims are offenses in which the offender and the "victim" engage in the act voluntarily. This category of offenses has been increasing steadily in recent years. Sometimes called "offenses against morality," these acts include adultery and fornication, prostitution, gambling, drug sales and use, and drunkenness, among others. Another expanding category is political offenses, which include any act that is viewed as a threat to the government. These activities may involve treason, sedition, espionage, sabotage, and bribery. None of these crimes are mala in se offenses because they are not necessarily evil. Many of those who engage in these activities believe that they are acting justly against an unjust government. As the history of the United States illustrates, today's revolutionary can sometimes become tomorrow's hero. Therefore, political crimes are not necessarily bad in themselves.

A third type of mala prohibita offense that has grown dramatically in recent years is criminality produced through the powers delegated by Congress or state legislators. These regulatory offenses are usually activities of a business or corporate nature that are viewed as a threat to public health, safety, or welfare. These include laws regulating pollution levels, workplace safety, the manufacture of unsafe products, and other aspects of business. They are crimes created by regulatory agencies as part of their effort to oversee certain activities of business enterprises. Regulatory offenses often change over time as acceptable levels of pollution, employee exposure to risk, and the allowable margin for safety in consumer products change correspondingly. Examples of regulatory agencies include the Federal Trade Commission, the Federal Communications Commission, the Consumer Product Safety Commission, the Food and Drug Administration, and the Environmental Protection Agency.

The increase in mala prohibita offenses has raised concern that the distinction between crime and merely inappropriate or offensive behaviors may be diminishing, a phenomenon called **overcriminalization.** This may dilute the moral force of the law if the law comes to be regarded as petty and intrusive rather than as a necessary means of social control.

overcriminalization
Conduct that is criminalized even though it does not cause great social harm and is not uniformly regarded as criminal conduct by many.

It can be seen, therefore, that mala in se offenses are common to all societies. They differ only in regard to the breadth of their definitions (e.g., including or excluding abortion from the definition of murder). Mala prohibita offenses vary widely among societies, over time, and sometimes even *within* societies. In the United States, for example, there is great variation in the extent to which gambling and marijuana use are considered crimes. Table 2.1 illustrates the three types of mala prohibita offenses and their differences.

Criminal Harm

Mala in se and mala prohibita offenses are distinct both in their substance and in the nature of the harm they cause. Mala prohibita offenses cause harm that violates moral, business, or political principles. In the case of victimless crimes the harm is usually moral and consensual in nature. Gambling, prostitution, and most

TABLE 2.1

A Typology of Mala Prohibita Offenses

TYPE OF OFFENSE	NATURE OF OFFENSE	EXAMPLES
Crime without victims	Offenses against morality involving consensual acts between offender and victim	Gambling, prostitution, drug offenses
Political offenses	Acts viewed as threats to the government	Espionage, bribery, treason
Regulatory offenses	Acts viewed as threats to public health, safety, and welfare	Food and drug labeling and usage warnings, product safety requirements

drug offenses are of this type. Unfairness in business is the typical harm in regulatory offenses. Price-fixing, bid-rigging, and manufacturing shortcuts violate the principles of free markets. Betrayal of a government principle is the harm caused by political offenses. Treason and sedition are examples. In each of these cases of mala prohibita offenses, *violation of principles* is the focus of concern.

For mala in se offenses the harm is more personal and direct. All variations of assault, rape, and homicide result in physical harm to the victim in addition to violation of generally accepted moral principles. Burglary and theft involve loss and violation of property in addition to transgression of moral rules.

Therefore, the seriousness of mala in se offenses is manifested by the physical loss or harm that they cause. Mala prohibita offenses involve violation of moral, business, or political principles, but they do not entail *direct physical loss or harm*. It is the harm caused by mala in se offenses that results in their central position in discussions of crime and justice.

Distinguishing Offensive from Criminal Behavior

As the case of Prohibition makes clear, the ability to *create* crime through the actions of government is cause for concern. In assessing current events or historical ones, how can we determine the extent to which changes in the law truly reflect social consensus or are merely the fruits of lobbying efforts that try to shape public sentiment? One way to determine this is to examine the enforcement of newly enacted laws. The 55-mile-per-hour speed limit is one example. It was enacted in the 1970s in an effort to conserve fuel and reduce highway fatalities, but it was not enforced, and eventually the speed limit was raised in most states. The point is that it is impossible to enforce a law if it is violated by large numbers of people. Other laws have had similar fates, but still others are actively enforced because the public wants them to be enforced.

In the continuing effort to establish the limits of acceptable behavior, the mala prohibita offenses of alcohol consumption, commercialized sex, gambling, and drug use have drawn the most attention over the years. In this section, therefore, we examine each of these types of offenses in turn.

Alcohol Consumption

Throughout the nation's history, alcohol consumption has been viewed alternately as a vice, an evil, a crime, or a leisure activity. As was described earlier, Prohibition served as a national experiment to see how the public would react to criminalizing liquor consumption. Its ultimate repeal is a testament to the fact that the law, by itself, cannot change behavior.

In recent years the attack on alcohol consumption began anew with the campaign mounted by Mothers Against Drunk Driving (MADD). MADD was founded by a mother whose teenage daughter had been killed in an automobile crash. The accident was caused by a man with two prior drunk-driving convictions who was out on bail on a third charge. MADD became a powerful political lobbying group because it addressed the already widespread belief that drunk driving was not adequately criminalized. The 1980s began the anti–drunk-driving era, in which some states increased penalties for drunk driving, establishing mandatory prison sentences and suspending the licenses of violators. In 1984, the federal government established rules that forced every state to raise its drinking age from 18 to 21. Drunk-driving awareness programs became common throughout the United States.

What are the results of these efforts to further criminalize drunk driving? It is true that the rate of traffic fatalities (per 100,000 miles driven) has fallen dramatically in the last twenty years, but it has been falling steadily since at least 1930. In that year there were nearly sixteen traffic deaths per 100,000 miles driven in the United States. By 1950, the rate had dropped to 7.6 deaths per 100,000 miles. In 1970, the rate was 4.9 and in 1990 it was 2.2.[14] The conclusion is that driving is far less lethal than ever before, the result of a trend that began long before the contemporary campaign against drunk driving. The extent to which the campaign contributed to this result is unclear. In 1930, the drinking age was 21; it subsequently dropped to 18 and then moved back to 21. Mandatory seatbelts, child safety seats, airbags, antilock brakes, and other safety features have undoubtedly reduced traffic deaths and injuries, but these are all innovations that occurred apart from the anti–drunk-driving crusade. In fact, the best data indicate that only 30 percent of traffic deaths are related to drunk driving.[15]

One problem with the anti–drunk-driving campaign is that it focuses on *driving after drinking,* rather than on *drinking* itself. Studies have found only about 10 percent of all drivers to be problem drinkers.[16] These individuals are unlikely to be deterred by increased penalties because they are *drunk* at the time of their offense, a time when one is least likely to consider the consequences of one's actions. It has been argued that "most people wouldn't be deterred by the threat of severe penalties because they aren't problem drinkers in the first place."[17] It is not surprising, therefore, that police roadblocks and other "crackdowns" in search of drunk drivers have had disappointing results. It is estimated that during peak drinking hours (Friday and Saturday nights) only 3 or 4 percent of all drivers are legally drunk.[18] Studies of police crackdowns on drunk driving in different cities and even different countries have shown them to have little or no deterrent effect.[19] Given the small proportion of drivers who are impaired, combined with the odds against apprehension (the estimated probability of being asked to submit to a breath test is one per million vehicle miles driven), even doubling the number of officers would not significantly increase the risk of apprehension.[20]

Whatever the causes, traffic deaths per miles driven are the lowest they have ever been. It is likely that reductions in the numbers of problem drinkers will have the greatest impact on both drunk driving and alcohol-related illnesses in the future. Addressing alcohol consumption as a personal health issue, rather than as a crime issue, may do more to decrease the incidence of problem drinking than any other strategy. In much the same way that cigarette smoking was reduced dramatically after it became a health issue (rather than being criminalized), it appears that once a "harmless, recreational" activity like drinking is seen as unhealthful, the definition of that behavior changes to "harmful and unnecessary," and fewer people engage in it. Thus, alternatives to criminalization can produce desirable behaviors that the law cannot.

Commercialized Sex

The selling of sex for money has existed at least as long as alcohol consumption, gambling, and the other "vices." Historically, prostitution was seen as an undesirable behavior, and that view continues today. The only disagreements lie in opinions about precisely *why* it is bad and about whether criminalization is the best way to address the problem.

During the 1800s, prostitution was criminalized throughout the nation: Either the behavior itself was criminalized or it was a crime to operate a brothel, engage in lewd behavior, or otherwise engage in consensual sex for pay. One hundred years ago, objections to prostitution largely followed moral and religious arguments. The same moral intolerance for alcohol that resulted in Prohibition also resulted in the Mann Act in 1910. This act prohibited "white slave traffic," meaning the interstate transportation of women for purposes of prostitution. The Act compared prostitution with slavery (obviously omitting the slavery of nonwhites).

In the law's first five years, more than 1,000 people were convicted of white slavery.[21] Most of these defendants were men, but not all of the prosecutions dealt with prostitution. Many involved "debauchery" and "immoral purposes"; the defendants were older married men with young girlfriends who happened to cross state lines and be reported by their spouses. One case involved two university students who had sex on the way home from a date.[22] Clearly, the Mann Act was not limited to prostitution; it aimed to suppress all nonmarital sex.

During the early 1900s, many cities created vice commissions, acting on the widespread belief that prostitution was an "evil" or a "plague."[23] Absolute intolerance was the remedy prescribed for this social ill. It took the form of attempts to shut down "red light" districts, periodic police raids, and the closing of suspected brothels. The result was the *displacement* of prostitution, not its elimination. Prostitutes went to different neighborhoods and took to street-walking. Thus, in some ways intolerance of prostitution actually made life worse for prostitutes by replacing madams in brothels with more abusive pimps on the street.

The Mann Act was not overhauled until 1986, although prosecutions under its provisions became infrequent long before that. Charlie Chaplin was acquitted of violating the Mann Act in 1944 but ultimately left the United States in protest; Chuck Berry was convicted under the Mann Act in 1962. By the end of the 1960s, however, there were only 36 prosecutions per year.[24] This decline in enforcement was the result of a growing feeling that the law should not be applied to consensual sex in personal relationships in which there is no question of payment.

The federal government ultimately limited prosecutions under the act to commercialized sex, and in 1986 the law was amended to focus on "transportation for illegal sexual activity and related crimes." This new law marked the end of a 75-year period in which federal vice prosecutions were characterized by accusations of "debauchery," "immoral purposes," and "white slavery." Not until the 1980s was the law limited to actual acts of prostitution.

In perhaps the most obvious illustration of the double standard in law, men were almost never arrested for prostitution, although they could be arrested for soliciting sex. Yet as one historian noted, "The customers were not creatures from outer space."[25] So few judges attempted to apply the law to men that the police

contemporary issues

Obscenity: Sex or Violence?

Obscenity and pornography constitute another "vice" with which the law has had difficulty over the years. To what extent should they be criminalized and, more importantly, what precisely *are* they?

The First Amendment to the United States Constitution, ratified in 1791, protects freedom of religion, freedom of the press, the right to assemble peacefully, and the right to petition the government; it also states that "Congress shall make no law . . . abridging the freedom of speech." The Supreme Court held early on that the First Amendment did not apply to *all* speech. The case of obscenity has been troublesome, however, because it is very difficult to define. As Justice Stewart of the Supreme Court remarked in 1964, "Perhaps I could never succeed in intelligibly" defining obscenity. "But I know it when I see it."[A]

THE MILLER CASE

The U.S. Supreme Court settled on the current legal definition of obscenity in the case of *Miller v. California*.[B] Marvin Miller had conducted a mass mailing to advertise four books, entitled *Intercourse, Man-Woman, Sex Orgies Illustrated,* and *An Illustrated History of Pornography.* The brochures consisted primarily of pictures and drawings "very explicitly depicting men and women in groups of two or more engaging in a variety of sexual activities, with genitals often prominently displayed." The legal action resulted from a complaint to the police from a person who had been sent five of these unsolicited brochures.

In its decision, the Supreme Court stated that obscenity exists when the average person, applying contemporary community standards, would find that the work (1) "taken as a whole, appeals to the prurient interest in sex," (2) portrays sexual conduct (specifically defined by state law) in a "patently offensive way," and (3) "taken as a whole, lacks serious literary, artistic, political, or scientific value." Examples of what state laws could define as obscene included "patently offensive representations of ultimate sexual acts, normal or perverted, actual or simulated" as well as "masturbation, excretory functions, and lewd exhibition of genitals."

The Court has decided more than thirty cases on obscenity-related issues since *Miller.*[C] These cases involved determinations of obscenity in showing adult films to an adult audience, the mainstream film *Carnal Knowledge,* a George Carlin monologue, child pornography cases, and reviews of state laws. The Court has not uniformly applied such concepts as "serious value," "prurient interest," and "community standards" set forth in *Miller,* illustrating the inadequacy of that definition of obscenity.

A NEW APPROACH TO AN OLD PROBLEM

Two different approaches might be taken to unravel the continuing complexities in current obscenity law. The first would legalize obscenity, prohibiting only its exposure to juveniles and nonconsenting adults. The second approach would be to move the focus of obscenity law from sex to violence.

The first approach was proposed by Justice Brennan in 1973 in his dissenting opinion (expressing the views of a four-justice minority) in *Paris Adult Theater I v. Slaton.*[D] Brennan proposed that the law not be permitted "to suppress sexually oriented material on the basis of their allegedly 'obscene contents'" unless the material was distributed or obtrusively exposed to juveniles or nonconsenting adults. This approach protects the First Amendment right of free speech while avoiding the vagueness inherent in general tests for obscenity. A similar proposal was recommended by the U.S. Commission on Obscenity and Pornography in 1970.[E]

A second approach to obscenity law would be to prohibit the depiction of gratuitous *violence,* rather than sex.[F] Depictions of violent, assaultive behavior that are exhibited without legal justification would be held objectionable and punishable under law. The legal justifications for the use of force (e.g., self-defense, defense of others, etc.) are well defined in existing law, as are the definitions of assault. Such a test for obscenity might include photographs or broadcasts depicting assaultive behavior committed by persons without legal justification. The only exception would be factual accounts of real events, which have informational or educational value. This definition of obscenity would avoid the problems inherent in determining the level of "offensiveness" of depictions of sex and focus instead on *assaultive* depictions of conduct, making concern about depictions of sex secondary to concern about depictions of violence.

NOTES

[A] *Jacobellis v. Ohio,* 84 S. Ct. 1676 (1964).

[B] *Miller v. California,* 93 S. Ct. 1243 (1973).

[C] Joseph F. Kobylka, *The Politics of Obscenity* (Westport, CT: Greenwood Press, 1991).

[D] *Paris Adult Theatre v. Slaton,* 93 S. Ct. 2662 (1973).

[E] U.S. Commission on Obscenity and Pornography, *Report* (Washington, D.C.: U.S. Government Printing Office, 1970).

[F] Jay S. Albanese, "Looking for a New Approach to an Old Problem," in R. Muraskin and A. R. Roberts, eds., *Visions for Change: Crime and Justice in the Twenty-First Century, 2nd. ed.* (Upper Saddle River, NJ: Prentice Hall, 1998), pp. 60–72.

were fearful of being sued for false arrest if they arrested males who solicited prostitutes.[26] This tradition of differential application of the law against prostitution continues today: Women arrested on charges of prostitution are often placed on probation or given short jail sentences, while their male patrons are either fined or, more often, are not arrested at all.

During the last thirty years the rise of the women's movement and the National Organization for Women (NOW) has cast prostitution in a new light. NOW condemned the exploitation of women but in 1971 came out in favor of decriminalizing prostitution.[27] Nevada licenses prostitution on a county-by-county basis in jurisdictions with fewer than 400,000 residents, but other states have not followed suit. It appears that public sentiment still favors the criminalization of prostitution, although this may be due to the lack of noncriminal alternatives that do not appear immoral to a large segment of the public.

Media and Criminal Justice

THE PEOPLE VS. LARRY FLYNT

A cynical statement often made by politicians is "Where you sit depends on where you stand." This saying implies that there is a political and social aspect to controversial issues, and that perspective is the key to take a position on any issue. Once a stand is taken by an individual, however, that position will further influence others' regard for that person.

This focus on *perspective* is often used as the basis for debating what "crime" is and how it should be defined. While there is no question that crime is a political and social construct, there will always be debate over where precisely an offensive act, picture, or word crosses the line into "crime." The question of what constitutes "obscenity" is perhaps one of the most controversial issues facing our criminal justice system today.

Supreme Court Justice Potter Stewart admitted in a 1964 case that the justices were challenged with defining "what may be indefinable":

> [U]nder the First and Fourteenth Amendments criminal laws in this area are constitutionally limited to hard-core pornography. I shall not today attempt further to define the kinds of materials I understand to be embraced within that shorthand description; and perhaps I could never succeed in intelligibly doing so. But I know it when I see it. . . .[A]

The 1996 movie *The People vs. Larry Flynt* stirred new interest in this age-old controversy with its biographical portrayal of Larry Flynt, who rose to fame in the 1970s as the strip-club proprietor who created *Hustler* magazine. The movie presents the prurient side of the unapologetic smut-peddler, while also focusing on the legal war Flynt waged over his right to publish the magazine. Under his claim of free speech protection, Flynt not only went to trial, but was incarcerated. In 1978, he was shot and paralyzed by an unknown assailant, leaving him wheelchair bound to this day.

Larry Flynt, publisher of *Hustler* magazine, appearing in court in 1998 on charges that he and his brother sold sexually explicit photos at their Cincinnati store. The 1996 movie *The People v. Larry Flynt* depicts some of Flynt's previous legal battles related to the content of his magazine.

Larry Flynt (played by Woody Harrelson) says in the movie: "If the First Amendment will protect a scumbag like me, then it will protect all of you. Because I am the worst."

As the movie reveals, a real-life Southern Baptist minister named Reverend Jerry Falwell filed a $40 million lawsuit because he was offended by Flynt's offensive parodies in *Hustler.* Flynt's arguments pointed out the dangers of censorship: Any newspaper risks offending with its editorial cartoons that make fun of public officials. Op-ed columns risk offending every day. Negative reviews of films offend the producers.

(continued)

As the logic goes, Falwell's televised sermons must surely offend atheists.

The portrayal of Flynt's life and legal battles is more than a documentary, and perhaps less accurate than the true story. Perhaps the most important scene in the film is a spectacular sequence in which Flynt's character tries to drive home the point that there is a fine line between "acceptable" and "unacceptable" violence and obscenity.

Standing on a stage with a huge screen in the background, Flynt narrates as, behind him, images of pornography are interspersed with photos of horrific war atrocities in a mesmerizing mosaic of offensive pictures. His point is well taken: After several minutes of this graphic depiction of nudity, torture, and violence, it is hard to tell the difference between the photos. Which, Flynt asks, is more obscene? It is an outlandish act of defiance, and serves to successfully rally supporters—at least in the movie—to his free-speech cause.

The political nature of crime is further revealed when Flynt wears an American flag as a diaper in a court appearance (where the judge is played by the *real* Larry Flynt to further challenge the viewer's perspective). He wears rude-message T-shirts and throws oranges at the judge, defying convention at every opportunity and justifying his disorderly conduct as freedom of expression. The rhetorical question might be asked: Why is it legal and acceptable to wear a rude-message T-shirt on the street, but not in a court of law? Does it become illegal at the threshold of the courthouse door, or only when the judge is offended?

The issue of whether pornography is a mala in se crime or a mala prohibita crime clearly begs the question of perspective in defining crime, particularly in the context of its political and social realities. *The People vs. Larry Flynt* provides a fascinating and historical, even obscene and offensive, look at the "gray areas" of crime that hinge on political context and social perspective.

MEDIA AND CRIMINAL JUSTICE QUESTION

Given the continuing controversy over when depiction of sex cross the line of obscenity, at what point would *you* draw the line between legal and illegal depictions of nudity and sex? How would you defend your view?

NOTE

[A]A. T. Mason and D. G. Stephenson, *American Constitutional Law, Introductory Essays and Selected Cases,* 10th ed. (Englewood Cliffs, NJ: Prentice Hall, 1994), p. 419.

Gambling

Gambling encompasses games of chance, in which the outcome is determined by luck rather than skill. Like prostitution, gambling has existed throughout recorded history. Biblical accounts of the Crucifixion include an anecdote about four soldiers who each wanted Jesus' robe. They resolved the dispute by saying, "Let's not tear it; let's throw dice to see who will get it."[28] Gambling was also popular among the Native Americans: The Onondaga and the Iroquois wagered using dice.[29] The Narragansett and the Chumash often gambled for days in games in which "the worldly goods of entire tribes might change hands."[30]

Lotteries were the most popular form of gambling in the American colonies. The Virginia Company of London was given permission to conduct lottery drawings in England to help fund its plantation in Virginia, yet at the same time it attempted to reduce gambling in Virginia. Reports of "gaming, idleness, and vice" were rampant, and antigambling ordinances became part of Jamestown's first legal code.[31] Nevertheless, gambling remained popular.

This particular dichotomy, in which gambling was encouraged for one purpose (public funding) but viewed as dissolute for another (recreation), provides an early illustration of how attitudes toward gambling have vacillated throughout history. The Puritans of Massachusetts saw gambling as an "appearance of evil" and therefore irreligious.[32] Like Virginia, Massachusetts and other colonies passed laws that attempted to limit or prohibit gambling, but gambling (especially card and dice games) continued in spite of the laws.[33] During the early 1700s, when funds were needed for public works (e.g., schools and roads), many northeastern colonies started lotteries to raise the required funds. This provides another example of how gambling has been viewed as either a vice or a virtue, depending on how the profits are used.

The ability of lotteries to raise money, especially among a public that rebelled against taxation, increased their popularity. In fact, most of the Ivy League colleges were first endowed with funds from lotteries. By 1800, there were approximately 2,000 authorized lotteries, and they were growing in size and scope.[34] Horse racing, cards, and dice games were also popular from colonial times on. These games were somewhat more limited than lotteries because fewer people were able to participate in any one race or game, whereas lotteries involved entire towns or states or, on several occasions, the entire nation. Many early colonies and states prohibited horse racing and card and dice games, but their popularity led to widespread disregard of the law.[35]

Gambling includes all games of chance in which the outcome is determined by luck rather than skill. Gambling has a long history as an illegal vice and more recently as a leisure activity in government approved games that raise revenues without raising taxes.

Like the drinking of alcoholic beverages, gambling was widely criticized in public while privately enjoyed as a form of recreation or social intercourse. Unlike drinking, however, gambling could be employed for socially constructive purposes (e.g, lotteries to build roads), whereas drinking, prostitution, and narcotics had no redeeming social value. The fact that gambling could be used for constructive purposes distinguished it from other vices. Nevertheless, those who gambled for recreational purposes were criticized. Thomas Jefferson publicly argued that "gambling corrupts our disposition," yet he gambled in private. In fact, while he was composing the Declaration of Independence he made notations in his personal log about winning and losing at backgammon, cards, and bingo.[36] Benjamin Franklin manufactured playing cards.

Widespread interest and participation in lotteries, cards, dice, and horse racing led to the commercialization of these enterprises. The growth of gambling halls, casinos, lottery brokers, and professional gamblers resulted in numerous reports of fixed games and races, marked cards, loaded dice, and dishonest players and operators. In the mid-1800s, the public's negative reaction to these reports led to a series of reforms that changed the image of gambling. Because there was less confidence that gambling could be carried out honestly, it was prohibited in many places, and gambling halls and other commercial gaming enterprises were criminalized. Some gaming businesses were closed as a consequence, but "many moved underground and operated by bribing law enforcement officials."[37] Hence, the beginnings of organized crime's involvement in gambling can be seen as the result of a successful campaign by reformers to prohibit gaming enterprises. Policy games (or "numbers") were invented to satisfy those who remained interested in the lotteries after they were banned in many states.

The growing intolerance for gambling continued into the early 1900s, fueled by public figures and religious leaders. Reform administrations in Buffalo, Chicago, Cleveland, Denver, Detroit, New Orleans, New York, Pittsburgh, and San Francisco raided gambling operations. These local efforts prompted a number of states to go further in prohibiting gambling. By 1910, Arizona, New Mexico, and Nevada had passed laws that even banned card-playing at home. Other states passed laws that made it easier to prosecute illegal gaming operators.[38]

By the 1930s, however, legalized gambling was making a return as a permissible form of recreation (or vice). Horse racing returned through a pari-mutuel betting system regulated by the states in which the betting odds and winnings depended on the total amount wagered and the distribution of bets among the horses. Lotteries were still prohibited, but they were reemerging in an institution that formerly sought their prohibition: churches. During the Depression era, churches turned to bingo and other lottery games as a way to raise funds. By 1940, it was estimated that nearly 25 percent of all Americans gambled on church lotteries.[39]

A second step in the association of gambling enterprises with organized crime occurred during Prohibition. During the 1920s and 1930s, bootleggers of illegal alcohol became intertwined with providers of illegal gaming. As historian Mark Haller explains, bootleggers and gambling entrepreneurs originally coexisted, because their customers overlapped, especially at the speakeasies created by Prohibition. Bootleggers ultimately succeeded in infiltrating the illegal gambling industry because they were younger, more violent, and sought "coordination of the nightlife and commercialized entertainment of a city."[40] Therefore, bootleggers (who existed as a result of Prohibition) eventually became involved in illegal gambling (which existed as a result of changes in the law) as another profitable way to serve their customers. It was this predictable expansion of the illegal bootlegging market that began the associations of notorious criminals such as Al Capone, Lucky Luciano, and Bugsy Siegel with illegal gambling.

Public sentiment toward gambling has been marked by indifference. Despite periodic scandals and moral crusades, the "now it's legal, now it's not" history of gambling reflects public attention to the issue rather than indignation. Today gambling enjoys renewed popularity and legitimacy, largely as a way to boost local economies without raising taxes. Lotteries are legal once again in most states, and in a majority of the states casino gambling has been approved or is under active review. Like alcohol consumption, gambling is tolerated as a social vice largely because of the government's ability to profit from it (mostly through taxation). It appears that the only difference between legal and illegal gambling is whether or not the state is running the game.

Drug Use

Unlike gambling, narcotics distribution and use were generally not a crime until late in the nineteenth century. Although drug use was always considered a vice, during the 1800s the only laws that addressed the consumption of drugs were those that criminalized opium, which was associated almost exclusively with Chinese immigrants. Around the turn of the century, several states passed laws against morphine and cocaine use, but these laws were directed largely at pharmacists and physicians.[41]

The situation changed dramatically in the early twentieth century as intolerance for all the vices peaked. In 1914, Congress passed the Harrison Narcotic Drug Act, which added cocaine to the list of drugs whose use was subject to severe restrictions. Prohibition began in 1920, and during the following decade far fewer arrests were made for narcotics use than for violations of the liquor laws. However, evidence of continuing concern with narcotics can be seen in the es-

FUTURE ISSUES

Why We Buy Guns

Gun ownership is popular in the United States. It is estimated that Americans possess more than 200 million firearms, a number that is said to increase by two million each year.[A] Investigators have attempted to find out why gun ownership is so widespread in light of conflicting views and evidence regarding the degree to which possession of a gun either helps people protect themselves or increases the possibility of accidental or criminal harm.

People usually own guns for one of three reasons: sporting purposes, self-protection, or crime. To date, most surveys have addressed only the possession of guns for self-protection. For obvious reasons, it is difficult to determine whether a person owns a gun in order to commit a crime. People who own guns for sporting purposes have been largely overlooked in gun studies until recent years.[B] This group may own guns for reasons unrelated to concern about crime.

A survey in Cincinnati found that both sport and protective gun ownership are highest among men, people with military experience, and people who were socialized into acceptance of guns and trained in their use at an early age. Interestingly, it was found that those who believed that their neighbors would take steps to protect them were *less* likely to own guns. This **informal collective security** implies that as mutual reliance within a neighborhood increases, "the need for self-protection through guns decreases."[C] This suggests that gun ownership is not necessarily a response to crime, and that communities with strong informal social support do more to enhance the feeling of personal safety than does gun ownership. Debates about gun ownership therefore might be refocused on the need for neighborhood support.

It has been found that many people own guns for sporting purposes unrelated to concern about crime. Communities with strong informal social support and cohesion are more likely to enhance personal feelings of safety than does gun ownership.

FUTURES QUESTION

If it is true that "informal collective security" within neighborhoods increases residents' perceptions of safety, what strategies would you propose to increase this collective security within neighborhoods?

NOTES

[A]Gary Kleck, *Point Blank: Guns and Violence in America* (New York: Aldine de Gruyter, 1991).

[B]Beth Bjerregaard and Alan J. Lizotte, "Gun Ownership and Gang Membership," *Journal of Criminal Law and Criminology,* vol. 86 (1995), pp. 37–58.

[C]Liqun Cao, Francis T. Cullen, and Bruce G. Link, "The Social Determinants of Gun Ownership: Self-Protection in an Urban Environment," *Criminology,* vol. 35 (1997), pp. 629–57; see also John Hagan, *Crime and Disrepute* (Thousand Oaks, CA: Pine Forge Press, 1994).

tablishment of the Federal Bureau of Narcotics (FBN) in 1930. The FBN led the crusade to add marijuana to the list of dangerous narcotics, a crusade that ultimately resulted in the Marijuana Tax Act of 1937.[42]

informal collective security
When neighborhood residents believe that neighbors will take steps to protect them when necessary.

The prohibition of narcotics has continued ever since, highlighted by the formation of the Drug Enforcement Administration in 1973 and the creation in 1989 of the position of "drug czar" to head the Office of National Drug Policy. These initiatives further promoted the criminalization of narcotics, increasing the penalties for violations and emphasizing law enforcement approaches to controlling the problem. It is interesting that despite the moderation of public attitudes toward other vices during the late twentieth century, narcotics are now criminalized more extensively than at any time in the nation's history (with the exception of marijuana laws in a few states).

FIGURE 2.1

Past-month users of any illicit drugs, cocaine, and marijuana, 1985 to 1995

SOURCE: National Household Survey on Drug Abuse, National Institute on Drug Abuse (1985–91). Substance Abuse and Mental Health Services Administration (1992–95).

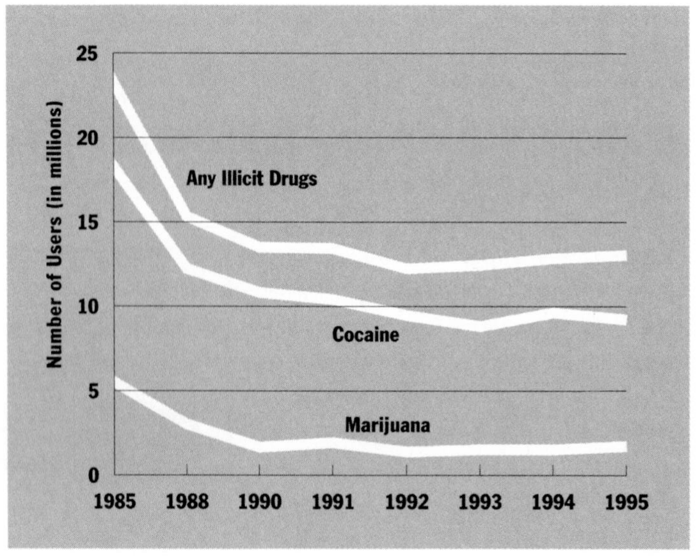

The evidence suggests that drug usage has decreased among most Americans in recent years but is much greater among the poor and addicted.[43] Figure 2.1 illustrates that approximately 6 percent of the population aged twelve and older (12.8 million people) used illegal drugs within the previous thirty days. Ten years earlier the number of drug users was twice that level. Ironically, the situation may well have been similar in the case of liquor usage during the Prohibition era. It is not clear that the intensive criminalization of narcotics has been responsible for changes in drug use, although it is undisputed that the illegal drug market has been exploited by organized crime, another unfortunate parallel to Prohibition. In the same way that alcohol use has declined in recent years as it has become a public health issue, drug use could also decline if it were defined in this way, rather than as a crime. In fact, several prominent conservatives have joined with liberals in advocating the legalization of drugs.[44] Legalization is unlikely to occur any time soon, however, since drugs still carry the same degree of stigma as prostitution. It is difficult to imagine elected representatives voting in favor of any kind of legalization plan as long as they are afraid to give the appearance of supporting drug use. Nevertheless, this stigma has been overcome in the case of gambling, so legalization of drugs may be a matter of time, combined with growing evidence of the ineffectiveness of police crackdowns, interdiction efforts, and eradication of drug production in source countries, as well as the high costs of long-term imprisonment.[45] It is interesting to speculate as to whether the contemporary war on drugs will be discussed seventy-five years from now in the same way that we speak of the Prohibition era seventy-five years ago.

Two problems of Prohibition during the 1920s mirror the impact of drug prohibitions in recent years: their impact on drug and alcohol use is not clear, and prohibition has helped organized crime dominate the illegal market.

In sum, the law reflects the moral views of society, but its purpose is to protect the public. The question remains: To what extent should undesirable behaviors be criminalized when they are engaged in consensually? We must be selective in the behaviors we choose to prohibit because overcriminalization can result in a cluttered, inefficient, and sometimes unjust criminal justice system.

Critical Thinking EXERCISE

Drug Use Forecasting

A government program consisting of urinanalysis and self-report information on drug use taken from a sample of arrestees in selected cities across the United States.

Drug Use Forecasting

The Drug Use Forecasting **(DUF) program began in 1987 under the auspices of the National Institute of Justice. The program consists of urinanalysis and self-report information taken from a sample of arrestees in twenty-four cities.[A] The self-report information consists of questions about the suspect's drug use history. The purpose of the program is to provide a measure of drug use among arrested crime suspects through systematic information about drug types, usage patterns, and trends over time.**

The information generated has been useful to policymakers, police, courts, and correctional agencies in understanding the scope of the problem and in the establishment and targeting of treatment programs to specific high-risk populations. The data have also been useful in increasing public knowledge and concern about the correspondence between drug use and crime.[B]

Figure 2.2 illustrates the extent of drug use among arrestees in the cities participating in the DUF program. On average, more than half of all arrestees test positive for drugs, a finding that holds true for both men and women. In many cities, more than 60 percent of arrestees test positive for drugs.

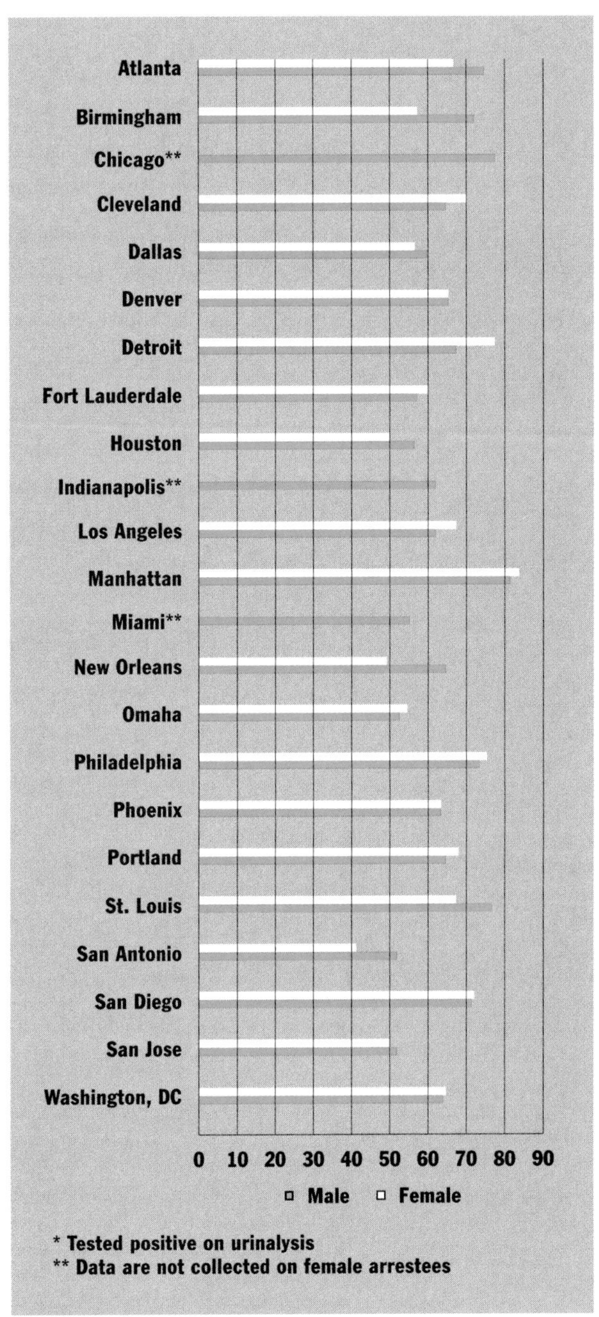

FIGURE 2.2

Drug use among booked arrestees, 1995

SOURCE: Drug Use Forecasting Program (Washington, D.C.: U.S. National Institute of Justice, 1996).

Critical Thinking Questions

1. **Why is it not necessarily true that the high incidence of drug use among arrestees means that drug use causes crime?**
2. **Is it fair for an arrestee to be forced to submit to urinanalysis before he or she has been convicted of a crime?**

Notes

[A]**Monique Smith, *Drug Use Forecasting: How Findings are Used* (Washington, D.C.: National Institute of Justice, 1993).**

[B]**Charles C. Foti, Jr., *The Effect of Drug Testing in New Orleans* (Washington, D.C.: National Institute of Justice, 1993).**

Critical Thinking EXERCISE

Binge Drinking

Despite the gains made in reducing alcohol-related traffic fatalities, other drinking behaviors remain a problem. Heavy episodic alcohol

use, or binge drinking, has been identified by the Harvard School of Public Health as "the single most serious public health problem confronting American colleges."[A]

In 1993, the Harvard Alcohol Study surveyed a nationally representative sample of college students and found that 44 percent were binge drinkers—the men reporting that they consumed five or more drinks in a row and the women four or more drinks in a row at least once in the two weeks before the survey. Twenty percent of students were found to be frequent binge drinkers, while only 16 percent abstained from drinking alcoholic beverages.[B] A 1997 follow-up survey found only a slight reduction in the proportion of binge drinkers (43 percent), and slight *increases* in both those who abstain (19 percent) and those who binge drink frequently (21 percent). A major predictor of college binge drinking was found to be students' alcohol use while in high school.

Binge drinkers in both the 1993 and 1997 surveys were at least five times more likely than non-binge drinkers to experience alcohol-related problems such as missing classes, fall behind in their work, forget where they were or what they did, get hurt or injured, damage property, or drive after drinking. In addition, there were secondhand effects of binge drinking on others, including having study or sleep interrupted (61 percent), having to take care of a drunken student (50 percent), or being insulted or humiliated (29 percent).

Despite the high level of public attention to responsible alcohol consumption in recent years, there appears to be little impact thus far on binge drinking by college students. For example, unchanged in the 1993 and 1997 surveys was the high rate at which residents of fraternities or sororities binge drink (81 percent).

Critical Thinking Questions

1. Why do you believe binge drinking by college students has not decreased, while alcohol consumption among the general public has declined?
2. What strategies do you believe would be effective in reducing binge drinking by college students?

Notes

[A]Henry Wechsler, George W. Dowdall, Gretchen Maenner, Jeana Gledhill-Hoyt, and Hang Lee, "Changes in Binge Drinking and Related Problems Among American College Students Between 1993 and 1997: Results of the Harvard School of Public Health College Alcohol Study," *Journal of American College Health,* vol. 47 (September, 1998), pp. 57–68.

[B]Henry Wechsler, George W. Dowdall, B. Moeykens, and S. Castillo, "Health and Behavioral Consequences of Binge Drinking in College: A National Survey of Students at 140 Campuses," *Journal of the American Medical Association,* vol. 272 (1994), pp. 1672–77.

Summary

ASPECTS OF CRIME

- As a society becomes larger and more complex, rules are required to ensure that citizens do not victimize or exploit one another.

- Forms of conduct that are prohibited by a society's rules are *crimes* and form the basis of *criminal law.*
- The criminal law punishes actions, not thoughts.
- The political nature of crime leads to efforts to criminalize or decriminalize certain behaviors, depending on public sentiment at the time.
- The Prohibition era showed that it is necessary to have true public support for laws if they are to be effective.
- *Mala in se* acts are considered evil in themselves, whereas *mala prohibita* offenses are the result of legislative decisions to prohibit certain undesirable behaviors.
- Mala prohibita offenses can be grouped into three categories: crimes without victims, political offenses, and regulatory offenses.

DISTINGUISHING OFFENSIVE FROM CRIMINAL BEHAVIOR

- Criminalization of drunk driving has had little effect on alcohol consumption.
- Efforts to eliminate prostitution have resulted in its displacement to other locations.
- Although gambling is widely viewed as a vice, it is also employed for socially constructive purposes.
- Criminalization of narcotics has expanded steadily during the twentieth century.

Key Terms

crime
criminal law
mala in se
mala prohibita
drug use forecasting
overcriminalization
informal collective security

Questions for Review and Discussion

1. What is the definition of a crime?
2. What is the role of intent in the definition of crime?
3. In what respects is crime political in nature?
4. What lessons can be drawn from the experience of Prohibition?
5. What is meant by the terms *mala in se* and *mala prohibita*?
6. What would be the possible effects of addressing alcohol and drug consumption as personal health issues rather than as crimes?
7. Why are men unlikely to be arrested for soliciting prostitutes?
8. How do governments justify the legalization of gambling in the form of lotteries and off-track betting?
9. What is meant by "overcriminalization"? Do you think this phenomenon has occurred in the United States?

Notes

[1]Rosabeth Moss Kanter, *Commitment and Community: Communes and Utopias in Sociological Perspective* (Cambridge, MA: Harvard University Press, 1972); Jay S. Albanese, *Justice, Privacy, and Crime Control* (Lanham, MD: University Press of America, 1984), pp. 46–56.

[2]Jay S. Albanese, "Tomorrow's Thieves," *The Futurist* (September–October 1988), pp. 24–8.

[3]William Preston, Jr., *Aliens and Dissenters: Federal Suppression of Radicals, 1903–1933* (Champaign: University of Illinois Press, 1963).

[4]Francis Russell, *Sacco and Vanzetti: The Case Resolved* (New York: Viking, 1986).

[5]Stanley I. Kutler, *The American Inquisition: Justice and Injustice in the Cold War* (New York: Hill & Wang, 1982).

[6]Melvin I. Urofsky, *A March of Liberty: A Constitutional History of the United States* (New York: McGraw-Hill, 1988), pp. 750ff.

[7]Lawrence M. Friedman, *Crime and Punishment in American History* (New York: Basic Books, 1993), p. 372.

[8]Steven E. Barkan, *Protectors on Trial: Criminal Justice in the Southern Civil Rights and Vietnam Antiwar Movement* (New Brunswick, NJ: Rutgers University Press, 1985).

[9]Friedman, p. 341.

[10]Mark H. Moore, "Actually, Prohibition was a Success," in R. L. Evans and I. M. Berent, eds., *Drug Legalization* (LaSalle, IL: Open Court Press, 1992).

Argues that Prohibition worked because of a decline in cirrhosis deaths during the early 1900s. The unreliability of the data and reporting methods of the period make both the statistics used and the conclusions drawn suspect.

[11]Ibid., p. 266.

[12]Jay S. Albanese, *Organized Crime in America,* 3rd ed. (Cincinnati: Anderson Publishing, 1996); Samuel Walker, *Popular Justice: A History of American Criminal Justice* (New York: Oxford University Press, 1980).

[13]Friedman, pp. 6–7.

[14]National Safety Council, *Accident Facts* (Washington, D.C.: National Safety Council, 1992).

[15]James B. Jacobs, *Drunk Driving: An American Dilemma* (Chicago: University of Chicago Press, 1989).

[16]Ibid., p. 48.

[17]Samuel Walker, *Sense and Nonsense about Crime and Drugs,* 3rd ed. (Belmont, CA: Wadsworth, 1994), p. 110.

[18]Jacobs, p. 47.

[19]H. Lawrence Ross, *Deterring the Drunk Driver,* revised ed. (Lexington, MA: Lexington Books, 1984).

[20]Ross, p. 33; Walker, p. 113.

[21]Ruth Rosen, *The Lost Sisterhood: Prostitution in America, 1900–1918* (Baltimore: Johns Hopkins University Press, 1982), p. 112.

[22]*Caminetti v. United States,* 242 U.S. 470 (1917); Marlene D. Beckman, "The White Slave Traffic: The Historical Impact of a Criminal Law Policy on Women," *Georgetown Law Journal,* vol. 72 (1984), p. 1111.

[23]Rosen, p. 15.

[24]Frederick K. Grittner, *White Slavery: Myth, Ideology and America Law* (New York: Free Press, 1990), pp. 150–65.

[25]Friedman, p. 331.

[26]George E. Worthington and Ruth Topping, "The Misdemeanant's Division of the Philadelphia Municipal Court," *Journal of Social Hygiene,* vol. 8 (1922), p. 22.

[27]Deborah Rhode, *Justice and Gender* (Cambridge, MA: Harvard University Press, 1989).

[28]Mark 15:24; Luke 23–34; John 19–24.

[29]Henry Chafetz, *Play the Devil: A History of Gambling in the United States from 1492 to 1955* (New York: Potter Publishing, 1960), p. 8.

[30]John Rosecrance, *Gambling without Guilt: The Legitimation of an American Pastime* (Belmont, CA: Brooks/Cole Publishing, 1988), p. 12.

[31]Ibid., pp. 12–3.

[32]Gilbert Geis, *Not the Law's Business* (New York: Schocken, 1979), p. 223.

[33]Chafetz, p. 17.

[34]Herbert Asbury, *Sucker's Progress: An Informal History of Gambling from the Colonies to Canfield* (first published in 1938) (Montclair, NJ: Patterson Smith, 1969), pp. 76–8.

[35]William H. P. Robertson, *The History of Thoroughbred Racing in America* (Englewood Cliffs, NJ: Prentice Hall, 1964), p. 8; Stephen Longstreet, *Win or Lose: A Social History of Gambling* (Indianapolis: Bobbs-Merrill, 1977).

[36]Longstreet, p. 37.

[37]Rosecrance, p. 23.

[38]Ibid., pp. 36–7.

[39]Ibid., p. 38.

[40]Mark H. Haller, "The Changing Structure of American Gambling in the Twentieth Century," *Journal of Social Issues*, vol. 35 (1979), p. 110.

[41]Friedman, pp. 137–8.

[42]David F. Musto, *The American Disease: Origins of Narcotic Control* (New York, 1973).

[43]Elliott Currie, *Reckoning: Drugs, the Cities, and the American Future* (New York: Hill & Wang, 1992).

[44]Kurt L. Schmoke, "Decriminalizing Drugs: It Just Might Work—and Nothing Else Does," in R. L. Evans and I. M. Berent, eds., *Drug Legalization* (LaSalle, IL: Open Court Press, 1992); Ethan A. Nadelmann, "Drug Prohibition in the United States: Costs, Consequences, and Alternatives," *Science*, vol. 245 (September 1989).

[45]Lawrence W. Sherman, "Police Crackdowns: Initial and Residual Deterrence," in M. Tonry and N. Morris, eds., *Crime and Justice: An Annual Review of Research* (Chicago: University of Chicago Press, 1990); U.S. Comptroller General, *Drug Control: Interdiction Efforts in Central America Have Had Little Impact on the Flow of Drugs* (Washington, D.C.: U.S. General Accounting Office, 1994); Samuel Walker, *Sense and Nonsense about Crime and Drugs*, 3rd ed. (Belmont, CA: Brooks/Cole, 1994), pp. 260–3.

For Further Reading

Jay S. Albanese, *Organized Crime in America*, 3rd ed. (Cincinnati: Anderson Publishing, 1996).

Lawrence M. Friedman, *Crime and Punishment in American History* (New York: Basic Books, 1993).

Jeffrey Reiman, *And the Poor Get Prison* (Boston: Allyn & Bacon, 1996).

U.S. Commission on Obscenity and Pornography, *Report* (Washington, D.C.: U.S. Government Printing Office, 1970).

chapter three

Measuring Crime

It is not the thief who is hanged,
but one who was caught stealing.

CZECH PROVERB

We are bombarded with reports of crime and violence nearly every day of our lives.

- Rap stars shot and killed for no apparent reason.
- More than sixty black church arsons with no known motive.
- Professional athletes stabbed and shot by stalking "fans."
- Child abuse cases rise to three million per year.
- Children who kill their parents are arrested in growing numbers.
- Brutal rapes involving acquaintances, spouses, and even children are reported more often.

Usually we read about it in the newspaper, see a report on television, or hear about it from friends; occasionally, we experience it ourselves. Judging from these sources, crime and violence are rampant. Rarely a day goes by without a news report about a senselessly violent murder, rape, or assault.

CHAPTER OUTLINE

It is difficult to know, however, whether crime and violence are actually increasing. Could the avalanche of crime news be due to more lurid reporting on more cable television channels and in more magazines, and exploitation by more politicians and more talk shows? If crime is really increasing, is it changing rapidly? How do current criminal incidents compare with those of the past? These important questions cannot be answered without an objective measure of rates of crime over time.

It is important to know the true extent of crime, for a number of reasons. First of all, people generally like to know the degree of risk they face so that they can evaluate for themselves how fearful or careful they should be. As the President's Crime Commission noted,

> **It is essential that society be able to tell when changes occur and what they are, that it be able to distinguish normal ups and downs from long-term trends. Whether the amount of crime is increasing or decreasing, and by how much, is an important question—for law enforcement, for the individual citizen who must run the risk of crime, and for the official who must plan and establish prevention and control programs.[1]**

As the Commission noted, policymakers also need to know the true extent of crime. Otherwise it is difficult to determine whether a program has achieved its goals.

Not all crimes are counted. The Federal Bureau of Investigation (FBI) tallies crimes reported to police and arrests made each year for eight types of offenses, and counts only arrests for nineteen other types of offenses. Although there are many other types of crime, most of the more serious forms of crime are included in the FBI's Uniform Crime Reports (UCR), discussed in the next section. The offenses for which detailed information is collected are criminal homicide, forcible rape, robbery, aggravated assault, burglary, larceny, motor vehicle theft, and arson; these constitute the FBI's Crime Index and therefore are known as Index crimes. The offenses for which only arrests are counted (known as Part II offenses) are simple assault; forgery and counterfeiting; fraud; embezzlement; buying, receiving, or possessing stolen property; vandalism; weapons offenses; prostitution and commercialized vice; other sex offenses; drug law violations; gambling; offenses against the family and children; driving under the influence; liquor law violations; drunkenness; disorderly conduct; vagrancy; curfew and loitering laws; and runaways.

The information in the UCR is of limited utility because it does not include data on people who commit crimes but are not apprehended. If, for the sake of argument, we assume that the number of people arrested for each offense approaches the number who actually commit that offense, arrest statistics can be used to show the most common types of crimes committed in the United States. Although this assumption may not be entirely justified, arrests provide at least some indication of which crimes are most problematic for society.

As it turns out, there has been little variation in the relative proportions of arrests for various crimes during the last twenty years. Table 3.1 illustrates how many people were arrested for each crime counted by the FBI during 1996. Several observations are apparent. First, the most common arrests are for relatively minor offenses. Driving under the influence, drunkenness, minor assaults, disorderly conduct, and liquor law violations account for more than a third of all arrests made by police each year. Second, the most serious crimes, such as arson, rape, and criminal homicide, appear to be the least common, judging from the number of arrests made. Third, while total arrests have tripled during the last twenty years (from 4.3 million to 15.1 million), the order of items in Table 3.1 has remained fairly constant. That is to say, the ten most common crimes today are the same as they were two decades ago.

Because serious crimes cause the most concern, despite their relative infrequency, definitions of the most serious offenses are presented here. (More extensive descriptions are provided later in the chapter.) These offenses can be categorized into two general groups: offenses against persons and offenses against property. The first four crimes (criminal homicide, forcible rape, robbery, and aggravated assault) involve violence against a person, whereas the latter four (burglary, arson, larceny, and motor vehicle theft) involve property.

Criminal homicide: All intentional killings (murder), as well as manslaughter (reckless or heat of passion killings), excluding suicide, negligent deaths, and justifiable homicide

Forcible rape: Sexual intercourse without effective consent

Robbery: Theft from a person using force or threat

Aggravated assault: A physical thrust against another person with intent to kill or cause severe bodily injury

Burglary: Unlawful entry into, or surreptitious remaining within, a building with intent to commit a crime inside that building

Arson: Intentional or reckless burning of property without the lawful consent of the owner

Larceny: Taking property from another person without using force or fraud, with intent to deprive the owner

Motor vehicle theft: Taking of a car, truck, or motorcycle without using force or fraud, with intent to deprive the owner

Equipped with an understanding of the common offenses for which people are arrested in the United States, and knowing the general direction of some of the more serious crimes committed, let us try to determine how often these crimes actually occur, whether or not someone is arrested for committing them.

TABLE 3.1

Frequency of Arrests in the United States

(numbers are rounded to the nearest thousand)

OFFENSES	NUMBER OF ARRESTS
1. Drug law violations	1,506,000
2. Larceny	1,486,000
3. Driving under the influence	1,467,000
4. Simple assault	1,329,000
5. Disorderly conduct	843,000
6. Drunkenness	719,000
7. Liquor law violations	677,000
8. Aggravated assault	522,000
9. Fraud	465,000
10. Burglary	365,000
11. Vandalism	321,000
12. Weapons offenses	216,000
13. Juvenile runaways	196,000
14. Loitering and curfew violations	185,000
15. Motor vehicle theft	175,000
16. Robbery	156,000
17. Stolen property	151,000
18. Offenses against the family	150,000
19. Forgery and counterfeiting	122,000
20. Prostitution	99,000
21. Other sex offenses (nonrape)	96,000
22. Forcible rape	33,000
23. Vagrancy	28,000
24. Criminal homicide	21,000
25. Gambling offenses	19,000
26. Arson	19,000
27. Embezzlement	16,000
Total arrests (1996)*	15,168,100

*There were nearly four million additional arrests for "other" nontraffic offenses.

SOURCE: Federal Bureau of Investigation, *Crime in the United States* (Washington, D.C.: U.S. Government Printing Office, published annually).

Trends in Crime Rates

The simplest questions are sometimes the most difficult to answer. One such question is, "Is the crime rate increasing or decreasing?" The only way to understand the difficulty of this question is to visualize a typical criminal incident. That description would portray an offender assaulting or stealing from a victim. Occasionally the police force would become involved, but usually only if the victim called them after the fact. A diagram of a typical crime of violence is presented

FIGURE 3.1
A typical crime against a person

in Figure 3.1. A diagram of a typical property crime would be similar, although it might substitute a house, garage, or purse for the person shown in Figure 3.1.

There are only three sources of information about the extent of crime because only three parties may be involved: offenders, victims, and police (in some cases witnesses may also be present). As Figure 3.1 illustrates, police are often involved after the fact. In addition, witnesses often are not available to provide an account of what occurred. Nevertheless, over the years attempts have been made to explore each of the three primary sources of information to see how well they capture the true extent of crime.

What the Police Say

In the United States, national crime statistics have been collected since 1930. Every time a crime is reported to the police, a notation of the incident is made. These incidents are compiled by local police and sent to the FBI in Washington, D.C. Each year, the FBI compiles these statistics and publishes them in its **Uniform Crime Reports** (UCR). Although this process was initiated in 1930 at the recommendation of the International Association of Chiefs of Police (IACP), it was not until 1958 that participation in this voluntary program by local (especially rural) police departments was sufficient to permit national crime estimates. The UCR now covers virtually all of the U.S. population.

Uniform Crime Reports
A compilation by the FBI of all crimes reported to the police in the United States.

There are, of course, many ways to count crime—by incident, victimization, arrest, conviction, and so forth. The Uniform Crime Reporting System collects information on *offenses known to police,* since these produce larger numbers than any other category or reportable crime information. Moreover, detailed information is collected for only seven types of offenses. Those types were selected on the basis of seriousness, frequency of occurrence, and likelihood of being reported to the police. They are criminal homicide, forcible rape, robbery, aggra-

contemporary issues

Drug-Abusing Women Offenders

Trends in crime are often reflected in arrest and incarceration trends. A national survey found that the majority of women arrested tested positive for at least one illicit drug, even though drug offenses account for only about 10 percent of the charges for which women are brought to court. This finding is supported by studies that show that many nondrug offenses for which women are arrested (i.e., burglary, fraud, larceny, and prostitution) are often committed to support drug habits.[A] Surveys of female arrestees and women in prison, or on probation and parole, have found remarkable results:

- *Health problems:* Many drug-abusing women are physically or mentally ill.[B]
- *Education and employment:* Most drug-involved women offenders are unemployed or have low-paying jobs. Most have not finished high school.[C]
- *Parenting:* Most drug-abusing women offenders are single mothers who receive little or no support from the children's fathers or other family members.[D]
- *Drug use history:* Most female offenders started using drugs at an early age, and many used drugs on a daily basis before their incarceration.[E]
- *Child neglect:* One study reported that 60 to 80 percent of child abuse and neglect cases came from substance-abusing families.[F]

A national survey of community-based programs for female offenders found that the long-term drug use that characterizes these women means that "a single treatment episode is rarely sufficient to produce more than limited short-term benefits."[G]

Even though only 10 percent of women brought to court are charged with drug offenses, the majority test positive for illicit drug use. Most have related problems regarding poor health, education, and parenting.

NOTES

[A]Y. I. Hser, C. Chou, and M. Douglas Anglin, "The Criminality of Female Narcotics Addicts: A Causal Modeling Approach," *Journal of Quantitative Criminology,* vol. 6 (1990), pp. 201–28.

[B]B. Daley and C. Przybycin, "Cocaine-Dependent Women Have Unique Treatment Needs," *Addiction Letter,* vol. 5 (1989).

[C]Jean Wellisch, M. Douglas Anglin, and Michael L. Prendergast, "Numbers and Characteristics of Drug-Abusing Women in the Criminal Justice System: Implications for Treatment," *Journal of Drug Issues,* vol. 23 (1993), pp. 7–30.

[D]P. Bekir, T. McLellan, A. R. Childress, and P. Gariti, "Role Reversals in Families of Substance Misusers: A Transgenerational Phenomenon," *International Journal of the Addictions,* vol. 28 (1993), pp. 613–30.

[E]See note C.

[F]H. Ramirez and C. Sosa, *Substance Abuse Forum Abstract* (Los Angeles County Department of Children's Services, 1991).

[G]Jean Wellisch, Michael L. Prendergast, and M. Douglas Anglin, *Drug-Abusing Women Offender: Results of a National Survey* (Washington, D.C.: National Institute of Justice, 1994), p. 6.

vated assault, burglary, larceny, and motor vehicle theft. Arson was added to the list in 1979. Taken together, these eight crimes are called the *Crime Index* inasmuch as they produce an indicator of the extent of serious crime in the United States. For these crimes, information on the age, sex, and race of suspects arrested on these charges is also collected.

The UCR also collects arrest data for nineteen other types of offenses, the "Part II" offenses mentioned earlier. Because the UCR collects only arrest information for those offenses (not all the instances reported to the police), their utility is limited in that we only know about offenders who are caught.

If the Uniform Crime Reports were our sole source of information about the true extent of crime, it is likely that our picture of the crime rate would be in-

The Uniform Crime Reports count all crimes reported to the police for eight crimes including criminal homicide, forcible rape, aggravated assault, robbery, burglary, larceny auto theft, and arson. The number of persons arrested are tallied for nineteen other offenses.

complete. First, only crimes reported to police are included in the UCR. As we will see, many crimes are not reported to the police. Changes in reporting procedures by local police departments also can produce "paper" increases in crime. History provides several clear examples of this phenomenon.

> **Perhaps the clearest illustration of the impact that changes in reporting systems can have is that shown by the history of such changes in New York City and Chicago. These cities are two of the nation's largest police jurisdictions, accounting in 1965 for 20 percent of all reported burglaries. Changes in their reporting systems have several times produced large paper increases of crime.**
>
> **Although Chicago, with about 3 million people, has remained a little less than half the size of New York City . . . it was reporting . . . about 8 times as many robberies as New York City until 1949, when the FBI discontinued publication of New York reports because it no longer believed them. In 1950 New York discontinued its practice of allowing precincts to handle complaints directly and installed a central reporting system, through which citizens had to route all calls.**
>
> **In the first year, robberies rose 400 percent and burglaries 1,300 percent, passing Chicago in volume for both offenses. In 1960 Chicago installed a central complaint bureau of its own, reporting thereafter several times more robberies then New York. In 1966 New York, which appeared to have had a sharp decline in robberies in the late fifties, again tightened its central controls and found a much higher number of offenses.[2]**

This problem of counting accurately still occurs today. In 1997, for example, the FBI announced that it was discarding the crime statistics submitted by the Philadelphia Police Department for the previous eighteen months. The statistics were inaccurate, and Philadelphia agreed to submit corrected figures to the *Uniform Crime Reports.*[3] In 1998, police officials in Atlanta, New York, and Boca Raton, Florida, were disciplined for falsely reporting crime statistics.[3a]

Another reason the UCR data may provide an incomplete summary of the extent of crime is that attempted crimes are included along with completed crimes. Moreover, the Index crimes do not provide an adequate representation of all serious crime. Corporate price-fixing, illegal dumping, and the manufacture of unsafe products are examples of crimes that cause harm and loss to a much greater extent than do the Index crimes, yet their impact is overlooked by the UCR system. (These more sophisticated crimes are discussed in detail in Chapter 17.)

The true extent of crime in the United States is a bit more difficult to determine than one might think. Table 3.2 provides a summary of crimes reported to police in the United States over a twenty-year period. This table, taken from the UCR, includes both the number of crimes reported to the police and the crime rate (i.e., number per 1,000 population). In 1973, for example, a total of 8,409,110 Index crimes were reported to the police. Twenty-three years later the number had increased to 13,473,580. The smaller numbers appearing under the reported offenses transform these numbers into rates. That is, the 2.5 million burglaries reported to police in 1996 meant that there were nearly 9.5 burglaries for every 1,000 people in the country.

crime rates
The number of crimes committed divided by the population at risk. This provides an indication of the risk of victimization per capita.

Crime rates are a much more reliable way to measure crime than mere numbers of crimes. This is because numbers do not account for changes in the pop-

TABLE 3.2

Serious Crimes Reported to Police in the United States

(number and rate per 1,000 population)

OFFENSES	1973	1980	1990	1996
Homicide	19,640 (0.094)	23,040 (0.102)	23,440 (0.094)	19,650 (0.074)
Rape	51,400 (0.245)	82,990 (0.368)	102,560 (0.412)	95,770 (0.361)
Robbery	384,220 (1.83)	565,840 (2.51)	639,270 (2.57)	537,050 (2.02)
Aggravated assault	420,650 (2.00)	654,960 (2.98)	1,054,860 (4.24)	1,029,810 (3.88)
Burglary	2,256,500 (12.2)	3,759,200 (16.8)	3,073,900 (12.4)	2,501,500 (9.43)
Larceny	4,347,900 (20.7)	7,112,700 (31.7)	7,945,700 (31.9)	7,894,600 (27.8)
Motor vehicle theft	928,800 (4.43)	1,114,700 (5.02)	1,635,900 (6.6)	1,395,200 (5.26)
Total U.S. population	209.9 million	225.3 million	249 million	265.3 million

SOURCE: Federal Bureau of Investigation, *Crime in the United States* (Washington, D.C.: U.S. Government Printing Office, published annually).

ulation, which can greatly affect the degree of risk faced by an individual. For instance, if there are one hundred people in your town and ten Index crimes were committed last year, your chances of being a victim (on average) would be one in ten. However, if your town has 1,000 people living in it and ten Index crimes are reported, the Uniform Crime Reports would show that the chances of being victimized in the first town are one in ten, but in the second town they are one in one hundred. Therefore, even though the numbers of crimes occurring are equivalent, the risk of being the victim of a crime can be very different, depending on the population of the jurisdiction.

Because the population of the United States has been increasing steadily (as displayed in the bottom row of Table 3.2), the use of mere numbers of crimes can be misleading. An actual example illustrates the point. Table 3.2 indicates that in 1973 there were 19,640 homicides reported to police in the United States. Twenty-three years later this number had grown to 19,650, an increase of 10. The 19,640 homicides in 1973 meant a rate of 0.094 per 1,000 people in the country (or 94 per 100,000 people). However, the 19,650 homicides in 1996 resulted in a *lower* homicide rate of 74 per 100,000. What this means is that, although the number of homicides increased slightly, the population grew proportionately faster than the number of homicides taking place. Table 3.2 indicates that the U.S. population grew from 209.9 million to 265.3 million over this twenty-three–year span, a greater rate of growth than the rate of increase in the number of homicides. As a result, there was a slight reduction in an individual's risk of being a victim of a homicide. When comparing changes in the extent of crime, therefore, it is important to rely only on crime rates, because they account for changes in the population at risk. Measuring risk, after all, is the purpose of counting crimes.

Until very recently, the measurement of crime was limited to crimes that were known to the police. However, it became apparent that not all crimes are reported. For example, some victims may fear embarrassment, public disclosure, or interrogation by the police. Some victims may know the offender and not want to inform police of his or her identity. For property crimes, a victim may feel that the value of the property taken is not worth the effort to get police involved. Some may not think the police can do anything about the crime. Further, some people simply fear or mistrust the police or are afraid of possible retaliation by the offender. Finally, some victims of crimes are engaging in criminal behavior themselves and therefore are reluctant to have any involvement with police. For all these reasons, it can be seen that police statistics, as collected by the Uniform Crime Reports, provide an incomplete picture of the true extent of crime.

What Victims Say

victimization
An incident in which a crime occurred against a victim. A representative sample of the U.S. population is surveyed annually to determine the extent of victimization and the extent to which these incidents were reported to police.

In 1967, the President's Crime Commission, recognizing the need for more accurate knowledge about the amount and kinds of crime, conducted the first national survey of crime **victimization.** A survey of 10,000 households (containing 33,000 people) was carried out in which people were asked whether they had been the victim of a crime during the past year and, if so, whether the crime had been reported to the police.

Since 1973, the National Crime Survey (NCS) has conducted interviews of more than 100,000 individuals from 50,000 households throughout the nation each year. People are asked to report anonymously whether they have been the victim of certain crimes during the past year. Participants in the survey are selected through a representative sampling of households across the country; every household therefore has an equal chance of being included in the survey. The findings are used to estimate the true extent of crime within a relatively small margin of error.

In each household, family members of at least twelve years of age are interviewed individually. These surveys elicit much more information than is gathered by the Uniform Crime Reports in that they include not only crime data but also information about the victim's age, sex, race, education level, and income; the extent of injury or loss suffered; any relationship with the offender; and whether or not the crime was reported to the police. As a result, victimization surveys have many more potential uses than do police statistics. To date, this information has been used for the following purposes:

1. To estimate the costs of victim compensation programs in determining whether such programs are economically feasible
2. To determine the kinds of special programs needed for elderly victims of crime, since their fear of crime remains high even though victimization rates are low among elderly citizens
3. To analyze the circumstance in cases of rape in order to better inform women about ways of preventing this crime[4]

Victimization surveys thus provide a great deal of information about criminal incidents that can serve as a basis for crime prevention programs.

Victimization surveys also provide a more complete picture of the risk posed by crime because they count both reported crimes and those not reported to police. For example, the 1967 survey consisted of interviews with 33,000 people and found only 14 rapes, 31 robberies, 71 aggravated assaults, 309 larcenies, and 68 motor vehicle thefts.[5] This shows that crime is relatively rare even when one counts crimes not reported to police. Since 1973, the sample has included 100,000 people and the survey has been conducted twice a year. The larger sample is used to ensure that enough crime is uncovered so that precise estimates can be made. By comparison, most public opinion polls interview a sample of less than 2,000 people to determine nationwide opinion on a particular subject. Fortunately, crimes are much less common than opinions.

While the Uniform Crime Reports collect a little information about all crimes known to police, victimization surveys collect extensive information about a representative sample of the population, whether or not the victimization was reported. The results of these surveys therefore are accurate within a specified degree of error.

When victimization surveys were first tested, there was concern about whether citizens who were interviewed would be truthful about their victimization experiences. To address this concern, pretests were conducted in Baltimore, San Jose, and Washington, D.C., in 1970 and 1971. In these test surveys, a sample of known victims were taken from the police files and interviewed (this is called a "reverse record check"). It was thought that if known victims did not report known crimes to interviewers, it was unlikely that unreported crimes would be shared with interviewers either.

A total of 983 victims in the three cities were selected from police files and interviewed. Overall, more than 70 percent of known assault, robbery, rape, burglary, or larceny victims reported their victimizations to the interviewers. Burglaries were reported to interviewers nearly 90 percent of the time, while fewer than 50 percent of assault victims reported the incident.

Individuals who failed to report a known crime were subsequently asked why they had not told the interviewer about it. Among the reasons given was forgetting. Crimes that had occurred up to three months before the interview were reported to interviewers 81 percent of the time, whereas crimes that had occurred ten to twelve months earlier were reported only 67 percent of the time. (As a result of this finding, victimization surveys are now conducted twice a year, using six-month reference periods.) It was also found that personal crimes of violence (rape, robbery, assault) committed by someone known to the victim were less likely to be reported than crimes committed by a stranger. For example, 84 percent of rapes by a stranger were reported to interviewers, as opposed to 54 percent of those committed by a nonstranger. Needless to say, there are other methodological issues involved in the administration of victimization surveys, but the important ones are those noted here.[6]

Like the Uniform Crime Reports, victimization surveys collect information about forcible rape, robbery, assault, burglary, larceny, and motor vehicle theft. (Murder victims, obviously, are not included in victim surveys.) For victimization surveys, forcible rape is defined in the same manner as it is for the Uniform Crime Reports, although the UCR counts only rapes of females. The NCS victimization surveys, however, count both simple (minor) assaults and aggravated assaults, while the UCR counts only aggravated assaults.

The crimes of robbery, burglary, larceny, and motor vehicle theft are counted somewhat differently in victimization surveys than they are in the Uniform Crime

TABLE 3.3

Crime Victimization in the United States

(number and rate per 1,000 population)

OFFENSES	1973	1980	1990	1996
Rape	156,000 (1.0)	174,000 (0.9)	130,000 (0.6)	98,000 (0.4)
Robbery	1,108,000 (6.7)	1,209,000 (6.6)	1,150,000 (5.7)	1,134,000 (5.2)
Aggravated assault	1,622,000 (10.1)	1,707,000 (9.3)	1,601,000 (7.9)	1,910,000 (8.8)
Household burglary	6,459,000 (91.7)	6,973,000 (84.3)	5,148,000 (53.8)	4,845,000 (47.2)
Larceny from the person	14,970,000 (91.1)	15,300,000 (83.0)	12,975,000 (63.8)	21,120,000 (205.7) (all larcenies)
Household larceny	7,537,000 (107.0)	10,490,000 (126.5)	8,304,000 (86.7)	Combined with other larcenies beginning 1993
Motor vehicle theft	1,344,000 (19.1)	1,381,000 (16.7)	1,968,000 (20.5)	1,387,000 (13.5)

SOURCE: Lisa D. Bastian, Craig Perkins, Patsy Klaus, and Cheryl Ringel, *Criminal Victimization* (Washington, D.C.: Bureau of Justice Statistics, published annually).

Reports. The UCR counts these crimes whether the victim is a private individual or a commercial establishment. Since victim surveys include only households, however, commercial robberies, burglaries, larcenies, and motor vehicle thefts are not counted. Therefore, bank and store robberies, nonresidential burglaries, and larcenies from commercial establishments are omitted from victim survey estimates. Further, the UCR definition of motor vehicle theft includes snowmobiles and golf carts, but the NCS victimization surveys do not.

Despite these differences, there is a fairly close correspondence between the definitions used in the UCR and victim surveys. As a result, it is possible to gather nationwide crime information from two points of view: that of the victim and that of the police.

Table 3.3 is a summary of nationwide victimization rates over a twenty-three-year period. As in the Uniform Crime Reports, both numbers of crimes and rates of victimization are presented. For example, the victimization surveys estimate that 1,108,000 robberies occurred in the United States in 1973. This means that there were approximately 6.7 robberies for every 1,000 citizens in the nation. In 1996, there were an estimated 1,134,000 million robberies, an increase of 26,000 robberies over twenty-three years. Nevertheless, **personal risk** declined to 5.2 robberies per 1,000 citizens because the population increased at a higher rate than the number of robberies. The risk of being a robbery victim therefore declined by 22 percent. Once again, it can be seen that the use of raw numbers of crimes is misleading because they provide no indication of changes in degree of personal risk.

personal risk
The purpose of measuring crime is to assess personal risk. This can be determined only through knowledge of crime rates.

Reconciling the Differences

A comparison of the extent of crime as reported in police statistics and victim surveys reveals significant differences. For instance, the Uniform Crime Reports in-

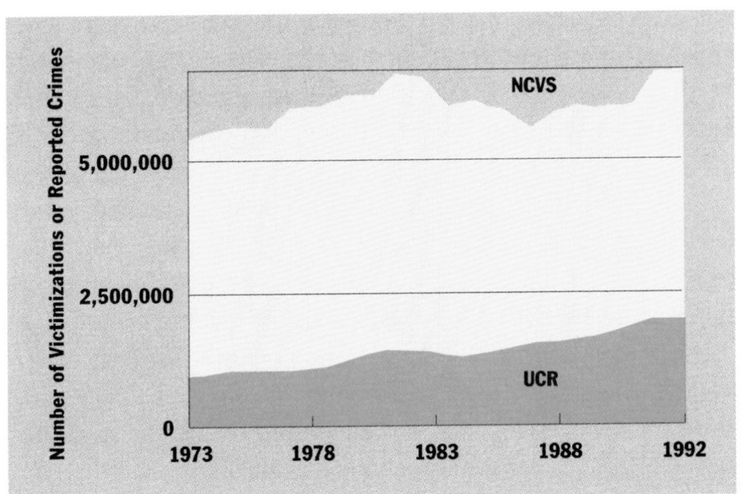

FIGURE 3.2

The volume of violent crime as measured by police statistics and victimization surveys

SOURCE: Marianne W. Zawitz et al., *Highlights from 20 Years of Surveying Crime Victims* (Washington, D.C.: Bureau of Justice Statistics, 1993).

FIGURE 3.3

Comparative frequency of crimes

SOURCE: Marianne W. Zawitz et al., *Highlights from 20 Years of Surveying Crime Victims* (Washington, D.C.: Bureau of Justice Statistics, 1993).

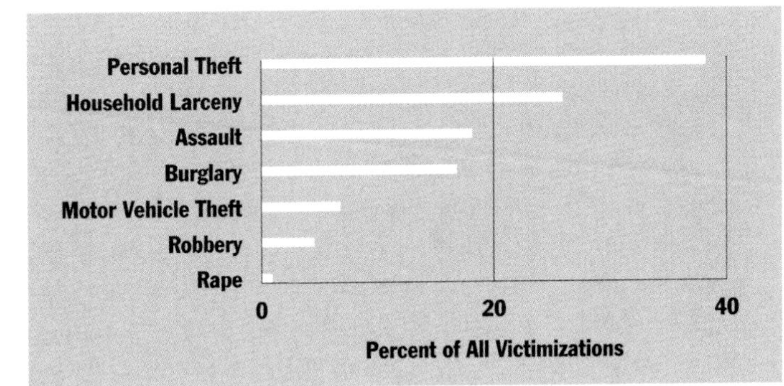

dicate that there were 95,770 reported cases of forcible rape in 1996, while victim surveys show 98,000 rapes, or 2,230 additional rapes. There were 537,050 reported robberies in 1996; victim surveys uncovered 1,134,000 robberies, more than double the number reported to police. The same is true for all the other crimes counted by both the UCR and victimization surveys. In every instance, victim surveys show that there is anywhere from 20 to 300 percent more serious crime than police statistics indicate. Taken as a whole, victim surveys annually uncover two to three times more crime than is reported in the Uniform Crime Reports. This is clearly one of the most significant findings of the victim surveys.

As Figure 3.2 illustrates, the volume of violent crime discovered from interviews with the general public is much greater than the volume reported to police. The same is true for property crimes, as can be seen from the data presented in Tables 3.2 and 3.3.

Nevertheless, violent crime is far less common than property crime. Approximately 80 percent of all the victimizations uncovered by victimization surveys are some form of larceny or burglary. Crimes against persons (rape, robbery, assault) constitute the remainder of the victimizations. This difference is displayed in Figure 3.3.

Table 3.4 provides a major part of the explanation for these differences. Victimization surveys reveal that, overall, 36 percent of all the crimes they count are reported to police, a percentage that has generally been increasing over the years. Therefore, police statistics provide a very incomplete picture of the true extent of serious crime in the United States. Larceny is the crime least likely

TABLE 3.4

Victimizations Reported to Police

TYPE OF CRIME	PERCENT REPORTED IN 1973	PERCENT REPORTED IN 1996
Crimes of violence (total)	46	41
Rape	49	32
Robbery	52	55
Aggravated assault	52	52
Simple assault	38	36
Crimes of theft		
Larceny	24	27
Household burglary	47	50
Motor vehicle theft	68	78
All crimes above (weighted average)	32	36

to be reported (about 27 percent of the time), while motor vehicle theft is the crime most likely to be reported (about 78 percent of the time). The high rate of reporting of auto theft is undoubtedly due to mandatory automobile insurance, which usually requires that a police report be submitted before the owner can make a claim.

The reasons for not reporting crimes to the police have been found to vary according to the nature of the crime. Figure 3.4 presents the reasons given in victimization surveys. The most common reasons for not reporting violent crimes are that the victim saw the incident as a private matter or that the offender was not successful in his or her attempt. The most common reasons for not reporting thefts are that the object was recovered, proof was lacking, the offender was unsuccessful, or the incident was reported to someone other than the police. For household crimes, the reasons are the same as those for thefts, with the additional reason that 10 to 12 percent of victims believed the police would not want to be bothered.

Crime	Most Frequent Reasons for Reporting Crimes To the Police
Violent Crime	
Rape	Prevent further crimes by offender, 23% Punish offender, 12% Prevent crime by offender against anyone,* 12%
Robbery	Recover property, 20% Prevent further crimes by offender, 12% Catch or find offender, 11%
Aggravated assault	Prevent further crimes by offender, 20% Stop or prevent this incident, 15% Because it was a crime, 14%
Simple assault	Prevent further crimes by offender, 25% Stop or prevent this incident, 17% Because it was a crime, 11%
Theft	
Personal larceny with contact	Recover property, 36% Because it was a crime, 18% Stop or prevent this incident, 9%
Personal larceny without contact	Recover property, 29% Because it was a crime, 19% Collect insurance, 9%
Household Crime	
Burglary	Recover property, 20% Prevent further crimes by offender, 13% Because it was a crime, 12%
Household larceny	Recover property, 27% Because it was a crime, 15% Prevent further crimes by offender, 11%
Motor vehicle theft	Recover property, 36% Because it was a crime, 12% Collect insurance, 12%

*Estimate is based on 10 or fewer sample cases.

FIGURE 3.4

Reasons why crimes are not reported to police

SOURCE: Marianne W. Zawitz et al., *Highlights from 20 Years of Surveying Victims* (Washington, D.C.: Bureau of Justice Statistics, 1993).

Another explanation of differences between UCR and victim survey findings lies in the way they count crimes. The UCR counts crimes against persons of any age, but victim surveys count personal victimizations (rape, robbery, assault) of individuals aged 12 and older. The reason for the exclusion of young people is that a primary purpose of crime statistics is to provide an indication of personal risk, and the chances of children being the victim of one of the crimes measured is very small. Also, young children are not reliable interview respondents. For purposes of consistency, however, victimization rates for personal crimes are computed for the total population over 12 years old. In this way victimization rates are not biased by the exclusion of young children.

TABLE 3.5

Crime Trends in the United States, 1973–1996

(rate per 1,000 population)

OFFENSES	UNIFORM CRIME REPORT	VICTIMIZATION SURVEYS
Homicide	−21%	n/a
Rape	+47%	−60%
Robbery	+10%	−22%
Aggravated assault	+94%	−13%
Burglary	−23%	−49%
Larceny (total)	+35%	−13% (1993–96 only)
Motor vehicle theft	+19%	−29%

SOURCE: Compiled from *Uniform Crime Report* and *Criminal Victimization* (published annually by the Federal Bureau of Investigation and Bureau of Justice Statistics, respectively).

Still another reason that UCR and victim survey crime statistics are not directly comparable is that the UCR computes property crime rates for the total population whereas victim surveys calculate property crime rates for the total number of households. For example, victimization surveys found that 4,845,000 household burglaries occurred in 1996. When computing the burglary rate, it makes little sense to compute this number for the total population because people cannot be burglarized. The only populations at risk for burglary are households and businesses. Therefore, burglary rates logically should be calculated for the total number of places able to be burglarized, which, in the case of victim surveys, is the total number of households.

Although the UCR and victimization surveys differ somewhat in the way they count crime, each is internally consistent. Therefore, it is possible to examine crime trends over a period of years. Table 3.5 summarizes trends in crime over twenty-three years beginning in 1973, when national victimization surveys were first conducted.

Table 3.5 makes it clear that police statistics indicate a dramatic rise in the rate of most crimes reported to police from 1973 to 1996. Only homicide and burglary show decreases, while the rates of other crimes have increased from 10 percent (robbery) to 94 percent (aggravated assault). Victimization surveys show a nearly opposite picture of crime trends: a decrease for every crime. The decreases in crime rates range from 13 percent (for robbery and larceny)[7] to a decrease of 60 percent (rape).

Both of these measures cannot be correct, and for the reasons given earlier, the crime figures provided by victimization surveys are the most accurate. The primary reason for this, of course, is that the UCR counts only crimes reported to the police, while victim surveys count both those reported and those not reported.[8]

What Offenders Say

A third possible source of information about the extent of crime is the offenders themselves. Efforts to conduct "self-report" surveys of offenders date from the

1940s.[9] The first studies attempted to identify differences between offenders who were caught and those who were not apprehended. Many subsequent self-report studies have been undertaken, but most use small samples of juveniles rather than representative samples of the entire U.S. population, as victimization surveys do.[10]

When one compares information from self-reports with crimes reported to police, several significant differences are apparent. Most important and consistent among the findings of the self-report studies are that virtually all juveniles break the law at one time or another, although only 10 to 20 percent are caught and arrested. Only a small proportion of all youth, however, engage in serious or frequent criminal behavior. Self-reports have also discovered that offenders are more evenly distributed by race and social class than police statistics would suggest.

There have been only two national self-report surveys, and these were limited to young people.[11] These surveys, like most self-reports, were designed to investigate the causes of delinquency, rather than estimate national crime trends.[12] These surveys usually do not include questions about many serious crimes, owing to the reluctance of respondents to report their involvement in such crimes. Therefore, they are weighted toward less serious offenses such as alcohol and drug use, truancy, and simple assaults. Also, the administration of self-reports has been confined mostly to schools, an environment that excludes some of the most serious and frequent offenders.

To date, self-reports have dealt primarily with characteristics of offenders. Questions could be added about victim selection, relationship, and description. Answers to these questions would help in developing crime prevention programs that aim to raise public awareness of the causes of victimization.

Crimes against Households

When one examines crimes against households (i.e., apartments and homes), victimization surveys can provide a precise estimate of risk. A household touched by crime is one that was victimized by burglary or theft, or in which a household member was robbed, raped, or assaulted, or from whom property was stolen (no matter where the crime occurred). Approximately 23 percent of households in the United States are touched by crime, and less than 5 percent of the incidents involve serious violent crimes. This reflects a steady decline in the risk of victimization since 1975, when these statistics were first gathered. Table 3.6 summarizes

TABLE 3.6

Percentage of Households Victimized by Crime

OFFENSES	1975	1992	1995
Violent crimes (rape, robbery, assault)	5.8%	5.0%	2.6%
Burglary	7.7%	4.2%	4.1%
Theft (from person or household)	26.6%	16.9%	16.4%
Motor vehicle theft	1.8%	2.0%	1.5%
Total (any crime above)	32.1%	22.6%	23.4%

SOURCE: Michael R. Rand, *Crime and the Nation's Households, 1992* (Washington, D.C.: Bureau of Justice Statistics, 1993) and Carol J. DeFrances and Steven K. Smith, *Perceptions of Neighborhood Crime, 1995* (Washington, D.C.: Bureau of Justice Statistics, 1998).

A household touched by crime is one that suffered a burglary or theft, or in which a household member was robbed, raped, or assaulted. The proportion of households touched by crime has dropped from one third to less than one fourth from the 1970s to the 1990s.

these changes. In 1975, approximately one in three households were touched by crime (6 percent involving violence). Twenty years later, fewer than one in four households were victimized.[13] Despite the increase in the total number of households, from 73.1 million in 1975 to 101.5 million in 1995, the risk of both violent and property crimes against household members dropped. In fact, the level of risk in 1995 was at its lowest point since the inception of this measure of victimization in 1975. Naturally, individual risk is affected greatly by place of residence, income, and size of household, but for the nation as a whole the risk of victimization has declined steadily over the past twenty years.

Violent Crimes

The violent crimes of homicide, rape, robbery, and assault lie at the heart of the public's fear of crime. Even though these constitute only 13 percent of all Index crimes reported to police, they can involve serious injury or death and are greatly feared. The crimes of rape, robbery, and assault comprise nearly 20 percent of all crimes counted by victimization surveys (whether reported or not). Essential information about these crimes includes the specific types of actions they incorporate and exclude, as well as the nature of the circumstances under which they occur. In this section we describe each of these categories of crime in detail.

criminal homicide
Murder or manslaughter.

murder
All intentional killings, as well as deaths that occur in the course of dangerous felonies.

Homicide

Criminal homicides include both murder and manslaughter. **Murder** includes all intentional killings, as well as deaths that occur in the course of dangerous felonies. A person who robs someone on the street, who dies from the shock, would be held liable for felony murder because he or she caused a death in the course of a dangerous felony. Likewise, if one aims to shoot a person but misses and kills his girlfriend instead, one is liable for murder for her death even though there was no intent to kill her. This is because a person's life was *intentionally* taken without lawful justification. All the elements of the crime are fulfilled. The law does not punish a person less severely because he or she is a poor shot.

manslaughter
A mitigated murder: causing a death recklessly, or intentionally under extenuating circumstances.

Manslaughter is a mitigated murder. It involves causing death recklessly or intentionally under extenuating circumstances. An example of a reckless death would be killing a pedestrian with one's car while drunk or speeding. In law, recklessness is conscious disregard of a substantial and unjustifiable risk. In this example, a reasonable person would know that it is difficult to control an automobile properly when one is speeding or drinking. This "reasonableness" standard is used throughout the criminal law to assess the culpability of an individual's conduct. Reckless manslaughter is punished less seriously than murder owing to the lower state of mind involved (recklessness versus intention).

Recklessness is distinguished from negligence, which is failure to be aware of a substantial and unjustifiable risk. Negligence is not subject to criminal prosecution, although a person can be sued in civil court for damages suffered as the result of negligent conduct.

There is a middle ground between negligence and recklessness called gross negligence. Gross negligence is failure to perceive a substantial and unjustifiable risk that is a "gross deviation" from the standard of care of a reasonable person. It is usually applied in cases involving fatal car accidents in which conduct, such as speeding, is not seen as serious enough to constitute recklessness but is more blameworthy than the negligence standard, to which only civil penalties apply. Gross negligence is the borderland of the criminal state of mind and is the least severely punished form of criminal homicide.

There are very limited circumstances in which intentional killings are punished as manslaughter rather than as murder. These circumstances are of two types: "heat of passion" killings and imperfect self-defense.

So-called heat of passion killings reduce murder to manslaughter only when the offender responds to an unlawful act in the sudden heat of passion (without time to cool off). Imperfect self-defense occurs when a person kills another while responding to an unlawful act with excessive or unnecessary force. If a husband walks in on his wife in bed with someone else and shoots her, he has responded to an unlawful act (adultery) with excessive force (death is not the penalty for adultery). Heat of passion cases often occur in troubled marital or cohabitation situations.[14] Reduction of a charge from murder to manslaughter only reduces the length of the possible sentence; it does not excuse the conduct.

The incidence of criminal homicide does not fluctuate widely. As Table 3.5 indicates, the *number* of homicides has fluctuated over the years, but between 1973 and 1996 the *rate* dropped owing to proportional increases in the population. Therefore, a person's risk of being the victim of a criminal homicide is slightly less today than it was two decades ago.

More than two-thirds of homicides are committed with guns and 13 percent with knives. According to the FBI, about 25 percent of all criminal homicides (in which the circumstances are known) are related to the commission of a felony, such as robbery that results in death. Nearly 45 percent of all homicides result from arguments, romantic triangles, and drug or alcohol-influenced brawls.[15]

Sexual Assault

Rape is sexual intercourse without effective consent. The term *sexual assault* is often used in order to accommodate homosexual rape; it includes both rape (forced vaginal intercourse) and sodomy (forced oral or anal sex). Victimization surveys include sodomy, and in the future the Uniform Crime Reports will include it in the definition of rape.

rape
Sexual intercourse without effective consent.

Intercourse is defined as any penetration, however slight. Any kind of physical force, including "terrorizing of the senses," suffices to establish lack of consent. Effective consent also is not present if the victim is a minor, mentally ill, mentally retarded, or physically helpless.

Statutory rape is nonforcible sexual intercourse with a minor, an offense that the law provides as a way of protecting young people from exploitation by older ones. Statutory rape is not included in the UCR or victimization surveys because of its consensual nature.

statutory rape
Nonforcible sexual intercourse with a minor.

According to victimization surveys, rapes of males accounted for 8 percent of all rapes. (Since victimization surveys are conducted among the general public, sexual assaults among the prison population are not included in this number.) In half of all cases of rape of a female, the victim knew the offender; in only 20 percent of all cases did the offender brandish a weapon. Just over half of female rape victims reported the incident to the police, a fact that was related to the presence of a weapon or injury rather than to the existence of a prior relationship. Interestingly, most female victims who fought back through words or actions believed that their efforts helped the situation rather than aggravating it.[16]

Assault

Simple assault is distinguished from aggravated assault by the nature of the offender's intent. **Simple assault** is a thrust against another person with the intention of injuring that person. **Aggravated assault** contains all these elements in addition to the intention to cause serious bodily harm or death. A "thrust" can be a punch, a gunshot, a threatening action that causes fear and anxiety, or any form of "offensive touching." Assault has been charged in cases involving spitting at another person and in cases involving fondling an individual without his or her consent. Aggravated assault is a felony; simple assault is punished less severely, as a misdemeanor.

simple assault
A thrust against another person with the intention of injuring that person.

aggravated assault
A thrust against another person with the intention to cause serious bodily harm or death.

Victimization surveys include data on simple assaults, accounting for some of the difference in the rates of assault reported in victim surveys and the Uniform Crime Reports. Still, aggravated assault is the most common crime of violence, accounting for more than 1 million reports to the police each year and more than 500,000 arrests.[17]

More than 20 percent of assaults of all kinds occur at or near the victim's home. Only about 7 percent occur inside a bar, restaurant, or nightclub. Only a third of aggravated assaults involve a gun; blunt objects cause more injury in assaults than any other type of weapon. As in the case of rape, more than 70 percent of victims who used words or actions in self-defense felt that their efforts helped the situation.[18]

Robbery

robbery
A theft from a person using threats or force.

Robbery is a combination of two other crimes: larceny (theft) and assault. It consists of theft from a person using threats or force. If only threats are employed, they must be serious enough to fulfill the element of assault in the crime of robbery. The threat must also involve *immediate* harm, precluding the victim from calling the police or taking other action to prevent the crime. Also, the number of victims in a given robbery incident determines the total number of robbery charges that can be brought against a defendant. Robbery is punished according to the amount of force used.

After assault, robbery is the most common violent crime. It provokes high levels of fear because 80 percent of robberies are committed by strangers. Approximately half of all robberies are committed by armed offenders (using guns about half the time). Nearly 35 percent of robbery victims are physically injured, although, again, most of those who used words or actions to resist their attacker believed that it helped.[19]

Property Crimes

Crimes against property account for the overwhelming majority (80–90 percent) of all serious crimes. It seems that stealing by stealth is more common than any other predatory crime. As a greater proportion of citizens have come to own more property of more kinds, burglary and larceny have come to be regarded as more serious crimes. The three main types of property crimes are burglary, larceny, and arson.

Burglary

burglary
Unlawful entry into a building in order to commit a crime while inside.

Burglary is unlawful entry into a building in order to commit a crime while inside. No breaking or force is required as long as the offender's presence is unlawful (i.e., involves trespass). In a case in Buffalo, a person entered a store during regular business hours and hid there when the store closed. Once everyone had left, he shopped at his leisure in the empty store, leaving his selections in a bin near the loading dock. When the store reopened in the morning, he planned to pose as a new customer and simply leave through the back door. However, a security guard noticed his selections by the loading dock and was waiting for him as he attempted to leave. In this case the person's entry into the store was legal, but he remained behind surreptitiously, making his action criminal trespass.

Burglaries of dwellings cause the greatest concern. Most burglaries have theft as their object, but burglaries can also occur for the purpose of assault. As was noted earlier, about five million household burglaries take place each year, representing about 4 percent of all U.S. households. Therefore, the odds of occurrence of household burglary are low. Only 30 percent of burglaries result in losses of $500 or more. More than 70 percent of burglaries with forced entry are reported to police, whereas only 42 percent of entries without force are reported.[20]

Larceny

larceny
Taking property of another person with the intent of depriving the owner.

Larceny is the most commonly occurring serious crime in the United States. It consists of taking the property of another person with the intent of depriving the owner. If force is used in a larceny, it becomes robbery. If deceit or trickery is used, the larceny becomes fraud, forgery, or embezzlement. The intention to deprive the owner is important because moving companies take people's property all the time, as do valets, dry cleaners, and people who borrow books from libraries. Their conduct does not constitute larceny because there is no intention to *deprive* the owner. Instead, the property is borrowed or loaned for a short period, usually in exchange for a service. Consent by the owner of the property is an absolute defense against charges of larceny.

The slightest movement of property can also be defined as "taking" under the law. If shoppers stuff silk underwear under their jackets but are stopped before leaving the store, they have "taken" the property and can be charged with larceny (even though they never made it out the door).[21] Treating the silk underwear in a manner inconsistent with the buyer's right to inspect merchandise and the store's ownership of the property constitutes larceny in this case.

More than twenty million larcenies occur each year; eight million of them involve property taken from households. Only about 333,000 involve pickpockets, while 152,000 involve purse snatchings. Larceny from the person without contact is the offense least likely to be reported to police, according to victimization surveys. The total loss from larceny each year is approximately $5.4 billion.[22]

Arson

arson
Burning property of another without the lawful consent of the owner.

Arson is burning of property without the lawful consent of the owner. As in the case of larceny, the lawful consent of the owner is an absolute defense against a charge of arson. Consent can be unlawful if the owner is a minor or mentally incompetent, or if consent is given with the intent of defrauding an insurance company.

Accidental fires do not constitute arson, although the law holds a person to the "reasonableness" standard in evaluating his or her decisions. A competent adult who starts a bonfire at a school pep rally only ten feet from the gymnasium could be charged with reckless arson if the gym burns down. This is because a reasonable person would know that he or she is disregarding a substantial and unjustifiable risk in starting a large fire next to a building. Reckless arsons are punished less severely than intentional arson.

More than 100,000 arsons are reported to police each year. Interestingly, only 56 percent of arsons occur in cities. Twenty percent take place in rural areas and the remainder in suburban locations. About 25 percent of arsons involve burnings of automobiles, and 33 percent involve residences. The remainder involve commercial and community properties. The average loss in an incident of arson was $11,000 in 1995.[23] For arson to be charged, it is not necessary for the entire structure or vehicle to be burned or destroyed. It must only be charred, or

Approximately half of all arrests for violent crimes are young people under the age of 25, more than 88 percent are male, and 55 percent are white.

damaged intentionally or recklessly in some way by fire or explosion, for the incident to be defined as arson.

Characteristics of Offenders and Victims

To evaluate the nature of criminal events, it is important to understand the types of people who are likely to become involved in such events either as victims or offenders. The Uniform Crime Reports include information about the age, sex, and race of those arrested. Victimization surveys also include this information, as well as data regarding location, neighborhood, and other relevant factors. In this section some key characteristics of crime victims and offenders are discussed.

Age

There is often little relation between an individual's fear of crime and the actual chances that he or she will be a victim of a crime. The elderly have been found to be most fearful of crime, yet they are victimized less often than any other age group. Table 3.7 summarizes the distribution of crime victims by age. The table indicates that people aged 65 or older are victimized at a rate of less than 3 per 1,000 for the crimes of rape, robbery, aggravated assault, and personal larceny. This is seventeen times lower than the victimization rate of sixteen- to nineteen-year-olds, the highest-risk group, for the same crimes. It appears that one of the advantages of aging is a reduction in the likelihood of being a crime victim. The risk is highest during the teenage and young adult years, but it drops dramatically after age twenty-five.

The reasons for these discrepancies by age are not difficult to understand. Young people are more active and mobile and expose themselves to risk more often. They also visit more dangerous places, at later hours, and take fewer se-

TABLE 3.7

Age Distribution of Crime Victims
(rate per 1,000 persons aged 12 and older)

AGE GROUP	RAPE/SEX ASSAULT	ROBBERY	AGGRAVATED ASSAULT	PERSONAL THEFT*
12–15	2.6	10	15.6	3.3
16–19	4.9	12	25.3	2.5
20–24	2.1	10	15.9	2.9
25–34	1.8	7.1	9.8	1.2
35–49	1.3	3.8	7.4	1.0
50–64	0.1	1.8	3.8	1.2
65 and older	0.0	1.1	0.8	0.7

*Includes pickpocketing and purse-snatching.

SOURCE: Compiled from Cheryl Ringel, *Criminal Victimization 1996* (Washington, D.C.: Bureau of Justice Statistics, 1997).

curity precautions than do older people. In fact, while they own considerably less property than older people, they expose themselves to risk much more often and, hence, are victimized more frequently.

Individuals arrested for Index crimes are tracked by the Uniform Crime Reports. The UCR reports that 18.3 percent of those arrested for Index crimes are under 18 and that 45 percent are under age 25. This does not vary much by type of crime, with 46 percent of violent crime arrests (including homicide) and 58 percent of property crime arrests involving individuals under age 25.[24] This suggests that a majority of Index crimes are committed by young people. Violent and property crimes require some combination of force or stealth, or both, and therefore are most easily carried out by young people. Older individuals who are disposed to violence or theft are much more likely to be arrested for forgery, fraud, embezzlement, and offenses against the family, crimes in which the victims either are tricked or have little chance of escape.

Gender

Eighty-eight percent of individuals arrested for violent crimes and 74 percent of those arrested for property crimes are male. Women are most frequently arrested for larceny, although they account for only 32 percent of larceny arrests.[25] It is clear that serious crimes are far more likely to be committed by men than by women.

The same is not true for victims, however. Victimization rates for men and women show that property crimes affect women almost as often as men. The rate of property crimes affecting men is 72 per 1,000 population; for women the rate is 64 per 1,000. Women are victimized by violent crimes at a rate of 25 per 1,000, whereas the rate for men is 40 per 1,000 population.[26] Except for the crime of rape, women are significantly less likely than men to be victims of serious crime. Women are only slightly more likely than men to experience thefts from the person with contact (i.e., purse-snatching and pickpocketing). This overrepresentation of women among crime victims, as compared to those arrested, suggests that for virtually all serious crimes men victimize women in disproportionate numbers.

Race and Ethnicity

Whites account for 63 percent of all arrests for Index crimes. This includes 55 percent of arrests for violent crimes and 65 percent of arrests for property crimes. On the other hand, whites and blacks are victimized by property crimes at the same rate, but blacks are significantly more likely to be the victims of violent crimes than are whites. These data are summarized in Table 3.8, which makes it clear that blacks are victimized by violent crimes at a rate almost 50 percent higher than the rate for whites.[27] Younger black males are at even higher risk. Black males aged 16 to 19 are victimized by violent crime almost twice as often as white males. Nevertheless, the arrest rate for whites is higher than that for blacks for violent crimes. For property crimes, whites are arrested more than twice as often as blacks, although white and black victimization rates for these crimes are identical.

Blacks are more often victimized by rape, robbery, and aggravated assault than are whites, although whites are more often victims of simple assault. When one examines the circumstances of these crimes, victimization surveys report that violent crimes involving black victims are twice as likely to be committed by offenders with guns as violent crimes with white victims (20 percent versus 11 percent). Nevertheless, 80 percent of all victimizations involve white-on-white or black-on-black incidents.[28]

Hispanics constitute a small, but growing, segment of victims of serious crimes. People of Hispanic origin constitute about 8 percent of the U.S. population. They are immigrants from Spanish-speaking countries such as Mexico (62 percent), Puerto Rico (13 percent), and Central and South America (12 percent). Their rate of victimization by violent crimes is 40 per 1,000 population, 33 percent higher than the rate for whites but 10 percent lower than that for blacks. Hispanics are victims of thefts at a rate comparable to the rates for blacks and whites.[29]

It should be kept in mind, of course, that race itself does not predispose a person to crime. In the United States, race and ethnicity are closely tied to age, income, and residence in cities (where crime rates are higher). Whites tend to be older and have higher incomes than blacks and Hispanics, whose median age

TABLE 3.8

Race of Victims and Offenders*

RACE	OFFENDERS: VIOLENT CRIME	VICTIMS: VIOLENT CRIME	OFFENDERS: PROPERTY CRIME	VICTIMS: PROPERTY CRIME
White	54%	30 per 1,000	66%	61 per 1,000
Black	45%	44 per 1,000	32%	61 per 1,000
Other	2%	23 per 1,000	2%	52 per 1,000

*Offenders: percent of total arrests; victims: rate per 1,000 population aged 12 and over.

SOURCE: Federal Bureau of Investigation, *Uniform Crime Report* (Washington, D.C.: U.S. Government Printing Office, published annually); Marianne W. Zawitz et al., *Highlights from 20 Years of Surveying Crime Victims* (Washington, D.C.: Bureau of Justice Statistics, 1993).

Media and Criminal Justice

NEW JERSEY DRIVE

In the early 1990s, newspaper headlines often featured stories about a growing crime phenomenon in Newark, New Jersey. Newark, it seemed, had become the unofficial car-theft capital of the world. While UCR statistics on auto theft—which are considered some of the most accurate data in the type I Index crimes—have not fluctuated dramatically in recent years, auto theft in Newark had taken on a whole new dimension.

In 1992, a Newark police officer shot a young black man who was "spinning donuts" in a stolen car directly in front of the officers. Apparently, the officer's mother's car had recently been stolen, although it is unclear if the officer suspected the shooting victim of being the same car thief. The incident sparked an all-out "gang war" between the car thieves and the police. Specialized "anti–auto-theft" sting units were established by the Newark police to combat the problem. Car thieves, who had previously stolen cars for either joyriding or "parting out" (sending autos to the "chop shop" for disassembly) had discovered a whole new motive for auto theft: revenge.

The 1995 movie *New Jersey Drive* provides a fictionalized account of the clash between the Newark police and its young inner-city residents. The main character of the movie, Jason Petty, is a young man torn between the values instilled by his mother and the peer pressure applied by his "posse" of friends. Jason can differentiate between stealing a car for a few hours of cruising through the projects and stealing a car for profit or revenge. It is clear that a person's "ride" offers tremendous status and acceptance in his ghetto neighborhood. However, when Jason's friends unknowingly steal a policeman's car and are ambushed by a police sting operation, Jason finds himself entering the vindictive game of stealing cars to defy and provoke the corrupt police.

While the officers in *New Jersey Drive* are portrayed as brutal and corrupt, the movie depicts the young car thieves as equally dangerous and retaliatory. Their reckless driving and baited police chases endanger the lives of all around them; countless cars are stolen and smashed in the process. Jason and his friend Midget actually steal a police cruiser for kicks, riding around and harassing motorists on the P.A. system.

The movie does not take sides on who is right and wrong in the senseless barrage of both property and violent crimes that results from the conflict between car thieves and police. Instead, it focuses on the hopelessness and boredom of the youths who live in an environment that feeds their need for thrills, and where police are clearly frustrated at their inability to cure the problem with mere law enforcement tactics. Clearly, the crime picture in Newark is far more complicated than statistics on a page: The more the police endeavor to stop the car theft problem with aggressive and proactive policing, the larger the problem becomes.

In the movie, the subterranean clash between police and car thieves escalates to a tragic ending in which no one wins, but the youth of Newark become wise to the reality of their seemingly harmless car-theft antics. The movie's message is made clear: Not the *numbers* of autos stolen in Newark, but rather the *reason* that the autos are stolen, are what make it the car-theft capital of the world.

The study of crime statistics is important in determining patterns and trends among different types of crimes, but is limited in its potential for answering the *why* behind the variations in crime rates. *New Jersey Drive* is an important film for portraying a real-world story that shows that increased law enforcement might actually exacerbate the crime problem, instead of driving crime down. A true crime picture, then, not only considers the methods of data collection and raw numbers retrieved, but allows us to conjecture about the causes of data fluctuations behind a crime such as auto theft.

MEDIA AND CRIMINAL JUSTICE QUESTION

Can you offer additional reasons for the high rate of car theft in Newark? How would you propose to lower thefts over the long term?

and income are lower. They are also more likely to live outside cities. These factors contribute greatly to the differences in rates of victimization by race.

The influence of income on the risk of victimization is illustrated by the fact that the risk of household burglary declines as income rises. Households with incomes below $15,000 per year are more than 25 percent more likely to be burglarized than those with incomes above $15,000. Households with incomes of $50,000 or more have the lowest burglary rates (41 per 1,000 households). The same is true for victims of violent crime. People with incomes below $15,000 are 25 percent more likely to be victimized than those who earn more. Likewise, rented dwellings are 75 percent more likely to be burglarized than homes that are owned by the resident (73 versus 42 per 1,000 households). Victimization surveys have found that household burglaries, larcenies, and motor vehicle thefts are between 33 and 55 percent higher in central cities than in the suburbs. Rates of violent crime are 40 percent higher in central cities than in suburbs or rural areas.[30] Therefore, differences in living conditions help explain the differences in victimization rates that are thought by some to be associated exclusively with race and ethnicity.

Other Types of Crime

Thus far we have considered only the most serious violent and property crimes. These crimes are the focus of much public concern and require close examination for that reason. Nevertheless, there are other types of crime that may pose greater threats both now and in the future. They can be grouped into six categories: white collar crime, computer crime, organized crime, serial murder, hate crimes, and terrorism. These offenses are examined in more detail in Chapters 16 and 17, but their essential elements are presented here.

White Collar Crime

white collar crimes
A generic term that encompasses crimes of fraud, crimes against public administration, and regulatory offenses.

White collar crimes are crimes of fraud that are usually carried out during the course of a legitimate occupation. In place of the force or stealth that is inherent in violent and property crimes, white collar crimes employ deceit in an effort to trick an unsuspecting victim. White collar crimes are of three types: crimes of fraud, crimes against public administration, and regulatory offenses.[31] Crimes of fraud have money as their object and include embezzlement, extortion, forgery, and fraud. Crimes against public administration attempt to impede government processes. These include bribery, obstruction of justice, official misconduct, and perjury. Regulatory offenses are violations that circumvent measures designed to protect public health, safety, or welfare in business, industry, and government.

It can be seen that *white collar crime* is a generic term that encompasses several specific types of crimes. Examples of each of these types are presented in Chapter 17.

Computer Crime

The United States has been completely infiltrated by computers. Most American households now own computers, as do the vast majority of businesses. In the very near future, computers will become as central to our lives at home as they already are at work for most people. The distinctions among computers, telephones, cable television, mail, libraries, and even simple conversations will become blurred as the computer becomes the central forum for all these activities.

The trend toward computerization creates opportunities for misuse, just as do all social and technological advances. Some people have found ways to use the computer as an *instrument* of theft, harassment, or extortion. Others have and will use computers as an *object*, causing damage to hardware and software or altering data in an unauthorized manner.[32]

These opportunities for misuse will grow in the future as computer usage increases. Trends in **computer crimes** and laws dealing with such crimes suggest that more can be done to anticipate the criminal opportunities created by a computerized society. These possibilities are discussed in Chapter 17.

Reputed organized crime figure John Gotti was convicted of participating in five murders in 1992. He was sentenced to life in prison.

Organized Crime

Organized crime encompasses a number of criminal activities, all revolving around the provision of illicit goods or services and the infiltration of legitimate business. Most organized crime emerges from the illicit desires of the public. As is noted in Chapter 2, Prohibition, drugs, and gambling have done much to create a "black market" in which a sizable portion of the public demands goods or services that the government has criminalized. Organized crime groups are funded primarily through these activities.[33]

The crime of conspiracy characterizes nearly all organized crime activity. Laws dealing with conspiracy make it illegal for two or more people to plan a crime. Other laws, such as the Racketeer Influenced and Corrupt Organization (RICO) provisions of the Organized Crime Control Act, bar people from engaging in an enterprise through a pattern of racketeering activity. These laws, and others, have a common purpose: to make it difficult to *organize* to violate the law. The success of these laws in combating organized crime is assessed later.

Serial Murder

Serial murder was once a rare event, but it has occurred much more frequently during the last two decades. One count of serial murder that took place during the 1980s and 1990s alone totaled more than one hundred and accounted for several hundred victims. **Serial murders** are sets of homicides in which three or more people are killed over a period of more than thirty days.[34] Usually one victim is killed at a time, unlike the case in **mass murder,** in which a number of people are killed in the same incident.

As was noted earlier, the FBI reports that nearly half of all murders involve relatives or acquaintances. This is generally not true in the case of serial murders, in which the victims are often strangers. Even though serial murders account only for an estimated 3 percent of all homicides, the overtones of stalking, strangers, slaughter, and sadistic cruelty make them more feared than traditional homicides.[35] In addition, serial murder appears to be much more common in the United States than elsewhere in the world.

Concern about serial murder as a "new" manifestation of homicide grew rapidly during the early 1980s. In 1983, the FBI established the Violent Crime Apprehension Program (VICAP), and in 1984, the National Center for the Analysis of Violent Crime (NCAVC) was formed. These programs focus explicitly on multiple killers.[36] Some believe that these programs may contribute to the serial murder scare, as unsolved murders may become labeled as "unsolved serial murders" without adequate proof.[37] Nevertheless, the large number of serial murderers apprehended in recent years is proof enough for many that a new, more devastating method of murder is occurring frequently enough to be feared.

computer crime
Unauthorized use of a computer to damage its hardware or software, or as an instrument of theft, harassment, or extortion.

organized crime
A generic term that encompasses the provision of illicit goods and services and the infiltration of legitimate business.

serial murder
Homicides in which three or more people are killed over a period of more than 30 days.

mass murder
Homicides in which a number of people are killed in the same criminal incident.

FUTURE ISSUES

Can We Predict How Violent the Future Will Be?

The three best predictors of crime are age, opportunity, and motivation. Most people who commit serious crimes are males, between the ages of 16 and 24, poor, and from a central city. Victimization surveys show that most victims have the same characteristics as their offenders. Age is one of the strongest predictors of serious violent and property crime because these crimes involve force or stealth, or both, and hence are more likely to be committed by younger people. Few 40-year-olds rob convenience stores, because to do so you have to be able to hop over the counter, hop back, and maybe outrun a pursuer. People between the ages of 16 and 24 are strong and agile and therefore are the most crime-prone age group. Victims also tend to be age 16 to 24 because they are out more often, for more hours, later at night, and in a greater diversity of neighborhoods and settings.

What, then, does the future hold for 16 to 24 year olds? This is a shrinking age group in the U.S. population. In 1970, the median age in America was 27, today it is 33, and it is expected to rise past 40 by the year 2020 as life expectancy increases and birth and immigration rates remain low.[38] These facts have led one criminologist to conclude that "there is no evidence that violent or property crimes will increase dramatically over the next two decades, and all indications would seem to be that the rates will actually undergo an overall decline."[39] This view corresponds with the findings of victimization surveys, which show a general decline in the rates of serious crime in recent years.

This forecast is subject to change, however, when one considers the possible impact of changes in opportunities and motivation for criminal activity in coming years. With regard to opportunities, the news is not good. As was noted earlier, serious crimes most often occur in central cities and involve poor people. Large pockets of poor inner-city dwellers, who are undereducated, unskilled, and underemployed, will contribute to serious crimes against persons and property. The National Commission on Children and the Children's Defense Fund report that 20 percent of all children in America are living below the poverty level.[40] Also, 29 percent of young people do not graduate from high school.[41] These facts do not bode well for the future of poverty, a factor closely associated with both serious criminal offenders and victims.

Added to economic opportunities for crime are those provided by technology. The popularity of portable equipment of all types—

Hate Crimes

hate crimes
Threats or assaults that are motivated by race, ethnicity, religion, or sexual orientation.

Hate (or "bias") **crimes** are those in which victims are threatened or assaulted solely because they are of a specific race, ethnicity, religion, or sexual orientation. During the 1980s, the number of hate crimes committed in the United States each year rose from fewer than 50 to nearly 250. This increase prompted the federal government to approve the 1990 Hate Crime Statistics Act, which requires the collection of data about these offenses. Before that time, hate crimes often were logged as assaults, murders, or other crimes, without specific recognition of their motivation. Virtually every state now has laws that deal specifically with hate crimes as a separate category of offense. The intolerance that underlies hate crimes is disturbing, especially in a society whose culture is only 200 years old and for which diversity was a founding principle.

Terrorism

Terrorism within the United States was not considered a serious problem by most observers until the World Trade Center bombing in 1993, followed by the bombing of the Oklahoma City federal building in 1995. These incidents opened

cellular telephones, computers and hand-held computer games, and tape and compact disc players, among many others—offers opportunities for theft, robbery, and misuse that did not exist a few years ago. Therefore, advances in technology often create opportunities for crime that are difficult to anticipate very far into the future.

The third important factor is motivation. Unless people are motivated to conform to law, there is little police can do to stop them. Police now catch only 20 percent of offenders who commit reported serious crimes, a rate that has declined somewhat over the years. Simply put, the odds of apprehension are low, have always been low, and are unlikely to increase any time soon. Therefore, the law counts on the fact that most people will choose not to break it. Decisions to commit crime are often based on values, ethics, and morals established early in life. Respect for others and their property is what keeps most of us law abiding, regardless of our economic background. These values are learned primarily through family and school role models.

Surveys of youth in custody find that 70 percent of all juveniles now in custody come from single-parent homes, 52 percent have a family member who has been incarcerated, 63 percent report regular drug use, 57 percent report regular alcohol use, and more than 85 percent have been arrested at least twice before and were arrested for the first time at age 12 or 13.[42] A 10-year study followed more than 1,000 children from age 3 to age 15. It found that preschool behavior problems were the single best predictor of antisocial behaviors appearing at age 11.[43] The best predictor of adult criminality is juvenile delinquency, and the best predictor of juvenile delinquency is behavior problems dating back to early childhood. Given the current status of the families of juveniles who are already in trouble, unless something is done to enhance the integrity of the family unit, the reduced numbers of teenagers and young adults in the population may not mean much in the face of a growing proportion of unguided, unsupervised, uneducated, and poor young people who lack respect for other people and their property.

FUTURES QUESTION

What strategies would you propose to reduce opportunities for crime in the future?

the eyes of many Americans to what the rest of the world already knew: A free society is an open target for extremists who wish to advance their views through violence.

Terrorism is defined as the use of violence for political ends. The violence is often accompanied by warnings or threats of certain consequences if desired political or governmental actions are not taken. Terrorist groups exist on both the ideological right and left, and many such groups exist throughout the world. In the United States terrorism has often been blamed on foreign nationals, but the Oklahoma City bombing led to the realization that terrorist acts may be committed by individuals and groups within society as well. The security problems posed by an open and free society in which some members believe that the government is oppressive and unfair have dangerous consequences for the government, for the terrorists themselves, and for many innocent victims. These issues are described in detail in Chapter 16.

terrorism
The use of violence for political purposes.

These many manifestations of crime, and concern about their incidence over time, fuel the continuing public concern about crime, violence, and justice in the United States. The remaining chapters of this book detail what we know about the causes and adjudication of these crimes. Ideas for long-term prevention strategies are highlighted throughout the book.

Critical Thinking EXERCISE

Homicide and State of Mind

The punishments for various forms of criminal homicide differ according to the state of mind of the offender at the time of the act. Because the result is always death, murder and manslaughter are distinguished by the nature of the offender's "guilty mind." In the following four scenarios that result in death, determine the construction worker's state of mind and whether he should be charged with murder or manslaughter.

1. **Clyde is a roofer working on a high-rise building. One day he sees a man walking on the street below who he knows is dating his former girlfriend. He picks up his hammer and drops it on the man, who dies as a result.**
2. **One day Clyde is bored, so he drops his hammer because he likes to watch people scatter. One unfortunate passerby is killed as a result of this action.**
3. **During an argument with a fellow worker, Clyde throws his hammer at him. The hammer misses the worker and falls to the street below, killing a pedestrian.**
4. **One day Clyde comes to work drunk and accidentally drops his hammer while attempting to drive a nail. A person on the street below is killed.**

Critical Thinking EXERCISE

The Elements of Crimes

Like all college and university students, Rico borrows books from the library to read and study. One day he borrows a book entitled *Criminal Justice,* and it changes his life. He decides not to return the book but to keep it instead.

- **Is this borrowing or larceny, and how are we to make the distinction?**

On her way home from class, Francesca orders fried chicken at the drive-through window of a fast-food outlet. When she drives up to the cashier's window, she pulls out a toy gun. The cashier grabs the bag of chicken back and closes the window. Francesca drives off but is later caught.

- **Should Francesca be charged with attempted armed robbery? Why or why not?**

Summary

TRENDS IN CRIME RATES

- Each year the FBI compiles statistics on crimes reported to the police and publishes them in its *Uniform Crime Reports* .
- The UCR collects detailed information for the seven most serious types of offenses and collects arrest information for nineteen "Part II" offenses.

- Victimization surveys provide information about crimes that are not reported to the police.
- Victim surveys reveal that the amount of serious crime is much higher than police statistics indicate.
- Surveys of offenders show that virtually all juveniles break the law at one time or another.
- Victimization surveys can provide a precise estimate of the risk of crimes against households.

VIOLENT CRIMES

- Murder includes all intentional killings as well as deaths that occur in the course of felonies; manslaughter involves causing death recklessly, or intentionally under extenuating circumstances.
- Rape is sexual intercourse without effective consent; statutory rape is nonforcible sexual intercourse with a minor.
- Assault is a thrust against another person with the intention of injuring that person.
- Robbery consists of larceny from a person using threats or force.

PROPERTY CRIMES

- Burglary is unlawful entry into a building in order to commit a crime while inside.
- Larceny consists of taking the property of another person with the intent of depriving the owner.
- Arson is burning of property without the consent of the owner.

CHARACTERISTICS OF OFFENDERS AND VICTIMS

- Rates of victimization are higher among teenagers and young adults than among older people; offenders also are most likely to be teenagers or young adults.
- The majority of offenders are male.
- Blacks are much more likely to be victimized by violent crimes than are whites.

OTHER TYPES OF CRIME

- Other types of crime that may pose greater threats in the future are white-collar crime, computer crime, organized crime, serial murder, hate crimes, and terrorism.

Key Terms

Uniform Crime Reports
crime rate
victimization
personal risk
criminal homicide
murder
manslaughter
rape
statutory rape
simple assault
aggravated assault
robbery
burglary
larceny
arson
white collar crimes
computer crime
organized crime
serial murder
mass murder
hate crimes
terrorism

Questions for Review and Discussion

1. Why does the UCR present an incomplete picture of the true extent of crime?
2. What advantages do victimization surveys have over the UCR?
3. What are the most common types of crime as revealed by victimization surveys?
4. What reasons do people give for not reporting crimes to the police?
5. What is meant by recklessness? By negligence?
6. In what circumstances are intentional killings punished as manslaughter rather than murder?

7. How does aggravated assault differ from simple assault?
8. What is the difference between larceny and robbery?
9. Why are both offenders and victims likely to be young?
10. What factors account for differences in rates of victimization by race?

Notes

[1]President's Commission on Law Enforcement and Administration of Justice, *Task Force Report: Crime and Its Impact—An Assessment* (Washington, D.C.: U.S. Government Printing Office, 1967), p. 19.

[2]Ibid., pp. 22–3.

[3]"FBI Deleting Statistics on Philadelphia Crime," *Richmond Times-Dispatch* (October 20, 1997), p. 2.

[3a]Fox Butterfield, "As Crime Falls, Pressure Rises to Alter Data," *New York Times* (August 3, 1998), p. 1.

[4]Patsy Klaus, *Measuring Crime* (Washington, D.C.: Bureau of Justice Statistics, 1981).

[5]James Garofalo and Michael J. Hindelang, *Introduction to the National Crime Survey* (Washington, D.C.: U.S. Government Printing Office, 1977).

[6]For a more detailed exposition of these methodological issues, see Wesley G. Skogan, *Issues in the Measurement of Victimization* (Washington, D.C.: U.S. Government Printing Office, 1981) and Richard F. Sparks, Hazel G. Genn, and David J. Dodd, *Surveying Victims* (New York: Wiley & Sons, 1977).

[7]Personal and household larceny were combined into a single category, "larceny," beginning in 1993.

[8]Ernest J. Eck and Lucius J. Riccio, "Relationship Between Reported Crime Rates and Victimization Survey Results: An Empirical and Analytical Study," *Journal of Criminal Justice,* vol. 7 (Winter, 1979).

[9]Austin L. Porterfield, *Youth in Trouble* (Fort Worth: Texas Christian University Press, 1946); J. S. Wallerstein and C. L. Wylie, "Our Law-Abiding Law-breakers," *National Probation* (March–April, 1947), pp. 107–12.

[10]See Jay S. Albanese, *Dealing with Delinquency: The Future of Juvenile Justice,* 2nd ed. (Chicago: Nelson-Hall, 1993), pp. 26–31.

[11]Delbert S. Elliott et al., *The Prevalence and Incidence of Delinquent Behavior,* 1976–1980 (Boulder, CO: Behavioral Research Institute, 1983); Martin Gold, *Delinquent Behavior in an American City* (Belmont, CA: Brooks/Cole, 1970); M. Gold and D. J. Reimer, "Changing Patterns of Delinquent Behavior among Americans 13–16 Years Old: 1967–1972," *Crime & Delinquency Literature* vol. 7 (1975), pp. 483–517.

[12]Robert M. O'Brien, *Crime and Victimization Data* (Beverly Hills, CA: Sage Publications, 1985), pp. 63–79.

[13]Michael R. Rand, *Crime and the Nation's Households, 1992* (Washington, D.C.: Bureau of Justice Statistics, 1993).

[14]See *State v. Ott,* 297 Or. 375 (S. Ct. Oregon 1984) and *State v. Gounagais,* 88 Wash. 304 (S. Ct. Washington 1915).

[15]Federal Bureau of Investigation, *Crime in the United States, 1995* (Washington, D.C.: U.S. Government Printing Office, 1996), p. 21.

[16]Ronet Bachman, *Violence Against Women* (Washington, D.C.: U.S. Government Printing Office, 1994); Marianne W. Zawitz et al., *Highlights from 20 Years of Surveying Crime Victims* (Washington, D.C.: Bureau of Justice Statistics, 1993).

[17]Federal Bureau of Investigation, *Crime in the United States, 1996* (Washington, D.C.: U.S. Government Printing Office, 1997).

[18]Bachman, p. 10; Zawitz, p. 11.

[19]Lisa D. Bastian, *Criminal Victimization in the United States, 1990* (Washington, D.C.: U.S. Government Printing Office, 1992); Zawitz, p. 10.

[20]Zawitz, p. 12.

[21]*Berry v. State,* 90 Wis. 2d 316 (S. Ct. Wisconsin 1979).

[22]Zawitz, p. 13.

[23]Federal Bureau of Investigation, 1996, p. 54.
[24]Compiled from Federal Bureau of Investigation, *Crime in the United States* (Washington, D.C.: U.S. Government Printing Office, 1996), pp. 218–9.
[25]Ibid.
[26]Ronet Bachman, *Violence Against Women* (Washington, D.C.: U.S. Government Printing Office, 1994).
[27]Lisa D. Bastian and Bruce M. Taylor, *Young Black Male Victims* (Washington, D.C.: Bureau of Justice Statistics, 1994).
[28]Catherine J. Whitaker, *Black Victims* (Washington, D.C.: Bureau of Justice Statistics, 1990).
[29]Lisa D. Bastian, *Hispanic Victims* (Washington, D.C.: Bureau of Justice Statistics, 1990).
[30]See studies on wealth by Edward Wolff and "Economic Disparities Greatest in the United States," *The Buffalo News* (April 17, 1995), p. D9.
[31]Jay Albanese, *White Collar Crime in America* (Englewood Cliffs, NJ: Prentice Hall, 1995).
[32]Jay S. Albanese and Robert D. Pursley, *Crime in America: Some Existing and Emerging Issues* (Englewood Cliffs, NJ: Prentice Hall, 1993), Chap. 2.
[33]Jay Albanese, *Organized Crime in America,* 3rd ed. (Cincinnati: Anderson Publishing, 1996).
[34]Ronald M. Holmes and Stephen T. Holmes, *Murder in America* (Thousand Oaks, CA: Sage Publications, 1994), p. 92.
[35]Victor E. Kappeler, Mark Blumberg, and Gary W. Potter, *The Mythology of Crime and Justice* (Prospect Heights, IL: Waveland Press, 1993), p. 60.
[36]S. G. Michaud and H. Aynesworth, "The FBI's New Psyche Squad," *The New York Times Magazine* (October 26, 1986).
[37]Kappeler, Blumberg, and Potter, p. 65.
[38]Gregory Spencer, *Projections of the Population of the United States by Age, Sex, and Race: 1988 to 2080,* U.S. Bureau of Census Current Population Reports, Series P-25, No. 1018 (Washington, D.C.: U.S. Government Printing Office, 1989).
[39]Chester L. Britt, "The Nature of Common Crime in the Year 2010," in J. Klofas and S. Stojkovic, eds., *Crime and Justice in the Year 2010* (Belmont, CA: Wadsworth, 1995), p. 99.
[40]William M. Welch, "Childhood Poverty of 20% Said to Put Nation at Risk," *The Buffalo News* (April 26, 1990), p. 14; Linda Kanamine, "Child Poverty Escalates at Alarming Rate," *USA Today* (June 3, 1991), p. 3.
[41]Jerry Zremski, "State Gets Low Marks on Children," *The Buffalo News* (February 2, 1991), p. 6.
[42]Allen Beck, Susan Kline, Lawrence Greenfield, *Survey of Youth in Custody* (Washington, D.C.: U.S. Government Printing Office, 1988); James Austin, Barry Krisberg, and Robert DeComo, *Juveniles Taken into Custody* (Washington, D.C., Office of Juvenile Justice and Delinquency Prevention, 1995).
[43]Jennifer L. White, Terrie E. Moffit, Felton Earles, Lee Robins, and Phil A. Silva, "How Can We Tell?: Predictors of Childhood Conduct Disorder and Adolescent Delinquency," *Criminology,* vol. 28 (1990), pp. 507–33.

For Further Reading

Thomas V. Brady, *Measuring What Matters—Part One: Measures of Crime, Fear, and Disorder* (Washington, D.C.: National Institute of Justice, 1996).

Criminal Victimization in the U.S. (Washington, D.C.: U.S. Bureau of Justice Statistics, published annually).

Federal Bureau of Investigation, *Uniform Crime Reports* (Washington, D.C.: U.S. Government Printing Office, published annually).

Steven F. Messner and Richard Rosenfeld, *Crime and the American Dream* (Belmont, CA: Wadsworth, 1994).

chapter four

Explanations of Crime

Society prepares the crime;
the criminal commits it.

HENRY THOMAS BUCKLE
(1821–1862)

CHAPTER OUTLINE

Contemporary accounts of crime and violence leave us wondering, "How could someone do such a thing?" Understanding the motives of criminal offenders is a central question in criminal justice because all attempts to prevent and control crime are based on assumptions about its causes. Consider these questions, all of which arise from recent highly publicized crimes:[1]

- How could a mother kill her own children?
- How could children kill their own parents?
- How can a rapist be punished severely, be released, and then do it again?
- How can young people commit brutal assaults without any provocation?

LA COUNTY
LA COUNTY

Questions such as these make it clear that we have a long way to go in understanding the causes of crime. Fortunately, during the twentieth century growing concern has led to a more systematic study of crime.

A related question is why crime rates vary dramatically among nations, states, cities, and even neighborhoods. For example, both Interpol (the International Criminal Police Organization) and the United Nations gather reported crime information from nations around the world.[2] These statistics reveal that the United States has approximately twice the murder rate of countries such as Canada, Australia, France, and Germany, and four times the murder rate of England, Italy, Norway, Spain, and Switzerland.[3] Comparisons of rates of other offenses are not as reliable, owing to differences in crime definitions and huge variations in the percent of crimes reported to authorities (see Chapter 16). It is clear, however, that rates of crime, especially murder, vary widely among nations. A close look at the causes of crime can help in determining what measures can be taken in attempting to reduce the incidence of serious crime in the United States and elsewhere.

The study of the causes of crime has not discovered a uniform explanation. Some have argued that a single explanation should be able to account for all criminality, while others believe that different explanations are required for different types of crime and offenders.[4] At present there are four general types of explanations of crime: classical, positivist, structural, and ethical.

Classical Explanations of Crime

classical school
The view that crime is the product of the rational exercise of free will guided by the pursuit of pleasure and minimizing pain.

The **classical school** of thought in criminology sees crime as resulting from the conscious exercise of an individual's free will. Classicists see people as hedonists: People pursue pleasure while attempting to minimize pain. Two of the best-known classicists, Cesare Beccaria and Jeremy Bentham, wrote during the eighteenth century.[5]

Classical thinking, sometimes called the free will school, dominated criminal codes during the nineteenth century because the law assumed that all people were equal in their capacity to guide their conduct rationally. If the law was violated, the punishment was based on the violation committed, rather than on the type of person who committed it. This punishment was designed to deter future misconduct by the offender and other members of society. Recent exponents of the classical explanation are Michael Gottfredson and Travis Hirschi, who believe that crime is a chosen course of conduct by individuals with low self-control, who are unable to defer immediate gratification of their desires.[6] Empirical studies continue to test the ability of classical explanations to account for the commission of crimes, but the results are inconsistent.[7]

Dissatisfaction with the classical school first appeared toward the end of the nineteenth century. Crime was still seen as a growing problem, and punishment of violators apparently was not deterring others from committing criminal acts—a perception that remains widespread today, some one hundred years later. The late 1900s also witnessed the rise of the scientific method and the beginnings of social science. Charles Darwin developed his theory of evolution through natural selection, publishing it in his famous work *The Origin of Species.*[8] Emile Durkheim observed differences in rates of suicide in different regions of France. He used these observations to develop a theory of social factors in suicide.[9] Both Darwin and Durkheim were pioneers in the use of the scientific method, in which knowledge is advanced through observation rather than by theorizing without first gathering data. This scientific approach to explanations gave rise to the positivist school of criminology.

Positivist Explanations of Crime

According to **positivism,** human behavior is determined by internal and external influences. Positivists maintain that these influences, which include biological, psychological, and/or social factors, determine individual behavior. Rather than seeing crime as the product of the rational exercise of free will, as classicists do, positivists see crime as largely determined by a variety of internal and external influences on a person. In many ways the positive school in criminology emphasizes "nurture" (i.e., factors in the individual's environment), whereas the classical school stresses "nature" (i.e., a presupposed "natural" state of seeking pleasure and avoiding pain).

positivism
The view that crime is determined by internal and external influences on a person.

Positivists believe that there are fundamental differences between criminals and noncriminals based on these internal and external influences, which may include personality imbalances, family role models, and peer group pressure, among many others. From the positivist perspective all people are *not* equal because the criminal act is seen as a symptom of an underlying problem rather than the problem itself, as the classicists see it. Instead of punishment, therefore, positivists see reform or rehabilitation of the offender as the best way to prevent future crime, either by changing the influences on an individual or by changing how he or she reacts to them.

Biological Determinism

The earliest positivists saw the roots of criminal behavior in biological attributes, an approach known as **biological determinism.** Cesare Lombroso (1835–1909) took body measurements of offenders in Italian prisons and concluded that they were "born criminals" with distinctive body measurements and skull sizes. On the basis of his measurements, Lombroso developed a theory of *atavism,* which suggested that "born criminals" were biological throwbacks to an earlier stage of human evolution.[10] However, in 1913, an English physician, Charles Goring, published the results of his measurements of 3,000 English convicts, which had been compared to similar measurements of a group of nonconvicts. Goring found no evidence of a distinct physical criminal type, thereby discrediting Lombroso's theory of atavism.[11]

biological determinism
The view that crime is the product of biological attributes that produce criminal behavior.

Biological determinism did not die with Lombroso. Studies that focus on the body build of delinquents have been followed by investigations of chromosomal abnormalities, glandular dysfunction, chemical imbalances, and nutritional deficiencies. As measurement methods and studies of subtle biological differences have improved, interest in biological influences on crime has grown. A number of criminologists now see links between certain biological features and a propen-

contemporary issues

Explaining Serial Murders

If one had to choose a single crime that has typified the violence and fear of crime in recent years, it might be serial murders. According to the U.S. Department of Justice, a total of 124 serial homicides occurred in the United States from 1795 to 1974. Since 1975, however, more than 331 serial murders have been committed.

This increase in serial murders is due in part to improvements in reporting practices over the years.[70] Such a large increase is not likely to be a mere statistical artifact, however. For example, between 1950 and 1970 only two cases of serial murder in the United States were found to involve ten or more victims (Charlie Starkweather and the Boston Strangler). Since 1971, however, there have been more than twenty-eight cases involving between ten and twenty victims, and at least nine involving more than twenty victims.[71] Therefore, serial murders appear to be becoming both more frequent *and* more serious. A completely accurate picture is unlikely to emerge, however, because police solve only about 70 percent of all homicides, and the proportion of unsolved cases that involve serial murders is difficult to estimate with accuracy.

Serial killer Jeffrey Dahmer confessed to murdering and dismembering 15–17 young men and boys. He was sentenced to 15 consecutive life sentences and was killed by a fellow inmate in 1994.

Serial murders have appeared in most industrialized societies, although the rate seems to be highest in the United States. This is probably a result of America's higher homicide rate in general. It is interesting to note, however, that serial murders in the United States appear to average more victims per murderer than serial murders in any other country.[72]

Serial murders lack the more understandable economic motives of property crimes, and even the motives arising from domestic quarrels that lead to so many single homicides. Serial murders are most often stranger-to-stranger crimes with vague motives. The typical serial killer is a white man between the ages of twenty-five and thirty-five. He usually targets strangers near his home or workplace, and rarely travels far from home to kill.[73] The West Coast states of the United States have experienced a disproportionate number of serial killings (about 40 percent of the total).[74] The fewest serial killings occur on the East Coast. This is interesting because most single murders occur in Southern states, but most serial murders are not committed there.

Many typologies of serial murders have been developed. One of these is summarized in Table 4.1. This typology was proposed by Ronald Holmes and James De Burger, who have identified four kinds of serial murders: visionary, mission, hedonistic, and power/control.[75] Visionary killers kill in response to imagined voices that command them to do so. Mission killers consciously attempt to eliminate

sity to engage in crime.[12] Studies of twins raised separately, for example, have compared the incidence of their delinquent behavior, and studies of adopted children have compared their criminality to that of their biological parents. These studies suggest that genetic factors play some role in delinquency, but it is not clear that biological factors outweigh environmental factors.[13] The Panel on the Understanding and Control of Violent Behavior of the National Academy of Sciences concluded that biological studies have "produced mixed results, suggesting at most a weak genetic influence on the chance of violent behavior."[14] Nevertheless, there is continuing interest in the interplay between biological predispositions and social influences on behavior. Such a biosocial approach at-

TABLE 4.1

A Typology of Serial Murderers

Visionary: The visionary serial killer is impelled to murder because he has heard voices or seen visions demanding that he kill a certain person or category of persons. For some the voice or vision is perceived to be that of a demon, for others it may be perceived as coming from God.

Mission: The mission serial killer has a conscious goal in his life to eliminate a certain identifiable group of people. He does not hear voices or see visions. He has a self-imposed duty to rid the world of a group of people who are "undesirable" or "unworthy" to live with other humans.

Hedonistic: The hedonistic serial killer simply kills for the thrill of it, because he enjoys it. The thrill becomes an end in itself. The lust murderer can be viewed as a subcategory of this type because of the sexual enjoyment experienced in the homicidal act. Anthropophagy, dismemberment, necrophilia, and other forms of sexual aberration are prevalent in this form of serial killing.

Power/control: The power or control serial killer receives gratification from the complete control of the victim. This type of murderer experiences pleasure and excitement not from sexual acts carried out on the victim, but from his belief that he has the power to do whatever he wishes to another human who is completely helpless to stop him.

SOURCE: Ronald M. Holmes and Stephen T. Holmes, *Murder in America*, pp. 119–26, copyright (©) 1994 by Sage Publications. Reprinted by permission of Sage Publications, Inc.

a certain type of "unworthy" person. Hedonistic killers obtain pleasure from the act. Power/control killers receive gratification from the control they exercise over the victim. These categories are not exhaustive, and the same authors have added two other categories for the rare cases of serial homicide by females. In some cases these women have been found to kill to achieve "comfort," usually by killing people they know for their money. Another type is the "disciple," who kills at the command of a charismatic leader who happens to be psychotic.[76]

Some criminologists have attempted to explain serial killings by examining their common features. For example, Joel Norris believes that certain biological or genetic traits are common to many serial killers. These traits include everything from earlobes adhering to one's head to a curved pinky finger.[77] Other scholars object to this biological approach because no documented study supports these predictions.[78] On the other hand, several researchers have discovered common features in the family backgrounds of serial killers. Violent punishment by parents and strong, overbearing mothers are frequently occurring features of the family histories of serial killers.[79] A "love-hate" relationship with their mother is thought to account for the large number of prostitutes among the victims of serial killers. Likewise, there are many cases involving weak or absent fathers, as well as cases in which the killers experienced suicidal tendencies that somehow become externalized, resulting in murder.

Fox and Levin find that the "overwhelming majority" of serial killers kill for the "thrill" of it. These murderers are sociopaths (antisocial personalities) who possess "a disorder of character rather than of the mind."[80] Rather than being insane, they simply act without conscience or feeling toward others. This "thrill" may be connected to sexual gratification, control, or a social "cause," corresponding to the typology presented in Table 4.1.

As serial murders become more common, our understanding of its nature and causes will improve. This will make it possible to develop screening tools that include factors that can assist in identifying individuals at high risk for such behavior.

tempts to link biological attributes such as prenatal complications, malnutrition, brain dysfunction, poor attention span, hyperactivity, and low IQ with social "triggers," such as abuse, neglect, poverty, and antisocial role models, that may result in criminal violence.[15]

Psychological Explanations

Psychological explanations of crime look inside the human psyche (or internalized controls) for the causes of crime. Instead of examining human physiology, psychologists look at how the human mind operates. The oldest, and most influential, psychological explanation of crime is based on the work of Sigmund Freud (1856–1939). Freud's psychoanalytic theory sees behavior as resulting from the interaction of the three components of the personality: id, ego, and superego. The **id** is defined as the primitive, instinctual drives of aggression and sex with which everyone is born. The **superego** acts as one's conscience, reflecting the values a person develops in the early years of life through interactions with family members. The **ego** mediates between the self-centered desires of the id and the learned values of the superego. The id, ego, and superego are theoretical constructs, of course; one cannot open someone's head and find them. Freud hypothesized their existence, attempting to demonstrate their presence through case studies of individuals' behavior.

id
According to Freud, the innate primitive, instinctual drives of aggression and sex.

superego
According to Freud, a personality construct that reflects the values learned early in life, acting as a conscience.

ego
According to Freud, personality construct that mediates between the desires of the id and the values of the superego.

Most explanations of crime based on Freud's theory see crime as resulting from faulty ego or superego structures that fail to control the id adequately. This results in personality imbalances, which produce deviant behavior. A weak, or defective, superego, for example, might result in "unsocialized aggressive behavior," in which a person has insufficient control over his or her aggressive or sexual instincts.[16] The conscience, in other words, is not sufficiently developed.

The ego and superego are said to develop by age six, and some psychologists believe that it is difficult, if not impossible, to correct the damage caused when the development of these components of the personality is inadequate because of poor family relationships or other negative experiences during the early years.[17] Studies of juvenile murderers have found many to be "volatile" and "explosive" and some to be mentally ill as a result of personality problems that began during early childhood.[18] A study of 210 chronic delinquents found that those who committed violent crimes were more than twice as likely to have been exposed to serious physical abuse and to violence involving weapons between the adults in their households.[19] Therefore, prior exposure to violence can trigger psychological reactions that produce greater risk of delinquent behavior in the future.

Another type of psychological theory focuses on **defense mechanisms** that shield the individual from anxiety or guilt. For example, a person may have an impulse that runs counter to his or her conscience, producing anxiety. By changing one's behavior, it is possible to neutralize these guilt feelings. There are several types of defense mechanisms, including displacement, reaction formation, and unconsciously intended side effects. **Displacement** occurs when one substitutes a target that subconsciously means the same thing as the intended target as when a man who is angry at his boss goes home and kicks his dog. Such displacement neutralizes the man's anxiety by substituting a "safe" target on which to vent his feelings. **Reaction formation** occurs when one denies an unacceptable part of one's personality by engaging in behavior that suggests the opposite. A man who engages in macho behaviors may do so as a reaction formation to counteract guilt caused by subconscious homosexual feelings.[20] *Unconsciously intended side effects* occur when an act is committed in a manner that makes it look as if the individual had a different motive. A person may shoplift so as to invite punishment and thereby relieve guilt felt about an unrelated action. This is done because the person cannot consciously admit the true motive owing to guilt or anxiety about it.

defense mechanism
A psychological adjustment that an individual makes in order to relieve anxiety or guilt.

displacement
A defense mechanism in which one substitutes a target that unconsciously means the same thing as the actual target.

reaction formation
A defense mechanism in which one denies an unacceptable part of one's personality by engaging in behavior that suggests the opposite.

None of these theories states that personality problems or defense mechanisms necessarily lead to criminal behavior. A person may neutralize guilt over feelings of greed by engaging in philanthropic activities. On the other hand, the same person might choose to steal covertly. This is one of the problems of psychological theories of crime. They have difficulty explaining the criminal *choice* as a way to resolve guilt or deal with aggressive impulses. Self-report studies have found that nearly all juveniles break the law at one time or another. If most crime is caused by psychological forces, why do these personality imbalances disappear in adulthood? Psychological theories, taken by themselves, have difficulty in explaining this.

Finally, psychological theories have not performed well in practice. Many studies have been conducted that assess personality characteristics in attempting to predict future involvement in crime. Reviews of hundreds of these studies have found little reliable evidence that personality tests or clinical interviews can predict criminal behavior accurately.[21]

Sociological Explanations

Sociological explanations of crime are more common than any other type. They arose largely from the inability of biological and psychological explanations to account for many types of crime that appeared to be "normal" reactions of people raised in dysfunctional families or neighborhoods.

Unlike biological or psychological explanations, which look at problems *within* the individual (whether physiological abnormalities or personality conflicts), sociological explanations look at *environmental* influences that affect the way people behave. Sociological explanations can be grouped into three types: those based on learning, blocked opportunity, or the social bond to conventional society.

THEORIES BASED ON LEARNING One of the earliest attempts to explain juvenile delinquency from the learning perspective was conducted by Clifford Shaw and Henry McKay. They observed that the areas of Chicago with high delinquency rates in 1900 to 1906 also had the highest rates in 1917 to 1923, even though the population of the area had changed completely. High- and low-delinquency areas were distinguished by the "standards and values" of the people in those areas, according to Shaw and McKay. High-delinquency areas were characterized by conflicting moral values, social disorganization, and decaying transitional neighborhoods. Conversely, low-delinquency areas were characterized by universal, conventional values and child-rearing practices. They found that most delinquent acts were committed in groups of two or three juveniles, and therefore concluded that the chief agencies for the transmission of delinquency were play groups and gangs.

Teenage gangs develop as a means of survival, friendship, and financial gain. When these groups recruit new members, the values and traditions are passed to the next generation. This process is called **cultural transmission.** Shaw and McKay believed that this was the reason why the high-delinquency areas remained the same over the years.[22] They concluded that delinquent gang membership might be a normal response to social conditions in slum areas. This is very different from the psychological approach, which sees troubled personalities as the cause of delinquency. Recent studies have provided further support for the

cultural transmission
The process through which criminal values or traditions are passed among generations in socially disorganized neighborhoods.

explanation of crime as resulting from "social disorganization" within neighborhoods. A study in England found that as a community is better organized (i.e., there are more local churches, committees, friendship networks, and the like), crime rates decrease.[23] An examination of sixty urban neighborhoods in the United States found similar results. This suggests that "both frequent and infrequent social interaction among neighbors is important for establishing community controls." A high percentage of residents who get together once a year or more has the strongest effect on crime rates.[24]

Another influential sociological theory based on learning was proposed by Edwin Sutherland in 1939. Sutherland believed that delinquent behavior is learned in much the same way that a person learns anything else. He called this process **differential association:** A person becomes criminal or delinquent when he or she associates more with people who condone violation of the law than with people who do not. These attitudes toward the law are learned from intimate personal groups such as family, friends, and peers. Although everybody is exposed to procriminal and anticriminal attitudes, the *proportions* in which one is exposed to these kinds of attitudes determine whether one will acquire those attitudes. Therefore, Sutherland does not speak of association with criminals or noncriminals but, rather, of association with those holding attitudes favorable to or tolerant of criminal behavior.[25] Subsequent researchers have investigated the link between juvenile associations and delinquency in order to determine how well the theory of differential association explains juvenile crime.[26] A study of chronic delinquents found that violent offenders were more likely to have experienced serious domestic violence and physical abuse. These juveniles were also more likely to believe that aggression has little impact on its victims and that it enhances one's self-image.[27] The results thus are mixed, suggesting that the theory is a better explanation of the spread of delinquency than of its ultimate cause.

differential association
The view that crime is learned when one disproportionately associates with those who condone law violation.

THEORIES BASED ON BLOCKED OPPORTUNITY In 1938, Robert Merton proposed a sociological theory of crime based on blocked opportunity.[28] Merton's explanation of deviant behavior was based on the concept of **anomie.** This concept was first used by Emile Durkheim in the late 1800s in his study of suicide. Durkheim defined anomie as "normlessness," a condition in which the rules that guide relations among people in society have broken down. What Merton did was to separate the components of anomie implied by Durkheim.

anomie
Normlessness, or lack of attachment to conventional social goals or means for attaining them.

Merton explained how *social goals and means* can produce anomie. Culturally defined social goals are widely shared beliefs within society. These include pursuit of a career, living in a comfortable home, and having a family. The acceptable means for achieving these goals include education, hard work at a job, and marriage. It is not socially acceptable to obtain these social goals by fraud, theft, or kidnapping. The existence of these deviant means for obtaining social goals is due to anomie, according to Merton. Anomie occurs when there is a gap between culturally defined goals and the acceptable means for reaching them. The larger the gap, the greater the deviance.

Although most people accept social goals and the acceptable means for obtaining them, some do not. For example, persons who have trouble achieving social goals such as education and a career might retreat to a life that rejects both the goals and accepted means (e.g., drug addicts). Others might become innovators and seek success in other ways. Still others might rebel and seek to change the goals themselves. Merton's explanation has intuitive appeal, although it offers no clue as to what causes a person to react in a particular way in response to anomie.

Another theory based on blocked opportunity was developed by Albert Cohen in 1955.[29] He attempted to explain senseless, purely negative acts, such as wanton vandalism, which probably are not learned. He believed that a person's self- image depends on how he or she is judged by others. If other people hold a person in low esteem, that person is likely to develop low self-esteem. In addition, the majority of people who judge juveniles are from the middle class (e.g., teachers, employers, the media) and therefore establish middle-class goals or "measuring rods" for juveniles to live up to. Lower-class juveniles are more likely to experience failure and frustration in meeting these goals than are middle- and upper-class juveniles. Cohen argued that lower-class juveniles resolve this frustration through reaction formation (one of the defense mechanisms discussed earlier), whereby they replace middle-class goals and norms with their own goals and norms. They gain status in their peer groups by aiming at goals that they *can* achieve, such as toughness or gang leadership. Such goals usually involve engaging in negative behavior for short-run gratification.

Richard Cloward and Lloyd Ohlin[30] agreed with Merton's claim that delinquency and crime result from lack of access to legitimate means for achieving goals. They believe, however, that even illegitimate means are unevenly distributed in society. As a result, some lower-class neighborhoods provide greater opportunity for illegal gain than do others. Unlike Cohen, Cloward and Ohlin do not believe that individuals substitute new goals; instead, they use illegitimate means to achieve accepted goals. Rather than getting a job and earning money to buy clothing, for example, an individual might steal them. Moreover, Cloward and Ohlin believe that not all delinquents can achieve success through illegitimate means because the opportunities for doing so are not available to everyone, just as there are differences in the opportunities available to individuals to achieve these goals by legitimate means.

Cloward and Ohlin describe three types of criminal subcultures that develop when youths cease to adhere to middle-class standards. Youths may become part of the adult *criminal* subculture, they may participate in the *conflict* subculture by forming fighting gangs that emphasize violence and status by coercion, or they may become part of the *retreatist* subculture when either no opportunities exist in the criminal subculture or status cannot be obtained in the conflict group. Therefore, Cloward and Ohlin maintain that not only are legitimate opportunities for success blocked for lower-class juveniles, but illegitimate opportunities can also be blocked, leading to the creation of one of these types of delinquent subcultures.

Another form of opportunity theory is called *routine activities theory*. This theory asserts that the likelihood of crime increases when three conditions occur simultaneously: (1) the presence of a motivated offender, (2) suitable targets available to victimize, and (3) the absence of guardians to deter the offender. As proposed by Lawrence Cohen and Marcus Felson, these three conditions occur as part of the "routine" activities of guardians and potential victims.[30a] Guardians can be police, family members, friends, or others in a position to prevent a crime.

The aftermath of Hurricane Andrew in Florida in 1992 was consistent with the tenets of routine activities theory, according to a study of the disaster.[30b] After the storm, there was a brief period without police protection of neighborhoods. Motivated offenders moved in, took advantage of the situation, and committed property crimes. The fact that there was comparatively little looting resulted from neighbors filling the void as guardians in the absence of police.

Routine activities theory is a theory to explain how one is victimized rather than a theory of crime. It does not address the crucial issue of why some people are motivated to commit crimes in the first place. Nevertheless, routine activities theory was influential during the 1980s and 1990s in explaining the circumstances of criminal incidents.[30c]

labeling theory
The view that when a person is labeled criminal through the adjudication process, further criminality is produced through negative public image and self-image.

LABELING THEORY Sociologist Howard Becker popularized **labeling theory** in his 1963 book *The Outsiders.* Originally put forth in 1951 by Edwin Lemert, labeling theory holds that "when society acts negatively to a particular individual (by adjudicating a person through the criminal justice system) by means of the 'label' (delinquent) . . . we actually encourage future delinquency." Thus, for Lemert and Becker the labeling process depends less on the behavior of the delinquent than it does on how others respond to their acts.[31] It is society's labeling of the individual (through adjudication as a delinquent) that promotes deviant behavior, rather than any action by the juvenile. For example, a juvenile who is suspended from school or adjudicated in court as a delinquent gains a bad reputation. This bad reputation lowers the behavioral expectations of others (i.e., teachers, parents, friends). The juvenile internalizes this reputation and acts in accord with it, resulting in more bad behavior, which everyone expects. According to this view, juveniles who are labeled as delinquents are actually encouraged to commit future acts of delinquency through the lowered expectations of others and a changed self-image. The more frequent and prolonged the individual's contacts with the juvenile justice system, the more likely it is that he or she will ultimately accept the delinquent label as a personal identity and perhaps enter a life of crime.

In a 1964 book, *Delinquency and Drift,* David Matza argued that most delinquents realize that what they do is wrong and feel guilty about it. They learn "techniques of neutralization" to rationalize their behavior, claiming that it was necessary for self-defense or that the victim deserved it. Matza believes that delinquency is episodic and that juveniles "drift" away from the rules of society (through neutralization techniques), but that they can also drift back.[32] Statistics indicate that most juveniles commit crimes, but they generally do not become adult criminals. Proponents of the concept of a delinquent subculture have difficulty explaining this phenomenon.

social bond
A person's attachment to others, commitment to conventional activities, involvement in those activities, and belief in widely shared moral values.

Strength of the Social Bond

The third type of sociological explanation of crime is based on the individual's bond to society. When that bond is weakened or broken, the constraints that society places on the individual are also weakened or broken. As a result, the person becomes more likely to break the law. A person's **social bond** to society has four primary elements: attachment to others, commitment to conventional ac-

The stronger the social bond an individual feels, the less likely he or she will engage in delinquency. The elements of this bond include attachment to others, commitment and involvement in conventional activities, and belief in widely shared moral values.

tivities, involvement in conventional activities, and belief in widely shared moral values.

In an attempt to test this theory, Travis Hirschi administered a self-report survey to 4,000 junior and senior high school students in California. He found that strong attachments to parents, commitment to values, involvement in school, and respect for police and law reduced the likelihood of delinquency. Replications of this study in Albany, New York, and elsewhere have generally supported Hirschi's results.[33]

It is clear that sociological explanations of crime far outnumber psychological or biological explanations. This is because a far greater number of social influences can be identified and measured. Also, each person's social environment is different and changes over time, making sociological explanations popular among positivists.

Structural Explanations of Crime

A third approach to explaining crime focuses less on individual behavior and more on the behavior of law. That is to say, social, political, and economic conditions cause certain behaviors to be defined as criminal. These conditions also cause the law to be applied in certain ways. As a result, a great deal of "marginal" criminal behavior is defined as crimes by the powerful as a way to control people who are perceived as "undesirable." Laws against gambling, loansharking, and vagrancy are examples of the way law is employed as a tool of social control, rather than as a means of protecting society from harm.

According to the **structural** or **conflict view,** the crime problem has deeper roots than the immediate environment or the pursuit of pleasure. The criminal law reflects the will of those in power, and behaviors that threaten the interests of the powerful are punished most severely.[34] This rationale is used to explain why prisons are filled largely with poor and powerless people, rather than with

structural/conflict view
The view that there is lack of consensus on basic values, so that crime is defined in such a way as to protect the interests of the powerful.

middle- and upper-class wrongdoers. Conflict theory sees little consensus within society on basic values, and therefore the interests of the powerful are imposed through the criminal law and the manner in which it is enforced.[35] This explanation of crime clearly has merit in explaining politically or ideologically motivated crimes that are committed to protest some social, economic, or political

Media and Criminal Justice

BOYZ N' THE HOOD

John Singleton was only twenty-one when he wrote and directed the largely autobiographical movie *Boyz N' the Hood* in 1991. Set in inner-city Central Los Angeles, the film follows the lives of three boys from childhood through their teenage years, offering a showcase of sociological factors that theorists claim contribute to criminality.

The film's main character, Tre, is the product of divorced parents, but is not necessarily from a "broken family." Tre's father is a hard-working disciplinarian, determined to teach his son right and wrong; his mother is a rising professional, determined to coparent her son even though she eschews the problems of the "hood" in which Tre is raised. It is assumed Tre will do his chores, be respectful, work for his material goods, and go to college. *Boyz N' the Hood* presents Tre as an endangered species in a neighborhood where gentrification, fatherless households, peer pressure, gang wars, and substance abuse are all clearly depicted as causes of crime.

Structural explanations for crime can be seen in every scene of the movie. Graffitted walls are riddled with bullet holes and sidewalks are stained with blood. Police tape cordons off trash-strewn lots, where children gather to discuss the latest drive-by shooting. Mothers are drug-addicted and unemployed, allowing unsupervised toddlers to wander into the streets. Facets of social ecology theory are seen in community fear and physical incivilities. Elija Anderson's "siege mentality," in which residents believe in a governmental plot to eradicate the inner-city minority population, is proposed in the argument of Tre's father, Furious Styles. Furious works as a mortgage broker for poor people, trying to help them buy their own meager homes so that foreign developers don't invade the community and buy up the real estate. In a speech to the residents of Compton, he points out that in their neighborhood there is a liquor store and gun shop on every corner, but that one would never find such shops in Beverly Hills.

Social Process theories can also be found in the movie. Albert Cohen's "middle class measuring rods" are illustrated when Tre's white teacher explains to the black children about how the Pilgrims were our forefathers. When young Tre argues that he believes the origin of all mankind is from Africa, the teacher deems him disruptive and he is suspended from school. Still, Tre uses his "reaction formation" to become what Cohen termed a "college boy." His friend Ricky, however, reacts to his blocked opportunities as a "corner boy" participating in minor crimes for peer acceptance while at the same time using his athletic ability as his ticket out of the hood. Ricky's brother Doughboy is clearly a "delinquent boy," a drop-out and ex-con who has no job, no college, and no future to sustain him. Doughboy hangs out, drinking and smoking with his friends, living each violent day as if it might be his last.

Labeling theory is shown in the self-fulfilling prophecies predicted by each boy's parents. Tre's parents reinforce him with education and values: Even in a world of police brutality and peer pressure. Tre knows he is good and does not succumb to the pull of his neighborhood. Ricky's mother tells the boy on a daily basis that he will become a football star, providing him with the reinforcement to pursue a football scholarship. Her other son, Doughboy, is reminded daily that he is fat, lazy, and worthless in his mother's eyes: "just like your father," she says.

Boyz N' the Hood is a virtual storyboard of crime theories. The movie's focus is not based in plot, but rather in the realities of a "hood" that proves to be a rich and fertile breeding ground for young criminals. Singleton ends his movie with a sobering statistic: One in twenty young black men in an inner-city neighborhood will die of gunshot wounds, most at the hands of other young black men. His movie shows some of these young men, both the victims and the perpetrators, but ends in a message of hope with his main character Tre. Tre serves as Singleton's message that there are success stories in the inner-city, that not all residents of the "hood" become part of their environment, and that early intervention is the key.

MEDIA AND CRIMINAL JUSTICE QUESTION

Which explanation of crime accounts for the crime depicted in *Boyz N' the Hood*? Defend your answer.

condition. People who publicly refuse to pay their federal income taxes, or who protest mandated changes in the school curriculum by refusing to send their children to school, provide examples of the conflict view. In both cases it might be said that there is conflict regarding basic values, and therefore the powerful (i.e., those who make the laws) have used their position to impose their values on society. On the other hand, the conflict view has little relevance in explaining murder, rape, robbery, assault, burglary, larceny, and many other crimes, which are rarely committed for ideological reasons.[36]

The structural view focuses, therefore, on the structure of society and how certain behaviors come to be defined as criminal. It also attempts to explain why the law is enforced selectively. It is less successful in explaining how and why individuals choose to violate the law under most circumstances.

The Ethical Explanation of Crime

Classicists explain crime in terms of the hedonistic nature of humans. Positivists emphasize the ways in which the social environment leads some people to commit crimes. Structuralists focus on the political forces that cause laws to be made and enforced in certain ways. The **ethical view** sees crime as a moral failure in decision-making. Simply stated, crime occurs when a person fails to *choose* the proper course of conduct owing to failure to appreciate its wrongfulness, rather than because of the possibility of being caught, as the classicists suggest. According to the ethical view, the positivist and classical views are inadequate. In their place, the following set of principles are proposed:

ethical view
The view that crime results when criminal acts bring pleasure, rather than guilt, owing to failure to learn how to prioritize values in difficult situations.

1. External factors play a role in influencing some people to engage in crime, although these factors by themselves do not *cause* crime (as positivists suggest).
2. A freely willed decision lies at the base of virtually all criminal behavior, but there is no hedonistic tendency to engage in crime that is controlled only through the possibility of apprehension (as classicists suggest).
3. Crime is caused by failure to appreciate the wrongfulness of criminal conduct (i.e., failure to appreciate its long-term impact on the offender and on the community or victim).

In this view, crime results when criminal acts bring pleasure rather than guilt. The key to understanding crime causation lies in discovering *how* people make noncriminal choices. Stated another way, where do people learn to make decisions in accord with legal and ethical principles?

Ethicists argue that most people are incapable of thinking through decisions in ethical terms because ethical principles are rarely included in the educational process.[37] Lacking education or experience in ethical decision-making, people often do what comes naturally: They base decisions on self-interest rather than on the greater interest of the community, they are concerned primarily with the short-term consequences of their decisions, and they confuse competing values such as honesty and loyalty. This is illustrated by individuals who derive pleasure from shortchanging a store clerk, shoplifting, gang crimes, vandalism, and other

TABLE 4.2

Four Approaches to Explaining Criminal Behavior

TYPE OF EXPLANATION	PRIMARY CAUSE OF CRIME	PRESCRIBED REMEDY
Classical	Free-will decision guided by hedonistic tendency to maximize pleasure and minimize pain	Deterrence through threat of apprehension and punishment
Positivist	Internal or external factors (e.g., biological, psychological, social, economic)	Rehabilitation or reform by changing these internal or external conditions, or changing someone's reaction to them
Structural	Political and economic conditions promote a culture of competitive individualism in which individual gain becomes more important than the social good	More equitable distribution of power and wealth in society, so that all individuals have a greater stake in a better society
Ethical	Free-will decision guided by ethical principles; illegal conduct fails to bring pleasure owing to its wrongfulness and empathy for the victim	Education and reinforcement in ethical decision-making from an early age; reduction of external factors that promote unethical decisions

crimes, rather than feeling guilt over the wrongful behavior and empathy for the victim. For example, a recent study of college students and prison inmates found the students were much more likely to feel bad or stressed about committing a crime, whereas the prison inmates were more likely to feel exhilarated or proud.[38] This suggests that appreciation of the wrongfulness of conduct (the basis for ethics) may be a bulwark against criminal behavior.

If positivists lay too much blame for crime on the doorstep of social and economic conditions, classicists give too much credence to the impact of threatened penalties, and structuralists place too much emphasis on economic inequality, an ethical approach would redirect the focus on external conditions and penalties to focus instead on *individual responsibility.* When ethical principles are internalized, criminal conduct is prevented because pleasure is no longer derived from crime, owing to the understanding and value placed on the crime's wrongfulness and impact.

Table 4.2 summarizes the major features of each of the four basic explanations of crime. The relationship between the identified causes and the prescribed solutions is highlighted.

Correlates of Crime

The tension among the classical, positivist, structural, and ethical explanations of crime lies in their emphasis. The positivist and structural explanations place most of the responsibility for crime on social factors that influence behavior. The classical and ethical explanations place most of the responsibility on individual decision-making. The classicists place more emphasis on how the likelihood of apprehension and the threat of penalties (i.e., pain) control the pursuit of pleasure (i.e., crime), whereas the ethical view places more emphasis on the fact that crime (i.e., victimizing others) does not bring pleasure to ethical individuals.

FUTURE ISSUES

Television Crime Dramas and the Causes of Homicide

Crime-oriented programs are among the most popular forms of entertainment on television. News magazines, televised trials, "reality" police shows, and crime dramas can be found every night on many different channels. Crime dramas are fictional and are created to entertain viewers. It is likely that fact-based crime shows also serve primarily to entertain rather than inform, owing to their propensity to feature the most sensational and violent cases. For many people however, a significant part of what they know about crime is derived from crime drama; most people do not have personal experience with violent crime.

Most crime dramas focus on the commission and solution of homicides. This runs counter to the fact that homicide is by far the least commonly committed serious crime. Television crime dramas also devote very little time to the causes of the criminal behavior depicted, often resorting to "blind passions, crazy plots, and references to magic, if not to clinical madness," while simultaneously placing great emphasis on careful, scientific gathering and analysis of evidence.[A] These contradictions between media images of crime and its reality have given rise to increasing criticism of the media's role in creating inaccurate public perceptions.[B]

In 1997, a study was published on the content of all episodes of regularly scheduled network television crime dramas over a period of six weeks. A total of sixty-nine programs were studied. (Movies, news broadcasts, reruns, magazine shows, "reality" police shows, and comedies that dealt with crime were excluded.) The study found that most programs left viewers "with the impression that homicides were the consequences of idiosyncratic behavior; the result of vague and indeterminate causes, often perpetrated by 'people who were killers'; and generally unconnected to events of the past or present that might otherwise account for the behavior."[C] The programs made virtually no attempt to account for the homicidal behavior in terms of the offender's social background, or past experiences, deprivations, or failure to develop moral values, and they did not consider the deterrent influences of the criminal law. In two thirds of the crime dramas reviewed, the most common plot motives were greed, mental illness, self-protection, murder for hire, vengeance, or a jilted friend or lover.

Such a portrayal of homicide suggests that it stems from individual characteristics and circumstances and that larger social factors are irrelevant. The viewer comes away with the notion that homicide offenders are different from other individuals. Rarely is an effort made to provide insight into why most people, when placed in similar situations, do not commit (or even consider) homicide. The result over the long term may be an aggravation of the view that law-abiding people are "us" and offenders are "them"—with no thought to the influences and motivations that are common to everyone.

FUTURES QUESTION

If many people base their views about the causes and prevention of homicide on television crime dramas, what will be the impact if an increasing number of these programs begin broadcasts on an increasing number of channels?

NOTES

[A]E. Mandel, *Delightful Murder* (Minneapolis: University of Minnesota Press, 1984), p. 43.

[B]Ray Surette, *The Media and Criminal Justice: Images and Reality* (Pacific Grove, CA: Brooks/Cole, 1992).

[C]David Fabianic, "Television Dramas and Homicide Causation," *Journal of Criminal Justice,* vol. 25 (1997), p. 200.

Regardless of one's perspective on the causes of crime, however, it is agreed that guns and drugs are very often associated with criminal activity. The disagreement occurs in determining precisely how to counteract these dangerous associations among crime, guns, and drugs.

Guns

Few issues in criminal justice provoke more boisterous debate than the connection between guns and crime. The incidence of crimes involving guns is extremely high, but it is not clear whether the absence of guns would necessarily reduce the rate of violent crimes. If all guns disappeared tomorrow, would violent crime disappear? Would it be significantly reduced?

Crime involves a decision by an individual. It is unlikely that a gun determines this decision, but it is possible that the presence of a gun would give a potential offender the "courage" to proceed with a crime that he or she might not otherwise commit. This is what much of the gun control debate is about. To what extent would better control of guns result in better control of crime? To answer this question we need accurate information about the incidence of crimes involving guns. We can then proceed to a review of various strategies for making it more difficult for criminals to obtain guns.

According to victimization surveys, 29 percent of victims of rape, robbery, and aggravated assault faced an offender with a firearm.[39] In 86 percent of these cases, the offender used a handgun. According to the Uniform Crime Reports, 70 percent of murders are committed with firearms,[40] and 81 percent of these involve handguns. It is clear that murder is the only crime of violence that is committed principally with guns, although handguns are the firearm of choice among criminals using weapons for all types of offenses.

Despite the relatively low rate of gun use for all violent crimes except murder, efforts to keep guns away from criminals are hotly debated. Proposals to reduce the availability of guns for criminal use most often involve one or more of the following: ban handguns altogether for most citizens, ban assault weapons, ban the carrying of weapons, ban certain kinds of bullets, and impose mandatory sentences for crimes using guns. A brief examination of these alternative proposals illustrates why they have had limited success.

Several cities have banned handguns for nearly all citizens except police officers; Washington, D.C., is the largest of these cities. However, the impact on crimes committed with handguns has been negligible,[41] for two reasons. The first is that local gun control laws are unlikely to be effective when guns are readily available in bordering jurisdictions. The classic case is that of John Hinckley, who bought a gun in another jurisdiction, brought it to Washington, and shot President Reagan. The second reason is that there are an estimated 70 million handguns in the United States. Even though most are owned by law-abiding citizens, guns often find their way into the hands of criminals.

During the last one hundred years, more than 220 million guns were manufactured in or imported to the United States. Since 1973 alone, more than 40 million handguns have been produced in the United States.[42] It is not known what percentage of these guns have been lost, seized, stolen, or destroyed, but it is reasonable to believe that most are still in working order. An indirect measure of the percentage of guns that are stolen can be obtained from interviews with inmates (admittedly, a sample consisting only of offenders who have been caught and incarcerated). A survey of inmates in state prisons found that 9 percent had stolen a gun, and 28 percent had acquired a gun illegally from a fence or drug dealer.[43] Interviews with juvenile and adult inmates in other studies have found that between 10 and 50 percent have stolen a gun at some point in their criminal career.[44] In fact, the FBI's National Crime Information Center listed more than 300,000 *reported* incidents of stolen guns, ammunition, cannons, and grenades in a single year.[45] Of the guns stolen, almost 60 percent were handguns. Thus,

Banning handguns for private citizens in some localities has not had significant impact on gun-related crimes because guns remain available in bordering jurisdictions. There are 70 million handguns already in circulation the United States, and public fear of crime remains high.

other than increasing the "black market" price for stolen handguns, attempts to ban handguns will have little impact in the foreseeable future.

A second proposal is to ban assault weapons. Such a ban is even less likely to lower crime rates because criminals rarely use these weapons to commit crimes. As noted earlier, 81 percent of murders with guns are committed with handguns, and most of the remainder do not involve assault weapons. Therefore, a ban on assault weapons would have extremely little impact on gun crimes, even if the assault weapons now in circulation could be effectively monitored, something that is not currently possible. The National Firearms Act requires that all automatic weapons be registered with the Bureau of Alcohol, Tobacco, and Firearms. In 1995, more than 240,000 automatic weapons were legally registered, and nearly 8 percent of these were reported as stolen.[46]

A third proposal is to severely restrict the unauthorized carrying of a handgun. The idea behind these laws is that handguns are easily carried and concealed. If this were not the case, perhaps fewer handgun crimes would occur. Interviews with convicted offenders show that many purchased a gun for self-defense, left home without intending to commit a crime, but ended up using the gun while committing a crime.[47] Beginning with Massachusetts, a number of states have made it illegal to carry a handgun without a special license. The penalty is a mandatory sentence of one year in prison simply for illegally carrying the weapon. In Massachusetts, gun crimes decreased after the law was enacted, but assaults with other kinds of weapons increased, suggesting a "substitution effect" in weapon choice. Also, murders and robberies with guns decreased in Boston, but they also decreased in cities without such prohibitions over the same period.[48] These findings suggest that guns are an *accompaniment* to crime rather than a causal influence.

A fourth proposal is to ban bullets. Such bans have been proposed several times, mostly in the context of armor-piercing bullets that would be dangerous to police. Since few criminals have been caught with such dangerous bullets and no police officer has yet been killed with them, it is not clear how common they really are.[49] The problem with this proposal is that bullets are easily manufactured at home by the enterprising hunter, private citizen, or criminal. Therefore, a ban on bullets "would stimulate a sizable cottage industry" in bullet-making.[50]

The fifth proposal is to impose mandatory sentences for crimes committed with guns. Many states and cities have passed laws increasing the penalties for these offenses. Evaluations of their impact reveal that these sentencing laws have had little effect because the criminals affected were already receiving severe sentences.[51] Simply stated, offenders who commit crimes with guns already receive severe sentences (for the robbery, assault, or murder they committed). The impact of a law that adds a year or two in prison is insignificant in comparison.

It is clear that these five frequently heard proposals are flawed, for a variety of reasons. The debate could focus instead on one fundamental issue: How can we keep guns out of the hands of juveniles, criminals, and the mentally ill? Provisions for background checks at the point of sale are minimal, the records that are supposedly checked (to determine criminality or mental illness) are incomplete, and many gun sales occur between private owners and hence are beyond the practical reach of regulation. Closer surveillance of gun sales would entail costs that American society appears unwilling to pay. The gun control debate therefore focuses almost entirely on criminal penalties. Contemporary proposals to sue gun manufacturers, require gun insurance, and establish gun-free zones around schools are replacing more serious discussion of the connection between guns and crime.[52] However, until point-of-sale checks (both retail and private) are monitored more effectively and the criminal and mental health records on which background checks are based are made more accurate, it will be impossible to keep guns away from criminals, juveniles, and the mentally ill.

Drugs and Alcohol

Like guns, drugs are an issue that is often raised in discussions of what to do about crime. The issue is twofold: To what extent are drugs and crime linked, and what is the best way to reduce the proportion of criminals who use drugs?

The number of adults arrested for violation of drug laws increased by 150 percent between 1980 and 1995.[53] Court commitments to state prisons for these violations have risen by 104 percent in recent years.[54] These figures illustrate a dramatic escalation in public concern about drug offenses, but they do not demonstrate a connection between drugs and crime. This is because the total number and penalties for drug law violations increased over the same period, and those arrested may have been entrepreneurs catering to the public demand for drugs, rather than drug users.

In 1987, the National Institute of Justice began the Drug Use Forecasting (DUF) program in New York City. By 1990, this program had expanded to twenty-three cities. Urine specimens are taken from a sample of arrestees in each city to determine what proportion of those arrested have already used drugs. More than half of male arrestees in each DUF city tested positive for drugs at the time of arrest.[55] A majority of women also tested positive for at least one drug, regardless of the crime for which they were arrested.[56] Although these figures do not necessarily mean that drugs *caused* the criminal activity in question, it suggests that drugs play some role in the lifestyle of the arrestee. Better-controlled studies have found that criminals who use drugs commit robberies and assaults more often than non–drug-using offenders.[57] Another study found that more than half of the murders that occur in New York City are drug-related (39 percent involved drug trafficking, 8 percent drug intoxication, 2 percent a theft to buy drugs; 4 percent involved more than one of these causes).[58]

Trained dogs are used to search vehicles for drugs at border crossings. More than 60 percent of jailed offenders used drugs regularly, and about 30 percent had used drugs at the time of the offense.

It appears that alcohol also plays an important role in crime, particularly violent crime. It has been found, for example, that chronic drinkers are more likely than nondrinkers to have histories of violent behavior. Tests have shown that drinking immediately preceded half of all violent crimes studied by researchers.[59]

Among offenders in jail for any crime, more than 75 percent have used drugs in the past, about 60 percent use drugs regularly, and about 30 percent had used drugs at the time of the offense. More than 56 percent of inmates state that they were under the influence of drugs or alcohol at the time of the offense.[60] The evidence is quite strong, therefore, that use of drugs and alcohol is correlated with criminal behavior. Proposals for reducing the use of drugs are intended to reduce either the supply of drugs or the demand for them.

Strategies to reduce the supply of drugs have included massive increases in arrests for drug crimes and prevention of the importation of drugs to the United States. Neither of these strategies has had a significant long-term impact. So-called police crackdowns or "sweeps," in which many arrests are made in a specific geographical area, have been found to have little effect. Although these crackdowns often reduce drug trafficking for short periods in the targeted areas, studies have found that drug markets are simply moved, and customers go elsewhere to purchase the product.[61] Strategies to prevent the import of drugs have been unsuccessful for related reasons. Source countries have little incentive to substitute less profitable crops for drug-producing plants such as coca and poppies, and the immense borders of the United States are difficult to monitor effectively.[62]

Demand reduction strategies focus on drug education, treatment, and punishment as methods to reduce the public's appetite for drugs. These efforts have shown sporadic success. In Maricopa County, Arizona, for example, a "zero tolerance" program was instituted to hold all drug users accountable for their behavior. In two years of operation, a drug task force made 730 arrests, 32 percent of which were for marijuana possession. A large number of cases that previously would have been dismissed were referred for drug treatment, thus "widening the net" of the criminal justice system by including more offenders of all types. The program did succeed in increasing the use of treatment as an alternative to prosecution in some cases, and a community-wide consensus was created regarding the seriousness of the drug problem.[63]

The Drug Abuse Resistance Program (DARE) attempts to reduce drug use through educational programs for students in kindergarten through high school. More than half the nation's school districts have adopted this program in at least one of their schools. An evaluation of DARE programs found that they had little effect on drug use, attitudes toward drugs, attitudes toward the police, and self-esteem. On the other hand, DARE programs did increase student knowledge about substance abuse.[64] A revised DARE program was begun in 1993, and it appears that more interactive learning strategies involving student role-playing and responding to case-based scenarios may prove more effective.

A study of drinking at college parties found that students who did not drink believed the risk of being caught was very high if they committed a crime. Those who drank most heavily condemned crime less strongly and believed the risk of being caught was low. A major implication of this research is that it may be possible to reduce crime by preventing heavy drinking.[65]

Treatment programs to reduce the drug-using population have had mixed results. Such programs are of two types: treatment with medications (i.e., other drugs, such as methadone), and behavioral programs that employ counseling and other techniques to reduce drug dependency. The differences between these two approaches are summarized in Table 4.3.

Perhaps the largest study of the impact of drug treatment tracked 10,000 patients receiving methadone maintenance, residential treatment, or outpatient treatment. Regardless of the type of treatment used, it was found that heroin use was reduced even three to five years after the treatment ended. The rate of serious crimes committed by these patients also dropped after treatment. Unfortunately, treatment for at least six months was necessary to overcome heroin addiction. In addition, no treatment program was found to have much success in reducing use of cocaine, which is more addictive than heroin.[66]

It appears that attempts to decrease drug use by reducing either supply or demand will require new ideas if they are to become more effective. Clearly, a reduction in demand would make a reduction in supply unnecessary. Even if the

TABLE 4.3

Summary of Drug Abuse Treatment Methods

Pharmacological modalities: treatment with prescribed medications

1. Agonist substitution: treatment with a medication that has pharmacological actions similar to the abused drug; methadone treatment of heroin addiction and nicotine chewing gum treatment of tobacco dependence are examples
   a. Maintenance: chronic treatment at a stabilized dosage; methadone maintenance is an example
   b. Detoxification: short-term treatment with progressively decreasing dosages to suppress withdrawal signs and symptoms following cessation of drug abuse
2. Antagonist treatment: treatment with a medication that blocks the pharmacological effects of the abused drug; naltrexone treatment of heroin addiction is an example
3. Symptomatic treatment: treatment with a medication whose pharmacological mechanism of action is not related to that of the abused drug, but whose effects might alter some of the symptoms of drug abuse; benzodiazepine hypnotic/tranquilizer treatment of the insomnia and anxiety associated with opioid withdrawal is an example

Behavioral modalities: treatment with nonpharmacological methods based on the learning of altered behavioral patterns

1. Verbal therapy: a broad range of counseling and psychotherapy approaches relying primarily on talking; provided in either individual or group formats
2. Contingency management: systematic scheduling of consequences to desirable or undesirable behavior so as to provide incentives for therapeutic behavior change; based on the experimentally derived operant psychology principles of Skinner
3. Conditioning therapy: systematic controlled exposure to drug-related stimuli in the absence of drug abuse so as to reduce or eliminate the learned ability to elicit feelings of drug withdrawal or drug craving; based on the experimentally derived classical conditioning psychology principles of Pavlov
4. Therapeutic community: relatively long-term (typically six months or longer) treatment in a closed residential setting emphasizing drug abstinence and the learning of new attitudes and behaviors toward drugs and toward others in society
5. Skill development: a broad range of interventions intended to teach specific skills in areas where deficits are thought to contribute to drug abuse vulnerability; vocational/employment skills, job-finding skills, social skills, assertiveness skills, and relaxation/stress management skills are examples
6. Peer support self-help groups: modeled after Alcoholics Anonymous, recovering abusers share their experiences and support one another in remaining drug-free; Narcotics Anonymous is an example

SOURCE: *Drug Abuse and Drug Abuse Research* (Rockville, MD: National Institute on Drug Abuse, 1991).

supply were somehow reduced, lingering demand would create new criminal opportunities such as we now find in the domestic manufacture of synthetic drugs through chemical combinations.[67] Despite these roadblocks, efforts are under way to reduce the demand and availability of drugs. The central role of the family is made clear by the fact that inmates whose parents abused drugs began using drugs themselves by age thirteen. If the parents did not abuse drugs or alcohol, the child did not use drugs until age sixteen.[68] An examination of community antidrug efforts in thirteen cities found that those with a broader scope (such as community education, family-support, and security programs) and those that forged cooperative partnerships with the local police had some impact regardless of the type of neighborhood involved.[69] Much of the hope for reducing drug use in American society is likely to emerge from these community efforts.

Critical Thinking EXERCISE

Explaining an Attempted Assassination

In 1981, John Hinckley stood outside the Hilton Hotel in Washington, D.C., as President Ronald Reagan left the hotel surrounded by police and Secret Service agents. Hinckley shot the President, and wounded several other people, from a distance of no more than twenty feet. He was quickly subdued and charged with attempted murder.

It soon became known that Hinckley had become obsessed with actress Jodie Foster after seeing her in the movie *Taxi Driver.* He had written her several letters, but it was clear that he had no chance of developing a relationship with her.

Critical Thinking Question

Assuming that you possess only this information, what psychological explanation could you use to explain Hinckley's shooting of the President, especially since there was absolutely no chance that he could avoid being caught?

President Ronald Reagan waves, then looks up before being pushed into a limousine by Secret Service agents after being shot outside a Washington Hotel by John Hinckley on March 30, 1981.

A Case Study of Delinquency

Following is an excerpt from the report of a probation officer in an actual case of delinquency. The juvenile's name is Waln Brown. The complainants are Waln's mother and his high school principal; the complaint is failure to obey the reasonable commands of his family and fighting in school (for which Waln was suspended).

> **Waln Brown is 15 years old, has above average intelligence, and is nearly six feet tall. He is extremely nervous and was a bed-wetter until age nine. Presently, he has acute acne.**
>
> **Waln's mother is an insistent, possessive, and very dominating personality. Mr. Brown is rather cool, calm, and fairly well collected. Of the two, he seems the most sensible. Mrs. Brown is inclined to be flighty, easily disturbed, and is emotionally unstable.**

Mrs. Brown's work hours are such that she has little time to spend with the children, and when she does devote a little time to them her nerves are frayed to the point where she makes rash judgements. Presently, Mrs. Brown is an emotionally sick woman. Waln has lacked an opportunity to associate with his father, and this has created unconscious hostilities toward his environment.

The trials and tribulations that Waln has gotten himself into are not too abnormal, nor have they been of the seriously antisocial kind. To our way of thinking, this environment could have produced a much more seriously delinquent youngster than we are currently dealing with. Actually, Waln is and has been, during the most impressionable period of his life, a rejected, over-dominated child, and at the moment he is striking back at society. And we are using these terms in their widest sense.

SOURCE: Waln Brown, *The Other Side of Delinquency* (New Brunswick, NJ: Rutgers University Press, 1983).

Critical Thinking Questions

1. **As a criminologist assigned to this case, what theory(s) of crime discussed in this chapter do you think best explain Waln's delinquency?**
2. **What disposition would you recommend in court, and how is it related to the causes you have identified?**

Summary

CLASSICAL EXPLANATIONS OF CRIME

- The classical school of thought in criminology sees crime as resulting from the conscious exercise of an individual's free will that is controlled by the threat of punishment.

POSITIVIST EXPLANATIONS OF CRIME

- The earliest positivists saw the roots of criminal behavior in biological attributes, an approach known as biological determinism.
- Psychological explanations look inside the human psyche (i.e., at internal controls) for the causes of crime.
- Some explanations of crime based on Freud's theory of personality see delinquency as resulting from the failure of the ego or superego to control the id; others focus on defense mechanisms that shield the individual from anxiety or guilt.
- Sociological explanations of crime focus on environmental influences that affect the way people behave.
- There are several types of sociological explanations, including theories based on learning, theories based on blocked opportunity, and labeling theory.

STRUCTURAL EXPLANATIONS OF CRIME

- Structural explanations focus on the selective formulation and application of the law rather than on the behavior of individuals.

THE ETHICAL EXPLANATION OF CRIME

- The ethical view sees crime as a moral failure in decision-making.

CORRELATES OF CRIME

- The incidence of crimes involving guns is extremely high, but it is not clear whether the absence of guns would necessarily reduce the rate of violent crimes.

- The main proposals for reducing the availability of guns for criminal use include banning handguns altogether, banning assault weapons, banning carrying of weapons, banning certain kinds of bullets, and imposing mandatory sentences for crimes using guns.
- There is strong evidence that use of drugs or alcohol is correlated with criminal behavior.
- Strategies to reduce the supply of drugs include massive increases in arrests for drug crimes and efforts to prevent the importation of drugs to the United States. Demand reduction strategies focus on drug education, treatment, and punishment.

Key Terms

classical school
positivism
biological determinism
id
superego
ego
defense mechanism
displacement
reaction formation
cultural transmission
differential association
anomie
labeling theory
social bond
structural/conflict view
ethical view

Questions for Review and Discussion

1. What is the main drawback of the classical explanation of crime?
2. What conclusions have been reached by recent studies of the connection between biological factors and criminal behavior?
3. What are some of the psychological defense mechanisms that have been linked to criminal behavior?
4. What did Sutherland mean by differential association?
5. Briefly describe Cloward and Ohlin's theory of blocked opportunity.
6. How does labeling theory explain juvenile delinquency?
7. How do structural explanations of crime differ from other types of explanations?
8. What is the central focus of the ethical view of crime?
9. What are the main proposals for reducing the availability of guns for criminal use? Why do they tend not to be very effective?
10. What strategies have been proposed to reduce the supply of drugs or the demand for them?

Notes

[1]Alfred Blumstein, "Violence by Young People: Why the Deadly Nexus?," *National Institute of Justice Journal* (August 1995), pp. 2–9; John M. Dawson and Patrick A. Langan, *Murder in Families* (Washington, D.C.: Bureau of Justice Statistics, 1994); John Ritter, "Parent-Killers: A Deadly Streak," *USA Today* (March 8, 1995), p. 3; Kevin Johnson, "Woman Charged in Kids' Fire Deaths, *USA Today* (August 23, 1994), p. 3; Barry Meier, "Sexual Predator Finding Sentence May Last Past Jail," *The New York Times* (February 22, 1995), p. 1.

[2]International crime statistics are still difficult to compare, but more efforts are being made to develop a reliable base of international crime data. See James P. Lynch, "Building Data Systems for Cross-National Comparisons of Crime and Criminal Justice Policy," *ICPSR Bulletin*, vol. 15 (February 1995), pp. 1–6.

[3]Interpol, *International Crime Statistics* (Lyons, France: Interpol General Secretariat, 1990).

[4]Compare the conclusions of Don C. Gibbons, "Talking about Crime: Observations on the Prospects for Causal Theory in Criminology," *Criminal Justice Research Bulletin*, vol. 7 (1992), pp. 1–10 with Michael R. Gottfredson and Travis Hirschi, *A General Theory of Crime* (Stanford, CA: Stanford University Press, 1990).

[5]For excerpts from the writings of Bentham and Beccaria, see Joseph E. Jacoby, *Classics of Criminology*, 2nd ed. (Prospect Heights, IL: Waveland Press, 1994).

[6]Michael R. Gottfredson and Travis Hirschi, *A General Theory of Crime* (Stanford, CA: Stanford University Press, 1990), pp. 90–1.

[7]Augustine Brannigan, "Self-Control, Social Control, and Evolutionary Psychology: Towards an Integrated Perspective on Crime," *Canadian Journal of Criminology*, vol. 39 (October 1997), pp. 403–31; T. David Evans, Francis T. Cullen, Velmer S. Burton, Jr., R. Gregory Dunaway, and Michael L. Benson, "The Social Consequences of Self-Control: Testing the General Theory of Crime," *Criminology*, vol. 35 (August 1997), pp. 475–501.

[8]Charles Darwin, *The Origin of Species* (New York: Modern Library, 1936).

[9]Emile Durkheim, *Suicide* (New York: Free Press, 1951).

[10]Cesare Lombroso and Gina Lombroso-Ferrero, *The Criminal Man* (Montclair, NJ: Patterson Smith, 1972).

[11]Charles Goring, *The English Convict* (London: Her Majesty's Stationery Office, 1913).

[12]R. J. Herrenstein, "Criminogenic Traits," and Patricia A. Brennan, Sarnoff A. Mednick, and Jan Voluka, "Biomedical Factors in Crime," in J. Q. Wilson and J. Petersilia, eds., *Crime* (San Francisco: ICS Press, 1995).

[13]Janet Katz and William J. Chambliss, "Biology and Crime," in J. Sheley, ed., *Criminology: Contemporary Handbook* (Belmont, CA: Wadsworth, 1991); Lee Ellis, "Genetics and Criminal Behavior," *Criminology*, vol. 20 (1982), pp. 43–66; William Gabrielli and Sarnoof Mednick, "Urban Environment, Genetics, and Crime," *Criminology*, vol. 22 (1984), pp. 645–53.

[14]Jeffrey A. Roth, "Understanding and Preventing Violence," *National Institute of Justice Research in Brief* (February 1994), p. 8; Albert J. Reiss and Jeffrey A. Roth, eds., *Understanding and Preventing Violence* (Washington, D.C.: National Academy Press, 1993).

[15]For a summary of this research, see Lee Ellis and Anthony Walsh, "Gene-Based Evolutionary Theories in Criminology," *Criminology*, vol. 37 (1997), pp. 229–76; Tim Friend, "Violence-Prone Men May be Both Born and Made," *USA Today* (December 14, 1994), p. 5D; Robert Wright, "The Biology of Violence," *The New Yorker* (March 13, 1995), pp. 68–77.

[16]Richard Jenkins and Lester F. Hewitt, *Fundamental Patterns of Maladjustment* (Springfield, IL: Thomas, 1947).

[17]William McCord and Joan McCord, *Psychopathy and Delinquency* (New York: Grune & Stratton, 1956).

[18]James Sorrells, "Kids Who Kill," *Crime and Delinquency*, vol. 23 (1977), pp. 312–20; Richard Rosner, Melvin Widerlight, M. Bernice Horner Rosner, and Rita Reis Wieczorek, "Adolescents Accused of Murder and Manslaughter: A Five-Year Descriptive Study," *Bulletin of the American Academy of Psychiatry and the Law*, vol. 7 (1979), pp. 342–51.

[19]Steven Spaccarelli, Blake Bowden, J. Douglas Coatsworth, Soni Kim, "Psychosocial Correlates of Male Sexual Aggression in a Chronic Delinquent Sample," *Criminal Justice and Behavior*, vol. 24 (March 1997), pp. 71–95.

[20]Albert K. Cohen, *Deviance and Control* (Englewood Cliffs, NJ: Prentice Hall, 1966).

[21]See Karl Schuessler and Donald Cressey, "Personality Characteristics of Criminals," *American Journal of Sociology* vol. 55 (1950), pp. 476–84; Gordon Waldo and Simon Dinitz, "Personality Attributes of the Criminal: An Analysis of Research Studies: 1950–1965," *Journal of Research in Crime and Delinquency*, vol. 4 (1967), pp. 185–201; David J. Tannenbaum, "Personality and Criminality: A Summary and Implications of the Literature," *American Sociological Review*, vol. 22 (1977), pp. 225–35.

[22]Clifford R. Shaw and Henry D. McKay, *Juvenile Delinquency and Urban Areas* (1932), reprint (Chicago: University of Chicago Press, 1969); Leo Carroll and Pamela Irving Jackson, "Inequality, Opportunity, and Crime Rates in Central Cities," *Criminology* vol. 21 (1983), pp. 178–94.

[23]Robert J. Sampson and W. Byron Groves, "Community Structure and Anomie: Testing Social Disorganization Theory," *American Journal of Sociology,* vol. 94 (1989), pp. 744–802.

[24]Paul E. Bellair, "Social Interaction and Community Crime: Examining the Importance of Neighborhood Networks," *Criminology,* vol. 35 (1997), pp. 677–703.

[25]Edwin H. Sutherland, *Principles of Criminology* (Philadelphia: Lippincott, 1939).

[26]Jack Gibbs, "The State of Criminological Theory," *Criminology,* vol. 25 (1987), pp. 821–40; Mark Warr and Mark Stafford, "The Influence of Delinquent Peers: What They Think or What They Do?", *Criminology,* vol. 29 (1991), pp. 851–66.

[27]Spaccarelli et al., "Psychosocial Correlates of Male Sexual Aggression in a Chronic Delinquent Sample," p. 92.

[28]Robert K. Merton, "Social Structure and Anomie," *American Sociological Review,* vol. 3 (1938), pp. 672–82.

[29]Albert K. Cohen, *Delinquent Boys: The Culture of the Gang,* reprint of 1955 edition (New York: Free Press, 1971).

[30]Richard A. Cloward and Lloyd E. Ohlin, *Delinquency and Opportunity: A Theory of Delinquent Gangs* (New York: The Free Press, 1960).

[30a]Lawrence E. Cohen and Marcus Felson, "Social Change and Crime Rate Trends: A Routine Activities Approach," *American Sociological Review,* vol. 44 (1979), pp. 588–601.

[30b]Paul F. Cromwell, Roger Dunham, Ronald Akers, and Lonn Lanza-Kaduce, "Routine Activities and Social Control in the Aftermath of a Natural Catastrophe," *European Journal on Criminal Policy and Research,* vol. 3 (1995), pp. 56–69.

[30c]Ronald V. Clarke and Marcus Felson, eds. *Routine Activities and Rational Choice* (New Brunswick, NJ: Transaction, 1993); Marcus Felson, *Crime & Everyday Life,* 2nd ed. (Thousand Oaks, CA: Pine Forge Press, 1998).

[31]Howard Becker, *The Outsiders: Studies in the Sociology of Deviance* (New York: The Free Press, 1963); Edwin M. Lemert, *Social Pathology: A Systematic Approach to the Theory of Sociopathic Behavior* (New York: McGraw-Hill, 1951).

[32]David Matza, *Delinquency and Drift* (New York: Wiley, 1964).

[33]Travis Hirschi, *Causes of Delinquency* (Berkeley: University of California Press, 1969); Michael J. Hindelang, "Causes of Delinquency: A Partial Replication and Exposition," *Social Problems*, vol. 20 (1973), pp. 470–87; LeGrande Gardiner and Donald Shoemaker, "Social Bonding and Delinquency: A Comparative Analysis," *Sociological Quarterly,* vol. 30 (1989), pp. 481–500.

[34]Jeffrey Reiman, *The Rich Get Richer and the Poor Get Prison: Ideology, Class, and Criminal Justice,* 3rd ed. (New York: Macmillan, 1990).

[35]Jeffrey Reiman, . . . *And the Poor Get Prison: Economic Bias in American Criminal Justice* (Boston: Allyn & Bacon, 1996).

[36]Ronald L. Akers, *Criminological Theories,* 2nd ed. (Los Angeles: Roxbury Publishing, 1997), pp. 157–8.

[37]Jay S. Albanese, *Dealing with Delinquency: The Future of Juvenile Justice,* 2nd ed. (Chicago: Nelson-Hall, 1993), pp. 61–4; Jay Albanese, *White Collar Crime in America* (Englewood Cliffs, NJ: Prentice Hall, 1995), pp. 105–9; Jay Albanese, *Organized Crime in America,* 3rd ed. (Cincinnati: Anderson Publishing, 1996), pp. 68–72.

[38]Peter B. Wood, "Nonsocial Reinforcement and Habitual Criminal Conduct: An Extension of Learning Theory," *Criminology,* vol. 35 (1997), pp. 335–66.

[39]Marianne W. Zawitz, *Guns Used in Crime* (Washington, D.C.: Bureau of Justice Statistics, 1995).

[40]Federal Bureau of Investigation, *Crime in the United States, 1993* (Washington, D.C.: U.S. Government Printing Office, 1994).

[41]Gary Kleck, *Point Blank: Guns and Violence in America* (New York: Aldine De Gruyter, 1991); Edward D. Jones, "The District of Columbia's 'Firearms Control Regulations Act of 1975': The Toughest Handgun Control Law in the United States—or Is It?," *The Annals,* vol. 455 (May 1981), pp. 138–49.

[42]Data from Bureau of Alcohol, Tobacco, and Firearms, cited in Zawitz, pp. 1–2.

[43]Allen Beck et al., *Survey of State Prison Inmates, 1991* (Washington, D.C.: Bureau of Justice Statistics, 1993), pp. 18–19.

[44]Joseph F. Sheley and James D. Wright, "Gun Acquisition and Possession in Selected Juvenile Samples," *Research in Brief* (Washington, D.C.: National Institute of Justice, 1993); James D. Wright and Peter H. Rossi, *Armed and Dangerous: A Survey of Felons and Their Firearms* (Hawthorne, NY: Aldine, 1986).

[45]Cited in Zawitz, p. 4.

[46]Cited in Zawitz, p. 5.

[47]James D. Wright and Peter H. Rossi, *Armed and Considered Dangerous: A Survey of Felons and Their Firearms* (New York: Aldine, 1986).

[48]Glenn L. Pierce and William J. Bowers, "The Bartley-Fox Gun Law's Short-Term Impact on Crime," *The Annals* vol. 455 (May 1981), pp. 120–37.

[49]Kleck, *Point Blank,* p. 82.

[50]Samuel Walker, *Sense and Nonsense about Crime and Drugs,* 3rd ed. (Belmont, CA: Wadsworth, 1994).

[51]Colin Loftin and David McDowall, "One with a Gun Gets You Two: Mandatory Sentencing and Firearms Violence in Detroit," *The Annals,* vol. 455 (May 1981), pp. 150–67; Alan Lizotte and Marjorie S. Zatz, "The Use and Abuse of Sentence Enhancement for Firearms Offenses in California," *Law and Contemporary Problems,* vol. 49 (1986), pp. 199–221.

[52]Dennis A. Hennigan, "Gun Makers are Liable," *USA Today* (March 27, 1995), p. 10; "Require Gun Insurance" *USA Today* (January 4, 1994), p. 10; Herb Kohl, "Keep Schools Gun-Free," *USA Today* (May 3, 1995), p. 10.

[53]Federal Bureau of Investigation, *Uniform Crime Report—1996* (Washington, D.C.: U.S. Government Printing Office, 1997).

[54]Allen J. Beck, *Prisoners in 1994* (Washington, D.C.: Bureau of Justice Statistics, 1995), p. 13.

[55]National Institute of Justice, *Arrestee Drug Use* (Washington, D.C.: National Institute of Justice, 1990).

[56]National Institute of Justice, *Drug Use Forecasting: 1993 Annual Report* (Washington, D.C.: U.S. Department of Justice, 1994).

[57]Jeffrey A. Roth, *Psychoactive Substances and Violence* (Washington, D.C.: National Institute of Justice, 1994).

[58]P. J. Goldstein, H. H. Brownstein, P. J. Ryan, and P. A. Bellucci, "Crack and Homicide in New York City, 1988: A Conceptually Based Event Analysis," *Contemporary Drug Problems,* vol. 16 (Winter 1989), pp. 651–87.

[59]Roth, p. 2.

[60]Caroline Wolf Harlow, *Drugs and Jail Inmates* (Washington, D.C.: Bureau of Justice Statistics, 1991).

[61]David M. Kennedy, *Closing the Market: Controlling the Drug Trade in Tampa, Florida* (Washington, D.C.: National Institute of Justice, 1993); Lawrence W. Sherman, "Police Crackdowns: Initial and Residual Deterrence," in M. Tonry and N. Morris, eds. *Crime and Justice: A Review of Research* (Chicago: University of Chicago Press, 1990).

[62]U.S. Comptroller General, *Drug Control: Interdiction Efforts in Central America Have Had Little Impact in the Flow of Drugs* (Washington, D.C.: U.S. General Accounting Office, 1994); U.S. Comptroller General, *Drug Control: Heavy Investment in Military Surveillance is Not Paying Off* (Washington, D.C.: U.S. General Accounting Office, 1993).

[63]John R. Hepburn, Wayne Johnston, and Scott Rodgers, *Do Drugs. Do Time: An Evaluation of the Maricopa County Demand Reduction Program* (Washington, D.C.: National Institute of Justice, 1994).

[64]Christopher Ringwalt et al., *Past and Future Directions of the D.A.R.E. Program: An Evaluation Review* (Research Triangle Park, NC: Research Triangle Institute, 1994).

[65]Lonn Lanza-Kadua, Donna M. Bishop, and Lawrence Winna, "Risk Benefit Calculations, Moral Evaluations, and Alcohol Use: Exploring the Alcohol-Crime Connection," *Crime & Delinquency,* vol. 43 (1997), pp. 222–39; see also, J. J. Thompson, "Plugging the Kegs: Students Benefit When Colleges Limit Excessive Drinking," *U.S. News & World Report* (January 26, 1998), pp. 63–7.

[66]R. L. Hubbard, *Drug Abuse Treatment: A National Study of Effectiveness* (Chapel Hill: University of North Carolina Press, 1989).

[67]Domestic Chemical Action Group, *Controlling Chemicals Used to Make Illegal Drugs: The Chemical Action Task Force and the Domestic Chemical Action Group* (Washington, D.C.: National Institute of Justice, 1993).

[68]Caroline Wolf Harlow, p. 7.

[69]Saul N. Weingart, Francis X. Hartmann, and David Osborne, *Case Studies of Community Anti-Drug Efforts* (Washington, D.C.: National Institute of Justice, 1994).

[70]Philip Jenkins, *Using Murder: The Social Construction of Serial Homicide* (New York: Aldine de Gruyter, 1994), pp. 22–9.

[71]Philip Jenkins, "Myth and Murder," in V. Kappeler, M. Blumberg, and G. Potter, *The Mythology of Crime and Criminal Justice* (Prospect Heights, IL: Waveland Press, 1993), pp. 53–70.

[72]Ibid.

[73]Eric W. Hickey, *Serial Murderers and Their Victims* (Pacific Grove, CA: Brooks/Cole, 1991).

[74]Jack Levin and James Alan Fox, *Mass Murder* (New York: Berkeley, 1991), p. 56; Jenkins, "Myth and Murder," p. 61.

[75]Ronald M. Holmes and James De Burger, *Serial Murder* (Newbury Park, CA: Sage Publications, 1988).

[76]Ronald M. Holmes and Stephen T. Holmes, *Murder in America* (Thousand Oaks, CA: Sage Publications, 1994), pp. 119–26.

[77]Joel Norris, *Serial Killers: The Growing Menace* (New York: Dolphin, 1988).

[78]Steven A. Egger, *Serial Murder: An Elusive Phenomenon* (New York: Praeger, 1990), p. 19; James Alan Fox and Jack Levin, *Overkill: Mass Murder and Serial Killing Exposed* (New York: Plenum, 1994), pp. 91–2.

[79]Donald T. Lunde, *Murder and Madness* (Stanford, CA: Stanford Alumni Association, 1976); W. S. Willie, *Citizens Who Commit Murder: A Psychiatric Study* (St. Louis: Warren Green, 1975); J. M. Reinhardt, *The Psychology of Strange Killers* (Springfield, IL: Charles C. Thomas, 1962).

[80]Fox and Levin, *Overkill: Mass Murder and Serial Killing Exposed,* pp. 18–9.

For Further Reading

Ronald L. Akers, *Criminological Theories,* 2nd ed. (Los Angeles: Roxbury Publishing, 1997).

Geoffrey Canada, *Fist Stick Knife Gun* (Boston: Beacon Press, 1996).

Elliott Currie, *Crime and Punishment in America* (New York: Holt, 1998).

Joseph E. Jacoby, ed., *Classics of Criminology,* 2nd ed. (Prospect Heights, IL: Waveland Press, 1994).

chapter five

Criminal Law

Remove justice, and what are kingdoms but gangs of criminals on a large scale?

ST. AUGUSTINE
(354–430 A.D.)

The proper role of law in regulating behavior is a subject of continuing debate. To what extent should the law be used to regulate behavior?

Consider the case of the father of a high school football player. Before a game he sharpened a buckle on his son's helmet. The buckle cut several opposing players, one of whom required twelve stitches. The reason for the father's action was that referees had not penalized opposing players for harming his son in an earlier game.[1] Is this conduct illegal or simply a case of bad judgment? Should the son be held accountable, or were the injuries entirely the father's fault?

These questions are fundamental to understanding criminal justice because the criminal law defines the outer boundaries of the criminal justice system. Police, courts, and corrections can take no action until a

CHAPTER OUTLINE

MEDICAL
EXAMINER

behavior has been criminalized. Understanding the nature, elements, and sources of criminal law provides a basis for comprehending how acts become defined as crimes, and how liability is imposed or excused under various circumstances.

The Nature of Criminal Law

civil law
Formal rules that regulate disputes between private parties.

criminal law
Formal rules designed to maintain social control.

The law can be divided into two basic categories: civil and criminal. **Civil law** is the set of formal rules that regulate disputes between private parties. Civil laws are concerned primarily with issues of personal injury and compensation. Most law is civil law, reflecting the large number and many types of disputes that can arise between individuals. **Criminal law,** on the other hand, is the set of formal rules for maintaining social control. Violations of criminal law are considered crimes against society because they break rules that have been established for the common good of society. In civil law, in contrast, no general societal interest is at stake.

Criminal cases are concerned primarily with issues of societal injury and the appropriate punishment of the offender. In fact, the nature of punishment is a basic difference between civil and criminal law. Only the government (which represents society) can use legitimate force against a person. Civil penalties are designed only to provide compensation to an injured party. In the case of the football helmet, both the father and the son can be charged with assault. Their actions fulfilled the elements of the crime (discussed in Chapter 2) by unlawfully causing injury to another. The buckle was sharpened by the father for a specific illegal purpose, and the son used the buckle in a menacing and dangerous way. They could be criminally punished by the government through fines or jail. In addition, players who were injured by the sharpened helmet buckle could bring civil suits against the father and son to seek compensation for their injuries. The difference between the criminal and civil cases would be in their objectives: punishment in one case and compensation in the other.

substantive criminal law
The specific behaviors prohibited under the criminal law.

procedural law
The rules for adjudication of individuals suspected of violating the law.

The criminal law can be further divided into two types. **Substantive criminal law** defines behaviors that are prohibited, and **procedural law** provides the rules for adjudication of cases involving those behaviors. For example, the precise definitions of rape, robbery, burglary, or assault are included in the substantive criminal law. The rules of criminal procedure (discussed in later chapters) are specified in procedural law. These procedural rules are designed to ensure fairness in arrests, searches, preliminary hearings, arraignments, trials, and every other stage of the criminal justice process. All states, as well as the federal government, have both a substantive and a procedural criminal law, which vary somewhat among jurisdictions. This chapter focuses on substantive criminal law.

Sources of Criminal Law

American criminal law is derived from British common law. Even though legal codes have existed for thousands of years in societies of all kinds, the structure of American law is modeled most closely on the British experience.[2] The common law was a body of unrecorded decisions made by judges in England during the Middle Ages. These decisions reflected the social values, customs, and beliefs of the period, and they were used as a basis for making decisions in subsequent cases. As time went by, these decisions were recorded and followed more formally, so that legal decisions were guided by case law rather than by rules established by legislatures.

When America was first colonized, British precedents and procedures were followed. Biblical principles were often relied on in court, as was the case in England. Nevertheless, living as they did in a wilderness thousands of miles from Europe, the colonists faced certain problems that did not exist in England.[3] This resulted in reliance on tighter legal rules created by local and state governments. This move toward regulating behavior by statute, rather than by court decisions, distinguishes American criminal law from its British foundations.

Today American criminal law has four main sources. The fundamental principles that guide the enactment of specific laws and the interpretations of courts are found in **constitutions.** The U.S. Constitution guides the formulation of federal law, and each state has a constitution that guides the passage of state law. If a contradiction arises between state and federal law, the U.S. Constitution supersedes any state law or constitution. For example, if Kansas passed a law making it a crime to criticize government officials, the law would be found unconstitutional by the courts. The First Amendment to the U.S. Constitution guarantees freedom of speech, and therefore such a law would be in violation of a constitutional principle and could not stand.

constitution
The fundamental principles of a society that guide the enactment of specific laws and the application of those laws by courts.

Another source of criminal law is statutes. **Statutes** are the specific laws passed by state legislatures or the U.S. Congress that prohibit or mandate certain acts. These laws are often systematically codified and compiled in a single volume called a **criminal code** or **penal code.** Legislatures can pass any law they desire as long as it does not violate a constitutional principle.

statute
Specific laws passed by legislatures that prohibit or mandate certain acts.

criminal (penal) code
A compilation of all the criminal laws of a jurisdiction.

A third source of criminal law is court decisions. These decisions, often called **case law,** involve judges' interpretations of laws passed by legislatures to determine their applicability in a given case or to clarify their meaning. In the United States, judges are required to follow previous decisions, or **precedents,** in order to maintain consistency regarding what is deemed lawful or unlawful. This precedent rule—formally termed *stare decisis*—is occasionally broken when judges believe that a reversal or modification is necessary because of changing social values. Reversals or modifications of earlier rulings are made by appellate courts.

case law
Judicial application and interpretation of laws as they apply in a given case.

precedent
Previous court decisions that are followed in current cases to ensure consistency in the application of the law.

A fourth source of criminal law is **administrative regulations.** These regulations have the force of criminal law inasmuch as they can provide for criminal penalties. They are written by regulatory agencies that have been empowered by legislatures to develop rules governing specific policy areas. Many regulatory agencies were established during the second half of the twentieth century to protect public health, safety, and welfare in an increasingly complex marketplace. The Food and Drug Administration was established to screen products to protect consumers. Similarly, the Environmental Protection Agency, Securities and Exchange Commission, and Consumer Product Safety Commission were established to promulgate rules to promote safety and consistency in dealing with pollution and waste, corporate transactions, and potentially dangerous products, respectively. If a regulatory agency wishes to add new rules, it must provide public notice of its intention and hold public hearings before the adoption of the rules. This permits public debate on proposed expansions of the scope of the law.

administrative regulations
Rules applied to organizations that are designed to protect public health, safety, and welfare in the marketplace.

If one were to collect all fifty-one federal and state constitutions, all fifty-one sets of statutes, all state and federal court decisions, and all state and federal administrative regulations, one would have a complete collection of all the criminal law in the United States. Unfortunately, the collection would soon be out of date because court decisions are made every day, and some of these decisions alter or modify existing law. Changes in statutes occur somewhat less often, and constitutions are changed only rarely.

consensus view
The view that law reflects society's consensus regarding behavior that is harmful enough to warrant government intervention.

conflict view
The view that an act becomes a crime only when it serves the interests of those in positions of power.

CONSENSUS AND CONFLICT The criminal law is said to arise from one of two primary circumstances: consensus or conflict. According to the **consensus view,** the criminal law reflects a society's consensus regarding behavior that is harmful enough to warrant government intervention. Emile Durkheim, a founder of sociology, declared in 1893 that an act is criminal "when it offends strong and defined states of the collective conscience."[4]

The **conflict view** asserts that an act becomes a crime only when it serves the interests of those holding positions of power. In this view, the criminal law is used to protect the property interests of the ruling class. The conflict view has been used to explain laws against vagrancy, loitering, and the vices. This view also attempts to explain the selective enforcement of laws against various racial, ethnic, and economic groups in terms of protecting the interests of the powerful, rather than protecting public safety in general.[5]

Examples can be found of both the consensus and conflict views. Criminal laws that have existed for centuries, such as those barring murder, assault, and larceny, clearly reflect wide social consensus regarding their harmfulness. On the other hand, newer laws such as those that severely penalize crack cocaine and juvenile law violations are directed primarily against the actions of poor and powerless groups in society. Nevertheless, the criminal law reflects social consensus in large measure, although, as seen in Chapter 8, discrimination in its enforcement is a continuing problem.

Limits of Criminal Law

Debates regarding the proper role of criminal law arise when definitions of crimes are not clear, are applied inconsistently, or appear to reach into constitutionally protected areas. In a famous case in Jacksonville, Florida, two men and two women riding in a car were stopped by police after they stopped near a used-car lot that had been broken into several times. They were charged with "prowling by auto."[6] The arrestees challenged this charge, which was part of Jacksonville's vagrancy ordinance. The U.S. Supreme Court held that the law was "void-for-vagueness." This means that the language in the law was so imprecise that a person of "ordinary intelligence" could not tell whether his or her acts were prohibited. As a result of this ruling, criminal laws must be written in very precise fashion, creating difficulties for cities attempting to legislate bans on "cruising."[7]

Another limit on the criminal law is determination of responsibility for its application. The Tenth Amendment to the U.S. Constitution gives states the power to pass laws. This "police power" enables a state to carry out its responsibility to protect health, safety, and morality. Some argue that the power to punish wrongdoers is vested in the legislature and that courts must stringently apply the law as written. Others argue that liberal, rather than strict, interpretation of statutes is necessary because no law can anticipate all the possible circumstances that may arise. Therefore, courts must be given enough leeway to apply the law to situations that were not foreseen by the legislature.

This debate continues today as legislatures pass broader laws covering more types of behaviors, but then complain about how courts apply those laws in specific cases. For example, consider laws that require motorcycle riders to wear helmets or automobile occupants to wear seatbelts. Whom do these laws protect? Do they infringe on the right of private citizens to be left alone? Clearly, it is important to protect young people, but what about protecting adults from the consequences of their own actions? Should an adult motorcycle or automobile driver be permitted to make an individual choice about safety gear? These are all valid questions that arise when the law attempts to protect "public health and safety" rather than trying to prevent a predatory harm, such as an assault or larceny, where the distinction between offender and victim is clear.[8] Using the reasoning behind helmet and seatbelt laws, could not cigarette smoking, obscene gestures, or alcohol consumption be prohibited? It is worthwhile to consider these questions in light of the discussion of Prohibition in Chapter 2.[9]

There is debate over the reach of the criminal law when it attempts to protect people from themselves, rather than from others. Mandatory motorcycle helmet laws, bicycle helmets, and seatbelt laws are believed by some to infringe on their right to privacy.

The Nature of Crime

When a legislature decides to create a new criminal law, the crime in question must contain several elements. Without any one of these elements, no crime can exist. If these elements are present, however, legislatures can choose to make any undesirable behavior illegal, as long as it does not violate a constitutional principle. This is why it is important for citizens to be informed of proposed new laws to determine whether the social goal to be accomplished will justify the possible infringement on individual liberty.

Perhaps the most important element of a crime is the **mens rea** or "guilty mind." The mens rea is a conscious decision to commit an unlawful act. It consists of more than just criminal intent because a person need not intend to commit a specific act but only to commit any act that is illegal. For example, in an argument with a lover one might draw a gun to shoot, but miss and hit an innocent bystander. This person would still be criminally liable for the death of the bystander even though he or she did not intend to kill her. The original intent to kill the lover meets the mens rea requirement because the individual intended to kill someone and did so. This person should not be punished less severely merely because he or she is a poor shot. The fact that the wrong target was hit does not negate the individual's guilty mind. Thus, mens rea connotes a guilty state of mind rather than merely criminal intent.

mens rea
The guilty mind or conscious decision to commit a criminal act.

A second element necessary for a crime is the act itself. The act, or **actus reus,** is the behavior that must be committed to meet the definition of the crime. No murder can occur without a death, and no arson can occur without a fire or

actus reus
The behavior that must be committed to meet the definition of a crime.

Most crimes require an action, or actus reus, to be committed. Nevertheless, the *failure* to act can incur liability in some cases such as failure to stop at a light, or failure to file an income tax return.

explosion. Intent to commit a crime is not sufficient for criminal liability without a specific act. Some kinds of criminal behavior require different types of acts, however. For example, *failure* to file a federal income tax return each year is a crime. In this case, the actus reus is the failure to file. As a result, actus reus can take the form of an act or of an *omission* of an act where there is a legal duty to act.

The third element of a crime is the "attendant circumstances" or causal link. That is, in order for a crime to occur, there must be a specific relationship between the act and the harm that results. For example, taking the life of another person does not always constitute criminal homicide. Homicide by police officers in the line of duty or by citizens in self-defense is viewed as justifiable. Only the unlawful or unjustifiable taking of the life of another constitutes criminal homicide. Likewise, the harm caused must follow directly from the illegal act. Intervening or superseding causes relieve one from criminal liability. If one assaults someone in a bar and that person is taken away by ambulance, one might escape liability for the victim's ultimate death if he or she is dropped by the ambulance crew or is left waiting in the emergency room for four hours before treatment is administered. In cases such as these, the court would determine the extent to which the intervening or superseding causes independently resulted in harm apart from the original assault.[10]

The circumstances or causation, together with the actus reus and mens rea, are referred to as the *elements of a crime*. Whenever a legislature defines a new form of criminal behavior, all three elements must be present. For example, a common definition of the crime of burglary is "the unauthorized entry, or surreptitious remaining in a building or occupied structure, for the purpose of committing a crime therein." The actus reus for this crime is the entry or remaining in a building, while the mens rea is "for the purpose of committing a crime therein." The attendant circumstances prescribe that the entry must be "unauthorized" or the remaining "surreptitious." Without each of these circumstances, there can be no burglary. In sum, the three elements of a crime tell us the conditions that must exist before a person can be found guilty of a particular crime.

Characteristics of Criminal Acts

The three elements of a crime—act, guilty mind, and attendant circumstances—can be more difficult to establish than is apparent at first glance. An act is required in order to confirm the existence of a guilty mind and to demonstrate the intention to carry it out. The question is *how much* of an act is necessary to incur criminal liability. Five characteristics of acts can invoke criminal liability: sufficiency, possession, statuses, voluntariness, and omissions.

SUFFICIENCY In a Utah case, the defendant fell asleep in his car on the shoulder of the highway. Police stopped, smelled alcohol on his breath, and arrested him for driving while intoxicated. His conviction was reversed by the Utah Supreme Court because the defendant was not in physical control of the vehicle at the time, as required by the law.[11] Clearly, the man probably drank, drove his car for a while, and then fell asleep. The case against him failed because he was not violating the law at the time of the arrest and because it is also possible that he

contemporary issues

Setting a Trap for Pornography

Keith Jacobson ordered two magazines entitled *Bare Boys* from a bookstore. The magazines contained photographs of nude preteen and teenage boys. Finding Jacobson's name on the bookstore's mailing list, the Postal Service and the Customs Service sent mail to him using the names of five different fictitious organizations and a bogus pen pal. The organizations claimed to represent citizens who were interested in sexual freedom and opposed to censorship. The proceeds from sales of publications were supposedly used to support lobbying efforts. Jacobson occasionally corresponded with the organizations, expressing his views of censorship and the "hysteria" surrounding child pornography.

The mail sent to Jacobson was designed to elicit a response that would violate the Child Protection Act of 1984, which bars individuals from receiving sexually explicit depictions of children through the mails. After receiving these mailings for more than two years, Jacobson ordered a magazine that depicted young boys engaging in sexual acts; he was arrested under the Child Protection Act. A search of his house revealed no sexually oriented materials except for the *Bare Boys* magazines and the government agencies' bogus mailings.

Although Jacobson claimed entrapment, he was convicted at trial. The appeal was heard by the U.S. Supreme Court, which based its decision on the subjective formulation of entrapment: The prosecution must prove beyond a reasonable doubt that the defendant was disposed to commit the criminal act *before* being approached by government agents.

The case of *Jacobson v. United States* (1992) involved the possession of child pornography in a sting operation where the government sold it to Jacobson and then arrested him for possessing it.

By the time Jacobson violated the law, he had been the target of twenty-six months of repeated mailings. Jacobson's earlier order of the *Bare Boys* magazines could not be used to show predisposition because this act was legal at the time of the order; moreover, Jacobson's uncontradicted testimony stated that he did not know the magazines would depict minors until they arrived in the mail.

The Supreme Court had previously held that a person's sexual inclinations, tastes, and fantasies are "beyond the reach of the government." In Jacobson's case, the government provoked and aggravated his interest in illegal sexually explicit materials and "exerted substantial pressure" on him to purchase them under the pretense that he was doing it as part of a fight against censorship. Jacobson's conviction was reversed.

SOURCE: *Jacobson v. United States,* 112 S. Ct. 1535 (1992).

drove while sober, pulled over, drank, and then feel asleep. In short, the act observed by the police was not sufficient to confirm the existence of a guilty mind. If the car was running, or parked on the traveled portion of the highway, this would have been sufficient to conclude that he was operating the automobile while drunk, even though the police arrived after he had fallen asleep.

POSSESSION Possession alone is sufficient to fulfill the act requirement. In a New Jersey case, the defendant and his brother had marijuana and LSD in a locked box in a closet. Both had access to the box, although both testified that the LSD did not belong to the defendant but to his brother. Should the defendant be held liable for items that were not on his person and did not belong to him? The court affirmed his conviction, holding that the elements of possession were fulfilled by the defendant: He knew of the existence and illegal nature of the object, and he had the opportunity to exercise control over it.[12] This is called **constructive possession.** It is distinguished from **actual possession,** in which the defendant has

constructive possession
A condition in which a person has the opportunity to exercise control over an object.

actual possession
A condition in which a person has exclusive control over an object.

A person may *constructively* possess an object under law without actually possessing it. This occurs most often in automobile searches when a suspect had the opportunity to exercise control over an object (e.g., a gun or drugs) in the car but did not have it on his or her person at the time of the stop.

exclusive control over an object (such as a concealed weapon), and it suffices to meet the act requirement.

STATUSES A particular status does not suffice to meet the act requirement. In a well-known California case, a man was convicted of a misdemeanor for being "addicted to the use of narcotics." His conviction was reversed on grounds that narcotics addiction has been held to be an illness, and people cannot be punished for being ill.[13] In other words, addiction is a status, not an act. A person can be convicted of buying, selling, or possessing narcotics because these are *acts*. The *status* of being an addict does not suffice for criminal punishment, however.

VOLUNTARINESS A fourth feature of criminal acts is that they must be both voluntary and conscious. Unconscious and involuntary acts are not subject to criminal penalties. In an unusual case, a handicapped passenger on a flight from the Bahamas to Luxembourg was found to possess a loaded pistol. The pilot redirected the flight to New York, where police arrested the passenger for possession of a gun without a license under New York law. The court held that the act was not voluntary because the aircraft was not scheduled to land in New York. Therefore, the passenger's presence in New York, and his possession of the gun there, was not a voluntary act and he had not committed a criminal act.[14]

OMISSIONS A fifth characteristic of the act requirement is that an omission suffices to meet the act requirement in situations in which there is a duty to act. In a child-abuse case in Pennsylvania, a woman with a five-year-old daughter lived with her boyfriend. The boyfriend regularly beat the child, ultimately causing her death. The court faced the question: Should the mother be held liable for failing to protect her child from the boyfriend's beatings? The court held that as a parent, the mother had a legal duty to protect her child, which she had failed to do.[15] Omissions most often incur criminal penalties in situations in which there is a legal or contractual duty to act. Failure to file income taxes and failure to obey traffic laws are two common examples.

The State of Mind Requirement

The state of mind requirement separates criminal from civil law. Criminal law requires *mens rea,* or a guilty mind, which is not required in civil law. Punishments for violations of criminal law are based on assessment of gradations of *mens rea*. In New York State, for example, there are three degrees of assault. Third-degree assault is causing an injury *recklessly*. Second-degree assault is causing *serious* injury recklessly, while first-degree assault is causing serious injury *with intent to cause* that injury. **Recklessness** connotes conscious disregard for a substantial and unjustifiable risk. It is punished because it fails to meet the standard of conduct of a *reasonable* person. (A hypothetical "reasonable person" is often used by the courts to assess whether a defendant's conduct is culpable or excusable.) **Intention** connotes conduct that is carried out *knowingly* or *purposely*. This indicates that the defendant either had a conscious intention to commit the act or was at least aware that the conduct would cause a certain result.

recklessness
Conscious disregard for a substantial and unjustifiable risk.

intention
Conduct that is carried out knowingly or purposely.

In an Ohio case, the defendant was upset when a man blew a horn at him while driving. The defendant took it upon himself to follow the other driver home and harass him, despite warnings that the other driver had a heart condition. Ultimately the other driver had a heart attack and died. The defendant was charged with manslaughter, and his conviction was affirmed. The court held that the death could be "reasonably anticipated by an ordinary prudent person."[16] The defendant had acted recklessly in this case, and his actions were the proximate (immediate) cause of the victim's death.

An individual's state of mind is central, therefore, to determining criminal responsibility. The more an act reflects planning, or behavior that deviates from the standard of a reasonable person, the more severe the punishment. This is distinguished from civil law, in which the objective is to obtain compensation for private injury and the defendant's state of mind is less relevant.

The Causation Requirement

An act must be shown to cause the particular harm suffered. In most cases this is not a problem, except when the act and the resulting harm are separated by time or place. Three conditions can characterize the relationship between the act and the harm suffered in order for the act to be considered a crime. These conditions are "but for" causation, proximate causation, and simultaneous causes.

In a Pennsylvania case, three men mugged a man named Markiw. Markiw suffered chest pains, was brought to a hospital, and died five days later. Should the muggers be held liable for robbery *and* murder? In this case the court ruled that Markiw's heart disease was aggravated by the mugging, and upheld a murder conviction.[17] "But for" the mugging (the act), the court ruled, Markiw would not have died so soon. The harm caused by a criminal act must always have occurred *because of* the act. This issue arises most commonly in homicide cases.

The act must also be the "proximate cause" of the result. That is to say, the harm must be sufficiently direct, logical, natural, and not dependent on the acts of others. In a Rochester, New York, case, Frank Stafford drank heavily and flashed $100 bills. Three other men at the bar decided to rob him. They offered him a ride, robbed him, and left him drunk and half undressed in the middle of the road. A truck came by and accidentally hit Stafford and killed him. Are the three robbers the proximate cause of Stafford's death? Even though the death was unintended, the court held that it "should have been foreseen" and was "reasonably related" to the robbers' actions. A conviction for murder was upheld.[18] What this means is that a defendant is responsible for the natural and probable consequences of his or her acts.[19] This causal chain is broken only by unforeseeable intervening and superseding causes, which did not occur in this case.

Simultaneous causes, which separately would cause the harm suffered, generally result in liability for *both* parties. For example, in a Kentucky case, Gibson drove into the country to try out a new pistol. He shot at a tree. Two men named Jones and Taylor heard the shots and confronted Gibson, arguing about the legality of his target practice. Shots were fired, and both Jones and Taylor shot Gibson once, killing him. Each wound was sufficient to cause death. Whose bullet killed the victim? Jones argued that he should not be held liable because there was no evidence to show that *his* bullet had killed Gibson. The court held, however, that whether a person actually inflicts the wound or contributes in some way to the harm, he or she is guilty.[20] Without such reasoning, both defendants would go free in such cases. Although simultaneous causation, and problems in establishing proximate or "but for" causation, are rare, they most often occur in homicide cases, which makes them significant issues in criminal law.

Defenses to Criminal Charges

criminal liability
Establishing the presence of the elements of a crime in a given case, thereby subjecting the accused person to criminal penalties.

In criminal cases, police and prosecutors attempt to establish **criminal liability.** This involves establishing the presence of the elements of the crime that subject the accused person to criminal penalties. Defendants, and defense lawyers working in their behalf, attempt to establish reasons why the act, guilty mind, or attendant circumstances do not apply. In many cases the defense will stipulate that the act and harm were both caused by the defendant, but that there is a valid excuse for the defendant's conduct. Acceptable legal defenses are of three general types: defenses related to mental illness, defenses involving force, and defenses involving justification or excuse.

Defenses Related to Mental Illness

Mental illness can play a role in a criminal case in two ways. First, it must be asked whether the defendant is sane enough to be placed on trial. Second, it must be established whether the defendant was sane at the time of the act.

A defendant must be mentally competent to stand trial in order to understand the legal proceedings against him or her. The legal standard for determining competency to stand trial was established nearly forty years ago, when the U.S. Supreme Court held that a person is incompetent to stand trial if he or she lacks the ability to consult with a lawyer with a reasonable degree of understanding *and* lacks a rational and factual understanding of the legal proceedings.[21]

A defendant who is found incompetent to stand trial does not go free. He or she can be committed to a mental institution and tried after having been restored to competency. Courts have held that a person may be held in a mental institution for "a reasonable period" to achieve competency to stand trial. Some courts have interpreted this period to be no more than the maximum sentence for the crime, if convicted.[22]

insanity defense
A claim that the defendant was not sane under law at the time of the act.

reasonableness standard
A standard under which persons are culpable for their actions if they understand the consequences of those actions. Young children and the mentally ill are generally not held culpable owing to their inability to reason effectively.

A more controversial application of mental illness to criminal law occurs when one attempts to determine whether a defendant was sane at the time of the act. A defense based on the claim that the defendant was not sane at the time of the act is referred to as the **insanity defense.** It is based on the principle that it is not desirable to punish people who are not blameworthy. Thus, the law treats young children and the mentally ill in the same way. Neither are held culpable for their actions because they do not understand the consequences of those actions; this is known as the **reasonableness standard.** The inability of young children or the mentally ill to reason or rationalize in a competent manner makes criminal punishment of their conduct both ineffective and illogical.

FUTURE ISSUES

Maternal Infanticide

Infant homicides (called infanticides) are among the rarest forms of homicide. Those committed by mothers are rarer still. Nevertheless, in 1994 the world's attention was focused on this issue when Susan Smith was convicted of drowning her two children.

According to the *Uniform Crime Reports,* approximately six hundred homicides of children under age five are committed each year. However, the U.S. Advisory Board on Child Abuse and Neglect estimates that nearly 2,000 infants and young children die from abuse or neglect each year.[A] Many of these cases involve maternal infanticide.

Postpartum psychosis is the medical label for irrational behavior that results from depression following childbirth, but little is known about the social circumstances that accompany such behavior.[B] In an important study, Martha Smithey interviewed fifteen Texas women who had been held legally responsible for the deaths of their own infants. She discovered that the women had been victims of prior sexual abuse or trauma at the hands of both relatives and strangers. They were also abused by their husbands. As mothers, they had little or no emotional support, and the fathers of the infants were abusive, unsupportive, or antagonistic.[C] The fathers also provided very little economic support. Figure 5.1 illustrates the factors associated with infanticides.

As Figure 5.1 illustrates, the lack of emotional or economic support from parents or fathers, combined with their antagonistic or abusive behaviors toward the mothers, resulted in significant emotional stress, substance abuse by the mothers, and ultimately infanticide. The substance abuse occurred as a mechanism to cope with the stress, and it interfered with rational judgment in the mother's actions toward the child.

FUTURES QUESTION

If it is true that 2,000 young children die each year at the hands of their parents or caregivers, and the parents are sometimes victims of abuse themselves, what would you propose as a way to break this cycle?

NOTES

[A] U.S. Advisory Board on Child Abuse and Neglect, *A Nation's Shame: Fatal Child Abuse and Neglect in the United States* (Washington, D.C.: U.S. Department of Health and Human Services, 1995).

[B] C. Dix, *The New Mother Syndrome: Coping with Post-Partum Stress and Depression* (New York: Doubleday, 1985).

[C] Martha Smithey, "Infant Homicide at the Hands of Mothers: Towards a Sociological Perspective," *Deviant Behavior,* vol. 18 (1997), pp. 255–72.

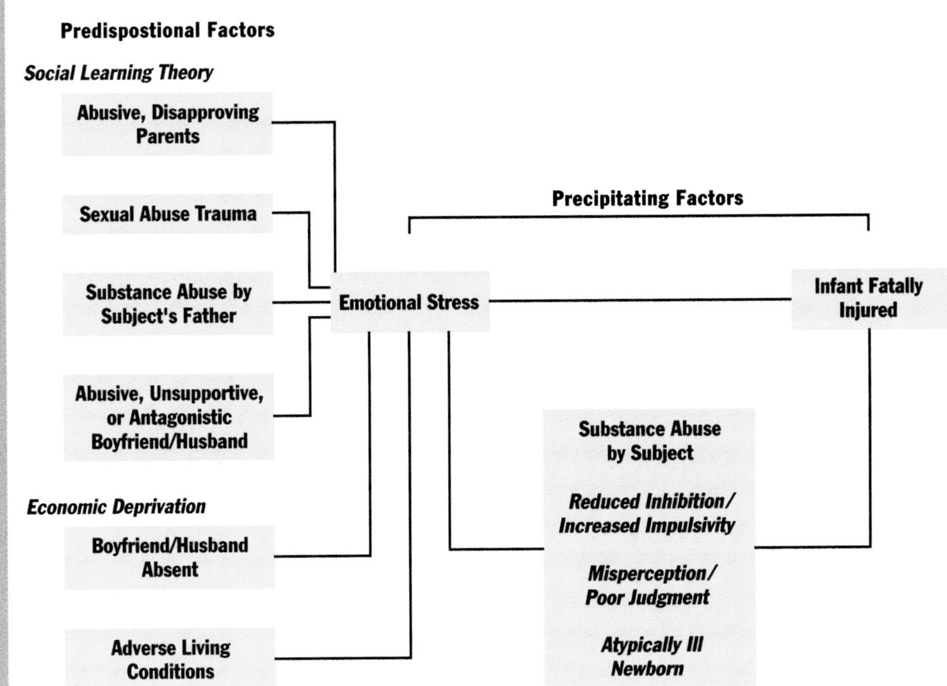

FIGURE 5.1

A conceptual model of infanticide

SOURCE: Martha Smithey, "Infant Homicide at the Hands of Mothers: Toward a Sociological Perspective," *Deviant Behavior,* vol. 18 (1997), pp. 255–72.

Over the years the courts have adopted several different formulations of the insanity defense. None has been satisfactory because in each instance the legal system finds itself asking a question that it cannot answer: What was the person's level of mental functioning at the time of the crime, and does it constitute insanity? This is ultimately a question of *mens rea* (or lack of it), and psychiatrists are unable to agree on a standard for determining the presence or absence of *mens rea* in any given case.

The insanity defense originated in England in 1843 in the case of Daniel M'Naghten. M'Naghten suffered from the delusion that the British prime minister, Sir Robert Peel, was going to have him killed. In order to frustrate this imagined conspiracy against him, M'Naghten went to the prime minister's house in an effort to kill him first. He killed the prime minister's secretary by mistake.

After a trial for murder, M'Naghten was found not guilty by reason of insanity. On appeal, England's highest court formulated the *M'Naghten rule,* which defined legal insanity for the first time. The definition of insanity focused on the *reasoning ability* of the defendant in determining whether he did not know the nature and quality of his act, or know that it was wrong, owing to a disease of the mind.[23]

In 1887, the *irresistible impulse* rule was adopted in Alabama, where a defendant was ruled to be insane if he or she had been "moved to action by an insane impulse controlling the will of judgment."[24] In 1954, the *Durham rule* was adopted in a federal court, which held that legal insanity occurs when the "unlawful act was the *product* of mental disease or defect."[25] This version of "but for" causation gave much credence to psychiatric courtroom testimony in determining whether a particular act was the "product" of mental illness.

In 1972, the test for legal insanity proposed by the American Law Institute in the Model Penal Code was adopted in federal courts. In this formulation legal insanity exists when a defendant "lacks substantial capacity to appreciate the wrongfulness of his conduct or to conform his conduct to the requirements of the law."[26] This definition of legal insanity modified earlier definitions, changing "know" to "appreciate" and "irresistible impulse" to "lacks substantial capacity." The Model Penal Code was adopted in all federal courts and in about half the states.

To the average person, this all appears quite subjective, and this has been true in practice. Prosecutors always seem able to find mental health experts who will argue that the defendant is mentally competent, while experts for the defense argue the reverse. Juries are often left to their own judgment in the battle of "dueling experts" in the courtroom. To the public, the insanity defense looks like a mechanism by which offenders "get away with murder." This has resulted in many calls for abolition of the insanity defense. Aside from the possibility that it might allow dangerous people to go free, the insanity defense has also created some ironic situations. During a trial, a prosecutor might argue that the defendant was sane at the time of the act. However, if the defendant is found not guilty by reason of insanity, the prosecutor would then have to make the reverse argument, claiming that the defendant was insane, in order to obtain a civil commitment to a mental institution. The opposite has occurred for the defense. In some cases the prosecution and defense have actually exchanged their psychiatric experts after a finding of not guilty by reason of insanity, because they were now making arguments regarding civil commitment that contradicted the arguments made during the criminal trial.

In practice, the insanity defense has not been invoked very often. Studies have found that the insanity plea is used in only 2 percent of cases that go to trial.[27] Moreover, this defense has rarely been successful. Judges and juries issue verdicts of not guilty by reason of insanity in only 2 to 5 percent of the cases in which it is attempted.[28] The number of people in mental hospitals who have been found not guilty by reason of insanity constitutes fewer than 1 percent of the inmates held in prisons who were found guilty of the crime with which they were charged.[29]

Interestingly, the debate over the insanity defense may be beside the point, as follow-up studies of insanity cases have found that the length of incarceration in prison of those found guilty was virtually the same as the length of incarceration in mental hospitals of those found not guilty by reason of insanity.[30] The U.S. Supreme Court has even found it constitutional to hold "insane" individuals in mental hospitals longer than they would have been held in prison if they had been convicted and sentenced.[31]

Nevertheless, dissatisfaction with the insanity defense has led to its abandonment in three states (Montana, Idaho, Utah). This appears to have had little impact in practice, however, as defendants who are likely to plead insanity have been found incompetent to stand trial. The result is that they are confined indefinitely to the same mental hospitals to which they would have been committed if they had been found not guilty by reason of insanity.[32]

In 1982, John Hinckley was found not guilty by reason of insanity in the attempted murder of President Reagan. Many believed that Hinckley "got away with murder," although he remains confined indefinitely at St. Elizabeth's Hospital in Washington, D.C. In response to public outrage at this finding, seventeen states adopted a new type of verdict called "guilty but mentally ill." This means that the defendant was not legally insane at the time of the offense but suffered from a disorder that may have affected the commission of the crime. If found guilty but mentally ill, an offender is sentenced to prison but given psychological treatment. This is a troublesome outcome for two reasons. First, most prisons have no facilities for treating mental illness, and such treatment is not often guaranteed or enforced as directed by the court.[33] Second, guilty but mentally ill findings appear to constitute punishment without *mens rea*. To punish someone who is mentally ill violates a fundamental assumption of criminal law: We cannot compare the conduct of a mentally ill person to the "reasonableness" standard. The finding of guilty but mentally ill thus does not appear to be a logical solution to the perceived problem of the insanity defense, other than to assuage public and political feelings about the certainty of punishment.

Defenses Involving Force

A person may use force for self-protection or to protect others, but as we will see shortly, the extent of that force is limited by law. Defenses involving force are of three types: self-defense, defense of others, and defense of property.

The battered woman syndrome is an extension of the law of self-defense. Victims who have suffered from an ongoing pattern of physical abuse have been exempted from liability when they strike out at their attackers in situations in which they are not imminently threatened with harm.

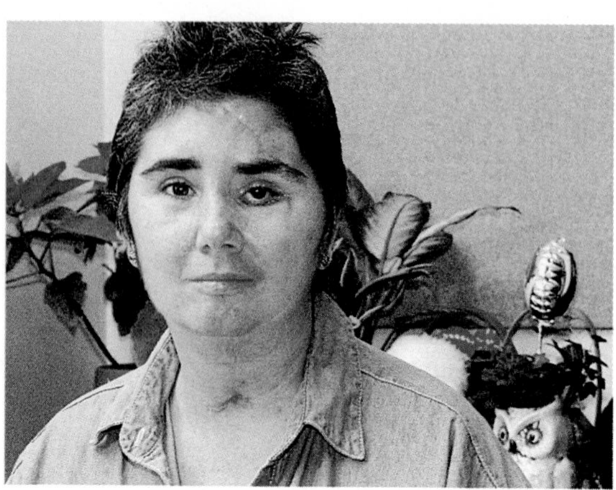

As a general rule, a person is permitted to use whatever force reasonably appears necessary, short of deadly force, to prevent immediate and unlawful harm to him- or herself. The right to kill in self-defense is permitted only to prevent imminent death or serious injury threatened by the attacker. Although the concept of self-defense is easily understood, problems can arise when the victim's *perception* of potential harm is not reasonable.

In a Louisiana case, a bar patron weighing 215 pounds threatened to kill the bartender, who weighed only 145 pounds, for refusing to serve him drinks after he had become intoxicated. The unarmed patron started to climb over the bar, and the bartender shot him. Clearly, the extent of force used by the bartender exceeded that used by the patron. However, the court ruled that the shooting was lawful because of the circumstances. The size and age of the parties, the threat of weapons, and the aggressiveness of the assault are all relevant in determining the reasonableness of the victim's behavior. In this case, the court believed that the patron's large size and irrational, aggressive behavior were enough to justify the bartender's belief that his life was in danger.[34]

Some states require a person who can safely retreat from danger to do so before using deadly force, on the principle that it is not reasonably necessary to use extreme force when danger can be avoided by running away. Other states see the issue differently, basing their self-defense laws on the belief that a person should not be required to run away from an aggressor. In no state, however, is a person required to retreat from an attack in his or her own home.

The dual issues of "reasonably necessary" force and no requirement of retreat in one's own home have collided in cases of spousal abuse. In one case, the defendant killed her husband by stabbing him with a pair of scissors. She was not in fear of immediate harm at the time of the act, but her husband had a history of assaulting her when he was drunk.[35] In another case, a woman set fire to her husband's bed while he was sleeping because he had beaten her severely and would not allow her to leave.[36] The rules of self-defense do not apply in these cases because of the absence of an immediate threat of harm. Nevertheless, many courts have permitted defendants in such cases to claim self-defense on grounds that an ongoing pattern of severe physical abuse constitutes a continual threat of harm. This has been called the **battered woman syndrome.** Some states have changed their laws to expand the application of

battered woman syndrome
An ongoing pattern of severe physical abuse that constitutes a continual threat of harm.

self-defense to situations in which women have been the victims of a pattern of physical abuse.

Laws permitting the use of force in defense of others are designed to encourage citizens to come to the aid of others. A person may use reasonable force to defend another person against unlawful force. The force used can be no more than what would be justified in self-defense. In one case an inmate in a Massachusetts prison attempted to rescue a fellow inmate from a severe beating by assaulting a corrections officer who was inflicting the beating. In determining whether the inmate's intervention was legally justified, the court held that defense of others "does not necessarily stop at the prison gates."[37]

The right to defend one's property by force is narrowly limited. In general, reasonable force, short of deadly force, can be used to protect property or prevent a crime. Deadly force in defense of property is permitted only in one's own home during a burglary or other dangerous felony, such as rape, kidnapping, or robbery. In a California case, a man had tools stolen from his garage. To prevent further thefts he rigged a pistol that would fire at the door if it was opened slightly. This contraption shot a 16-year-old in the face during an attempted theft. The garage owner was convicted of assault because "deadly mechanical devices are without mercy or discretion."[38] They place at risk children, firefighters, and others who might enter the garage for reasons other than theft. Deadly force in defense of property is not permitted unless the victim is in imminent danger of serious bodily harm (in which case the rules for self-defense would apply).

Defenses Involving Justification or Excuse

In certain cases defendants admit to unlawful conduct, but an overriding justification or excuse makes their actions lawful. Five defenses of this type are discussed here: duress, necessity, mistake of fact, ignorance of law, and entrapment.

DURESS Three conditions must be met for a claim of **duress** to succeed as a defense. The defendant must have engaged in a criminal act because of a threat of serious bodily harm by another person. In addition, the threat must be immediate and without reasonable possibility for escape. In many jurisdictions the defense of duress is disallowed if the defendant intentionally or recklessly placed him- or herself in a situation subject to duress. (The defense of duress is called *coercion* or *compulsion* in some jurisdictions.)

duress
A defense in which a person claims to have engaged in criminal conduct because of a threat of immediate and serious bodily harm by another person.

In a Washington, D.C., case, Clifford Bailey and James Cogdell escaped from jail, claiming that there had been "various threats and beatings directed at them." In addition, conditions at the jail were deplorable:

> **Inmates . . . and on occasion the guards . . . set fire to trash, bedding, and other objects thrown from the cells. According to the inmates, the guards simply allowed the fires to burn until they went out. . . . [And] poor ventilation caused the smoke to collect and linger in the cellblock.[39]**

The defendants also testified that the guards had subjected them to beatings and death threats and that medical attention was inadequate. In response to the charge of escape, they claimed the defense of duress, citing the horrible conditions they had endured in prison.

The book and movie *Alive* depict a situation similar to that 100 years ago in England where two men were tried for murder after they had been lost at sea and killed and ate a boy in order to survive.

The U.S. Supreme Court held that duress was not applicable in this case because the defendants had made no "bona fide effort to surrender or return to custody as soon as the claimed duress or necessity had lost its coercive force."[39] (The defendants were at large for a month or more.) Criminal acts committed while an individual is under immediate, serious, and nonreckless duress are excused only while the coercive threats are in force. Once the duress has ended, no further criminal conduct is excused.

NECESSITY In a classic case from the late 1800s, two men and an eighteen-year-old boy were shipwrecked and adrift at sea in a raft for twenty days. After a week without food or water, and with little hope of rescue, the two men decided to kill the boy and eat him so that they could survive. They reasoned that the boy had no family responsibilities whereas they did, making the boy more expendable. The two men were rescued four days later.

Were the men guilty of homicide, or could their behavior be excused? They claimed the defense of necessity, which holds that a defendant has engaged in otherwise criminal behavior because of the forces of nature. In this case the men were convicted of homicide and sentenced to death, sentences that were later commuted to six months in prison. The court held that people may not save themselves at the expense of another.[40] The defense of necessity is successful only in cases in which the necessity is great, no reasonable alternative exists, and the harm done is less than the harm avoided. In this case, since a death was caused to prevent another death, the defense was not applicable.

Necessity is called the "choice of evils" in the Model Penal Code. This conveys the principle that harm is done in these cases and that the defense is allowed only where the correct choice between degrees of harm is made. That choice must always be the lesser evil. In a Colorado case an attorney's claim of necessity in response to a charge of speeding was rejected since his claim that he was late for a court hearing because of delays in a previous hearing elsewhere "failed to establish that he did not cause the situation or that his injuries would outweigh the consequences of his conduct."[41] Nevertheless, one can imagine a circumstance in which speeding might be excused, such as a passenger suffering a medical emergency. Here again, the balance between the lesser of two evils lies at the heart of the defense of necessity.

IGNORANCE OR MISTAKE OF FACT Mistake or ignorance of fact can serve as a defense if it negates the state of mind required for the crime. The mistake or ignorance must be both honest and reasonable. If a woman mistakenly picks up a purse that is very similar to her own and walks off with it, she could claim mistake of fact in response to a charge of larceny. The mistake of fact is a defense because it negates the *mens rea* element of the crime of larceny. A court would assess the circumstances to determine whether the mistake was both honest and reasonable.

An exception to this rule is made for strict liability offenses. These offenses can be committed without *mens rea* and still be punished with criminal penalties. They are limited to conduct that poses grave threats to public health, safety, or welfare. The government uses strict liability to impose high standards of conduct in business and industry in order to prevent contamination of food, protect employees in dangerous work environments, and so on.

An interesting example is the law against bigamy. Both English common law and rulings in some states have upheld bigamy charges even when the defendant has been shown to have a reasonable belief that a prior marriage ended in divorce or the death of the previous spouse.[42] This is because bigamy laws are often written as strict liability offenses, in which no *mens rea* is required. Strict liability offenses are exceptions to the guilty mind requirement and therefore rarely occur.[43] In cases such as bigamy, engaging in the criminal conduct, however reasonable the circumstances, still incurs a criminal penalty.

IGNORANCE OR MISTAKE OF LAW Ignorance of the law has rarely been sufficient to excuse criminal conduct. It is permitted as a defense only in situations in which the law is not widely known and a person cannot be expected to be aware of a particular law. These situations are not common because citizens are generally expected to know the law and a claim of ignorance could be used to excuse virtually any type of illegal conduct. In a California case, Neva Snyder claimed that her conviction for possession of a firearm as a convicted felon should be overturned. She mistakenly believed that her prior conviction for marijuana sales was only a misdemeanor. Since the court held that she was "presumed to know" what the law is, her mistake was not reasonable.[44]

In another case, an offender failed to register under a local ordinance requiring convicted persons to do so. The U.S. Supreme Court reversed the conviction, stating that ignorance of law could be used as an excuse in this case.[45] Thus, if the ignorance or mistake is reasonable under the circumstances, and there is no evidence that the defendant should have known of the illegality of the conduct, ignorance or mistake of law is a defense.[46]

Media and Criminal Justice

THE ADVOCATE

An examination of our criminal justice system always returns to the sources of criminal law, for without the law there could be no law violators for the system to process. The origins of U.S. criminal law are historically based in the feudal landlord system of Western Europe, evolving from the common law systems of countries such as England and France.

Based on a true story and set in fifteenth century France, the 1993 movie *The Advocate* (also known as *The Hour of the Pig*) bears a plot so unbelievable that it might be mistaken for a comedy. The story revolves around a lawyer from Paris, the "advocate" Richard Courtois, who leaves the big city and journeys to the provinces, where he attempts to use his city logic in a country court where archaic common law continues to reign. The crusty old magistrate is simply a puppet of the local landlord, who pays all the courtroom actors to make sure things are done exactly the way they have always been done.

The opening scene of the movie features a peasant and a she-ass on the gallows and nooses around both the man's and the donkey's necks, in preparation for hanging. The crime of both, it is learned, is "unnatural sexual acts." Just as the lever is about to be pulled, a messenger arrives with a letter of reprieve. Unfortunately for the peasant, the pardon is for the she-ass. The letter defends the good character of the donkey, who was "violated without consent" and declares her free "without stain to her character."

In medieval France, the viewer soon sees, an animal is considered as culpable as a human for its "crimes." Advocate Courtois serves as the equivalent to today's public defender, charged with providing legal advocacy for anyone (or thing) charged in the land baron's court. In his first case, he must defend a local woman charged with witchcraft. In the landlord's court, precedent dictates that a witch is a witch, and rats can testify in court, but not Jews. Logic is secondary to custom.

Courtois soon finds his most challenging case when he is told he must defend a pig. The pig is charged with killing a young boy, but it also belongs to the Gypsy family whom the villagers fear and despise. The Gypsies need their pig to survive, and know that the pig is falsely accused. The ideas that the seizure and imminent execution of the pig for murder is really about getting rid of the Gypsies is a fact that the land baron barely tries to hide from idealistic Courtois. The point is that it is the landlord's court, that the pig fits the description of the murderer, and that this is simply how things are done in provincial France.

The movie would be comical if it weren't so disturbingly accurate in its portrayal of common law. The frustration experienced by Courtois is that of a rational man, whose legal perspective is based in democracy and statutory law. He is a Renaissance man trapped in the waning Middle Ages, during which religion and superstition were the basic tenets of the law, and the power went unquestionably to the feudal lords. *The Advocate* does an excellent job of revealing the ridiculousness of early common law, but is careful to show that legal manipulations by both prosecutors and defense attorneys (which would today be considered unethical and corrupt) were an integral, even expected, part of the medieval legal system.

There is plenty of humor in *The Advocate,* but the message turns serious when the clever Courtois uses the provincial common law to his own end in defense of the innocent pig. The movie is based on the actual writings of the real Courtois, who, horrified by the hypocrisy and superstition that provided the basis for his defense of the pig, documented his experiences as a country advocate upon returning to Paris in the late 1400s.

MEDIA AND CRIMINAL JUSTICE QUESTION

Identify and apply specific elements of contemporary criminal law that would prohibit some of the conduct depicted in *The Advocate.*

entrapment
A defense designed to prevent the government from manufacturing crime by setting traps for unwary citizens.

ENTRAPMENT The traditional or *subjective formulation* of the defense of **entrapment** was established by the U.S. Supreme Court in 1932. Sorrells was approached by an undercover police officer who had been in his military unit during World War I. The two men got into a discussion of old times, and at several points in the conversation the undercover police officer asked Sorrells if he could obtain some liquor for him (an act that was illegal at the time). Sorrells said no to the first two requests, but after the third request, Sorrells left and brought back some liquor, not knowing that his friend was now a police officer.

Sorrells was arrested, tried, and convicted of possession and sale of liquor. He appealed the conviction. In its decision, the Supreme Court held that a question is raised when "the criminal design originates with the officials of the government, and they implant in the mind of an innocent person the disposition to commit the alleged offense and induce its commission in order that they may prosecute." The Supreme Court found that the undercover officer's actions amounted to entrapment because "entrapment exists if the defendant was not predisposed to commit the crimes in question, and his intent originated with the officials of the government."[47] Since it focuses on the defendant's frame of mind, this is known as the subjective formulation of the entrapment defense.

The purpose of the entrapment defense is to prevent the government from "manufacturing" crime by setting traps for unwary citizens. The government's role in committing a crime can, of course, range from trivial to very influential. The precise role necessary for entrapment to occur has been the subject of much scrutiny, especially as police undercover tactics have become more common. It should be noted that the entrapment defense is aimed strictly at misconduct on the part of the government. If a private citizen, not associated with the government, entraps another into committing an offense, the entrapment defense is not available.

A second formulation of the entrapment defense, adopted in the Model Penal Code and in about half the states, focuses on the conduct of police and its potential to trap innocent persons. This standard is called the *objective formulation* and can be stated as follows:

> **Entrapment occurs when government agents induce or encourage another person to engage in criminal behavior by knowingly making false representations about the lawfulness of the conduct or by employing methods that create a substantial risk that such an offense will be committed by innocent [i.e., unpredisposed] persons.**

The primary difference between the two formulations is that the objective standard shifts attention *away* from the prior record and predisposition of the defendant and *toward* the conduct of the police. Both formulations address the danger of inducing innocent persons to commit crimes, but under the objective standard the predisposition of the defendant is irrelevant.

The significance of this difference is made clear by an actual case. An undercover police officer went to Russell's home, claiming that he wanted to sell methamphetamine. The officer offered to supply an essential ingredient of the illegal drug in return for half the amount manufactured. The officer's actual aim, however, was to locate the manufacturing laboratory, and therefore he demanded to see where the drug was actually made. Russell took the officer to the factory, and the officer eventually supplied him with the necessary ingredient to manufacture the drug. Russell and his associates were later arrested for the manufacture and sale of a controlled dangerous substance. Russell claimed that he had been entrapped.

Using the subjective formulation of entrapment, the U.S. Supreme Court upheld Russell's conviction, stating that

> **It does not seem particularly desirable for the law to grant complete immunity from prosecution to one who himself planned to commit a crime, and then committed it, simply because government undercover agents subjected him to inducements which might have seduced a hypothetical individual who was not so predisposed.[48]**

The Court's focus on the predisposition of the defendant, rather than on the conduct of the government agent, guided its decision. Three of the justices dissented, however, urging adoption of the objective standard for entrapment. They believed that a reasonable application of the objective standard in this case would have resulted in a finding of entrapment.

> **Since . . . it does not matter whether the respondent was predisposed to commit the offense of which he was convicted, the focus must be, rather, on the conduct of the undercover agent. . . . In these circumstances, the agent's undertaking to supply this ingredient to the respondent, thus making it possible for the government to prosecute him for manufacturing an illicit drug with it, was, I think, precisely the type of governmental conduct that the entrapment defense is meant to prevent.**

It is easy to see from the Court's opinion in this case, as well as from the dissent, that use of the subjective versus the objective standard to establish entrapment can lead to very different conclusions based on the same set of facts.

In sum, government agents "in their zeal to enforce the law . . . may not originate a criminal design" that creates the disposition to commit a criminal act "and then induce commission of the crime so that the government may prosecute."[49] This is what the entrapment defense is designed to prevent. The split among the states in adopting the objective versus the subjective formulation of the entrapment defense is a primary reason why entrapment, and some police undercover tactics, remain controversial issues.

Three important features of the criminal law have been highlighted in this chapter: the decision to criminalize a behavior, the elements of a crime, and the defenses that excuse criminal conduct in certain circumstances. The decision to criminalize sets the limits of the criminal law and makes clear its social purposes. The elements of crimes provide citizens with fair warning of how specific behaviors will be interpreted by the justice system. The allowable defenses to crimes show us that exceptions are necessary to ensure that the law is applied in a fair manner.

Banning Pit Bulls

Several cities have imposed ownership bans on pit bulls, a breed of aggressive dogs that sometimes attack humans. In one city a proposed law read, "Existing pit bulls must be registered, tat-

tooed for identification, and neutered. No new pit bulls may be brought into the city. Owners must be at least 18 years of age and carry $100,000 insurance."

These laws are vigorously opposed by groups such as "People for Pit Bulls," which argue that the laws are discriminatory (against a single type of dog) and a violation of privacy. They claim that the dogs do not pose enough of a danger to justify the laws and are entitled to reproductive freedom. They also point out that the laws discriminate against poor owners (who cannot afford the insurance).

Critical Thinking Questions

You are an attorney hired by the city to defend a new ordinance like the one just cited.

1. What are the limits on police power to establish this law?
2. On what grounds would you defend the law?
3. What is the likelihood of a successful defense of this law? Explain your answer.

Hinckley, Kaczynski, and Legal Insanity

Beginning in adolescence, John Hinckley was an introvert. As a young adult he became intensely interested in the film *Taxi Driver,* which featured an alienated, violent cab driver who became a hero after rescuing a young prostitute (played by Jodie Foster). Hinckley unsuccessfully tried to begin a relationship with Jodie Foster. He became a drifter, stalked President Carter, contemplated suicide, wrote to Foster about his plan to assassinate President Reagan, and then shot the President in broad daylight outside a Washington hotel. At trial Hinckley was found not guilty by reason of insanity. He remains confined indefinitely in a mental hospital.

Theodore Kaczynski held a Ph.D. in mathematics. He left his job and moved to a remote shack in the woods, where he lived for twenty years in the most primitive conditions. During this time he developed strong attitudes against prominent individuals (especially university professors) whose views he did not share. Kaczynski mailed a series of "package bombs" that resulted in three deaths and two injuries. He was put on trial for these acts. He was also a suspect in eleven other bombing cases that caused twenty-one additional injuries. A prosecution psychiatrist concluded that Kaczynski suffered from paranoid schizophrenia, which causes delusions and the potential for violence. Kaczynski pleaded guilty and was sentenced to life imprisonment without the possibility of parole.

Critical Thinking Question

Putting aside the outcomes in the actual cases, make an argument for the opposite finding: Why should Hinckley have been convicted and Kaczynksi found not guilty by reason of insanity, given what you know about the defendants and about legal definitions of insanity?

Summary

THE NATURE OF CRIMINAL LAW

- Civil law is the set of formal rules that regulate disputes between private parties. Criminal law is the set of formal rules designed to maintain social control.
- Substantive criminal law defines behaviors that are prohibited, while procedural law provides the rules for adjudication of cases involving those behaviors.
- The four main sources of criminal law are constitutions, statutes, case law, and administrative regulations.

THE NATURE OF CRIME

- No crime can exist without three elements: *mens rea* ("guilty mind"), *actus reus* (a specific behavior), and attendant circumstances (a specific relationship between the act and the harm that results).
- Five characteristics of acts can invoke criminal sanctions: sufficiency, possession, statuses, voluntariness, and omissions.
- Punishments for violations of criminal law are based on assessment of the offender's state of mind, including degree of recklessness (conscious disregard for a substantial and unjustifiable risk) and intent (whether the act was carried out knowingly or purposely).
- For an act to be considered a crime, the harm suffered must have occurred *because of* the act ("but for" causation) and the act must be the proximate or direct cause of the harm. Simultaneous causes generally result in liability for both parties.

DEFENSES TO CRIMINAL CHARGES

- A defense based on the claim that the defendant was not sane at the time of the act is referred to as the insanity defense. Although the Model Penal Code proposes a specific test for legal insanity, in practice the determination of insanity is highly subjective. Some states have adopted a finding of "guilty but mentally ill."
- Defenses involving force are of three types: self-defense, defense of others, and defense of property.
- Defenses involving justification or excuse include duress, necessity, mistake of fact, ignorance of law, and entrapment.
- The subjective formulation of the entrapment defense focuses on the defendant's state of mind; the objective formulation focuses on the conduct of police and its potential to trap innocent persons.

Key Terms

civil law
criminal law
substantive criminal law
procedural law
constitution
statute
criminal (penal) code
case law
precedent
administrative regulations
consensus view
conflict view
mens rea
actus reus
constructive possession
actual possession
recklessness
intention
criminal liability
insanity defense
reasonableness standard
battered woman syndrome
duress
entrapment

Questions for Review and Discussion

1. Distinguish between civil and criminal law and give an example of each.
2. Name and describe the four main sources of criminal law.
3. What is meant by *mens rea* and *actus reus*?
4. Describe the five characteristics of acts that can be sufficient to invoke criminal sanctions.
5. Define recklessness and intent. How do these terms relate to the determination of *mens rea*?
6. What three conditions must characterize the relationship between an act and the harm suffered in order for the act to be considered a crime?
7. How has the legal definition of insanity changed since the M'Naghten case of 1843?
8. What degree of force is permitted in defense of property in one's own home during a dangerous felony?
9. What conditions must be met for a claim of duress to succeed as a defense?
10. Distinguish between the subjective and objective formulations of the entrapment defense.

Notes

[1]"Father Says He Sharpened Son's Buckle," *The Associated Press* (October 23, 1996).

[2]Lawrence M. Friedman, *A History of American Criminal Law* (New York: Simon & Schuster, 1973).

[3]Lawrence M. Friedman, *Crime and Punishment in American History* (New York: Basic Books, 1993), pp. 22–3.

[4]Emile Durkheim, *The Division of Labor in Society* (New York: The Free Press, 1893), p. 80.

[5]William J. Chambliss and Thomas F. Courtless, *Criminal Law, Criminology, and Criminal Justice* (Belmont, CA: Brooks/Cole, 1992), pp. 12–32.

[6]*Papachristou v. Jacksonville,* 92 S. Ct. 839 (1972). See also *State v. Palendrano,* 120 N.J. Superior 336 (1972).

[7]Deborah Sharp, "Cruising Taking a Bruising in Miami Beach," *USA Today* (September 1, 1993), p. 9; Richard Price, "Party May Soon be Over for Dance on Wheels," *USA Today* (March 16, 1990), p. 7.

[8]Richard Price, "Helmet Law Jolts Motorcyclists," *USA Today* (December 31, 1991), p. 3; Jeanne DeQuine, "Miami Case Tests Child Car-Seat Laws," *USA Today* (April 29, 1991), p. 3; Haya El Nasser, "Seat-belt Case Takes Law to Limit," *USA Today* (October 16, 1990), p. 3.

[9]Jonathan Schonsheck, *On Criminalization: An Essay in the Philosophy of Criminal Law* (Boston: Kluwer Academic, 1994).

[10]See Joel Samaha, *Criminal Law,* 3rd ed. (St. Paul, MN: West Publishing, 1994); Thomas J. Gardner and Terry M. Anderson, *Criminal Law: Principles and Cases* (St. Paul, MN: West Publishing, 1992).

[11]*State v. Bugger,* 25 Utah 2d 404, Sup. Ct. of Utah (1971).

[12]*State v. McMenamin,* 133 N.J. Superior 521 (1975).

[13]*Robinson v. California,* 82 S. Ct. 1417 (1962). See also *Powell v. Texas,* 88 S. Ct. 2145 (1968).

[14]*People v. Newton,* 340 N.Y.S. 2d 277, Sup. Ct. (1973).

[15]*Commonwealth v. Howard,* 265 Pa. Superior 535 (1979); *Jones v. United States,* 308 F. 2d 307, D.C. Cir. (1962).

[16]*State v. Nosis,* 22 Ohio App. 2d 16, Ct. Appeals of Ohio (1969).

[17]*Commonwealth v. Cotton,* 338 Pa. Superior 20 (1984).

[18]*People v. Kibbe,* 362 N.Y.S. 2d, Ct. Appeals (1974). See also *State v. Lassiter,* 197 N.J. Superior 2 (1984).

[19]See H. L. A. Hart and A. M. Honore, "Causation in the Law," Law Quarterly Review, vol. 72 (1956), pp. 58–90. Reprinted in J. L. Coleman, ed., *Crimes and Punishments,* vol. 4 (New York: Garland, 1994), pp. 194–269.

[20]*Jones v. Commonwealth,* 281 S. W. 2d 920, Ct. App. Ky. (1955).

[21]*Dusky v. United States,* 80 S. Ct. 788 (1960).

[22]See *Jackson v. Indiana,* 92 S. Ct. 1845 (1972).

[23]*M'Naghten's Case,* 8 Eng. Rep. 718 (1843).

[24]*Parsons v. State,* 81 Ala. 577 (1887).

[25]*Durham v. United States,* 214 F. 2d 862, D.C. Cir. (1954).

[26]*U.S. v. Brawner,* 471 F. 2d 969, D.C. Cir. (1972).

[27]Norval Morris, *Madness and the Criminal Law* (Chicago: University of Chicago Press, 1982).

[28]See Henry J. Steadman, *Beating a Rap?* (Chicago: University of Chicago Press, 1979); Samuel Walker, *Sense and Nonsense about Crime,* 2nd ed. (Monterey, CA: Brooks/Cole, 1989).

[29]Norval Morris, *Insanity Defense* (Washington, D.C.: National Institute of Justice, 1979).

[30]See Henry J. Steadman, Margaret A. McGreevy, and Joseph P. Morrisey, *Before and After Hinckley: Evaluating Insanity Defense Reform* (New York: Guilford Press, 1993).

[31]*Jones v. United States,* 103 S. Ct. 3043 (1983).

[32]Gordon Witkin, "What Does It Take to be Crazy?," *U.S. News & World Report* (January 12, 1998), p. 7.

[33]Debra T. Landis, "'Guilty But Mentally Ill' Statutes: Validity and Construction," 71 *American Law Reports* 702, 1991.

[34]*Mullin v. Pence,* 390 So. 2d 803, Ct. App. La. (1974).

[35]*State v. Kelly,* 97 N.J. 178 (1978).

[36]Faith McNulty, *The Burning Bed* (New York: Bantam, 1981).

[37]*Commonwealth v. Martin,* 369 Mass. 640, Sup. Ct. (1976).

[38]*People v. Ceballos,* 12 Cal. 3d 470, Sup. Ct. (1974).

[39]*U.S. v. Bailey,* 100 S. Ct. 624 (1980). See *U.S. v. Webb,* 747 F. 2d 278, cert. denied 105 S. Ct. 1222 (1984).

[40]*Regina v. Dudley and Stephens,* 14 Q.B.D. 273 (1884).

[41]*People v. Dover,* 790 P. 2d 834 Col. Sup. Ct. (1990).

[42]*Crown v. Tolson,* 23 Q.B.D. 168 (1889); *Stuart v. Commonwealth,* 11 Va. App. 216 (1990).

[43]Kenneth W. Simons, "When is Strict Liability Just?," *Journal of Criminal Law and Criminology,* vol. 87 (1997), pp. 1075–1137.

[44]*People v. Snyder,* 186 Cal. Rptr. 485 (1982).

[45]*Lambert v. California,* 78 S. Ct. 240 (1957).

[46]Douglas Husak and Andrew von Hirsch, "Culpability and Mistake of Law," in S. Shute, J. Gardner, and J. Horder, eds., *Action and Value in Criminal Law* (New York: Oxford University Press, 1993), pp. 157–74.

[47]*Sorrells v. United States,* 53 S. Ct. 210 (1932).

[48]*U.S. v. Russell,* 93 S. Ct. 1637 (1973).

[49]Ibid.

For Further Reading

Annette Carrel, *It's the Law* (New York: Volcano Press, 1994).
Alan Dershowitz, *The Abuse Excuse* (Boston: Little, Brown, 1995).
H.L.A. Hart, *The Concept of Law,* 2nd ed. (New York: Oxford University Press, 1997).
John C. Klotter and Terry D. Edwards, *Criminal Law,* 5th ed. (Cincinnati: Anderson Publishing, 1998).

chapter six

The Criminal Justice System

Laws were made to prevent the strong from always having their way.

OVID
(43 B.C.–17 A.D.)

CHAPTER OUTLINE

- Pulling people out of cars at gunpoint.
- Roughing up those who don't speak English.
- Frisking citizens for no clear reason.
- Conducting searches in an abusive manner.
- Selectively harassing minorities.
- Using force without provocation.

As one neighborhood organizer said, "In the beginning we all wanted the police to bomb the crack houses, but now it's backfiring at the cost of the community. I think the cops have been given free rein to intimidate people at large."[1] The specific complaints against police are listed above, and they all resulted from an effort to *reduce* crime in New York City.

SHERIFF DEPARTMENT
LIVINGSTON CO.

New York City experienced a remarkable drop in the crime rate during the late 1990s. It was attributed in part to more aggressive police tactics against minor offenses that affect the quality of life: drinking in public, playing loud music, urinating in public, jumping subway turnstiles, loitering. It turned out that many of those arrested for these minor crimes were also wanted for more serious crimes. However, these aggressive police tactics involved stopping people on the street and requesting identification, conducting drug sweeps of entire neighborhoods, and frisking people. These tactics drew considerable criticism because they necessarily created at least temporary infringements of the privacy of many innocent persons. Complaints against police grew considerably in New York; Pittsburgh; Charlotte; Washington, D.C.; and elsewhere, alleging overly aggressive police tactics. These charges are serious, and they reflect a dilemma that lies at the heart of the American criminal justice system: What is the best way to balance the right of individuals to be left alone with the community's interest in apprehending criminals?

This dilemma is most evident in the case of police because of their continual interaction with the public. However, the balance between individual and community interests must also be struck in the decision to formally charge a person with a crime, in the determination of guilt or innocence at trial, and in sentencing and parole release decisions. The entire criminal justice system is designed to provide a mechanism for achieving this balance in a just manner. There are agencies, laws, and procedures devoted to this task, but they sometimes fall short of achieving their goal.

Origins of the Criminal Justice System

Perhaps the most important thing to remember in learning about the American system of justice is that there is no such thing as the criminal justice "system." No mention of a criminal justice system appears in the Constitution or in any federal or state law. In reality, the criminal justice system is a string of more than 55,000 independent government agencies set up to deal with different aspects of crime and the treatment of offenders.

The agencies of criminal justice have no legal obligation to cooperate with one another, and they often do not. The only thing they have in common is the fact that they all deal with the same clientele: crime suspects, people accused of crimes, and offenders. It is because of their relative lack of cooperation that they are sometimes called a "nonsystem" of criminal justice.[2] For example, a city may hire more police officers, who will contribute to an increase in the overall number of arrests. This results in more cases being brought to court, more adjudications of guilt, and more offenders sentenced to probation and prison. The need for more prosecutors, defense lawyers, judges, courtrooms, probation officers, and prison space created by the increase in police and arrests is rarely accounted for. This lack of "system-wide" thinking has hurt both the efficiency and effectiveness of criminal justice in the United States throughout the nation's history.

It is important to keep the idea of a "system" in mind, because we will see that anything done by one criminal justice agency invariably affects the others. Therefore, despite the fact that the various criminal justice agencies were not set up as a system, they must attempt to act together if justice is to be achieved. In fact, many of the problems of criminal justice are caused by the failure of the various criminal justice agencies to act as a system. Throughout this book, therefore, the term *criminal justice system* is used to emphasize the importance of cooperation among criminal justice agencies.

Over the course of history, societies have been fairly consistent in the way they handle criminal justice. First, the members of societies place authority in the hands of a government to act on their behalf. When some members do not follow the codified rules—that is, the laws—the government often establishes an agency that is responsible for making sure that the laws are obeyed. In American society this enforcement function is performed by the police.

Next, societies often set up agencies to arbitrate in these matters. That is, if a person has an excuse or justification for violating the law, how do we determine whether it is a valid one? In American society this arbitration function is performed by the courts.

Finally, when an assessment of blame or responsibility is made, a penalty or punishment is administered to the offender and compensation is sometimes given to the victim. In American society this is carried out by the corrections system. Thus, it is rather easy to see how a system of justice evolves in a society to resolve disputes. The need for rules and a method to enforce those rules, together with a way to evaluate justifications for rule violations and the administration of penalties, are all necessary to serve the common good. These fundamental components of criminal justice are required to resolve the sometimes conflicting interests of individual citizens in ways that serve the wider public interest.

The agencies of law enforcement, the courts, and corrections comprise what we loosely call the criminal justice system. In the United States there are two levels of criminal justice systems: state and federal. Each state has its own set of criminal justice agencies, and the federal government has a criminal justice system that handles concerns that apply to some or all of the states. Therefore, there are actually fifty-one criminal justice systems in the United States.

Justice in the Colonial Period

Our modern system of criminal justice is a product of evolutionary changes such as those just described. It has evolved as American society has developed mechanisms for establishing rules, enforcing them, determining responsibility for violations, and deciding on appropriate remedies.

Early America was a sparsely populated domain that extended from New Hampshire to Georgia, and was no more than two hundred miles wide. Unlike the situation today, in which paid professionals make, enforce, and adjudicate the law and carry out penalties, "colonial justice was a business of amateurs."[3] The first police force was not established until 1845, lawyers often played no role in the justice process, and cases were usually decided by lay magistrates. This made justice "democratic" in that it was communal in nature, protecting the perceived shared rights of the community. This was unlike the system in England, which was dominated by aristocrats enforcing the law against the less privileged.[4]

Religion and sin played a significant role in colonial justice, inasmuch as crime and sin were viewed as essentially the same. In many ways religion formed

Religion formed the basis for justice in Colonial times. Shame and repentance characterized this period rather than the modern day emphasis on punishment or treatment.

the basis for colonial justice. Colonial criminal codes often defined crime in biblical terms, and blasphemy, profanity, and violations of the Sabbath were seen as serious offenses and punished severely. This religious orientation manifested itself in corrections as well. Rather than punishment or treatment, which typify the modern era, shame and repentance characterized the colonial period. Punishments were used to "lead" a violator toward repentance and to serve as an example to others.[5] Therefore, the stocks, whipping, and the ducking stool were used as methods of shaming rather than as punishment for its own sake.[6] In the modern era we still expect offenders to express remorse for their actions, even though such expressions make little difference in terms of punishment or forgiveness.

As the shared values of a common religious tradition were dissipated by rapid population growth, geographical expansion, and a lessening of the role of religion in the lives of citizens, the law gradually came to be relied on more and more often to enforce a standard of morality that previously had been the province of religion. The result was a dramatic increase in both the number of laws and the number of law violators, a trend that continues today. Simply stated, the more widely shared cultural and religious traditions one finds in a society, the less reliance is placed on the law to maintain the boundaries of acceptable behavior. The police, courts, and corrections are poor substitutes for the internalized controls that are the product of cultural traditions and religious beliefs.

The development of the criminal justice system as we know it today resulted from this historical progression from small, religiously and culturally similar communities to larger towns and cities with more diverse populations in which religious tenets were less dominant. As can be seen in the next chapter, the first police departments were established in cities where individual responsibility for security broke down. This invariably occurred when population growth and increasing diversity weakened responsibility among the citizens, resulting in an "everyone for himself or herself" mentality. This created the need for criminal justice agencies to maintain order and public safety. These agencies appeared in one city after another and gradually expanded to become state and federal agencies.[7]

The Evolution of Due Process

The criminal justice process is no longer a simple one run by amateurs. The many legal steps and procedures that have been added are designed to achieve two goals: accuracy and fairness. These are the essential elements of due process, a legal protection included in the U.S. Constitution that guarantees all citizens the right to be adjudicated under the law. This protection from arbitrary and unjust treatment became more important as those making, enforcing, and adjudicating laws increasingly became strangers in a more populated and urban nation. As strong religious values weakened, a common moral fiber could no longer be counted on to promote conformity to laws.

contemporary issues

Unauthorized Access to Criminal History Records

The National Crime Information Center (NCIC) is the world's largest, most sophisticated computerized criminal justice information system. It consists of a central computer at FBI headquarters that is connected to a network of federal and state computer systems. NCIC provides access to more than twenty-four million records in fourteen files. The largest file is the criminal history file, with seventeen million records. The other files contain information in categories such as wanted persons, missing persons, and stolen vehicles. Nearly 20,000 federal, state, and local criminal justice agencies in the United States and Canada can access NCIC directly from nearly 100,000 computer terminals. The FBI assigns a nine-character code to each user to control access.

A review by the General Accounting Office (GAO), the investigative arm of Congress, found that the NCIC is vulnerable to misuse by "insiders" who use their authorized access inappropriately. This misuse can take the form of selling information to private investigators or altering or deleting information in NCIC records. For example, a computer operator in a Texas district attorney's office obtained NCIC criminal history information and gave it to her boyfriend, who sold it to private investigators. A former Arizona police officer obtained NCIC information from three friends in different police agencies in order to locate his estranged girlfriend and murder her. In New York, a law enforcement employee obtained NCIC criminal history information and disclosed it to a local politician to be used against opponents. In all, some sixty-two instances of NCIC abuses were uncovered by the GAO, all of them involving insiders.

These documented incidents, together with misuses reported in FBI audits and GAO interviews, led the GAO to make recommendations for improved NCIC security. The recommendations include the following:

1. Specific access controls, such as unique passwords, should be required for access and to identify authorized users.
2. Federal laws should be passed that are designed to deter misuse of the NCIC by imposing stronger sanctions.
3. State and local user agencies should enhance their security measures through more rigorous identification, authentication, and audit procedures.

The U.S. Department of Justice and the FBI agreed with these recommendations, and new security measures are planned for an upgraded NCIC 2000 system. Nevertheless, without mandatory improvements in security at the state and local levels, where most abuses have occurred in the past, efforts to enhance security measures will not be very effective.

SOURCE: U.S. Comptroller General, *National Crime Information Center* (Washington, D.C.: U.S. General Accounting Office, 1993).

Accuracy is a fundamental goal because confidence in the outcome is pivotal if a criminal justice system is to survive. If the public did not believe that the findings of the criminal justice process were accurate, they would lose confidence in the system, turn to private forms of justice, and eventually look for new forms of government.

Fairness is closely related to accuracy. Fairness in the justice process refers to the balance between the government's interest in apprehending crime suspects and the public's interest in avoiding unnecessary government interference in the lives of individuals. The establishment of thresholds for government intervention, such as probable cause (discussed in Chapter 9), are designed to achieve a *fair* balance between the sometimes conflicting interests of the government and individual citizens.

Some have held that the criminal justice process has other functions besides accuracy and fairness. It is claimed, for example, that crime control is an important function.[8] However, there is little reliable evidence to suggest that the criminal justice system deters offenders or reforms those who pass through it. It has also been argued that overemphasis on accuracy and fairness interferes with the system's ability to deter or prevent crime.[9] Not only is this a speculative view, but it is impractical as well, since it is unlikely that a nation born only two hundred years ago out of violent revolution would be willing to lower the legal thresholds established to preserve accuracy and fairness in the balance between government and citizen. Indeed, Americans have long been suspicious of government. This suspicion dates back to the Revolution and to the philosophy of John Locke, which holds that government exists not by divine right or by force, but only by the consent of the governed, who may alter or abolish the government if it acts in a manner inconsistent with the natural rights of citizens.[10] It should be remembered that an important cause of the American Revolution was the widespread perception that British government procedures were arbitrary and unfair.[11]

The relative emphasis placed on the goals of accuracy, fairness, or crime control remains relevant today. The criticism of New York City Police Department tactics cited at the beginning of this chapter illustrates that neither law enforcement nor criminal justice is a simple concept. They both involve the rights and interests of the innocent, the guilty, those victimized, and those empowered to enforce the law. These competing concerns are highlighted throughout this book.

The Agencies of Criminal Justice

The contemporary structure of law enforcement, courts, and corrections institutionalizes basic notions of how law should be enforced and adjudicated, and the manner in which one should deal with violators. As the various agencies of criminal justice are described, it should be kept in mind that this structure is largely an outgrowth of the nation's history. The United States was founded in the aftermath of a revolution against the British government, which was seen as arbitrary, undemocratic, and far too strong. This experience has guided the establishment of criminal justice agencies, which have been granted the power to intrude into the lives of citizens only under certain specified circumstances. Also, many criminal justice agencies exist on the local level to enhance local control and prevent these agencies from becoming too powerful or abusive.

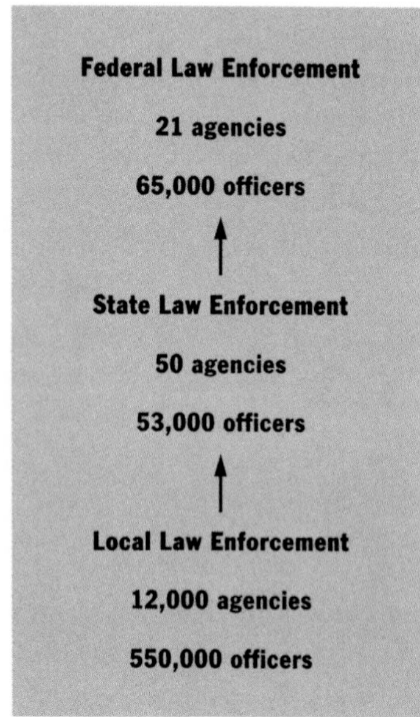

FIGURE 6.1
Law enforcement in the United States

Law Enforcement

Law enforcement agencies exist at all levels of government: federal, state, and local. In each case, however, their duties are the same. We generally expect law enforcement agencies to perform four tasks: protect people and their rights, apprehend those who violate laws, prevent crimes, and provide social services. The first two responsibilities are traditionally associated with the function of policing, that is, enforcing the law by apprehending violators and thereby protecting citizens. As we will see later, in recent years the last two duties have become more prominent aspects of law enforcement.

The only difference between law enforcement agencies at different levels of government is in the types of laws they enforce. Federal law enforcement officers are charged with enforcing federal laws, state police enforce state laws, and local police must enforce both state and local laws. As can be seen in Figure 6.1, the vast majority of police agencies and police officers are at the local level of government. This reflects the evolution of policing in the United States and the historical suspicion of larger, more powerful government agencies.

Courts

Just as two types of criminal justice systems exist in the United States, state and federal, there are also two court systems. In criminal courts, legal responsibility is determined through interpretation of the law in relation to the circumstances of individual cases. There are more than 17,000 courts and related agencies in the United States; most of them operate at the state and local levels. These courts can be grouped into three basic categories, depending on the level of jurisdiction. These include courts of limited jurisdiction, general jurisdiction, and appellate jurisdiction. Courts can also be classified by their legal jurisdiction, which determines the types of cases they are allowed to hear.

Generally speaking, the U.S. court system comprises a federal court system (to interpret federal law) and a state court system (to interpret state and local laws). Like the state courts, the federal court system has three levels of jurisdiction. Courts of **limited jurisdiction** have narrow legal authority and may arbitrate only in certain types of disputes. They include municipal courts and special courts such as tax courts and surrogate courts. In each case the court's scope of authority is narrowly circumscribed. Courts of **general jurisdiction** are usually referred to as trial courts. These are the courts in which trials for felonies and civil cases occur. There is no uniform name for these courts across the country; they are called county courts, circuit courts, and even supreme courts in some jurisdictions. The highest level of jurisdiction is **appellate jurisdiction.** Appellate courts review specific legal issues raised by cases in courts with general jurisdiction. An appellate court may reverse a conviction in a criminal case, but any retrial that might occur would take place in the court of general jurisdiction in which the case was originally tried. Figure 6.2 illustrates the court system structure. As is shown in this figure, a case moves from a trial court to a court of appellate jurisdiction.

limited jurisdiction
The jurisdiction of courts that have narrow legal authority over specific types of matters (e.g., surrogate court, tax court).

general jurisdiction
The jurisdiction of courts where most trials for felonies occur, as well as trials in major civil cases.

appellate jurisdiction
The jurisdiction of a court that reviews specific legal issues raised in trial courts.

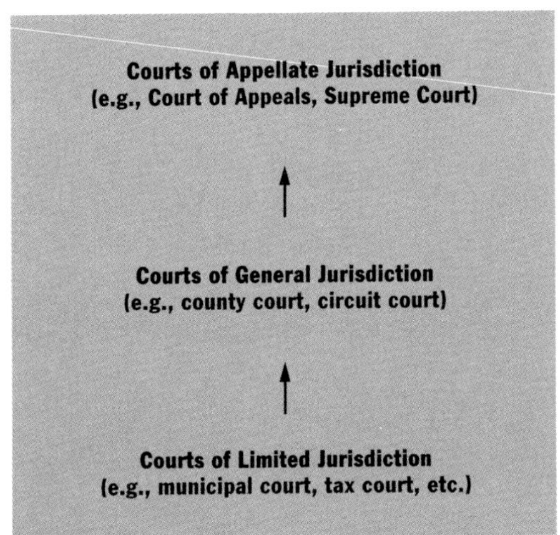

FIGURE 6.2
The court process

This sequence occurs in every state and in the federal court system, although the names of the courts vary.

Corrections

Like law enforcement, the correctional system exists at all three levels of government: local, state, and federal. All told, there are more than 6,000 correctional facilities in the United States. Of these, nearly 3,400 are local jails, of which the vast majority are administered by counties. Usually operated by the county sheriff, local jails are used to detain adults awaiting trial and offenders serving sentences of one year or less.

When offenders convicted in state courts are sentenced to periods of imprisonment, they are usually sent to the state correctional system. The state system includes prisons and prison farms and camps, as well as community-based facilities such as halfway houses, work release centers, and drug/alcohol treatment facilities. Of all the offenders sentenced to state correctional systems, the vast majority (95 percent) are incarcerated in prisons or other locked facilities. State facilities also hold nearly 60 percent of all persons incarcerated in the United States on a given day.

Many offenders are placed on probation, which involves serving a sentence in the community under the supervision of a probation officer. There are more than three million offenders on probation in the United States, compared to 500,000 in jail and one million in prison.[12] These numbers are all at record levels and provide an indication of the extent to which the correctional system is used to deal with offenders.

This overview of the agencies of criminal justice has omitted "linking" agencies, such as the prosecutor and defense counsel, that serve to link law enforcement and the courts. Also omitted are parole agencies. These agencies are considered in later chapters.

It is useful to think of the criminal justice process as a filter. The law, police, courts, and corrections each capture their share of law violators. The law casts the widest net, given the large number of behaviors that are illegal. The police arrest some law violators, depending on priorities, resources, and other factors discussed in Chapter 8. At the preliminary hearing, a judge evaluates the police officer's arrest decision, and so on. A diagram of this criminal justice filter is presented in Figure 6.3.

As is illustrated in Figure 6.3, the criminal law and decisions at the stages of arrest, preliminary hearing, grand jury, arraignment, trial, and sentencing represent the major decision points in the criminal justice process. Each step acts as a filter, pushing through serious cases that also have sufficient evidence to prove them. When cases are not serious, or there is insufficient evidence for prosecution, the case is filtered out. Sometimes a serious case makes it a long way through the system, only to end in an acquittal at trial because the evidence was weak. At other times, a nonserious case may make it to a preliminary hearing or grand jury, where a judge or jury may determine that the case is not worthy of further prosecution. The purpose of the filters, therefore, is to provide multiple opportunities for the system to correct itself as a case moves through it. Because of the many actors involved (politicians, police, prosecutors, judges, and juries),

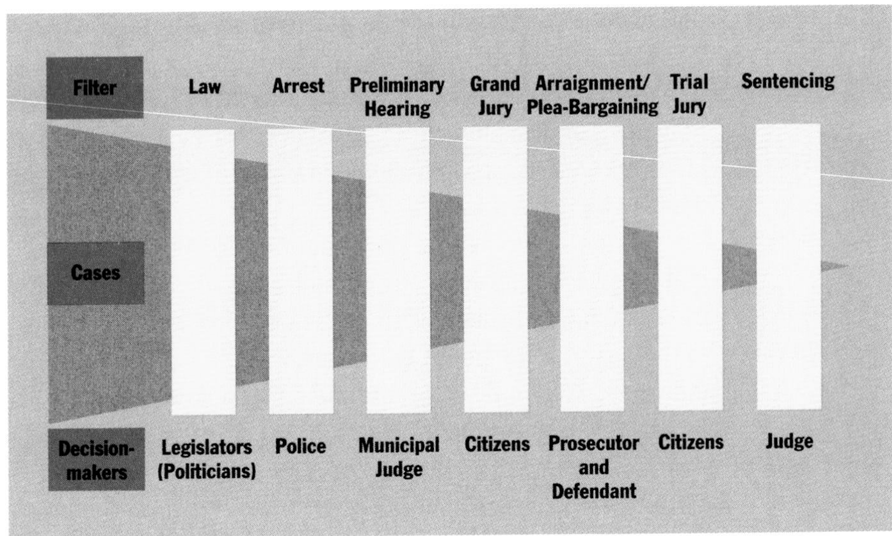

FIGURE 6.3
The criminal justice filter

there is room for confusion or error in any given case. The rules of criminal procedure provide a way to ensure that most offenders whose cases make it all the way through the system are actually guilty.

Criminal Procedure

Criminal procedure is a crucial part of criminal justice. It is here that a citizen becomes a suspect, and perhaps a defendant and a convicted offender. The power of the government is vast compared to the resources of a private citizen, and therefore it is extremely important that criminal procedures safeguard the rights of individuals in the adjudication process. An interesting example is the case of Terry Nichols, who was charged with conspiracy and murder for the planning and execution of the 1995 bombing of the federal office building in Oklahoma City. Nichols was associated with Timothy McVeigh, who was convicted of murder in the bombings. Nichols was not in Oklahoma City at the time of the bombing, however.[13] In view of the horror of the most deadly terrorist act in the history of the United States, an objective presentation and evaluation of the evidence against Nichols had to occur under the law of criminal procedure. Without criminal procedure to guide the inquiry into guilt or innocence, public sentiment and outrage can result in unfair verdicts and gross injustices. In the case of Terry Nichols, the jury considered his role in the crime and convicted him of conspiracy and involuntary manslaughter, clearing him of murder charges. He was sentenced to life in prison.

Law, Investigation, Arrest

The first requirement of any criminal justice process is, of course, a suspected violation of law. This, in turn, requires the existence of a specific criminal law. In other words, the law makes possible all the subsequent steps in the process. For example, an individual who possesses marijuana may come to the attention of

Police need probable cause to make an arrest. This standard, stated in the Fourth Amendment, requires police investigation to show a reasonable link between a specific person and a particular illegal act.

police and be subject to the criminal justice process. If it is not illegal to possess marijuana, however, the criminal justice system plays no role. Therefore, the criminal law provides the raw material that feeds the criminal justice process. As the number of laws increases, so does the potential number of cases to be handled by the system.

If one breaks the law, however, there is still no guarantee that one will be subject to the criminal justice process. Not only must one break the law, but one's actions must be made known to the police. If the police do not know of the criminal act, the individual will not be subject to the criminal justice process. In order to continue through the system, therefore, we will assume that the police find out about the illegal conduct.

The first action to be taken by the police will be an investigation. The investigation may be the most important part of a case once it enters the criminal justice process. Although it seems obvious, the first fact to be ascertained is whether or not a crime has been committed. Naturally, if a police officer hears a gunshot, enters the room, and finds a body on the floor with a person standing over it holding a smoking gun, it is safe to assume that a crime may have been committed. However, in most instances police respond to calls from citizens *after* a crime has been committed; only rarely do they see a serious crime in progress. As a result, police often must reconstruct an incident from the accounts of victims and witnesses in order to determine whether a crime was actually committed. As it turns out, many of the complaints to which police respond are unfounded: Property reported stolen is actually misplaced or lost, suspicious noises outside are not burglars, and suspicious persons reported to police have committed no crime.

Once it is established that a crime has been committed, evidence is collected to support the case and a search for the offender is begun. From this point, two possible outcomes can result from the investigation: arrest or no arrest.

If the police do not find a suspect, no arrest is made and the case remains "open" until a suspect is found. Continuing investigations are conducted by police detectives. One of the most serious problems facing police is a low rate of solving (or "clearing") crimes through an arrest. For the criminal justice process to continue, however, a suspect must be found. When this occurs, he or she is placed under arrest. An **arrest** involves taking a suspected law violator into custody for the purpose of prosecution. To carry out a valid arrest, a police officer must have **probable cause** to believe that a specific person committed a particular illegal act. This requires a reasonable link between the person and the crime. The police officer must have more than suspicion as a basis for linking a person to an act, but does not have to be certain beyond a reasonable doubt. The concept of probable cause is taken from the Fourth Amendment to the U.S. Constitution, which is discussed further in Chapter 9.

arrest
Taking a suspect into custody for the purpose of prosecution.

probable cause
A reasonable link between a particular person and a specific crime.

booking
An official administrative record of an arrest.

citation (summons)
A written notice to appear in court.

Following an arrest, the suspect is booked. **Booking** is a procedure in which an official record of the arrest is made. Fingerprints and photographs of the suspect are usually taken at this point. For minor offenses, such as traffic violations, a citation is issued and the suspect is not taken into custody. A **citation** (or **summons**) is a written notice to appear in court. It documents the offense charged, the person suspected, and the time and place at which the person must appear in court. If the person charged signs the citation, thereby agreeing to appear in court, he or she is entitled to be released pending the court appearance.

Initial Appearance and Preliminary Hearing

After an arrest and booking, the suspect must be brought before a judge within a reasonable period of time. In many states the time limit is forty-eight hours, excluding Sundays and holidays. This limit was established in response to past injustices in which arrestees were held in jail for long periods without knowledge of the charges against them and without an opportunity to post bail. At the initial appearance, which usually takes place in municipal court, the arrestee is given formal notice of the charge(s) for which he or she is being held. The suspect is also informed of his or her legal rights, such as the right to legal counsel and the protection against self-incrimination. These rights are heard for the second time, since the U.S. Supreme Court has ruled that suspects must be given notice of basic legal rights at the time that they are taken into custody (see Chapter 9).

The judge also sets **bail** at the initial appearance. Bail is simply a way of ensuring that the arrestee will appear in court for trial. An arrestee who posts bail remains free pending the court appearance. Bail is posted in the form of cash or its equivalent. For instance, if the judge sets bail at $1,000, a person with access to that amount of money will go free until trial. A property owner with equity of $2,000 also has sufficient collateral for release on bail. (Most states require collateral to be double the cash amount because of changing real estate values and to cover the cost of converting the property to cash if bail is forfeited.) Most of those who are arrested do not have money or property in these amounts, however, and must rely on bail bondsmen to post bail for them; this is known as a **surety.** For a fee, the bail bondsman will post bail for the arrestee. When the arrestee appears for trial, the court gives the money back to the bondsman, who charges the arrestee 10 percent of that amount for the use of the money.

bail
An insurance policy designed to ensure that an accused person will appear at trial.

surety
The posting of bail by someone other than the accused (usually a bondsman).

Sometimes, if the risk of forfeiture appears too great, a bail bondsman will refuse to post bail. In such cases, unless the arrestee can obtain money from other sources, he or she will be held in custody until the criminal proceedings have been completed. Thus, because the bail system relies exclusively on cash or its equivalent, it discriminates against poor people. As a result, the overwhelming majority of those in jail awaiting trial are poor.

Most states allow judges to release suspects *on their own recognizance.* This means that a judge can release a suspect pending trial after receiving a written promise to appear in court. It is within the judge's discretion, however, to later require bail or to increase the bail amount. In setting bail the judge may consider the seriousness of the crime charged, a prior criminal record, employment history, family ties, and financial burdens or obligations.

If the crime charged is within the jurisdiction of a municipal court, the arrestee may also be asked to make a plea at the initial appearance. For minor crimes, this appearance is sometimes called an **arraignment.** The judge then sets a date for trial in municipal court.

arraignment
An appearance before a judge at which the accused is given legal rights and enters a plea.

Let us assume, however, that the offense charged is a serious crime. In these cases the criminal procedure is more extensive. The distinction between serious and nonserious crimes is related to the possible sentences that can be imposed. Serious crimes that are punishable by incarceration for more than one year are called **felonies** in most states. Less serious crimes that are punishable by imprisonment for one year or less are called **misdemeanors.** Municipal courts usually have jurisdiction to hold trials in misdemeanor cases; felony cases must be heard in higher (general jurisdiction) courts.

felony
A serious crime punishable by more than one year in prison.

misdemeanor
A less serious crime punishable by one year or less in jail.

Up to this point in the process, the suspect has been arrested, has been booked, and has made an initial appearance before a judge. There has been no discussion of the strength of the evidence in the case. Evidence is first discussed at the next step of criminal justice procedure, the preliminary hearing.

A preliminary hearing (or "probable cause" hearing) is an appearance before a judge to determine whether probable cause exists to hold the arrestee for trial. The hearing usually takes place in municipal court. On behalf of the police, the prosecutor presents evidence against the accused person. The arrestee is present and may be represented by an attorney, who has the right to cross-examine witnesses and present exculpatory evidence showing that the defendant is innocent. If the judge is convinced that there is probable cause to believe that a crime has been committed and that the person charged committed it, the case is bound over for trial. If the judge does not find the evidence convincing enough to establish probable cause, the complaint is dismissed and the defendant is released. Although the defendant can waive the preliminary hearing, most defendants do not because the hearing provides an opportunity to assess the strength of the prosecutor's case against them.

Before a defendant can stand trial, he or she must be formally accused on the basis of a determination of probable cause. This can occur in either of two ways. An **information** is a formal accusation filed by the prosecutor based on the findings of the preliminary hearing. An **indictment** is also a formal accusation, but it requires the concurrence of a grand jury.

information
A formal accusation of a crime filed by a prosecutor on the basis of a preliminary hearing.

indictment
A "true bill" of a grand jury that formally charges a person with a crime.

grand jury
A group of citizens who hear evidence from a prosecutor to determine whether probable cause exists to formally charge a person with a crime.

Grand Jury, Indictment, Arraignment

A **grand jury** consists of a group of citizens who hear the evidence presented by a prosecutor in order to determine whether probable cause exists to hold a person for trial. It was originated in England to prevent the holding of accused persons without justification. Following this common law tradition, grand juries in the United States consist of between sixteen and twenty-three people, who are usually selected from voter registration rolls in the same way as members of trial juries. Evidence is presented by the prosecutor, and members of the grand jury can question witnesses. The defendant is not permitted to attend grand jury proceedings, and all grand jury hearings are secret. The nonrepresentation of the accused in grand jury proceedings has drawn considerable criticism.

The secrecy of grand jury proceedings, together with the absence of defense counsel, can lead to abuses. Abraham Blumberg has reported that grand juries often act as a "rubber stamp" for prosecutors, "since in practice grand juries tend to ratify the charges that are presented to them."[14] This occurs because the pros-

FUTURE ISSUES

Blame and Believability in Rape Cases

The processing of rape cases through the criminal justice system is said to be strongly influenced by a tendency to blame the victim. Whether or not the victim was drinking, hitchhiking, had a "bad" reputation, had a prior sexual relationship with the offender, or reported the crime promptly have all been identified as influencing the prosecution of these cases.[A] A study was conducted in Detroit to determine the extent to which characteristics of the victim affected the processing of aggravated versus simple rapes. Aggravated rapes were those involving strangers, multiple offenders, a weapon, or injury. Cases without any of these characteristics were considered simple rapes.

The researchers found that aggravated rapes were more likely to occur away from home and to produce physical evidence of the crime, but the two kinds of rapes did not differ significantly in any other way. Both simple and aggravated rapes were equally likely to be prosecuted, and characteristics of the victim appeared to play no role in the outcome of the case. The investigators found that "walking alone late at night, hitchhiking, and accompanying a man to his home apparently did not lead a victim to be blamed for precipitating a rape."[B] If these findings hold true in other cities, we can conclude that the processing of rape cases through the criminal justice system is based on the offender's conduct rather than that of the victim.

FUTURES QUESTION

How would you explain the findings of this study, given the differences in the severity of the crimes?

Rapes committed by strangers that involve serious physical injury have been found to occur away from home. A study of these cases found little evidence of "blaming the victim" for engaging in high-risk conduct that may have precipitated the rape. Prosecutions and convictions did not appear to turn on the victim's conduct.

NOTES

[A]Wayne A. Kerstetter, "Gateway to Justice: Police and Prosecutorial Response to Sexual Assaults Against Women," *Journal of Criminal Law and Criminology,* vol. 81 (1990), pp. 267–313; Susan Estrich, *Real Rape* (Cambridge, MA: Harvard University Press, 1987).

[B]Julie Horney and Cassia Spohn, "The Influence of Blame and Believability Factors on the Processing of Simple versus Aggravated Rape Cases," *Criminology,* vol. 34 (1996), pp. 135–62.

ecutor presents evidence and arguments that are not opposed by the suspect. Also, questions about a suspect's political beliefs or associations can be used to influence a grand jury. There are several other problems with grand jury proceedings: A prosecutor who does not obtain an indictment can simply try again with another grand jury, "leaked" media announcements of grand jury investigations are sometimes used to cast doubt on the character of the suspect, and most states do not require a prosecutor to present known evidence that might show that the accused is innocent.[15] These criticisms were renewed in 1998 with the grand jury investigation of President Clinton's alleged liaison with a White House intern. The intern's mother and secret service agents assigned to the White House were subpoenaed to testify before the grand jury. There were numerous leaks to the media about the content of secret grand jury testimony. Many observers saw these actions as attempts to intimidate certain individuals rather than efforts to discover the truth.[16]

If a majority of the members of a grand jury believe that there is probable cause to hold the accused for trial, they issue a "true bill" in which the accused is formally charged with the crime. A true bill is equivalent to an indictment.

If a majority of the grand jury members do not believe that there is enough evidence against the accused to establish probable cause, the charges are dismissed. This is called a "no bill," meaning that no indictment is forthcoming. It is possible, however, for a grand jury proceeding to begin before a person has even been arrested. If the grand jury votes to indict, a judge can issue a warrant for the person's arrest based on the grand jury's finding of probable cause. This proceeding, called a *secret indictment,* is carried out when knowledge of a pending investigation would cause a suspect to flee the jurisdiction or alter his or her conduct.

Grand juries are still used in about half the states. The Supreme Court has permitted the states to use preliminary hearings in lieu of grand jury proceedings, making it likely that the latter will be used even less often in the future. Until grand jury proceedings attain greater public confidence, visibility, and consistent fairness, they will remain "an artifact of the past, serving more as an adjunct of prosecutorial power than a buffer between an arrogant state and the powerless individual."[17]

Once a grand jury votes to indict, or an information has been drawn up after a preliminary hearing, the defendant is arraigned. An arraignment takes place before a judge, who reads the information or indictment to the suspect, formally notifying him or her of the charge or charges. The judge again formally notifies the defendant of his or her constitutional rights, such as the right to a trial by jury, the right to have legal counsel at trial, and the right to cross-examine witnesses. If it is an issue in the case, the defendant's competency to stand trial is assessed, and the court appoints legal counsel for the defendant if he or she cannot afford to retain a lawyer. Finally, the judge asks the defendant to make a **plea.**

plea
A defendant's formal answer to a charge against him or her.

Defendants generally have four alternatives in making a plea: They can plead guilty, nolo contendere, no plea, or not guilty. If a defendant pleads guilty (which rarely occurs without negotiations with the prosecutor), the judge will set a date for sentencing. Nolo contendere means "no contest" and is treated as a plea of guilty. In states where nolo pleas are permitted, it is up to the judge to accept or disallow such a plea. If a defendant pleads nolo contendere, the judge must first accept the plea. A nolo plea may not be used against a defendant in a later civil suit.

Former Vice President Spiro Agnew provides perhaps the best-known case of a nolo plea. Agnew's plea of "no contest" to charges of accepting illegal kickbacks as governor of Maryland protected him from having his plea used against him in civil suits brought by residents of Maryland or other injured parties. Those seeking damages had to offer independent proof that he had accepted kickbacks, without relying on his plea.[18]

If a defendant chooses to make no plea, the case is treated as if he or she had pleaded not guilty. "No plea" is sometimes entered when a defendant has not yet had an opportunity to discuss the case with his or her attorney. Finally, when a defendant pleads "not guilty" (which most accused people do at their arraignment), the judge sets a date for trial.

Trial, Conviction, Sentencing

After the arraignment a trial takes place, provided that the defendant does not decide to plead guilty at some point before the trial. A defendant can plead guilty at any time, and by doing so waives the right to a trial. There are two types of trial formats. In a **bench trial** the prosecutor and defense counsel make their arguments to a judge, who determines guilt or innocence. A **jury trial** is similar except that guilt or innocence is determined by a jury. In a jury trial the judge is present only to rule on issues of law or procedure.

bench trial
A trial in which a judge determines guilt or innocence.

jury trial
A trial in which a jury determines guilt or innocence.

Whether a case is heard at a bench or jury trial, the standard of proof is the same. To arrive at a verdict of guilty, a judge or jury must believe "beyond a reasonable doubt" that the defendant committed the crime.[19] This is the highest standard of proof in American jurisprudence. It should be kept in mind, however, that while "beyond a reasonable doubt" is not the same as 100 percent certainty, it is a much higher standard than probable cause. Some doubt can remain, but only reasonable doubts can result in a verdict of not guilty.

The precise meaning of "beyond a reasonable doubt" has been the subject of much debate. Legislatures and court decisions have defined this term differently. Some jurisdictions define reasonable doubt as "a serious and substantial doubt," while others define it as "a doubt based on reason." In a Nebraska case the judge used "actual and substantial doubt" to explain the meaning of "beyond a reasonable doubt" to a jury. On appeal, the U.S. Supreme Court admitted that the Nebraska definition was ambiguous but upheld the constitutionality of the judge's explanation.[20] This issue is critical because it deals with jurors' comprehension of the burden of proof when a defendant's liberty is at stake. Table 6.1 summarizes the definitions of "beyond a reasonable doubt" used in various states. As is shown in Table 6.1, a wide variety of phrases are used to define "beyond a reasonable doubt." Some of these are quite vague ("doubt based on reason"), whereas others appear to require proof beyond *all* doubt ("moral certainty of guilt"). The Supreme Court has been reluctant to prescribe a uniform definition, and the result is wide disparity in terminology and meaning among the states.[21]

Unlike a grand jury, a **trial jury** most often consists of twelve citizens, who in most states must unanimously agree on a verdict of guilt. If only eleven of the twelve agree that the evidence indicates guilt beyond a reasonable doubt, the verdict must be "not guilty." A finding of not guilty is an **acquittal,** and it means that no further legal action can be taken against the accused person on the charge in question. A finding of guilt by a judge or jury is a **conviction.** Only at this point can a defendant be termed an *offender.* An offender can challenge the conviction only on appeal to a higher court, attempting to show that errors may have been made in law or procedure in the case. While most appeals are unsuccessful, those that succeed usually result in a new trial.

trial jury
A group of citizens (usually twelve) who decide on the guilt or innocence of a defendant.

acquittal
A finding of not guilty after trial.

conviction
A finding of guilt by a judge, jury, or plea.

Upon a finding of guilty, the judge sets a date for sentencing. In sentencing, the judge decides what he or she believes to be the most appropriate punishment,

TABLE 6.1

Classification of States according to Definition of Reasonable Doubt

"HESITATE TO ACT IN IMPORTANT AFFAIRS OF LIFE" OR "WILLING TO ACT IN IMPORTANT AFFAIRS OF LIFE"	"DOUBT BASED ON REASON" OR "DOUBT BASED ON A VALID REASON" OR "DOUBT BASED ON REASON AND COMMON SENSE"	"ACTUAL AND SUBSTANTIAL DOUBT" OR "SERIOUS AND SUBSTANTIAL DOUBT" OR "FAIR AND ACTUAL DOUBT"	"DOUBT THAT CAN BE ARTICULATED" OR "DOUBT FOR WHICH A REASON CAN BE GIVEN" OR "AN INABILITY TO LET THE MIND REST EASILY UPON THE CERTAINTY OF YOUR VERDICT"	"MORAL CERTAINTY OF GUILT" OR "FIRMLY CONVINCED OF GUILT"	NO DEFINITION PROVIDED OR NO DEFINITION REQUIRED OR NO DEFINITION PERMITTED
Alaska	Connecticut	Alabama	Florida	Alabama	Kansas
Arkansas	Florida	Arkansas	New York	Arizona	Kentucky
Colorado	Hawaii	California	Tennessee	California	Louisiana
Connecticut	Michigan	Delaware		Georgia	Mississippi
Florida	Missouri	Idaho		Hawaii	New Jersey
Idaho	Nevada	Indiana		Iowa	North Dakota
Indiana	New Hampshire	Massachusetts		Massachusetts	Oklahoma
Maine	New Mexico	Nebraska		Minnesota	Washington
Maryland	New York	Nevada		Missouri	Wyoming
Massachusetts	North Carolina	Virginia		Montana	
Michigan	North Dakota			Nebraska	
Minnesota	Oregon				
Montana	Rhode Island				
New Mexico	South Dakota				
North Dakota	Utah				
Ohio	Vermont				
Oregon	West Virginia				
Pennsylvania	Washington				
South Carolina	Wisconsin				
Texas					
West Virginia					
Wisconsin					

SOURCE: Craig Hemmens, Kathryn E. Scarborough, and Rolando Del Carmen, "Grave Doubts about 'Reasonable Doubt': Confusion in State and Federal Courts," *Journal of Criminal Justice*, vol. 25 (1997), pp. 231–54.

given the type of crime and offender. The judge's discretion is guided only by the minimum and maximum sentence for the crime as set by law. If the penalty established by law for a certain crime is one to ten years in prison, a judge can sentence a convicted offender to any term between one and ten years. A sentence outside this range would be a violation of law and would require resentencing.

In deciding on an appropriate sentence, the judge will often ask the probation department to conduct a presentence investigation of the offender. This investigation seeks information regarding the offender's personal and social background, his or her criminal record, and any other information that may help the judge match the sentence to the offender. Information that indicates a history of drug or alcohol abuse or knowledge that an offender has dependents may influence the judge's decision.

At the sentencing hearing, the judge can fine the offender, impose a sentence of incarceration, or place the offender on probation, depending on the type of crime involved. In **probation,** the offender serves his or her sentence in the community, under the supervision of a probation officer employed by the court. Although the use of incarceration has been increasing steadily in recent years, probation remains the most widely utilized sentencing alternative in criminal court. **Incarceration** serves to segregate offenders from the rest of the community in jails or prisons in order to rehabilitate, incapacitate, or punish them and deter others from committing similar crimes. (Trends in criminal sentences are discussed further in Chapter 13.)

probation
A sentence served in the community under the supervision of a probation officer.

incarceration
Segregation of offenders from society in a correctional institution.

After serving part of a sentence of incarceration, an offender may be placed on **parole.** This final step in the criminal justice process occurs when an offender sentenced to incarceration is released before completion of the sentence so that he or she can serve the remainder of the term under the supervision of a parole officer in the community. Parole is designed to assist the offender in readjusting to life and work in society after serving time in prison.

parole
A conditional release from incarceration to serve the remainder of the sentence under supervision in the community.

Appeals

Appeals are an often misunderstood part of the criminal justice process. Appellate courts are seen as hovering "over the shoulder" of trial court judges, reversing their decision, and imposing their own brand of justice at a much later time and often in a different city. The far-removed presence of appellate courts promotes misunderstanding of their nature and functions. It is important to understand, for example, that appellate courts never hear new trials or sentence offenders.

appeal
A review of a criminal conviction by a higher court on grounds of law or procedure.

Once convicted, an offender can appeal the conviction to an appellate court. The appeal is a written statement, called a *brief,* that explains the alleged legal errors made during the trial. The appellate court, consisting of a panel of several judges, reviews the brief and the trial transcript. If the court finds that there is no basis for the appeal, the appeal is dismissed. If the court finds grounds for the appeal, it holds a hearing in which the defense attorney and the prosecutor present arguments on the issue raised in the brief. This is not a retrial, but a hearing on a single legal issue. For example, the appeal discussed earlier (*Victor v. Nebraska*) dealt with the legal meaning of proof "beyond a reasonable doubt." The U.S. Supreme Court heard arguments on that issue only.[22] The evidence presented at trial, the defendant's background, the length of the sentence, and all other aspects of the case were not relevant to the appeal and were not argued.

Some time after the hearing, the appellate court justices discuss the issue and vote either to affirm the conviction by leaving it undisturbed or to reverse the conviction by overturning it because of the significant legal error made during the trial. Occasionally an appellate court will find "harmless error," meaning that a legal error was made during the trial but was not serious enough to affect the fairness of the trial.[23] That was the Supreme Court's finding in *Victor v. Nebraska.*

Most appeals are unsuccessful, and the defendant usually has little recourse but to accept the trial court's verdict unless a violation of a constitutional right is alleged, in which case the defendant may appeal to the federal courts. Here again, however, appeals are usually unsuccessful.

In the rare case in which a conviction is reversed, the case usually is retried in the original court of general jurisdiction. For example, if a confession is ruled

Media and Criminal Justice

CRIMINAL JUSTICE

A study of the American criminal justice system, with its focus on due process, always allows that some guilty people will go free because there is not probable cause for an arrest, or they cannot be proved guilty beyond a reasonable doubt in a court of law. Is it possible, however, that a truly innocent person, perhaps a person with a prior criminal record who has been mistakenly identified by a crack-addicted robbery victim, might plead guilty out of desperation?

The 1990 HBO movie *Criminal Justice* has a simple title, but the story questions whether our system emphasizes *criminal* more than *justice.* The plot revolves around a young black man named Jesse Williams, who is picked up by police for the robbery and slashing of a young Hispanic girl in his neighborhood. The viewer sees that the victim is a prostitute and drug user, but the police and prosecutor conveniently ignore any factors that might impeach her, as she is the only witness to the crime.

Jesse is open about his prior record, cooperating with police and insisting that he has "gone straight." However, the victim's positive identification of Jesse in a police lineup immediately begins the wheels of criminal procedure turning.

Before his initial appearance, Jesse is granted a court-appointed attorney. Jesse's attorney knows the system well, and is not surprised when Jesse insists he is not guilty. In a preliminary hearing, the judge refuses to exclude the shaky lineup and Jesse finds himself facing serious charges. His lawyer advises him to take a plea bargain in the face of some very strong evidence, but Jesse insists that the girl who identified him won't appear if there is a trial. He refuses a plea bargain, deciding to take his chances in court.

In the grand jury, the victim recounts with conviction that Jesse Williams robbed and slashed her, but she lies when asked about her drug use and purpose for being in the crack house where the crime occurred. Jesse is indicted and the trial is scheduled.

Criminal Justice provides an excellent play-by-play portrayal of criminal procedure in the American court system. The prosecutor is clear about her mandate: get criminals like Jesse off the streets, even if it means cutting a deal. The public defender is equally convinced that Jesse should take a deal rather than face harsh sentencing after trial. The judge is concerned only about expediency and a high rate of case processing. After a long voire dire process, the jury just wants to get the case over with.

But what about Jesse? His insistence on going to trial appears to be based more on his belief that the victim won't appear in court than on the idea that he didn't commit the crime. The movie's pinnacle moment occurs when the jury is convened, the trial begins, and the victim finally enters the room to testify. Jesse's reaction, and the consequences that follow, leave the viewer with more questions than answers about our system.

The postscript of the film points out that more than 98 percent of cases in the Brooklyn, New York, court system are resolved by plea-bargaining. The implication, of course, is that surely some of those must be victims of a system that does not have the time or resources to offer people trials.

MEDIA AND CRIMINAL JUSTICE QUESTION

Why did the prosecutor, defense attorney, and judge all assume that the defendant was guilty in this case? Are there measures that could be taken to prevent such assumptions?

to be defective on appeal, a new trial may occur, but the confession used in the original trial may not be used in the retrial. Other evidence of guilt, independent of the confession, must be produced. The decision to retry a case is within the discretion of the prosecutor. Such a retrial is not considered a violation of the double jeopardy clause of the Fifth Amendment, which prohibits a defendant from being tried twice for the same crime. The reversal of the conviction renders the initial trial a **mistrial,** and the retrial is considered the first trial under law, as the first attempt was found legally invalid.

mistrial
A trial outcome that is legally invalid owing to errors of law or procedure.

Some have alleged that appeals impair the deterrent effect of the criminal justice system because punishments are not finalized until a lengthy appeals process has been completed. Former Supreme Court Chief Justice Warren Burger argued that appellate review should be accomplished more quickly, within eight weeks of a conviction. He also urged the establishment of limits on the number of appeals that may be made by the same defendant in the same case, and several states and the federal government have established such limits.[24]

In the United States nearly $300 per person is spent each year on the justice system. Most of this annual total of $74 billion is paid by state and local governments who use it to pay and equip police, and to build and staff courts and prisons.

The Cost of Justice

Justice is expensive. Each year, federal, state, and local governments spend $74 billion on the civil and criminal justice system agencies, or $299 per person. This translates into seven cents for each dollar spent by local governments, six cents for each dollar spent by state governments, and less than one cent of every dollar spent by the federal government.[25] All this money, of course, is provided by taxpayers. Because most justice agencies are operated by state and local governments, their justice expenditures account for 87 percent of all justice dollars.

Why is the cost of justice so high? The primary reason is increasing spending on prisons and police. State spending to build new prisons has increased by 612 percent, twice as fast as spending to operate prisons, which rose by 328 percent. Spending on police protection was significantly greater than spending on corrections, accounting for nearly $32 billion of the $74 billion total.[26] The high cost of police is due to the fact that there are more police agencies than any other type of justice agency. Most police officers (77 percent) are employees of local governments, which spend 73 percent of all police protection dollars.

Increased spending on police and prisons reflects the decisions of legislatures, which appropriate funds to these agencies because the public either actively encourages them or does not object strongly. The high levels of fear of crime, documented in Chapter 1, have put pressure on legislators to "do something" about this problem. Spending on police and prisons is a popular way to "do something" because these agencies already exist and have clear legal mandates. Spending on more innovative programs, such as delinquency prevention and family intervention initiatives, is less popular because these are not established political institutions.

These trends are a source of concern inasmuch as spending on justice agencies increased by 24 percent in only five years. In addition, 1.7 million people are employed in the civil and criminal justice systems combined for a total payroll of $4.3 billion. These costs are not likely to be reduced in the near future. Calls for police service have increased, jails are filled beyond their capacity, police departments are increasing staffing, and prosecutors report that they are unable to keep up with case loads.[27] Prosecutors, public defenders, judges, trial court administrators, and probation, parole, and correctional administrators all believe that the current system is not achieving its goals. The time appears ripe for innovations in adjudication and sentencing, a subject that is discussed further in Chapters 11 and 13.

Critical Thinking EXERCISE

Justice on the Carolina Frontier (1764)

Before the American Revolution the backcountry of South Carolina was a lawless place. Because of its remoteness, criminals could operate with impunity. Following is an excerpt from a petition from the Reverend Charles Woodmason to the British government on behalf of the people of his community:

> **That for many years past, the back parts of this province have been infested with an infernal gang of villains, who have committed such horrid depredations on our properties and estates, such insults on the persons of many settlers, and perpetrated such shocking outrages throughout the back settlements as is past description.**
>
> **Our large stocks of cattle are either stolen and destroyed, our cow pens are broken up, and all our valuable horses are carried off. Houses have been burned by these rogues, and families stripped and turned naked into the wood. Stores have been broken open and rifled by them. Private houses have been plundered. . . . Married women have been ravished, virgins deflowered, and other unheard of cruelties committed by these barbarous ruffians, who . . . have hereby reduced numbers of individuals to poverty. . . .**
>
> **No trading persons (or others) with money or goods, no responsible persons and traders dare keep cash or any valuable articles by them. Nor can women stir abroad but with a guard, or in terror. . . . Merchants' stores are obliged to be kept constantly guarded (which enhances the price of goods). And thus we live not as under a British government . . . but as if we were in Hungary or Germany, and in a state of war . . . obliged to be constantly on the watch and on our guard against these intruders and having it not in our power to call what we possess our own, not even for an hour; as being liable daily and hourly to be stripped of our property.**
>
> **Representations of these grievances and vexations have often been made by use to those in power, but without redress. . . .**

SOURCE: Charles Woodmason, "Lawlessness on the South Carolina Frontier," (1764), in *The Annals of America,* vol. 2 (Chicago: Encyclopedia Britannica, 1976), pp. 185–95.

Critical Thinking Questions

1. **How would you respond to this petition to make the community a more just place, knowing that the population is small and cannot afford a police force?**

2. In the actual petition, Charles Woodmason requested the establishment of a better court system and local jails; a printed criminal code, requiring public officials to carry out their duty under penalty of law; the founding of public schools; and the establishment of parishes with ministers. Which of these requests would have had the most immediate impact on the situation in South Carolina?
3. Which of Woodmason's requests would have the greatest impact over the long term?

Critical Thinking EXERCISE

Prior Record of Defendants and Juror Prejudice

John Adamson was convicted of murder in California. He had prior convictions for robbery, burglary, and larceny. Prior convictions cannot be introduced as evidence unless the defendant takes the witness stand in his own behalf. Then the prosecutor can introduce the prior convictions in an effort to discredit his testimony.

Adamson wanted to testify in his own behalf, but was afraid that the prosecutor would use the opportunity to prejudice the jury by talking about Adamson's past, rather than his current charges. On the other hand, if he failed to testify, the prosecutor could prejudice the jury by inferring that his refusal to testify was due to his guilt on the current charges. Adamson's situation was especially serious because there were no other witnesses who could testify about the crime.

Adamson appealed his conviction, arguing that this situation forces an accused person who is a repeat offender "to choose between the risk of having his prior offenses disclosed to the jury or of having it draw harmful inferences" from the evidence presented by the prosecution about the murder charge. This is especially serious when the defendant may be the only one able to explain or deny the prosecutor's allegations about the circumstances of the crime or the offender.

SOURCE: *Adamson v. California,* 67 S. Ct. 1672 (1947).

Critical Thinking Questions

1. Why do you believe evidence of prior crimes is excluded from criminal trials?
2. Adamson argued on appeal that his right to due process under the Fourteenth Amendment was violated by forcing him into a "no win" situation in which he had to choose between exposing his past crime to the jury or allowing the prosecutor to implicate him in criminal activities without any response or explanation. In considering the objectives of accuracy and fairness discussed earlier, how should the U.S. Supreme Court rule in Adamson's case?

Summary

ORIGINS OF THE CRIMINAL JUSTICE SYSTEM

- Because there are more than 55,000 independent criminal justice agencies that often do not cooperate with one another, the American criminal justice "system" is often called a nonsystem.
- A system of justice evolves in a society in order to enforce rules, resolve disputes, and administer punishment. In the United States this occurred in the Colonial period, as small, religiously and culturally similar communities evolved into larger towns and cities with more diverse populations.
- The criminal justice process has two fundamental goals: fairness and accuracy.

THE AGENCIES OF CRIMINAL JUSTICE

- The main types of criminal justice agencies are law enforcement agencies, courts (including trial and appeals courts), and correctional systems. All three types are found at all three levels of government.

CRIMINAL PROCEDURE

- The criminal justice process begins with a violation of law that is made known to the police. The police conduct an investigation, which may or may not lead to the arrest and booking of a suspect.
- At the initial appearance the arrestee is given formal notice of the charge(s) for which he or she is being held and informed of his or her legal rights; in addition, the judge sets bail. This step is followed by a preliminary hearing to determine whether there is probable cause to believe that a crime has been committed and that the person charged committed it.
- A grand jury consists of a group of citizens who hear the evidence presented by a prosecutor in order to determine whether probable cause exists to hold a person for trial, in which case it will issue a true bill or indictment in which the accused person is formally charged with the crime.
- At an arraignment a judge reads the information or indictment and notifies the defendant of his or her constitutional rights. The defendant then makes a plea of guilty, nolo contendere, no plea, or not guilty.
- In a bench trial the prosecutor and defense make their arguments to a judge, who determines guilt or innocence. A jury trial is similar except that guilt or innocence is determined by a trial jury of twelve citizens. A finding of not guilty is an acquittal; a finding of guilty is a conviction.
- In the case of a guilty verdict the judge sets a date for sentencing and may ask the probation department to conduct a presentence investigation of the offender. At the sentencing hearing the judge can fine the offender, impose a sentence of incarceration, or place the offender on probation.
- A convicted offender can appeal the conviction to an appellate court consisting of a panel of several justices, who may vote either to affirm the conviction or to reverse it, that is, to overturn it because a significant legal error was made during the trial.

THE COST OF JUSTICE

- Criminal justice is expensive. A major reason for the cost of justice is a significant increase in spending on prisons and police in recent years.

Key Terms

limited jurisdiction
general jurisdiction
appellate jurisdiction
arrest
probable cause
booking
citation
summons
bail
surety
arraignment
felony
misdemeanor
information
indictment
grand jury
plea
bench trial
jury trial
trial jury
acquittal
conviction
probation
incarceration
parole
appeal
mistrial

Questions for Review and Discussion

1. Why is the criminal justice system sometimes referred to as a "nonsystem"?
2. What social conditions contributed to the evolution of the criminal justice system in the United States?
3. What are the two main goals of the criminal justice system?
4. Name the three basic types of criminal justice agencies and their primary functions.
5. What are the steps in the criminal justice process, assuming that an offender undergoes the entire process from violation to punishment?
6. What is bail, and what purpose does it serve?
7. Distinguish between a grand jury and a trial jury.
8. What standard of proof must be met for a jury to arrive at a verdict of guilty?
9. What is an appeal?
10. Why has the cost of justice risen so dramatically in recent years?

Notes

[1]Larry Reibstein, "NYPD Black and Blue," *Newsweek* (June 2, 1997), p. 67.

[2]Daniel L. Skoler, *Governmental Structuring of Criminal Justice Services: Organizing the Non-System* (Washington, D.C.: U.S. Government Printing Office, 1978).

[3]Lawrence M. Friedman, *Crime and Punishment in American History* (New York: Basic Books, 1993), p. 27.

[4]Ibid., p. 3; Peter Charles Hoffer and William B. Scott, eds., *Criminal Proceedings in Colonial Virginia* (Athens: University of Georgia Press, 1984).

[5]Bradley Chapin, *Criminal Justice in Colonial America, 1606–1660* (Athens: University of Georgia Press, 1983).

[6]See Herbert A. Johnson and Nancy Travis Wolfe, *History of Criminal Justice*, 2nd ed. (Cincinnati: Anderson Publishing, 1996).

[7]Abram Chayes, "How the Constitution Establishes Justice," in R. A. Goldwin and W. A. Schambra, eds., *The Constitution, the Courts, and the Quest for Justice* (Washington, D.C.: American Enterprise Institute, 1989), pp. 25–39; F. Thornton Miller, *Juries and Judges Versus the Law: Virginia's Provincial Legal Perspective, 1783–1828* (Charlottesville: University Press of Virginia, 1994); Francis A. Allen, *The Habits of Legality: Criminal Justice and the Rule of Law* (New York: Oxford University Press, 1996); Ronald Dworkin, *Freedom's Law: The Moral Reading of the American Consti-*

tution (Cambridge, MA: Harvard University Press, 1996); Stephen B. Presser, *Recapturing the Constitution: Race, Religion, and Abortion Reconsidered* (Washington, D.C.: Regery, 1994); Cass R. Sunstein, *The Partial Constitution* (Cambridge, MA: Harvard University Press, 1993).

[8]Herbert Packer, *The Limits of the Criminal Sanction* (Standard, CA: Stanford University Press, 1968).

[9]Charles L. Gould, "The Criminal Justice System Favors Offenders," in Bonnie Szumski, ed., *Criminal Justice: Opposing Viewpoints* (St. Paul, MN: Greenhaven Press, 1987), pp. 33–9.

[10]John Locke, *Concerning the True Original Extent and End of Civil Government* (Chicago: Encyclopaedia Britannica, 1952).

[11]George H. Smith, *The American Revolution* (Nashville, TN: Knowledge Products, 1979); Leonard W. Levy, *Seasoned Judgments: The American Constitution, Rights, and History* (New Brunswick, NJ: Transaction, 1995).

[12]Allen J. Beck et al., *Correctional Populations in the United States* (Washington, D.C.: Bureau of Justice Statistics, 1997).

[13]Jonah Blank, "Guilty—But Just How Guilty?," *U.S. News & World Report* (January 12, 1998), p. 21.

[14]Abraham S. Blumberg, *Criminal Justice: Issues and Ironies,* 2nd ed. (New York: New Viewpoints, 1979).

[15]Marvin E. Frankel and Garry P. Naftalis, *The Grand Jury* (New York: Hill & Wang, 1977).

[16]Judy Keen and Gary Fields, "Deal Sought on Guards' Testimony," *USA Today* (February 13, 1998), p. 1; Walter Shapiro, "Loneliest Job in the World—Except for All the Lawyers," *USA Today* (February 13, 1998), p. 6.

[17]Blumberg, p. 144.

[18]See Spiro T. Agnew, *Go Quietly . . . Or Else* (New York: William Morrow, 1980).

[19]Ronald L. Carlson, *Criminal Justice Procedure,* 5th ed. (Cincinnati: Anderson Publishing, 1996), p. 177.

[20]*Victor v. Nebraska,* 114 S. Ct. 1239 (1994).

[21]Craig Hemmens, Kathryn E. Scarborough, and Rolando V. Del Carmen, "Grave Doubts about 'Reasonable Doubt': Confusion in State and Federal Courts," *Journal of Criminal Justice,* vol. 25 (1997), pp. 231–54.

[22]*Victor v. Nebraska,* 114 S. Ct. 1239 (1994).

[23]Gilbert B. Stuckey, *Procedures in the Justice System,* 5th ed. (New York: Macmillan, 1996), p. 242.

[24]Warren E. Burger, "The Legal System Gives Too Much Protection to Criminals" (speech delivered to the American Bar Association in 1981), in Bonnie Szumski, ed., *Criminal Justice: Opposing Viewpoints* (St. Paul, MN: Greenhaven Press, 1987), pp. 102–7.

[25]Sue A. Lindgren, *Justice Expenditure and Employment* (Washington, D.C.: Bureau of Justice Statistics, 1995).

[26]Ibid.

[27]Barbara A. Webster and J. Thomas McEwen, *Assessing Criminal Justice Needs* (Washington, D.C.: National Institute of Justice, 1992); Tom McEwen, *National Assessment Program: 1994 Survey Results* (Washington, D.C.: National Institute of Justice, 1995).

For Further Reading

Jim McGee and Brian Duffy, *Main Justice* (New York: Touchstone, 1997).
David L. Protess and Robert Warden, *A Promise of Justice: The 14 Year Fight to Save Four Innocent Men* (New York: Hyperion, 1998).
Terry Sullivan, *Killer Clown: John Wayne Gacy* (New York: Kensington, 1991).

chapter seven

Origins and Organization of Law Enforcement

No man is entitled to the blessings of freedom unless he be vigilant in its preservation.

DOUGLAS MACARTHUR
(1880–1964)

CHAPTER OUTLINE

- A drunk stumbles down the street late at night, slowly making his way home.
- A juvenile is out on the corner at 11 P.M. on a school night.
- A man urinates against a building on a deserted street.
- A young person panhandles, begging for loose change.
- A woman, dressed provocatively, loiters under a street lamp.

These behaviors are not terribly serious, yet they each contribute to a perception of social disorder in the community. Each of the actions listed is a misdemeanor at best, but it creates concern, fear, and changes in behavior. Fewer people go out at night, certain areas are viewed as unsafe, and

DCFD
I'M
Hungry
Change
Job
Veryfine

the level of mutual suspicion in the community increases. In recent years considerable attention has been given to these "quality of life" issues. There is growing recognition of the ways in which they contribute to more serious criminal behavior.[1]

In many cities police are changing the way they enforce the law. They no longer react only to serious crime but increasingly attempt to maintain a sense of order through enforcement of "disorderly" behaviors such as those just listed. The appropriate role of police in society has been debated for many years. Contemporary thinking and discussion about police work emanate from long-standing assumptions about the proper role of law enforcement in American life.

Community Protection before Police

To understand why public policing was invented in the first place, it is helpful to think about what would happen if it was suddenly eliminated. It is unlikely that rates of murder, rape, and assault would increase dramatically if police did not exist. Instead, property crimes, such as burglary and larceny, would probably become more prevalent rather quickly. The reason for this is that moral strictures against crimes of violence are much stronger than those against property crimes. It is much easier to rationalize a theft than an assault. In fact property crimes occur about ten times more frequently than crimes of violence.

If crimes against property would be committed more frequently if police did not exist, it follows that property owners would be most interested in preventing those crimes. Long before police departments were formally established, less formal measures of self-protection were used by property owners who could afford them. These measures are illustrated by the **mutual pledge system** that was prevalent in Britain during the Middle Ages. Alfred the Great (870–901) established an organized system of community self-responsibility in which everyone in the community was responsible for everyone else. Communities were divided into ten-family groups called "tithings." Cities as we know them did not exist, so each tithing was responsible for maintaining peace within its own boundaries. "It was each citizen's duty to raise the 'hue and cry' when a crime was committed, to collect his neighbors and to pursue a criminal who fled from the district. If such a group failed to apprehend a lawbreaker, all were fined by the Crown."[2] This system of mutual responsibility and shared penalties was designed to ensure that all members of the community made a conscientious effort to control crime.

mutual pledge system
A system of community self-responsibility that existed in Britain during the Middle Ages in which residents were held responsible for the conduct of their neighbors.

constable
A citizen in charge of weapons and equipment for one hundred families in his geographical area. In England constables were appointed by a local nobleman beginning around the year 900.

shire reeve
An official appointed by the British Crown who was responsible for overseeing the constables and several hundred families in a given area (called a "shire"). The modern word *sheriff* is derived from this term.

Every ten tithings, or one hundred families, comprised a "hundred" and was headed by a **constable** (who was appointed by a local nobleman to be in charge of weapons and equipment). The hundreds, in turn, were grouped together to form a "shire" (about the equivalent of a county). For each shire the Crown appointed a supervisor called a **shire reeve,** from which the modern term "sheriff" is derived.

The Watch and Ward System

Another advance toward an organized system of policing was made during the reign of Edward I (1272–1307). The Statute of Winchester, enacted in 1285, established the **watch and ward system** to aid constables in their law enforcement efforts.[3] This system also emphasized community responsibility for crime control. Men from each town were required to take turns standing watch at night. If any criminals were apprehended, they were turned over to the constable for trial the following day.

In 1326, Edward II established the position of **justice of the peace,** who assisted the sheriff in enforcing the law. Eventually this role shifted to adjudication of cases in court, while the sheriffs retained their local peacekeeping function.

This system of law enforcement, based on the mutual pledge and supplemented by the watch and ward, was in effect for several hundred years, but gradually it lost community support and declined. This decline has been described as follows:

> **What was everybody's business became nobody's duty, and the citizens who were bound by law to take their turn at police work gradually evaded personal police service by paying others to do the work for them. . . . [The substitutes] were usually ill-paid and ignorant men, often too old to be in any sense efficient.[4]**

In the sixteenth century the advent of "bellmen," who watched for fires, relieved the watchman of that duty. However, this did little to prevent crime, as watchmen were generally incompetent, sometimes drank on the job, and eventually came to be ridiculed. Consider the situation as it existed in London at that time:

> **During the 16th and 17th centuries, there was no question in the minds of Londoners that they lived in a dangerous place which was ill-protected by their watchmen. The destruction of the city wall and the gates allowed them to give all their attention to the town and its people, but this did not lead to any improvement. The watchmen generally were considered to be incompetent and cowardly. By the mid-17th century they had acquired the derisive name of "Charlies." It was a common sport of rich young men of the time to taunt and terrorize them, to wreck the watchhouses, and occasionally to murder the watchmen. The large rattles they carried to signal for help were little comfort since they knew their colleagues were not dependable; the watchmen spent a good deal of time discreetly concealed from the public.**

Jonathan Rubinstein describes the citizens' reactions to these circumstances, noting that there was no public outcry to change the watch and ward system. Since there were no lights in the city, homeowners were required to place a candle on the street in front of their houses at night. This rule was not enforced, and as a result the streets were dark and considered dangerous. Those who could afford to do so hired guards and armed themselves. Women never went out on the street unaccompanied. Those who could not afford these self-protective measures were often victimized.[5] Given this situation, in which the rich could buy protection for themselves and the poor were being victimized in unsafe streets, a catalyst was needed—some unanticipated influence or event that would galvanize the poor to act. That catalyst was gin.

watch and ward system
A system established in 1285 to aid constables in their law enforcement efforts. Men from each town were required to take turns standing watch at night. Crime suspects were turned over to the constable.

justice of the peace
An office established by Edward II in 1326 to assist the sheriff in enforcing the law. Eventually the role of the justice of the peace shifted to adjudication, while the sheriffs retained their local peacekeeping function.

Media and Criminal Justice

THE UNTOUCHABLES

In the chronology of events that caused our modern police system to evolve from the "watch and ward" system, Prohibition has been deemed one of the darkest eras for law enforcement. The 1987 film *The Untouchables* features a fictionalized account of some very real characters in policing history: gangster Al Capone and his organized crime mob and federal agent Elliot Ness and his motley crew of crime fighters.

The story is set in 1930s Chicago, where, after ten years of prohibition on alcohol production and sales, the mob had become quite astute at smuggling gin and paying off police to ignore their illegal activity. Having entered the Depression, it was a rare officer who could resist the mob's bribes, which had become an expected fringe benefit of the job. Elliot Ness and his agents were called "The Untouchables" because they advocated a code of professionalism and ethics that was beyond reproach and "untouchable" to the mob.

The film offers an excellent account of a very important turning point in the history of policing. Special Agent Elliot Ness is considered a laughing stock to local police when he begins his attack on organized crime; indeed, even the FBI seem intent on having Ness fail. Ness realizes early that if he wants to get the cooperation of local police, he will have to learn the ropes through a "real" police officer. He finds an ally in a seasoned Irish cop named Malone, who explains to Ness that he'd better get used to the idea of using violence to fight violence.

Even Ness knows his limits, however. When Malone asks "What are your prepared to do?" Ness replies, "Everything within the law."

In one telling scene, a Capone mobster is captured for gin-running at the Canadian border, but he refuses to cooperate with Ness' interrogation. The gangster doesn't know that his partner has already been shot dead, and that the body is lying on the porch outside the cabin where he's being questioned. Disgusted with the gangster's defiant attitude, Malone walks outside, grabs the corpse, and props it up against the wall beside the window. He shakes the man violently, yelling that if the man doesn't talk, he's going to be shot. After a moment of silence, Malone puts a bullet through the corpse and lets it drop. Inside, Ness is horrified by this outrageous tactic—but his mobster is now talking.

Such scenes provide insight into the history of policing by illustrating the social, economic, and political factors that caused police corruption in the 1920s and 30s, and ultimately led to the rise of organized crime. The Wickersham Commission would later determine that the only way to battle the overwhelming problem of police corruption in the United States was to repeal Prohibition. This, coupled with the efforts of real-life agents such as Ness, sent a clear message that the country needed a new breed of "untouchable" and ethical officers. Ness and his contemporaries were responsible for beginning a progressive era of policing that would eventually contribute to the professionalization of our modern police forces.

MEDIA AND CRIMINAL JUSTICE QUESTION

What were the important factors that contributed to the high levels of police corruption during the Prohibition era?

The Invention of Gin

The catalyst that provoked a more organized effort toward the establishment of public policing was the invention of gin by a Dutch chemist during the seventeenth century. The British government encouraged the manufacture of gin as a way to deal with grain surpluses, while also making a profit. Gin was much cheaper than brandy and much more potent than beer, wine, or ale. Sales of gin skyrocketed; between 1727 and 1743, consumption more than doubled. According to one historian,

> **Within a few decades, London was awash in an orgy of drinking which has probably not been matched in history. By 1725 there were more than 7,000 gin shops in London and drink was sold as a sideline by numerous shopkeepers and peddlers. For a penny anyone could drink all day in any "flash house" and get a**

> **straw pallet in a back room to sleep it off. . . . Public drunkenness became a commonplace sight, and drink-crazed mobs often roamed through the city. The streets of London, never safe, were now filled with people whose behavior was unpredictable and occasionally quite violent. Not surprisingly, the gin craze was accompanied by a great rise in violent crimes and theft.[6]**

Rather than deal with the cause of the problem, the government "got tough" on offenders. Street lighting was improved, more watchmen were hired, and the penalties for many crimes were dramatically increased. Individual citizens also began arming themselves and stayed off the streets at night. In addition, the rich began to move away from areas where poor people lived.

The Gin Act, passed in 1736, attempted to limit the availability of gin by establishing extremely high licensing fees for all gin sellers and manufacturers and providing rewards for information leading to the conviction of unlicensed distillers or retailers. These measures had little positive effect. Constables overlooked violations, informers were beaten or murdered, and, although the Act was in force for seven years and resulted in 10,000 prosecutions, only three licenses were sold. There was no reduction in the consumption of gin.[7] Clearly, the Gin Act did not accomplish what it was designed to do.

Consumption of gin was reduced only when taxes were increased, resulting in higher prices. The problems associated with gin were alleviated, but fear of crime did not decline correspondingly.

> **Although the gin craze abated, the fear of crime and the belief that it continued to increase did not. Members of Parliament continued to be accompanied to and from sessions by linkmen [bodyguards], and bulletproof coaches were advertised to thwart the highwaymen who plagued travelers on the roads to the city. In 1776 the Lord Mayor of London was robbed at gunpoint, and within the decade two of England's great nobles, the Duke of York and the Prince of Wales, were mugged as they walked in the city during the day. In the same period, the Great Seal of England was stolen from the house of the Lord Chancellor and melted down for the silver. There was a growing demand for protection, and private societies for the enforcement of law flourished.[8]**

In 1748, in response to growing concern, Henry Fielding proposed that the watch and ward system be centralized. He organized a private agency that patrolled the streets rather than staying at the watchboxes. He also organized a mounted patrol, the Bow Street Runners, to guard highways. The Runners quickly established a reputation for their ability to catch criminals.[9] Although this system declined after Fielding's death, he is credited with being the first person to propose the idea of a mobile police force.

Despite the success of the Bow Street Runners, fear of crime continued to increase. The Gordon Riots of 1780 produced serious mob violence in London, but the notion of a centralized police agency still was not widely accepted. There was fear, particularly among the wealthy who controlled the constables, that a centralized police agency would become too strong and abuse its power.

Finally, in response to the urging of legal reformer and philosopher Jeremy Bentham and the lobbying of English statesman Sir Robert Peel, the **Metropolitan Police of London** was established in 1829. The force, also referred to as the

Metropolitan Police of London
The first organized police department in London, established in 1829. The popular English name for police officers, "bobbies," comes from Sir Robert Peel, a founder of the Metropolitan Police.

New Police or the preventive police, was seen "as a civilizing instrument whose effort and example would make possible more harmonious relations among city people."[10] The popular English name for police officers, "bobbies," comes from the name of the founder of the Metropolitan Police, Robert Peel.

The basis of this new police force was very different from that of the watch and ward system. The city was to be patrolled by officers who were assigned specific territories (or beats). The watch and ward system had made it clear that strict supervision was required to ensure that officers would actually perform their duties and not sleep, drink, or loaf on the job. Robert Peel sought to provide inspiration by employing military principles in organizing what had traditionally been a civilian force.[11] Thus, the Metropolitan Police were distinguished by their patrolling of specific areas and by their paramilitary organization, which was designed to maintain discipline.

The New Police were not without problems, however. Poorly supervised patrol officers often drank or slept on the job, and there was a general lack of discipline. The first police commissioner was Colonel Charles Rowan, a former military officer. In order to maintain discipline, he instituted severe penalties for even minor infractions. For most violations the officer was dismissed from the force. As a result, during the early years of the Metropolitan Police more than a third of the force was discharged each year.[12]

Police in the United States

Despite the problems experienced in England, the American Colonies repeated the British experience. As early as 1636, Boston had night watchmen to protect warehouses and homes. This approach was imitated in other Eastern cities. As in England, the night watch was supervised by constables at the local level and by sheriffs at the county level.

The night watchmen were poorly paid, poorly supervised, and known for drinking and falling asleep on the job. Perhaps the most widespread criticism, however, was the same one that plagued the British watch and ward system: The watchmen did nothing to prevent crime.[13]

After the American Revolution no further efforts were made to establish a full-time police force. Most Americans saw a police force as the equivalent of a standing domestic army, because the British had used their army to enforce their laws in the Colonies. This was an important issue at the Constitutional Convention.[14] It was believed that a police force would lead to the same kinds of oppression and abuse that the Colonists had come to America to escape.

It was not until 1838 that Boston created a daytime police force to supplement the night watch. This occurred only after major riots in 1834, 1835, and 1837.[15] The Boston police forces were separate agencies, however, and there was intense rivalry between the day and night forces. New York was the first city to create a unified day and night police force (and to abolish the night watch). The New York City Police Department, established in 1845, was unique in its payment of low salaries, its use of uniforms to distinguish police officers from other citizens, and its paramilitary organization. New York's example was soon followed by other cities, including Chicago (1851), New Orleans, Cincinnati (1852), Philadelphia (1855), Newark (1857), and Baltimore (1857). By 1900, nearly every city of any size had established a full-time police force.

Most of the new police forces assigned officers to specific territories. At first the officers resisted wearing uniforms because they felt demeaned by them. There were other, more serious problems as well:

> **These first formal police forces in American cities were faced with many of the problems that police continue to confront today. Police officers became objects of disrespect. The need for larger staffs required the police to compromise personnel standards in order to fill the ranks. And police salaries were among the lowest in local government service, a factor which precluded attracting sufficient numbers of high standard candidates. It is small wonder that the police were not respected, were not notably successful, and were not noted for their visibility and progressiveness.[16]**

These problems of low pay, disrespect, and ineffectiveness existed for a number of reasons. First, the military model of organization was not well suited to police work. Unlike the soldier, the police officer is primarily a solitary worker, and military discipline is most effective for people who work together in a group. Second, police officers have the contradictory tasks of both protecting and arresting their employers: the public. Citizens expect the police to protect them, but they become irate when they are stopped, questioned, or arrested. Third, police forces were often used as a source of political patronage and control, and police work therefore became associated with corrupt politics.[17]

Efforts to improve police efficiency and discipline were impeded by problems of communication. During much of the 1800s, there were no police telephones or callboxes, and those that existed could be sabotaged by officers who did not wish to be bothered by their superiors.[18] In fact, it was not until 1929 that the first two-way radio was installed in a patrol car.

The Progressive Era

The early decades of the twentieth century saw the beginnings of a movement toward police professionalism. The progressive era was marked by renewed concern about crime resulting from the passage of the Eighteenth Amendment (Prohibition), which led to extensive illegal manufacturing and distribution of alcoholic beverages. This period was characterized by criticism of corruption and inefficiency in social institutions, and by recommendations for change that centered on better management and training. Government concern was manifested as early as 1919 with the formation of the Chicago Crime Commission; similar commissions were created to investigate crime in twenty-four states. In addition, two national crime commissions were established: the National Crime Commission in 1925 and the Wickersham Commission in 1931. These commissions focused on improved operation of the criminal justice system as the best way to reduce crime. They recommended a number of reforms in police operations.

> **The dominant concern of the crime commissions and those who conducted the crime surveys was to find ways to bring criminals to justice more swiftly and certainly. The first agency in the criminal justice system responsible for this**

task was the police. Professionalization of the police came to be defined in terms of those changes in police organization, administration, and technology that would improve the efficiency of the police in the deterrence and apprehension of criminals. Police officials measured progress toward police professionalism in terms of expansion of police services, development of scientific methods of criminal investigation and identification, police training, communications, transportation, police records, police selection, executive tenure, and police organizational growth.[19]

progressive era for policing A period of reform that began during the early twentieth century and emphasized efficiency, professionalism, and improved technology as ways to improve the quality of policing.

In short, the themes of the **progressive era for policing** were efficiency, professionalism, and improved technology.

Police Professionalism

During this period a dedicated effort was made to transform police work from an undesirable job into an attractive career. A leader in the movement to improve police professionalism was August Vollmer, Chief of Police in Berkeley, California, from 1905 to 1932. He established the first crime detection laboratory in the United States, and John Larson invented the polygraph while working for Vollmer. This period also saw the inauguration of investigative techniques such as fingerprint identification, firearms identification, toxicology, document examination, and other methods that had not been used in American policing before 1900.[20]

Police professionalism was also enhanced by improved selection and training procedures. In 1900, the only criteria used to select police officers were physical fitness and political influence. After World War I psychological and intelligence tests began to be employed; these "revealed a shockingly low level of intelligence and psychological fitness among police personnel."[21] A 1934 survey estimated that only 20,000 of the 134,000 police officers in the country participated in any kind of training program. As Vollmer pointed out, however, twenty-five years earlier training programs for police did not exist at all.[22] The problem continues today as classroom training and written testing of police recruits have come under fire. These training and assessment methods are not good predictors of successful performance on the job. As a result, there is now a move toward "authentic assessment" of police candidates, which consists of rating their ability to carry out actual job-related tasks.[23] This reflects a continuing emphasis on the progressive idea of improved professionalism and training.

Innovations in equipment also contributed to improved police work during the twentieth century. In 1930, there were fewer than 1,000 patrol cars in the entire country. By 1966, there were more than 200,000 radio-equipped cars. The advent of the patrol car, the two-way radio, and the telephone had dramatic effects on American policing.[24] These technological advances enabled police to patrol much larger geographical areas, respond to calls more quickly, and generally increase their accessibility to the public.

The human element of police professionalism has not always kept pace. Female officers, minority officers, and new tactical approaches to policing have not always won ready acceptance. A 1997 study in a Midwestern city found de facto segregation of officers by race, as well as sexual harassment and marginalization of women. Although no single factor was found to cause the lack of integration of women and blacks, organizational policies within the department and entrenched attitudes were apparent.[25] Findings such as these have led to a growing emphasis on research within police agencies. Such ongoing research promotes police departments becoming "learning organizations" that are more dynamic and better able to respond to social and technological change. This research must go beyond statistical descriptions and examine changes in the behavior of the police and society and the impact of those changes.[26] In this way, efforts to improve police professionalism will not be subverted by negative attitudes or archaic organizational policies.

Reliance on Technology

In recent decades improvements in police communications and technology have backfired to a certain extent. Following the lead of police in other countries, American police have made it easier to contact them through the introduction of the 911 emergency phone number, nontoll telephones, and remote communications equipment. The public makes use of these innovations so frequently that police efficiency has suffered. As one observer explains,

> **These efforts have been so successful that they threaten to overturn the traditional conceptions of police work and to undermine the efficiency and purpose of street patrols. Since New York City introduced its emergency number in July 1968, the average number of calls each day to the police has risen from 12,000 to 17,000, and it is still climbing. In Philadelphia, a city one-fourth the size of New York, during a 14-hour period of a Friday in June 1971, more than 8,000 emergency calls were received. During peak periods, patrolmen are often unable to handle all of their assignments. They are so busy answering calls that they have no time to patrol these territories.[27]**

The volume of 911 calls has increased dramatically in recent years. An increasing number of these calls do not involve emergencies, which reduces police effectiveness in responding to truly serious crimes.

During the 1990s, this problem has become even more serious. The number of 911 calls made each day in the United States is estimated at 268,000. By the year 2005 New York City alone will receive an estimated 12.5 million 911 calls annually.[28]

The problem lies not only in the growing volume of calls to the police. An increasing proportion of 911 calls do not involve emergencies. Also, the growing use of cellular phones has resulted in eighteen million additional 911 calls each year from locations that are difficult to trace, and undertrained and poorly paid dispatchers have contributed to several tragedies as a result of failure to respond.[29] Better training of dispatchers, new fiberoptic systems designed to handle a higher volume of calls, and the use of alternate, nonemergency numbers are some recent initiatives designed to address the dramatic increase in emergency calls. One researcher concludes that the increase in violent crime reported by the *Uniform Crime Reports* over the past two decades is due to better police record-keeping rather than to real changes in the levels of crime.[30]

The influence of the media on police has also been dramatic. The ability of media to access police records (through the Freedom of Information Act), and the use of remote video cameras, automobiles, and even helicopters to film police in action, have all contributed to changes in the way police behave. According to police researcher Peter Manning, police engage in "reflexivity," in which their choices are influenced by the anticipated responses of others. Those responses, in turn, are shaped by how police decisions are portrayed in the media.[31] For example, news footage of police beating a motorist, as in the Rodney King incident, is repeated and analyzed many times. This blurs the line between unusual and everyday police actions and can confuse or mislead the public and policymakers. According to Manning, the police are countering this extensive media coverage with media of their own. Increasingly, they are relying on surveillance videos and video cameras in patrol cars in an effort to present their own version of typical police conduct.

The growing reliance on technology, coupled with the increasing demand for police services, began to peak during the 1960s, when concern about crime was also at an all-time high.[32] This concern manifested itself in a series of government investigations. Between 1967 and 1973, there were no fewer than seven national crime commissions.[33] Among their recommendations were improvements in police professionalism, training, and technology. In 1968, the Law Enforcement Assistance Administration (LEAA) was set up within the U.S. Department of Justice to allocate money to improve the efficiency and effectiveness of the criminal justice system. Between 1968 and 1977, the LEAA spent over $6 billion on crime control programs and college education for police officers. Much of the money was spent on weaponry, riot control equipment, helicopters, SWAT equipment, and other equipment for police. This occurred despite the fact that the use of such equipment had resulted in violent outcomes and widespread criticism of the police during the civil rights and antiwar protests of the late 1960s and early 1970s.[34] A 1977 article from the *New York Times* illustrates the problem:

> **The Attorney General has publicly criticized such LEAA-financed activities as the $250,000 development of a shoe to accommodate a pistol that could be shot through the toe. And (the Attorney General) was reportedly upset when he learned that the agency, which is financing about 55,000 programs, was planning to spend $2.5 million for a brochure telling local police departments how to apply for agency funds.[35]**

The expenditure of money on questionable items, coupled with poor or nonexistent evaluations to assess the effectiveness of the programs funded, led to growing criticism of the LEAA. By the late 1970s, there was a move to abolish the LEAA and discontinue federal aid to local law enforcement. The LEAA was finally abolished in the early 1980s. Law enforcement now is almost entirely the responsibility of local governments, although the federal government plays a role in the allocation of funds. For example, federal highway and transportation funds are increasingly allocated to states on the basis of their enforcement of laws involving drunk driving, acceptable blood alcohol levels, and speed limits, as compared to standards imposed by the federal government. In this way the federal government manages to control some aspects of local law enforcement.

The Dilemma of Policing

From the ambivalence in establishing an organized police system to the reluctance to centralize it and make it more efficient, the ability of police to apprehend criminals and reduce the fear of crime has been hampered. On one hand is the need to organize law enforcement efforts in a more efficient way. On the other hand is reluctance to provide the resources and authority that are required if a system of property protection is to be effective.

When public policing was eventually established in England and, later, in the United States, those societies were unwilling to invest the resources and training necessary to create an efficient law enforcement system. As a result, law enforcement is carried out by municipalities, which are often ill-equipped to deal efficiently or effectively with crime. In the United States today, only 1 percent of the 18,000 law enforcement agencies are at the state or federal level. As the President's Crime Commission stated more than thirty years ago, "A fundamental problem confronting law enforcement today is that of fragmented crime repression efforts resulting from the large number of uncoordinated local governments and law enforcement agencies."[36] A 1996 investigation came to a similar conclusion regarding federal police, citing a "need for greater coordination of the numerous agencies involved in federal law enforcement."[37]

The need for coordination has been a problem throughout the history of policing in the United States, even though the amount of resources devoted to the task has increased dramatically in recent years. A study of eighty-eight large cities found that police expenditures per capita (adjusted for inflation) have nearly quadrupled since 1938. In addition, the proportion of city budgets allocated to police grew steadily, from 8 percent in 1940 to 14 percent in 1980. The number of police employees has increased by 170 percent since 1932.[38] There is no single explanation for this expansion in police strength, although concern about crime in general increased markedly during this period.[39] However, this growing police presence must be organized more efficiently if it is to be fully effective. An example of this problem is the enforcement of drug laws. A person who sells crack cocaine in any city could be under surveillance and arrested by the city police, state police, FBI, or Drug Enforcement Administration (DEA). Other agencies could also be involved if certain other circumstances are present, such as the possession of weapons, terrorist purposes, or affiliation with organized crime. Such overlapping jurisdictions sometimes result in several law enforcement agencies investigating the same suspects for the same crimes. Thus, additional resources alone have not improved the efficiency of policing. It will take greater recognition of the limits of political boundaries and jurisdictions to make law enforcement more effective.

Back to Community Policing

Recently there has been a trend back toward **community policing.** The central tenet of community policing is a service-oriented style of law enforcement, as opposed to the traditional focus on serious street crimes. Table 7.1 summarizes the major differences between community policing and traditional law enforcement.

community policing
A service-oriented style of law enforcement that focuses on disorder in the community, crime prevention, and fear reduction.

TABLE 7.1

Traditional vs. Community-Based Policing

	CRIMINAL JUSTICE SYSTEM	COMMUNITY-BASED PREVENTION
The crime problem	Index crime: the more serious the crime, as determined by traditional measures, the more energy criminal justice agencies should expend dealing with it	Disorder, fear, serious crime: seriousness determined by context, neighborhood priorities, and the extent to which problems destabilize neighborhoods and communities
Priorities in crime control	Apprehend and process offenders	Prevent and control crime, restore and maintain order, reduce citizen fear
Role of citizens	Aid police: since crime control is best left to criminal justice professionals, citizens "aid" professionals in controlling serious crime by calling police, being good witnesses, and testifying against wrongdoers; all else is vigilantism	Citizens are key: control of disorder, fear, and crime has its origins in the "small change" of neighborhood life; citizens set standards for the neighborhood and maintain order; police and other criminal justice agencies support and aid citizens, especially in emergencies
Police, prosecutors, courts, and corrections: structure	Centralized organization	Decentralized agencies: allow for flexible responses to local problems and needs
Methods	Process individual cases: when crimes occur	Problem-solving approach: identify and solve larger problems within which individual cases are embedded
Use of discretion	Discouraged, unrecognized: assumption that little guidance is needed for law enforcement processing; clear and precise rules and regulations developed as required; attempt to limit/eradicate discretion with mandatory arrest and prosecution policies, determinate sentences	Fundamental and important to crime-control efforts: controls developed through statements of legislative intent; carefully crafted laws that address the complexity of issues; formulation of guidelines, procedures, rules, and regulations with input from citizens and line police officers
Order vs. Liberty interests	Individual liberty interest predominate: most nonviolent deviance should be tolerated in the name of individual liberty interests	Balanced: liberty interests not absolute, but balanced against need to maintain basic levels of order for neighborhoods and communities to function
Public–private relationship	Police neutral and removed: should intrude into community life as little as possible	Police act on behalf of community: are intimately involved in local life, but also act justly, equitably, in accord with established legal principles

SOURCE: Reprinted with the permission of The Free Press, a Division of Simon & Schuster from FIXING BROKEN WINDOWS: Restoring Order and Reducing Crime in Our Communities by George L. Kelling and Catherine M. Coles. Copyright © 1996 by George L. Kelling and Catherine M. Coles.

Community-based policing differs from the traditional approach in eight distinct ways.[40] Community policing focuses more broadly on disorder in the community, crime prevention and fear reduction, and community support in organized prevention and enforcement efforts. On the other hand, traditional policing focuses exclusively on serious crime and the apprehension of offenders; citizens are involved only to the extent that they can help police carry out their law-enforcement role. Traditional policing responds to crimes after they occur, whereas community policing attempts to solve underlying problems that ultimately result in crimes. Perhaps most important is the difference in the attitudes of police officers: They are neutral and detached in the traditional model, but in the community policing model they act in conjunction with citizens.

Despite this trend, national surveys of police departments have found that they continue to embrace the crime control model of enforcement. Most states continue to view law enforcement as more important than community service.[41] A survey of police departments employing one hundred or more officers found that the announced change to a community policing philosophy did not alter the departments' organizational structure in any significant way.[42] In addition, it is not clear whether the media will help or hinder community policing in their quest for immediate news and their penchant for paying less attention to community trends than to immediate crises.[43]

The Organization of Law Enforcement

Owing to the fear of a strong central government that existed at the time of the nation's founding, the Constitution has no provision for a national police force with broad enforcement powers, as is the case in many other countries. Instead, there are many different agencies at each level of government that specialize in the enforcement of certain types of laws. Most of these are at the local level.

Local Police

The vast majority of police agencies are found at the local level of government. In fact, of the nearly 18,000 police agencies in the United States, more than 17,000 are operated by municipal and other local governments.[44] Most of these are the police departments of municipalities, but local law enforcement also includes county sheriffs and special police agencies such as park, airport, transit, and university police. Local police departments have nearly 500,000 full-time employees, about 80 percent of whom are police officers. The remaining 20 percent are civilian employees of police departments.[45]

Local police primarily enforce applicable state laws, but they also enforce local ordinances and traffic laws and investigate accidents and suspected crimes. Sheriffs provide police protection and investigate crimes in jurisdictions within their county that lack their own police forces; they also serve court papers, maintain order in courtrooms, and operate county jail facilities.[46]

The local nature of American policing is further illustrated by the fact that nearly two thirds of local police and sheriffs' departments employ fewer than ten full-time officers. Of this number, nearly 2,000 departments have only one full-time officer or only part-time officers.[47] The number of officers is related to the size of the population served. In towns with populations of 2,500 or less, the typical police department has three sworn full-time officers. As towns develop into cities, their police departments also grow: Towns with populations of 2,500 to 10,000 have police departments with an average of ten full-time sworn officers, and the numbers are higher in cities with populations of 100,000 to 250,000, which average 266 full-time sworn officers.[48]

An interesting trend is the growth of police paramilitary units at the local level. These units function as military special-operations teams that respond to hostage situations, bomb threats, and similar situations that require a show of force. They are typically equipped with submachine guns, semiautomatic shotguns, sniper rifles, flash-bang grenades, night vision equipment, and battering rams. A national survey of small cities with 25,000 to 50,000 residents found that 65 percent of departments had a SWAT team, often outfitted with the latest armor and weaponry.[49] Between 1985 and 1995, the number of paramilitary units within small city police departments increased by 157 percent. These units averaged only 106 hours of formal training per officer per year, compared to an average of 225 hours of formal training in medium-sized to large police departments.[50] The need for paramilitary units in smaller jurisdictions is infrequent, and the low level of training poses a serious hazard, given the destructive potential of high-powered weaponry.

FUTURE ISSUES

Preventing Subway Crime

Washington, D.C., opened its Metro subway system in 1976. Since then the number of crimes occurring there has been much lower than anticipated. A comparison of crime rates in the Metro with those in the subway systems of Atlanta, Boston, and Chicago found that the Metro's crime rates are significantly lower.

The Metro incorporates numerous features that reduce the opportunity for crime compared to other subway systems.[A] These crime prevention features include target hardening, access control, reducing criminal opportunities, and increasing the risk of apprehension. The Metro's seats, windows, and platform walls are constructed with materials that are highly resistant to graffiti and vandalism. The number of stairways from the street to underground is limited, and the Metro closes during early-morning hours. Stairways are located at both ends of each platform to disperse passengers, reducing opportunities for jostling and pickpocketing. The Metro deliberately omitted restrooms, lockers, excess benches, and food vendors to discourage loitering and litter.

Increasing the risk of apprehension is another key feature of the Metro. Fare cards are used rather than tokens; the cards must be inserted in a turnstile upon both entrance and exit. This greatly reduces the likelihood of fare evasion. All Metro stations have at least eight surveillance cameras, and police are asked to take immediate action against "quality of life" violations such as loud radios, eating, drinking, and smoking. The platforms have few pillars to reduce possible cover for criminals, and high ceilings to enhance visibility. Public telephones are located at the entrance and exit of each station in order to reduce the waiting time for passengers who need to be picked up. Train schedules are also matched to rider demand in order to reduce waiting time. All graffiti is removed within twenty-four hours.

The Metro train system in Washington, D.C., has the lowest crime rate of any major city subway system. This is because it is equipped with crime prevention features that control access, reduce criminal opportunities, and increase the likelihood of apprehension.

An examination of the Metro's features concluded that they effectively reduce criminal opportunities.[B] Even though studies have found that crime is lower on subways than on the street, public fear is still higher underground.[C] The success of the Metro in controlling subway crime has implications for the prevention of crime on the streets as well.

FUTURES QUESTION

If crime prevention is achieved through close attention to design features in subways, what can be changed to reduce crime and fear on city streets?

NOTES

[A]Nancy G. La Vigne, *Visibility and Vigilance: Metro's Situational Approach to Preventing Subway Crime* (Washington, D.C.: National Institute of Justice, 1997).

[B]Ibid., p. 9

[C]Dennis J. Kenney, *Crime, Fear, and the New York City Subways: The Role of Citizen Action* (New York: Praeger, 1987).

State Police

Every state except Hawaii has a state police force. These agencies were created in response to the need for law enforcement on roads that pass between municipalities. State police are, of course, different from local and federal police agencies in that they enforce state laws exclusively. Most states also have specialized law enforcement agencies similar to those at the federal level. State departments of environmental protection, alcohol control, and other specialized units are common.

In all, state police departments have approximately 80,000 full-time employees, of whom about 70 percent are sworn officers. These departments vary widely in size. The largest state police department is the California Highway Patrol, with 6,000 sworn officers; the smallest is the North Dakota Highway Patrol, with 115 full-time officers.[51]

All state police departments are responsible for traffic law enforcement and accident investigation. Nearly all are engaged primarily in highway patrol activities. Only about half have the authority to conduct investigative work. The focus on highway patrol is evidenced by the fact that in the nation as a whole there are ninety-eight police cars (marked and unmarked) for every one hundred sworn state police officers.[52]

Given the ease with which people, planes, cars, and electronic communications can traverse local boundaries, multijurisdictional crimes are becoming more common. Police agencies respect geographical boundaries, but criminals do not. The creation of **multijurisdictional task forces** allows for pooling of evidence, personnel, and expertise while reducing unnecessary duplication of effort. A recent study of eight cities found that each had a combined federal, state, and local law enforcement task force that focused on some combination of drug crimes, weapons, and violent crimes. The Metropolitan Richmond Task Force in Virginia includes detectives from the DEA; the Richmond Police Department; the Virginia State Police; the Henrico, Chesterfield, and Hanover County Police Departments; and the City of Petersburg. Two major task force investigations culminated in 1995 with the conviction of twenty members of two drug-trafficking organizations. Similarly, the Cold Homicide Task Force was formed in 1994 and involves the FBI, Virginia State Police, and Richmond Police Department. The task force identified an East Coast drug organization as responsible for twelve homicides in New York City and Virginia. Thus, although task forces deal with only a small proportion of all the crimes that occur in an area, they often pursue complicated cases requiring resources that no single agency can devote.[53]

multijurisdictional task forces Multiagency efforts designed to combat multijurisdictional crimes, allowing for pooling of evidence, personnel, and expertise while reducing unnecessary duplication of effort.

Federal Law Enforcement Agencies

There are nearly 70,000 federal law enforcement officers in the United States, and they are employed by seventeen different agencies. These officers are authorized to carry firearms and make arrests in investigating violations of federal law. Unlike state police agencies, few federal agencies engage in patrol work; most perform exclusively investigative functions.

Federal law enforcement agencies can enforce only laws enacted by Congress. Congress has the power to coin money, for example, and hence has delegated law enforcement authority to the U.S. Treasury Department. The Treasury Department is responsible for the printing of currency and therefore is also responsible for enforcing federal laws against counterfeiting and forgery. This function is performed by the Secret Service (which has the ancillary task of protecting the President). In addition, the Treasury Department is responsible for collecting federal income taxes, preventing contraband from entering the United States, and regulating the sale and distribution of alcohol, tobacco, and firearms. As a result, the Treasury Department houses the enforcement division of the Internal Revenue Service, the Customs Service, and the Bureau of Alcohol, Tobacco, and Firearms.

Four federal agencies employ 58 percent of all federal law enforcement officers. The largest agency is the Immigration and Naturalization Service (INS), with 12,400 agents and officers who protect the nation's borders against illegal immigration. Within the INS is the Border Patrol (4,200 officers), which monitors 145 border stations around the country.[54] The U.S. Customs Service has nearly 10,000 agents, and is responsible for investigating contraband that enters or leaves the United States. The Federal Bureau of Investigation (10,400 agents) is responsible for enforcing more than 250 federal laws that are not specifically designated to another federal agency. The FBI thus is a "catch-all" agency and has the widest jurisdiction of any federal law enforcement agency. Finally, the Federal Bureau of Prisons employs more than 11,000 corrections officers, who maintain security at all U.S. correctional facilities for convicted offenders and for defendants awaiting trial.

The remaining federal law enforcement agencies employ fewer than 4,000 officers each; the smallest is the U.S. Fish and Wildlife Service, which employs only 620 agents. Table 7.2 presents a summary of all federal law enforcement agencies that employ more than five hundred full-time officers with authority to carry firearms and make arrests.

Partly because the historical evolution of policing in America began at the local level, and because most federal agencies do not engage in patrol work, the organization of police in the United States is skewed heavily toward local police. For example, the New York City Police Department, with more than 28,000 officers, is nearly three times the size of the FBI. Likewise, the Chicago Police Department

TABLE 7.2

Federal Law Enforcement Agencies

AGENCY	NUMBER OF OFFICERS	PRIMARY RESPONSIBILITY
U.S. Customs Service	9,700	Investigates contraband entering or leaving country
Federal Bureau of Investigation	10,400	Enforces 250 federal laws not specifically designated to other agencies
Federal Bureau of Prisons	11,300	Corrections officers in federal jails and prisons
Immigration and Naturalization Service	12,400	Border Patrol and investigation of illegal aliens at ports of entry
Administrative Office of U.S. Courts	2,800	Federal probation and parole officers
Internal Revenue Service	3,800	Investigates tax fraud
U.S. Postal Inspection Service	3,600	Investigates crimes committed using the mails
Drug Enforcement Administration	2,900	Investigates federal narcotics crimes
U.S. Secret Service	3,200	Investigates counterfeiting and federal computer fraud; provides security for federal officials
National Park Service	2,100	Police services for the U.S. park system
U.S. Marshals Service	2,700	Provides security in federal courtrooms; finds fugitives; transports prisoners; manages witness security program and federal forfeitures
Bureau of Alcohol, Tobacco and Firearms	1,900	Investigates illegal forearm, explosive use; enforces federal alcohol, tobacco regulations
U.S. Capitol Police	1,000	Police services for U.S. Capitol
Tennessee Valley Authority	740	Police services for TVA facilities
U.S. Forest Service	619	Protects national forest land, animals, natural resources, and visitors
General Services Administration—Federal Protective Services	643	Security for federal buildings and property
U.S. Fish and Wildlife Service	869	Enforces federal laws relating to hunting and fishing

SOURCE: Adapted from Brian A. Reaves, *Federal Law Enforcement Officers* (Washington, D.C.: Bureau of Justice Statistics, 1994); Brian A. Reaves, *Federal Law Enforcement Officers* (Washington, D.C.: Bureau of Justice Statistics, 1997).

(12,000 officers), the Los Angeles Police Department (7,700), the Philadelphia Police Department (6,000), the Houston Police Department (5,000), and other large city police departments are larger than most federal law enforcement agencies.

The Movement toward Private Policing

Private security is growing at an incredible rate. There are now twice as many private security officers as there are police officers in the United States (Figure 7.1). In an interesting reversal of history, public policing, which arose because of the ineffectiveness of private security measures, is now faced with a movement back toward privatization. Private security has been assuming law enforcement tasks because of the inability of public police to adapt quickly to major social or technological changes. These changes have resulted in new manifestations of crime, spurring private entrepreneurs to offer protective services to those who can afford them. This response has played a significant role in the continuing growth of private security.[55]

A review of historical events provides several examples of this trend. The development of an interstate railroad system during the mid-1800s created opportunities for theft, robberies, and vandalism that were beyond the capacity of public police agencies to control. Because regional policing and regulatory enforcement agencies were not yet developed, local police agencies were not well equipped to deal with multijurisdictional crimes. In 1855, Allan Pinkerton was hired by six railroads to provide police protection over a five-state region. Within the next few years, Pinkerton extended his activities into areas that were normally the responsibility of municipal police by providing detective services and an evening patrol for businesses in the Chicago area.[56]

In 1844, Samuel Morse invented the telegraph, which not only revolutionized communications but also provided the means to detect burglaries electronically through the use of relays. In 1858, an entrepreneur named Edwin Holmes seized the opportunity to establish the first central-office burglar alarm. He later founded Holmes Protection, Inc., a private security agency that is still operating today. In 1874, American District Telegraph (ADT) was established to provide protective services through the use of messengers and telegraph lines.[57] Today, private security agencies continue to maintain a larger proportion of the central burglar alarm market than do police departments.

The 1850s also saw social changes resulting from an expanding population and increasing distance between population centers. Robberies, thefts, and unreliable delivery of goods led Perry Brink to form a truck and package delivery service in 1859. Brink later expanded into armored-car services, delivering his first payroll in 1891; today Brink's is the largest agency of its kind in the United States, with annual revenues of over $100 million.[58]

FIGURE 7.1

Trends in private security and law enforcement employment

SOURCE: William Cunningham, J. Strauchs, and Clifford W. VanMeter, *The Hallcrest Report II: Private Security Trends 1990–2000* (Boston: Butterworth-Heinemann, 1990).

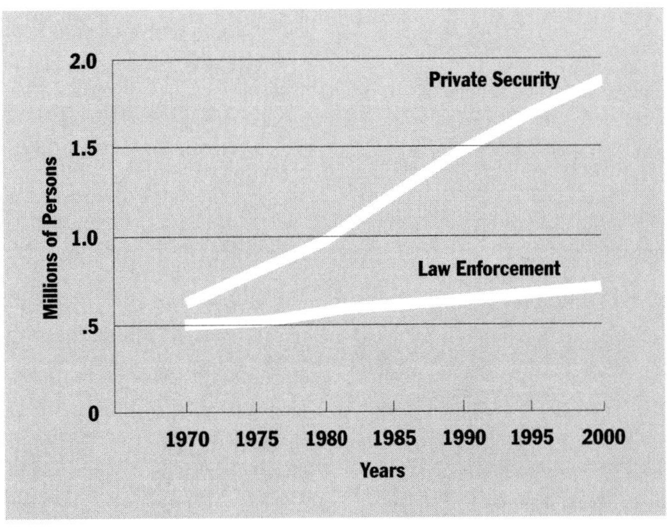

The private security industry has been assuming tasks previously entrusted to police due to its ability to more quickly adapt to technological or social changes. Examples include private security domination of the alarm business, airport screening, shopping malls, college campus security, and executive protection for corporations.

In 1909, a former U.S. Secret Service agent, William Burns, formed the International Detective Agency, which eventually grew to become "the sole investigating agency for the American Banking Association and . . . the second largest [to Pinkerton's] contract guard and investigative service in the United States."[59] It now employs more than 30,000 people.

During the 1960s, the deterioration of central cities caused many urban residents to move to the suburbs. The resulting changes in public shopping patterns accelerated the development of enclosed shopping malls in suburban locations. This, in turn, led to the utilization of private protective services on a large scale. Virtually all enclosed malls now have private security forces.

The late 1960s also witnessed widespread demonstrations and uprisings on college campuses. These protests were not handled adequately by local police. According to a RAND Corporation study, many colleges and universities have doubled or tripled their expenditures on private security since then.[60] Increasing incidents of robberies, assaults, and theft on college campuses, together with new national requirements for reporting of campus crime, have kept campus security forces at the forefront of a growing industry. Today campus law enforcement expenditures average $109 per student.[61]

During the late 1960s and early 1970s, there was a dramatic increase in the number of people using air transportation, largely owing to the increasing capacity of the airline industry and the decreasing cost of air travel. Between 1963 and 1967, there were only four attempted skyjackings in the United States. From 1968 to 1972, there were 134 aircraft hijacking attempts. In addition, a large number of bomb threats were made against aircraft in the United States and elsewhere. In response to this situation, the Federal Aviation Administration (FAA) began compulsory point-of-departure screening of airline passengers in 1972. This screening for weapons and explosives is the responsibility of the airlines and is carried out primarily by contract security firms. Similar procedures have been established in other countries and are also conducted by private security agencies.[62] After the shooting of two Capitol police officers in Washington, D.C., in 1998,

contemporary issues

Campus Law Enforcement

Campus security is a growing industry as crime on college campuses has become a national concern. This attention is the result of a number of highly publicized homicides at universities, as well as the problem of "binge" drinking and reckless deaths on college campuses. Today, three fourths of four-year colleges and universities with more than 2,500 students employ sworn police officers who have general arrest powers under state or local law. Nearly 11,000 full-time sworn officers serve these colleges and universities, plus 9,000 additional full-time campus security personnel who are not sworn officers.

The backgrounds and training requirements of campus security officers vary widely. Most sworn campus police officers are armed, including 95 percent of security personnel serving campuses with 20,000 or more students. One fourth of campuses contract for private security services, most involving private security companies. Training for new officers ranges from less than four hundred to more than nine hundred hours. Similarly, 30 percent of campus security agencies require that new officers have some college education, but only 2 percent require a four-year degree.

Campus security officers engage in a variety of tasks, from investigation of serious crime to enforcement of parking regulations. The tasks of campus security personnel are summarized in Figure 7.2.

As Figure 7.2 indicates, most campus security agencies are responsible for alarm monitoring, building lockup, investigation of serious crimes, personal safety escorts, stadium security, parking, and traffic enforcement. A smaller number handle medical center or nuclear facility security.

The vast majority (85 percent) of campus law enforcement agencies operate general crime prevention programs. These programs are designed to increase awareness of criminal opportunities and reduce the risk of victimization. Two thirds of campus police agencies have education programs for date rape prevention, and half have programs for prevention of drug and alcohol abuse. If cities and towns placed the same degree of emphasis on crime awareness and prevention programs that college campuses do, would levels of crime be as low there as they are on college campuses?

SOURCE: Brian A. Reaves, *Campus Law Enforcement* (Washington, D.C.: Bureau of Justice Statistics, 1996).

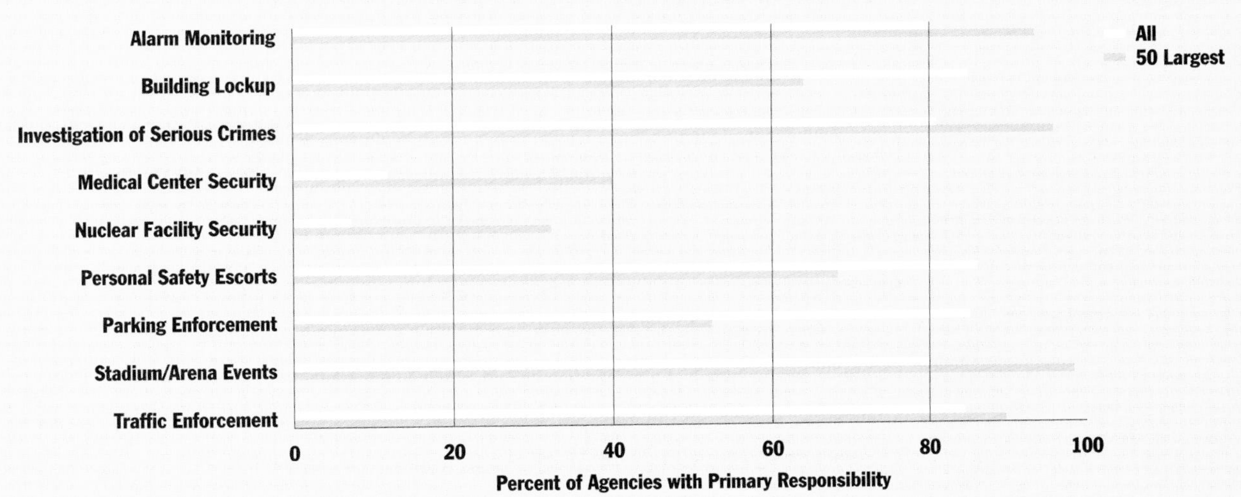

FIGURE 7.2

Tasks performed by campus law enforcement personnel

SOURCE: Brian A. Reaves, *Campus Law Enforcement* (Washington, D.C.: Bureau of Justice Statistics, 1996).

new technology is being considered to make it more difficult to evade weapons screening and to reduce potential risk to bystanders and security agents.[62a]

In recent years the expanding frontiers of international business have also increased the scale and influence of U.S. multinational corporations. A new manifestation of crime that has resulted from this growth is terrorist threats and kidnapping of corporate executives and their families. It is estimated that businesses paid more than $250 million in ransoms during the 1970s alone.[63] As a result, there are now an estimated 20,000 private security personnel involved in executive protection.

There is every reason to believe that private security will continue to grow and to assume tasks that were previously the responsibility of public law enforcement. Increasing reliance on nuclear power, greater frequency of terrorist acts, more sophisticated weapons, and the drug epidemic are creating opportunities for new forms of crime that police are ill equipped to control. The ultimate result of these trends may be continued shrinkage of the domain of public police and increased reliance on private protection services. In addition, the relatively high cost of public police may lead to consolidation and, in some cases, elimination of these agencies.[64]

The United States is not the only nation that is undergoing a trend toward privatization. Similar trends can be seen in Australia, Canada, England, and Wales.[65] It remains to be seen whether public law enforcement will embrace aspects of privatization that can benefit their communities, and whether private security agencies can perform police tasks in a consistently efficient, effective, and accountable manner.

Critical Thinking EXERCISE

An estimated 1,200 horses are used in law enforcement, primarily in large cities. Mounted patrols can cover larger areas than foot patrols, have greater visibility, promote greater citizen interaction, and horses cost less to buy and maintain than squad cars.

Dogs and Horses in Law Enforcement

The use of animals in law enforcement is a rapidly growing phenomenon. There are nearly 5,200 police dogs in the United States. Ninety percent of police departments that serve populations of 100,000 or more use dogs for police work; two thirds of all local police officers are employed in departments that use dogs.[A] Dogs are used primarily for investigative purposes—to track suspects and detect narcotics. Evidence uncovered by trained police dogs may be used in court.

An estimated 1,200 horses are used in law enforcement. Like dogs, horses are more commonly used in large jurisdictions than in small ones. Nearly 85 percent of large cities have mounted patrols, and more cities of all sizes are establishing them.[B] Historically, horses were used primarily to control crowds and patrol rough terrain. Today they are being used in routine neighborhood patrols. Mounted patrols cover more area than foot patrols, have greater visibility, provide good community relations, and cost less to purchase and maintain than squad cars.

Critical Thinking Questions

1. **Why do you believe the use of mounted patrols decreased in the first place, and why do you think it is making a resurgence now?**
2. **Mounted officers appear to have greater success in community relations than officers in squad cars or even those on bicycles. Why do you think this is so?**
3. **How do you think dogs came to be used in investigative work, and why are they still used for such work?**

Notes

[A]Brian A. Reaves, *Local Police Departments* (Washington, D.C.: Bureau of Justice Statistics, 1996), p. 17.

[B]Andrea L. Mays, "Cops on the Hoof Beat," *USA Today* (August 13, 1996), p. 14.

The Cyclical Nature of Community Policing

Before the establishment of full-time police in the 1800s, private citizens were largely responsible for protecting their own property. With advances in police professionalism and technology, the public has come to rely on the police for this service. The dramatic growth in calls for police service over the years testifies to this reliance.

Increased calls to police have diminished their effectiveness in solving crimes (less than 20 percent of serious crimes are now "closed" by an arrest). Community policing attempts to reintroduce the public as a significant player in crime control. It has been defined as "a collaboration between the police and the community that identifies and solves community problems."[A] Recognizing that many crimes stem from poor and disorganized neighborhoods, community policing is designed to incorporate members of the community as "active allies in the effort to enhance the safety and quality of neighborhoods" so that police are "no longer the sole guardians of law and order."[B] It is ironic that in 150 years the United States has evolved from a crime prevention system in which private citizens fended for themselves to one in which they are almost totally dependent on police. The trend is now being reversed.

The nature of community policing varies in different jurisdictions, but the theme is the same: assigning a neighborhood patrol officer who gets to know the local residents, building trust between police officers and citizens, devoting time to solving problems before they develop into crimes. This approach to law enforcement makes citizens partners with the police in controlling crime, rather than passive recipients of police services.

Evaluations of the effectiveness of community policing strategies have found mixed results thus far. On the positive side, citizens in many neighborhoods have reported a more positive view of police and of the crime situation in their area. On the negative side, community policing has had no clear effects on crime rates, it has proved difficult to involve neighborhood organizations in the programs, and within police departments there appears to be some resistance to community policing strategies.[C]

Critical Thinking Questions

1. Why do you believe the public's attitude toward police often improves in neighborhoods where community policing is practiced?
2. Why do you think community policing has not had a dramatic impact on crime?
3. What forces within police departments may provoke resistance to the idea of community policing?

Notes

[A]Bureau of Justice Assistance, *Understanding Community Policing* (Washington, D.C.: Office of Justice Programs, 1994), p. vii.

[B]Ibid.

[C]Gary W. Cordner, "Community Policing: Elements and Effects," *Police Forum,* vol. 5 (July 1995), pp. 1–8; Susan Sadd and Randolph M. Grinc, *Implementation Challenges in Community Policing: Innovative Neighborhood-Oriented Policing in Eight Cities* (Washington, D.C.: National Institute of Justice, 1996); Wesley G. Skogan, *Community Policing in Chicago: Year Two* (Washington, D.C.: National Institute of Justice, 1995); Stephen D. Mastrofski, Roger B. Parks, Albert J. Reiss, and Robert E. Warden, *Policing Neighborhoods: A Report from Indianapolis* (Washington, D.C.: National Institute of Justice, 1998).

Summary

COMMUNITY PROTECTION BEFORE POLICE

- Before police departments were formally established, less formal measures of self-protection were used. In the mutual pledge system, everyone in the community was responsible for everyone else. In the watch and ward system, men from each town were required to take turns standing watch at night.
- The invention of gin was a catalyst for the establishment of public policing. Although the gin craze abated, the fear of crime did not. This led to the creation of the Bow Street Runners, a private agency that patrolled the streets.
- The first police force was established in London in 1829. Police officers patrolled specific areas and were organized in a paramilitary fashion to maintain discipline.

POLICE IN THE UNITED STATES

- The first daytime police force in the United States was established in Boston in 1838; New York was the first city to create a unified day and night police force. By 1900, nearly every city of any size had established a full-time police force.
- Urban police forces were plagued by problems of low pay, disrespect, and ineffectiveness. During the progressive era there was a movement toward police efficiency, professionalism, and improved technology.
- Police effectiveness was increased through improved investigative techniques and better selection and training procedures.
- Innovations in equipment also contributed to improved police work. However, the introduction of an emergency phone number led to unanticipated problems because of an extremely high volume of calls.

THE ORGANIZATION OF LAW ENFORCEMENT

- Policing faces a dilemma: There is a need to organize law enforcement efforts in a more efficient way. However, there is also reluctance to provide the necessary resources and authority.
- The vast majority of police agencies are found at the local level of government. Local police enforce applicable state laws, local ordinances, and traffic laws; they also investigate accidents and suspected crimes.
- State police agencies enforce state laws and investigate accidents. They include specialized law enforcement agencies for such purposes as alcohol control.
- There are seventeen different federal law agencies that enforce laws enacted by Congress. The largest federal agencies are the U.S. Customs Service, the Federal Bureau of Investigation, the Federal Bureau of Prisons, and the Immigration and Naturalization Service.

Key Terms

mutual pledge system
constable
shire reeve
watch and ward system
justice of the peace
progressive era for policing
community policing
multijurisdictional task forces

Questions for Review and Discussion

1. What systems for community protection evolved before the establishment of formal police departments?
2. Why did the invention of gin act as a catalyst for the establishment of public policing?
3. What were some of the problems faced by early police forces?
4. How was police professionalism enhanced in the early decades of the twentieth century?
5. Why is growing reliance on technology a problem for police operations today?
6. Why is law enforcement carried out largely by municipalities in the United States?
7. What are the primary activities of local and state police forces?
8. What are the major federal law enforcement agencies, and what are their responsibilities?

Notes

[1]George L. Kelling and Catherine M. Coles, *Fixing Broken Windows: Restoring Order and Reducing Crime in Our Communities* (New York: Touchstone, 1997).

[2]President's Commission on Law Enforcement and Administration of Justice, *Task Force Report: The Police* (Washington, D.C.: U.S. Government Printing Office, 1967), p. 3.

[3]Harold T. Amidon, "Law Enforcement: From 'The Beginning' to the English Bobby," *Journal of Police Science and Administration*, vol. 5 (September 1977), pp. 355–67.

[4]President's Commission, p. 4.

[5]Jonathan Rubinstein, *City Police* (New York: Ballantine, 1974), pp. 4–5.

[6]Rubinstein, p. 6.

[7]M. Dorothy George, *London Life in the Eighteenth Century* (New York: Capricorn Books, 1925).

[8]Rubinstein, pp. 8–9.

[9]Amidon, p. 366.

[10]Rubinstein, p. 10.

[11]Ibid.

[12]Rubinstein, p. 11.

[13]Center for Research on Criminal Justice, *The Iron Fist and the Velvet Glove*, revised ed. (Berkeley, CA: Center for Research on Criminal Justice, 1977), p. 22.

[14]George Smith, *The United States Constitution* (Nashville, TN: Knowledge Products, 1987).

[15]Roger Lane, *Policing the City: Boston, 1822–1885* (Cambridge, MA: Harvard University Press, 1971); Center for Research on Criminal Justice, *The Iron Fist and the Velvet Glove*, revised ed. (Berkeley: Center for Research on Criminal Justice, 1977).

[16]President's Commission, p. 5.

[17]Carl B. Klockars, *The Idea of Police* (Beverly Hills, CA: Sage Publications, 1985).

[18]Rubinstein, pp. 15–20.

[19]Nathan Douthit, "Enforcement and Nonenforcement Roles in Policing: A Historical Inquiry," *Journal of Police Science and Administration*, vol. 3 (September 1975), p. 339.

[20]Harry Soderman, "Science and Criminal Investigation," *The Annals*, vol. 146 (1929), pp. 237–48.

[21]Douthit, p. 341.

[22]August Vollmer, "Police Progress in the Last Twenty-five Years," *Journal of Criminal Law, Criminology, and Police Science,* vol. 24 (1933), pp. 161–75.

[23]Clifford E. Thermer, "Authentic Assessment for Performance-Based Police Training," *Police Forum,* vol. 7 (July 1997), pp. 1–5.

[24]See Samuel Walker, *A Critical History of Police Reform* (Lexington, MA: Lexington Books, 1977).

[25]Robin N. Haarr, "Patterns of Interaction in a Police Patrol Bureau: Race and Gender Barriers to Integration," *Justice Quarterly,* vol. 14 (March 1997), pp. 53–85.

[26]William A. Geller, "Suppose We Were Really Serious about Police Departments Becoming 'Learning Organizations'?," *National Institute of Justice Journal,* no. 234 (December 1997), pp. 2–8.

[27]Rubinstein, p. 22.

[28]Gordon Witkin with Monika Guttman, "This is 911 . . . Please Hold," *U.S. News & World Report* (June 17, 1996), pp. 31–8.

[29]Ibid.

[30]Robert M. O'Brien, "Police Productivity and Crime Rates: 1973–1992," *Criminology,* vol. 34 (May 1996), pp. 183–207.

[31]Peter K. Manning, "Policing and Reflection," *Police Forum,* vol. 6 (October 1996), pp. 1–5.

[32]James O. Finckenauer, "Crime as a National Political Issue: 1964–76, From Law and Order to Domestic Tranquility," *Crime & Delinquency,* vol. 24 (January 1978), pp. 1–23.

[33]These commissions are listed in Chapter 1 in the discussion of government concern about crime.

[34]See National Advisory Commission on Civil Disorders (1968) and President's Commission on Campus Unrest (1970).

[35]Wendell Rawls, "Justice Department May Seek Special Revenue Sharing to Replace Anti-Crime Grants," *New York Times* (June 30, 1977), p. 30.

[36]President's Commission, p. 68.

[37]U.S. Comptroller General, *Federal Law Enforcement* (Washington, D.C.: U.S. General Accounting Office, 1996), p. 8.

[38]Craig Uchida and Robert Goldberg, *Police Employment and Expenditure Trends* (Washington, D.C.: Bureau of Justice Statistics, 1986); *The Municipal Year Book 1997* (Washington, D.C.: International City/County Management Association, 1997).

[39]Mahesh K. Nalla, Michael J. Lynch, and Michael J. Leiber, "Determinants of Police Growth in Phoenix, 1950–1988," *Justice Quarterly,* vol. 14 (March 1997), pp. 115–43.

[40]Kelling and Coles, pp. 240–1.

[41]Jihong Zhao and Quint C. Thurman, "Community Policing: Where are We Now?," *Crime and Delinquency,* vol. 43 (July 1997), pp. 345–57; Velmer Burton, James Frank, Robert Langworthy, and Troy Barker, "The Prescribed Roles of Police in a Free Society: Analyzing State Legal Codes," *Justice Quarterly,* vol. 10 (1994), pp. 683–95.

[42]Edward R. Maguire, "Structural Change in Large Municipal Police Organizations During the Community Policing Era," *Justice Quarterly,* vol. 14 (September 1997), pp. 547–76.

[43]Joanne Ziembo-Bogl, "Exploring the Function of the Media in Community Policing," *Police Forum,* vol. 8 (January 1998), pp. 1–12.

[44]Brian A. Reaves, *Census of State and Local Law Enforcement Agencies* (Washington, D.C.: Bureau of Justice Statistics, 1993).

[45]Brian A. Reaves, *Local Police Departments* (Washington, D.C.: Bureau of Justice Statistics, 1996).

[46]Brian A. Reaves, *State and Local Police Departments* (Washington, D.C.: Bureau of Justice Statistics, 1992); Brian A. Reaves, *Sheriffs' Departments* (Washington, D.C.: Bureau of Justice Statistics, 1992).

[47]Reaves, *Census of State and Local Law Enforcement Agencies,* p. 9.

[48]Reaves, *Local Police Departments,* p. 2.

[49]Peter B. Kraska and Louis J. Cubellis, "Militarizing Mayberry and Beyond: Making Sense of American Paramilitary Policing," *Justice Quarterly*, vol. 14 (December 1997), pp. 607–29.

[50]Peter B. Kraska and Victor E. Kappeler, "Militarizing American Police: The Rise and Normalization of Paramilitary Units," *Social Problems*, vol. 44 (1997), pp. 1–18.

[51]Reaves, *State and Local Police Departments*, p. 10.

[52]Ibid., p. 12.

[53]Pamela K. Lattimore et al., *Homicide in Eight U.S. Cities: Trends, Context, and Policy Implications* (Washington, D.C.: National Institute of Justice, 1997), pp. 125–9.

[54]U.S. Comptroller General, *Border Patrol: Staffing and Enforcement Activities* (Washington, D.C.: U.S. General Accounting Office, 1996).

[55]Jay S. Albanese, "The Future of Policing: A Private Concern?," *Police Studies: The International Review of Police Development*, vol. 8 (1986), pp. 86–91.

[56]Samuel Walker, *A Critical History of Police Reform* (Lexington, MA: Lexington Books, 1977), p. 30.

[57]National Advisory Committee on Criminal Justice Standards and Goals, *Report of the Task Force on Private Security* (Cincinnati: Anderson Publishing, 1977).

[58]James S. Kakalik and Sorrel Wildhorn, *The Private Police: Security and Danger* (New York: Crane Russak, 1977), p. 75.

[59]William Cunningham, John J. Strauchs, and Clifford W. Van Meter, *The Hallcrest Report II: Private Security Trends 1970–2000* (Boston: Butterworth-Heinemann, 1990), p. 295.

[60]Kakalik and Wildhorn, 1977.

[61]Brian A. Reaves, *Campus Law Enforcement Agencies* (Washington, D.C.: Bureau of Justice Statistics, 1996), p. 2.

[62]Hilary Draper, *Private Police* (Atlantic Highlands, NJ: Humanities Press, 1978), pp. 85–9.

[62a]Peter Cary, "Shootout at the Capitol," *U.S. News & World Report* (August 3, 1998), p. 19.

[63]William C. Cunningham and Todd H. Taylor, *Crime and Protection in America: A Study of Private Security and Law Enforcement Resources and Relationships* (Washington, D.C.: U.S. Government Printing Office, 1985), p. 7.

[64]John T. Krimmel, "The Northern York County Police Consolidation Experience: An Analysis of Consolidation of Police Services in Eight Pennsylvania Rural Communities," *Policing: An International Journal of Police Strategies and Management*, vol. 20 (1997), pp. 497–507.

[65]T. Lyons, G. O. Burton, and R. C. Sonnichsen, "Law Enforcement Views on Future Policing Issues," in D. J. Loree, ed., *Future Issues in Policing: Symposium Proceedings* (Ottawa: Canadian Police College, 1989), pp. 17–33; B. MacRae, "Robbery, Responses and the Future," in D. Challinger, ed., *Armed Robbery: Proceedings of a Seminar* (Australian Institute of Criminology) (Washington, D.C.: National Institute of Justice, 1989); N. South, "Reconstructing Policing: Differentiation and Contradiction in Post-War Private and Public Policing," in R. Matthews, ed., *Privatizing Criminal Justice* (London: Sage Publications, 1989), pp. 76–104; A. A. Vass and K. Menzies, "Community Service Order as a Public and Private Enterprise," *British Journal of Criminology*, vol. 29 (1989), pp. 255–72.

For Further Reading

George L. Kelling and Catherine M. Coles, *Fixing Broken Windows: Restoring Order and Reducing Crime in Our Communities* (New York: Touchstone, 1997).

Jonathan Rubinstein, *City Police* (New York: Ballantine, 1973).

Ralph A. Weisheit, David N. Falcone, L. Edward Wells, *Crime and Policing in Rural and Small-Town America* (Prospect Heights, IL: Waveland Press, 1998).

chapter eight

Police Discretion and Behavior

Law has never made men a whit more just.

HENRY DAVID THOREAU
(1817–1862)

In 1998, forty-four police officers from northern Ohio were arrested on cocaine distribution charges, the largest number of officers ever arrested in a single day in U.S. history. In addition, more than five hundred convictions have resulted from federal investigations of police corruption since 1994.[1] Scandals in all parts of the country have emerged as police power is misused in a variety of ways:

- A police employee is caught filing $600,000 in fraudulent income tax returns in the names of individuals arrested by the department.
- A police officer is caught selling confidential information from police files to private detectives.
- Several police officers are found to beat crime suspects in custody without cause.
- A sixty-nine–count indictment alleges that a small city police department is so corrupt that it has become a racketeering gang.

CHAPTER OUTLINE

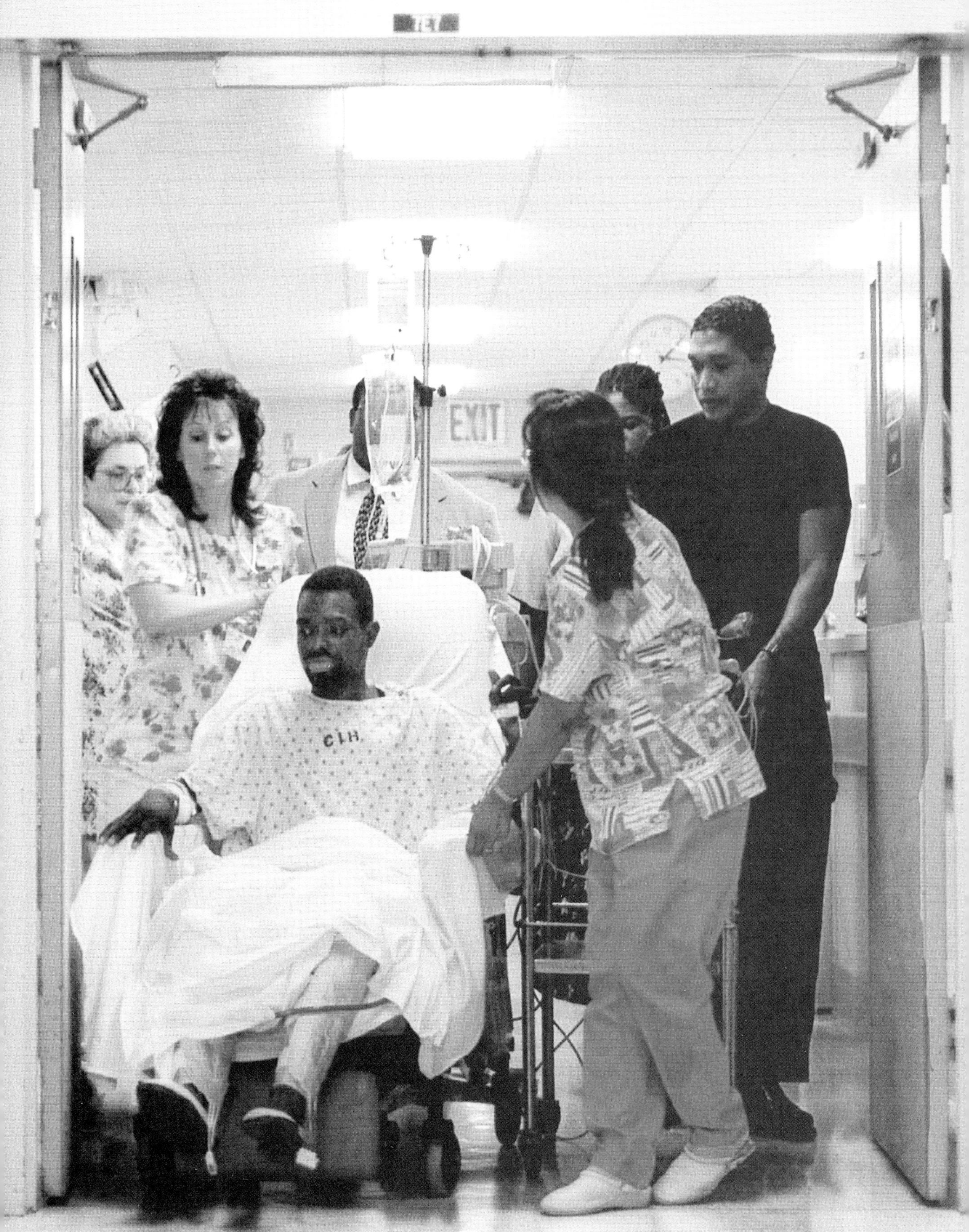
TRAUMA/SURGICAL INTENSIVE CARE
EXIT
CIH

Reports of police corruption occur with regularity even though police professionalism has improved dramatically over the years. Police are trained more extensively now than at any time in American history. Two questions lie at the foundation of this dilemma: Why do police abuse their discretion, and does police work attract or promote certain kinds of personality characteristics that promote abusive actions?

For many people, the police are the closest contact they ever have with the criminal justice system. It is not surprising, therefore, that when the system is examined or criticized, police take on a central role. As a result, improvement of the criminal justice system is often considered synonymous with improvement of police.

The primary task of police is law enforcement. That job description is not as clear as it may seen, however. If you were the mayor of your town, how would you want the police to enforce the law? Would you have them give a ticket to anyone who does not make a full stop at a stop sign? What about people who drive at 35 mph in a 30 mph zone? Would you arrest teenagers hanging out in a mall for loitering? What soon becomes evident is that the laws in the criminal code are quite specific, but it is far less clear how the police should act in particular situations. Although we can agree that use of excessive force and police corruption are wrong, determining the proper role of police on the continuum between nonintervention and lawlessness can be difficult.

The Outer Limits of Law Enforcement

Nearly forty years ago Joseph Goldstein recognized that a police officer's decision to place a suspect under arrest "largely determines the outer limits of law enforcement."[2] There has been renewed interest in this claim recently as police have been shown to possess greater latitude in deciding whether to arrest than was once believed. Although police officers are sworn to enforce the law, they choose to take official action only part of the time. This is the essence of police discretion: the ability to choose between arrest and nonarrest solely on the basis of the officer's judgment. In many cases an officer warns, reprimands, or releases a person rather than making an arrest. Traffic violations, gambling offenses, prostitution, violations of liquor laws, and minor assaults are examples of crimes for which police often exercise discretion.

This situation upsets some people, who feel that the police are not performing their job as they should. Others believe that full enforcement of the laws is not desired by the public (who would feel harassed), the courts (which are already overloaded), the police (who would be bogged down by court appearances), or the legislature (which may not have intended certain laws to be enforced fully). In any event, police do not have the resources that would be necessary to process each case, even if an arrest was made every time one was possible. As a result, police engage in an unwritten policy of **selective enforcement,** meaning that not all laws are fully enforced.

selective enforcement
An unwritten policy in which police are not required to fully enforce all laws as written.

As Goldstein pointed out, "the mandate of full enforcement, under circumstances which compel selective enforcement, has placed the municipal police in an intolerable position" in which some laws are enforced and some are not, depending on the police officer involved, the situation, the offense, and other, possibly arbitrary, factors.[3] Whenever discretion is exercised in such important matters (such as the denial of a person's liberty through arrest) without clear or consistent objectives, unfairness and discrimination become possible. The proper exercise of discretion, therefore, is perhaps the most important issue in police and community relations.[4]

Since the issue of discretion came to prominence, researchers have focused largely on the range and appropriateness of factors that influence a police officer's decision to arrest. For example, Nathan Goldman examined 1,083 contacts between police and juveniles in four Pennsylvania cities and found that 64 percent of the encounters resulted in no legal action being taken. He discovered that police arrest rates varied from 12 per 1,000 juveniles to nearly 50, depending on the city.[5] Irving Piliavin and Scott Briar found that the demeanor of juveniles was the most important factor in a police officer's decision to take them into custody.[6] Robert Terry examined the race, sex, and social class of juveniles in police encounters. He found that social class and race were not significant factors in the decision, but that women were likely to be handled slightly more severely than men, even when the seriousness of the offense and the juvenile's prior record were taken into account.[7] In Washington, D.C., Donald Black and Albert Reiss found that neither race nor demeanor made a difference in police decision-making. Rather, the complainant's preference (i.e., whether they are insistent or indifferent to arrest of the suspect) was found to be the most important factor.[8] This study was replicated in a large, unnamed Midwestern city with the same results.[9] More recent studies continue to find conflicting results regarding the influence of a suspect's demeanor in arrest situations.[10]

A number of studies have asked police officers to respond to hypothetical scenarios of drunk-driving situations, disorderly conduct, and other offenses to determine whether the factors leading to the arrest/nonarrest decision could be identified. These studies have assessed the age, education, experience, type of offense, race, and sex of the officer as well as similar attributes of the offender.[11] The results have been mixed, yielding disjointed and sometimes contradictory results, which make it difficult to draw conclusions regarding the importance of various factors in the exercise of police discretion.

Although these studies help us understand the nature and scope of police discretion, they do not explain how discretion is used in some situations and not in others. There are several reasons for this:

- Most of these studies examine only a few factors that may influence police decision-making and do not attempt to explain it comprehensively.
- Most do not cover a wide enough range of offenses to account adequately for discretion in serious versus nonserious cases.
- Studies reporting on factors influencing police decisions in one city may not hold true for police decisions in other cities.
- Many studies rely on responses to hypothetical scenarios rather than actual observations of police work.
- Even factors that are found to be important in police discretion cannot be used to make accurate predictions more than 25 percent of the time.

The search for possible factors that could affect police decisions could go on forever. After race, sex, demeanor, seriousness of offense, education, and experience have been examined, many other factors remain to be considered. Why not compare a police officer's marital status, upbringing, birth order, or IQ with similar attributes of suspects? Nearly forty years of empirical research along these lines produced little information that would be useful for policy development, other than the fact that some kind of policy was needed.

The Call for Reform

Thirty years ago the President's Crime Commission Task Force on Police noted that the arrest decision "continues to be informal, and, as a consequence, may very well serve to complicate rather than solve important social problems."[12] The Commission went on to recommend that police departments "should develop and enunciate policies that give police personnel specific guidance for the common situations requiring police discretion."[13]

In 1973, the National Advisory Commission on Criminal Justice Standards and Goals also called for specific guidelines, recommending "comprehensive policy statements that publicly establish the limits of discretion, that provide guidelines for its exercise within those limits, and that eliminate discriminatory enforcement of the law."[14] In 1974, the American Bar Association and the International Association of Chiefs of Police (ABA-IACP) jointly published standards for policing in urban areas. Their report stated that

> **Police discretion can best be structured and controlled through the process of administrative rule-making by police agencies. Police administrators should, therefore, give the highest priority to the formulation of administrative rules governing the exercise of discretion, particularly in the areas of selective enforcement, investigative techniques, and enforcement methods.[15]**

As these excerpts illustrate, the mandate for police decision-making policy has been clearly stated. However, it is not clear *how* this policy will be developed or what its contents will be, given the conflicting research findings. Nevertheless, the advantages of systematically drafting policy in this manner have been recognized by the President's Crime Commission:

> **This would remove from individual policemen some of the burden of having to make important decisions ad hoc, in a matter of seconds. It would create a body of standards that would help make the supervision and evaluation of the work of the individual policeman consistent. It would help courts understand the issues at stake when police procedures are challenged and lessen the likelihood of inappropriate judicial restriction being placed on police work.[16]**

For all of these reasons, such a policy would do much to improve the validity and consistency of discretionary acts by police. Until we can explain how police exercise their discretion in making arrests, however, attempts to formulate decision-making policy can be little more than hit-or-miss propositions.

A comprehensive effort to develop a model for the use of police discretion was conducted by Richard Sykes, James Fox, and John Clark, who noticed that previous work has examined police discretion from one of two perspectives: as

Studies of police discretion have found that the more serious the crime and the more impolite the suspect, the greater the likelihood that an arrest will occur. Department arrest policy was not shown to have a decisive impact on arrest decisions.

a product of either formal criteria (serious law violation or department policy) or informal criteria (factors such as demeanor or education). They hypothesized that police consider these factors in a particular order: (1) legal (perceived seriousness), (2) policy (departmental priorities), (3) demeanor (disrespect shown by the suspect), and (4) safety (danger to the officer).[17] According to this model, the more serious the crime, the higher the departmental priority, the more disrespect shown by the suspect, and the greater the danger to the officer, the greater the likelihood that an arrest will occur. For example, a nonserious crime such as disorderly conduct would not be expected to result in an arrest unless it was identified by the department as an enforcement priority or the suspect was disrespectful or reacted violently to the officer. On the other hand, if the crime is sufficiently serious, an arrest may take place regardless of whether the other factors are present.

To test this explanation, the researchers arranged for five observers to ride with police for over a year in three different Midwestern locations. One site was a city with a population of about 500,000, and two were residential suburbs with populations of about 25,000 each. All together, the observers recorded a total of 3,323 encounters between police and citizens. Only about 16 percent of these encounters involved offenses other than routine traffic violations. This finding confirms the conclusion of other studies that the overwhelming majority of police work does not involve crime-related matters.[18]

Of the 520 remaining encounters, 28 percent did not involve law violations (such as calls about suspicious persons), and therefore police had no discretion to arrest in these cases. Arrests actually occurred in only 27 percent of the 374 cases for which an arrest was possible. Therefore, police had to be considering factors other than law violation in the 73 percent of cases in which they could have made an arrest but did not.

Police department policy also did not appear to have a significant impact on whether police made an arrest. First, the police departments observed did not have many explicit policies, except that offense reports were required in cases of suspected crimes against property or persons. Second, of the fifty-five suspected crimes in these categories, 65 percent did not result in an arrest (except in the case of felonies).

The researchers also examined nonlegal factors. They assessed the effect of demeanor in 282 cases of suspected misdemeanors and found a strong relationship between demeanor and likelihood of arrest. Citizens who were polite were arrested about 10 percent of the time, while those who were impolite to a degree "much greater than average" were arrested 41 percent of the time. Similarly, citizens who showed no anger were arrested about 9 percent of the time, whereas 23 percent of those who displayed anger were arrested. The researchers also assessed the effects of threats to the officer's safety. They found, however, that "the incidence of violence or threatened violence was so low as to make conclusions difficult."[19]

Formulating an Arrest Policy

Criticisms of police arrest decisions are common. Research has shown that a variety of factors affect these decisions. The research just described suggests that arrests are guided by the seriousness of the offense, department policy, and the suspect's demeanor. Recently, David Klinger argued that police discretion is tied to local crime rates. As crime increases, deviant acts must be more serious if they are to result in formal action by police.[20]

Most studies have found that explicit department policy to guide the use of discretion is rare. For example, a department that believes it is appropriate to consider the complainant's preference, or that wishes to keep loiterers off the street, should state these priorities in specific terms rather than leaving the arrest decision up to the individual officer's unguided judgment. Police discretion can be controlled through greater specificity in department policies and priorities and also by departments being more explicit about what factors should *not* be considered in arrest decisions (e.g., demeanor).

The idea of developing decision-making policy on the basis of a specification of current practice is not new. Corresponding efforts have been made in parole decision-making and in sentencing policy.[21] Although police decision-making often requires spontaneous judgments, a properly developed policy based on an understanding of current practice, together with input regarding factors that police *ought* to consider, should help promote consistent and defensible police decisions.

Styles of Policing

Management of police discretion is a major concern of police supervisors. It is difficult to balance the competing goals of protecting the community and not interfering unduly in the lives of citizens. Three "styles" of policing have been identified that characterize different approaches to the management of police discretion: the watchman style, the legalistic style, and the service style.[22]

The watchman style of policing emphasizes the maintenance of order. Order is threatened by both serious and nonserious but disruptive crimes. Therefore, police may use both formal (arrest) and informal (warnings or threats) methods to maintain order. The watchman style is characteristic in lower-class neighborhoods, where police intervention is seen as necessary to control behavior. The Christopher Commission, which investigated the Los Angeles Police Department after the beating of Rodney King, observed that the police in Los Angeles emphasized crime control over crime prevention, thereby distancing themselves from the community they served.[23]

Three styles of policing have been identified: the watchman style emphasizes the maintenance of order, the legalistic style focuses strictly on violations of the law, while the service style attempts to solve problems that might lead to crime, such as loitering, intoxication, and domestic arguments.

The legalistic style of policing focuses more strictly on law violations, rather than on the maintenance of order. This more limited approach to policing is largely reactive. The police respond to calls for service, act only if there is probable cause of serious law violation, and generally avoid intervention in problems that do not constitute violations.

The service style of policing approaches law enforcement from a broad problem-solving perspective. Police seek to correct problems that are symptomatic of crime, such as loitering, public intoxication, and domestic arguments. These social problems are addressed both through direct intervention and through referrals to other social agencies.[24] This style of policing is found most often in middle- and upper-class neighborhoods, and it avoids legal processing of minor offenders to the extent possible.

The style of policing employed by a department depends largely on the chief's preferences and, in larger cities, on those of the precinct commander, as well as on the responsiveness of the neighborhood. To reflect their different emphases, these three styles have been termed the *neighbor* (watchman), *soldier* (legalistic), and *teacher* (service) *styles.*[25] The nature of the public's reaction to local police often corresponds to the style of policing employed.[26] Public hostility is more common in watchman-style police departments because of their emphasis on order rather than service. Nevertheless, the personalities of the officers involved also play a significant role in the use of discretion, regardless of the style of policing characteristic of the department.

The Police Personality

Police officers have often been accused of being cynical or having a "bad attitude" toward the public they serve. These attitudes are thought to influence police arrest decisions and contribute to poor community relations, corruption, and brutality. To what extent do police officers acquire personality characteristics that are unique to their job? Are there many types of police personalities? Are police significantly different from the general public? Most importantly, do certain personality characteristics affect a police officer's discretion and performance on the job?

Studies of Police Cynicism

The term *police personality* simply refers to a value orientation that is specific to police officers or to certain types of police officers. Police officers have often been charged with being cynical, that is, believing that human conduct is motivated entirely by self-interest. A cynical person attributes all actions to selfish motives and has a pessimistic outlook on human behavior.

cynicism
A belief that human conduct is motivated entirely by self-interest. A cynical person attributes all actions to selfish motives and has a pessimistic outlook on human behavior.

The pioneering study of police **cynicism** was conducted by Arthur Niederhoffer. Niederhoffer was a New York City police officer for twenty years before he earned a Ph.D. in sociology and began a teaching career. He was the first researcher to attempt to quantify police cynicism and explain its origins and variation among police officers.

Niederhoffer claimed that it is possible to distinguish between two types of police cynicism: that directed against people in general and that aimed at the police system itself. He believed that general cynicism is endemic to police officers of all ranks and dispositions and that cynicism toward the police system is common among patrol officers but not among "professional" police officers. In his view, professional police officers do not become cynical toward the police system because they hope to transform the system and eventually control it.

anomie
A "normlessness" or lack of attachment felt by some people toward their society.

The origins of cynicism, according to Niederhoffer, were a by-product of **anomie** in the social structure. This term was coined by sociologist Emile Durkheim in the late 1800s to describe a "normlessness" or lack of attachment felt by some people toward their society. As Niederhoffer explained, "As the cynic becomes increasingly pessimistic and misanthropic, he finds it easier to reduce his commitment to the social system and its values. If the patrolman remains a 'loner,' his isolation may lead to psychological anomie and even to suicide."[27] Niederhoffer supported his view by pointing out that suicide rates are 50 percent higher among police officers than in the general population. He also believed, however, that police cynicism could either cause anomie or be caused by it.

According to Niederhoffer, all police officers enter a law enforcement career with an attitude of professionalism and commitment, but soon experience failure or frustration, or both, on the job. This leads to disenchantment, resulting in cynicism for some but renewed commitment for others. Niederhoffer believed the degree of cynicism experienced by an officer is determined by age and length of experience on the job.

Niederhoffer developed a questionnaire to assess levels of cynicism and administered it to 220 male officers in the New York City Police Department at various stages of their careers. The questionnaire contained twenty statements, each with three response choices. It is shown in Table 8.1.

Choice "a" was the altruistic or noncynical response, choice "b" was a neutral response, and choice "c" indicated a cynical response. The altruistic response received a score of 1, the neutral response a score of 3, and the cynical response a score of 5. Therefore, the lowest possible score one could receive was 20, while the highest (i.e., most cynical) was 100. As Table 8.2 indicates, the most cynical group consisted of patrol officers with two to twelve years of experience (a score of 66.5). The least cynical group consisted of officers on their first day on the job.

Niederhoffer found that the most cynical officers reached that point after seven to ten years of service. As Table 8.2 illustrates, cynicism is not strictly a function of experience on the job. Newly appointed officers were less cynical than officers with even a small amount of experience. Superiors were less cynical than patrolmen, college-educated patrolmen were more cynical than other patrolmen, and officers became less cynical as they approached retirement.

TABLE 8.1

Niederhoffer's Police Cynicism Questionnaire

For each of the following items, please place the letter of the statement which, in your opinion, is most nearly correct on the line at the left.

_____ 1. The average police superior is . . .
a. Very interested in the welfare of his subordinates.
b. Somewhat concerned about the welfare of his subordinates.
c. Mostly concerned with his own problems.

_____ 2. The average departmental complaint is a result of . . .
a. The superior's dedication to proper standards of efficiency.
b. Some personal friction between superior and subordinate.
c. The pressure on superior from higher authority to give out complaints.

_____ 3. The average arrest is made because . . .
a. The patrolman is dedicated to perform his duty properly.
b. A complainant insisted on it.
c. The officer could not avoid it without getting into trouble.

_____ 4. The best arrests are made . . .
a. As a result of hard work and intelligent dedication to duty.
b. As a result of good information from an informer.
c. Coming from the "coop."

_____ 5. A college degree as a requirement for appointment to the police department . . .
a. Would result in a much more efficient police department.
b. Would cause friction and possibly do more harm than good.
c. Would let into the department men who are probably ill-suited for police work.

_____ 6. When you get to know the department from the inside, you begin to feel that . . .
a. It is a very efficient, smoothly operating organization.
b. It is hardly any different from other civil service organizations.
c. It is a wonder that it does one half as well as it does.

_____ 7. Police Academy training of recruits . . .
a. Does a very fine job of preparing the recruit for life in the precinct.
b. Cannot overcome the contradictions between theory and practice.
c. Might well be cut in half. The recruit has to learn all over when he is assigned to a precinct.

_____ 8. Professionalization of police work . . .
a. Is already here for many groups of policemen.
b. May come in the future.
c. Is a dream. It will not come in the foreseeable future.

_____ 9. When a patrolman appears at the police department Trial Room . . .
a. He knows that he is getting a fair and impartial trial with legal safeguards.
b. The outcome depends as much on the personal impression he leaves with the trial commissioner as it does on the merits of the case.
c. He will probably be found guilty even when he has a good defense.

_____ 10. The average policeman is . . .
a. Dedicated to high ideals of police service and would not hesitate to perform police duty even though he may have to work overtime.
b. Trying to perform eight hours of duty without getting into trouble.
c. Just as interested in promoting private contacts as he is in performing police work.

_____ 11. The Rules and Regulations of police work . . .
a. Are fair and sensible in regulating conduct on and off duty.
b. Create a problem that it is very difficult to perform an active tour of duty without violating some rules and regulations.
c. Are so restrictive and contradictory that the average policeman just uses common sense on the job, and does not worry about rules and regulations.

_____ 12. The youth problem is best handled by police who are . . .
a. Trained in a social service approach.
b. The average patrolman on post.
c. By mobile, strong-arm Youth Squads who are ready to take strong action.

_____ 13. The majority of special assignments in the police department . . .
a. Are a result of careful consideration of the man's background and qualifications, and depend on merit.
b. Are being handled as capably as you could expect in a large civil service organization.
c. Depend on whom you know, not on merit.

_____ 14. The average detective . . .
a. Has special qualifications and is superior to a patrolman in intelligence and dedication to duty.
b. Is just about the same as the average patrolman.
c. Is a little chesty and thinks he is a little better than a patrolman.

_____ 15. Police department summonses are issued by policemen . . .
a. As part of a sensible pattern of enforcement.
b. On the basis of their own ideas of right and wrong driving.
c. Because a patrolman knows he must meet his quota even if this is not official.

_____ 16. The public . . .
a. Shows a lot of respect for policemen.
b. Considers policemen average civil service workers.
c. Considers policemen very low as far as prestige goes.

_____ 17. The public . . .
a. Is eager to cooperate with policemen to help them perform their duty.
b. Usually has to be forced to cooperate with policemen.
c. Is more apt to obstruct police work, if it can, than cooperate.

_____ 18. Policemen . . .
a. Understand human behavior as well as psychologists and sociologists because they get so much experience in real life.
b. Have no more talent in understanding human behavior than any average person.
c. Have a peculiar view of human nature because of the misery and cruelty of life which they see every day.

_____ 19. The newspapers in general . . .
a. Try to help police departments by giving prominent coverage to items favorable to police.
b. Just report the news impartially whether or not it concerns the police.
c. Seem to enjoy giving an unfavorable slant to news concerning the police and prominently play up to police misdeeds rather than virtues.

_____ 20. Testifying in court . . .
a. Policemen receive real cooperation and are treated fairly by court personnel.
b. Police witnesses are treated no differently from civilian witnesses.
c. Too often the policemen are treated as criminals when they take the witness stand.

SOURCE: From BEHIND THE SHIELD: POLICE IN URBAN SOCIETY by Arthur Niederhofer. Copyright © 1967 by Arthur Niederhofer. Used by permission of Doubleday, a division of Bantam Doubleday Dell Publishing Group, Inc.

TABLE 8.2

Cynicism and Police Experience

EXPERIENCE	CYNICISM SCORE
Controls on first day	42.6
Recruits 2–3 months on job	60.3
Patrolmen 2–6 years on job	64.1
Patrolmen 7–10 years	69.1
Patrolmen 11–14 years	62.9
Patrolmen 15–19 years	62.5

SOURCE: Arthur Niederhoffer, *Behind the Shield* (Garden City, NY: Anchor Books, 1967).

Niederhoffer's survey had two unanticipated results: Unmarried patrolmen had the highest cynicism scores of any group (73.4), and increasing age was not associated with increasing cynicism, as had been predicted. Nevertheless, the study documented a sharp rise in cynical attitudes among police officers that begins very early and subsides near the end of a career but never returns to the original low level.

Niederhoffer's cynicism scale was a pioneering effort inasmuch as it was the first attempt to quantify police cynicism. A number of subsequent efforts have been made to validate and challenge his model. G. Marie Wilt and James Bannon administered Niederhoffer's questionnaire to 577 officers of the Detroit Police Department and obtained somewhat lower scores than those recorded in New York City police officers. Nevertheless, the results of the two surveys were similar in many respects. Wilt and Bannon believed that noticeable increases in the cynicism scores of police recruits during their first few weeks of training in both Detroit and New York might be due to the cynicism of experienced officers teaching at the police academy. The recruits may simply "desire to emulate experienced officers in an effort to shed their status as novices."[28]

Robert Regoli and other researchers have since applied Niederhoffer's cynicism scale on police in Washington and Idaho. They found five distinctly different types of cynicism: cynicism about the public, about dedication to duty, about police solidarity, about organizational functions, and about training and education. Regoli concluded that "because the attitude was found to be multidimensional, it is possible that police can be cynical toward one aspect of the occupation and not others, or toward any combination of aspects simultaneously."[29] Regoli and Poole offered a modified version of Niederhoffer's scale.[30]

Further examinations of the dimensions of cynicism have been conducted with police officers, supervisors, and chiefs. Niederhoffer's scale was found to measure several different dimensions of cynicism, although length of tenure as chief and size of the department were associated with lower cynicism. In sum, Niederhoffer's efforts to quantify cynicism have been confounded by problems of measuring it accurately.[31]

All these investigations of police cynicism leave one question unanswered: Is police work the only, or even the primary, source of police cynicism? As Niederhoffer recognized in 1967, "Still the lingering doubt persists. Is it not likely that there is something unusual about an individual who chooses to become a policeman?"[32] Those who choose to become police officers may have personality characteristics that make them more susceptible to cynicism.

The Working Personality

Jerome Skolnick examined police attitudes and discretion in a medium-sized city that he called Westville. Like Niederhoffer, Skolnick believed that the police officer's "working personality" grows out of his or her social environment rather than being a product of preexisting personality traits. Skolnick maintained that the "police personality" emerges from several aspects of police work—in particular, danger, isolation, and authority. He believed that danger causes police officers to be more wary of people in general, making them more suspicious. Suspicious people tend to isolate themselves from others, and Skolnick believed that police officers do this as well, making them undesirable as friends. With regard to authority, Skolnick recognized that police have authority to direct and restrain citizens, but this authority is often challenged. This reinforces the officer's perception of danger and further isolates him or her from the rest of society.

This link between danger and suspicion, coupled with constant challenges to their authority, may lead police officers to react to "vague indications of danger suggested by appearance." These perceptions are reinforced, according to Skolnick, by the police system, which encourages sensitivity to danger. Skolnick administered a questionnaire to 224 police officers in Westville, asking them which type of police assignment they would most prefer. The responses indicated that confining and routine jobs were considered least desirable, while the most potentially dangerous jobs were preferred. "Thus the police officer, as a personality, may well enjoy the possibility of danger, especially its associated excitement, while fearing it at the same time."[33] A similar finding was discovered in a survey of ninety-one officers from five different police departments, which found that "even though the officers surveyed did not perceive physical injury as an everyday happening . . . nearly four-fifths of the sample believed that they worked at a dangerous job, and . . . two-thirds thought that policing was more dangerous than other kinds of employment."[34]

Skolnick asked the officers to state (in order) the two most serious problems faced by police. The most common problems cited were relations with the public and racial problems. In fact, the officers believed that, both on and off the job, the public generally has negative, or at least nonsupportive, views of the police. According to Skolnick, this feeling of isolation increases police solidarity as officers are more likely to associate with one another than with people in other occupations. The officers he studied socialized primarily with other officers, and 35 percent of their close friends were other officers.

The element of authority was also found to play a role in the police officer's social isolation. Traffic citations were cited as an example. Police officers generally did not like to give traffic tickets because of the hostility they encountered as a result. The following passage describes how this process operates:

> **Although traffic patrol plays a major role in separating police officers from the respectable community, other of their tasks also have this consequence. Traffic patrol is only the most obvious illustration of the police officer's general responsibility for maintaining public order, which also includes keeping order at public accidents, sporting events, and political rallies. These activities share one feature: The officer is called upon to *direct* ordinary citizens and therefore to restrain their freedom of action. Resenting the restraint, the average citizen in such a situation typically thinks something along the lines of, "He is supposed to catch crooks: why is he bothering me?" Thus the citizen stresses the "dangerous" portion of the police officer's role while belittling the officer's authority.[35]**

According to Skolnick, therefore, the perceived danger of the police officer's job, together with frequent challenges to his or her authority and a perceived lack of public support, results in police solidarity and isolation from others. Like Niederhoffer, Skolnick believes that the police officer's "working personality" emerges from the job and work environment, rather than from preexisting personality traits.

Studies of police attitudes have found that job experiences rather than pre-existing personality traits often produce cynicism, authoritarianism, and other undesirable attitudes. Officers with higher levels of education have been found to display these attitudes less often and to perform better on the job.

Sources of Police Attitudes

Police attitudes come from one of two sources. One group of investigators, including Niederhoffer and Skolnick, subscribe to the "socialization model." That is, they view the police personality as a product of the demands of police work. An alternative explanation, classified as the "predispositional model," holds that the police personality is a product of the personality traits of the individual officer.[36]

To assess the validity of the predispositional model, Richard Bennett and Theodore Greenstein administered a survey that asks people to assign priorities to the values that serve as guiding principles in their lives.[37] The list included such principles as a comfortable life, an exciting life, a sense of accomplishment, equality, freedom, and happiness. The respondents were students at a state university. They were divided into three groups: police officers, police science majors, and non–police science majors. It was expected that the police officers and police science majors (who were seriously contemplating careers in law enforcement) would have similar value orientations. Interestingly, however, the opposite was the case. The data "strongly suggest that police science majors have value systems nearly identical to those of students not majoring in police science. . . . On the other hand, police science majors' value systems are markedly divergent from the value systems of experienced police officers."[38] Therefore, the researchers rejected the predisposition hypothesis as an explanation of the police personality.

An important implication of this study is that efforts to reduce the "value gap" between the police and the community should take the form of new training procedures rather than selective recruitment based on personality characteristics. In addition, training programs should probably focus on social and legal aspects of the job (such as the proper use of discretion) rather than on personal values, because there appears to be no significant difference between the personal values of police officers and those of ordinary citizens.

These findings gained further support in a study conducted in England that compared three groups: male constables with more than two years of experience, new recruits with less than seven days on the job, and male working-class civilians. The researchers found that "police recruits have similar values to those of the population from which they are recruited, whereas there are more differences between the values of experienced policemen and the community."[39] As in the earlier study, the researchers found no empirical support for the predisposition model. It appears that police officers acquire their attitudes from their work environment and that people who choose a police career do not differ from the general population in personality characteristics.[40]

Other personality screening tests have been unable to identify preexisting characteristics of a police personality. Popular screening tests, such as the Minnesota Multiphasic Personality Inventory (MMPI) and the California Psychological Inventory (CPI), have been unable to predict the on-the-job success of police applicants, although some differences between police candidates and the general population have been found in a few samples.[41] Likewise, other personality screening devices have been unable to identify the reasons that some people become police officers or to explain why some are successful and some are not.[42] Nevertheless, more than 90 percent of large police departments use psychological tests and interviews in the officer selection process, despite clear evidence that police attitudes are a result of socialization on the job.[43]

Education and Attitudes

Since the predisposition model has been discredited, most investigators have focused on how police officers react to their environment, with a view toward inhibiting the development of cynical, suspicious, or authoritarian attitudes. The most commonly recommended strategy to reduce undesirable police attitudes is college education.[44] As a result, several investigators have attempted to examine the effect of higher education on police attitudes.

Alexander Smith, Bernard Locke, and William Walker conducted a series of three studies of education and attitudes at John Jay College of Criminal Justice in New York City. They looked specifically at the effect of college education on authoritarianism. An **authoritarian** person is one who favors blind obedience to authority; a characteristic statement by such an individual might be, "You should listen to me because I tell you to."

authoritarian
A person who favors blind obedience to authority.

In the first study, the authors compared the attitudes of officers entering college with those of officers who chose not to attend college. They found that police who go to college are significantly less authoritarian than those who do not.[45] The second study compared the attitudes of college freshmen who were police officers to those who were not. Again, they found that "the police officer enrolled in college scores significantly lower on the 'authoritarianism' scale than does his fellow student who is not a police officer."[46] The third study compared the attitudes of police officers who were college graduates with the attitudes of police who had not attended college. The two groups were matched according to age and experience. The researchers found that college education made a considerable difference in the development of authoritarian attitudes.[47] In sum, the findings of each of these studies are consistent. Police officers who are attracted to college or are attending college appear to be less authoritarian than nonpolice at the same educational level. Likewise, police officers who graduate with a Bachelor's degree appear to be less authoritarian than officers of similar age and experience who do not have a college education.

A questionnaire mailed to one hundred officers of the Royal Canadian Mounted Police (the federal police of Canada) compared four groups of officers who differed in age, experience, and education. They were each administered the authoritarianism scale used by Smith, Locke, and Walker, as well as a liberal-conservative scale and a "rigid-flexible" personality test. The findings were remarkable. Senior police officers who were not college graduates were characterized by authoritarian, conservative, and rigid attitudes, whereas college-educated officers did not have these attitudes.[48] It appears, therefore, that authoritarian attitudes are more likely to be found in officers without a college education who have been on the job a long time. These studies do much to reveal the relationship between higher education and police attitudes, but they leave open the question of whether a police officer's attitudes make any difference in his or her performance.

Attitudes and Performance

This review of research on the "police personality" leaves us with an important question: Does it really matter what a police officer's attitudes are? That is, do attitudes affect performance on the job?

contemporary issues

The Performance of Policewomen

Several investigations have compared the performance of male and female officers. In a controlled comparison conducted by the Police Foundation, eighty-six new female officers were matched with eighty-six new male officers in Washington, D.C. Performance measures ranging from driving skills to quality of arrests were used in the evaluation.[A] The performance assessment was made by trained male and female observers, who rode with the new officers on patrol. Other information was obtained from supervisors' ratings and department records.

For nine of the indicators, no significant difference was found between the male and female officers. These indicators included the length of time it took to handle an incident, the proportion of arrests that resulted in prosecution, the way threatening situations were handled, the use of sick leave, the frequency of injury on the job, and citizen satisfaction with the way an incident was handled.

Differences were discovered, however, in the five remaining performance indicators. First, it was found that men made more arrests and gave more traffic citations than did women, even accounting for the fact that women were more often given inside assignments. Second, the Chief's Survey ratings, made by the officer's patrol sergeant, rated men "above average" in street patrol and in handling violence, whereas women were generally rated "average." Likewise, the Official's Survey, completed by captains and lieutenants, rated male officers as more competent than female officers in general street patrol and in handling violent incidents. Fourth, it took women longer than men to pass the driving skills test (six weeks, compared to one month for the men). According to the evaluators, this might be due to the fact that the women had less previous driving experience than the men and made somewhat greater use of compact cars for personal use, causing greater difficulty in handling full-size police cars. Fifth, it was found that "unbecoming conduct" occurred at different rates among the men and women. Men were more likely to engage in both mild and serious misconduct, whereas women were more likely to be tardy.

Studies have found that the performance of women as police officers is comparable to that of men, although they appear to be resented by some male officers. Female officers constitute 9 percent of all sworn officers in the United States, and 3 percent of all police supervisory positions.

In a final aspect of this evaluation, the Police Foundation conducted a telephone interview of a representative sample of 129 citizens. It was found that regardless of age or sex, citizens generally approved of policewomen on patrol. They also felt that there was little difference between the performance of male and female officers. The citizens were moderately skeptical about a female officer's ability to handle a violent situation, but they believed that a male–female team would be better able to handle fights between male and female citizens. Respondents also felt that female officers would show slightly more respect toward citizens than would male officers.

The Police Foundation concluded that women appeared to handle violent incidents as well as men (despite the ratings of superior officers).[B] The evaluation also showed that the overall performance of men and women was similar, and that the differences often were counterbalancing. That is, men made more arrests, but they also en-

dogmatism
An attitude characterized by tenacious adherence to one's opinions even though they may be unwarranted and based on insufficiently examined premises.

These questions were addressed in a study of the effects of **dogmatism** on the performance of 118 patrol officers in Lincoln, Nebraska. Dogmatism is closely associated with authoritarianism. A dogmatic person is one who is positive about his or her opinions even though they may be unwarranted. A dogmatic viewpoint is one that is based on insufficiently examined premises. The dogmatism scale used in this study was developed by Milton Rokeach, who also developed the authoritarianism and value orientation scales discussed earlier.[49]

The study examined the officers' levels of education, their scores on the dogmatism scale, and their job performance as measured by ratings using the International Association of Chiefs of Police (IACP) evaluation system. Twenty factors from this scale were considered, ranging from attendance to initiative to effec-

gaged in more "serious unbecoming conduct" than did women. The evaluators reached the following conclusions:

> **The men and women studied for this report performed patrol work in a generally similar manner. They responded to similar types of calls for police service while on patrol and encountered similar proportions of citizens who were dangerous, upset, drunk or violent . . . There were no reported incidents which cast serious doubt on the ability of women to perform patrol work satisfactorily, and in fact this study includes reports of some incidents in which individual women performed quite well in difficult circumstances . . . In sum, the study shows that sex is not a bona fide occupational qualification for doing police patrol work.[C]**

Subsequent investigations of the performance of female versus male officers have had similar findings. In St. Louis, New York City, Japan, Israel, and other jurisdictions, it has been found that female officers perform police tasks as competently as do male officers, but that female officers in the United States "encounter interactional barriers and gendered images that establish them as outsiders, sexual objects, targets of men's resentment, and competitors who threaten to change the rules of officer interaction."[D] Despite the satisfactory performance of female officers, these attitudes may be responsible for the slow assimilation of women in policing. Female officers constitute only 9 percent of all sworn officers in the United States, and only 3 percent of officers in supervisory positions are women.

NOTES

[A]Peter B. Bloch and Deborah Anderson, *Policewomen on Patrol: Final Report* (Washington, D.C.: Police Foundation, 1974).

[B]Ibid., p. 61.

[C]Ibid., p. 2.

[D]Susan Ehrlich Martin and Nancy C. Jurik, *Doing Justice, Doing Gender: Women in Law Enforcement Occupations* (Thousand Oaks, CA: Sage Publications, 1996), p. 73; Lewis J. Sherman, "An Evaluation of Policewomen on Patrol in a Suburban Police Department," *Journal of Police Science and Administration*, vol. 3 (December 1975), pp. 434–8; Joyce L. Sichel, Lucy N. Friedman, Janet C. Quint, and Michael E. Smith, *Women on Patrol: A Pilot Study of Police Performance in New York City* (Washington, D.C.: U.S. Department of Justice, 1978); Anthony V. Bouza, "Women in Policing," *FBI Law Enforcement Bulletin*, vol. 44 (1975), pp. 2–7; Susan Ehrlich Martin, *Breaking and Entering: Policewomen on Patrol* (Berkeley: University of California Press, 1980); Bernadette Jones Palombo, "Attitudes, Training, Performance and Retention of Female and Minority Police Officers," in G. T. Felkenes and P. C. Unsinger, eds., *Diversity, Affirmative Action and Law Enforcement* (Springfield, IL: Charles C Thomas, 1992), pp. 76–9; Donna C. Hale and Stacey M. Myland, "Dragons and Dinosaurs: The Plight of Patrol Women," *Police Forum*, vol. 3 (April 1993); Daniel Bell, "Policewomen: Myths and Reality," *Journal of Police Science and Administration*, vol. 10 (March 1982), pp. 112–20; Peter Horne, *Women in Law Enforcement*, 2nd ed. (Springfield, IL: Charles C Thomas, 1980); Sean A. Grennan, "Findings on the Roles of Officer Gender in Violent Encounters with Citizens," *Journal of Police Science and Administration*, vol. 15 (1987); Kerry Segrave, *Policewomen: A History* (Jefferson, NC: McFarland & Company, 1995); Susan Ehrlich Martin, "Women on the Move?: A Report on the Status of Women in Policing," *Women & Criminal Justice*, vol. 1 (1989), pp. 21–40.

tiveness on the job. The results showed that officers with higher levels of education had more open belief systems and performed in a more satisfactory manner than those with less education.[50] Age, length of experience, and college major did not affect this relationship. This finding is extremely important because it reveals the links among education, attitudes, and performance, and shows how a college education plays a direct role in this relationship (i.e., the more college education officers had attained, the less dogmatic their attitudes were and the higher their job performance was rated by their supervisors).

In recent years numerous studies have examined the relationship between attitudes and performance. Most of them have focused on successful performance in the police training academy, although some have assessed performance

Pursuit Driving

Police have traditionally had considerable discretion in their decision to pursue a suspect. This discretion has come under increasing scrutiny in recent years because of incidents in which police chases resulted in accidents and the deaths of suspects, police, and innocent bystanders. The National Highway Safety Administration estimates that more than 250 people are killed each year and another 20,000 injured as a result of high-speed pursuits by police.[A]

A review of police pursuits found that many are unnecessary. In Miami–Dade County, a review of all 488 police pursuits that occurred between 1990 and 1994 found that only 35 percent involved suspected felonies. Forty-five percent of the pursuits were initiated for traffic violations.[B] The findings in other cities were similar: In Omaha, only 40 percent of pursuits involved suspected felonies; in Aiken County, South Carolina, 43 percent were felony pursuits.

More than 90 percent of police departments have written policies that govern pursuits, although fewer than a third regularly collect pursuit statistics.[C] In addition, the average time devoted to driving training at police academies is less than fourteen hours. In-service training adds three additional hours per year. This training is suspect, however, because it focuses on the mechanics of police pursuit and defensive driving, rather than on the decision to engage in a pursuit. As police expert Geoffrey Alpert has observed, "It is shameful for our law enforcement agencies to expect their officers to make proper and appropriate decisions with minimal or no training."[D]

FUTURES QUESTION

Why do you believe that the police pursuit decision has not been systematically addressed until recently, and under what circumstances do you think police should engage in a pursuit?

NOTES

[A]Louis P. Mitchell, "High Speed Pursuits," *Criminal Justice: The Americas*, vol. 2 (January 1990), p. 18.

[B]Geoffrey P. Alpert, "Pursuit Driving: Planning Policies and Action from Agency, Officer, and Public Information," *Police Forum* (January 1997), pp. 1–12.

[C]Geoffrey P. Alpert, "Analyzing Police Pursuit," *Criminal Law Bulletin*, vol. 27 (July–August 1991), pp. 358–67.

[D]"Pursuit Driving," p. 3.

after several years on the job. The results have been mixed. Psychological tests have been found to "predict a greater number of officers' . . . job performance than would be expected by chance alone," but not by much.[51] The reliability and validity of various psychological tests and interviews are not often high[52]; nevertheless, there is additional evidence that higher educational levels are associated with higher academy scores.[53]

Clearly, additional investigations are needed to develop more reliable methods for assessing personality characteristics and examining their relationship to police performance over longer periods. Only through further research will the subtle relationship between attitudes and behavior be clarified.

When Police Make Bad Decisions

Every encounter between a police officer and citizen involves a decision. As was discussed earlier, if the behavior is serious enough, the officer will arrest the offender. In the vast majority of cases, however, the officer has considerable discretion in choosing a course of action. Sometimes police are offered money or other inducements to take no official action or to release a suspect. If a police officer accepts such money or favors in exchange for a specific legal duty, he or she has committed an act of corruption.

Forms of Police Corruption

There are three forms of police corruption: nonfeasance, misfeasance, and malfeasance. **Nonfeasance** involves failure to perform a legal duty, **misfeasance** is failure to perform a legal duty in a proper manner, and **malfeasance** is commission of an illegal act. For example, an officer who sees a car swerving down the road can legitimately pull it over. If the driver hands the officer his license with a $50 bill clipped to it and the officer takes it, does not write out a ticket, and then proceeds to search the driver by tearing off his clothes, the officer is guilty of nonfeasance (in failing to write a ticket), misfeasance (in conducting a search improperly), and malfeasance (in accepting a bribe).

nonfeasance
A form of police corruption involving failure to perform a legal duty.

misfeasance
A form of police corruption involving failure to perform a legal duty in a proper manner.

malfeasance
A form of police corruption involving commission of an illegal act.

It can be seen that malfeasance is a form of corruption, whereas nonfeasance and misfeasance do not always constitute corruption. Many police departments set enforcement priorities and ignore petty offenses in favor of serious crimes. Under these circumstances nonfeasance in certain situations represents department policy rather than an individual failure to perform a legal duty. Likewise, misfeasance is not always considered corruption. If an officer conducts a search in violation of legal rules, it may reflect improper understanding of the law rather than a willful attempt to circumvent it.

A general definition of police corruption thus should reflect the possibility of various types of official wrongdoing. **Police corruption** consists of illegal acts or omissions by police officers in the line of duty who, by virtue of their official position, receive (or intend to receive) any gain for themselves or others. The important elements of this definition are the illegal acts or omissions, the fact that they occur while the officer is on duty, and the intent to receive a reward for these acts. Fundamentally, therefore, police corruption is misuse of authority for personal gain.

police corruption
Illegal acts or omissions of acts by police officers who, by virtue of their official position, receive (or intend to receive) any gain for themselves or others.

Explanations of Corruption

Several investigators have offered useful explanations of police corruption, some of which focus on individual officers, some on departmental problems, and others on problems external to the department.[54] Individual explanations see the particular officer as the primary problem. Supporters of this view claim that if a few "rotten apples" were eliminated, police corruption would disappear. For example, some officers are seen as being of "low moral caliber." Such an officer might feel that he or she is underpaid, is unjustly maligned by the public, and receives no recognition for good work, and might therefore be unable to resist temptation. Another type of corrupt officer would be one who misuses authority for selfish ends. Such behavior might emerge from thoughts such as, "I might as well make the most of the situation" (e.g., an offer of a bribe). This type of officer may actively seek opportunities for illicit payoffs, justifying this activity with a rationalization such as low pay or lack of recognition.[55] The case of Michael Dowd of the New York City Police Department is a recent example of a "bad

The Mollen Commission investigation of police corruption in New York City included testimony from Michael Dowd, who was one of nearly 50 officers arrested during 1994 and 1995 on charges of brutality, drug trafficking, extortion, and civil rights violations.

apple." Dowd was found to be organizing raids on the apartments of drug dealers in order to steal cash and narcotics.[56] His behavior was featured in the Mollen Commission's investigation of corruption in New York City during the mid-1990s.

Explanations that focus on the individual officer are popular, but most experts reject the "rotten apples" explanation of corruption because it fails to explain how individual officers become corrupt or why police corruption is so widespread, and it does not account for differences between departments, or within a particular department over time. As one investigator notes, if corruption is to be explained in terms of a few "bad" people, then some departments must have attracted a disproportionately high number of rotten apples over long periods.[57] This is illustrated in the case of Michael Dowd, who was one of nearly fifty officers who were arrested in New York City during 1994 and 1995 on charges of brutality, drug trafficking, extortion, and civil rights violations.[58] Another drawback, noted by the Knapp Commission in its investigation of corruption in the New York City Police Department during the 1970s, is that the "rotten apple" theory can become an excuse for command officers to deny that a serious problem exists.[59]

A second type of explanation of police corruption is the "departmental" explanation. If corruption cannot be explained in terms of a few bad apples, then the barrel itself must be examined. An example of this approach is the "deviant police subculture" hypothesis. According to this view, small groups of officers within a department might have a similar outlook regarding their commitment to the job and the support they receive from superiors. If these officers feel uncommitted and unsupported, their outlook and values will be reinforced by others in the group, which may lead to cynicism or lack of commitment to the job, opening the door to corruption.[60] In New Orleans, for example, between 1993 and 1995 more than fifty police officers were charged with offenses that included

Media and Criminal Justice

RUSH

In the 1970s, the films *Serpico* and *Prince of the City* received a great deal of attention for their stories of "good cops gone bad." The plots were different, but the message was the same: In policing, do the ends justify the means? Is it really such a terrible crime to take drugs away from a small-time dealer and trade those drugs to a desperate addict for information that would lead the cop to the big drug kingpin? Such questions become even more disturbing when it is realized that the movies were based on the true stories of real New York City police officers. Today, the real Serpico still appears before NYPD police commissions, arguing that honest cops cannot survive in a department where the blue curtain of secrecy remains in place.

In the past twenty years, many films have been made that depict the problems that occur when a police officer's working personality takes over his or her life. The suspicion, cynicism, hostility, and emphasis on getting "the collar" at any cost begin to affect officer discretion and behavior. Movies such as *Internal Affairs* (1990), *One Good Cop* (1991), *Deep Cover* (1992), *The Bad Lieutenant* (1992), and *Donnie Brasco* (1997) all offer vivid portrayals of the dangers of police subculture: "Going native" in undercover work, using brutality to control criminals who have no fear of the system, accepting bribes or sexual favors to ignore crime, and trading contraband to further the goals of law enforcement, are all very real dangers in police subculture.

The 1992 movie *Rush* provides a shocking look at the lives of two Texas narcotics officers who, in the interest of capturing drug dealers, eventually find themselves drug-addicted. The story, written by Kim Wozencraft, is much like its 1970s predecessors in that it is based on actual events. In *Rush,* an experienced narc named Raynor trains a new police recruit, Kristen, in the world of undercover operations. The cultural transmission of the police subculture is not even subtle; Raynor basically tells Kristen to forget everything she's been taught in the academy. One of her first lessons in "real" police work is learning how to use a hyperdermic needle on herself to shoot up heroin.

Some of the most disturbing scenes are those in which the officers are faced with a common dilemma in undercover work. They must shoot up drugs in front of the people they are investigating in order to gain their trust and infiltrate the drug operation. There is no way to fake it, and they don't. But at what point do Raynor and Kristen cross the line? Is it when they first engage in drug use to ingratiate themselves with the criminals, when they become addicted, when they refuse to seek help, or when they begin to enjoy it?

In *Rush,* Raynor and Kristen choose their undercover work because they like the challenge and the danger. Or is it because they can break the law without actually being "criminals"? In the end, they behave more like criminals who just happened to be employed as cops. Interestingly, their police supervisor knows that they have become drug-addicted, but dismisses it as an occupational hazard, a necessary tragedy.

Rush, and the other films of this genre, graphically reveal the subculture and process by which well-meaning cops become the people they have sworn to defeat.

MEDIA AND CRIMINAL JUSTICE QUESTION

What are the significant factors that police officers must weigh in undercover operations as portrayed in *Rush*? Which factors do you believe should be overriding concerns?

rape, assault, drug trafficking, and murder.[61] This suggests the existence of an organized subculture within the department that condoned illegal behavior.

Another version of this explanation focuses on secrecy within the department. A questionnaire administered by William Westley revealed that three fourths of the officers surveyed would not report their partners if they engaged in a corrupt activity; moreover, officers would perjure themselves rather than testify against their partners. When he asked them their reasons, Westley found that if the unwritten code of secrecy within the police organization was violated, the officer would be regarded as a "stool pigeon" or "outcast," even though he or she would be reporting illegal behavior.[62]

Departmental explanations have been investigated in several studies.[63] It is clear from the findings that certain conditions within a department can be conducive to corruption. As the Pennsylvania Crime Commission found in its investigation of corruption in the Philadelphia Police Department, "Systematic corruption does not occur in a vacuum. Officers succumb to pressures within the department," such as illegal conduct by fellow officers and failure by superiors to take action against "open and widespread violations" of the law and of department policy.[64] The 1994 Mollen Commission in New York City found that rather than merely overlooking the illicit behavior of other officers, groups of officers were acting as criminal gangs.[65]

A third explanation of corruption focuses on factors external to the department, especially government actions that make honest policing more difficult. For example, laws prohibiting such behaviors as gambling, drug use, and prostitution are difficult to enforce because there is no complainant except the government (represented by the police). As a result, police are mandated to enforce laws that neither the offender nor the "victim" wish to have enforced. As a result, "the law enforcement system is placed in the middle of two conflicting demands. On the one hand, it is their job to enforce the law, albeit with discretion; on the other hand, there is considerable disagreement as to whether or not certain particular activities should be declared criminal."[66] In such a situation police may "look the other way," or be paid to do so. Also, when arrests are made in gambling, drug, or prostitution cases and the offenders are treated leniently in the courts, it becomes easier for police to become corrupt because neither the public nor the criminal justice system appears to be serious about enforcing the law.

A second category of externally caused corruption results from a weak or ineffective local government. When government is unwilling or unable to oversee or manage its police force, the operation of the department becomes haphazard and corruption often results. In addition, corruption in the local government can spread to the police department through the need for "protection" of illegal activities. A study of police corruption in three cities found that corruption was made possible by informal systems that allow politicians to influence personnel decisions within the department: "By determining who will occupy key positions of power within a department, and by making as many members of the . . . department as possible obligated to the politicians, political leaders can impose their own goals on the department—including protection of vice for the financial benefit of the political party in power or of the party leaders themselves."[67]

Other investigators have found that corruption can result from the "political climate" of the city.[68] An example is the case of Chicago, in which a new police chief was appointed in 1998. The previous chief was forced to resign after it was discovered that he had maintained a close friendship with a convicted felon. The Chicago Police Department was faced with accusations that police brutality was endemic, in addition to the fact that officers had been charged with taking bribes and selling drugs. Clearly there was a pervasive culture of corruption, although the police union blamed local politicians for placing political interests above the law.[69] In a similar vein, the City of Philadelphia also appointed a new police chief in 1998 to "improve the performance of a 7,000-officer force that has been troubled over the years by numerous accusations of brutality, graft and . . . ineptitude."[70]

In both cases, there was a long history of political interference in department affairs, combined with brutality against citizens and corruption involving the vices.

Preventing Corruption

The most effective prevention strategies are those that are based on carefully identified causes. If one finds that corruption in a particular department involves only a few officers, several control strategies may be appropriate. Examples include close monitoring of complaints against the police, making all police hirings and dismissals more visible to serve as an example and deterrent, and making sure police officers do not get into debt. Other, longer-term strategies include more exhaustive background checks of recruits, periodic retraining of all police, and measures aimed at enhancing professionalism by allowing for leaves for study or specialized training. These sorts of strategies are likely to work because they attempt to improve the commitment of individual officers to the ideals and values of a law enforcement career.

If corruption is found to be due to problems in the department itself, a different set of control strategies would be appropriate. For example, establishing civilian review boards to hear complaints against the department and enhancing career mobility within the department may help prevent hidden corruption. Likewise, procedures to ensure the fair and confidential hearing of personnel matters within the department and to guarantee that promotions are based on qualifications, rather than on patronage, can help prevent political considerations from inhibiting honest police work.

When corruption is found to be due to external, governmental factors, the most fruitful strategies are those that improve police supervision and decision-making. Supervision of officers can be improved by making sure that only qualified police and government officials are given supervisory responsibilities. Similarly, decriminalization of certain undesirable behaviors would eliminate opportunities for corruption by removing "victimless" crimes from police jurisdiction.

In its New York City investigation, the Knapp Commission found that the most important source of police corruption was control of the city's gambling, narcotics, loansharking, and illegal sex-related enterprises. The next most important source was "legitimate business seeking to ease its way through the maze of City ordinances and regulations."[71] In this case changes in laws and regulations could have a substantial impact on police corruption. The Knapp Commission noted that, "The laws against gambling, prostitution, and the conduct of certain business activities on the Sabbath all contribute to the prevalence of police corruption."[72] One expert has concluded that without "a public commitment . . . to realistic vice laws . . . the elimination of police corruption will not occur."[73]

Police Performance

Most people agree that the primary job of police is law enforcement. Given the necessity of selective enforcement, it is also generally agreed that police should devote most of their efforts to preventing and controlling crime. A question arises, however, when we want to assess whether or not police are performing their task effectively. How should we evaluate police performance in controlling crime?

Responding to Crime

One commonly used indicator of police performance is the crime rate. If the crime rate is going up in a town, its residents may claim that the police are not controlling crime effectively. Is this a fair indicator of police performance?

The manner in which police enforce the law is the key to evaluating their performance in controlling crime. However, police are primarily a *reactive* force. As noted in Chapter 2, only about a third of all serious crimes are reported to the police; the police therefore can react to only a third of the serious criminal incidents that take place. In the vast majority of cases, police are informed of an incident *after* it occurs by a complaining victim, a witness, or an alarm. (A study of police response time found that only about 6 percent of callers reported crimes while they were in progress.[74]) It is difficult to hold police responsible for increases in the crime rate when they are not called for most crimes and if, when they are called, it is only after the incident has ended.

Another factor to consider is that there are a number of things that may cause the crime rate to rise. An increase in the proportion of young people in the population, higher rates of long-term unemployment, widespread drug use, and other factors may all play a role. What is striking about these conditions is that police have no control over them. Thus, the crime rate is not a useful indicator of police effectiveness.

The number of officers is also inadequate as an indicator. Police forces in the United States range in strength from 1 to 55 officers per 1,000 residents. In cities with populations of 250,000 or more, police departments vary in size from 1.7 to 7 officers per 1,000 citizens. There is no evidence that the presence of more officers has any effect on the crime rate in a city. The number of police officers per 1,000 Americans rose from 1.6 to 2.6 over the last twenty years. During the same period the reported crime rate rose 436 percent (from 1 serious crime per 1,000 to nearly 6 per 1,000).

Another commonly used measure of police performance is the proportion of crimes cleared by arrest, that is, the proportion of "open" cases that are "closed" or solved by an arrest. It could be argued that because we know the number of crimes reported to the police, we can determine how well they perform by looking at the number of cases they solve.

Table 8.3 presents a list of police clearance rates for Index crimes. These figures show that approximately 21 percent of all crimes were cleared by arrest, meaning that one in five reported Index crimes led to an arrest. (The overall total is low because property crimes occur nearly ten times more frequently than crimes of violence.)

Clearance rates also have drawbacks when used as an indicator of police performance. Low clearance rates are often due to other factors besides poor police work. Some crimes are not cleared because police cannot spend an unlimited amount of time on an unsolved case. New crimes occur every day, and the police are forced to move on to the next case. Moreover, clearance rates are lowest for property offenses, which are the least likely to be solved. Because burglary,

TABLE 8.3

Crimes Cleared by Arrest

TYPE OF CRIME	PERCENT CLEARED
Murder	67
Forcible rape	52
Robbery	27
Aggravated assault	58
Burglary	14
Larceny	20
Motor vehicle theft	14
Arson	15
Overall clearance rate	21

SOURCE: Federal Bureau of Investigation, *Uniform Crime Reports, 1996* (Washington, D.C.: U.S. Government Printing Office, 1997).

larceny, motor vehicle theft, and arson occur without the knowledge or presence of the owner, there is often a significant lag between the time that the crime occurs and the time when police are informed of it. Analyses of police investigations have found that the older the crime, the lower its chances of being solved.[75]

If clearances were used to evaluate police performance, an artificial increase in the clearance rate might result. For example, if a police department had fifty unsolved burglaries and managed to catch a burglar in the act last night, there would be an incentive to charge the suspect with fifty-one burglaries in order to close all the open cases, even though the evidence supported only one charge of burglary.

If clearance rates are not a good measure of police performance, why not use arrests as an indicator of effectiveness in controlling crime? In a given year more than twelve million arrests are made in the United States. If one hundred arrests are made in one town in a year, however, what does that indicate? It could be that one hundred people were arrested once, or perhaps one person was arrested one hundred times. Moreover, arrests provide no indication of how many cases were dismissed in court owing to insufficient evidence, illegal searches, or other problems. Thus, by themselves arrests do not offer a good measure of police performance.

Still another possible indicator of police performance is the number of arrests resulting in convictions. In a typical year about 80 percent of all individuals arrested are prosecuted. Of these, about 25 percent are acquitted or dismissed, and approximately 75 percent (or 60 percent of those arrested) are convicted on the same or a lesser charge.[76] The reasons for acquittals, dismissals, or reduced charges may have nothing to do with police work, however. They may involve reluctant victims or witnesses, incompetent counsel, errors in court procedure, or any number of circumstances that are beyond police control.

The best indicator of police performance is *arrests resulting in prosecutions.* Prosecutors will not bring a case to court unless it involves a meaningful charge resulting from a legal arrest and is based on sufficient evidence. Beyond this, further criminal justice processing is the responsibility of the prosecutor. Therefore, using arrests resulting in prosecutions as a measure of police performance overcomes the limitations of using number of arrests or number of arrests resulting in convictions. In sum, the evaluation of police performance is an important concern and should be based only on valid, reliable, and representative indicators of police efforts to control crime.

Noncriminal Matters

Evaluation of police performance in controlling crime assumes that the police spend most of their time in these endeavors. However, in reality this is not the case. Examinations of calls for police service in a number of cities, such as Tampa, Rochester, and St. Louis, have found that the vast majority of police time is devoted to noncriminal matters. It is not unusual for police to spend more than three-fourths of their working day responding to calls that have nothing to do with crime.[77]

There are two major reasons for such requests: (1) Often police are the only social service agency that is available 24 hours a day, and (2) the police will deal with the social problems of the poor and disadvantaged, groups that are not served by many other agencies. As a result, police devote the vast majority of their time to social service tasks.

If they are to concentrate on criminal matters, it has been proposed that police must be relieved of some noncriminal tasks. Such an approach is used in New Zealand, where a Traffic Control Corps (TCC) was established in 1935 to deal with matters such as speeding, parking, minor accidents, and directing traffic. In serious traffic situations, such as those involving injury, the TCC turns suspects over to the police for prosecution. The TCC is separate from the police and, because of its specialized function, does not require its personnel to meet the strict physical and training standards that must be met by police officers. The TCC has also reduced the ill will that often occurs in traffic stops by police.[78]

Another way to reduce police time spent on noncriminal matters is "problem-oriented" or community policing, in which effectiveness is increased by addressing underlying problems that give rise to criminal incidents, rather than merely reacting to the incidents themselves.[79] For example, a concentration of burglaries, larcenies, loiterers, or vandalism in a particular neighborhood may be a result of poor lighting, a local school problem, or other difficulties that can be remedied with proper analysis of the problem.[80]

The large number of arrests for offenses involving consensual acts, such as drug use, drunkenness, liquor law violations, gambling, vagrancy, and prostitution, reflect a law enforcement response to problems that are essentially medical, social, or sexual in nature. Offenses such as these might be handled by other agencies that are better able to deal with crimes that are largely symptoms of other underlying problems. Leaving the police with jurisdiction over fewer, more serious offenses may produce a more efficient response to predatory crimes. Such a strategy may also have an impact on organized crime, which profits from organizing a variety of consensual, but illegal, behaviors.

In addition to these three approaches, other alternatives have been suggested, such as increased use of civilians in noncriminal tasks and greater innovation in police investigative methods and in the organization of police departments.[81] If such policies are implemented, law enforcement will be better able to fulfill its potential for both crime control and community service.

Critical Thinking EXERCISE

Responding to Spousal Abuse

One of the important lessons of the O. J. Simpson trial was the need for improved police response to domestic violence. Yet many experts believed that the police response to these incidents had already been greatly improved.

The watershed was an incident that resulted in the case of *Thurman v. The City of Torrington, Connecticut.*[A] In this case a woman had been repeatedly and severely abused and threatened by her former husband, who was no longer living with her. The Torrington Police Department failed to enforce a court order prohibiting the husband from harassing her. After an attack in

which her husband nearly killed her, Thurman sued the police department for negligence and for violation of her civil rights. She won the case and was awarded a settlement of $2 million.

The Torrington case dramatically changed the way police exercise discretion in cases of domestic violence. Police departments, and their insurers, realized that their potential legal accountability made a new policy mandatory. However, the question remained: How *should* police handle domestic violence cases? As one former police chief remarked, "The chief's responsibility is to take whatever legal measures he believes wisest, based on something other than seat-of-the-pants feelings."[B]

Today 93 percent of large local police agencies and more than three fourths of sheriff's departments have written policies concerning domestic disputes. Nearly half of these agencies also have special units to deal with domestic violence.[C]

The precise actions taken by police vary by state, and sometimes even by locality. Fourteen states now have laws requiring that arrests be made in domestic violence situations. This was done in response to a study in Milwaukee, which found that when police made arrests the number of subsequent complaints was reduced. This finding is controversial, however, because it has not been found to hold in other locations, and the decline in subsequent complaints may be due to intimidation by the arrested spouse rather than to the deterrent impact of an arrest.[D]

Victims report that police respond to more than three-fourths of domestic incidents by coming to the scene, although they appear to respond more quickly to victimizations by strangers than to victimizations by intimates.[E] This points to a problem in current police policies. Even in jurisdictions where police are required to arrest the offender when responding to episodes of domestic violence, they often do not do so. Some officers believe that they will place the victim in more danger by making an arrest. In other cases police departments may give these types of situations low priority or may assume that the victim will not follow through with a complaint.[F] Therefore, many cases of domestic violence continue to be handled informally.

It has been observed that police are aware of households that are at high risk of a serious domestic assault (owing to a history of complaints), but that their focus on case-by-case responses prevents effective police action *before* such an assault.[G] It appears that paying greater attention to problem *households,* rather than just responding to assaultive *incidents,* may hold the best prospects for long-term prevention.

Critical Thinking Questions

1. How do you explain the different results found in various studies of the impact of arrests in domestic violence cases?
2. How do you explain the fact that 90 percent of all domestic violence cases involve men assaulting women? Why is the proportion not closer to 50 percent?
3. Why do you think society is reluctant to target problem households rather than simply having police respond to specific incidents of domestic assault?

Notes

[A]595 F. Suppl. 1521 (1985).

[B]Anthony Bouza, "Responding to Domestic Violence," in M. Steinman, ed., *Woman Battering: Policy Responses* (Cincinnati: Anderson Publishing, 1991), p. 201.

[C]Marianne W. Zawitz, *Violence Between Intimates* (Washington, D.C.: Bureau of Justice Statistics, 1994).

[D]Jannell D. Schmidt and Lawrence W. Sherman, "Does Arrest Deter Domestic Violence?," in E. S. Buzawa and C. G. Buzawa, *Do Arrests and Restraining Orders Work?* (Thousand Oaks, CA: Sage Publications, 1996), pp. 43–53; Jeffrey Fagan, *The Criminalization of Domestic Violence: Promises and Limits* (Washington, D.C.: National Institute of Justice, 1996); Loretta J. Stalans and Arthur J. Lurigio, "Responding to Violence Against Women," *Crime & Delinquency,* vol. 41 (October 1995), pp. 387–98; J. W. E. Sheptycki, *Innovations in Policing Domestic Violence* (Brookfield, VT: Avebury, 1993).

[E]Zawitz, p. 5.

[F]See Eve S. Buzawa, Thomas L. Austin, and Carl G. Buzawa, "The Role of Arrest in Domestic Versus Stranger Assault: Is There a Difference?," in E. S. Buzawa and C. G. Buzawa, *Do Arrests and Restraining Orders Work?* (Thousand Oaks, CA: Sage Publications, 1996), p. 152.

[G]Lawrence W. Sherman, Jannell D. Schmidt, and Daniel P. Rogan, *Policing Domestic Violence: Experiments and Dilemmas* (New York: The Free Press, 1992); Shelly Feuer Domash, "Putting the Cuffs on Domestic Abusers," *Police* (January 1998), pp. 46–7.

Critical Thinking EXERCISE

Changing the Police Culture in 1913

In 1913, a New York City crime reporter noticed that a peculiar culture within the New York City Police Department promoted unprofessional conduct. Consider his comments in light of major events in the evolution of police during this century.

> The average patrolman, as a matter of fact, had small chance to become an officer in the department. There was an inherited aristocracy of crookedness which rose, generation after generation, to take the higher offices of the force. . . . Over a long period of years this police system has established its traditions, which it hands down from one generation to another. These traditions form a strange code of ethics. . . . Saloon keepers and gamblers may be taxed for the privilege of breaking the law. They are a part of the "necessary evil" in a great city, as is prostitution. . . . And so, by gradual and natural steps, the solidarity of the underworld is built up. The gambler is a thief, the thief is a "cadet"; the prostitute, part wife, part business partner, part slave of her man. And the vice promoters and the slum politicians and the crooked policemen are all a part of the same class. . . .
>
> [Here are] the statistics concerning the men who entered the New York Police Force in 1912. Of 421 appointed, 4 out of every 5 were born in New York City. The average age on entering the force was 24 years, and about 2 out of every 3 were married. Only 2 of the 421 had an education reaching through high school; the remainder had gone no further than the grammar grades.
>
> They were drawn from a great variety of occupations—more than a quarter of them from positions like those of drivers and motormen—and nearly all of the remainder were

drawn from work of a grade somewhat above that of the common laborer. . . . About one-third of these men had been arrested, nearly all for the minor offenses in which active, city-bred youths of their class are most apt to be concerned—the commonest charge being that of disorderly conduct.

The police, in short, are drawn from the boys brought up on the streets of New York. They know the poorer population as no reformer can ever know it; for they are part of it.

In the older Police Force, the patrolman was assigned, whenever possible, to the district he grew up in. And, to some extent, he is still. To the patrolman observing an offense, someone has said, the practical question far too often is: "Shall I take my friend's money or send him to jail?" . . .

As a matter of fact, the Police Force has never originated any movement toward improvement in administering the law—especially in that greatest of all questions, the suppression of criminal immorality—of its own accord. This has always been the province of the outsider—of the reformer with the up-country ideals of human conduct.

SOURCE: George K. Turner, "The Puzzle of the Underworld," *McClure's* (July 1913).

Critical Thinking Questions

1. **What changes in law enforcement since 1913 have improved the situation described here?**
2. **What evidence is there that vestiges of the police culture described in 1913 still exist?**
3. **What changes would you suggest to make policing more professional than it now is?**

Summary

THE OUTER LIMITS OF LAW ENFORCEMENT

- Police engage in selective enforcement, meaning that not all laws are fully enforced.
- Various factors that might affect police discretion have been investigated, but the results are not conclusive.
- Although many calls have been made for a specific policy to govern police decision-making, there are no clear guidelines for developing such a policy.
- According to the sociolegal theory of police discretion, it is necessary to specify the types of situations in which police have wide discretion to act. Only then can a policy to guide all police decision-making be developed.

THE POLICE PERSONALITY

- Niederhoffer found that the degree of cynicism experienced by an officer is determined by age and length of experience on the job. Other studies have found that police cynicism has several dimensions, but they leave unanswered the question of whether police work is the only source of police cynicism.
- According to Skolnick, the perceived danger of the police officer's job, together with frequent challenges to his or her authority and a perceived lack of public support, results in police solidarity and isolation from others.
- Research findings have disproved the predisposition hypothesis, which states that the police personality is a product of previously existing traits.
- Authoritarian attitudes are more likely to be found in officers without a college education who have been on the job a long time. Officers with less education have also been found to be more dogmatic than those with higher levels of education.

WHEN POLICE MAKE BAD DECISIONS

- There are three forms of police corruption: nonfeasance (failure to perform a legal duty), misfeasance (failure to perform a legal duty in a proper manner), and malfeasance (commission of an illegal act).
- Some explanations of corruption focus on individual "rotten apples" while others focus on "the barrel"—the whole department. Most experts reject individual explanations and suggest that there is a deviant police subculture or that corruption results from secrecy within departments.
- Still other explanations look to external factors such as laws that are difficult to enforce or a weak local government.
- Preventing corruption depends on careful identification of its causes.

POLICE PERFORMANCE

- Various measures of police response to crime have been used, but most problems stem from the fact that the police are primarily reactive and are unable to spend unlimited time on unsolved cases.
- These problems can be overcome by using the number of arrests that result in prosecutions as an indicator of police performance.
- Police spend a great deal of time on noncriminal matters. Some of those matters could be handled by specialized agencies such as New Zealand's Traffic Control Corps, allowing the police to devote more time to law enforcement.

Key Terms

selective enforcement
cynicism
anomie
authoritarian
dogmatism
nonfeasance
misfeasance
malfeasance
police corruption

Questions for Review and Discussion

1. What is meant by selective enforcement?
2. Why is it difficult to formulate a clear policy to guide police decision-making?
3. What are the key findings of research on police cynicism?
4. What two factors were identified by Skolnick as leading to the development of the police personality?
5. Why has the predisposition hypothesis been discredited as an explanation of the formation of the police personality?
6. In what way does college education influence authoritarianism in police officers?
7. How do police officers' attitudes affect their performance?
8. What are the three forms of police corruption? Give an example of each.
9. What are the three main types of explanations of police corruption?
10. What can be done to prevent police corruption?
11. What numerical measure is the best indicator of police performance in crime control?
12. What can be done to relieve police of noncriminal tasks so that they can devote more time to crime control?

Notes

[1]Warren Cohen, "The Feds Make a Cop Drug Bust," *U.S. News & World Report* (February 2, 1998), p. 36; Kevin Johnson, "42 Law Officers Arrested in Sting," *USA Today* (January 22, 1998), p. 3.

[2]Joseph Goldstein, "Police Discretion Not to Invoke the Criminal Process: Low-Visibility Decisions in the Administration of Justice," *Yale Law Journal,* vol. 69 (1960), p. 543.

[3]Ibid., p. 580.

[4]David L. Carter and Louis A. Radelet, *The Police in the Community,* 6th ed. (Upper Saddle River, NJ: Prentice Hall, 1999), p. 73.

[5]Nathan Goldman, *The Differential Selection of Juvenile Offenders for Court Appearance* (Hackensack, NJ: National Council on Crime & Delinquency, 1963).

[6]Irving Piliavin and Scott Briar, "Police Encounters with Juveniles," *American Sociological Review,* vol. 70 (September 1964), pp. 206–14.

[7]Robert M. Terry, "Discrimination in the Handling of Juvenile Offenders by Social Control Agencies," *Journal of Research in Crime & Delinquency,* vol. 4 (1967), pp. 218–30.

[8]Donald J. Black and Albert J. Reiss, "Police Control of Juveniles," *American Sociological Review,* vol. 35 (1970), pp. 63–77.

[9]Richard J. Lundman, Richard E. Sykes, and John P. Clark, "Police Control of Juveniles: A Replication," *Journal of Research in Crime & Delinquency,* vol. 15 (1978), pp. 74–91.

[10]David A. Klinger, "More on Demeanor and Arrest in Dade County," *Criminology,* vol. 34 (February 1996), pp. 61–82; Robert E. Worden and Robin L. Shephard, "Demeanor, Crime, and Police Behavior: A Reexamination of the Police Services Study Data," *Criminology,* vol. 34 (February 1996), pp. 83–105.

[11]James O. Finckenauer, "Higher Education and Police Discretion," *Journal of Police Science and Administration,* vol. 3 (1975), pp. 450–65; Wayne R. LaFave, *Arrest: The Decision to Take a Suspect into Custody* (Boston: Little, Brown, 1965); James O. Finckenauer, "Some Factors in Police Discretion and Decisionmaking," *Journal of Criminal Justice,* vol. 4 (1976), pp. 29–46; Imogene L. Moyer, "Demeanor, Sex, and Race in Police Processing," *Journal of Criminal Justice,* vol. 9 (1981), pp. 235–46; Dennis D. Powell, "A Study of Police Discretion in Six Southern Cities," *Journal of Police Science and Administration,* vol. 17 (1990), pp. 1–7; Stephen D. Mastrofski, Robert E. Worden, and Jeffrey B. Snipes, "Law Enforcement in a Time of Community Policing," *Criminology,* vol. 33 (1995), pp. 539–63; David A. Klinger, Demeanor or Crime?: Why 'Hostile' Citizens are More Likely to be Arrested," *Criminology,* vol. 32 (1994), pp. 475–93; Richard J. Lundman, "Demeanor or Crime?: The Midwest Police-Citizen Encounters Study," *Criminology,* vol. 32 (1994), pp. 631–56.

[12]President's Commission on Law Enforcement and Administration of Justice, *Task Force Report on Police* (Washington, D.C.: U.S. Government Printing Office, 1967), p. 22.

[13]President's Commission on Law Enforcement and Administration of Justice, *The Challenge of Crime in a Free Society* (Washington, D.C.: U.S. Government Printing Office, 1967), p. 103.

[14]National Advisory Commission on Criminal Justice Standards and Goals, *Report on Police* (Washington, D.C.: U.S. Government Printing Office, 1973), p. 21.

[15]American Bar Association, *The Urban Police Function* (Gaithersburg, MD: International Association of Chiefs of Police, 1974), p. 8.

[16]President's Commission on Law Enforcement and Administration of Justice, *The Challenge of Crime in a Free Society,* p. 271.

[17]Richard E. Sykes, James E. Fox, and John P. Clark, "A Socio-Legal Theory of Police Discretion," in A. Niederhoffer and A. Blumberg, eds., *The Ambivalent Force,* 2nd ed. (Hinsdale, IL: Dryden Press, 1976), pp. 171–83.

[18]George Autunes and Eric J. Scott, "Calling the Cops: Police Telephone Operators and Citizen Calls for Service," *Journal of Criminal Justice,* vol. 9 (1981), pp. 165–80; Elaine Cumming, Ian Cumming, and Laura Edell, "Policeman, Philosopher, Guide, and Friend," *Social Problems,* vol. 12 (1965), pp. 197–205.

[19]Sykes, Fox, and Clark, p. 179.

[20]David A. Klinger, "Negotiating Order in Patrol Work: An Ecological Theory of Police Response to Deviance," *Criminology,* vol. 35 (May 1997), pp. 277–306.

[21]Don M. Gottfredson, Leslie T. Wilkins, and Peter B. Hoffman, *Guidelines for Parole and Sentencing Policy: A Policy Control Method* (Lexington, MA: Lexington Books, 1978).

[22]James Q. Wilson, *Varieties of Police Behavior* (Cambridge, MA: Harvard University Press, 1968).

[23]Independent Commission on the Los Angeles Police Department, *Report of the Independent Commission on the Los Angeles Police Department* (1991).

[24]Robert C. Davis and Bruce G. Taylor, "A Proactive Response to Family Violence: The Results of a Randomized Experiment," *Criminology,* vol. 35 (May 1997), pp. 307–33.

[25]Roy R. Roberg and Jack Kuykendall, *Police Organization and Management: Behavior, Theory, and Process* (Pacific Grove, CA: Brooks/Cole, 1990), p. 41.

[26]Douglas W. Perez, *The Paradoxes of Police Work* (Incline Village, NV: Copperhouse Publishing, 1997).

[27]Arthur Niederhoffer, *Behind the Shield: The Police in Urban Society* (Garden City, NY: Anchor Books, 1967), p. 101.

[28]G. Marie Wilt and James D. Bannon, "Cynicism or Realism: A Critique of Niederhoffer's Research into Police Attitudes," *Journal of Police Science and Administration,* vol. 4 (March 1976), p. 40.

[29]Robert M. Regoli, An Empirical Assessment of Niederhoffer's Police Cynicism Scale," *Journal of Criminal Justice,* vol. 4 (1976), pp. 231–41.

[30]Robert M. Regoli and Eric D. Poole, "Measurement of Police Cynicism: A Factor Scaling Approach," *Journal of Criminal Justice,* vol. 7 (1979), pp. 37–51.

[31]Robert M. Regoli, Eric D. Poole, and John D. Hewitt, "Refining Police Cynicism Theory: An Empirical Assessment, Evaluation, and Implications," in D. M. Peterson, ed., *Police Work: Strategies and Outcomes in Law Enforcement* (Beverly Hills, CA: Sage Publications, 1979), pp. 59–68; John P. Crank, Robert G. Culbertson, Eric D. Poole, and Robert M. Regoli, "The Measurement of Cynicism Among Police Chiefs," *Journal of Criminal Justice,* vol. 15 (1987), pp. 37–48; Robert H. Langworthy, "Police Cynicism: What We Know from the Niederhoffer Scale," *Journal of Criminal Justice,* vol. 15 (1987), pp. 17–35.

[32]Niederhoffer, pp. 107–8.

[33]Jerome H. Skolnick, *Justice Without Trial: Law Enforcement in Democratic Society,* 3rd ed. (New York: Macmillan, 1994), p. 46.

[34]Francis T. Cullen, Bruce G. Link, Lawrence F. Travis, and Terrence Lemming, "Paradox in Policing: A Note on Perceptions of Danger," *Journal of Police Science and Administration,* vol. 11 (December 1983), pp. 457–62.

[35]Skolnick, p. 54.

[36]Richard S. Bennett and Theodore Greenstein, "The Police Personality: A Test of the Predispositional Model," *Journal of Police Science and Administration,* vol. 3 (1975), pp. 439–45.

[37]Milton Rokeach, *The Nature of Human Values* (New York: The Free Press, 1973).

[38]Bennett and Greenstein, p. 444.

[39]Raymond Cochrane and Anthony J. P. Butler, "The Values of Police Officers, Recruits, and Civilians in England," *Journal of Police Science and Administration,* vol. 8 (June 1980), pp. 205–11.

[40]S. J. Saxe and M. Reiser, "A Comparison of Three Police Applicant Groups Using the MMPI," *Journal of Police Science and Administration,* vol. 4 (December 1976), pp. 419–25; L. S. Schoenfeld, J. C. Kobos, and I. R. Phinney, "Screening Police Applicants: A Study of Reliability with the MMPI," *Psychological Reports,* vol. 47 (1980), pp. 419–25; Edward E. Johnson, "Psychological Tests Used in Assessing a Sample of Police and Fire Fighter Candidates," *Journal of Police Science and Administration,* vol. 11 (December 1983), pp. 430–3; Jack Aylward, "Psychological Testing and Police Selection," *Journal of Police Science and Administration,* vol. 3 (Spring 1975), pp. 201–10.

[41]Bruce N. Carpenter and Susan M. Raza, "Personality Characteristics of Police Applicants: Comparisons Across Subgroups and with Other Populations," *Journal of Police Science and Administration,* vol. 15 (March 1987), pp. 10–17; Joseph Putti, Samuel Aryee, and Tan Seck Kang, "Personal Values of Recruits and Officers in a Law Enforcement Agency: An Exploratory Study," *Journal of Police Science and Administration,* vol. 16 (1988), pp. 249–54; Stephen B. Perrott and Donald M. Taylor, "Attitudinal Differences Between Police Constables and Their Supervisors," *Criminal Justice & Behavior,* vol. 22 (September 1995), pp. 326–39; Jennifer M. Brown and Elizabeth A. Campbell, *Stress and Policing* (New York: John Wiley & Sons, 1994).

[42]David Lester, "Why Do People Become Police Officers?: A Study of Reasons and Their Predictions of Success," *Journal of Police Science and Administration,* vol. 11 (June 1983), pp. 170–4; Deirdre Hiatt and George E. Hargrave, "Predicting Job Performance Problems with Psychological Screening," *Journal of Police Science and Administration,* vol. 16 (1988), pp. 122–5; Joyce I. McQuilkin, Vickey L. Russell, Alan G. Frost, and Wayne R. Faust, "Psychological Test Validity for Selecting Law Enforcement Officer," *Journal of Police Science and Administration,* vol. 17 (1990), pp. 289–94.

[43]Beth Sanders, Thomas Hughes, and Robert Langworthy, "Police Office Recruitment and Selection: A Survey of Major Police Departments in the U.S.," *Police Forum,* vol. 5 (October 1995), pp. 1–4; Philip Ash, Karen B. Slora, and Cynthia F. Britton, "Police Agency Selection Practices," *Journal of Police Science and Administration,* vol. 17 (1990), pp. 258–69.

[44]Matt L. Rodriguez, "Increasing Importance of Higher Education in Police Human Resource Development Programs," *CJ The Americas,* vol. 8 (April–May 1995), pp. 1–9.

[45]Alexander B. Smith, Bernard Locke, and William F. Walker, "Authoritarianism in College and Non-College Oriented Police," *Journal of Criminal Law, Criminology, and Police Science,* vol. 58 (Spring 1967), pp. 128–32.

[46]Alexander B. Smith, Bernard Locke, and William F. Walker, "Authoritarianism in Police College Students and Non-Police College Students," *Journal of Criminal Law, Criminology, and Police Science,* vol. 59 (Fall 1968), pp. 440–3.

[47]Alexander B. Smith, Bernard Locke, and Abe Fenster, "Authoritarianism in Policemen Who are College Graduates and Non-College Police," *Journal of Criminal Law, Criminology, and Police Science,* vol. 61 (Summer 1969), pp. 313–5.

[48]A. F. Dalley, "University vs. Non-University Graduated Policemen: A Study of Police Attitudes," *Journal of Police Science and Administration,* vol. 3 (December 1975), pp. 458–68.

[49]Milton Rokeach, *The Open and Closed Mind* (New York: Basic Books, 1960).

[50]Roy R. Roberg, "An Analysis of the Relationship Among Higher Education, Belief Systems, and Job Performance of Patrol Officers," *Journal of Police Science and Administration,* vol. 6 (September 1978), pp. 336–44.

[51]Bruce W. Topp and Frederic A. Powell, "A Short-Form Dogmatism Scale for Use in Field Studies," *Social Forces,* vol. 44 (December 1965), pp. 211–14.

[52]George Pugh, "The California Psychological Inventory and Police Selection," *Journal of Police Science and Administration,* vol. 13 (June 1985), pp. 172–7.

[53]Elizabeth J. Shusman, Robin E. Inwald, and Hilary Knatz, "A Cross-Validation Study of Police Recruit Performance as Predicted by the IPI and MMPI," *Journal of Police Science and Administration,* vol. 15 (June 1987), pp. 162–8; Gerald Gruber, "The Police Applicant Test: A Predictive Validity Study," *Journal of Police Science and Administration,* vol. 14 (June 1986), pp. 121–9; G. Milkovich and W. Glueck, *Personnel/Human Resource Management* (Plano,TX: Business Publications, 1985); George E. Hargrave and Deidre Hiatt, "Law Enforcement Selection with the Interview, MMPI, and CPI: A Study of Reliability and Validity," *Journal of Police Science and Administration,* vol. 15 (June 1987), pp. 110–17; Anthony R. Moriarty and Mark W.

Field, *Police Officer Selection* (Springfield, IL: Charles C Thomas, 1994). See also Mary Ann Wycoff and Timothy N. Oettmeier, *Evaluating Patrol Office Performance Under Community Policing* (Washington, D.C.: National Institute of Justice, 1994); Joseph E. Talley and Lisa D. Hinz, *Performance Prediction of Public Safety and Law Enforcement Personnel* (Springfield, IL: Charles C Thomas, 1990).

[54]Mark Pogrebin and Burton Atkins, "Probable Causes for Police Corruption: Some Theories," *Journal of Criminal Justice*, vol. 4 (1976), pp. 9–16; Samuel Walker, *The Police in America* (New York: McGraw-Hill, 1983).

[55]Herman Goldstein, *Policing in a Free Society* (Cambridge, MA: Ballinger, 1977); Virgil Peterson, "The Chicago Police Scandals," *Atlantic* (October 1960), pp. 58–64; Howard S. Cohen and Michael Feldberg, *Power and Restraint: The Moral Dimension of Police Work* (New York: Praeger, 1991); Edwin J. Delattre, *Character & Cops: Ethics in Policing*, 3rd ed. (Washington, D.C.: AEI Press, 1996); Steve Herbert, "Morality in Law Enforcement: Chasing 'Bad Guys' with the Los Angeles Police Department," *Law & Society Review*, vol. 30 (1996), pp. 799–817.

[56]Gordon Witkin, "When the Bad Guys are Cops," *Newsweek* (September 11, 1995), pp. 20–2; Mike McAlary, *Good Cop Bad Cop* (New York: Pocket Books, 1994).

[57]Walker, p. 181.

[58]Witkin, pp. 20–2; Tom Morganthau, "Why Good Cops Go Bad," *Newsweek* (December 19, 1994), p. 34.

[59]Knapp Commission, *Report on Police Corruption* (New York: George Braziller, 1972), p. 6.

[60]John Kleinig, *The Ethics of Policing* (New York: Cambridge University Press, 1996).

[61]Witkin, p. 22.

[62]William A. Westley, *Violence and the Police* (Cambridge, MA: MIT Press, 1970).

[63]Albert J. Reiss, *Police and the Public* (New Haven: Yale University Press, 1971); J. Roebuck and T. Barker, "A Typology of Police Corruption," *Social Problems*, vol. 21 (1974), pp. 423–7; E. Stoddard, "The Informal Code of Police Deviancy: Group Approach to Blue Coat Crime," *Journal of Criminal Law, Criminology, and Police Science*, vol. 59 (1968), pp. 201–13; Report of the Commission on Police Integrity (Chicago, 1997).

[64]Pennsylvania Crime Commission, *Report on Police Corruption and the Quality of Law Enforcement in Philadelphia* (St. Davids: Pennsylvania Crime Commission, 1974).

[65]Morganthau, p. 34.

[66]William Chambliss and R. Seidman, *Law, Order, and Power* (Reading, MA: Addison-Wesley, 1971), p. 490.

[67]Lawrence W. Sherman, *Scandal and Reform: Controlling Police Corruption* (Berkeley: University of California Press, 1978), p. 35.

[68]John A. Gardiner, *The Politics of Corruption: Organized Crime in an American City* (New York: Russell Sage, 1970); Chambliss and Seidman, *Law, Order, and Power;* Knapp Commission, *Report on Police Corruption.*

[69]Dirk Johnson, "Popular Detective will Head Chicago Police," *The New York Times* (February 19, 1998), p. 2.

[70]B. Drummond Ayres, Jr., "Former New York Official to Lead Philadelphia Police," *The New York Times* (February 19, 1998), p. 16.

[71]Knapp Commission, p. 68.

[72]Ibid., p. 18.

[73]Edward A. Malloy, *The Ethics of Law Enforcement and Criminal Punishment* (Lanham, MD: University Press of America, 1982), p. 45.

[74]Marianne W. Zawitz, ed., *Report to the Nation on Crime and Justice*, 2nd ed. (Washington, D.C.: Bureau of Justice Statistics, 1988).

[75]Peter Greenwood, Jan M. Chaiken, and Joan Petersilia, *The Criminal Investigation Process* (Lexington, MA: Lexington Books, 1977); John E. Eck, *Solving Crimes: The Investigation of Burglary and Robbery* (Washington, D.C.: Police Executive Research Forum, 1983).

[76]Jacob Perez, *Tracking Offenders* (Washington, D.C.: Bureau of Justice Statistics, 1991).

[77]George Autunes and Eric J. Scott, "Calling the Cops: Police Telephone Operators and Citizen Calls for Service," *Journal of Criminal Justice,* vol. 9 (1981); David H. Bayley, *Police for the Future* (New York: Oxford University Press, 1994), Chap. 2; Elaine Cumming, Ian Cumming, and Laura Edell, "Policemen as Philosopher, Guide and Friend," *Social Problems,* vol. 12 (1965).

[78]Norval Morris and Gordon Hawkins, *Letter to the President on Crime Control* (Chicago: University of Chicago Press, 1977).

[79]William Spelman and John E. Eck, *Problem-Oriented Policing* (Washington, D.C.: National Institute of Justice, 1987).

[80]Lorraine Green Mazerolle and William Terrill, "Problem-Oriented Policing in Public Housing: Identifying the Distribution of Problem Places," *Policing: An International Journal of Police Strategies and Management,* vol. 20 (1997), pp. 235–55; Richard H. Ward, "On the Cutting Edge: Policing Research Shows Changes," *Criminal Justice: The Americas,* vol. 1 (August–September 1988), p. 1.

[81]Vergil L. Williams and Raymond O. Sumrall, "Productivity Measures in the Criminal Investigation Function," *Journal of Criminal Justice,* vol. 10 (1982); David H. Bayley, *Police for the Future* (New York: Oxford University Press, 1994); Peter B. Bloch and James Bell, *Managing Investigations: The Rochester System* (Washington, D.C.: The Police Foundation, 1976).

For Further Reading

Edwin J. Delattre, *Character & Cops: Ethics in Policing,* 3rd ed. (Washington, D.C.: AEI Press, 1996).

Harvey Rachlin, *The Making of a Cop* (New York: Pocket Books, 1991).

Wesley G. Skogan and Susan M. Martnett, *Community Policing: Chicago Style* (New York: Oxford University Press, 1997).

chapter nine

Police and the Rule of Law

They that can give up essential liberty to obtain a little temporary safety deserve neither liberty nor safety.

BENJAMIN FRANKLIN
(1706–1790)

Baltimore police officers obtained a warrant to search the apartment of Lawrence McWebb for marijuana and drug paraphernalia. The warrant stated that McWebb's was the only apartment on the third floor, but in fact there were two apartments. During their search of McWebb's apartment, the officers entered the other apartment, believing that it was part of McWebb's dwelling. They found narcotics only in the second apartment, which was occupied by Harold Garrison. Garrison was charged with narcotics possession despite the fact that police had probable cause and a warrant to search only McWebb's apartment.[1]

CHAPTER OUTLINE

TABLE 9.1

Bill of Rights Provisions Relating to Police

AMENDMENT	GUARANTEE
Fourth	Protection against unreasonable searches and seizures
Fourth	No warrants but upon probable cause
Fifth	Shall not be compelled to be a witness against oneself
Fifth and Fourteenth	Life, liberty, and property shall not be deprived without due process of law
Eighth	Cruel and unusual punishments shall not be inflicted

Was this a lawful search of Garrison's apartment? Should the evidence found in his apartment be used against him? These questions lie at the heart of the conflict between an individual's right to privacy and the government's interest in apprehending criminals. The answers may be found in interpretations of the provisions and principles set forth in the United States Constitution more than two hundred years ago. This chapter reviews principles from the Constitution as they apply to police actions that affect the liberty of citizens.

Procedural Law

Procedural law is a very important part of the criminal justice process because it specifies how people accused of crimes will be treated. Like substantive law, the provisions of criminal procedure are guided by the principles of the United States Constitution. The Bill of Rights—the first ten amendments to the Constitution—details many of the requirements for adjudication, such as arrests, warrants, searches, trials, lawyers, punishment, and other important aspects of criminal procedure. The purpose of the Bill of Rights is to protect the individual citizen against arbitrary use of power by the government (Table 9.1).

Although the Bill of Rights was added to the Constitution more than two hundred years ago, it had little impact on the administration of justice until the 1960s. This situation existed because the majority of all criminal law is state law, while the Constitution is a federal document. For much of the nation's history the Bill of Rights was interpreted as protecting citizens against mistreatment by the federal government, rather than by state or local governments. After the Civil War, however, the Fourteenth Amendment was added to the Constitution. It states that

> **No State shall make or enforce any law which shall abridge the privileges or immunities of citizens of the United States; nor shall any State deprive any person of life, liberty, or property, without due process of law; nor deny any person within its jurisdiction the equal protection of the laws.**

Most people have read the Fourteenth Amendment to mean that the Bill of Rights applies to the states, but it was not until the 1960s that the U.S. Supreme Court interpreted it in this way. The important clause in this amendment is "due process of law," which means that individuals cannot be denied their rights as citizens without adjudication according to law. A number of Supreme Court decisions during the last thirty-five years illustrate the importance of due process in the American system of criminal justice.

The Fourth Amendment

Perhaps the most intrusive authority possessed by police is their ability to search citizens and their belongings and to seize their possessions. When a suspect is arrested, a search is often conducted. Questions often arise regarding the scope of the authority to search, its limits, and the circumstances in which a search may or may not be appropriate.

When these questions are raised in a particular case, they inevitably refer back to a single source: the Fourth Amendment to the Constitution. This amendment provides the guidelines and underlying principles for all law and policy regarding search and seizures by police:

> **The right of people to be secure in their persons, houses, papers, and effects, against unreasonable searches and seizures, shall not be violated, and no warrants shall issue but upon probable cause, supported by oath or affirmation, and particularly describing the place to be searched, and the persons or things to be seized.**

Individuals thus are protected against searches and seizures conducted without a warrant specifying "probable cause." This provision goes back to the nation's early years, when fear of an oppressive government was high. Indeed, this was an important factor in the American Revolution. The ability of British soldiers to enter homes in America and seize property at will played a significant role in the Colonists' movement toward independence. Without the protection of the Fourth Amendment, government agents could conduct searches in an arbitrary fashion. The Fourth Amendment created a standard—probable cause—by which the privacy of individuals would be protected.

Probable cause has been interpreted to mean a reasonable link between a specific person and a particular crime, given the "totality of circumstances."[2] It is a lower standard of proof than that required to convict at trial (i.e., proof beyond a reasonable doubt), but it is higher than the standard required to frisk a suspect (i.e., reasonable suspicion). If police have evidence that establishes probable cause, they write it in a sworn statement (i.e., statement supported by "oath or affirmation"). When a judge signs this statement, it becomes a **warrant.** Issuance of a warrant indicates that the judge agrees with the officer's assessment of the evidence. It also means that there is little chance of the evidence being thrown out of court at a later date, since the judge approved the warrant *before* the search.

probable cause
The legal threshold required to arrest and search an individual; a reasonable link between a specific person and a particular crime.

warrant
A sworn statement by police that attests to the existence of probable cause in a given case; it is signed by a judge who agrees with the officer's assessment of the facts.

As explained in Chapter 6, the U.S. Supreme Court interprets the meaning of the Constitution in a given case. The Supreme Court's decisions are significant because its rulings become law everywhere in the United States. As the scenario at the beginning of the chapter suggests, in some situations the authority of the police to search a suspect and seize property is unclear. The Supreme Court has attempted to provide guidelines for applying the provisions of the Fourth Amendment in circumstances too numerous to be anticipated by laws that must be general in nature.

Frisks versus Searches

For many years the police, the courts, and the public have been uncertain about the scope of a police officer's authority to stop a suspect when there are no grounds for arrest. Although it is common practice for officers to stop and question citizens, until about thirty years ago it was not clear whether the police actually had this right and, if they did, what its limits were.

The case that established the legal authority and limits for a "stop and frisk" was *Terry v. Ohio.*[3] The case involved a Cleveland police officer who had been a

The Fourth Amendment to the Constitution provides the underlying principles that guide all law and policy regarding stops, searches, and seizures by the police.

plainclothes detective for thirty-five years and had patrolled a certain section of the downtown area for shoplifters and pickpockets for nearly thirty years.

The officer saw three men repeatedly walk slowly past a store window and suspected that they were "casing" the store for a robbery. He identified himself as a police officer and proceeded to ask them several questions, to which they "mumbled something" in response. The officer then grabbed one of the men, turned him around, and "patted him down." He felt something in the man's left breast pocket and removed it; it was a .38-caliber revolver. He proceeded to pat down the outer garments of the other men and found another pistol on one of them. The men were charged with carrying concealed weapons in violation of the law.

In court, the men claimed that the officer had no probable cause to search them. Therefore, the search was illegal and the guns should not be admitted as evidence against them. On appeal, the U.S. Supreme Court agreed that the police officer did not have probable cause to conduct a search, but the gun possession charge was allowed to stand.

frisk
A patting-down of the outer clothing of a suspect based on reasonable suspicion, designed to protect a police officer from attack with a weapon while an inquiry is being made.

search
An exploratory inspection of a person or property based on probable cause of law violation.

The Court distinguished between a "stop" and an "arrest" and between a "frisk" and a "search." A **frisk** was defined as a patting-down of outer clothing, whereas a **search** is an exploratory search for evidence. The Court held that a frisk is essential to the proper performance of a police officer's investigative duties, for without it "the answer to the police officer may be a bullet, and a loaded pistol discovered during the frisk is admissible [as evidence]." As a result, the two men were convicted of illegally carrying concealed weapons. The Court concluded that the experienced officer's observations were "enough to make it quite reasonable to fear that they were armed; and nothing in their response to his hailing them, identifying himself as a police officer, and asking their names served to dispel that reasonable belief." The officer's actions were not "the product of a volatile or inventive imagination, or undertaken simply as an act of harassment; the record evidences the tempered act of a policeman who in the course of an investigation had to make a quick decision as to how to protect himself and others from possible danger, and took limited steps to do so."

According to the Supreme Court, frisks are limited to a search for weapons that may pose an immediate threat to the officer's safety. The Court concluded that cases such as these must be decided on the basis of their own facts, but generally, police officers who observe unusual conduct that leads them to conclude that criminal activity may be afoot, and that the persons involved may be armed and dangerous, are entitled to conduct "a carefully limited search of the outer clothing of such persons in an attempt to discover weapons" that might be used to assault them. Such a frisk was held to be reasonable under the Fourth Amendment, and any weapons seized may be introduced in evidence.

The decision in *Terry v. Ohio* lowered the threshold required for police to take action against a suspect. Before 1968, police could search only if they had probable cause. After *Terry,* police could conduct a frisk of a person's outer clothing to search for weapons if they had only "reasonable suspicion." **Reasonable suspicion** is a lower standard of evidence than probable cause, and therefore the scope of the search permitted is less intrusive.[4]

reasonable suspicion
A situation in which a police officer has good reason to believe that criminal activity may be occurring; this permits a brief investigative inquiry of the suspect.

The "reasonable suspicion" threshold was criticized within the Supreme Court itself. Probable cause is part of the Constitution and has a long history. The reasonable suspicion concept was invented in 1968, and it is less clear how it should be defined and applied. The dissenting justices argued that, "To give the police greater power than a magistrate is to take a long step down the totalitarian path." They noted that probable cause is determined by a judge when he or she signs a warrant or evaluates an arrest in court. Reasonable suspicion, they argued, gives police a judicial function in that it allows them to act against someone without probable cause. The Justices feared that a police state could result if police are given too much power.

The Supreme Court's statement in *Terry* that each case of this kind must be "decided on its own facts" opened the door for other cases to be appealed on questions such as: How long can a stop continue? What facts comprise "reasonable suspicion"? Can an automobile be "frisked"?

STOP AND FRISK OF AUTOMOBILES Fifteen years after *Terry,* the Supreme Court ruled on whether "stop and frisk" could be applied to automobiles. After stopping a driver for speeding and reckless driving, police noticed a hunting knife on the floor of the car. The officers subjected the suspect to a patdown search but found no weapons. One of the officers then shone his flashlight into the car and saw something protruding from under the armrest on the front seat. He lifted the armrest and saw an open pouch that contained what looked like marijuana. The suspect was arrested and the car impounded; a later search found more marijuana in the trunk.

The Supreme Court had previously held that police may order people out of a car during a stop for a traffic violation, and may frisk those persons for weapons if there is a reasonable belief that they are armed and dangerous.[5] Acting on an informant's tip, police can also reach into a car and pull a gun from the driver's waistband even when the gun was not seen from outside the car. The Court believed that police should have this power because of the hazards they face in roadside encounters.[6]

Relying on these precedents, the Court held in *Michigan v. Long* that the limited search of a car for concealed weapons is permissible if the officer has a rea-

The U.S. Supreme Court has interpreted the Fourth Amendment to allow police to stop automobiles and frisk individuals based on a "reasonable suspicion" standard.

sonable belief, based on specific facts, that the suspect is dangerous and may gain immediate control of weapons.[7] If the officer finds contraband other than weapons during this limited search, he or she "clearly cannot be required to ignore the contraband, and the Fourth Amendment does not require its suppression in such circumstances."

Citing the facts of this case (it was a late hour in a rural area; Long was speeding, swerved into a ditch, appeared to be drunk, and did not immediately answer the officers' questions), the Court noted that "Long was not frisked until the officers observed that there was a large knife in the interior of the car into which Long was about to re-enter." Regarding the search, the Court concluded that it was restricted to areas to which Long would have access and that could contain a weapon. This decision gives police the authority to search a car without probable cause, as long as they possess a "reasonable belief" that the occupant is armed.

In another type of "automobile frisk," two New York City police officers saw a man speeding in a car with a cracked windshield. The officers stopped him, and he left the car and approached one of the officers. The other officer opened the car door to look for the vehicle identification number (VIN), which is located on the doorjamb of older cars. When he did not find the number, the officer reached into the car to move papers on the dashboard to see if the VIN was located there. As he did so, he saw the handle of a gun protruding from underneath the driver's seat. He seized the gun and arrested the suspect.

The New York State Court of Appeals excluded the gun from evidence, holding that there was no reason to search a car that was stopped for traffic violations. The U.S. Supreme Court reversed the ruling, noting the important role of the VIN in the regulation of automobiles and stating that "there was no reasonable expectation of privacy in the VIN." The justices also noted that the officers had seen the defendant commit two traffic violations, so they may have had reason to be concerned for their safety.[8]

Stop and frisk is a common police practice. A 1996 survey asked citizens if they had been suspects in a police encounter in the past year. An estimated 4.4 million people reported having been questioned by police as possible suspects.

Of this group, 740,000 (17 percent) have been patted-down by police.[9] The results of these encounters are summarized in Figure 9.1. About 30 percent of those who were patted-down by police were handcuffed, and nearly 40 percent of the encounters resulted in force being use or threatened. The need for appropriate legal guidelines for the conduct of stop and frisks is critical, given their widespread use as a police investigative tool.

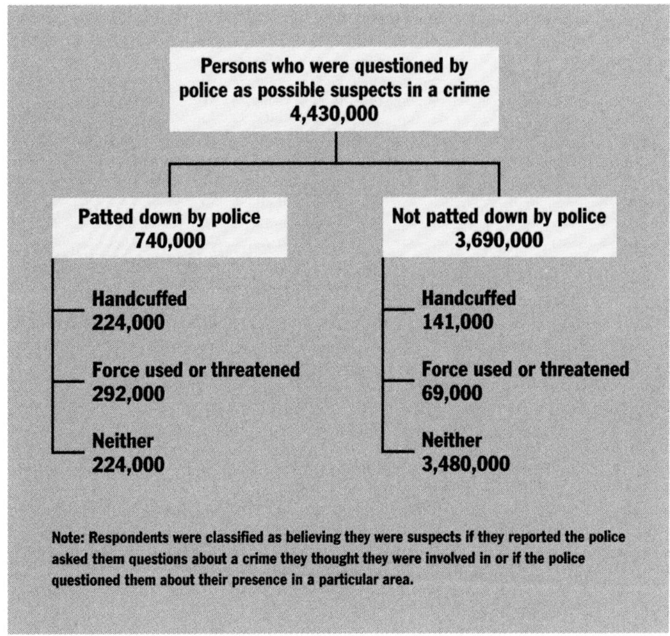

FIGURE 9.1
Prevalence of frisks by police

SOURCE: Lawrence A. Greenfeld, Patrick A. Langan, and Steven K. Smith, *Police Use of Force: Collection of National Data* (Washington, D.C.: Bureau of Justice Statistics, 1997).

THE LIMITS OF STOP AND FRISK The Supreme Court is still wrestling with the question of limits on "frisks" for weapons. In *Florida v. Royer* the Court held that police had gone beyond the limits of an investigatory stop when a suspect who matched the profile of a "drug courier" was asked to accompany police to a small room for questioning. The police did not indicate that he was free to go, even though they did not have probable cause to arrest him.[10] In *United States v. Place*, the Court held that detention of a traveler's luggage is allowed under *Terry* and that detection by a trained narcotics dog is not a search under the Fourth Amendment; however, detaining luggage for ninety minutes is unreasonable under the Fourth Amendment.[11]

These cases point to the difference between a stop for purposes of further investigation and a "seizure." Seizure of property occurs when there is some meaningful interference with the individual's possession of that property.[12] In a 1997 case, police moved a bag from the overhead compartment on a bus to the seat to allow a drug-sniffing dog to smell it. It took a short time to accomplish this and it did not impair the owner's access to the bag, making the stop reasonable under the Fourth Amendment.[13] The Supreme Court has held that a 20-minute investigatory stop, conducted pursuant to the guidelines set forth in *Terry* without unnecessary delay, is reasonable under the Fourth Amendment.[14] Therefore, physical movement of property does not constitute a seizure, although keeping it from the owner for an extended period, or destroying it, does.[15]

In 1993, the U.S. Supreme Court held in *Minnesota v. Dickerson* that a frisk that goes beyond a pat-down search is not permissible because of its limited purpose and scope. In this case an officer felt a small lump in a suspect's pocket, which the officer then examined with his fingers and determined to be cocaine wrapped in cellophane. The Court held that once the officer concluded that the lump was not a weapon, the continued examination constituted a search without probable cause. It was disallowed because it was unrelated to the purpose of the frisk: to protect an officer's safety.[16]

A common point in all these cases is that the line between a frisk and search becomes blurred when the potential danger to the officer is not evident and the search goes beyond a pat-down for weapons. The next sections explain the legal rules that have been developed to regulate full exploratory searches for evidence.

The Exclusionary Rule: *Mapp v. Ohio*

The landmark case that applied the provisions of the Fourth Amendment to searches was decided in 1961. Three Cleveland police officers had arrived at Dolree Mapp's residence in response to information that a person wanted in connection with a recent bombing was hiding there. The officers knocked on the door and demanded entrance. After telephoning her attorney, Mapp refused to admit them without a search warrant. The police left the scene.

Three hours later the police (now numbering at least seven officers) again tried to enter Mapp's house. An officer knocked on the door, and when Mapp did not answer immediately, they forced one of the doors and gained entry. Mapp, who was halfway down the stairs, demanded to see a warrant. One of the officers held up a piece of paper that he claimed was a warrant. Mapp grabbed the paper and stuffed it into her blouse. After a struggle the police recovered the piece of paper and handcuffed Mapp because she had been "belligerent" during their recovery of the "warrant."

Meanwhile Mapp's attorney arrived, but the officers would not let him enter the house or see his client. Mapp was then forcibly taken upstairs to her bedroom, where the police searched a dresser, closet, and suitcases. They also searched several other rooms, including the basement, where they found a trunk that contained obscene materials. Mapp was arrested for possession of those materials.

At trial, it was discovered that the police had never obtained a search warrant for the search of Mapp's residence. Nevertheless, Mapp was convicted of illegal possession of obscene materials. The conviction was appealed, and the case eventually reached U.S. Supreme Court.

The Supreme Court had ruled in 1914 that illegally seized evidence could not be used in federal prosecutions.[17] In 1949, the Court held that the Fourth Amendment protected individuals from both state and federal actions, but it did not extend the exclusionary rule to the states.[18] It was not until the *Mapp* case that the Supreme Court held that since the Fourth Amendment's right of privacy is enforceable in states through the due process clause of the Fourteenth Amendment, the exclusionary rule applies to both state and federal prosecutions. A growing interest in civil rights combined with concern for due process in actions by police resulted in this decision.[19] The *Mapp* decision therefore applied the exclusionary rule to the States. The **exclusionary rule** holds that illegally seized evidence must be excluded from trials. Searches conducted without probable cause (or without a warrant where one is required) are illegal. Mapp's conviction in Ohio was reversed on the ground that her residence had been searched in violation of the Fourth Amendment. The Court explained the ruling as follows:

exclusionary rule
A legal principle holding that illegally seized evidence must be excluded from use in trials.

> **Our holding that the exclusionary rule is an essential part of both the Fourth and Fourteenth Amendments is not only the logical dictate of prior cases, but it also makes very good sense. There is no war between the Constitution and common sense. Presently, a federal prosecutor may make no use of evidence illegally seized, but a State's attorney across the street may, although he supposedly is operating under the enforceable provisions of the same Amendment. Thus the State, by admitting evidence unlawfully seized, served to encourage the disobedience to the Federal Constitution which it is bound to uphold.**

Police may seize contraband with or without a warrant, provided they have probable cause and meet the standards set forth by the Supreme Court.

In the *Mapp* case the police officers were required to possess a warrant in order to search Mapp's house legally. Because they did not have a warrant, their presence in her home was illegal under the Fourth Amendment. Therefore, any evidence they found was obtained illegally. No matter what the officers found in Mapp's house, it could not be used in court because their presence there was illegal.

Searches with Warrants

The ruling in *Mapp v. Ohio* remained intact for nearly twenty-five years. During the 1980s, however, a trend toward greater conservatism in American society resulted in a change in the composition of the U.S. Supreme Court through presidential appointments of new justices. The result was a shift in the balance between the individual's interest in privacy and the government's interest in apprehending criminals. Although the exclusionary rule still exists, the number of exceptions to the rule has grown.

The first and most significant exception was created in 1984 in the case of *U.S. v. Leon.*[20] Police in Burbank, California, initiated a drug-trafficking investigation of Leon on the basis of a tip from a confidential informant. After conducting a surveillance of his activities, the police applied for a warrant to search three residences and Leon's cars for drug-related items. The warrant application was reviewed by several deputy district attorneys, and the warrant was signed by a state court judge. The searches found large quantities of drugs, and Leon was indicted for federal drug offenses.

Leon filed a motion to suppress the evidence because the search warrant was invalid—the surveillance of Leon did not actually produce the probable cause needed for a warrant or search. A federal judge granted the motion to exclude the evidence from trial on the ground that the original affidavit was insufficient to establish probable cause. The court recognized that the police officers had acted in good faith, but the search and seizure violated the exclusionary rule and the evidence therefore could not be used at trial.

contemporary issues

Does the Exclusionary Rule Handcuff the Police?

Since the U.S. Supreme Court's decision in *Mapp v. Ohio* nearly forty years ago, there has been much debate over the desirability of the exclusionary rule. Supporters of the rule maintain that the *Mapp* case illustrates how citizens need the rule if they are to be protected against police misconduct. Without the protection provided by the exclusionary rule, there would be nothing to prevent police from making illegal searches in the hope of finding some kind of incriminating evidence. The potential for harassment of citizens would be great. On the other hand, opponents argue that the exclusionary rule makes it possible for criminals to go free. Just because a search is conducted illegally, all the evidence found is excluded from use at trial. Such a sweeping rule may "handcuff" the police in obtaining evidence against criminals.

This debate has prompted a number of empirical investigations to determine the relative merits of the exclusionary rule. Are many suspects released because searches are found to be illegal? Is there any evidence that the exclusionary rule deters police from making illegal searches?

Sheldon Krantz and his colleagues examined the effect of the exclusionary rule in 512 drug and gambling cases in Boston. They found that the rule was used to exclude evidence in only 2 percent of those cases.[A] The U.S. General Accounting Office assessed the impact of the exclusionary rule in federal court. A review of 2,804 cases found that the rule had been invoked successfully in only 1.3 percent of the cases.[B]

The National Institute of Justice conducted an exhaustive study of the exclusionary rule in California. The researchers examined felony cases over a three-year period and found that once a case reached trial, fewer than one half of 1 percent (0.4 percent) were dismissed because of the exclusionary rule, although there was some variation by jurisdiction and by type of crime.[C] Thus, as one expert noted, the impact of the exclusionary rule on violent crime was "infinitesimal."[D] Nevertheless, the rule appeared to have some effect in drug cases, in which police rarely have a complainant whom they can rely on to establish probable cause for search and arrest. More than 70 percent of all cases that were rejected because of search and seizure problems were drug cases. Although the exclusionary rule affects only drug cases in any significant way, the overall impact of the rule, based on empirical investigations conducted in different parts of the country, is that it results in dismissal of fewer than 2 percent of all cases. It is difficult to maintain, therefore, that the exclusionary rule significantly impairs the ability of police to apprehend criminals.

Nevertheless, the debate has continued. Despite evidence to the contrary, opponents of the exclusionary rule still argue that it significantly affects arrests. Interestingly, the Supreme Court anticipated this debate in the *Mapp* case:

> **Because [the Fourth Amendment protection of privacy] is enforceable in the same manner and to like effect as other basic rights secured by the Due Process Clause, we can no longer permit it to be revocable at the whim of any police officer who, in the name of law enforcement itself, chooses to suspend its enjoyment. Our decision, founded on reason and truth, gives to the individual no more than that which the Constitution guarantees him, to the police officer no less than that which honest law enforcement is entitled, and, to the courts, that judicial integrity so necessary in the true administration of justice.**

The Court argued that the exclusionary rule guarantees a constitutional right to individuals and grants to the government only the authority it needs if it is to carry out police functions with integrity.

The composition of the Supreme Court has changed greatly in the decades since the *Mapp* decision. The result has been a shift in views regarding the proper balance between the right to privacy and the government's desire to apprehend crime suspects. The Court has moved from enforcing a clear exclusionary rule to creating a number of exceptions in which searches may be made without a warrant or without a valid warrant under a variety of circumstances.

NOTES

[A] Sheldon Krantz, Bernard Gilman, Charles G. Benda, Carol Rogoff Hallstrom, and Gail J. Nadworny, *Police Policymaking* (Lexington, MA: Lexington Books, 1979).

[B] U.S. Comptroller General, *The Impact of the Exclusionary Rule on Federal Criminal Prosecutions* (Washington, D.C.: U.S. Government Printing Office, 1979).

[C] Robert W. Burkhart, Shirley Melnicoe, Annelsely K. Schmidt, Linda J. McKay, and Cheryl Martorana, *The Effects of the Exclusionary Rule: A Study in California* (Washington, D.C.: National Institute of Justice, 1982).

[D] James J. Fyfe, "The NIJ Study of the Exclusionary Rule," *Criminal Law Bulletin*, vol. 19 (May–June 1983), pp. 253–60.

The case eventually reached the U.S. Supreme Court, which established a **"good faith" exception** to the exclusionary rule. The Court based the exception on three arguments. First, it held that "the exclusionary rule is designed to deter police misconduct rather than to punish the errors of judges." The rationale was that it did not seem fair to penalize police for the error of the state court judge in signing the defective warrant. Second, the Court argued that such an exception would not defeat the purpose of the exclusionary rule. Police acted reasonably in this case, and the intent of the exclusionary rule is not to deter reasonable police conduct. Finally, the Court said that the exclusionary rule still applies if police act improperly. That is, if police mislead a judge by using false information in a warrant application, the exclusionary rule would apply and any evidence seized on the basis of that warrant would be excluded at trial.

"good faith" exception
A rule stating that illegally seized evidence may be introduced at trial even if police conducted a search based on a search warrant that later turned out to be invalid owing to a judge's error.

Three Justices dissented from this decision, and their opinion captures the essence of the ongoing debate over exceptions to the exclusionary rule. The dissent argued that an exception to the exclusionary rule for judicial errors begs the question. How can a search and seizure be "reasonable" (because it was conducted in good faith) but "unreasonable" (because probable cause did not exist) at the same time? The Fourth Amendment does not discuss intent on the part of the police. Either probable cause exists or it does not, making a search either reasonable or unlawful.

The dissent also believed that such an exception would encourage police and judicial misconduct. "Even when the police know their warrant application is probably insufficient, they retain an incentive to submit it to a magistrate, on the chance that he might take the bait." The good faith exception "implicitly tells magistrates that they need not take much care in reviewing warrant applications, since their mistakes will from now on have virtually no consequence: If their decision to issue a warrant was correct, the evidence will be admitted; if their decision was incorrect but the police relied in good faith on the warrant, the evidence will also be admitted."

Even though the majority of the Justices conceded that the exclusionary rule may deter police misconduct, the Court concluded that the Fourth Amendment does not prohibit the use of evidence obtained on the basis of a search warrant that was later found to be invalid. However, the good faith exception does not apply when a judge is found to have "abandoned his detached or neutral role" or when police officers are "dishonest or reckless in preparing their affidavit" or did not reasonably believe that probable cause existed.[21]

In a number of subsequent cases the Court attempted to refine the limits of this exception and create new exceptions for searches and seizures under law. For example, the Court held that inmates have no reasonable expectation of privacy in a prison cell and therefore are not protected by the Fourth Amendment.[22] Neither probable cause nor warrants are required to search inmates or seize their property. In a case involving the search of a high school student's purse, the Court held that the Fourth Amendment applies to school officials but that probable cause is not needed for searching students because of a "substantial need" to maintain order in schools.[23] In the case summarized at the beginning of the chapter, police mistakenly searched the wrong apartment without probable cause and found drugs there. The evidence was allowed at trial because the police error was an "honest mistake." Once again the Supreme Court relied on the intent of the officers, rather than on the presence of probable cause, thereby creating what has been called the "honest mistake" exception.[24]

Since then there have been additional cases in which the U.S. Supreme Court has permitted the use of evidence seized by police that would have been excluded under the rule applied in *Mapp v. Ohio.* The Court's reliance on reasonable police activity, rather than on strict application of the probable cause standard of the Fourth Amendment, characterizes the changing rules of search and seizure during the last twenty-five years. The result has been an expansion of the authority of government officials to search citizens.

Searches without Warrants

The ability of police officers to search suspects without a warrant emerged from the need for police to protect themselves and prevent the destruction of evidence in street encounters. It is not practical, timely, or safe to obtain a warrant to search someone who has just been arrested for a violent crime. As a result, the U.S. Supreme Court has interpreted the Fourth Amendment phrase "no warrants shall issue but upon probable cause" to mean that warrants must be based on probable cause, *not* that a warrant is the only way to establish probable cause. The Fourth Amendment as a whole has been interpreted to mean that citizens are protected against "unreasonable searches and seizures." Therefore, police are permitted to search without a warrant under circumstances in which it is "reasonable" to do so.

Over the years the Supreme Court has delineated five general types of situations in which searches can reasonably be conducted without a warrant. These exceptions to the warrant requirement include searches incident to a lawful arrest, with voluntary consent, of evidence in plain view, of automobiles and their contents, and of open fields and abandoned property.

SEARCHES INCIDENT TO A LAWFUL ARREST The case that established the authority of police to conduct a warrantless search incident to a lawful arrest was *Chimel v. California.*[25] Police officers went to Chimel's home with a warrant to arrest him for the burglary of a coin shop. Chimel was not home, but his wife allowed the police to enter and wait for his return. When Chimel arrived, the police showed him the warrant placing him under arrest and proceeded to search the house. They found the coins that he was suspected of stealing and used them as evidence to convict him of burglary. On appeal, the Supreme Court overturned the conviction on the ground that the search of Chimel's entire house was unreasonable under the Fourth Amendment.

> **When an arrest is made, it is reasonable for the arresting officer to search the person arrested in order to remove any weapons the [suspect] might seek to use in order to resist arrest or effect his escape. Otherwise, the officer's safety might well be endangered, and the arrest itself frustrated. In addition, it is entirely reasonable for the arresting officer to search for and seize any evidence on the arrestee's person in order to prevent its concealment or destruction. And**

> **the area into which an arrestee might reach in order to grab a weapon or evidentiary items must, of course, be governed by a like rule. A gun on a table or in a drawer in front of one who is arrested can be as dangerous to the arresting officer as one concealed in the clothing of the person arrested. There is ample justification, therefore, for a search of the arrestee's person and the area "within his immediate control"—construing that phrase to mean the area from within which he might gain possession of a weapon or destructible evidence.**

The Court's finding in *Chimel* allows for a search incident to a lawful arrest for two purposes: to remove weapons and to seize evidence that might be concealed or destroyed. In order to accomplish these purposes, the police officer is permitted to search the arrestee and the area "within his immediate control."

The difficulty of defining the area "within his immediate control" has resulted in a large number of cases that have attempted to delimit this area in different situations. Most of these cases have involved automobiles. A significant case of this kind was *U.S. v. Robinson,*[26] in which a Washington, D.C., police officer saw Robinson driving a Cadillac down the street. The officer recalled that he had stopped Robinson just four days earlier and knew that his license had been revoked. The officer pulled him over and placed him under arrest for driving without a license and for obtaining a permit under false pretenses.

In accordance with department policy, the officer conducted a search of the driver that consisted of a patting-down of his outer clothing. The officer felt something in Robinson's left breast pocket. In the words of the officer, "As I felt the package I could feel objects in the package but I couldn't tell what they were. . . . I knew they weren't cigarettes." The police officer opened the crumpled cigarette package and found fourteen gelatin capsules of white powder that proved to be heroin. The heroin seized from Robinson was admitted into evidence and resulted in his conviction for narcotics possession.

Robinson argued on appeal that the search and seizure were unlawful. If the officer did not believe that the object he felt in Robinson's shirt was a weapon of any sort, it should not have been seized. This reasoning was based on the Supreme Court's ruling in *Chimel,* which allowed for such warrantless searches only in order to protect the officer from injury or prevent the destruction of evidence of crime. Because the offense was only a traffic infraction, the search could not be justified on the ground that the "fruits of the crime" might be destroyed.

The Supreme Court rejected these arguments and held that "a search incident to the arrest requires no additional justification" beyond the probable cause required for the arrest. When a lawful arrest occurs and the suspect is taken into custody, therefore, "a full search of the person is not only an exception to the warrant requirement of the Fourth Amendment, but is also a 'reasonable' search under that Amendment."

The decision in *Robinson* clearly expands the scope of allowable searches incident to arrest. The dissenting opinion captures the nature of the debate within the Court, which continues today. The question is whether the decision allows police to use traffic arrests as a pretext to conduct a search. "Would it be reasonable for a police officer, because of the possibility that a razor blade was hidden somewhere in the wallet, to open it, remove all the contents, and examine each item carefully?" the dissent asked. "Or suppose a lawyer lawfully arrested for a traffic violation is found to have a sealed envelope on his person. Would it be permissible for the arresting officer to tear open the envelope in order to make sure that it did not contain a clandestine weapon—perhaps a pin or a razor blade?"

Since the decision in *Robinson,* the Supreme Court has heard a number of other cases concerning the limits of a search incident to a lawful arrest. In *U.S. v. Chadwick*[27] the Court ruled that police may seize luggage and other personal property incident to arrest, but once they gain control of it, they cannot search it without a warrant unless there is danger to the officer or a chance that evidence will be destroyed. In *New York v. Belton*[28] the Court modified its earlier decisions in both *Robinson* and *Chadwick* by allowing police to search the passenger compartment of an automobile as well as the contents of any containers there immediately following an arrest. In 1996, the Supreme Court summarized its current position in *Pennsylvania v. Labron,* stating that when there is probable cause that a car holds contraband and the car can move, the police have authority to search it without a warrant. These cases clearly have reduced the restrictions on police in conducting searches incident to an arrest.

SEARCHES WITH VOLUNTARY CONSENT Another well-established exception to the warrant requirement occurs when a search is made with the consent of the suspect. The primary concern here is the voluntariness of the consent. In the landmark case of *Schneckloth v. Bustamonte,*[29] a police officer in Sunnyvale, California, stopped a car that had only one working headlight. Six men were in the car. The driver could not produce a driver's license. The other two men in the front seat were Joe Alcala and Robert Bustamonte. Alcala explained that the car belonged to his brother. When the officer asked if he could search the car, Alcala said, "Sure, go ahead." The officer asked if the trunk could be opened, and it was opened for him. Under the rear seat the officer found three checks that had previously been reported stolen from a car wash. The checks were used as evidence in a trial in which Alcala and Bustamonte were convicted of possessing stolen checks. The question on appeal was whether the consent to search given by Alcala was truly voluntary.

The distinction between a voluntary and involuntary search is extremely important in this case, since the police did not have probable cause to conduct a search without consent. As was noted earlier, the decision in *Robinson* held that searches incident to arrest are allowable only after a "custodial" arrest in which a suspect may be taken into custody (rather than for minor offenses for which summonses are given). In the *Bustamonte* case, the car was stopped because of a burned-out headlight, for which the police could only issue a summons; they had no option to make a custodial arrest. Therefore, no search could take place unless consent was given.

The U.S. Supreme Court held that the search was consensual and that the evidence discovered was therefore admissible in court. It held that consent must be "voluntarily given, and not the result of duress or coercion, express or implied," and that voluntariness is "to be determined from all the circumstances." Significantly, the Court held that the suspect does not have to be told of his or her right to refuse the police request to search.

Again, there was a dissenting opinion in this case. It stated that "an individual can effectively waive [the Fourth Amendment protection against searches and seizures] even though he is totally ignorant of the fact that, in the absence of his consent, such invasions of his privacy would be constitutionally prohibited. It wholly escapes me how our citizens can meaningfully be said to have waived something as precious as a constitutional guarantee without ever being aware of its existence." In sum, are not searches in these circumstances taking advantage of a person's ignorance of his or her rights under the Constitution? As the dissent asserted, "The capacity to choose necessarily depends upon knowledge that there is a choice to be made."

The Supreme Court's decision in *Schneckloth* was followed by several others that further refined the scope of consent searches. In *U.S. v. Matlock*, the Court held that permission to search can be given by "a third party who possess[es] common authority over or other significant relationship to the premises or effects sought to be inspected."[30] The Court defined "common authority" as persons who have joint access or control of the property to be searched. This allows co-occupants and landlords to consent to searches in dwellings that they share or rent to others. In *U.S. v. Watson*, the Court held that a consent to search is not automatically involuntary if the person giving consent is in custody or under arrest.[31] In *Florida v. Jimeno*, the Court held that permission granted to search a car extends to closed containers within the car.[32] The Court ruled in *Ohio v. Robinette* that people stopped for traffic violations do not have to be told they are free to go before their consent to search can be recognized as voluntary.[32a]

In sum, warrantless searches may be conducted with consent, provided that the consent is voluntary and the person giving consent has the capacity to do so. The scope of a consent search is, of course, limited to the exact meaning of the permission given or the consent statement (if written permission is provided).

PLAIN VIEW SEARCHES The right of police to search items without a warrant that are in "plain view" is another well-established exception to the warrant requirement. The nature of this exception was explained in the Supreme Court's decision in *Coolidge v. New Hampshire*.[33] The Court specified two conditions for a plain view search: The police officer's presence where the plain view search is made must be lawful, and the discovery must be inadvertent. If police have probable cause before the search, they must obtain a warrant.

The Court established clearly a third condition for plain view searches in *Texas v. Brown*.[34] It held that police do not have to be "absolutely certain" that evidence is incriminating before they make a plain view search. In this case, during a routine traffic stop a police officer seized an opaque green party balloon (which was knotted), together with several small vials, white powder, and empty balloons that were in the automobile. The Court held that the circumstances established probable cause for arrest for possession of an illegal substance, even though the officer was not certain that the balloon he had seized contained an illicit substance. The Court restated its position in a 1994 case in which it found that there is no need to obtain a warrant if an object's shape, characteristics, or other circumstances make its contents obvious.[35]

The evidence seized in a plain view search must be "open to view." If the evidence is hidden, police cannot claim that a search was conducted using the "plain view" exception to the warrant requirement. Nevertheless, in this case federal agents were found not to need a warrant before the test of a suspected drug because the package was first opened by a private individual rather than a police officer, revealing the presence of illegal narcotics. Therefore, since the package was not "searched" or "seized" by the government, the evidence was confiscated under the plain view doctrine.[36]

In still another variation of the "plain view" exception, police entered an apartment from which a bullet had been fired that had hit a man on the floor below. While searching for the weapon and the shooter, an officer noticed two sets of expensive stereo components that he suspected were stolen. The officer recorded their serial numbers (an action that required that the stereo components be moved) and telephoned them to headquarters. The turntable had apparently been stolen, and therefore the officer seized it and arrested the suspect. The U.S. Supreme Court found that recording the serial numbers was not a "seizure" under the Fourth Amendment because it "did not meaningfully interfere with the suspect's possessory interest." Nevertheless, the movement of the equipment to record the numbers "did constitute a search separate and apart from the [shooting incident]" that was the original purpose of the officer's presence in the apartment. The Court held that the "plain view" doctrine does not apply here because the officer lacked probable cause to believe that the stereo equipment was stolen.[37]

In 1990, in *Horton v. California*, the Court reversed itself, stating that inadvertent discovery of evidence is "not a necessary condition" of plain view searches, although it characterizes most searches of this kind.[38] In a 1995 case it held that a person has no reasonable expectation of privacy in the visible interior of his or her car, even if the interior is inspected by police with a flashlight from outside the car.[39] As in other types of searches with and without warrants, it can be seen that in recent years the Court has relaxed earlier restrictions and allowed police to search under a wider variety of circumstances.

SEARCHES OF AUTOMOBILES AND THEIR CONTENTS Perhaps no other area of constitutional law has drawn as much attention in recent years as searches by police conducted after they have stopped a car for a traffic violation. There have been a large number of cases involving warrantless searches of vehicles. These cases have centered on the justification for the traffic stop, the allowable scope of the search, and subsequent searches conducted once a car has been impounded by police. In this section several significant cases that illustrate the complexity of the law in this area are reviewed.

The so-called automobile exception to the warrant requirement was established in 1925 in the case of *Carroll v. United States*.[40] The defendants, George Carroll and John Kiro, were arrested and convicted of transporting sixty-eight quarts of whiskey and gin in an automobile in violation of the National Prohibition Act. They challenged their convictions on the ground that the search and seizure of the illicit liquor were conducted in violation of the Fourth Amendment. The defendants claimed that, because the search was made without a warrant, the evidence discovered in the search should be excluded. In ruling on the appeal, the Supreme Court clarified a legal point it had made in 1914, stating that once a person has been lawfully arrested, "whatever is found upon his person or in his control which it is unlawful for him to have and which may be used to prove the offense may be seized and held as evidence in the prosecution."[41]

In the case of *Chambers v. Maroney*[42] the Supreme Court expanded the power of police to search an automobile without a warrant. It held that police do not have to obtain a warrant to search a car that was stopped on a highway and has been impounded and taken off the street, provided that they have probable cause to search the car. The Court saw "no difference between on the one hand seizing and holding a car before presenting the probable cause issue to a magistrate and on the other hand carrying out an immediate search without a warrant." If probable causes exists, both searches are reasonable. In this case the Court eliminated one of the initial justifications for a warrantless search—that it is allowable only when it is not possible or timely to obtain a search warrant. It held that this is not a requirement for a warrantless search because the probable cause was as valid at the station house as it was on the highway. The Court reiterated this finding in *Michigan v. Thomas.*[43] It held that after police had found contraband in the glove compartment of Thomas's car they had probable cause to conduct a warrantless search of the entire car, even though both the car and its occupants were already in police custody. Therefore, a vehicle does not necessarily have to be "moving" or even capable of moving for a warrantless search to be lawful.

In recent years the scope of the automobile exception has been expanded further. The Supreme Court has held that a warrantless search of a car to make an inventory of its contents does not violate the Fourth Amendment, even though the car was impounded for parking violations.[44] In another case, the Court ruled that once a vehicle has been lawfully stopped, the officer may order the driver out of the vehicle in order to protect the officer's safety. This applies even to drivers stopped for a traffic violation.[45] In still another case, the Court held that once police had impounded a van (after the driver was stopped for being under the influence of alcohol) they were permitted to conduct an inventory search of the van's contents, including the contents of a closed backpack in which illegal drugs were found.[46]

The Supreme Court has placed a limit on police stops of motor vehicles that are pulled over for no reason. It held that an automobile cannot be stopped unless there is a "reasonable suspicion" that the occupants are violating traffic or criminal law. The Court believed that random automobile stops could lead to arbitrary or discriminatory law enforcement. However, it did not rule out the use of "roadblock" stops, because such stops do not permit discriminatory use of police authority.[47] Nevertheless, in a 1995 case a traffic stop based on an erroneous computer readout stating that the person was wanted by the police was upheld. A clerical error had caused the false report, and hence the traffic stop without probable cause.[48] However, criminal evidence was found in the vehicle. As in *U.S. v. Leon,* the Court held that exclusion of the evidence would penalize police for a clerical (or judge's) error, overlooking the fact that it is the suspect, not the police, who is penalized in these circumstances.

The next sequence of cases heard by the Supreme Court involved the scope of the search allowed *within* a legally stopped automobile. In *Arkansas v. Sanders* the Court held that police must obtain a warrant to search luggage inside a legally stopped and searched automobile.[49] Two years later the Court examined this issue again in a case in which two packages were found in a stopped vehicle "wrapped in green opaque plastic." The Court held that a closed piece of luggage may not be searched without a warrant, no matter where it was found, because the Fourth Amendment protects persons and their effects whether they are "personal" or "impersonal."[50]

In 1982, in *Ross v. United States,* the Supreme Court changed its position and made perhaps its most sweeping decision regarding searches during automobile stops.[51] Police had pulled over a car driven by Albert Ross, whose appearance matched an informant's description of a drug dealer. They searched Ross, and in the process they noticed a bullet on the car's front seat. They then searched the interior of the car and found a pistol in the glove compartment. Ross was arrested and handcuffed. An officer took his keys and opened the trunk, where he found a closed brown paper bag. He opened the bag and discovered a number of glassine bags containing a white powder. Ross's car was then taken to the police station and searched more thoroughly. A zippered red leather pouch was found in the trunk containing $3,200 in cash. The police laboratory later determined that the powder in the paper bag was heroin. No warrant was obtained for any of these searches or seizures.

The case was appealed to the Supreme Court, and in its decision the Court reversed its previous ruling in *Robbins v. California* and *Arkansas v. Sanders.* It held that "if probable cause justifies the search of a lawfully stopped vehicle, it justifies the search of every part of the vehicle and its contents that may conceal the object of the search." This decision justified the search in terms of where the probable cause might lead, rather than the type of package found by police.

A strongly worded dissenting opinion stated that the *Ross* decision made a police officer's opinion equivalent to that of a "neutral and detached" judge in determining probable cause. It argued that the decision gave higher priority to police expediency in conducting automobile searches than to protecting the private property of citizens. In the words of the dissenting justices,

> **This case will have profound implications for the privacy of citizens traveling in automobiles, as the Court well understands. . . . A closed paper bag, a tool box, a knapsack, a suitcase, and an attache case can alike be searched without the protection of a neutral magistrate, based only on the rarely disturbed decision of a police officer that he has probable cause to search for contraband in the vehicle. . . . A rule so broad that all citizens lose vital Fourth Amendment protection is no cause for celebration.**

In the years since the *Ross* decision, however, the Supreme Court has continued to expand the scope of automobile searches that may be conducted without a warrant. In 1991, in *California v. Acevedo,* the Court allowed a warrantless search of a container in a car with probable cause, even if there is no probable cause to search the car itself.[52] In a Florida case, the Court held that a search of a car without a warrant eight hours after the car had been impounded was lawful, noting that the justification for the warrantless search did not disappear after the car had been impounded.[53] In another case, the Court upheld a warrantless search of a car three days after its seizure, holding that there is no requirement that a warrantless search be conducted immediately after the seizure.[54] It is clear from these cases that since 1925, when the automobile exception to the warrant requirement was established, the allowable scope of such searches has been broadened significantly.

OPEN FIELDS AND ABANDONED PROPERTY The fifth exception to the warrant requirement allows for searches of "open fields." Both open fields and abandoned property have been found not to be protected by the Fourth Amendment. An issue that has been the subject of much debate is how to determine where property protected by the Fourth Amendment ends and "open fields" begin.

The open fields exception was first recognized in 1924 in the case of *Hester v. United States.*[55] Police officers suspected that liquor was being manufactured illegally at Hester's home. When they became aware of the presence of the officers, Hester and an associate fled across an open field, carrying bottles. An officer pursued the two men, who dropped their bottles when the officer fired his pistol. The bottles were recovered and were found to contain illegally distilled whiskey. Although the officers did not have a search warrant or an arrest warrant, the Supreme Court upheld the men's convictions, holding that "there was no seizure in the sense of the law when the officers examined the contents of each bottle after it had been abandoned."

Since this decision, the meaning of "houses" under the Fourth Amendment has been extended to include the grounds and buildings immediately surrounding a home. This area is known as the "curtilage" of a home. Therefore, the Fourth Amendment applies to homes and their curtilage, but not to open fields outside this area. There are no precise guidelines for determining where curtilage ends and open fields begin.

In a Kentucky case, narcotics officers ignored a "No Trespassing" sign and a locked gate and entered private property. They found marijuana being grown on the property more than a mile from the owner's house. The Supreme Court upheld the warrantless seizure of the marijuana, reasoning that open fields are not the setting for intimate activities that the Fourth Amendment is intended to protect against government interference or surveillance. Even though the officers' search constituted criminal trespass, the Court believed that property ownership is only one element in determining whether a reasonable expectation of privacy exists.[56] The dissenting Justices found this decision "startling" because the police had trespassed on clearly marked private property. They stated:

> **Neither a public telephone booth nor a conversation conducted therein can fairly be described as a person, house, paper, or effect; yet we have held that the Fourth Amendment forbids the police without a warrant to eavesdrop on such a conversation. Nor can it plausibly be argued that an office or commercial establishment is covered by the plain language of the Amendment; yet we have held that such premises are entitled to constitutional protection if they are marked in a fashion that alerts the public to the fact that they are private.**

These dissenters pointed out that the Court's decision made it difficult for police to decide how far curtilage extends.

More recent cases have further expanded the scope of open fields searches. In *California v. Ciraolo,* for example, police flew an airplane over private property at 1,000 feet in response to an anonymous tip that marijuana was being grown in the yard. Warrantless ground-level surveillance was not possible because two fences surrounded the property. The marijuana plants were easily identified by air and a search warrant was obtained on the basis of this identification, which was supported by a photograph taken from the air. The suspect was arrested and marijuana plants were seized. The Supreme Court upheld this search and seizure, holding that "the Fourth Amendment simply does not require the police traveling in the public airways at this altitude to obtain a warrant in order to observe what is visible to the naked eye."[57]

A similar finding was reached in a case in which Drug Enforcement Administration agents had crossed several fences to approach a barn about fifty yards away from a house whose owner was suspected of manufacturing narcotics. The police stopped at the locked gate to the barn and shone a flashlight inside; there they saw what they believed was a drug laboratory. The Supreme Court held that the area around the barn was not within the curtilage of the house. It was some distance away and did not lie within a fence surrounding the house; the barn was not being used as part of the house, and the livestock corral fences "did little to protect the barn areas from observation." Therefore, the search was held to be valid because the illegal material was observed from open fields. That is, "shining a flashlight into a protected area without probable cause to search the area is permissible."[58] Like many other recent decisions of federal courts, this ruling expanded the authority of police to conduct searches without judicial warrants.[59]

The Fifth Amendment

The Fourth Amendment, as we have seen, deals primarily with arrest, search, and seizure. After an arrest and search have been carried out, however, the police have the authority to interrogate the arrested person. Interrogations are not specifically mentioned in the Constitution, but the limits of official interrogations are implied in the Fifth Amendment:

> **No person shall be held to answer for a capital, or otherwise infamous crime, unless on a presentment or indictment of a Grand Jury, except in cases arising in the land or naval forces, or in the Militia, when in actual service in time of War or public danger; nor shall any person be subject for the same offense to be twice put in jeopardy of life or limb; nor shall be compelled in any criminal case to be a witness against himself, nor be deprived of life, liberty, or property, without due process of law; nor shall private property be taken for public use, without just compensation.**

The Fifth Amendment mentions interrogations only when it states that no person can be "compelled in any criminal case to be a witness against himself." The Supreme Court has determined "criminal case" to be any official government investigation of suspected criminal behavior.

The inclusion of this phrase in the Fifth Amendment was a reaction to the Court of the Star Chamber, which was established by Henry VII in 1487. Sedition and heresy trials were conducted in this court, which allowed for forced testimony. This inquisitional system resulted in confessions due to torture rather than guilt. It was not until the sixteenth century that England guaranteed individuals protection from forced testimony against themselves.

This history of arbitrary and malicious accusatory practices led the framers of the Constitution to include in the Fifth Amendment specific provisions for grand juries, protection against double jeopardy, and protection against self-

Media and Criminal Justice

THE STAR CHAMBER

The name of the 1983 film, *The Star Chamber,* comes from an English court in the mid-1600s that was composed primarily of lawyers and judges to supplement the regular common-law courts. Popular in its day, it was eventually abolished because in meting out arbitrary justice, it undermined the protections of democracy.

In the film, a modern-day star chamber is established by a group of judges who meet in a secretive, backroom court and reevaluate rape and murder cases that they have had to legally dismiss based on "technicalities." Like the cynical cops whose innocent blunders necessitate that the guilty go free, these judges are frustrated with the limits of the law.

In one case, the gun used in a crime is tossed by the perpetrator into a garbage can as he flees from police. The police see the gun go into the trash container, but have been trained in procedural law to know that the contents of the container are the property of the owner, and are thus protected from a warrantless search and seizure. Luckily, a sanitation truck is on its way up the street; the officers cleverly wait for the trash can to be routinely emptied into the city's garbage truck, and then remove the evidence from the garbage in the truck's rear trough. At the trial, the perpetrator's lawyer successfully argues that evidence from the search should be excluded, because the truck's scoop had not been lowered before the removal of the gun. The judge has no choice but to admit that the garbage in the trough had not been mixed with all the other garbage, thus constituting an illegal search of private property.

In another case, seasoned patrol officers find themselves pulling over a suspicious van, using a radio report of unpaid parking tickets on the license plate as their probable cause. Citing the phantom smell of marijuana smoke as their basis for searching the vehicle, they find the bloody sneaker of a recently missing child, and immediately arrest the van's occupants for the child's murder. In court, it is learned that the defendant's parking tickets were indeed paid on time, but that a backlog in computer data entry had caused the dispatcher to relay outdated information on the vehicle to the arresting officers. Once the basis for the pullover is excluded, the consequent fruits of the illegal search also have to be excluded.

These vignettes provide the basis for the movie's panel of judges who create their own star chamber. The participants believe that justice has been lost to the stacks of law books and case precedents to which they must adhere. To the judges, the legal system isn't working anymore, and it is up to them to make sure true justice prevails. They collectively rule that the accused they have set free in a court of law are indeed actually guilty, and dispatch professional hitmen to serve the interests of justice.

The Star Chamber does consider the ultimate question: What if the judges of the star chamber are wrong? In the end, the film allows that any system of justice in our complex society has flaws, but that due process is a necessary evil in balancing the costs.

MEDIA AND CRIMINAL JUSTICE QUESTION

Explain why you believe the two police searches described here are legal or illegal under current law.

incrimination. The Fifth Amendment has had its greatest impact on interrogations and confessions obtained by the police.

The *Miranda* Warning

The landmark case in which the United States Supreme Court applied the Fifth Amendment to specific police procedures was *Miranda v. Arizona.*[60] Ernesto Miranda was arrested at his home and taken to the Phoenix police station. A rape victim identified him as her assailant. He was then taken into a police interrogation room and questioned by two officers. (The layout of a typical interrogation room is shown in Figure 9.2.) Two hours later the officers emerged from the room

FIGURE 9.2

Layout of the interview room in the Denver Police Department

SOURCE: William A. Geller, *Videotaping Interrogations and Confessions* (Washington, D.C.: National Institute of Justice, 1993), p. 8.

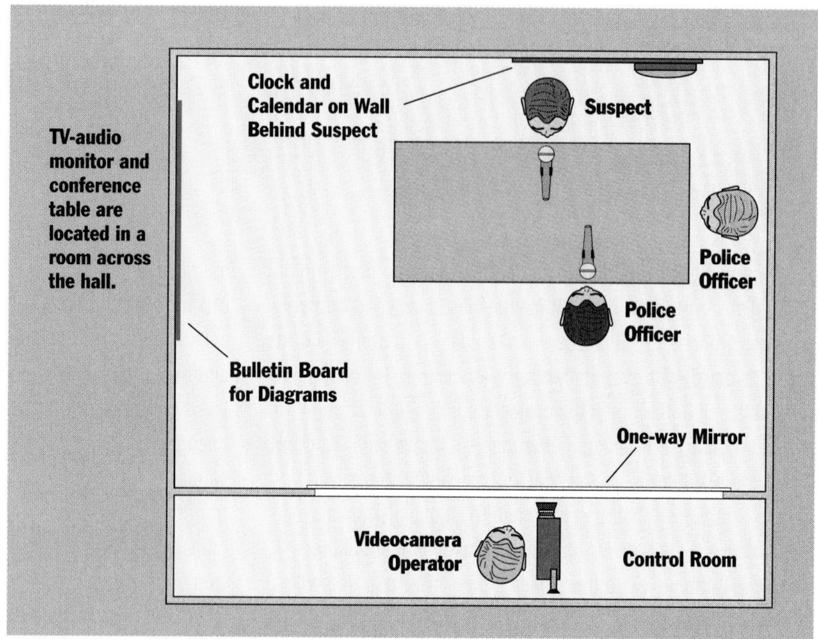

with a written confession signed by Miranda. A typed paragraph at the top of the confession said that it has been made voluntarily "with full knowledge of my legal rights, understanding any statement I make may be used against me."

At his trial, the officers admitted that Miranda had not been told that he had the right to have an attorney present during the interrogation. Nevertheless, the written confession was admitted into evidence. Miranda was found guilty of kidnapping and rape and was sentenced to twenty to thirty years in prison. He appealed his conviction, but the appeal was denied on the ground that he did not specifically request legal counsel at the interrogation. The case was finally appealed to the U.S. Supreme Court.

The Supreme Court took special notice of the typed paragraph at the top of Miranda's signed confession stating that it had been made "with full knowledge of my legal rights." As the Court noted, Miranda was uneducated, indigent, and "a seriously disturbed individual with pronounced sexual fantasies." Moreover, no one other than the police had been present during his interrogation. The Court believed that these circumstances cast doubt on whether the confession was truly voluntary.

> **The current practice of incommunicado interrogation is at odds with one of our nation's most cherished principles—that an individual may not be compelled to incriminate himself. Unless adequate protective devices are employed to dispel the compulsion inherent in custodial surroundings, no statement obtained from the defendant can truly be a product of free choice.**

Using this rationale, the Supreme Court overturned Miranda's conviction, stating that the confession was inadmissible as evidence. The Court held that "the mere fact that he signed a statement which contained a typed-in clause stating that he had 'full knowledge' of his 'legal rights' does not approach the knowing and intelligent waiver required to relinquish constitutional rights."

In order to ensure this protection from self-incrimination in future cases, the Supreme Court said that once a suspect is taken into custody, he or she must receive a five-point warning, known as the **Miranda warning:**

Miranda warning
A five-point warning derived from the case of *Miranda v. Arizona*. Its purpose is to provide fair notice to crime suspects of their basic constitutional rights.

- The suspect must be warned before any questioning that he or she has the right to remain silent.
- Any statements made by the person can be used in a court of law.
- The suspect has the right to the presence of an attorney.
- If the person cannot afford an attorney, one will be appointed before questioning begins.
- Opportunity to exercise these rights must be afforded to the suspect throughout the interrogation. After such warnings have been given, a person may knowingly and intelligently waive these rights and agree to answer questions or make a statement.

This warning is required when an individual is taken into custody and is subjected to questioning (for this is when the privilege against self-incrimination is jeopardized). Although the *Miranda* decision set specific guidelines for the conduct of police interrogations, it does not prohibit them in any way. The Court's only objective was to ensure fairness in nonvoluntary interrogations. As the Court observed, "There is no requirement that police stop a person who enters a police station and states that he wishes to confess a crime, or a person who calls the police to offer a confession or any other statement he desires to make. Volunteered statements of any kind are not barred by the Fifth Amendment and their admissibility [as evidence] is not affected by our holding today."

The *Miranda* decision ensures that those who are ignorant of the law will be given the same understanding of their constitutional protections as those who already understand their rights under the law. It added specific legal protections beyond the Court's decision two years earlier in *Escobedo v. Illinois*, which guaranteed a suspect in custody the right to an attorney when the investigation began to focus on him or her.[61] In that case the suspect was interrogated by police for fifteen hours, released, and rearrested eleven days later. Escobedo's attorney arrived at the police station for the second interrogation, but the police would not allow the attorney to see his client until the police had finished their questioning. It was during this second interrogation that Escobedo made incriminating statements. The Supreme Court reversed Escobedo's conviction, holding that he was

The purpose of the Miranda warning is to ensure that those who are ignorant of their rights under the Constitution have the same opportunities to defend themselves as those possessing such knowledge.

in custody as a suspect in a crime, was interrogated by police, and had requested to speak with his lawyer and was denied access. The Supreme Court's decision in *Miranda* two years after the *Escobedo* decision added that specific warnings should be required at police interrogations in order to deter this kind of police conduct.

The Erosion of *Miranda*

As with search and seizure cases, the emphasis shifted in court decisions of cases involving police interrogations during the 1980s and 1990s. Changing social views regarding the rights of suspects, corresponding with the appointment of more conservative Justices to the U.S. Supreme Court, have combined to chip away at the rules set forth by the Court during the 1960s.

In the 1980 case of *Rhode Island v. Innis,* a suspect in the robbery of a cab driver was captured by police and informed of his *Miranda* rights. The suspect indicated that he wanted to speak with a lawyer before talking to police. While en route to the police station with the suspect in the back seat, two of the officers engaged in a conversation about the missing gun. One of the officers stated that there were "a lot of handicapped children running around in this area" because a school for such children was located nearby, and "God forbid one of them might find a weapon with shells and they might hurt themselves." The suspect interrupted the conversation, stating that if they turned the car around he would show them where the gun was located "because of the kids in the area in the school." This case reached the Supreme Court, which was asked to determine whether the officers' conduct was the functional equivalent of interrogation.

The Supreme Court made it clear that the *Miranda* warnings apply during the "functional equivalent" of questioning, which consists of words or questions by police that are "reasonably likely to elicit an incriminating response from the suspect." This case is significant because it was the first time the Court addressed the meaning of interrogation under the *Miranda* rule.

The Court was divided in this case. The dissenting Justices argued that once a suspect asks for counsel, the choice to cut off questioning must be "scrupulously honored." They declared that the officers' appeal to the suspect's conscience was a "classic interrogation technique." Further, they concluded that if the officers' actions do not constitute the functional equivalent of interrogation, police will be "free to exert . . . pressure on him despite his request for counsel, so long as they are careful not to punctuate their statements with question marks."

The majority of the Justices did not agree with this view. Instead, they found that police "cannot be held accountable for the unforeseen results of their words or actions." They also found "nothing in the record to suggest that the officers were aware that the respondent was peculiarly susceptible to an appeal to his conscience." Finally, they found that the conversation in the police car "consisted of no more than a few off-hand remarks" and that the police did not carry on a "lengthy harangue" in the suspect's presence. These circumstances led the majority to conclude that the defendant had not been interrogated in a way that violated the *Miranda* rule. The Supreme Court concluded that in order for a violation of *Miranda* to take place, "It must also be established that a suspect's incriminating response was the product of words or actions on the part of the police that they should have known were reasonably likely to elicit an incriminating response."[62] This decision narrows the scope of the *Miranda* warning by applying it only to direct questioning by police or to situations in which their actions are "reasonably likely" to result in the suspect's self-incrimination. In a 1993 case, the U.S. Court of Appeals ruled that having a suspect point to the location of cocaine during a search of his residence was the functional equivalent of interrogation.[63]

THE PUBLIC SAFETY EXCEPTION In a landmark New York case, a woman approached two police officers on patrol and told them that she had just been raped. She described her assailant and said that he had just entered a nearby supermarket and was carrying a gun. While one of the officers radioed for assistance, the other entered the store and spotted a man named Benjamin Quarles, who matched the description of the assailant. The suspect spotted the officer and ran to the rear of the store as the officer pursued him with his gun drawn. The officer momentarily lost sight of the suspect but soon saw him again. He then ordered the suspect to stop and put his hands over his head. He frisked the suspect and discovered that he was wearing an empty shoulder holster. After handcuffing him, the officer asked him where the gun was. The suspect nodded toward some empty cartons and said, "The gun is over there." The officer retrieved the gun, arrested the suspect, and read him his *Miranda* rights.

The case reached the U.S. Supreme Court because the officer's first question to the handcuffed suspect was likely to be incriminating. If the suspect's statement, which gave the location of the gun, was obtained illegally (without benefit of the *Miranda* warning), it should be excluded from trial, as should the gun that was discovered as a result of the illegally obtained statement. A majority of the Justices held that "overriding considerations of public safety justify the officer's failure to provide *Miranda* warnings before he asked questions devoted to locating the abandoned weapon."[64] This decision created the **public safety exception** to the *Miranda* warning. The exception was justified on the ground that it would be allowed only in cases involving "questions reasonably prompted by a concern for public safety." The justices also believed that the cost of not finding the evidence in such cases is greater than the risk of compulsory self-incrimination. They reasoned that the exception would not pose a burden on police because the *Miranda* warning can be avoided only when there is a threat to the officer or the public.

public safety exception
A rule stating that police do not have to provide the *Miranda* warning to suspects when circumstances indicate public safety would be jeopardized.

In a sharply worded dissent, three Justices stated that at the time of the officer's question to Quarles, "there was no evidence that the interrogation was prompted by the arresting officers' concern for the public's safety." Because the incident took place after midnight, there were no customers or employees "wandering about the store in danger of coming across Quarles' discarded weapon." Second, they found that the "public safety" exception contains a "fundamental constitutional defect." An examination of the original Miranda case led them to conclude that "*Miranda* was not a decision about public safety; it was a decision about coerced confessions." A public safety exception does not reduce the degree of coercion in compelled statements. As a result, the public safety exception violates the Fifth Amendment because it allows coerced confessions to be used in court. Third, the dissenters believed that such an exception to the *Miranda* warning would impose a great burden on police who must determine the scope of this exception, resulting in many "hair-splitting" distinctions and uncertainty in the application of the law. This is because determining whether public safety is threatened would rely more on the subjective intentions of police officers than on objective facts.

THE LIMITS OF INTERROGATION Beginning in the 1980s, the Supreme Court decided many cases that provided additional exceptions to the *Miranda* rule. In *South Dakota v. Neville,* the Court held that it is not "fundamentally unfair" to use a defendant's refusal to take a blood-alcohol test as evidence of guilt. This refusal, if used as evidence, does not violate the protection against self-incrimination.[65] In *Oregon v. Bradshaw,* the Court held that after the accused makes a knowing and intelligent waiver of the right to counsel, his or her statements may be used as evidence if the accused initiates further conversation.[66] The Court found in another case that a probation officer seeking incriminating evidence is not required to give the *Miranda* warning to a probationer.[67] Further, roadside questioning of a motorist who was detained in a routine traffic stop was determined not to constitute a "custodial interrogation" for the purposes of *Miranda.*[68]

In *Oregon v. Elstad,* the Supreme Court ruled that the Fifth Amendment does not require the suppression of a confession made after a valid waiver of *Miranda* rights solely because the police had obtained an earlier voluntary, but unwarned, admission from the suspect.[69] In *Moran v. Burbine,* a suspect waived his right to an attorney while his sister contacted a lawyer, who called the police and told them not to interrogate the suspect before his arrival. The police questioned the suspect anyway and used his statements to obtain a conviction. Although the Supreme Court shared a "distaste for the deliberate misleading of [the attorney]," it held that the *Miranda* rule does not forbid police deception of an *attorney* because this has "no relevance at all to the degree of compulsion experienced by the defendant during interrogation," which is the purpose of the *Miranda* decision.[70] In a related case, police arrested a man for purchasing stolen firearms but questioned him about a murder. The Supreme Court held that "mere silence by law enforcement officials as to the subject matter of an interrogation is not 'trickery' sufficient to invalidate a suspect's waiver of *Miranda* rights." The constitutionality of the interrogation was upheld.[71]

Cases appealed during the 1990s generally have continued this trend. In *Illinois v. Perkins,* the use of jailhouse police informants who elicit incriminating statements from incarcerated suspects was found not to constitute a custodial interrogation and therefore did not violate the *Miranda* rule.[72] However, in 1990 the Supreme Court reaffirmed the principle it had set forth in *Escobedo,* that once a suspect invokes the right to counsel, police may not reinitiate their interrogation without a lawyer present.[73]

These cases characterize the direction of U.S. Supreme Court decisions in recent years. Despite the fact that empirical studies have found the *Miranda* decision to have little effect on police work, the Supreme Court has continually given police greater latitude to stray from the strict language of the *Miranda* finding. In

FUTURE ISSUES

An Appropriate Remedy for Police Misconduct?

Much of the controversy over improper police searches, interrogations, and use of force focuses on finding an appropriate remedy. Should police be criminally punished or civilly sued, have their cases thrown out of court, or suffer some other consequence if they are found to have engaged in misconduct?

Some argue that police officers should be punished as individuals for engaging in improper conduct in the course of their duties. In view of the extensive screening of police applicants, their training requirements, and the authority they hold over the liberty of other citizens, police should be held to a high standard of conduct. On the other hand, police are often asked to make quick decisions without knowing all the facts. Is it fair to punish them for decisions that are reasonable but incorrect?

Over the years court decisions have attempted to reach a middle ground. It has been held that government officials (including police) enjoy "qualified immunity" when performing discretionary functions on the job. This means that they are shielded from liability "if their conduct does not violate clearly established statutory or constitutional rights of which a reasonable person should have known."[A]

It has also been argued that the exclusionary rule is too permissive because it can allow a guilty person to go free, as in the *Miranda* case. Should police misconduct benefit the suspect? One alternative is to fine or suspend a police officer who makes improper decisions that a "reasonable" officer would not make under the same circumstances. This leads to the question of whether fines or suspension are appropriate or sufficient punishment for improper conduct.

In a majority of states, police officers who abuse their powers may be subject to "decertification proceedings" that strip them of the ability to work as police unless they are recertified at a later date.[B] This might serve as a greater deterrent to police misconduct, but it does not directly address the effects of past misconduct.

QUESTIONS

1. Would it be a good idea to allow new rules (such as the *Miranda* warning) enacted by the courts to apply only to *future* cases, rather than allowing a guilty person to go free?
2. If police officers were fined, suspended, or decertified for making certain kinds of improper decisions, how would such actions serve the interests of justice?

NOTES

[A] *Harlow v. Fitzgerald,* 457 U.S. 800 (1982).

[B] Roger Goldman and Steven Puro, "Decertification of Police: An Alternative to Traditional Remedies for Police Misconduct," *Hastings Constitutional Law Quarterly,* vol. 15 (1987), pp. 45–80; Steven Puro, Roger Goldman, and William C. Smith, "Police Decertification: Changing Patterns Among the States, 1985–1995," *Policing: An International Journal of Police Strategies & Management,* vol. 20 (1997), pp. 481–96.

doing so the Court has created a host of conditions and exceptions to the *Miranda* rule that create uncertainty in its application. Freedom from self-incrimination has been made secondary to the freedom of the government to search and question individuals suspected of crimes.

Uncertainty in the law and practice of confessions has caused many police departments to videotape interrogations and confessions. This is done in order to provide an objective record of the interrogation that can be referred to in responding to challenges from defense attorneys, and to reduce doubt about the voluntary nature of confessions. One study estimates that more than 60 percent of all large police agencies in the United States now videotape interrogations or confessions in at least some types of cases.[74] One impact of videotaping is that police agencies believe that their interrogations of suspects have improved since the videotaping began.

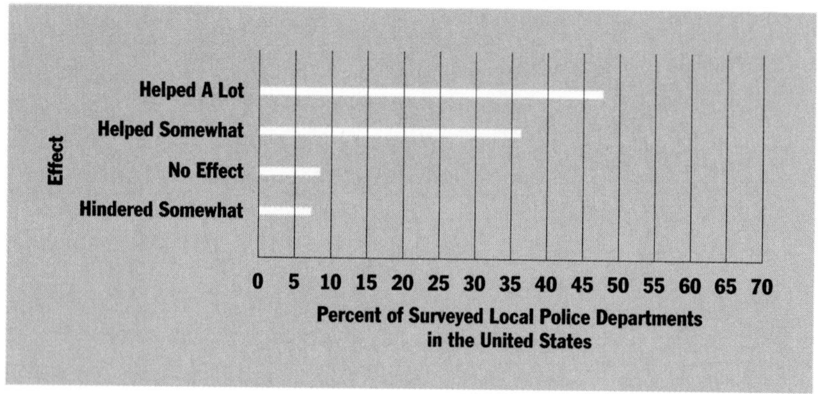

FIGURE 9.3

The effect of videotaping on the quality of police interrogations

SOURCE: William A. Geller, *Videotaping Interrogations and Confessions* (Washington, D.C.: National Institute of Justice, 1993), p. 5.

As Figure 9.3 illustrates, 85 percent of police departments surveyed believe that videotaping improves the quality of interrogations. This occurs because investigators are better prepared for interviews with suspects, knowing that their questioning will later be viewed by others. Also, monitoring by supervisors and use of videotapes in police training have encouraged greater diligence in the conduct of interrogations.

Use of Deadly Force

There is growing controversy about the legitimate use of force by police against citizens. When is the shooting of a suspect by police reasonable? When should the use of deadly force be prohibited? Do police discriminate in their use of force? In this section we examine the extent of police shootings, the nature of the victims, and the constitutionality of deadly force laws.

Legal Justification

The legal justification for police use of deadly force stems from English common law. Under common law an arresting officer could use deadly force to prevent the escape of a fleeing felon, but *not* to prevent the escape of a fleeing suspect who committed a misdemeanor. The reason for this distinction was that in the fifteenth century most felonies were punishable by death. Death could be imposed for the crimes of arson, murder, manslaughter, rape, robbery, burglary, sodomy, escape from prison, and larceny, among other offenses.

This common law "fleeing felon" rule was adopted in the United States. Since then, the number of crimes that are considered felonies has risen dramatically, while the use of capital punishment has dropped significantly. As a result, by the late nineteenth century the historical justification for the fleeing felon rule had disappeared.

The distinction between misdemeanors and felonies also is no longer obvious for many offenses. The difference between felony larceny and misdemeanor larceny, for instance, is the value of the property taken. A police officer operating under the fleeing felon rule cannot readily determine whether a larceny suspect has stolen enough property to be a fleeing felon rather than a fleeing misdemeanant.

Victims of Police Shootings

The National Center for Health Statistics collects information on "deaths by legal intervention," that is, civilian fatalities caused by police. During the 1950s, police were responsible for a total of 240 homicides in the nation as a whole. Between 1968 and 1976, this number increased to 342.[75] A 1991 survey of city police departments found that citizens were shot and killed at a rate of nearly one person for every 1,000 sworn officers.[76] It is believed, however, that homicides by police are underreported by 25 to 50 percent. In some cases medical authorities are inaccurate in determining the cause of death or deliberately omit mention of police involvement. Some deaths may be reported incorrectly because of ambiguity in the definitions of police homicides. Upon examination of death records from the California Department of Health over a seven-year period, Lawrence Sherman and Robert Langworthy found official records of 257 homicides by police. To check this figure, they asked the police departments themselves for the number of police homicides that had occurred in each jurisdiction. This yielded a total of 544 homicides for the same period. Thus, the actual number of civilian deaths caused by police shootings may be significantly higher than "official" statistics indicate.[77]

The Violent Crime Control and Law Enforcement Act of 1994 requires the Attorney General to obtain data on the use of excessive force by law enforcement officers. In order to gather this information, a national survey of citizens aged twelve and older was conducted during 1996. This survey made it possible for the first time to estimate the prevalence of the use of force in police–citizen encounters. The results indicate that nearly 21 percent (forty-five million) of people aged twelve and older had face-to-face contact with a police officer during 1996. An estimated 500,000 million people were handcuffed, hit, held, pushed, choked, threatened with a flashlight, restrained by a police dog, threatened or sprayed with a chemical or pepper spray, or threatened with a gun. About 60 percent of these individuals had aroused police suspicion according to their own admission.[78] Figure 9.4 summarizes these results.

It can be seen that about 1 in 5 citizens had contact with a police officer during 1996 and about 1 in 430 alleged that police threatened or used force against them. Future surveys will undoubtedly provide greater detail regarding these encounters and allow for the study of trends over time.

A primary objection to the use of deadly force by police is that they appear to shoot blacks significantly more often than whites, leading to charges of racial discrimination. A large number of investigations, conducted in many different cities, have found that blacks are shot by police two to four times more often than one would expect, given their proportion of the city's population.[79] Arnold Binder and Peter Scharf suggest that a more reliable indicator of discrimination in police shootings is comparison of the rate of shootings of blacks with their arrest rate for violent felonies (compared to whites). Binder and Scharf argue that "police as a general rule do not shoot college professors [white or black], physicians [white or black], infants [white or black], shopkeepers [white or black], and so on." Police do, however, shoot at felons (white or black). Binder and Scharf examined arrest rates for violent crimes by race of suspect and found that the pro-

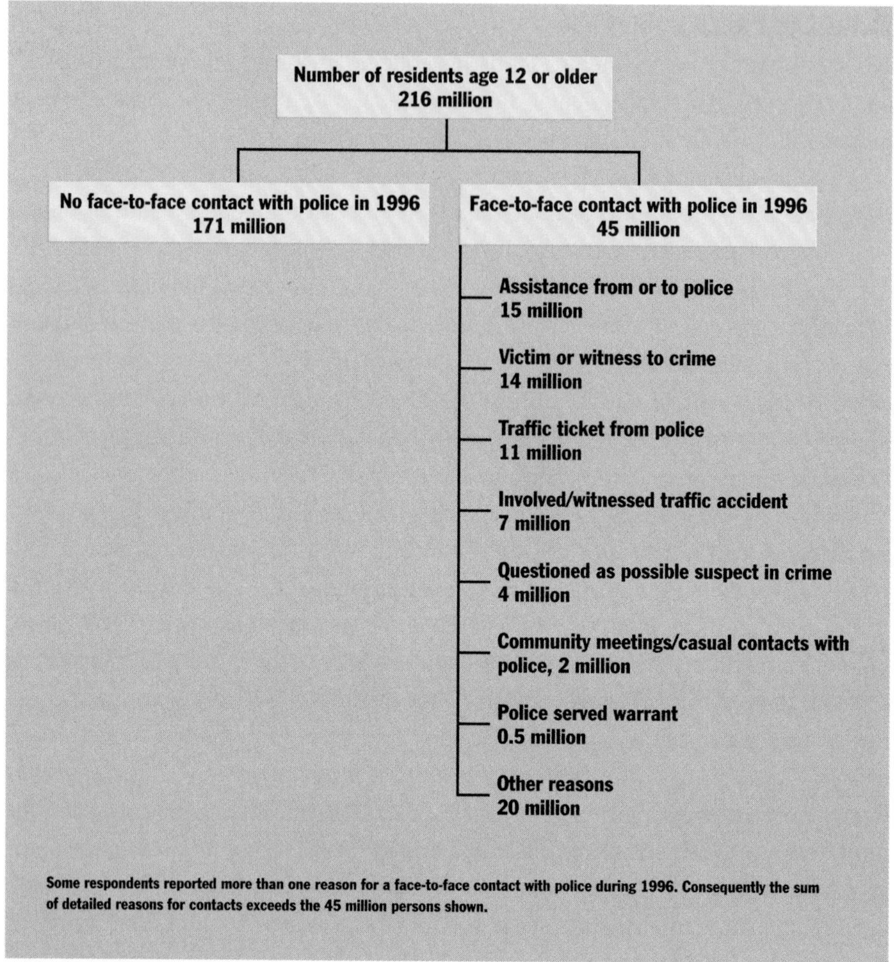

FIGURE 9.4

Number or residents age 12 or older with face-to-face contact with police during 1996, by reason for contact

SOURCE: Lawrence A. Greenfeld, Patrick A. Langan, and Steven K. Smith, *Police Use of Force: Collection of National Data* (Washington, D.C.: Bureau of Justice Statistics, 1997).

portion of blacks shot by police closely mirrored the proportion of people arrested for serious crimes who were black.[80]

Another way to determine possible racial discrimination is to examine the situational factors present in police shootings of all types. Mark Blumberg found no situational differences between white and black shooting victims in Atlanta and Kansas City.[81] A similar finding was reported in New York City.[82] On the other hand, studies in Los Angeles, Chicago, and Memphis found police more likely to shoot blacks than whites under similar circumstances.[83] As Blumberg has noted, this variation in findings among cities "underscores the need to examine this issue on a city-by-city basis."[84] Potential discrimination in police shooting decisions remains an important issue for study and policy. These efforts will be assisted by national surveys of police–citizen encounters conducted under the mandate of the Violent Crime Control and Law Enforcement Act of 1994.

Contemporary Deadly Force Laws

A significant element of the controversy over police use of deadly force was the lack of a uniform national standard governing the use of force by police. In 1980, a review of state laws found that eight states allowed deadly force only in defense of life or when the suspect has threatened deadly force or shows a substantial likelihood of doing so. Ten states permitted deadly force by police only against individuals suspected of violent crimes, whereas thirty-two states allowed police to shoot any "fleeing felon" (including unarmed suspects fleeing from nonviolent felonies).[85]

The primary reason for the fleeing felon rule is deterrence. It is argued that the authority of police to shoot unarmed, nonviolent suspects would deter future felonies. This belief has been tested by comparing crime rates in cities with differing rates of police shootings. A review of these investigations concluded that "nothing in the research to date suggests that a high frequency of police shooting reduces crime rates in any way."[86]

A further justification for the fleeing felon rule is that it increases the rate of apprehension of nonviolent felony suspects who might otherwise escape. As one investigator discovered, however, to apprehend by shooting even 1 percent of suspects in the nonviolent felonies reported to police in a year, police would have to "increase the rate at which they shot people during that year by fifty-fold."[87] This is because shootings are extremely rare in nonviolent circumstances.

The debate over the use of deadly force changed dramatically in 1985 with the U.S. Supreme Court's ruling in *Tennessee v. Garner.* The facts of this case illustrate the dilemma posed by the fleeing felon rule.

Responding to a "prowler inside call," two Memphis police officers saw a woman standing on her porch and gesturing toward an adjacent house. She told them that she had heard glass breaking and that "they" or "someone" was breaking in next door. While one officer radioed the police station, the other went behind the house. The officer heard a door slam and saw someone run across the backyard. The fleeing suspect, Edward Garner, stopped at a six-foot-high chain link fence at the edge of the yard. The officer was able to see Garner's face and hands with his flashlight. He saw no sign of a weapon and was "reasonably sure" that Garner was unarmed. While Garner crouched at the base of the fence, the officer called out, "Police, halt!", and took a few steps toward him. Garner then began to climb over the fence. Convinced that Garner would escape if he made it over the fence, the officer shot him. The bullet hit Garner in the back of the head and killed him. Ten dollars and a purse taken from the house were found on his body.

The Supreme Court held that the use of deadly force is subject to the Fourth Amendment because such a use of force "restrains the freedom of a person to walk away," and that person is therefore "seized." Using the rationale employed in all search and seizure cases, the Court attempted to evaluate the constitutionality of the officer's action by balancing the extent of the intrusion against the government's interest in apprehending people suspected of crimes. The Court found the fleeing felon law to be unconstitutional.

> **The use of deadly force to prevent the escape of all felony suspects, whatever the circumstances, is constitutionally unreasonable. It is not better that all**

> **felony suspects die than that they escape. Where the suspect poses no immediate threat to the officer and no threat to others, the harm resulting from failing to apprehend him does not justify the use of deadly force to do so. . . . A police officer may not seize an unarmed, nondangerous suspect by shooting him dead.[88]**

This decision struck down all fleeing felon laws in the United States. Police are constitutionally justified in using deadly force to stop a suspect only "if the suspect threatens the officer with a weapon or there is probable cause to believe that he has committed a crime involving the infliction or threatened infliction of serious physical harm." In the latter instance, police may use deadly force to prevent the suspect from escaping after some warning has been given "where feasible."

The Supreme Court admitted that there are practical difficulties in assessing the suspect's dangerousness, but pointed out that "similarly difficult judgments must be made by the police in equally uncertain circumstances [such as stop and frisk]." The Justices also found evidence to show that during the previous ten years "only 3.8% of all burglaries involved violent crime." As a result, they believed that burglars cannot be presumed to be dangerous and therefore be subjected to deadly force unless additional aggravating conditions are present.

Today the use of deadly force by police has been greatly reduced. Many police departments have enacted policies that restrict the use of force according to *Tennessee v. Garner* and define "dangerousness" in specific terms to guide the decisions of police officers. The frequency with which deadly force is used now appears to be related to the extent to which departments help their officers by limiting allowable use of force to specifically defined circumstances.[89]

Police Brutality

The 1991 Rodney King incident did more to focus public attention on use of force by police than has any other event in recent history. Rodney King, a 25-year-old black man, was stopped by Los Angeles police for alleged violation of motor vehicle laws. He was subjected to a beating that lasted several minutes, in which he was shocked twice with "stun" guns and struck numerous times with nightsticks and fists by four officers while twenty-one others watched. He suffered multiple skull fractures, a crushed cheekbone, lost teeth, and a broken ankle. What made this incident vivid was the fact that a private citizen had captured it on a home video camera. The video footage was replayed numerous times on news broadcasts.

police brutality
Use of excessive physical force by police in carrying out their duties.

In an era of growing police professionalism, this incident looked like a step backward and was a clear instance of police brutality. **Police brutality** occurs when police use excessive physical force in carrying out their duties. Many observers, including some police officials, saw the Rodney King incident as a case of excessive and intolerable behavior on the part of police.[90] In the same year other incidents of alleged excessive force by police (which were not videotaped) resulted in indictments and convictions in Memphis and New York City.[91] In the Rodney King

The Rodney King incident in Los Angeles focused attention on the use of force by police because it was videotaped by a private citizen and replayed numerous times on television.

case, the first trial ended in acquittal of the police officers; the announcement of this verdict was followed by several days of rioting in Los Angeles.

In all these cases the question is the same: What are the limits on the use of force by police in arresting and subduing citizens? The U.S. Supreme Court had addressed this issue in the 1989 case *Graham v. Connor.* It held that police officers may be held liable under the Fourth Amendment when they use excessive force.[92] In this case police handcuffed a suspect, refusing to allow him to explain that he had passed out because he was diabetic. While he was in their custody, the officers attacked him and inflicted injuries, including cut wrists, ear damage, and a broken foot. This use of force was held to be excessive according to an "objective reasonableness" standard, judged from the perspective of a reasonable officer on the scene. In the Rodney King case, many citizens found it difficult to accept explanations by police that their use of force was "reasonable" and necessary to subdue the suspect because the videotape appeared to speak for itself. In 1993, in a second trial, two Los Angeles police officers were ultimately convicted for violating King's constitutional rights. The following year, the City of Los Angeles settled a civil suit for damages suffered by King, who was awarded $3.8 million.

The Supreme Court's decision in *Graham* sets forth four kinds of factors that must be considered in evaluating the reasonableness of police use of force: the immediacy of the threat to the officer, the severity of the crime alleged, whether the suspect is resisting arrest, and whether the suspect is attempting to escape from custody. When applied objectively, these standards protect a reasonable police officer from harm while also protecting suspects from unreasonable use of force by police.

Critical Thinking EXERCISE

Civil Suits against Police

In 1998, New York City agreed to pay nearly $3 million to settle a lawsuit filed by the family of a man who died after being held in an illegal chokehold by a police officer. The officer was acquitted of negligent homicide but was convicted in federal court of violating the man's civil rights.[A] The officer faces a prison sentence. Clearly, the consequences of police conduct on both civil and criminal liability can be significant.

Police officers and their departments are increasingly being sued for damages. This is due in part to the general trend in America to pursue compensation through lawsuits. Police are especially susceptible to lawsuits given their authority over the liberty of others and their ability to use force to insure compliance with the law under certain circumstances. Most lawsuits against police involve claims of false arrest, negligence, or excessive use of force.

The U.S. Supreme Court has held that a police officer can be sued for false arrest or false imprisonment "when a reasonably well-trained officer, under the same circumstances" would have known that probable cause did not exist for the arrest. This liability holds even if the officer has a warrant signed by a judge, because the judge's incompetence in not recognizing the lack of probable cause cannot excuse the officer's conduct.[B]

Police have been sued for negligence when there is a failure to be aware of a substantial and unjustifiable risk posed by their conduct. These lawsuits usually involve high-speed pursuits for non-serious crimes in which bystanders or suspects have been injured or killed, and cases in which a lack of adequate training "amounts to deliberate indifference to the rights of persons" police encounter. The Supreme Court has held that when poor training is the result of a conscious or deliberate choice, police may be held liable for civil damages. In that particular case, a suspect in custody at the police station slumped to the floor several times, but the police never called for medical assistance. Subsequently, the suspect had to be hospitalized.[C] In a 1997 decision, the Supreme Court made it clear that only deliberate indifference to obvious consequences can result in a successful civil suit against police.[D]

Lawsuits brought in federal court often allege violation of Section 1983 of Title 42 of the United States Code. This law prohibits anyone from denying others their constitutional rights to life, liberty, or property without due process of law. This type of suit has occurred most often in cases of alleged excessive use of force. The consequences of the use of deadly force has spurred a move toward development of less-than-lethal methods to stop and subdue suspects, such as chemical sprays, tranquilizer darts, and electric shock devices.[E] As these new devices are developed, it will be important for extensive police training to occur in their proper use for they may open another avenue of litigation against police.

A study published in 1998 investigated what police administrators might do to avoid civil lawsuits against their departments. This survey of 248 police departments discovered 3 factors that are associated with fewer civil suits lodged against police departments: community policing, minority recruitment, and citizen review.

As community-oriented policing programs were adopted, lawsuits declined quite markedly in those departments. Also, stronger interest in minority recruitment of police officers and citizen involvement in handling complaints against police were associated with fewer civil suits. As study author John Worrall concluded, research like this can help police agencies to make "preemptive and preventive administrative decisions" that make a difference in the lives of both police and the public.[F]

Critical Thinking Questions

1. What do you believe lawsuits against police have been increasing in recent years?
2. What strategies might best protect police from future lawsuits?

Notes

[A]"New York Pays $3 Million to Police Victim Kin," *Associated Press Online,* (October 2, 1998).

[B]*Malley v. Briggs,* 106 S. Ct. 1092 (1986).

[C]*City of Canton, Ohio v. Harris,* 109 S. Ct. 1197 (1989).

[D]*Board of the County Commissioners of Bryan County, Oklahoma v. Brown,* 117 S. Ct. 1382 (1997).

[E]Steven M. Edwards, John Granfield, and Jamie Onnen, *Evaluation of Pepper Spray* (Washington, D.C.: National Institute of Justice, 1997).

[F]John L. Worrall, "Administrative Determinants of Civil Liability Lawsuits against Municipal Police Departments: An Exploratory Analysis," *Crime & Delinquency,* vol. 44 (April 1998), p. 295.

Unannounced Entry

Four police officers went to the home of Sharlene Wilson in Hot Springs, Arkansas, to serve a search warrant for narcotics. When they arrived, they saw an unlocked screen door and entered without knocking. They identified themselves as police, stated that they had a warrant, and searched the house, where they found illegal drugs. Wilson was convicted of drug possession, receiving a sentence of thirty-two years in prison.

Wilson appealed her conviction, arguing that the police officers failed to "knock and announce" their presence and purpose before entering her home. In 1995, the U.S. Supreme Court heard this case and ruled for the first time that the "knock and announce" principle is part of the Fourth Amendment protection against unreasonable searches and seizures.[A] At the same time, the Court said that this principle is not "inflexible" and that circumstances may create justifiable exceptions to this rule. In a 1997 decision, the Court left the "no knock" decision up to lower courts, but stated that a reasonable suspicion by police that knocking would be dangerous or inhibit their investigation justifies an unannounced entry.[B]

British common law often cited the maxim that "a man's home is his castle," meaning that an individual enjoys the maximum protection from interference from others, including the gov-

ernment, when in his or her home. The "knock and announce" principle can be traced to common law. It requires that a police officer identify him- or herself as a police officer, demand entry and inform the occupants of the warrant, and give the occupants an opportunity to open the door before he or she enters forcibly.

A review of state laws reveals two general approaches to this issue: the blanket approach and the particularity approach.[C] The *blanket approach* is used by eight states and holds that when police officers have probable cause to search for drugs, the knock and announce rule may be ignored. This approach is based on the assumption that people with illegal drugs can flush them down the toilet once they know the police are at the door. The *particularity approach,* used in forty states, requires police to follow the knock and announce rule unless they can show specific facts indicating that the occupants of a home are engaging in the destruction of evidence (the sounds of people running, toilets flushing, etc.). The difference is that the latter approach requires police to show that the suspects are actually attempting to destroy evidence rather than that they simply possess the ability to do so. Of the forty states that use the particularity approach, however, thirty permit certain exceptions. Two states have no specific knock and announce law. As one expert has observed, "Leaving it to the lower courts virtually ensures that the Supreme Court has not heard the last of this issue."[D]

Critical Thinking Question

What do you believe should be an appropriate "knock and announce" policy in balancing the interests of the individual's right to privacy and the state's interest in apprehending criminals?

Notes

[A]*Wilson v. Arkansas,* 115 S. Ct. 1914 (1995).

[B]*Richards v. Wisconsin,* 117 S. Ct. 1416 (1997).

[C]"Announcement in Police Entries," *Yale Law Journal,* vol. 80 (1970), p. 139; "The Knock and Announce Rule: A New Approach to the Destruction of Evidence Exception," *Columbia Law Review,* vol. 93 (1993), p. 685.

[D]Craig Hemmens, "The Police, The Fourth Amendment, and Unannounced Entry: *Wilson v. Arkansas,*" *Criminal Law Bulletin* (January–February, 1997), p. 53.

Summary

PROCEDURAL LAW

- Many important aspects of criminal procedure are detailed in the Bill of Rights, the first ten amendments to the U.S. Constitution.
- Only since the 1960s have the provisions of the Bill of Rights been applied to the states as well as to the federal government.

THE FOURTH AMENDMENT

- The Fourth Amendment protects individuals from searches and seizures conducted without a warrant specifying probable cause.

- A *frisk* is a patting-down of an individual's outer clothing, whereas a *search* is an exploratory search for evidence. Frisks are limited to a search for weapons that may pose an immediate threat to the officer's safety.
- Numerous Supreme Court rulings have specified the conditions under which police may search a vehicle or containers within it. Automobiles may be searched without probable cause if officers possess a reasonable belief that the occupant is armed.
- The exclusionary rule holds that illegally seized evidence must be excluded from trials. The "good faith" exception to this rule occurs when police conduct a search on the basis of a warrant that is later found to be defective.
- Searches may be conducted without a warrant if they are incident to a lawful arrest, are conducted with voluntary consent, or involve evidence in plain view, automobiles and their contents, or open fields and abandoned property. However, the Supreme Court has set specific limits on the circumstances in which such searches may be undertaken.

THE FIFTH AMENDMENT

- The Fifth Amendment provides for grand juries, protection against double jeopardy, and protection from self-incrimination. It has had its greatest impact on interrogations and confessions obtained by the police.
- To ensure protection against self-incrimination, suspects taken into custody must be read the *Miranda* warning, which states that the suspect has the right to remain silent and to have an attorney present during questioning.
- The Supreme Court has established some exceptions to the *Miranda* rule. These include the public safety exception, in which a suspect may be asked questions prompted by concern for public safety before being read the *Miranda* warning.

USE OF DEADLY FORCE

- Research on civilian fatalities due to police shootings has found that such incidents are underreported.
- There is evidence that police shoot blacks significantly more often than whites. However, this may be due to a higher number of situations involving black suspects.
- The Supreme Court has ruled that police may use deadly force to stop a suspect only if the suspect threatens the officer with a weapon or there is probable cause to believe that the suspect is dangerous.

POLICE BRUTALITY

- Police brutality occurs when police use excessive physical force in carrying out their duties.
- Police officers may be held liable under the Fourth Amendment when they use excessive force.
- The use of force is excessive only if it goes beyond "objective reasonableness," judged from the perspective of a reasonable officer on the scene.

Key Terms

probable cause
warrant
frisk
search
reasonable suspicion
exclusionary rule
Miranda warning
"good faith" exception
public safety exception
police brutality

Questions for Review and Discussion

1. What limits does the Fourth Amendment place on searches and seizures by police?
2. What is the difference between a frisk and a search?
3. What is meant by the "reasonable suspicion" standard?
4. What is the exclusionary rule, and what are some exceptions to that rule?
5. In what kinds of situations may a search be conducted without a warrant?
6. What protections are provided by the Fifth Amendment?
7. What is the *Miranda* rule, and what exceptions to the rule have been allowed by the Supreme Court?
8. What justification is there for the use of deadly force by police?
9. Is there evidence of discrimination in the frequency with which police shoot blacks as compared to whites?
10. What actions have police departments taken to prevent incidents of police brutality?

Notes

[1]*Maryland v. Garrison*, 107 S. Ct. 1013 (1987).
[2]*Illinois v. Gates*, 426 U.S. 318 (1982).
[3]88 S. Ct. 1868 (1968). (See also the related cases of *Sibron v. New York*, 88 S. Ct. 1902 [1968] and *Peters v. New York*, 88 S. Ct. 1904 [1968].)
[4]*Alabama v. White*, 496 U.S. 325 (1990); see also *Ornelas v. United States*, 116 S. Ct. 1657 (1996).
[5]*Pennsylvania v. Mimms*, 98 S. Ct. 330 (1977); see also *Maryland v. Wilson*, 117 S. Ct. 882 (1997).
[6]*Adams v. Williams*, 92 S. Ct. 1921 (1972).
[7]*Michigan v. Long*, 103 S. Ct. 3469 (1983).
[8]*New York v. Class*, 106 S. Ct. 960 (1986).
[9]Lawrence A. Greenfeld, Patrick A. Langan, and Steven K. Smith, *Police Use of Force: Collection of National Data* (Washington, D.C.: Bureau of Justice Statistics, 1997), p. 13.
[10]103 S. Ct. 1319 (1983).
[11]103 S. Ct. 2637 (1983).
[12]*Saldal v. Cook County*, 113 S. Ct. 538 (1992).
[13]*U.S. v. Gant*, 112 F. 3d 239 (1997). See also *U.S. v. Hary*, 961 F. 2d 1361 (1992) cert. denied 113 S. Ct. 238.
[14]*United States v. Sharpe*, 105 S. Ct. 1568 (1985).
[15]*Fuller v. Vines*, 36 F. 3d 65 (1994) cert. denied 115 S. Ct. 1361; *Bills v. Agetine*, 958 F. 2d 697 (1992) cert. denied 116 S. Ct. 179.
[16]*Minnesota v. Dickerson*, 113 S. Ct. 2130 (1993).
[17]*Weeks v. United States*, 34 S. Ct. 341 (1914).
[18]*Wolf v. Colorado*, 338 U.S. 25 (1949); Henry J. Abraham, *Freedom and the Court: Civil Rights and Liberties in the United States* (New York: Oxford University Press, 1977).
[19]*Rochin v. California*, 342 U.S. 165 (1952); *Rea v. United States*, 350 U.S. 214 (1956).
[20]*U.S. v. Leon*, 104 S. Ct. 3405 (1984) and *Massachusetts v. Sheppard*, 104 S. Ct. 3424 (1984).
[21]Robert L. Misner, "Limiting *Leon:* A Mistake of Law Analogy," *Journal of Criminal Law and Criminology*, vol. 77 (Fall 1986), pp. 507–45.
[22]*Hudson v. Palmer*, 104 S. Ct. 3194 (1984).
[23]*New Jersey v. T.L.O.*, 105 S. Ct. 733 (1985).
[24]*Maryland v. Garrison*, 107 S. Ct. 1013 (1987).
[25]89 S. Ct. 2034 (1969).

[26]94 S. Ct. 467 (1973). See also *Gustafson v. Florida*, 94 S. Ct. 488 (1973).
[27]97 S. Ct. 2476 (1977).
[28]101 S. Ct. 2860 (1981). See also *Pennsylvania v. Labron*, 116 S. Ct. 2485 (1996).
[29]93 S. Ct. 2041 (1973).
[30]*U.S. v. Matlock*, 94 S. Ct. 988 (1974).
[31]96 S. Ct. 820 (1976).
[32]111 S. Ct. 1801 (1991).
[32a]*Ohio v. Robinette*, 117 S. Ct. 417 (1996).
[33]91 S. Ct. 2022 (1971).
[34]103 S. Ct. 2317 (1983).
[35]*U.S. v. Robles*, 37 F. 3d 1260 (1994) cert. denied 117 S. Ct. 319 (1996).
[36]*United States v. Jacobson*, 104 S. Ct. 1652 (1984).
[37]*Arizona v. Hicks*, 107 S. Ct. 1149 (1987).
[38]496 U.S. 120 (1990).
[39]*U.S. v. Hatten*, 68 F. 3d 257 (1995) cert. denied 116 S. Ct. 1026.
[40]45 S. Ct. 280 (1925).
[41]*Weeks v. United States*, 34 S. Ct. 341 (1914).
[42]90 S. Ct. 1975 (1970).
[43]102 S. Ct. 3079 (1982).
[44]*South Dakota v. Opperman*, 96 S. Ct. 3092 (1976).
[45]*Pennsylvania v. Mimms*, 98 S. Ct. 330 (1977).
[46]*Colorado v. Bertine*, 107 S. Ct. 738 (1987).
[47]*Delaware v. Prouse*, 99 S. Ct. 1391 (1979).
[48]*Arizona v. Evans*, 115 S. Ct. 209 (1995).
[49]99 S. Ct. 2586 (1979).
[50]*Robbins v. California*, 101 S. Ct. 2841 (1981).
[51]102 S. Ct. 2157 (1982).
[52]*California v. Acevedo*, 111 S. Ct. 1982 (1991). See also *Brown v. United States*, 116 S. Ct. 1769 (1996).
[53]*Florida v. Meyers*, 104 S. Ct. 1852 (1985).
[54]*United States v. Johns*, 105 S. Ct. 881 (1985).
[55]44 S. Ct. 445 (1924).
[56]*Oliver v. United States*, 104 S. Ct. 1735 (1984).
[57]106 S. Ct. 1809 (1986).
[58]107 S. Ct. 1134 (1987).
[59]*U.S. v. Gorman*, 104 F. 3d 272 (1996); *U.S. v. Van Damme*, 48 F. 3d 461 (1995).
[60]86 S. Ct. 1602 (1966).
[61]378 U.S. 478 (1964).
[62]*Rhode Island v. Innis*, 100 S. Ct. 1682 (1980).
[63]*U.S. v. Finch*, 998 F. 2d 349 (1993); see also *U.S. v. Menesses*, 962 F. 2d 420 (1992) where the court ruled that a confession induced by the assurance that there will be no prosecution is not voluntary.
[64]*New York v. Quarles*, 104 S. Ct. 2626 (1984).
[65]103 S. Ct. 916 (1983).
[66]103 S. Ct. 2830 (1983).
[67]*Minnesota v. Murphy*, 104 S. Ct. 1136 (1984).
[68]*Berkimer v. McCarty*, 104 S. Ct. 3138 (1984).
[69]105 S. Ct. 1285 (1985).
[70]*Moran v. Burbine*, 106 S. Ct.1135 (1986).
[71]*Colorado v. Spring*, 107 S. Ct. 851 (1987); see also *Clabourne v. Lewis*, 64 F. 3d 1373 (1995).
[72]111 S. Ct. 1121 (1990).
[73]*Minnick v. Mississippi*, 111 S. Ct. 486 (1990).
[74]William A. Geller, *Videotaping Interrogations and Confessions* (Washington, D.C.: National Institute of Justice, 1993).

[75]Gerald D. Robin, "Justifiable Homicide by Police Officers," *Journal of Criminal Law, Criminology, and Police Science* (June 1963), pp. 225–31; Arthur L. Kobler, "Police Homicide in a Democracy," *Journal of Social Issues,* vol. 31 (1975), pp. 163–91; Cynthia G. Sulton and Phillip Cooper, "Summary of Research on the Police Use of Deadly Force," in R. Brenner and M. Kravitz, eds., *A Community Concern: Police Use of Deadly Force* (Washington, D.C.: U.S. Government Printing Office, 1979).

[76]Anthony M. Pate and Lorie A. Fridell, *Police Use of Force: Official Reports, Citizens' Complaints, and Legal Consequences* (Washington, D.C.: Police Foundation, 1993).

[77]Lawrence W. Sherman and Robert H. Langworthy, "Measuring Homicide by Police Officers," *Journal of Criminal Law and Criminology* (Winter 1979), pp. 546–60; Tom McEwen, *National Data Collection on Police Use of Force* (Washington, D.C.: Bureau of Justice Statistics, 1996).

[78]Lawrence A. Greenfeld, Patrick A. Langan, and Steven K. Smith, *Police Use of Force: Collection of National Data* (Washington, D.C.: Bureau of Justice Statistics, 1997).

[79]James J. Fyfe, *Shots Fired: An Examination of New York City Police Firearms Discharges* (Albany: State University of New York at Albany, Ph.D. Dissertation, 1978); Richard W. Harding and Richard P. Fahey, "Killings by Chicago Police," *Southern California Law Review* (March 1973), pp. 284–315; Marshall W. Meyer, "Police Shooting at Minorities: The Case of Los Angeles," *The Annals* (November 1980), pp. 98–110; C. H. Milton, J. W. Hallack, J. Lardner, and G. L. Abrecht, *Police Use of Deadly Force* (Washington, D.C.: Police Foundation, 1977); Robin, 1963.

[80]Arnold Binder and Peter Scharf, "Deadly Force in Law Enforcement," *Crime & Delinquency,* vol. 28 (January 1982), pp. 1–23.

[81]Mark Blumberg, "Race and Police Shootings: An Analysis in Two Cities," in J. Fyfe, ed., *Contemporary Issues in Law Enforcement* (Beverly Hills, CA: Sage Publications, 1981).

[82]James J. Fyfe, "Blind Justice: Police Shootings in Memphis," *Journal of Criminal Law and Criminology,* vol. 83 (Summer 1982).

[83]Jerome H. Skolnick and James J. Fyfe, *Above the Law: Police and the Excessive Use of Force* (New York: The Free Press, 1993); William A. Geller and Hans Toch, eds., *And Justice for All: Understanding and Controlling Police Abuse of Force* (Washington, D.C.: Police Executive Research Forum, 1995); Geoffrey P. Alpert and Lorie A. Fridell, *Police Vehicles and Firearms: Instruments of Deadly Force* (Prospect Heights, IL: Waveland Press, 1992).

[84]Mark Blumberg, "Research on Police Use of Deadly Force: The State of the Art," in A. Blumberg and E. Niederhoffer, eds., *The Ambivalent Force: Perspectives on the Police,* 3rd ed. (New York: Holt, Rinehart, and Winston, 1985), p. 344.

[85]Lawrence W. Sherman, "Execution without Trial: Police Homicide and the Constitution," *Vanderbilt Law Review* (January 1980), pp. 71–100.

[86]James J. Fyfe, "Observations on Police Deadly Force," *Crime & Delinquency,* vol. 27 (July 1981), pp. 376–89; Robert N. Brenner and Marjorie Kravitz, eds., *A Community Concern: Police Use of Deadly Force.*

[87]Fyfe, 1981, p. 381.

[88]*Tennessee v. Garner,* 105 S. Ct. 1694 (1985).

[89]James J. Fyfe, "Police Use of Deadly Force: Research and Reform," *Justice Quarterly,* vol. 5 (June 1988), pp. 165–205; U.S. Comptroller General, *Use of Force* (Washington, D.C.: U.S. General Accounting Office, 1996); Jerome H. Skolnick and James J. Fyfe, *Above the Law: Police and the Excessive Use of Force.*

[90]Lance Morrow, "Rough Justice," *Time* (April 1, 1991), pp. 16–17; Richard Lacayo, "Law and Disorder," *Time* (April 1, 1991), pp. 18–21.

[91]Ibid.

[92]490 U.S. 396 (1989).

For Further Reading

Anthony V. Bouza, *The Police Mystique* (New York: Plenum, 1990).
Steven G. Brandl and David E. Barlow, eds., *Classics in Policing* (Cincinnati: Anderson Publishing, 1996).
Jerome H. Skolnick and James J. Fyfe, *Above the Law: Police and the Excessive Use of Force* (New York: The Free Press, 1993).

chapter ten

The Origins and Organization of Courts

Laws are a dead letter without courts to expound and define their true meaning and operation.

ALEXANDER HAMILTON
(1755–1804)

CHAPTER OUTLINE

In 1995, O. J. Simpson, a successful and popular former football player, was charged with brutally killing his estranged wife and another man with a knife. Circumstantial evidence, such as shoeprints and blood, seemed to incriminate him. However, no eyewitnesses came forward, no murder weapon was recovered, Simpson had no apparent motive, and questions were raised about whether someone had tampered with the physical evidence. The O. J. Simpson case was unique in many ways. Most notably, it is rare for such a popular celebrity to be a defendant in a murder trial. It is

also rare that so little conclusive physical evidence links a particular person with a murder of this nature.

The physical evidence provided probable cause to arrest and indict Simpson, but it was not clear whether it would be sufficient to establish proof beyond a reasonable doubt and thus convince a jury to convict him. The police, prosecutors, and victims' families believed that the evidence was sufficient to convict Simpson, but neither Simpson nor his attorneys felt that it was persuasive. In the United States, a criminal trial such as Simpson's provides a public forum in which both the prosecution and the defense can put forward their strongest arguments before a neutral and detached third party: a judge or jury. This is the system that the nation's founders believed to be the best way to achieve truth and justice.

The History of Criminal Courts

Murder cases such as the one just described are not typical. Of the more than eleven million arrests made each year, far fewer than 1 percent are for murder. The overwhelming majority of court cases involve misdemeanors, because those are the offenses that are committed most often and for which most arrests are made. When one examines the historical record of both misdemeanor and felony trials and compares it to contemporary court proceedings, one finds some striking similarities as well as differences.

First, it appears that celebrated cases such as Simpson's have occurred in the past. Consider a case from two centuries ago. In 1800, the body of Gulielma Sands was found in a well. Her cousin, Catherine Ring, was suspected of having committed the crime because she lived with Sands. A coroner had concluded that the death was due to willful murder, and there were no other suspects. Ring was indicted for the murder, but she had an alibi, as well as the assistance of a "dream team" of defense attorneys that included Alexander Hamilton and Aaron Burr (who were among the best-known Americans at that time). It was a long trial involving seventy-five witnesses. The trial procedure was similar to the present system, though less cumbersome, and, in another striking similarity to the Simpson case, the jury returned a verdict of acquittal after only five minutes.[1] Both the Ring and the Simpson trials are not typical, however: Murders are uncommon, murder trials are rare, and long, celebrated murder cases are rarer still.

Second, the absence of lawyers is notable in most trials, including felonies, before the mid-twentieth century. Defense attorneys were not required in most types of cases until 1963, when the U.S. Supreme Court ruled in *Gideon v. Wainwright* that indigent defendants charged with felonies are guaranteed the right to have an attorney at trial, a right that has since been expanded to most other stages of criminal procedure. It took the Supreme Court nearly two hundred years to interpret the Sixth Amendment "right to counsel" to apply to all defendants, even poor ones. Most earlier trials, for both felonies and misdemeanors, took place without the accused being represented by a lawyer.

Third, there has historically been a distinct tendency for misdemeanor cases to be handled in an "amateur" or nonprofessional fashion. As in today's "People's Court," individuals, often neighbors, brought small claims against each other without benefit of legal counsel on either side. Minor criminal cases were treated

To Kill a Mockingbird **provides a fictional protrayal of a criminal trial illustrating similarities and differences in the manner in which criminal cases are handled compared to today.**

the same way until the late twentieth century. A century ago many cities had local aldermen or justices of the peace who would hear and decide cases for a fee. Their role is very similar to that of today's local judges, except that aldermen were untrained in the law and were not paid a salary. As one historian has written, "In some ways a (minor) criminal case was not much more than a civil suit with a government subsidy." Further, although no such penalty as banishment existed, the historical record has frequent references to local aldermen and magistrates telling minor offenders to "get out of town."[2] The nature of justice was indeed informal in cases that involved minor crimes, and in many ways this is still true, although in the last thirty years the presence of legal counsel in these cases has become much more common.

Fourth, when it came to felony cases—robbery, burglary, larceny, and assault—the court system has always been more formal and the criminal procedure more elaborate. The United States modeled its grand jury system on that of England, which required that a group of citizens find probable cause before a felony case could go to trial. This resulted in more deliberation on the merits of a case. Since then, the U.S. Supreme Court has granted states the right to determine probable cause using other procedures, such as preliminary hearings.[3] The right to a trial by jury is guaranteed in the Bill of Rights, but until recent years it was reserved for serious cases.

Historically, juries consisted of white men. Even after the Civil War, some states excluded blacks from juries until the U.S. Supreme Court specifically ruled against such prohibitions in 1879.[4] Also, in the past, people were generally reluctant to serve on juries, a situation that remains unchanged today. Historical records reveal that citizens have consistently attempted to evade jury service despite the belief that a jury system is fundamental to a fair trial.[5]

Fifth, the role of the defendant in criminal cases has changed dramatically over the years. Until the late 1800s, a defendant had no say in his or her own case. Defendants could not act as witnesses or take the stand in their own defense. Beginning just over a century ago, both the states and the federal government permitted defendants to testify under oath. This made the role of defendants and defense counsel more significant because a defendant could take an active role rather than being limited to reacting indirectly to the prosecution's allegations. Today defendants are expected to testify, and those who do not are often seen as having something to hide.

Before the nation's founding, each colony had its own court system. Under the Constitution the states retained significant powers. Among these were the powers to create, enforce, and apply laws. During the Colonial period punishments were generally more severe, and the death penalty was permitted for virtually all felonies, including such crimes as stealing crops, sacrilege, sodomy, and trading with Indians.[6] This severity stemmed from the uncertainty and dangerousness of frontier life and from the association of crime with sin. Civil laws were often used to enforce moral and religious behavior. Fines and imprisonment also were employed to punish such behaviors as blasphemy, failure to attend church, and violation of accepted religious practices.

During the American Revolution the courts were increasingly used as a forum to fight "unjust" laws imposed by England. Most of these laws involved taxation of the Colonies for paper, tea, and imports of various kinds, as well as Colonial trade with non-English nations and colonies. Smuggling was very common because of shortages of desired goods and the high taxes imposed by England on goods obtained by legitimate means. There were many cases of customs officials being harassed, threatened, and beaten, but few juries were willing to convict alleged assailants. During their trials it was argued that the imposition of taxes on the Colonies without Colonial representation in the British Parliament was unjust. At the time, juries were permitted to address the legitimacy of a law rather than focusing solely on the act itself, as is the case today.[7] The British responded by using naval and army forces to search commercial vessels, blockade ports, and search the homes and businesses of individuals suspected of smuggling.[8] In many ways, therefore, the American Revolution was more about taxes and their enforcement than it was about political independence.

The establishment of the United States in the late eighteenth century, combined with a rapidly growing population that included immigrants from many nations and a resultant rapid growth of urban centers, created a need for more courts with specialized tasks. Differing legal and social cultures often clashed, requiring court systems that could decide disputes neutrally. The heavy use of the court system today occurs for the same reason: The United States is still a relatively young society, it still attracts immigrants from all over the world, and diverse urban centers continue to grow. These factors produce disagreements on a wide variety of issues, often leading to court battles.

The Organization of Contemporary Courts

The court system lies at the heart of the American system of justice. It is where police, prosecutors, and victims square off against defendants and defense counsel to determine liability for crimes. Before a trial takes place, all that exists are allegations and suspected crimes. The only proof required prior to trial is probable cause, the standard set forth in the Fourth Amendment to the Constitution, which was added to protect citizens from the warrantless searches suffered by the Colonists under British rule. In order to convict a defendant at trial, a higher standard of proof must be met, usually requiring the concurrence of a jury. This higher standard ensures that only individuals who *are in fact guilty* are punished, not those who we believe *might be guilty*. It also serves to maintain high levels of public confidence in the accuracy and fairness of the system and of the government it represents.

State Court Systems

The vast majority of criminal cases are heard in state courts because most felonies are defined by state laws. For example, murder is generally a violation of state law (unless one kills the President of the United States). Robbery is also a violation of state law (unless it is a robbery of a federally insured bank). The definitions of murder, robbery, and other crimes are quite similar among the states, but significant differences are often seen as well. These include differences in the variations and degrees of crimes, the nature of aggravating or mitigating circumstances, and the penalties that may be imposed. These differences are permitted under the Tenth Amendment to the Constitution, which grants police power to the states.

State courts interpret only state law. Courts in each state are organized in a similar manner. There are three levels of jurisdiction: limited, general, and appellate. These are found in all state court systems, but each state determines how its system is organized. Therefore, the names of the courts and their precise jurisdictions vary somewhat from one state to another.

Figure 10.1 diagrams the court system in the Commonwealth of Virginia. Cases flow from the lower courts (at the bottom of the diagram) upward to the court of last resort. General district courts and juvenile and domestic relations courts have restricted jurisdiction over a specific range of matters; circuit courts are the general trial courts, and the court of appeals and the Supreme Court of Virginia are the two appellate courts in the state.

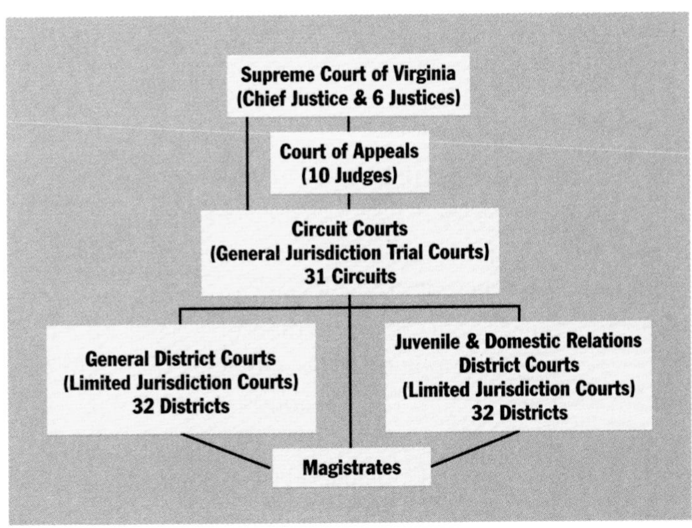

FIGURE 10.1
The Virginia state court structure
SOURCE: http://www.courts.state.va.us/cib/cib.htm

limited jurisdiction
The jurisdiction of a court whose legal authority is restricted to certain specific types of cases.

In all states, the lowest (i.e., most restricted) courts are the courts of **limited jurisdiction.** Their legal authority is restricted to certain specific types of cases. These courts usually exist in every county in the state. For example, small claims courts hear only civil cases that involve amounts of less than $10,000. Surrogate courts hear cases that involve probate of wills, administration of estates, and adoptions. Family courts hear matters involving children and the family, such as cases that involve juvenile delinquency, child protection, status offenders, foster care placement, paternity suits, family offenses, support of dependent relatives, and adoptions. Municipal courts include all city, town, village, and district courts. These courts handle trials for minor criminal and civil cases, traffic and motor vehicle violations, and ordinance violations, and conduct probable cause hearings for felonies.

Each type of limited jurisdiction court is permitted to hear only a narrow range of alleged offenses. Most of them hear civil cases. Only a small part of the family court case load consists of juvenile delinquency cases. Likewise, much of the case load of municipal courts is civil in nature. The entire case load of small claims courts and surrogate courts is civil in nature, involving disputes between private parties.

general jurisdiction
The jurisdiction of a trial court whose authority covers a broad spectrum of cases.

appellate courts
A court that hears appeals from lower courts.

Courts of **general jurisdiction** are often referred to as trial courts. Most felony trials are held at this level. These courts have different names. In sixteen states they are called circuit courts, fifteen states call them district courts, twelve call them superior courts, four use a combination of names, and three use other names. There is usually one felony court per county, for a nationwide total of 3,235.[9] These courts have jurisdiction to hear felony trials and civil suits involving amounts that are too large to be handled in small claims court.

At the highest level of state court systems are **appellate courts.** These courts hear appeals from courts of general jurisdiction. Appellate courts usually have a panel of three to nine judges who hear arguments in cases that are appealed to them from lower courts. Trials are not held in appellate courts, only arguments on specific legal issues. For example, in the *Miranda* case the appellate courts heard arguments about whether or not his confession had been obtained voluntarily. Other aspects of the case that were part of the trial (e.g., the victim's identification of the defendant) were not reconsidered because they were not a basis for the appeal. If an appellate court believes that an error was made in law or procedure in a court of general jurisdiction, the case is referred back to that court for retrial. Most states also have a higher appellate court known as a supreme court. The state supreme court is the court of last resort for appeals from lower courts in that state.

Contemporary criminal courts are located centrally to provide the greatest public access. Courts have three levels of jurisdiction: limited, general, and appellate.

The Federal Court System

The federal court system parallels the state court systems. Federal courts exist at three levels of jurisdiction, but they only hear cases that involve alleged violations of federal laws. In most instances federal laws are designed to prevent misconduct that occurs in more than one state. Interstate transportation of stolen property, kidnapping across state lines, and some forms of drug trafficking are examples. Figure 10.2 diagrams the federal court system in the United States. As with state courts, there is a case flow from courts of limited jurisdiction to courts of general jurisdiction to appellate courts.

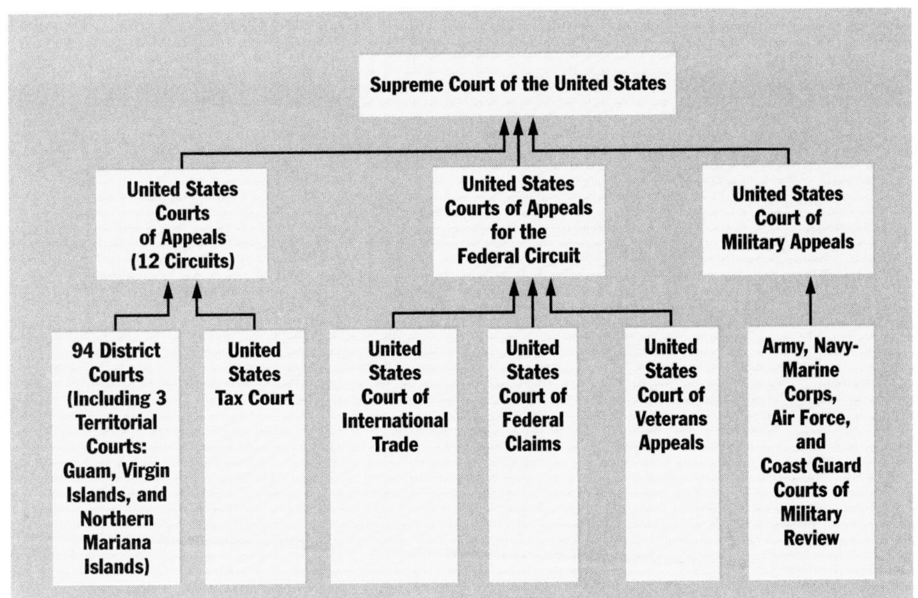

FIGURE 10.2
The federal court system
SOURCE: http://www.uscourts.gov/understanding_courts/gifs/figure1.gif

The U.S. Court of Claims, U.S. customs courts, and the U.S. Tax Court are examples of federal courts. The titles of these courts indicate their limited jurisdictions. Many of these courts were created by Congress and are therefore called legislative courts. Congress has greater control over courts that they created than over courts created by the Constitution. The jurisdiction of legislative courts and the terms of office for judges can be changed by an act of Congress. In constitutional courts, the authority of the courts does not rely on legislative acts.

The federal courts of general jurisdiction are the **U.S. district courts.** These courts have unlimited original jurisdiction in both civil and criminal matters and are the courts where most federal trials take place. The trials in the Oklahoma City bombing case occurred in federal courts because the crime was an attack on a federal building that resulted in the death of federal agents. In addition, these courts hear appeals from the courts of limited jurisdiction. There are ninety-four U.S. district courts in the United States, with at least one in each state. They are located throughout the country so that they can hear cases that involve alleged violations of federal law wherever they may occur. Larger states may have several federal district courts.

U.S. district courts
Federal trial courts of general jurisdiction.

Above the courts of general jurisdiction are the appellate courts. In the federal system, as in many states, there are two levels of appellate courts. The first level is the intermediate appellate court, which reviews the judgment of the trial courts. These decisions, in turn, may be reviewed by a court of last resort. On the federal level, the intermediate appellate courts are the **U.S. courts of appeals.** There are thirteen of these courts located throughout the United States in each federal judicial district.

U.S. courts of appeals
Intermediate federal appellate courts.

Figure 10.3 illustrates the composition of each federal judicial district. It shows how each district groups three or more states; all federal appeals from those states are directed to the court of appeals in that circuit.

FIGURE 10.3

The number and composition of federal judicial circuits

SOURCE: http://www.uscourts.gov/understanding_courts/gifs/map.gif

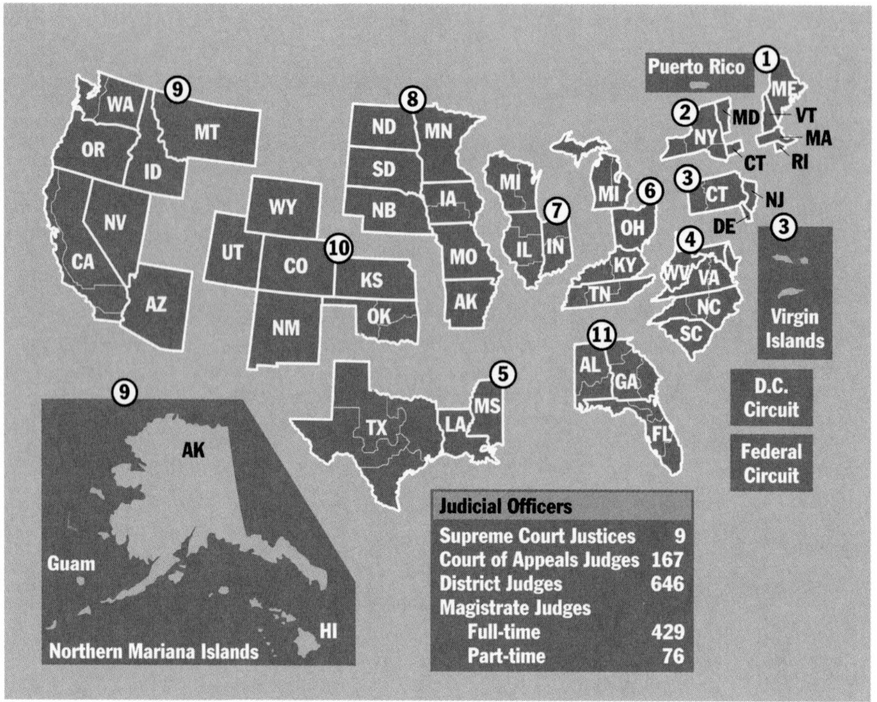

U.S. Supreme Court The highest court in the United States, which hears final appeals in cases that involve federal law, suits between states, and interpretations of the U.S. Constitution.

The courts of appeals were created in 1891 to take some of the burden off the nation's court of last resort, the **U.S. Supreme Court.** The U.S. Supreme Court can hear on appeal any case involving federal law, suits between states, and cases involving interpretations of the U.S. Constitution. The decisions of the U.S. Supreme Court cannot be appealed further, and the Supreme Court can also choose *not* to review a case if it so desires. In fact, each year more than 5,000 cases reach the U.S. Supreme Court and more than three-fourths of them are not heard. When this happens, the previous court's ruling stands as the final decision.

There are four types of cases in which the U.S. Supreme Court *must* render an opinion; all involve interpretations of the U.S. Constitution:

1. When an act of Congress has been found unconstitutional in a lower federal court
2. When a state supreme court has found a federal law unconstitutional
3. When a U.S. court of appeals has found a state law unconstitutional
4. When a constitutional challenge of a state law has been upheld by a state supreme court

writ of certiorari A legal order from the U.S. Supreme Court stating that a lower court must forward the record of a particular case for review.

The U.S. Supreme Court's ability to choose which cases it will hear is known as *certiorari.* This term is derived from the **writ of certiorari,** which is a legal order from the U.S. Supreme Court stating that a lower court must "forward the record" of a particular case for review. Such a writ is issued when four or more Justices of the U.S. Supreme Court believe that the legal issues presented in the case merit review.

The decisions of the Supreme Court are made by a majority vote of the nine Justices, who are appointed for life by the President with the consent of the Senate. The far-reaching powers of the Supreme Court were not included in Article

III of the U.S. Constitution, which created the Court. Rather they were established in the 1803 case of *Marbury v. Madison,* in which the Court claimed the authority to review the constitutionality of acts of Congress.[10] When Thomas Jefferson defeated incumbent John Adams in the Presidential election of 1800, Congress and President Adams created many new federal judgeships and appointed new judges just before Adams left office. They also reduced the number of U.S. Supreme Court Justices by one. This was done in an attempt to limit Jefferson's ability to appoint judges of his own choosing once he took office. This conflict reached the Supreme Court when Secretary of State James Madison would not deliver commissions to several new judges appointed by Adams, including William Marbury. In response to this situation Chief Justice John Marshall led the U.S. Supreme Court in ruling that Congress had exceeded its power and acted unconstitutionally. This case established the principle of **judicial review** of legislative acts. The *Marbury* ruling is considered one of the most significant court decisions in U.S. history, for it specifies how the balance of powers operates and clarifies the extent of the Supreme Court's authority.

judicial review
The U.S. Supreme Court's authority to review the constitutionality of acts of Congress.

Court Administration

Courts handle a large volume of cases each year, and in recent years there have been large increases in the numbers of cases filed. This reflects the growth of the population, increases in arrest rates, and an increasingly litigious society that resorts to the courts more often than ever before to resolve disputes. The dramatic growth in case loads has placed tremendous strain on many courts. The situation was made even worse in 1974, when Congress passed the Speedy Trial Act. This act requires that all criminal cases be brought to trial within 100 days; if they are not, they will be dismissed. The rationale for the act is that the Sixth Amendment requires "a speedy and public trial" and that delays in court often work against the interests of the accused, who may be in jail awaiting adjudication of the case. The result has been an increase in the speed with which criminal cases are brought to trial, along with a dramatic slowing in the processing of civil cases, which are not covered by the act. This is why it often takes several years for a civil case to reach the trial stage. In addition, criminal cases take up a great deal of court time. Every criminal case requires an initial appearance, a preliminary hearing or grand jury, arraignment, and possibly a trial and an appeal. Courts must be highly organized to handle so many court appearances and to determine the need for and availability of judges, courtrooms, court clerks, stenographers, sheriff's deputies, and other participants in the adjudication process.

The problem of rising case loads is serious in federal courts, where the volume of cases has nearly tripled over the last twenty years. In 1991, the average federal trial judge handled 401 cases. In 1997, the number was 470. Part of the problem is judicial vacancies. There are more than one hundred unfilled positions for federal judges because of disagreement between the President and the Senate (controlled by the opposing political party) about suitable candidates. In 1994, 101 new federal judges were approved. In 1996 and 1997, only a total of fifty-three were confirmed. Another factor that contributes to high federal case loads is the "federalizing" of crimes that were previously handled by the states.[11] Over the last two decades, Congress has dramatically increased the number of federal

TABLE 10.1

Number of Criminal Cases Filed in U.S. District Courts

YEAR	NUMBER OF CASES FILED
1980	27,910
1985	38,546
1990	47,962
1996	47,146

SOURCE: Administrative Office of the United States Courts, *Annual Report to the Director* (Washington, D.C.: U.S. Government Printing Office, published annually).

crimes, especially drug and gun offenses. Therefore, crimes that were once handled exclusively in state courts are increasingly being tried as violations of federal law. Table 10.1 illustrates the dramatic increase in criminal cases filed in U.S. district courts. In 1980, a total of 27,910 cases were filed; in 1996, 47,146 cases were filed.

Most states, as well as the federal government, have **court administrators** whose job is to manage these tasks. The first state court administrator is said to have been appointed more than fifty years ago,[12] but only in the last twenty-five years has systematic attention been given to court scheduling, budgeting, and security.[13]

Court administrators generally have Master's degrees in management or related fields, and their task is to ensure that courts operate as efficiently as possible within the constraints of budget, case load, and available personnel and physical facilities. This task is complex because most courts receive their funding from a combination of local, state, and federal sources. Court administrators also serve as liaisons between state and federal legislatures and the court system. They project the impact of new laws on court case loads and budgets, and coordinate the training of judges and other court personnel. The federal court system is administered by the Administrative Office of the U.S. Courts in Washington, D.C., whereas state court systems are administered by a similar state-level agency headed by a senior judge or a court administrator, or both.

court administrator
A person who manages court case loads with reference to the availability of judges, courtrooms, jurors, clerks, stenographers, courtroom security, and court budgeting.

Court administration has become a science as models have been developed to estimate case loads and predict the impact of changes in law, policy, and personnel.[14] These models consist of mathematical equations that describe the relationships among budgets, staff, workload, and agencies. Proposed increases in law enforcement hiring, for example, can be projected to produce increases in arrests, arraignments, preliminary hearings, trials, appeals, and so on. Likewise, changes in law and policy can have similar effects that will affect the entire criminal justice system. Because of finite resources of courts, changes in other parts of the system can now be anticipated and built into the budgeting process.

Participants in the Judicial Process

There are four main types of participants in the judicial process: prosecutors, defense counsel, judges and juries, and victims and witnesses. The roles of and interactions among these participants determine the nature and quality of the justice produced by the adjudication process. It is important, therefore, to understand how these participants can and should interact in convicting the guilty, exonerating the innocent, and protecting the community.

Prosecutors

prosecutor
An elected or appointed official who represents the community in bringing charges against an accused person.

Prosecutors are also called district, county, state, or commonwealth attorneys, depending on the state. Regardless of the title, their task is the same: to represent the community in bringing charges against an accused person. The job of the prosecutor is constrained by three factors: popularity, case load, and relationships with other actors in the adjudication process.

First, most prosecutors are elected (and some are appointed by the governor), and therefore they are encouraged to make "popular" prosecution decisions that in some cases may run counter to the ideals of justice. For example, prosecution to the full extent of the law of a college student caught with a small amount of marijuana may be unwarranted, but failure to do so may be used by political opponents as evidence that the prosecutor is "soft on crime." Likewise, a prosecutor may not believe that a first offender deserves the maximum penalty for a robbery or assault, but uninformed public or political pressure may encourage the prosecutor to pursue the maximum sentence anyway. Thus, a prosecutor must be able to deal effectively with demands for action that are not in the best interests of justice. As the standards of the American Bar Association state, the "duty of the prosecutor is to seek justice, not merely convict."[15]

Second, case load pressures often force prosecutors to make decisions based on expediency rather than justice. A prosecutor in a jurisdiction where many serious crimes occur may have to choose which cases to prosecute to the full extent of the law and which ones to plea-bargain. There may not be enough prosecutors to handle all the cases being filed in criminal court. Therefore, priorities must be set, meaning that some cases will be given superficial attention in order to free prosecutors to focus more fully on others. The result is that violent crimes, which are relatively rare, usually receive full attention, whereas the more common crimes against property are handled outside the courtroom in plea-bargains. (Plea-bargaining is discussed in Chapter 11.) This leads to accusations of "assembly-line justice" in which cases often end in reduced sentences.

Third, prosecutors must maintain good relationships with the other participants in the adjudication process: police, judges, juries, defense counsel, victims, and witnesses. Most cases are brought to prosecutors by the police, and police officers serve as witnesses in the majority of them. Therefore, prosecutors need the police to provide valid evidence and to serve as reliable witnesses. Since cases in which the evidence is weak ultimately result in dismissal or acquittal, prosecutors must work closely with police to ensure that time and effort are not wasted by either party. Prosecutors need judges to rule on the admissibility of evidence and decide guilt or innocence in nonjury trials. They also want judges to follow their recommendations in sentencing decisions. Prosecutors must maintain good relationships with defense counsel because most cases end in plea-bargains, and both sides must be willing to reach an agreement. They must also communicate well with juries, victims, and witnesses. Victims and witnesses provide evidence that may be crucial in determining guilt or innocence. It is important that they understand the judicial process, be forewarned about what they may face in court, and be supported throughout the process. Prosecutors thus must be able to communicate issues of fact and law clearly and reasonably. (Prosecutors are discussed further in Chapter 11.)

Defense Counsel

Defense attorneys represent the legal rights of the accused in criminal proceedings. Contrary to the image portrayed in some notorious cases, their task is not to get the best "deal" for their client. Instead, it is to ensure that their client's legal rights are protected. This is accomplished by examining the evidence used

defense attorney
An attorney who represents the legal rights of the accused in criminal or civil proceedings.

Defense attorneys have a difficult task in which strong advocacy of the legal rights of the defendant can be construed as a desire to win the case at any cost.

to establish probable cause and assessing the strength of the evidence to be used to prove guilt beyond a reasonable doubt. This sometimes brings defense counsel into conflict with police, prosecutors, victims, and witnesses who believe that they are being "attacked" by the defense. However, an effective defense attorney will use his or her skills to examine the reliability and validity of the evidence produced by police, prosecutors, victims, and witnesses, rather than attack anyone *as an individual.* This is a difficult task, and strong advocacy of the legal rights of a defendant is sometimes blurred with the desire to "win at all costs." Nevertheless, the role of a defense attorney is a crucial one, for without it there would be less certainty in the adjudication process. Without high levels of certainty in court findings of guilt or innocence, the public might lose faith in the justice system and in the government it represents. (Defense counsel is discussed further in Chapter 12.)

judge
A person who objectively assesses the strength of a case and rules on issues of law and procedure, and in many instances determines the disposition of a case.

Judges

The role of **judges** in the criminal justice process is pivotal in upholding the rights of the accused and arbitrating between the prosecution and the defense in a criminal case. From the initial appearance through sentencing, the task of judges is to objectively assess the strength of a case, rule on issues of law and procedure, and sometimes determine the ultimate disposition of a case.

contemporary issues

Dispute Resolution outside the Courtroom

A predictable response to increasing court case loads has been to resolve more disputes outside the courtroom. Historically, this has meant reliance on plea-bargaining, but this approach still involves the full adjudication process, from prosecution to defense representation to sentencing. Another approach, dispute resolution, involves handling complaints entirely outside the judicial process. Typically, this entails getting both sides to agree to a settlement determined by a mediator or arbiter appointed by the court.

The incentives for dispute resolution are three: A dispute can be resolved more quickly, less expensively, and often with a settlement that is more mutually agreeable than one that is likely to emerge from the normal adjudication process. For example, a teenager who spray paints his name on the walls of a school gymnasium can be charged with vandalism and placed on probation or perhaps incarcerated. A dispute resolution procedure would seek to resolve the complaint outside the court process. This might involve a "teen court" composed of students from the teenager's school that would advise the juvenile court judge regarding alternatives that the defendant's peers believe are proportional to the offense. It could also involve an advisory committee of local citizens that would impose a sentence such as cleaning up the paint, agreeing to undergo counseling, or other penalties that permit the community to address its own problems in ways it sees as fair, proportional, and locally controlled.

Dispute resolution works most effectively for first-time and minor offenders who commit "disorderly" offenses that are nonviolent yet disruptive and sometimes threatening to the community, such as loitering, vandalism, theft, and public nuisance offenses. In Hawaii, for example, it was found that different cultural, ethnic, and neighborhood groups sometimes have different views regarding appropriate responses to these types of misconduct.[A] Dispute resolution gives neighborhoods a greater voice in dealing with misconduct that occurs in their own communities.

A variation on dispute resolution is community prosecution, an approach that has been used on an experimental basis in several counties around the nation. Responding to the demands of neighborhood groups, assistant district attorneys (ADAs) are assigned to specific neighborhoods, where they intervene in disorderly behavior (vandalism, prostitution, drug sales, loitering, etc.). The ADAs bring affected parties together to negotiate solutions where feasible, make it easier for property owners to arrest trespassers and use civil eviction to remove undesirable tenants, and close properties that are found to violate local ordinances.[B] Community prosecution efforts force prosecutors to work on a neighborhood level, acting as problem-solvers rather than merely as processors of criminal cases. These efforts have helped local communities respond more effectively to crimes that erode the quality of life in the neighborhood.

Community prosecution uses assistant district attorneys to resolve problems in neighborhoods. They act as mediators to bring affected parties together, and they also enforce local ordinances and disorderly behavior offenses to improve the neighborhood environment.

A parallel development is community courts. These are decentralized courts that respond directly to neighborhood concerns rather than waiting for serious crimes to occur. Community courts are being instituted in localities around the country. They have several common features. Many have "satellite" courtrooms in problem neighborhoods; these are designed to forge a stronger connection between unruly conduct and the adjudication process. Many courts have formed citizens' advisory committees, use citizen volunteers, and have established teen courts, school outreach programs, and other programs that involve the community more closely in the adjudication process.[C]

Dispute resolution, community prosecution, and community courts are related ideas that attempt to accomplish three key objectives: address nonserious crimes more quickly, permit organized community input into the adjudication and sentencing processes, and establish a court presence and understanding at the neighborhood level. These initiatives, if widely adopted, will increase confidence in the judicial process by reflecting the values of the local community.

NOTES

[A] Sharon Rodgers, "The Future of Cultural Forms of Dispute Resolution in the Formal Legal System," *Futures Research Quarterly,* vol. 9 (Winter 1993), pp. 41–9.

[B] Barbara Boland, "What is Community Prosecution?," *National Institute of Justice Journal* (August 1996), pp. 35–40.

[C] David B. Rottman, "Community Courts: Prospects and Limits," *National Institute of Justice Journal* (August 1996), pp. 46–51.

Judges (sometimes called "magistrates" in courts of limited jurisdiction) are selected in one of five ways, depending on the state. In six states, judges are appointed by the governor, usually with the consent of the state legislature. This is similar to the selection process for federal judges, who are appointed by the President with the approval of the U.S. Senate. In two states, judges are selected by the state legislature alone. Nonpartisan elections (in which candidates are not affiliated with any political party) are held in thirteen states, and eight other states elect judges in partisan elections. In ten states, judges are chosen by a merit selection process. Eleven states use various combinations of these five methods, depending on the type of judicial vacancy to be filled.

Strengths and weaknesses are associated with each of these methods of selection, and the diversity of methods used by the states indicates a lack of consensus on which method is best. Selection of judges by election gives the public direct input into the selection process, but at the same time it may pressure a judge who is seeking election or reelection to make "popular" decisions rather than ones based on principles of justice. Political appointments by the governor or legislature sometimes result in the selection of a judge who is well connected politically but lacks some of the credentials that one might wish to see in a judge. Merit selection was designed to overcome the drawbacks of both election and appointment of judges.

merit selection plan
A method for selecting judges that involves a combination of appointment and election.

The Missouri **merit selection plan** was initiated in 1940. When a judicial vacancy occurs, a nominating commission composed of citizens and attorneys recommends three candidates to the governor, who must appoint one of those candidates. After the appointed judge has served on the bench for a year, a public referendum is held in which the voters decide, "Shall Judge Z remain in office?" If a majority votes "yes," the judge completes his or her term of office; a "no" vote starts the process all over again. The merit selection system was designed to remove judicial candidates from the political arena while allowing the public to confirm or unseat a judge after one year. Although it is not a foolproof system, it overcomes some of the problems associated with both elections and appointments. The procedure has been approved by both the American Bar Association and the American Judicature Society.

Regardless of the selection method used, judges play a significant role in the adjudication process. They serve as an informed, neutral party, ruling on issues of fact and law throughout the court process. Even in cases in which the evidence of guilt appears overwhelming, the judge must ensure that the defendant's legal rights have been adequately safeguarded by the defense and that the community's interests have been effectively represented by the prosecution.

In recent decades two important reforms—state court unification and the establishment of U.S. magistrates—have increased the quality of the judicial system. Courts had been criticized for the use of nonlawyers in judicial roles, especially in local "justice of the peace" courts in small jurisdictions. Local court procedures were idiosyncratic, giving unfair advantages to local attorneys practicing in those courts. Local courts were found to be more interested in generating revenue by imposing fines than in seeking justice.[16] During the 1960s and 1970s, several national commissions recommended the abolition of many local courts and the creation of unified lower courts of limited and general jurisdiction. In addition, uniform procedures for these courts were developed in order to reduce confusion about legal rules, mandate legal training for judges, provide for

Preventing Child Sexual Abuse

The U.S. Department of Health and Human Services reports that about 140,000 new cases of child sexual abuse occur every year.[A] These cases account for a small but increasing proportion of court case filings in both family and criminal court. Three fourths of the victims are sexually abused by someone they know, and about one third are under age seven.[B] These facts have resulted in the development of sexual abuse prevention programs aimed at preschool and elementary school children. By 1990, nearly half of the states required school-based child sexual abuse programs, which are designed to increase awareness of child sexual abuse and provide training in ways to increase personal safety.[C]

An assessment of 135 abuse prevention programs did not find any direct evidence that they are effective in preventing the occurrence of child sexual abuse.[D] Although many of the studies had methodological flaws, they clearly showed that children have difficulty grasping the idea that they could be abused by a family member. On the other hand, programs are effective in teaching children to say no or to leave the scene of potential abuse. This suggests that children can learn avoidance behaviors but lack the understanding to apply them when needed.

FUTURES QUESTION

Can you propose a way to prevent child sexual abuse other than through in-school programs?

NOTES

[A]U.S. Department of Health and Human Services, National Center on Child Abuse and Neglect, *Child Maltreatment 1994* (Washington, D.C.: U.S. Government Printing Office, 1996).

[B]S. Wurtele, "Sexual Abuse," in R. T. Ammerman and M. Hersen, eds., *Handbook of Prevention and Treatment with Children and Adolescents: Intervention in the Real World Context* (New York: Wiley, 1997).

[C]J. Kohl, "School-Based Child Sexual Abuse Prevention Programs," *Journal of Family Violence,* vol. 8 (1993), pp. 137–50.

[D]U.S. Comptroller General, *Preventing Child Sexual Abuse: Research Inconclusive about Effectiveness of Child Education Programs* (Washington, D.C.: U.S. General Accounting Office, 1996), p. 3.

rotation of judges among courts, and bring about other reforms.[17] Many states have streamlined their court systems to some extent, but few have completely unified their courts. Texas, for example, still has more than 2,000 courts of limited jurisdiction. Nevertheless, the court unification movement has helped standardize court jurisdiction, procedure, and personnel qualifications in many states.

The second important reform was the establishment of **U.S. magistrate judges** by Congress in 1968. These magistrates are appointed by U.S. district court judges; they hold pretrial hearings as well as trials for minor civil and criminal offenses. They replaced U.S. commissioners, who were not required to be trained lawyers (and many were not). Like the court unification movement in the state courts, the establishment of legally trained magistrates served to enhance and standardize the quality of justice in the lower federal courts.

U.S. magistrate judge
An official appointed by U.S. district court judges to conduct pretrial hearings and trials for minor civil and criminal offenses in federal court.

Victims and Witnesses

Victims and witnesses have sometimes been called the "forgotten players" in the criminal justice process because they are specifically represented by no one. The police and prosecutor represent the community at large, the defense represents the accused, and the judge is a neutral third party.

The parents of Polly Klaas were in the courtroom when Richard Allen Davis was sentenced to death in 1996 for the murder of their daughter.

The adjudication process is designed in this manner because violations of criminal law are viewed as violations of the rules of *social order.* It is society at large, not just the victim, that is harmed by an assault or robbery. Therefore, the prosecutor represents the entire jurisdiction and not just the victims or witnesses in a particular case.

In recent years efforts have been made to give victims and witnesses a greater role in the criminal justice process, usually at sentencing and at parole hearings, where they are permitted to voice their concerns. It is important to keep in mind, however, that the criminal justice process is not designed to settle private disputes between victims and offenders. That is the purpose of civil law. It may be argued that greater input by victims and witnesses in criminal proceedings serves to blur the distinction between criminal and civil proceedings.

Nevertheless, there have been cases in which victims and witnesses have not been appropriately informed of the progress of criminal proceedings or the pending release of offenders from prison. Also, until recently the impact of crime on victims has received little recognition.[18] In gang-dominated neighborhoods, for example, there are high levels of victim and witness intimidation.[19] Such intimidation occurs most often in relation to violent crimes and involves people with some previous connection with the defendant; many are young, and many are illegal immigrants. Explicit threats, physical violence, and property damage have been reported in these cases.

In response, prosecutors have requested high bail and aggressively prosecuted reported attempts at intimidation. In recent years new strategies have been developed, such as emergency relocation and support of victims and witnesses, more extensive pretrial and courtroom security measures, and coordination with other agencies that provide support services.[20] Today there are more than 8,000 organizations that provide counseling, transportation to court, temporary housing, and advocacy services for victims.[21] To the extent that the victim's rights movement has helped keep victims informed, aware, and protected during the adjudication process, it has accomplished a useful public service.

In addition to this movement to provide services to victims, there is a national push for a constitutional amendment to protect victims' rights. The proposed amendment is supported by the U.S. President.[22] Sometimes crime victims and families are excluded from trials where they may be called as witnesses, and there is a perception that defendants' rights are given more attention than the concerns of victims. The proposed amendment would guarantee

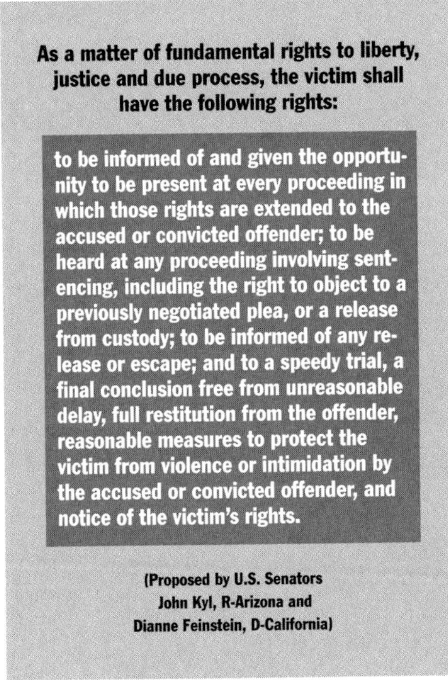
As a matter of fundamental rights to liberty, justice and due process, the victim shall have the following rights:

to be informed of and given the opportunity to be present at every proceeding in which those rights are extended to the accused or convicted offender; to be heard at any proceeding involving sentencing, including the right to object to a previously negotiated plea, or a release from custody; to be informed of any release or escape; and to a speedy trial, a final conclusion free from unreasonable delay, full restitution from the offender, reasonable measures to protect the victim from violence or intimidation by the accused or convicted offender, and notice of the victim's rights.

(Proposed by U.S. Senators John Kyl, R-Arizona and Dianne Feinstein, D-California)

FIGURE 10.4
Proposed constitutional amendment to guarantee victims' rights

victims the right to restitution and to be heard during plea-bargaining, at trial, at sentencing, and at parole hearings.

One version of the proposed constitutional amendment is presented in Figure 10.4. This version would give victims legal authority to object to plea-bargaining, guarantee a speedy trial, require full restitution by the offender, and provide for "reasonable measures" to protect the victim when necessary. Some prosecutors fear that this amendment, if passed, would give victims "veto power." Others have expressed concern about victims being present during trials in which they later appear as witnesses. They might then be able to shape their testimony according to the version of events presented by earlier witnesses.[23] Despite these potential problems, continuing concern with fair and equal treatment of victims in the criminal justice process will keep the victim's rights movement alive for years to come.

The Future of the Court System

The court system lies at the center of the justice system, for it is here that justice is most clearly carried out. Police and prosecutors work to assemble evidence of guilt. Defense attorneys closely scrutinize this evidence on behalf of the accused. Only in court, with a judge serving as referee, does an objective assessment of the facts and law occur. Without neutral and detached courts and judges, there would be no forum in which the rights of the community could be balanced against those of the accused.

There is both good and bad news in assessing the future of the court system. The good news includes improved judicial quality, specialized courts, and alternatives to the courtroom for certain kinds of cases. Judges are better qualified now than at any time in the nation's history. Virtually all are required to hold law

Media and Criminal Justice

THE THIN BLUE LINE

In 1978, a Dallas police officer was shot dead by someone inside a car he had stopped on a minor traffic violation. A young drifter with no previous criminal record, Randall Adams, was convicted of the murder. A Texas teenager named David Harris was allegedly in the car at the time of the shooting, and implicated Adams as the shooter. Adams was given the death penalty, and Harris was set free.

The story of Adams and Harris is true. The documentary Errol Morris made about them in 1988, *The Thin Blue Line,* has become a landmark in the study of the American criminal justice system. It is famous not just for its report of a fascinating case but because of its actual role in securing justice for a wrongly convicted man.

In the film, the director interviewed Adams and Harris (who was serving time for an unrelated murder) from prison, but he assembled a fascinating cast of key witnesses and courtroom players from the actual case. Randall Adams was prosecuted for the officer's murder by a state's attorney who was famous for never once losing a case. Adams was given a psychiatric examination by a court-appointed psychologist dubbed "Dr. Death" because he *always* ruled that the convict was a sociopath who would repeat his crimes and therefore deserved to die. The eyewitnesses who fingered Adams are revealed as mercenary liars who testified in a desperate attempt to obtain reward money. The most shocking revelation, however, comes from star witness David Harris, who as a 16-year-old was too young for the death penalty, and as a local resident did not make nearly as good a scapegoat as the transient Randall Adams.

The Thin Blue Line is an amazing movie not because it is based on a true story but because the true story is being uncovered as the documentary unfolds. The viewer is drawn into the case as it is examined and reenacted, hearing various versions of events from the accused, the police, the lawyers, the witnesses, and the judges who actually played a role in the case as it progressed to the Supreme Court. At the end, director Morris manages to elicit a truth that the court process never discovered. In the director's final interview with David Harris, the young man cryptically implies that he was responsible for the murder of Officer Woods. When asked if Adams is innocent, Harris simply replies, "I'm sure that he is." Asked how he can be sure, Harris says, "Because I'm the one that knows."

The story of *The Thin Blue Line* is rich in detail about the court system and its players, but it is horrifying in its implications. At the time of its release, Adams had been sitting on death row in a Texas prison for eleven years for a crime that he apparently did not commit. On the basis of the information uncovered by Morris in *The Thin Blue Line,* the case was reopened and Adams was eventually exonerated and released.

MEDIA AND CRIMINAL JUSTICE QUESTION

What new or revised procedures can you suggest that would reduce the number of erroneous convictions in criminal cases?

degrees, and legal education is more standardized today than it was in the past. This makes for a high standard of legal knowledge throughout most of the United States, except in some local justice of the peace courts, which still do not require legal training for judges.

Second, specialized courts have emerged to deal more effectively with the problem of drug-related crime. The drug court movement began during the late 1980s in response to the dramatic growth in drug-related cases. As is illustrated in Figure 10.5, the most frequently charged felonies in the nation's seventy-five largest counties are drug offenses, accounting for more than a third of all defendants. The purpose of these drug courts is to hold the defendant or offender "personally and publicly accountable for treatment progress."[24] Begun in Miami and now found in more than twenty other jurisdictions, the drug court is coordinated by the judge, who works with the prosecutor, defense, and drug treatment personnel to select an appropriate treatment; address issues of housing,

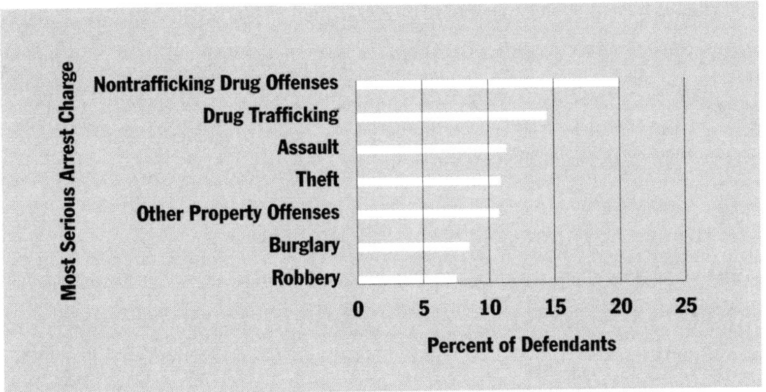

FIGURE 10.5
The most frequently charged offenses of felony defendants in the seventy-five largest counties

SOURCE: Brian A. Reaves, *Felony Defendants in Large Urban Counties* (Washington, D.C.: Bureau of Justice Statistics, 1998).

employment, or other barriers to progress; and monitor the offender's progress. Figure 10.6 illustrates two models of drug courts. One involves treatment after adjudication; the other entails treatment while prosecution is deferred.

An evaluation of Miami's felony drug court found that fewer defendants were incarcerated, but also that fewer drug cases were dropped during adjudication and offenders were arrested less frequently.[25] Nevertheless, some challenges

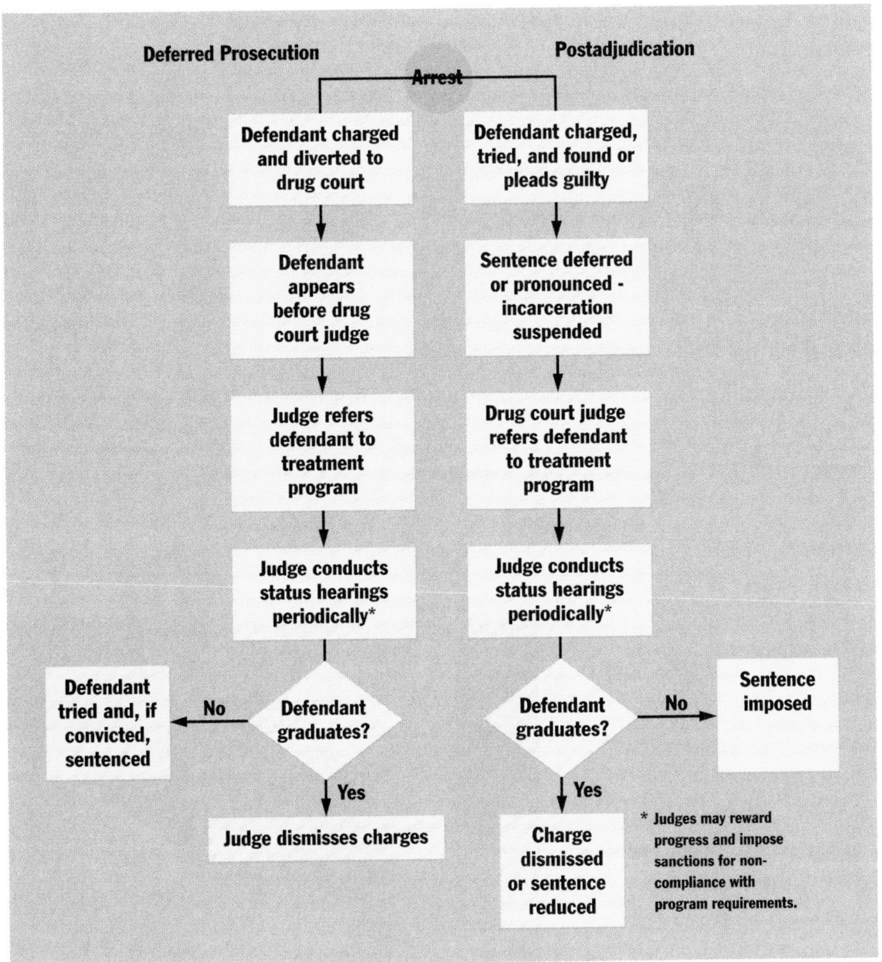

FIGURE 10.6
Two drug court models

SOURCE: U.S. Comptroller General, *Drug Courts: Overview of Growth, Characteristics, and Results* (Washington, D.C.: U.S. General Accounting Office, 1997).

remain, including the need for accurate information about defendants, proper screening of offenders to be referred to drug court, and the availability of different types of drug treatment for different kinds of drug abuse. In 1994, realizing the need to supplement existing police and corrections approaches, Congress passed the Violent Crime Control and Law Enforcement Act to support local and state drug courts.

The use of drug courts builds on the experiences of drug night courts and expedited processing of drug cases in selected cities. These approaches have been developed in an effort to handle the expanding drug case load by increasing hours of operation and handling these cases in a more timely fashion.[26] Drug courts concentrate drug cases and expertise in a single courtroom and thereby reduce the length of time from arrest to disposition while reducing the case loads of general felony courts.[27] Their goals are consistency in the handling of drug cases, timeliness in adjudication, and reduction of offender recidivism by addressing underlying drug addictions.

In addition to the changes just described, there is a growing trend toward the use of alternatives to the formal adjudication process. Mediation and pretrial intervention programs have been instituted in response to high case loads, but they also reflect a change in philosophy from "adjudication at any cost" to "justice at lower cost." These alternatives allow defendants to complete restitution or rehabilitation programs in exchange for holding their cases in abeyance. Once the restitution or rehabilitation is completed, the charges are dropped. In other programs, the victim and the accused mutually agree on an appropriate remedy outside of court.

Taking this trend one step further are efforts to prevent disputes from arising in the first place. The Resolving Conflict Creatively Program (RCCP) in New York City is a school-based program designed to teach young people how to resolve conflicts peacefully. The goal is to reduce violence, delinquency, and court appearances by young people by equipping them with the skills needed to make more rational decisions in dealing with conflict. Workshops teach about cooperation, appreciating diversity, being aware of bias, and specific skills for avoiding and deescalating conflicts.[28] An evaluation found that most students in the program "learn the key concepts and are able to apply them when responding to hypothetical conflicts." In addition, the participating students report fewer fights and less name-calling behavior compared to a matched group of nonparticipants.

The Resolving Conflict Creatively program is a school-based program in New York designed to teach young people how to resolve conflicts peacefully.

Finally, teachers in the program have been found to be "more willing to let students take responsibility for solving their own conflicts."[29] Efforts like the RCCP program may hold the long-term solution to crowded courts by disseminating the skills required for avoiding conflicts or resolving them *before* civil or criminal misconduct occurs.

There is also some ominous news for the future. The bad news involves ever-increasing case loads, judicial training, and court security. Despite higher levels of legal education, judicial training can be improved further. There are many judges who have legal training but no specific training in the skills required of a judge. Many have experience as prosecutors or defense counsel, but these are quite different roles from that of a neutral and detached arbiter in a criminal case. The Federal Judicial Center, established in 1967, is responsible for judicial education and research in the federal courts.[30] Unfortunately, not all states have similar organized systems for judicial training. Standardized judicial training is important for maintaining high levels of competence and public confidence in the adjudication process.

Second, court case loads continue to grow at an alarming rate. Both new criminal charges and appeals from adjudicated cases have increased tenfold in recent years, with no end in sight. In state courts, which handle more than 95 percent of the total volume of cases, nearly ninety million new cases are filed each year. Over the last three decades the largest increases have been in criminal cases (up 35 percent), juvenile cases (up 59 percent), and domestic relations cases (up 65 percent).[31] Despite a growing trend toward the use of mediation and pretrial intervention programs, new cases far outstrip the capacity of these programs to deal with them.

As the U.S. population grows, it is reasonable to expect the numbers of arrests and cases filed to increase as well. One of the largest sources of higher case loads is drug cases. The increase in laws and law enforcement in this area over the last two decades has led to thousands of arrests and prosecutions throughout the nation. As was noted earlier, specialized drug courts have been created in some areas, but the need is clear: More judges and more courtrooms will be required for the foreseeable future.

Third, courts are increasingly targeted for attack by criminals. Such cases have increased over the last twenty years. In 1979, a person connected with defendants in a pending drug case shot and killed a U.S. district court judge as he entered his car at home in Texas. In 1989, an offender appealing a conviction for possessing a pipe bomb sent one to the Alabama residence of a U.S. court of appeals judge, who was killed when the bomb exploded. In 1992, a defendant in a Chicago bank robbery slipped free of his handcuffs, grabbed the gun of a deputy marshal, and fatally shot him and another court security officer. These and other instances of attacks on court personnel are designed to disrupt the adjudication process. There have been three assassinations of judges and several killings and woundings of marshals and other court personnel. In addition to these outright attacks, many threats are made against judges,[32] and nearly 400,000 concealed guns and knives are confiscated annually at federal courthouses. A survey of federal judges found that 86 percent felt secure in the courtroom owing to rigorous screening procedures at courthouses. Only 42 percent felt secure elsewhere, however.[33] Indeed, most assaults and killings of judges have occurred outside the courthouse.

Despite the challenges posed by court security, increasing case loads, and judicial training, there is evidence that a number of states are responding by engaging in long-range court planning.[34] This will enable courts to develop strategic plans for handling the issues they face and to present convincing arguments for government to fund programs designed to address these issues.

Critical Thinking EXERCISE

Frivolity in the Courts

Some observers argue that the justice process has been compromised by the dramatic rise in the number of cases filed in both civil and criminal court. A survey of the seventy-five largest counties in the United States found 378,000 tort cases resolved in a single year.[A] These cases involved injury or loss due to noncriminal negligence or intention. A majority (60 percent) involved automobile accidents, followed by liability for injury due to unsafe business premises (17 percent). The cases took an average of more than nineteen months to complete. Interestingly, only 3 percent of the cases were resolved at trial. Seventy-three percent were settled out of court, and the nature and details of these settlements usually are not made public.

Critics have alleged that these settlements are often unjust, citing instances of six-figure settlements in cases in which little or no harm was done. These include one case in which a customer successfully sued McDonald's after she spilled hot coffee on her lap. A woman received a large settlement from an amusement park after being injured in a bumper-car collision, even though the jury found the park only 1 percent liable and the driver who drove the other bumper car (her husband) 85 percent liable.[B]

Examples such as these have provoked criticism of a civil court system that promotes opportunistic and frivolous suits by individuals and attorneys in the hope of "jackpot" settlements.[C] Proposed reforms include disciplining lawyers who file frivolous suits, making the losing party in a civil suit pay all the court costs incurred by both sides (as is done in other countries), eliminating the "deep pockets" principle that allows wealthy defendants to be held liable for the full cost of a settlement regardless of their degree of responsibility, and limiting the amount of punitive damages that can be awarded.[D]

In criminal cases an analogous development has occurred. Courts are increasingly used to resolve disputes between private parties, such as filings for trespass, harassment, and public nuisances. In such cases the courts are used as a forum to settle disputes between neighbors, friends, and family members who cannot resolve them on their own. The result is case load "clutter," in which court calendars are crowded with cases that involve no threat to the community or to society at large. Instead, courts are increasingly misused to resolve problems between private parties—on government time and at the taxpayer's expense.

Critical Thinking Questions

1. **Why do you believe states and the federal government have been slow to introduce reforms in the litigation process such as those described here?**

2. If these reforms are not enacted, what other methods could be used to reduce the number of frivolous case filings?

Notes

[A]Steven K. Smith, Carol J. DeFrances, and Patrick A. Langan, *Tort Cases in Large Counties* (Washington, D.C.: U.S. Bureau of Justice Statistics, 1995).

[B]"Step Right Up, Place Your Bets in Casino-style Courts," *USA Today* (March 6, 1995), p. 10A.

[C]Walter K. Olson, *The Litigation Explosion* (New York: Plume, 1992).

[D]Philip K. Howard, *The Death of Common Sense* (New York: Random House, 1994).

Limiting Criminal Appeals

The adjudication process is undermined when there are long delays between the commission of a crime and the imposition of a sentence. Many people view the growth in the number of appeals filed by convicted offenders as an example.

An appeal simply argues that an error of law or procedure was made in a case and that a new trial is warranted. Although 80 percent of appeals are unsuccessful, they delay punishment while the appeal is heard by an appellate court.[A] A common kind of appeal is a writ of habeas corpus, which requires that a prisoner be brought before a judge to determine whether he or she is incarcerated lawfully (i.e., no legal error has been made). The number of habeas corpus petitions filed has increased dramatically over the years, even though only about 3 percent result in a new trial or the release of an offender. Although the odds of success are low, the large volume of appeals from criminal trials adds to already mushrooming case loads.

During the 1990s, the U.S. Supreme Court has made rulings that limit an offender's right to appeal. The Court has held that an offender is entitled to federal appeal from a state court finding only when "actual prejudice" can be shown to result from failure to appeal in a state court, or "when a fundamental miscarriage of justice would result" without a review of the case.[B] This ruling limits the circumstances in which an offender can have a state case reviewed in federal court for legal errors.

In 1993, the U.S. Supreme Court held that an offender who has been sentenced to death for murder is not entitled to a federal order for a new state trial because new evidence is not automatic grounds for a new trial.[C] This holding also makes it more difficult for an offender to have a state court conviction reviewed by a federal court.[D] The outcome in practice has been fewer appeals accepted for review. In death penalty cases, in which numerous appeals are common, the ruling has resulted in more executions per year than at any time since the 1930s.

Critical Thinking Questions

1. Can you think of any negative consequences of limiting the number of appeals made by offenders, as the U.S. Supreme Court has done in recent years?
2. What are at least two positive consequences of limits on appeals?

3. How would you evaluate the relative strengths of the positive and negative consequences of limiting criminal appeals?

Notes

[A]Joy A. Chaper and Roger A. Hanson, *Understanding Reversible Error in Criminal Appeals* (Williamsburg, VA: National Center for State Courts, 1989).

[B]*Kenney v. Tamayo-Reyes,* 504 U.S. 1 (1992).

[C]*Herrera v. Collins,* 113 S. Ct. 853 (1993).

[D]Robert D. Pursley, "The Federal Habeas Corpus Process: Unraveling the Issues," *Criminal Justice Policy Review,* vol. 7 (1995), pp. 115–41.

Summary

THE HISTORY OF CRIMINAL COURTS

- Although celebrated cases have occurred on occasion in the past, in many cases lawyers were absent from the trial. Misdemeanor cases were handled in a nonprofessional fashion, while the processing of felonies tended to be more formal.
- Until the late 1800s, a defendant could not act as a witness or take the stand in his or her own defense. Today defendants are permitted to testify under oath.

THE ORGANIZATION OF CONTEMPORARY COURTS

- The vast majority of criminal cases are heard in state courts because most felonies are defined by state laws.
- There are three levels of jurisdiction: limited, general, and appellate. These are found in all state court systems, but each state determines how its system is organized.
- The legal authority of courts of limited jurisdiction is restricted to certain specific types of cases. Courts of general jurisdiction are often referred to as trial courts, and most felony trials are held at this level. Appellate courts hear appeals from courts of general jurisdiction.
- The federal court system parallels the state court systems. There are courts of limited jurisdiction such as the U.S. Court of Claims. There are also courts of general jurisdiction, the U.S. district courts; these are located throughout the country and hear cases that involve alleged violations of federal law.
- There are two levels of appellate courts. The intermediate level consists of U.S. courts of appeals. The highest level is the U.S. Supreme Court.
- All cases heard by the U.S. Supreme Court involve interpretations of the U.S. Constitution. The Court can choose which cases it will hear through a procedure termed *certiorari;* a *writ of certiorari* is issued when four or more Justices believe that the legal issues presented in a case merit review.
- The decisions of the U.S. Supreme Court are made by a majority vote of the nine Justices, who are appointed for life by the President with the consent of the Senate.
- Most states, as well as the federal government, have court administrators whose job is to handle court appearances and determine the need for and availability of court personnel.

PARTICIPANTS IN THE JUDICIAL PROCESS

- Prosecutors represent the community in bringing charges against an accused person. Most prosecutors are elected officials and therefore may feel pressure to make "popular" prosecution decisions. Other influences on prosecutors' decisions include case load pressures and the need to maintain good relations with other actors in the adjudication process.

- Defense attorneys represent the legal rights of the accused in criminal proceedings. They examine the evidence used to establish probable cause and assess the strength of the evidence that will be used to prove guilt.
- The task of judges is to objectively assess the strength of a case, rule on issues of law and procedure, and sometimes determine the ultimate disposition of a case. Judges are selected in a variety of ways, including appointment, nonpartisan election, and merit selection.
- Two recent reforms—state court unification and the establishment of U.S. magistrates—have improved the quality of the judicial system.
- Victims and witnesses are not represented by specific actors in the adjudication process. In recent years efforts have been made to give them a greater role in the process, usually at sentencing and at parole hearings.
- A proposed constitutional amendment would give victims legal authority to object to plea-bargaining, guarantee victims a speedy trial, require full restitution by the offender, and provide protection of victims when necessary.

THE FUTURE OF THE COURT SYSTEM

- Improved judicial quality, specialized courts, and alternatives to the courtroom are good news for the future of the court system.
- Challenges faced by the court system include ever-increasing case loads, the need to improve judicial training, and issues of court security.

Key Terms

limited jurisdiction
general jurisdiction
appellate court
U.S. district courts
U.S. courts of appeals
U.S. Supreme Court
writ of certiorari
judicial review
court administrator
prosecutor
defense attorney
judge
merit selection plan
U.S. magistrate judge

Questions for Review and Discussion

1. What are some of the most important differences between the way trials were conducted in the past and the way they are conducted today?
2. How are state court systems organized?
3. What are U.S. district courts?
4. What kinds of cases are heard by the U.S. Supreme Court?
5. What are the functions of a court administrator?
6. Describe the four main types of participants in the judicial process.
7. What are some of the ways in which judges are selected in different states?
8. What is meant by state court unification?
9. What initiatives have been taken to give victims and witnesses a greater role in the criminal justice process?
10. What are the major challenges facing the justice system in the future?

Notes

[1]Julius Goebel, Jr., ed., *The Law and Practice of Alexander Hamilton: Documents and Commentary* (New York: Columbia University Press, 1964).

[2]Lawrence M. Friedman, *Crime and Punishment in American History* (New York: Basic Books, 1993), p. 239.

[3]*Hurtado v. California*, 110 U.S. 516 (1884).

[4]*Strauder v. West Virginia* (1879).

[5]Friedman, pp. 245–50.

[6]Herbert A. Johnson and Nancy Travis Wolfe, *History of Criminal Justice*, 2nd ed. (Cincinnati: Anderson Publishing, 1996), pp. 81, 112.

[7]Peter Hoffer, *Law and People in Colonial America* (Baltimore: Johns Hopkins University Press, 1992).

[8]Johnson and Wolfe, p. 113.

[9]Patrick Langan, *State Felony Courts and Felony Laws* (Washington, D.C.: Bureau of Justice Statistics, 1987).

[10]1 Cr. 138 (1803).

[11]Ted Guest, "Making a Case for Judges," *U.S. News & World Report* (January 12, 1998), p. 29.

[12]H. Ted Rubin, *The Courts: Fulcrum of the Justice System* (Pacific Palisades, CA: Goodyear Publishing, 1976).

[13]Charles Swanson and Susan Talarico, eds., *Court Administration: Issues and Responses* (Athens: University of Georgia Press, 1987).

[14]U.S. Comptroller General, *Federal Criminal Justice System: A Model to Estimate System Workload* (Washington, D.C.: U.S. General Accounting Office, 1991).

[15]American Bar Association, *ABA Standards for Criminal Justice* (Washington, D.C.: American Bar Association, 1992), Standard 3-1.

[16]Thomas Henderson and Cornelius Kerwin, *Structuring Justice: The Implications of Court Unification Reforms* (Washington, D.C.: National Institute of Justice, 1984).

[17]American Bar Association, *ABA Standards Relating to Court Organization* (Chicago: American Bar Association, 1990).

[18]Ted R. Miller, Mark A. Cohen, and Brian Wiersema, *Victim Costs and Consequences: A New Look* (Washington, D.C.: National Institute of Justice, 1996).

[19]Kerry Murphy Healey, *Victim and Witness Intimidation: New Developments and Emerging Responses* (Washington, D.C.: National Institute of Justice, 1995).

[20]Ibid.

[21]Office for Victims of Crime, *Victims of Crime Act Crime Victims Fund* (Washington, D.C.: U.S. Department of Justice, 1996).

[22]Tony Mauro and Bill Nichols, "Obligation of a Fair Trial vs. Victims' Rights," *USA Today* (June 26, 1996), p. 8.

[23]Ibid.

[24]*The Drug Court Movement* (Washington, D.C.: National Institute of Justice, 1995).

[25]John S. Goldkamp and Doris Weiland, *Assessing the Impact of Dade County's Felony Drug Court* (Washington, D.C.: National Institute of Justice, 1993).

[26]American Bar Association, *Drug Night Courts: The Cook County Experience* (Washington, D.C.: Bureau of Justice Assistance, 1994).

[27]Steven Belenko and Tamara Dumankovsky, *Special Drug Courts* (Washington, D.C.: Bureau of Justice Assistance, 1993).

[28]William DeJong, *Building the Peace: The Resolving Conflict Creatively Program* (Washington, D.C.: National Institute of Justice, 1996); Donna Crawford and Richard Bodine, *Conflict Resolution Education* (Washington, D.C.: Office of Juvenile Justice and Delinquency Prevention, 1996).

[29]Ibid., p. 11.

[30]U.S. Comptroller General, *The Federal Judiciary: Observations on Selected Issues* (Washington, D.C.: U.S. General Accounting Office, 1995).

[31]National Center for State Courts, *Annual Report* (Washington, D.C.: National Center for State Courts, 1996).

[32]U.S. Comptroller General, *Federal Judicial Security* (Washington, D.C.: U.S. General Accounting Office, 1994).

[33]Ibid.
[34]Sohail Inayatullah, ed., "The Futures of State Courts," *Futures Research Quarterly* vol. 10 (Spring 1994), pp. 5–80.

For Further Reading

Barrett McGurn, *America's Court: The Supreme Court and the People* (Golden, CO: Fulcrum Publishing, 1997).

Elaine Pascoe, *America's Courts on Trial: Questioning Our Legal System* (New York: Millbrook Press, 1997).

Richard A. Posner, *The Federal Courts: Challenge and Reform* (Cambridge, MA: Harvard University Press, 1997).

chapter eleven

Prosecution, Pleas, and Trials

Laws too gentle are seldom obeyed; too severe, seldom executed.

BENJAMIN FRANKLIN
(1706–1790)

CHAPTER OUTLINE

Police are called to the scene where an inebriated husband is assaulting his wife. They arrest the man and charge him with assault, possession of narcotics, and possession of a weapon. When they have completed the arrest report, it is forwarded to the prosecutor for evaluation. The prosecutor may decide to prosecute on all the arrest charges, drop some of them, reduce the charges, or not prosecute the case at all. The latter might occur if there were obvious and grave errors in the conduct of the police in the case, or if the offense took place in an area with a high volume of felony cases, forcing the prosecutor to set priorities in deciding which cases will be adjudicated to the full extent of the law. If the prosecutor decides not to

Bronco Evidence
23

prosecute a case, the judge and jury cannot serve any function and the arrest is meaningless.

The Prosecutor's Role

The prosecutor is the only actor in the criminal justice system who is concerned with all aspects of criminal justice processing. From arrest through disposition, he or she makes decisions that greatly affect the outcome of a case. The scope of this discretion is rarely defined by statute, but it dramatically affects the operation of the criminal justice system.

Prosecutors also represent the public in their actions, whether they work at the federal, state, or county level. Because violations of the criminal law are crimes against society, prosecutors represent their jurisdiction, not victims or other individuals. Federal prosecutors are called U.S. attorneys; state prosecutors are called state, district, or commonwealth attorneys; and local prosecutors are called district attorneys, commonwealth attorneys, or county prosecutors. Most prosecutions occur at the state or county level: Of the nearly one million felony convictions each year in the United States, only 5 percent occur in federal courts.[1]

There are few limits on how prosecutors can carry out their role. As an example, the Manhattan district attorney in New York City has established a narcotics eviction program. In response to complaints from tenants in poor neighborhoods, the district attorney asks landlords to begin eviction proceedings against tenants who are using drugs or allowing others to use their apartments to sell drugs. If the landlord does not act, the district attorney initiates eviction proceedings under New York's real estate law, which prohibits the use of any premises for the conduct of illegal activity. Allegations of such use are supported by evidence produced by police searches of the premises. In one case, a 68-year-old woman was living with two daughters who were selling drugs. The judge allowed the mother to remain in the apartment but barred the daughters from returning there. In six years the program has removed more than 2,000 drug users and dealers from both residential and commercial buildings.[2]

Prosecutorial Discretion

Prosecutors are granted considerable discretion in the manner in which they enforce the law. As was just noted, they can set priorities, concentrate on certain types of cases, and avoid other cases entirely. A good way to assess the extent of prosecutorial discretion is to see how a prosecutor's decisions can affect the adjudication of a single case as it proceeds through the system. Let us assume that police have arrested a suspect on a charge of armed robbery. They turn over the case to the prosecutor, who decides whether the case will be prosecuted and what charges will be pressed. In the case of armed robbery, for example, assault, larceny, and weapons charges could be filed in addition to the robbery charge. This is because each of these crimes is a component of armed robbery. These additional charges are called **necessarily included offenses** (or "lesser" included of-

necessarily (or "lesser") included offenses
Crimes that are included as part of another, more serious, offense.

fenses) because they are, by definition, included as part of the other (more serious) offense.

After charges have been filed, the prosecutor can decide not to press the charges any further or to reduce the charge in exchange for a guilty plea. When the charge is not pressed further, it is called **nolle prosequi (or nol. pros.).** Such a decision is entirely within the prosecutor's discretion. Exchanging a reduced charge for a guilty plea is a form of plea-bargaining. Once a defendant has pleaded guilty or been convicted in court, the prosecutor usually recommends a particular sentence to the judge.

Prosecutors have broad discretion is deciding whether or not a case will be prosecuted and, if so, on which specific charges. Prosecutors also make sentencing recommendations to the judge.

This sequence of decisions shows that the prosecutor has considerable discretion at every major decision point in the criminal justice process. From determining whether the police decision to arrest was appropriate, to determining the charge(s) to be filed, to recommending bail, to playing a role in whether or not a defendant goes to trial, to influencing the judge's sentencing decision, the prosecutor's discretion is the most far-reaching in the criminal justice system.

The scope of the prosecutor's discretion continues to expand. Mandatory minimum sentence and truth in sentencing laws have resulted in reduced flexibility in the sentencing choices available to judges. For example, many states have laws that require mandatory sentences of one year or more for possession of a handgun without a permit. A prosecutor may choose to prosecute a first offender, who is not seen as deserving to spend a year in prison, with a lesser crime such as disorderly conduct or trespass, which does not carry a mandatory sentence. On the other hand, the prosecutor may wish to charge the first offender with illegal gun-carrying in order to deter others from committing the same crime, or as part of a campaign for reelection. Therefore, a prosecutor's choice of the precise charge, and whether that charge carries a mandatory sentence, controls the sentencing decision as well. This shifting of sentencing authority from the judge to the prosecutor has been criticized for placing too much power in the hands of one person.[3]

nolle prosequi (or nol. pros.)
A decision by a prosecutor not to press charges.

Selection of Prosecutors

There are more than 8,000 state, county, and local prosecutors in the United States. About a third of them handle felony cases in state trial courts; the others primarily deal with misdemeanor cases.[4] Most prosecutors are county officials, as is illustrated in Table 11.1. Approximately 70 percent of chief prosecutors hold full-time salaried positions. The typical prosecutor's office has two assistant prosecuting attorneys in addition to the chief prosecutor, although this number varies widely according to the size of the jurisdiction. In jurisdictions with populations of 500,000 or more, there are, on average, sixty-four assistant prosecutors.[5]

Depending on the state, prosecutors are either appointed or elected. There has been a continuing debate over which method of selection is preferable, although all but five states now elect prosecutors.[6] Supporters of appointment of prosecutors point out that appointment reduces the possibility of overzealous or lackluster prosecutions of unpopular or controversial cases for election-related reasons. For example, it is alleged that cases involving high-profile defendants are pursued more often during election years.[7] Also, elections are based on the assumption that the public knows how to evaluate a competent performance by a prosecutor. Election campaigns, however, often become contests over who will be the "toughest" prosecutor.

Supporters of election of prosecutors believe that elections provide regular opportunities for the public to express approval or disapproval of a prosecutor's policies. They also claim that appointments to the position of prosecutor may be based on political considerations, resulting in appointments of politically well-connected individuals who may not have the background or experience to be effective prosecutors on behalf of a jurisdiction.

In some states, special prosecutors can be appointed to investigate extraordinary crimes. They are appointed by the governor to investigate multijurisdictional crimes that involve a potential conflict of interest on the part of the state attorney general (who is part of the state government). In these cases the offense usually involves allegations of misconduct on the part of a government official or agency. Therefore, an outside "special" prosecutor is appointed to conduct an independent objective evaluation of the evidence.

TABLE 11.1

Chief Prosecutors Who Handle Felony Cases in State Courts

STATE	NUMBER OF CHIEF PROSECUTORS	TITLE	AREAS OF JURISDICTION
Alabama	40	District Attorney*	Judicial circuits
Alaska	13	District Attorney	Regional districts
Arizona	15	County Attorney	Counties
Arkansas	24	Prosecuting Attorney	Judicial circuits
California	58	District Attorney	Counties, city/county government of San Francisco
Colorado	22	District Attorney	Judicial circuits
Connecticut	12	State's Attorney	Judicial districts that are county- and city-based
Delaware	1	Attorney General	Attorney General as primary duties for the entire State
District of Columbia	1	U.S. Attorney	U.S. Attorney has jurisdiction over adult felony and misdemeanor cases
Florida	20	State's Attorney	Judicial circuits
Georgia	46	District Attorney	Judicial circuits
Hawaii	4	Prosecuting Attorney	Counties
Idaho	44	Prosecuting Attorney	Counties
Illinois	102	State's Attorney	Counties
Indiana	90	Prosecuting Attorney	Judicial circuits
Iowa	99	County Attorney	Counties
Kansas	105	County Attorney Called District Attorney in 5 counties	Counties
Kentucky	56	Commonwealth's Attorney	Judicial circuits
Louisiana	41	District Attorney	Judicial districts, Orleans Parish
Maine	8	District Attorney	Geographical districts
Maryland	24	State's Attorney	Counties, Baltimore City
Massachusetts	11	District Attorney	Geographical districts
Michigan	83	Prosecuting Attorney	Counties
Minnesota	87	County Attorney	Counties
Mississippi	22	District Attorney	Judicial districts
Missouri	115	Prosecuting Attorney Called Circuit Attorney in City of St. Louis	Counties Counties, City of St. Louis

*One circuit in Alabama has an elected assistant prosecutor.

**Salt Lake County, Utah, has both a district attorney, who handles felony cases, and a county attorney, who handles civil and city ordinance violations.

INDEPENDENT COUNSEL In the early 1980s, Congress passed legislation that created the Office of the Independent Counsel. This federal office was formed in response to allegations of misconduct by officials in the executive branch of the federal government. Several officials in the Reagan administration were convicted of lying to Congress. Independent counsel Lawrence Walsh spent $35 million in pursuing the Iran–Contra investigation.[8] Since then, numerous independent counsel investigations have been authorized. The best known is that conducted by Kenneth Starr, whose investigation of President Clinton's real estate dealings as Governor of Arkansas expanded into an investigation of alleged sexual misconduct in the White House.

Many observers expressed concern about the scope of the independent counsel's authority when Starr arranged for a friend of a White House intern to wear a concealed microphone to surreptitiously tape conversations, and when he subpoenaed the intern's mother to testify before a grand jury about her conversations with her own daughter. The independent counsel was seeking evidence of

STATE	NUMBER OF CHIEF PROSECUTORS	TITLE	AREAS OF JURISDICTION
Montana	56	County Attorney	Counties
Nebraska	93	County Attorney	Counties
Nevada	17	District Attorney	Counties, Carson City
New Hampshire	10	County Attorney	Counties
New Jersey	21	County Prosecutor	Counties
New Mexico	14	District Attorney	Judicial districts
New York	62	District Attorney	Counties, 5 boroughs of New York City
North Carolina	38	District Attorney	Prosecutorial districts
North Dakota	53	State's Attorney	Counties
Ohio	88	Prosecuting Attorney	Counties
Oklahoma	27	District Attorney	Judicial districts
Oregon	36	District Attorney	Counties
Pennsylvania	67	District Attorney	Counties, city/county government of Philadelphia
Rhode Island	1	Attorney General	Attorney General has primary duties for entire State
South Carolina	16	Solicitor	Judicial circuits
South Dakota	66	State's Attorney	Counties
Tennessee	31	District Attorney General	Judicial districts
Texas	152	District Attorney, Criminal District Attorney, and County and District Attorney	Counties, judicial districts
Utah	29	County Attorney**	Counties
Vermont	14	State's Attorney	Counties
Virginia	121	Commonwealth's Attorney	Counties, 26 independent cities
Washington	39	Prosecuting Attorney	Counties
West Virginia	55	Prosecuting Attorney	Counties
Wisconsin	71	District Attorney	Counties (2 counties that share a district attorney)
Wyoming	23	District Attorney County and Prosecuting Attorney	Judicial districts Counties where office of a district attorney has not been created
Total	2,343		

SOURCES: *1994 National Directory of Prosecutors, The American Bench*, 7th ed., information was also provided directly to Bureau of Justice Statistics by selected state prosecutor coordinators' offices; Carol J. DeFrances, Steven K. Smith, and Louise van der Does, *Prosecutors in State Courts* (Washington, D.C.: Bureau of Justice Statistics, 1996).

contemporary issues

Selective Prosecution of High-Rate Offenders

Many of the most serious offenders are also repeat offenders. Often they are habitual, high-rate, and/or dangerous offenders who commit a larger proportion of crimes than their numbers would warrant. In a growing number of jurisdictions, prosecutors have established formal or informal guidelines under which these offenders are prosecuted on an individualized basis. In two thirds of all prosecutor's offices, a system known as *vertical prosecution* is employed. For at least certain kinds of cases (such as sexual assault or drug cases), a prosecutor stays with the same case through sentencing.[A]

Selective prosecution ensures that the case receives special attention, charges are not reduced, and long sentences are recommended in order to incapacitate the offender. A national survey found that a significant proportion of prosecutor's offices had prosecuted at least one case of domestic violence (88 percent), stalking (68 percent), elder abuse (41 percent), hate crime (29 percent), or environmental pollution (26 percent) during the year.[B]

An examination of selective prosecution efforts in several counties found that written criteria for defining what constitutes a career criminal serve to promote consistency in prosecutors' judgments about which cases should be handled differently.[C] A problem arises, however, in determining which offenders are "dangerous" or "high-rate" early in their criminal careers. Some factors that are commonly believed to be associated with high-rate offending actually are not. Display of a weapon, alcoholism, prior arrests for drug offenses, prior probation or parole revocation, and previous incarceration have not been found to be associated with high-rate offending.[D] On the other hand, some defendants are arrested for less serious offenses (such as larceny or burglary of an empty building), yet their prior record indicates a high rate of violent offenses. These defendants cannot be selectively prosecuted because the most recent offense does not carry a severe penalty.

To be effective, selective prosecution must overcome at least two major hurdles: obtaining accurate knowledge of which factors are in fact associated with repeat and violent offenses, and arresting those offenders early in their careers for a serious offense that warrants selective prosecution. There are many repeat offenders. Two thirds of felony defendants have a felony arrest record, and more than a third are on bail, probation, or parole at the time that they are charged with a new crime.[E] Nearly 20 percent of felony offenders are convicted of two or more felonies that arise from a single case.[F] Multiple felonies in a single case might include robbery and murder; kidnapping and assault; burglary, theft, and assault; or some other combination of crimes that occur as part of a single incident. In addition, more than 96 percent of all prosecutor's offices use a defendant's criminal history during the course of pretrial negotiations and at sentencing.[G]

Continuing research is needed to ensure that typologies of career criminals are based on factual data and not on "folk wisdom" that is inaccurate or outdated. Also, there must be safeguards to ensure that individuals who are predicted to be high-rate offenders are not handled differently without proof that they have committed prior offenses. The criminal justice system permits punishment only for crimes committed in the past, not for crimes contemplated in the future. Yet if they are armed with reliable information about past patterns of criminal activity, prosecutors have a strong argument for enhanced sentencing based on the offender's past and the behavior of other criminals with similar backgrounds.

NOTES

[A]Carol J. DeFrances, Steven K. Smith, and Louise van der Does, *Prosecutors in State Courts* (Washington, D.C.: Bureau of Justice Statistics, 1996).

[B]Ibid., p. 3.

[C]Marcia R. Chaiken and Jan M. Chaiken, *Priority Prosecution of High-Rate Dangerous Offenders* (Washington, D.C.: National Institute of Justice, 1991), p. 4.

[D]Ibid., p. 6.

[E]Brian A. Reaves and Pheny Z. Smith, *Felony Defendants in Large Urban Counties* (Washington, D.C.: Bureau of Justice Statistics, 1995).

[F]Patrick A. Langan and Jodi M. Brown, *Felony Sentences in State Courts* (Washington, D.C.: Bureau of Justice Statistics, 1997), p. 6.

[G]DeFrances, Smith, and van der Does, p. 6.

presidential involvement in obstruction of justice or encouragement of perjury, but these intrusive tactics were widely criticized.[9] It has also been argued that the strong-arm tactics used by prosecutors in this case would result in disciplinary proceedings if they were used by a private attorney representing a client.[10] The law that created the independent counsel mandates that any evidence gathered

Independent counsel Kenneth Starr began his investigation of President Clinton's possible involvement in the Whitewater land deal in Arkansas, but turned his attention to the Monica Lewinsky investigation in 1998.

must be given to Congress, but no guidance is provided about when that evidence should be given or in what form.[11] As a result, Starr was criticized for an investigation that lasted more than five years (as of 1998) and cost more than $40 million. It can be seen that the power of a prosecutor can be far-reaching and that a precise definition of the scope of that authority is crucial.

PROSECUTORIAL MISCONDUCT There is also growing concern regarding the conduct of prosecutors once they are in office. In one well-known case, a prosecutor concealed from the jury in a murder case the fact that red stains on the defendant's clothing were paint, not blood.[12] There are documented instances in which prosecutors have attempted to sway juries with appeals to inadmissible evidence, prejudice, or inflammatory statements.[13] In other cases, prosecutors have retried defendants several times after their cases have been dropped or dismissed. In a Louisiana case, a man was tried five times for murder.[14] Nevertheless, the U.S. Supreme Court has granted prosecutors absolute immunity from being sued for misconduct in the courtroom, even if the misconduct is intentional. The Court made this ruling in a case in which a prosecutor was sued for knowingly using perjured testimony that resulted in an innocent person being convicted and incarcerated for nine years.[15] It held that without absolute immunity, prosecutors risked "harassment by unfounded litigation" that would make it difficult to carry out their duties effectively.

Nevertheless, prosecutors have only limited immunity against being sued for actions taken outside the courtroom. For example, in a case involving a prosecutor's decision to authorize a warrantless wiretap, he was not granted absolute immunity.[16] In another case, a prosecutor was found to have fabricated evidence by "shopping around" for a favorable expert witness and making false statements to the press. Here again the prosecutor was not granted absolute immunity.[17] The pattern in these cases shows that prosecutors enjoy absolute immunity in courtroom actions but only limited immunity for investigative actions such as advice and direction to the police.[18] One former prosecutor has recommended that civil

FUTURE ISSUES

Prosecuting False Statements

In 1934, Congress passed a law that made it a crime to lie to federal officials. This "false statements" statute was intended to prevent industries from lying to government regulatory agencies on matters involving compliance with the law. This law has increasingly been used against people who have committed no crime, yet have lied about their actions to a federal official. For example, Henry Cisneros, former U.S. Secretary of Housing and Urban Development, admitted during his background investigation that he had given money to his ex-mistress (which is not a crime). He lied to the FBI about the amount and duration of the payments. He is the first person ever prosecuted on charges of lying during a background check. Cisneros resigned from his cabinet post and faces a possible prison term if convicted.[A] According to legal scholar Paul Rothstein, "It smacks of entrapment to ask people questions about their sex lives and then, when they lie, prosecute them for the lie."[B]

In 1998, Ronald Blackley, a high-ranking official in the U.S. Department of Agriculture, was sentenced to twenty-seven months in prison for lies he told about $22,000 that he received from former business associates who had dealings with the Department of Agriculture. Blackley was not charged with taking the money; his crime was failing to disclose the income and lying about it to investigators.

Linda Tripp, a Pentagon employee, wore a concealed microphone to tape-record conversations with her friend, Monica Lewinsky, during the independent counsel's investigation of President Clinton. It was reported that, in her Pentagon background check, Tripp failed to reveal that she had been arrested for shoplifting at age nineteen, even though the charges had been dropped. If she knowingly lied, she can be prosecuted for making a false statement to a federal official.

An independent counsel was appointed to investigate Secretary of the Interior Bruce Babbitt for falsely denying to Congress that he had lied to a lobbyist, even though lying to a lobbyist is not a crime. As a former independent counsel observes, "You're seeing more and more prosecutions now of lies in which there is no underlying criminal conduct."[C]

FUTURES QUESTION

Should there be limits on the extent to which individuals can be prosecuted for lying when they are lying about noncriminal conduct?

NOTES

[A]Paul Glastris, " 'False Statements': The Flubber of All Laws," *U.S. News & World Report* (March 30, 1998), pp. 25–6.

[B]Ibid., p. 26; JoAnn Gambale and Jeffrey E. Richardson, "False Statements," *American Criminal Law Review,* vol. 30 (Spring 1993), pp. 659–83.

[C]Ibid.

penalties be imposed on prosecutors for misconduct and that appellate courts discipline prosecutors as they do defense attorneys in order to curb this kind of professional misconduct.[19] It is unethical for a prosecutor to bring a case when it is known that the defendant is innocent. Closer scrutiny and enforcement of ethical standards can serve as a means of controlling prosecutorial misconduct.

Diversion of Cases

diversion programs
Alternatives to the formal criminal justice process that occur after charging but before adjudication; they attempt to achieve a noncriminal disposition of the case.

Another important decision made by prosecutors is to divert some offenders out of the adjudication process. **Diversion programs** are alternatives to the formal criminal justice process that occur after charging but before adjudication; they attempt to achieve a noncriminal disposition of the case. Sixty-three percent of all prosecutor's offices in the United States have a diversion program for first-time offenders.[20]

A common type of diversion program is pretrial intervention (PTI). Where such programs exist, any offender can apply to the prosecutor for admission to the program. If the nature of the offense and the offender's background are such that little risk will be posed to the community, the prosecutor suspends prosecution of the case for one year. During this time the prosecutor can require the offender to make restitution to the victim, attend drug or alcohol treatment programs, or perform voluntary service to the community. After one year, if the offender has not gotten into further legal trouble the prosecutor will move to dismiss the case. If the offender fails to live up to the prosecutor's expectations, the case is resumed and passes through the normal adjudication process. Pretrial intervention gives first-time offenders and people who have committed misdemeanors or property crimes an opportunity to show that they can be rehabilitated. They also reduce court costs and case loads.

On the other hand, diversion programs have been criticized by those who feel that prosecutors who want to compile a good record for their office may recommend diversion only for offenders with the greatest chance of completing the program successfully. As a result, people who could benefit from diversion may be denied access to the program. Also, prosecutors may be tempted to encourage participation in diversion programs when the case is weak or when they would not otherwise have prosecuted the case. In this sense, diversion may *increase* rather than decrease the number of people who are subject to the criminal justice process, because, without diversion, the case might never have been prosecuted.[21]

Less formal efforts at diversion take the form of conditional sentences. Most prosecutors now recommend a wide range of "intermediate sanctions" that involve neither incarceration nor probation. More than three fourths of all prosecutor's offices report resolving some cases by recommending alcohol or drug rehabilitation, community service, counseling, or restitution.[22] These kinds of dispositions are designed to deter future misconduct more effectively by addressing the underlying causes of the unlawful behavior.

The evidence indicates that, despite the criticisms just mentioned, most felony cases result in prosecution. An analysis of prosecutions in eight states found that for every one hundred persons arrested for a felony, eighty-one were prosecuted. On the other hand, only fifty-nine were convicted, thirty-nine received jail or prison sentences, and only ten were imprisoned for more than one year.[23] What is not clear is why some of the cases were not prosecuted and why so many suspects escaped conviction and prison sentences.

Plea-Bargaining

Plea-bargaining occurs when a prosecutor agrees to press a less serious charge, drop some charges, or recommend a less severe sentence if the defendant agrees to plead guilty. Prosecutors often claim that plea-bargaining is a necessary evil that enables them to deal with large case loads. Others claim that it is merely an administrative convenience. To understand this debate, it is important to know the history, nature, and extent of plea-bargaining.

plea-bargaining
An arrangement in which a prosecutor agrees to press a less serious charge, drop some charges, or recommend a less severe sentence if the defendant agrees to plead guilty.

The History of Plea-Bargaining

Milton Heumann conducted a study to determine how recently plea-bargaining became a common practice in the United States. He examined trial rates for felonies in Connecticut Superior Court from 1880 to 1954 and found that the percentage of cases that went to trial averaged about 9 percent throughout this seventy-five–year period.[24] That is to say, only 9 percent of all dispositions were the result of a trial—meaning that 91 percent of the cases were resolved through guilty pleas. Heumann then looked at Connecticut trial rates from 1966 to 1973 and found that at no time did they exceed 10 percent.

High rates of plea-bargaining have been found in studies in other locations as well. An examination by Abraham Blumberg of trial rates in a metropolitan court covered twenty-five years. He found no significant variation in the frequency of trials over the years, and the trial rate never exceeded 10 percent.[25] A study by Kathleen Brosi found that the average trial rate in thirteen counties across the country was also under 10 percent.[26,27] Similarly, a study of felony defendants in the seventy-five largest counties in the United States found that more than 90 percent pleaded guilty and did not go to trial.[28] National surveys of prosecutor's offices in the United States found that the proportion of guilty pleas changed little in the period studied: from 91 percent of all felony convictions in 1988 to 89 percent in 1994.[29] It appears, therefore, that plea-bargaining is not a recent phenomenon and that it is widely used to resolve cases in jurisdictions of all types.

Plea-Bargaining Today

Contrary to what one might expect, courts with low case loads have been found to have lower trial rates than courts with high case loads.[30] The same finding was reported in a report on plea-bargaining in fourteen counties.[31] Counties with high rates of plea-bargaining often were found to have lower case loads than counties with low rates of plea-bargaining. To try to explain this, Heumann interviewed a number of prosecutors, judges, and defendants. He discovered that most cases do not involve substantial legal or factual issues, and that the risks of going to trial (and possibly losing) are quite high. Therefore, many prosecutors, defense counsel, and suspects feel that it is to their advantage to plead guilty rather than go to trial. Thus, plea-bargaining appears to result from factors other than high case loads.

In a controversial case, prosecutors in Ontario, Canada, offered a plea bargain to the wife of Paul Bernado, who was charged with the abduction, rape, torture, and murder of two teenaged girls inside their home. Even though there was evidence that the wife had participated in the killings and a judge found the plea bargain "distasteful," the plea was accepted because it was believed to be the only way to make a case against the husband.[32] However, sixteen months later videotapes were discovered that depicted the brutal rape and torture of the victims. More than 300,000 citizens signed petitions protesting the plea bargain agreement, but it could not be changed after the fact. The wife received a 12-year sentence and Bernado received a life term.[33] Thus, plea-bargaining can backfire if it is carried out before a thorough investigation is conducted, and sensational cases such as this one, though rare, inflame the public's belief that offenders are getting a "deal" and that prosecutors are not representing the community's interests effectively.

It is widely believed that plea-bargaining is much more prevalent in urban than in rural areas. One study compared trial rates and population density in twenty states and found no relationship between them.[34] In fact, trial rates varied by as much as 300 percent in jurisdictions with virtually identical populations. Therefore, large populations do not appear to account for high rates of plea-bargaining.

Public officials have often claimed that if prosecutors had smaller case loads the number of trials would increase. However, a study by the New York State Office of Court Administration does not support this conclusion.[35] It compared two counties in one state, one with a high rate of trials, the other with a low rate. The results are summarized in Table 11.2. In Cayuga County the proportion of cases that went to trial was only 2 percent, but the case load was less than half of that in Manhattan. More prosecutors would, of course, reduce the average case load per prosecutor, but it does not appear that lower case loads will necessarily increase the proportion of trials.

There is, then, no evidence to suggest that plea-bargaining is a new phenomenon or that it developed simply as a response to limited resources. While resource limitations undoubtedly set an upper limit on the trial rate, the evidence does not support the conclusion that increasing the number of prosecutors would reduce the level of plea-bargaining.

An investigation by Boland, Brady, Tyson, and Bassler examined felony arrests in fourteen counties across the country. They found that 50 percent of all cases were either dismissed or rejected by the prosecutor because of lack of sufficient evidence or other reasons. Forty-five percent ended in guilty pleas and only 5 percent went to trial.[36] Table 11.3 presents findings from a similar study conducted in the nation's seventy-five largest urban counties.

Table 11.3 indicates that, on average, the likelihood of a case going to trial is between 4 and 8 percent. It also shows that 36 percent of violent crimes and 22 percent of property crimes are either rejected by the prosecutor or dismissed by the judge before trial. The question that remains is, Why are so many cases lost along the way?

TABLE 11.2

Prosecutor Case Loads and Trial Rates in Two Counties

	MANHATTAN	CAYUGA COUNTY
Trial rate	7%	2%
Average case load (per prosecutor)	151	63

SOURCE: State of New York Judicial Conference and Office of Court Administration.

TABLE 11.3

Processing of Felony Cases

CRIMINAL PROCEDURE	VIOLENT CRIME	PROPERTY CRIME
Total felony defendants	100%	100%
Cases rejected by prosecutor or dismissed by court	36%	22%
Diversion from prosecution	2%	2%
Guilty pleas	52%	72%
Trials	8%	4%
Acquittal	2%	1%
Jail or prison sentence	76% of those convicted	63% of those convicted

SOURCE: Compiled from Brian A. Reaves, *Felony Defendants in Large Urban Counties* (Washington, D.C.: Bureau of Justice Statistics, 1998).

One of the first studies to address this issue was conducted by the Vera Institute of Justice. In this study, randomly selected case files of felony arrests in New York City were followed to their ultimate disposition. For a small subsample of those cases, participants were interviewed. Of the fifty-three robbery cases that were examined in detail, only one went to trial and just fifteen resulted in felony sentences.[37] Although it appears that justice was not carried out in these cases, a closer look reveals that 43 percent of the robberies involved a prior relationship between the victim and the defendant, which would greatly reduce the possibility of a conviction at trial. Of the robberies that remained, 87 percent resulted in convictions and 67 percent in a jail or prison sentence. Offenders who managed to avoid felony sentences by pleading guilty to a lesser charge did so primarily because of lack of interest on the part of the victim or because the victim had a criminal record or was engaging in criminal conduct (such as prostitution or drug-dealing). Even including the prior-relationship robberies, however, 98 percent of offenders with a criminal record were sentenced to jail. In a national survey of prosecutor's offices, the most frequently given reasons for case dismissals were search and seizure problems and unavailability of witnesses. In a large proportion of these cases, prosecutors declined to prosecute because of reluctance on the part of the victim (74 percent) or a witness (58 percent).[38]

The Vera Institute study also looked at the effect of court congestion on leniency in sentencing. It found that, rather than leading to more lenient sentences, congestion caused pretrial delays and custody, thereby inducing pleas by several defendants who probably would have been acquitted if they had gone to trial. Studies in several different jurisdictions found that judges tend to equalize the significance of lesser pleas by imposing a relatively longer sentence on the reduced charge, and questioned whether making a plea benefits the defendant in any way.[39,40] Likewise, some courts have permitted longer sentences in plea bargains by taking dismissed charges into consideration.[41,42,43]

Overreliance on plea-bargaining can result in abuses. In a 1995 case, a prosecutor in Ulster County, New York, authorized a "fake" plea bargain with a defendant. The prosecutor asked the defendant to lead him to a kidnapped girl, who was found dead. The prosecutor claimed that since the girl had been killed during the kidnapping, the plea bargain was voided. The ethics and constitutionality of such a move have been questioned.[44] In a related vein, some courts have allowed defendants who plea bargained to be reindicted if their sentence is subsequently overturned on other grounds. These courts see the plea bargain as an obligation to serve the full sentence, rather than as an obligation to plead guilty.[45] Thus, it can be seen that the contractual nature of plea bargains is being questioned when the plea "deal" changes after the agreement has been made.

In sum, there is a growing body of evidence suggesting that plea-bargaining is not due to overcrowded courts, overburdened prosecutors, or urban density. Further, it does not usually result in lenient sentences. In fact, plea-bargaining appears to be the result of two overriding factors: (1) Most cases involve few issues of fact or law because the evidence against the defendant either is present or is not, and (2) going to trial carries high risks for both sides; even an "open and shut" case can be lost at trial because of poor performance by witnesses, and the defendant knows that even a case with weak evidence can be decided in favor of the prosecution. Therefore, plea-bargaining occurs so often because it helps both the prosecution and the defense obtain a predictable outcome in an otherwise uncertain process.

Should Plea-Bargaining Be Abolished?

Plea-bargaining has many undesirable features. Plea negotiations between the prosecution and the defense are conducted in private, the rights of the accused and the interests of the community are not visibly balanced (as occurs in trials), and the public may believe that justice is not achieved. In 1973, these features led the National Advisory Commission on Criminal Justice Standards and Goals to recommend "that as soon as possible, but not later than 1978, negotiations between defendants and prosecutors concerning concessions to be made in return for guilty pleas be abolished."[46]

This recommendation formed the basis for several ill-fated efforts to eliminate plea-bargaining. Perhaps the best-evaluated effort involved New York State's drug laws. Under these laws the possession or sale of heroin or other narcotics was punished by mandatory minimum prison sentences of one to fifteen years, with maximum sentences ranging up to life imprisonment. If released, offenders were placed on parole for the rest of their lives, and pleas to lesser charges were not permitted.

The New York City Bar Association conducted an evaluation of the impact of this law on drug offenders. Researchers compared arrests, indictments, and convictions in 1972 (a year before the law was passed) and in 1975 (more than a year after it had taken effect). The results are summarized in Table 11.4. The figures show that, rather than increasing drug arrests, indictments, and convictions, the drug laws had the opposite effect. Arrests decreased, indictments fell, the proportion of arrests leading to indictments fell, and the number of convictions fell by almost one-half.[47]

Mandatory sentences, combined with policies that forbid plea-bargaining, appear to simply shift discretion to other parts of the criminal justice system. As Arthur Rosset and Donald Cressey have observed, "Efforts to eliminate discretionary decisions or to limit them substantially seem bound to fail because there must be a place in the courthouse both for the rule of law and for discretion."[48] Knowing that arrests, indictments, and convictions could lead to very severe penalties, police officers, grand juries, and trial juries are more reluctant to arrest, indict, or convict offenders who they believe do not deserve such harsh penalties.

Nevertheless, the New York experience has been repeated elsewhere, and for other crimes besides drug possession or sale. H. Lawrence Ross[49] has evaluated the effects of establishing mandatory penalties for drunk driving; David Rossman and his associates[50] and Colin Loftin, Milton Heumann, and David McDowall[51] have examined the impact of mandatory sentences for gun law violations. The results are remarkably similar: When discretion is removed from one part of the system, it is replaced by greater use of discretion in other parts.

In Massachusetts, for example, the Bartley–Fox gun law, which went into effect in 1975, provided for a mandatory one-

TABLE 11.4

The Impact of New York's Tougher Drug Laws

	YEAR BEFORE LAW ENACTED	TWO YEARS AFTER ENACTMENT
Number of arrests	19,269	15,941
Number of indictments	7,528	4,283
Indictment rate	39%	27%
Number of convictions	6,033	3,147
Conviction rate	86%	79%

SOURCE: Compiled from Association of the Bar of the City of New York, *The Nation's Toughest Drug Law: Evaluating the New York Experience* (Washington, D.C.: Drug Abuse Council, 1977).

Mandatory sentences and policies forbidding plea-bargaining have been found to shift discretion to police, grand juries, and trial juries who make their decisions more carefully when charging or sentencing a person.

year jail sentence for individuals convicted of illegally carrying a firearm. This law was copied by many other states. However, a comparison of arrests and convictions one year before and one year after the law took effect found that arrests dropped considerably, the conviction rate fell from 49 percent to 22 percent, and appeals for new trials in gun cases jumped from 20 percent to 95 percent.[52]

Similar results occurred when Alaska banned plea-bargaining, also in 1975. The new policy prohibited charge-bargaining as well as sentence-bargaining. An evaluation of this policy found that "the conviction and sentencing of persons charged with serious crimes of violence such as murder, rape, robbery, and felonious assault appeared to be completely unaffected by the change in policy."[53] California is the only state where voters have insisted on and obtained a plea ban, and the impact can be expected to be the same as in other jurisdictions.[54]

Given the consistent findings regarding the effects of mandatory sentences and policies prohibiting plea-bargaining, some general conclusions can be drawn. First, a restrictive plea-bargaining policy usually leads to a restrictive case-screening policy, and therefore fewer cases—the stronger ones—are prosecuted. Second, when sentences are mandatory, the bargaining focuses instead on the charges to be brought against the accused person. Third, when no–plea-bargaining polices *and* mandatory sentences are combined, fewer arrests, fewer indictments, and fewer convictions, and more dismissals, trials, and appeals result. Fourth, researchers have not found the harsh penalties to have a deterrent effect on commission of the offenses covered by these policies. Nevertheless, calls for abolition of plea-bargaining continue, and this trend has led to proposals for changing the way that plea-bargaining is conducted.[55]

Alternatives to Plea-Bargaining

Various ways to eliminate the undesirable aspects of plea-bargaining have been suggested. These include public negotiations, time limitations, more visible negotiations, better case-screening procedures, and reviews of plea agreements by judges and victims. The National Advisory Commission has called for a time limit on all plea negotiations; after a certain period, only pleas to the original charge would be permitted. In the view of the Commission, such a procedure would prevent unnecessary delays, which sometimes result in unwise pleas by defendants who are in jail awaiting trial. Felony cases are typically concluded in four to seven months, which can be a long time for a defendant awaiting trial in jail.[56]

In several cities a pretrial settlement conference is used. Before a trial is held, the prosecutor, defendant, counsel, and judge meet to discuss a plea. The arresting officer and the victim are invited to attend these sessions. No plea negotiations can take place outside this setting. Of course, so as not to prejudice a judge or jury, these discussions are not admissible as evidence if a trial eventually results. Therefore, trials are reserved for the few cases in which no settlement can be reached. This procedure makes the plea-bargaining process more visible, and a neutral party (the judge) is present to ensure that the rights of the defendant and the need to protect the community are properly balanced. Experimentation with this procedure has produced encouraging results.[57]

Another proposal is that prosecutors adopt more effective screening procedures in order to eliminate cases that are unlikely to be prosecuted successfully. A national survey of prosecutors found that the most frequent pretrial problem is "inadequate police preparation of crime reports."[58] Respondents noted that police provide insufficient details regarding proof to support arrests and are slow to give information about the defendant's background. A subsequent national survey of prosecutors had similar findings.[59] The extremely high proportion of cases involving prior relationships between the victim and the defendant clearly shows the need for greater effort in this regard. Moreover, better case screening is becoming mandatory as court case loads include more drug offenders. Throughout the nation, more than 30 percent of the felony court case load consists of cases that involve drug traffickers (19 percent) and possessors (13 percent).[60] It is important to distinguish between major and minor drug cases so as to use criminal justice resources more effectively. An investigation conducted in fourteen jurisdictions found that fewer pleas and more trials occurred in counties that were more selective in screening arrests and in rejecting certain cases.[61]

What Happens at Trial?

The trial is the centerpiece of the adjudication process, although, as we have seen, it is not used very often to decide cases. Trials serve an educational purpose for both jurors and the public in understanding how a balance is achieved between protection of the community and protection of the rights of the individual. The detailed procedures of a criminal trial are designed to ensure that this balance is reached in every case.[62]

The American system of criminal adjudication has often been criticized for the time it sometimes takes to proceed from arrest to final disposition of the case. Delays in the adjudication procedure cause the process to take even more time. Most felony cases are completed within three months after the arrest, although cases involving trials take twice as long.[63] For the nation as a whole, the average time from arrest to sentencing is about seven months.[64]

An example of a delay is a **continuance,** a court-authorized postponement to give the prosecution or defense more time to prepare its case. Judges have the discretion to grant continuances for several valid reasons. Whether the reason is to allow the defense to locate a witness, prepare motions, or obtain medical reports, continuances ensure that the most complete information is available for a criminal proceeding. Prosecutors can also obtain continuances, but in most states they

continuance
A court-authorized postponement of a case to allow the prosecution or defense more time to prepare its case.

are constitutionally required to be ready for trial within six months. Exceptions are permitted only when the delays are caused by the defense for valid reasons.

As it turns out, most continuances are requested by, and granted to, the defense, because by the time of indictment the prosecution has already prepared much of its case. The defense needs more time to examine the evidence. In addition, delays usually benefit the defendant more than the prosecution. Delays may frustrate or disillusion victims and witnesses, or they may calm community sentiment in well-publicized cases. (Cases that are highly publicized before the trial make it much more difficult to obtain an impartial jury.) On the other hand, delays cause suffering for defendants who cannot make bail and must await trial in jail.

discovery
A process that entitles a suspect to review certain information gathered by the prosecutor.

Another cause of delays is a process called **discovery.** This process entitles a suspect to have access to certain information that has been gathered by the prosecutor. For example, suspects have the right to see the results of blood tests or transcripts of interrogations conducted by the police or prosecutor in preparing the case for trial. In its examination of the prosecutor's evidence, the defense may find *exculpatory evidence,* that is, evidence that tends to show the innocence of the defendant. This evidence might consist of statements taken by police from victims or witnesses that show uncertainty about the identity of the offender. With this information, defense counsel can assess the strength of the prosecution's case and decide whether there is any benefit in going to trial or pleading guilty.

Even though more than 90 percent of criminal cases are resolved through guilty pleas, actual trials offer the greatest protection of individual legal and constitutional guarantees. This is because of the close attention given to balancing the interests of the community and the offender at each step.

When a trial takes place, it begins with the selection of a jury. The right to a jury dates from the Magna Carta, and it is incorporated into both Article III of the Constitution and the Sixth Amendment, which states that "in all criminal prosecutions, the accused shall enjoy the right to a speedy and public trial by an impartial jury." The jury pool is typically selected from voter registration, property tax, or motor vehicle records. This process has been widely criticized because it excludes people who do not vote, own property, or drive cars.[65] Nevertheless, other methods of sampling have not been found to be more effective in choosing a jury pool that is representative of the entire community.[66] The U.S. Supreme Court has held that it is not necessary for every jury to contain a representative cross section of the community by race, gender, religion, economic status, or other attributes. Instead, the Court held that jurors may not be *excluded* on the basis of these characteristics. In subsequent cases the Court overturned convictions in cases in which blacks or men were purposely excluded from juries.[67] A 1994 case involved in a paternity suit in which the mother was suing the purported father. During jury selection, nine of the mother's ten *peremptory challenges,* which permit removal of prospective jurors from consideration without cause, had been used to strike men from the jury panel. The Supreme Court held that this use of peremptory challenges was unconstitutional because it attempted to exclude an entire class of potential jurors.[68]

Once the jury pool has been selected, the process of *voir dire* begins. In this process, the judges, prosecutor, and defense counsel screen potential jurors by asking them certain kinds of questions. In order to prevent the inclusion of bi-

Media and Criminal Justice

INDICTMENT: THE MCMARTIN TRIAL

In July 1983, the mother of a boy who attended a well-regarded day care center in Manhattan Beach, California, called the police and reported that her son had a "red bottom." On the basis of the child's mention of Ray Buckey, a young man who worked at the McMartin Preschool, the mother alleged that her son had been a victim of sexual abuse, and demanded a police investigation.

In the following months Ray Buckey, his mother Peggy, and his grandmother Virginia McMartin were arrested, questioned, and released because of lack of evidence. However, a local television reporter made highly inflammatory reports about the police investigation on the news, repeating the claims of sexual abuse and, later, implying that satanism was involved in the case.

Indictment: The McMartin Trial (HBO, 1995) is a docudrama about the longest trial in American history. The trial lasted more than eight years and cost more than $16 million. Called the "O. J. Simpson trial of its time," the McMartin trial was the first to be televised live. *Indictment* explores the factors that led to this lengthy and highly publicized trial, in which some of the accused individuals remained in jail for more than six years without ever being convicted.

The movie carefully examines the events that unfolded after the accusations were made against the McMartin Preschool workers, showing how public hysteria prompted the Los Angeles County District Attorney to convene a grand jury. The grand jury, fueled by media attention to the alleged "child molesters," returned indictments on Buckey, his mother, his grandmother, his sister, and three female teachers.

Through the years, the prosecutors labor under great public pressure to build their case, but as their evidence begins to fall apart it becomes clear that many of the allegations are false. Their expert witness, who interviewed the alleged victims, is revealed to be an unlicensed therapist who used the power of suggestion to elicit the desired responses. Re-interviews of the first alleged victim and his mother indicate that the mother is psychologically unstable and that the boy may have been molested by his own father. As the investigation continues, some children are heard to report outlandish, obviously fabricated stories of beheading giraffes, watching pornography, and drinking babies' blood at the preschool. The prosecutorial team is unsure of how to proceed after such discoveries and, fearing negative public opinion if the charges are dropped, use their discretion to ignore exculpatory evidence.

Indictment presents the famous trial in a manner that implies that the prosecutorial team engaged in misconduct and breech of ethics. The message, however, is not so much about the players in the trial as about how public opinion can make puppets of district attorneys. In the movie, the prosecutors are depicted as servants of the people, allowing public pressure to influence prosecutorial decisions.

In the end, many of the charges were dropped and none of the accused was found guilty. Still, the accused are thought of as child molesters to this day, perhaps only because of a discretionary "witch hunt" by prosecutors.

MEDIA AND CRIMINAL JUSTICE QUESTION

What measures would you suggest to reduce the susceptibility of prosecutors to public hysteria on issues such as alleged child molestation?

ased jurors, both the prosecution and the defense can use *challenges for cause* to disqualify jurors whose background or statements may be prejudicial to the prosecution or defense. In addition, both the prosecution and the defense are entitled to a specific number of peremptory challenges. Peremptory challenges have their origin in British common law, although only recently have so-called jury selection consultants been used in high-profile cases. These experts examine nonverbal cues such as body language, eye contact, and dress to predict whether a particular juror may be sympathetic to the prosecution or defense. There is no evidence that these methods of juror selection have any validity, although stereotypes persist regarding the influence of age, gender, religion, and other attributes on a juror's attitudes.[69] Critics of the practice of using jury consultants have proposed barring nonlawyers from giving advice to either the prosecution or the defense during jury selection.[70]

The size of juries varies by state. All states require twelve-member juries in capital cases (i.e., those in which the death penalty can be applied), but six states allow for juries of less than twelve jurors in felony trials. The U.S. Supreme Court has left the size of juries up to the states, although it has held that a five-member jury is unconstitutional.[71] Thus, states have juries that range in size from six to twelve members. In rare circumstances the jury is *sequestered,* meaning that jurors are housed in a hotel for the duration of the trial and newspaper and television coverage of the case is closely monitored. Sequestration is expensive and occurs only in cases in which public opinion is very strong or divisive or the security of jurors is in question, that is, if there have been threats against jurors or attempts to bribe them.

After a jury has been selected, the prosecution makes an opening statement in which it outlines its case against the defendant. It is here that the state summarizes the evidence it will use to show the defendant's guilt. Next, the defense counsel makes an opening argument that states why the defendant should be exonerated of the crime. The evidence that will be used to support this position is summarized.

The body of the trial consists of presentation of the prosecutor's evidence and the statements of witnesses, followed by presentation of the case for the defense. Because the state is prosecuting an individual in a criminal case, the burden of proof is on the prosecution to prove guilt beyond a reasonable doubt.

The steps in a criminal case are presented in Figure 11.1. The pretrial steps are discussed in Chapter 6. The steps of a trial are elaborate because accuracy and the truth have been found to result most often when both sides have a fair opportunity to present their views.

Witnesses and physical evidence form the substance of all criminal cases. Witnesses are always sworn in by a court officer, usually a sheriff's deputy. *Swearing in* obliges the witness to be truthful; false statements can result in a charge of perjury. The first round of questions asked by the prosecutor to his or her own witnesses in a criminal case are called the *direct examination,* as are questions asked by the defense counsel to defense witnesses. The types of witnesses and physical evidence that can be used are explicitly defined in the rules of evidence of each state. *Circumstantial evidence* is a form of indirect evidence that is often used in criminal trials. Such evidence permits the jury to arrive at a conclusion by reasonable inference. For example, the witnessing of a person walking down the street with two sticks of dynamite just before an explosion is circumstantial evidence that the person might be involved in the incident. This form of evidence is very important when direct eyewitness evidence is lacking.

Once the prosecution has conducted a direct examination of its witnesses, the defense may *cross-examine* the prosecution witnesses in an effort to assess the validity of their statements by checking for inconsistencies, contradictions, or uncertainty. The prosecution may follow the defense cross-examination with a *redirect examination* in order to clarify issues that were cast in doubt by the defense's questions. Next, the defense may follow once again with a *re-cross-examination.* This procedure continues for each of the state's witnesses.

The defense then begins by calling its witnesses, and the process proceeds in reverse, with the prosecution cross-examining defense witnesses; this is followed by re-direct questioning by the defense and re–cross-examination by the prosecutor. At several points throughout the trial, the prosecution or defense may raise *objections* to questions posed by the other side because they are alleged to violate the rules of evidence. These objections usually relate to whether or not the information sought is material to the case and was obtained in accordance with the law. The judge's role is to rule on these objections according to the laws of the state. If the objection is *sustained,* the questioner must withdraw the question and the jury must disregard it and any response that was made by the witness. If the objection is *overruled,* the question is deemed proper and the questioning continues.

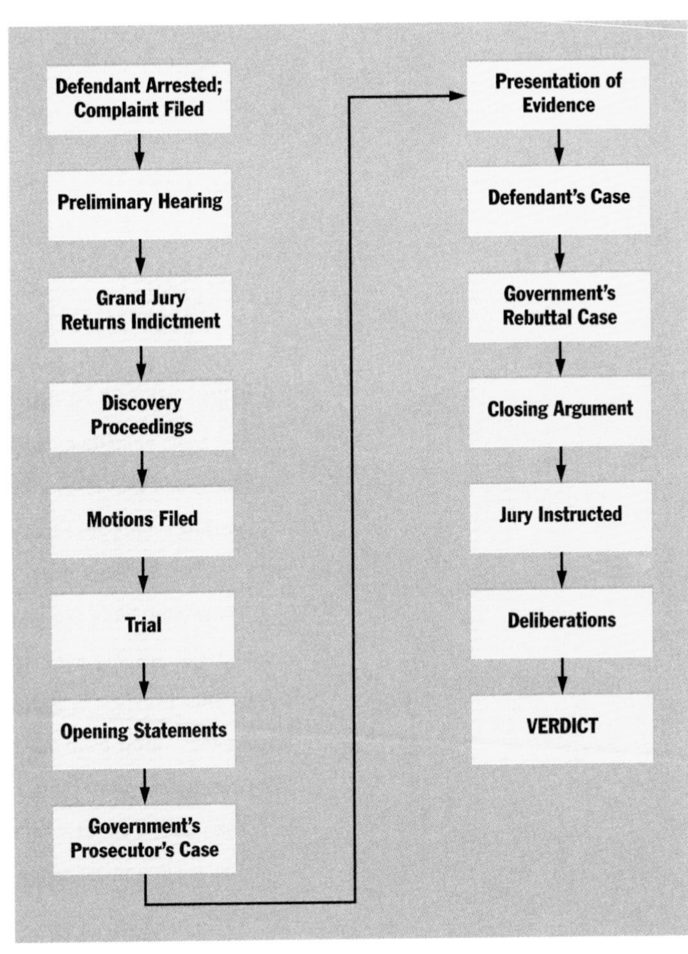

FIGURE 11.1

Progression of a case through trial

SOURCE: http://www.uscourts.gov/understanding_courts/gifs/figure4.gif

If the defendant desires, he or she can request a bench trial before a judge, rather than a jury trial. In a *bench trial,* the judge determines guilt or innocence; in a *jury trial,* the jury performs this task. According to the U.S. Supreme Court, jury trials must be available when the crime carries a sentence of over six months of imprisonment.[72]

When all the evidence has been presented, the prosecution and defense make final arguments to the jury summarizing the evidence they have presented. This is followed by the judge's instruction to the jury, in which the elements of the crime are explained, together with the degree of proof required—that is, proof beyond a reasonable doubt. The jury then deliberates until it has agreed on a verdict. In nearly all states unanimous jury verdicts are required in criminal cases.

In rare cases (less than 6 percent of all cases), a jury is unable to agree on a decision of guilt or innocence.[73] This is called a *hung jury,* and it means that the defendant can be tried again before a different jury. **Jury nullification** occurs when a defendant is acquitted in the face of facts that demonstrate guilt. Some people believe that the jury that acquitted O. J. Simpson of murder engaged in jury nullification, but sloppy evidence-gathering by police and lies told by witnesses led some jurors to conclude that Simpson was not guilty beyond a reasonable doubt.

jury nullification
Acquittal of a defendant despite facts that show guilt.

When a jury reaches a verdict of guilty, the defendant stands convicted of the crime alleged. He or she is then sentenced by the judge within the limits established by law. It is common for both the prosecutor and defense counsel to make recommendations to the judge regarding an appropriate sentence. (Sentencing is the subject of Chapter 13.)

The central role of the prosecutor is evident throughout the trial process. This authority supplements the prosecutor's discretion in earlier stages. As the representative of the public in his or her jurisdiction, the prosecutor is responsible for evaluating a criminal arrest in terms of probable cause, deciding whether to take the case to trial, proving the charges beyond a reasonable doubt, and seeing that justice is done throughout the adjudication process and at sentencing.

Critical Thinking EXERCISE

An Angel on Her Shoulder at the O. J. Simpson Case

Criminal trials sometimes appear more concerned with winning and losing than with doing justice. Radio and television talk shows report trials on a "play-by-play" basis that resembles the way sporting events are reported. "Who is winning today?" "Did the defense score any points today?" "Is the judge (referee) acting in a neutral fashion?"

These questions are more appropriate during the World Series than they are during a criminal trial, yet they are heard more and more often as trials increasingly become public spectacles. This situation is aggravated when prosecutors and defense counsel hold "mini–press conferences" after each day of the trial, an unfortunate development that encourages sports-like coverage. In some countries, such as Canada, the prosecution and defense are forbidden to speak publicly about a case while it is in progress. In the United States, this prohibition occurs only when a judge specifically orders it, an action that actually seems to heighten media interest.

The much-publicized O. J. Simpson case illustrates several current problems in criminal justice. At least one of these problems relates to the prosecution. At the beginning of the trial, prosecutor Marcia Clark wore an angel pin similar to one worn by members of the victims' families. She defended her action as a "very small and tasteful show of support."[A] However, the judge asked her to remove the pin. Such personal identification with the victim confuses the role of an attorney in a civil case (who represents a single client) with the role of a prosecutor (who represents the entire jurisdiction). The prosecutor's role is to seek justice on behalf of the community, not to avenge the victim's loss. This is an important distinction that is increasingly overlooked. As Justice Sutherland of the U.S. Supreme Court stated more than sixty years ago, the role of the prosecutor "is not that he shall win a case, but that justice shall be done."[B]

Questions

1. **What do you believe would be the reaction if public statements about ongoing trial proceedings outside the courtroom were prohibited in all cases?**
2. **What are some ways in which attorneys, the media, and the public can focus attention on the search for justice rather than portraying a trial as a win–lose situation?**

Notes

[A]Tony Mauro, "Flap Over Angel Pin Points to Larger Issue," *USA Today* (February 2, 1995), p. 3.
[B]*Berger v. United States,* 295 U.S. 88 (1935).

Critical Thinking EXERCISE

Spouse Murders

The nature of murders committed in the United States has changed in recent years. In 1975, 23 percent of all homicides were reported to have been committed by close relatives. By 1985, this figure had dropped to 17 percent, and in 1995 it stood at 11 percent of all homicides.[A] There has been a corresponding increase in homicides committed by strangers. Despite this trend, murder among intimates continues to receive a disproportionate amount of attention.

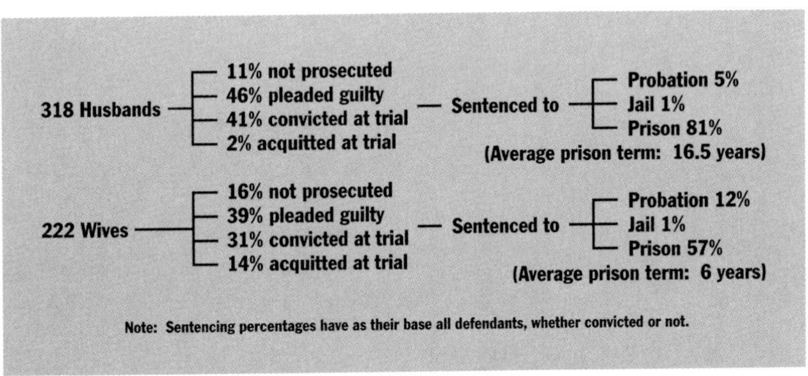

FIGURE 11.2
Spouse murder cases

SOURCE: Patrick A. Langan and John M. Dawson, *Spouse Murder Defendants in Large Urban Counties* (Washington, D.C.: Bureau of Justice Statistics, 1995).

An analysis of spouse murder in the seventy-five largest counties in the United States found interesting differences between the adjudication of female and male defendants (Figure 11.2). (It should be noted that spouse abuse has become so common that 88 percent of all prosecutor's offices reported prosecuting at least one case of domestic violence during 1994.[B]) Of the 540 spouse homicides analyzed, 318 involved husbands who killed their wives and 222 involved wives charged with murdering their husbands.[C] Of the 540 defendants, 80 percent ultimately were convicted of killing their spouse, although there was a gender difference: Seventy percent of wives versus 87 percent of husbands were convicted.

There was a similar difference in the sentences received. Wives were more than twice as likely to receive probation sentences (12 versus 5 percent), and 57 percent of wives received prison sentences, compared to 81 percent of husbands. Convicted wives also received prison sentences that were approximately 10 years shorter on average than those imposed on husbands (6 years versus 16.5 years).

Evidence from prosecutors' files reveals that wives are much more likely to have been assaulted by their spouse on previous occasions. Likewise, there is evidence that wives are more likely to have been provoked by their husbands through threats or intimidation. No explanation has been found for the significant differences in prison terms between husbands and wives, even when cases involving provocation are accounted for.

Critical Thinking Questions

1. Why do you believe that it is more common for husbands to murder wives than the reverse?
2. Why do you believe that significantly more husbands who have been convicted of killing their wives receive prison terms, and longer sentences, than wives who have been convicted of murdering their husbands?

Notes

[A]Federal Bureau of Investigation, *Uniform Crime Report* (Washington, D.C.: U.S. Government Printing Office, issued annually).

[B]Carol J. DeFrances, Steven K. Smith, and Louise van der Does, *Prosecutors in State Courts* (Washington, D.C.: Bureau of Justice Statistics, 1996).

[C]Patrick A. Langan and John M. Dawson, *Spouse Murder Defendants in Large Urban Counties* (Washington, D.C.: Bureau of Justice Statistics, 1995).

Summary

THE PROSECUTOR'S ROLE

- Because violations of the criminal law are crimes against society, prosecutors represent their jurisdiction, not victims or other individuals.
- Prosecutors have a great deal of discretion in deciding whether a case will be prosecuted and what charges will be pressed.
- Depending on the state, prosecutors are either appointed or elected. Approximately 70 percent of chief prosecutors hold full-time salaried positions.
- Prosecutors sometimes divert offenders to diversion programs, which are alternatives to the formal criminal justice process that attempt to achieve noncriminal disposition of cases.

PLEA-BARGAINING

- Plea-bargaining occurs when a prosecutor agrees to press a less serious charge, drop some charges, or recommend a less severe sentence if the defendant agrees to plead guilty.
- Historical records show that plea-bargaining has long been used in jurisdictions of all types.
- Critics of plea-bargaining point out that it takes place in private, the rights of the accused and the interests of the community are not adequately protected, and the public may believe that justice is not achieved. However, efforts to eliminate the practice have been unsuccessful.
- Proposals to eliminate undesirable aspects of plea-bargaining include time limits, more public negotiations, better case-screening procedures, and reviews by plea agreements by panels of judges.

WHAT HAPPENS AT TRIAL?

- Over 90 percent of criminal cases are resolved through guilty pleas.
- When a trial takes place, it begins with the selection of a jury, which usually consists of twelve members and two alternates.
- After a jury has been selected, the prosecution and defense counsel make opening statements. The body of the trial consists of presentation of the prosecutor's evidence and the statements of witnesses, followed by presentation of the case for the defense.
- When all the evidence has been presented, the prosecution and defense make their final arguments to the jury. This is followed by the judge's instruction to the jury.
- In order for a defendant to be found guilty, the jury must agree unanimously that guilt has been proven beyond a reasonable doubt.

Key Terms

necessarily included offense
nolle prosequi
diversion program
plea-bargaining
continuance
discovery
jury nullification

Questions for Review and Discussion

1. Who is represented by the prosecutor in a criminal case?
2. What degree of discretion do prosecutors have in the disposition of cases? Explain.
3. What are the arguments against appointment versus election of prosecutors?
4. What are diversion programs? Give an example of such a program.
5. What is plea-bargaining? How long has it been used in the United States?
6. What are some undesirable features of plea-bargaining?
7. What happens when mandatory sentences are combined with policies that forbid plea-bargaining?
8. What are some proposed alternatives to plea-bargaining?
9. List the sequence of events in a typical criminal trial.
10. What is required for a jury to reach a verdict of guilty?

Notes

[1]Patrick A. Langan, *Felony Sentences in the United States* (Washington, D.C.: Bureau of Justice Statistics, 1996).

[2]Peter Finn, *The Manhattan District Attorney's Narcotics Eviction Program* (Washington, D.C.: National Institute of Justice, 1995).

[3]Steven R. Donziger, ed., *The Real War on Crime: Report of the National Criminal Justice Commission* (New York: HarperPerennial, 1996), pp. 183–4.

[4]Carol J. DeFrances, Steven K. Smith, and Louise van der Does, *Prosecutors in State Courts* (Washington, D.C.: Bureau of Justice Statistics, 1996).

[5]Ibid., p. 2.

[6]Ibid., and see Marianne W. Zawitz, *Report to the Nation on Crime and Justice*, 2nd ed. (Washington, D.C.: Bureau of Justice Statistics, 1988).

[7]Comments of several defense attorneys appearing on *Rivera Live* on CNBC television, May 29, 1997, in reference to the sexual harassment case of *Paula Jones v. President Clinton*, and the prosecution of sportscaster Marv Albert.

[8]Constance Johnson, "High Crimes and Special Prosecutors," *U.S. News & World Report* (November 8, 1993), p. 47.

[9]Mortimer B. Zuckerman, "Has Mr. Starr No Shame?," *U.S. News & World Report* (April 6, 1998), p. 74; Barry A. Bohrer, "President Clinton is no Mafia Chieftain," *The National Law Journal*, vol. 20 (March 2, 1998), p. 23; Paul Glastris, "'False Statements': The Flubber of all Laws," *U.S. News & World Report* (March 30, 1998), pp. 25–6.

[10]Harvey Silvergate, "Prosecutors Tread Where Defenders Daren't Go," *The National Law Journal*, vol. 20 (February 16, 1998), p. 21.

[11]Douglas Stanglin, "Starr Weighs His Options," *U.S. News & World Report* (May 4, 1998), p. 9.

[12]*Miller v. Pate*, 386 U.S. 1 (1967).

[13]See Albert Alschuler, "Courtroom Misconduct by Prosecutors and Trial Judges," *Texas Law Review*, vol. 50 (1972), pp. 627–35.

[14]Pamela Coyle, "Tried and Tried Again: Defense Lawyers Say the D. A. Went Too Far Prosecuting a Louisiana Man Five Times for Murder," *ABA Journal*, vol. 84 (April 1998), p. 38.

[15]*Imbler v. Pachtman*, 424 U.S. 409 (1976).

[16]*Mitchell v. Forsyth*, 472 U.S. 511 (1985); 515 U.S. 304 (1995).

[17]*Buckley v. Fitzsimmons*, 509 U.S. 259 (1993).

[18]Erwin Chemerinsky, "Prosecutorial Immunity: The Interpretation Continues," *Trial*, vol. 34 (March 1998), p. 80.

[19]Bennett L. Gershman, "Why Prosecutors Misbehave," in P. F. Cromwell and R. G. Dunham, eds., *Crime and Justice in America: Present Realities and Future Prospects* (Upper Saddle River, NJ: Prentice Hall, 1997), pp. 192–200.

[20]DeFrances, Smith, and van der Does, 1996.

[21]Gennaro F. Vito and Deborah G. Wilson, *The American Juvenile Justice System* (Thousand Oaks, CA: Sage Publications, 1985), pp. 22–5.

[22]DeFrances, Smith, and van der Does, p. 4.

[23]Jacob Perez, *Tracking Offenders* (Washington, D.C.: Bureau of Justice Statistics, 1991).

[24]Milton Heumann, "A Note of Plea-Bargaining and Case Pressure," *Law & Society Review* vol. 9 (Spring 1975).

[25]Abraham S. Blumberg, *Criminal Justice: Issues and Ironies* (New York: New Viewpoints, 1979).

[26]Kathleen B. Brosi, *A Cross-City Comparison of Felony Case Processing* (Washington, D.C.: U.S. Government Printing Office, 1979).

[27]Barbara Boland and Brian Forst, *The Prevalence of Guilty Pleas* (Washington, D.C.: U.S. Bureau of Justice Statistics, 1984).

[28]Brian A. Reaves and Pheny Z. Smith, *Felony Defendants in Large Urban Counties* (Washington, D.C.: Bureau of Justice Statistics, 1995).

[29]Patrick A. Langan and Jodi M. Brown, *Felony Sentences in State Courts* (Washington, D.C.: Bureau of Justice Statistics, 1997), p. 7.

[30]Heumann, p. 218.

[31]Boland and Forst, 1984.

[32]"Clearing the Homolka Deal," *Maclean's*, vol. 109 (April 1, 1996), p. 27.

[33]"Questioning Homolka's Deal," *Maclean's*, vol. 110 (April 28, 1997), p. 21.

[34]H. Miller, *Plea-Bargaining in the United States* (Washington, D.C.: Georgetown University Law Center, 1977).

[35]State of New York, The Judicial Conference and Office of Court Administration, *Twenty-Second Annual Report*, 1977.

[36]Barbara Boland, E. Brady, H. Tyson, and J. Bassler, *The Prosecution of Felony Arrests* (Washington, D.C.: Bureau of Justice Statistics, 1983).

[37]Vera Institute of Justice, *Felony Arrests*, revised ed. (New York: Longman, 1981).

[38]DeFrances, Smith, and van der Does, 1996.

[39]Brosi, 1979.

[40]Boland, Brady, Tyson, and Bassler, 1983.

[41]H. J. Shin, "Do Lesser Pleas Pay?: Accommodations in the Sentencing and Parole Process," *Journal of Criminal Justice*, vol. 1 (1973).

[42]T. Dungsworth, *Plea-Bargaining: Who Gains? Who Loses?* (Washington, D.C.: Institute for Law and Social Research, 1978).

[43]Eric R. Komitee, "Bargains without Benefits: Do the Sentencing Guidelines Permit Upward Departures to Redress the Dismissal of Charges Pursuant to Plea Bargains?," *New York University Law Review*, vol. 70 (April 1995), pp. 166–95.

[44]David E. Rovella, "Fake Plea Bargain in Death Case Raises Concerns," *The National Law Journal*, vol. 18 (October 9, 1995), p. 13.

[45]Ty Alper, "The Danger of Winning: Contract Law Ramifications of Successful Bailey Challenges for Plea-Convicted Defendants," *New York University Law Review*, vol. 72 (October 1997), pp. 841–81.

[46]National Advisory Committee on Criminal Justice Standards and Goals, *A National Strategy to Reduce Crime* (New York: Avon, 1975).

[47]Association of the Bar of the City of New York, *The Nation's Toughest Drug Law: Evaluating the New York Experience* (Washington, D.C.: Drug Abuse Council, 1977).

[48]Arthur Rosset and Donald R. Cressey, *Justice by Consent: Plea-bargains in the American Courthouse* (Philadelphia: Lippincott, 1976), p. 161.

[49]H. Lawrence Ross, "The Neutralization of Severe Penalties: Some Traffic Studies," *Law & Society Review*, vol. 10 (1976).

[50]David Rossman, Paul Froyd, Glen L. Pierce, John McDevitt, and William J. Bowers, "Massachusetts Mandatory Minimum Sentence Gun Law: Enforcement, Prosecution, and Defense Impact," *Criminal Law Bulletin*, vol. 16 (March–April 1980).

[51]Colin Loftin, Milton Heumann, and David McDowall, "Mandatory Sentencing and Firearms Violence: Evaluating an Alternative to Gun Control," *Law & Society Review,* vol. 17 (1983).

[52]Rossman et al., 1980.

[53]Michael L. Rubinstein, Steven H. Clarke, and Theresa J. White, *Alaska Bans Plea Bargaining* (Washington, D.C.: U.S. Government Printing Office, 1980).

[54]Andrew Blum, "'No Plea' Policies Sprout Across U.S.," *The National Law Journal,* vol. 19 (September 9, 1996), p. 1.

[55]Marcus Dirk Dubber, "American Plea Bargains, German Lay Judges, and the Crisis of Criminal Procedure," *Stanford Law Review,* vol. 49 (February 1997), pp. 547–605.

[56]Barbara Boland, *Felony Case-Processing Time* (Washington, D.C.: Bureau of Justice Statistics, 1986); Langan and Brown, 1997.

[57]Wayne A. Kerstetter and Anne M. Heinz, *Pre-Trial Settlement Conference: An Evaluation* (Washington, D.C.: U.S. Government Printing Office, 1979); Debra S. Emmelman, "Trial by Plea Bargain: Case Settlement as a Product of Recursive Decisionmaking," *Law & Society Review,* vol. 30 (June 1996), pp. 335–60.

[58]Hugh Nugent and J. Thomas McEwen, *Prosecutor's National Assessment of Needs* (Washington, D.C.: National Institute of Justice, 1988).

[59]DeFrances, Smith, and van der Does, p. 5.

[60]Langan and Brown, 1997.

[61]Boland and Forst, 1984.

[62]Michael E. Tigar, "Trials Teach Lessons of Rights and Responsibilities," *The National Law Journal,* vol. 19 (November 18, 1996), p. 19.

[63]Brian Reaves, *Felony Defendants in Large Urban Counties* (Washington, D.C.: Bureau of Justice Statistics, 1990).

[64]Langan and Brown, p. 7.

[65]James P. Levine, *Juries and Politics* (Pacific Grove, CA: Brooks/Cole, 1992); Charles J. Ogletree, "Just Say No! A Proposal to Eliminate Racially Discriminatory Uses of Peremptory Challenges," *American Criminal Law Review,* vol. 31 (1994), pp. 1099–151.

[66]Hiroshi Fukurai, Edgar W. Butler, and Richard Krooth, "Cross-Sectional Jury Representation or Systematic Jury Representation? Simple Random and Cluster Sampling Strategies in Jury Selection," *Journal of Criminal Justice,* vol. 19 (1991), pp. 31–48.

[67]*Thiel v. Southern Pacific Company,* 328 U.S. 217 (1945); *Batson v. Kentucky,* 106 S. Ct. 1712 (1986); Audrey M. Fried, "Fulfilling the Promise of Batson: Protecting Jurors from the Use of Race-Based Peremptory Challenges by Defense Counsel," *University of Chicago Law Review,* vol. 64 (Fall 1997), pp. 1311–36.

[68]*J. E. B. v. Alabama ex rel. T. B.,* 114 S. Ct. 1419 (1994).

[69]Rita J. Simon, *The Jury: Its Role in American Society* (Lexington, MA: Lexington Books, 1980); D. Suggs and B. D. Sales, "Using Communication Cues to Evaluate Prospective Jurors in the *Voir Dire,*" *Arizona Law Review,* vol. 20 (1978), pp. 629–42.

[70]Andrew Blum, "Jury Consultants Targeted: Illinois Bill Would Bar Non-Lawyers from Advising," *The National Law Journal,* vol. 18 (November 20, 1995), p. 6.

[71]*Ballew v. Georgia,* 435 U.S. 223 (1978).

[72]*Blanton v. North Las Vegas,* 489 U.S. 538 (1989).

[73]Melvyn B. Zerman, *Beyond a Reasonable Doubt: Inside the American Jury System* (New York: Crowell, 1981).

For Further Reading

Steven R. Donziger, ed., *The Real War on Crime* (New York: HarperPerennial, 1996).

George P. Fletcher, *With Justice for Some: Protecting Victims' Rights in Criminal Trials* (Reading, MA: Addison-Wesley, 1996).

H. Richard Uviller, *Virtual Justice: The Flawed Prosecution of Crime in America* (New Haven: Yale University Press, 1996).

chapter twelve

Criminal Defense

No, I don't want evidence that you can use in court. I want the truth.

JOHN WINTON
(1975)

In 1998, Darrell Harris was placed on trial for killing three people and seriously wounding a fourth at a Brooklyn social club. It was the first capital punishment case to be tried after New York State reinstated the death penalty in 1995. Harris was charged with robbing the victims of $200 and then killing them because he wanted no witnesses to his crime. His defense attorney claimed that Harris had "lost control and snapped" during this incident because he suffered from posttraumatic stress disorder from the "combat-like" work conditions in the jails when he worked as a corrections officer.[1] In addition, Harris's attorney argued that Harris's mental health was affected by a chaotic and abusive childhood; spinal meningitis, which had caused brain damage; cocaine and alcohol abuse; and failure to hold a

CHAPTER OUTLINE

job. Two days before the homicides occurred, Harris was fired from his job as a security guard. He also had discovered that his car had been towed. In 1991, he had resigned from his job as a corrections officer after failing a drug test.

Most of these claims bear little relationship to the charges filed, and they feed the perception that defense attorneys focus less on seeking the truth than on exonerating their client at any cost. Cases such as these raise other questions as well: What is the proper role of a defense attorney? What is the scope of the right to have defense counsel? What are the limits on proper representation of the accused? This chapter addresses each of these questions.

The Sixth Amendment

The Sixth Amendment to the U.S. Constitution deals specifically with the rights of people accused of crimes. It states that

> **In all criminal prosecutions, the accused shall enjoy the right to a speedy and public trial, by an impartial jury of the State and district wherein the crime shall have been committed, which district shall have been previously ascertained by law, and to be informed of the nature and cause of the accusation; to be confronted with the witnesses against him; to have compulsory process for obtaining witnesses in his favor, and to have the Assistance of Counsel for his defence.**

The right to have the assistance of counsel has attracted a great deal of attention over the years. Do all defendants have this right? Does it apply to all crimes? At what stage of criminal procedure does it become effective? What kind of counsel does it guarantee?

The Scope of the Right to Counsel

The scope of the right to counsel has been defined by the U.S. Supreme Court in a series of cases involving the interpretation and application of the Sixth Amendment. The Court applied the right to counsel narrowly at first but has expanded it significantly over the last thirty years. In 1932, the Court held in *Powell v. Alabama* that legal counsel is guaranteed to defendants who are indigent, charged with a capital crime, or unable to represent themselves owing to ignorance, illiteracy, or low intelligence.[2] The case involved nine young black men who were accused of raping two white women. The Court reversed their convictions, although they were retried with the assistance of counsel and four of the nine defendants were convicted (even though one of the victims recanted the charges of rape). Six years after the *Powell* decision, in *Johnson v. Zerbst*, the Supreme Court extended the right to counsel to *all* indigent felony defendants in *federal* cases, but did not extend the right to state cases (where most felony trials take place).[3] The Court justified this position in the 1942 case *Betts v. Brady*, stating that the right to counsel is not a fundamental right in noncapital cases unless special circumstances, such as mental illness or lack of education, are present.[4] Nevertheless, many states did not follow the guidelines set forth in *Betts*, and attorneys often were not provided even in cases that warranted it. In 1963, this situation culminated in the

Media and Criminal Justice

PRIMAL FEAR

Many of the most famous American defense attorneys have said that they never ask their clients whether or not they are guilty because it doesn't matter. The job of a defense attorney is a simple mission: Consider the case against the accused and do one's utmost to test the strength of that case on any grounds available.

The 1996 psychological thriller *Primal Fear* features an arrogant but aggressive defense attorney named Martin Vail who is torn between the fight for justice and his own need for fame. When Vail sees an evening TV news story about a prominent Catholic priest who has been found murdered in his underwear, he immediately seeks to defend the shy young man accused of the crime. His new client, Aaron, insists that he is innocent, that he was in the room shortly before the cleric was murdered, but that he also remembers someone else being there. He claims to have blacked out, perhaps having been attacked by the murderer. As a good defense attorney, Vail doesn't care. He explains to Aaron that whether or not he committed the murder is immaterial to the defense of the case.

To prepare his defense, Vail launches an investigation that reveals that the murdered archbishop was involved in land deals that lost millions of dollars and left many powerful investors angry. The priest had received many death threats. Is it possible that Aaron is being framed for what was actually a mob hit?

At first Vail's motivation is to grab headlines and bolster his image. As the facts unfold, however, Vail begins to realize that he may actually be defending a truly innocent person. It is discovered that the murdered archbishop was involved in sexually exploitative relationships with Aaron and other young men at the orphanage, and Vail finds himself emotionally involved in the case, suddenly determined to help the innocent boy find justice.

Vail's defense must take a sudden turn, however, when the court-appointed psychologist discovers that Aaron has a dual-personality disorder and that a "bad" Aaron may have committed the crime. Unfortunately for Vail, the trial has already begun and his defense strategy has been launched; it is too late to enter a plea of insanity. The movie's climax occurs when Vail manages to coax the unsuspecting Aaron into revealing his "bad" alter ego on the witness stand: In a sudden violent outburst, Aaron's dark side is exposed to the jury, and a mistrial is declared.

The most riveting scene of *Primal Fear*, however, is not Vail's successful Perry Mason–style defense of Aaron in the courtroom. Rather, it is the last scene of the movie, in which Vail must face the truth about who actually killed the archbishop. After one final meeting with the vindicated Aaron, Vail is shown leaving the courthouse in shock, trying to absorb the ramifications of what he has done.

Primal Fear was made to be more entertaining than educational, but it still offers insight into a situation that defense attorneys must face every day: defending a person who may or may not be guilty, and living with the consequences of doing so.

MEDIA AND CRIMINAL JUSTICE QUESTION

Should the guilt or innocence of a defendant affect how a defense attorney handles the case?

case *Gideon v. Wainwright*, which produced one of the Supreme Court's most significant decisions.

Clarence Earl Gideon was charged with breaking into a poolroom in Panama City, Florida. A witness claimed to have seen him through the broken poolroom window at 5:30 A.M. A cigarette machine and jukebox were broken into, and coins were taken. A "small amount of beer and some wine" were also taken.[5] This offense was a felony under Florida law. Appearing in court without funds and without a lawyer, Gideon asked the court to appoint counsel for him, whereupon the following exchange took place:

> **The Court: Mr. Gideon, I am sorry, but I cannot appoint counsel to represent you in this case. Under the laws of the State of Florida, the only time the Court can appoint Counsel to represent a Defendant is when that person is charged with a**

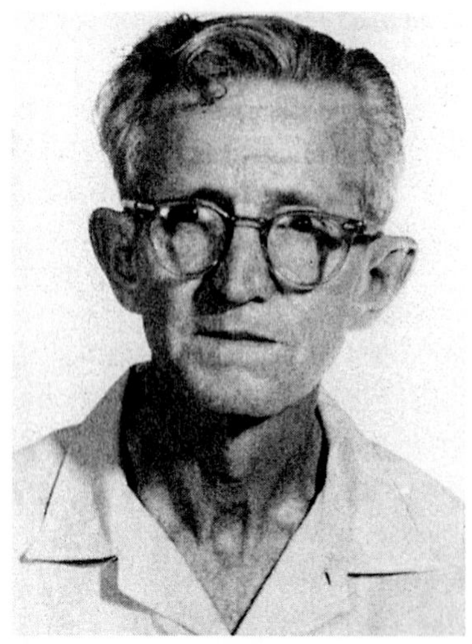

Clarence Earl Gideon's handwritten appeal to the U.S. Supreme Court led to a landmark decision guaranteeing indigents charged with felonies the right to legal counsel at trial.

> **capital offense. I am sorry, but I will have to deny your request to appoint Counsel to defend you in this case.**
>
> **The Defendant: The United States Supreme Court says I am entitled to be represented by Counsel.**

Gideon was forced to conduct his own defense at trial, and as the Supreme Court later said, he performed "about as well as could be expected from a layman. He made an opening statement to the jury, cross-examined the State's witnesses, presented witnesses in his own defense, declined to testify himself, and made a short argument emphasizing his innocence to the charge."

Nevertheless, the jury returned a verdict of guilty, and Gideon was sentenced to five years in state prison. From prison he filed a handwritten habeas corpus petition challenging his conviction and sentence on the ground that the trial court's refusal to appoint counsel for him denied him rights that were "guaranteed by the Constitution and the Bill of Rights of the United States Government."

In considering the petition, the Supreme Court noted that the government spends large amounts of money on lawyers to prosecute defendants and that defendants who have money hire the best lawyers they can find to represent them. The Court concluded:

> **That government hires lawyers to prosecute and defendants who have money hire lawyers to defend are the strongest indications of the widespread belief that lawyers in criminal courts are necessities, not luxuries. The right of one charged with crime to counsel may not be deemed fundamental and essential to fair trials in some countries, but it is in ours. From the very beginning, our state and national constitutions and laws have laid great emphasis on procedural and substantive safeguards designed to assure fair trials before impartial tribunals in which every defendant stands equal before the law. This noble ideal cannot be realized if the poor man charged with crime has to face his accusers without a lawyer to assist him.[6]**

The Court went on to quote Justice Sutherland's opinion from a 1932 case, *Powell v. Alabama*. It held that the right to be heard in court would be "of little value if it did not comprehend the right to be heard by counsel."

> **Even the intelligent and educated layman has small and sometimes no skill in the science of law. If charged with crime, he is incapable, generally, of determining for himself whether the indictment is good or bad. He is unfamiliar with the rules of evidence. Left without the aid of counsel he may be put on trial without a proper charge, and convicted upon incompetent evidence, or evidence irrelevant to the issue or otherwise inadmissible. He lacks both the skill and knowledge adequately to prepare his defense, even though he have a perfect one. He requires the guiding hand of counsel at every step in the proceedings against him. Without it, though he be not guilty, he faces the danger of conviction because he does not know how to establish his innocence.[7]**

Following this line of argument, the Court made the right to counsel during felony trials binding on all the states. Questions remained, however, regarding the scope of this right. Would it extend to misdemeanor cases? What about nontrial proceedings? Beginning in 1963, the same year as the *Gideon* decision, the Court extended the right to counsel to other stages of the criminal justice process in order to ensure fair and impartial treatment of individuals accused of crimes. The Sixth Amendment right to counsel now applies to crime suspects who are questioned while in police custody,[8] to preliminary hearings,[9] to the first appeal after conviction,[10] to police lineups,[11] to juvenile delinquency proceedings,[12] and to suspects charged with misdemeanors when imprisonment may result.[13] The latter case, *Argersinger v. Hamlin*, is particularly important because in it the Court established a general rule in considering the right to counsel. It held that in situations in which a person can be deprived of liberty, the right to counsel exists. This means that a defendant has the right to counsel in any criminal trial in which imprisonment for even one day can result.[14]

TABLE 12.1

Times at Which Jail Inmates Awaiting Trial First Talked with a Lawyer

FIRST MET WITH LAWYER	HIRED COUNSEL	APPOINTED COUNSEL
Before admission to jail	28%	13%
First week after admission	41%	34%
Second week after admission	10%	15%
More than 2 weeks after admission	19%	34%
Don't know	3%	4%
Number of inmates	68,409	230,599

SOURCE: James J. Stephan and Louis W. Jankowski, *Survey of Jail Inmates* (Washington, D.C.: Bureau of Justice Statistics, 1992).

The impact of these decisions illustrates their importance. Table 12.1 summarizes the findings of a survey of jail inmates awaiting trial in the United States. As the table indicates, of those who hired their own legal counsel, 69 percent first spoke with their attorney either before they were jailed or during the first week thereafter. Of those for whom counsel was provided by the government, only 47 percent spoke with a lawyer that early in the process. The timing of access to legal counsel can be critical, because at this time interrogations and statements are often made that can influence the outcome of a case. This survey of jail inmates also shows the significance of the Supreme Court decisions guaranteeing legal counsel to indigent defendants. More than 77 percent of all inmates received appointed counsel, revealing the large proportion of defendants who are poor.

Ineffective Assistance of Counsel

A defendant is entitled not only to legal counsel but to *effective* counsel. In 1970, the Supreme Court ruled that defendants are entitled "to the effective assistance of competent counsel."[15] Questions can arise as to whether the legal advice given to a defendant is defective to such a degree that the defendant's case is hampered by poor legal assistance. An actual case, *Strickland v. Washington*, illustrates this issue.

Over a ten-day period David Leroy Washington committed a series of crimes, including theft, kidnapping, assaults, torture, and three brutal stabbing murders. After his two accomplices were arrested, Washington surrendered to police and gave a lengthy statement in which he confessed to one of the criminal incidents. The State of Florida indicted Washington for kidnapping and murder and appointed an experienced criminal lawyer to represent him.

Washington's appointed counsel pursued pretrial motions but cut his efforts short when he learned that, against his advice, Washington had confessed to another of the murders. Washington waived his right to a jury trial, again acting against his counsel's advice, and pleaded guilty to all charges, including the three capital murder charges.

While entering his plea, Washington told the judge that he had no significant prior criminal record and that at the time of the crime spree he was under extreme stress caused by his inability to support his family. He also stated that he accepted responsibility for the crimes. The judge told Washington that he had "a great deal of respect for people who are willing to step forward and admit their responsibility," but he postponed sentencing.

In preparing for the sentencing hearing, Washington's lawyer spoke with his client about his background and spoke on the telephone with his wife and mother. His counsel did not seek any other character witnesses for him. He did not request a psychiatric examination, since his conversations with Washington gave no indications of psychological problems. He successfully excluded Washington's criminal record from consideration in sentencing by not requesting a presentence report. Such a report would have found that Washington did indeed have a significant criminal history.

At the sentencing hearing, the counsel argued that Washington's surrender, confession, offer to testify against a codefendant, and remorse and acceptance of responsibility justified sparing him from the death penalty. He also argued that Washington had no history of criminal activity and that he had committed the crimes under extreme mental or emotional disturbance. Washington was characterized as "fundamentally a good person who had briefly gone badly wrong in extremely stressful circumstances."[16]

In determining whether the death sentence was appropriate, the judge found several aggravating circumstances and no mitigating ones. He found that all three murders had been cruel, involving repeated stabbings; all had been committed during the course of robberies; and all had been committed in order to avoid detection and arrest. Despite the lack of evidence of prior convictions, the judge held that Washington had at least engaged in a course of stealing and was not suffering from extreme mental or emotional disturbance, and that his participation in the crimes was significant and not dominated by an accomplice. Washington was sentenced to death.

On appeal, Washington argued that he had received ineffective assistance of counsel in violation of the Sixth Amendment. Among other claims, he argued that his attorney's failure to request a psychiatric report, present character witnesses, and seek a presentence report had adversely affected his chances of receiving a less severe sentence. The Supreme Court ruled that when ineffective assistance of counsel is claimed, "the defendant must show that counsel's representation fell below an objective standard of reasonableness." In addition, the defendant must show "that there is a reasonable probability that, but for counsel's unprofessional errors, the result of the proceeding would have been different." In reviewing the facts of Washington's case, the Court determined that "the conduct of respondent's counsel at and before his sentencing proceeding cannot be found unreasonable." Moreover, it held that even if his attorney's conduct was unreasonable, the case was not affected to an extent that would warrant setting aside his death sentence.[17]

In a dissenting opinion, Justice Thurgood Marshall argued that the standard of "reasonably effective assistance" is too ambiguous. He also pointed out that it is often difficult to determine whether the outcome of a case would have been different if the defense lawyer had been more competent. Finally, the Sixth Amendment's guarantee of effective assistance of counsel exists "not only to reduce the chance that innocent persons will be convicted" but also to ensure that

Media and Criminal Justice

RIVER'S EDGE

In the early 1980s, an Oregon teenager killed his girlfriend and left her naked body lying on a riverbank. The murder itself was not what made headlines; instead, it was the fact that several of the murderer's high school friends went out to the river over the course of several days to poke and stare at the dead body. As word of the crime spread, more people came to see the body, but none of them called the police to report it.

The event was considered by many journalists to be symptomatic of a wider moral breakdown in society. This message is clearly the basis for the 1987 movie *River's Edge,* which recreates the famous murder while also focusing on the societal factors that contributed to the teens' behavior. Family, schools, peers, and police are all included in this portrait of what is wrong with American society. The film allows viewers to feel the horror that the teenagers obviously did not.

The young murderer, Sampson, is a learning-disabled boy who lives with an invalid aunt whom he spoon-feeds while reading Dr. Seuss books. He tells his friends that he killed his girlfriend Jamie because she was "talking trash" about his mother, but there is no mention of where his real parents are. Sampson's best friend is Layne, a pill-popping rebel who is far more interested in concealing the crime than Sampson is. For Layne, group loyalty is the only possible means of survival.

Another friend, Matt, is torn between group loyalty and doing right. His goal is autonomy—freedom from his abusive stepfather, absentee mother, whining little sister, and angry little brother. When Matt finally reports the crime to the police, he is interrogated like a suspect. His mother, assuming that he is in some sort of trouble, complains about having to miss work in order to pick him up from the police station. To escape from the hassles of his family life, Matt smokes marijuana regularly. At one point he smokes a joint in front of his mother. When she asks where he got it, he responds, "Don't worry, it's not yours."

River's Edge portrays suburban youth as aimless and lost. They go to school only when they feel like it, and waste their days drinking, smoking, and playing video games. They roam around all night without their parents' knowledge or care, driving nowhere, stealing six-packs, having sex, and befriending drug suppliers. One young girl asks, as she stares at Jamie's purple body, if maybe they should care. After all, she reasons, Jamie was their friend. Layne explains, however, that Sampson had his reasons, and that is enough to pacify the group mentality.

Matt's younger brother Tim is a 12-year-old who shoots fish in a barrel for fun and dismembers his younger sister's doll just to upset the child. He runs off at night from a mother who is too tired to go after him, and with another young cohort he steals a car, breaks into a house and assaults its occupant, takes several bags of marijuana and a gun, and then threatens to kill Matt for "ratting out" Sampson. With all these characters, *River's Edge* offers much commentary on the breakdown of the American family. It paints an ominous portrait of a generation of future criminals who do, and feel, nothing.

MEDIA AND CRIMINAL JUSTICE QUESTION

If you were a defense attorney, what approach would you take in defending Sampson against the charge of murder?

convictions result "only through fundamentally fair procedures." Marshall argued that once a defense lawyer's performance departs from constitutionally prescribed standards, due process is denied and a new trial is required, whether or not the defendant "suffered demonstrable prejudice."[18]

In sum, under current law, crime suspects and defendants are permitted to consult attorneys at most stages of the criminal justice process. The level of assistance provided must be "objectively reasonable, considering all the circumstances," and for an appeal to be sustained, it must be shown that without counsel's errors the outcome of the trial would probably have been different. The latter clearly is quite difficult to prove, and even demonstrating that legal counsel committed grave errors is insufficient by itself to prove that counsel's assistance was ineffective.

The Nature of Criminal Defense

The Bill of Rights and U.S. Supreme Court decisions express principles and aspirations for the role that government and law should play in the lives of citizens. These aspirations are not always realized in actual practice. The way criminal law is practiced, the reasons that most attorneys are not criminal attorneys, and the quality of legal representation are important issues in criminal defense in the United States.

The Practice of Criminal Law

The role of defense attorneys is to represent individuals accused of crimes. It is interesting to note, however, that the vast majority of lawyers are not criminal lawyers. In fact, of the more than 750,000 lawyers in the United States (with an additional 30,000 graduating from law school each year), only about 6 percent practice criminal law, and only 2 percent deal exclusively with criminal cases. This is so despite the fact that there is one lawyer for every 329 people in the United States, a far greater proportion than in any other nation. This ratio has nearly doubled since 1960[19] and translates into 281 lawyers for every 100,000 people in the United States, compared to 111 per 100,000 in Germany, 82 per 100,000 in England, and 11 per 100,000 in Japan.[20]

The reasons that most attorneys are not involved in criminal law are many. As defense attorney Seymour Wishman was told many times, "You spend most of your time with monsters," "you're in and out of depressing places like prisons all day long," "the pay isn't extraordinary," and "you're looked down upon."[21] A key factor is that most defendants are poor; as a result, relatively little money is made defending crime suspects (at least in comparison to other areas of law). Some defense lawyers dislike visiting police stations, jails, and prisons. In addition, the public sometimes views defense attorneys as trying to subvert justice by successfully defending guilty people.[22] Public opinion polls show little confidence in lawyers, especially defense lawyers.[23] As a result, lawyers who choose careers as criminal attorneys are in a distinct minority. However, with the dramatic rise in the number of attorneys graduating from law schools in recent years, it appears certain that there will be no dearth of lawyers to handle criminal defense in the future.

assigned counsel
Private attorney who is appointed by the court on a case-by-case basis from a list of available attorneys.

contract attorney
Private attorney, firm, or local bar association that provides legal representation to indigents for a specific period contracted with the county.

public defender
Salaried attorney who is paid by the government to represent indigents charged with crimes.

The Cost and Quality of Defense Lawyers

The notion that many criminal defendants are indigents is supported by the fact that three fourths of prison inmates were represented by court-appointed attorneys.[24,25] In order to meet the representation requirement, most states provide assigned counsel, contract attorney programs, or public defender services to indigents charged with crimes. **Assigned counsel** are private attorneys who are appointed by the court on a case-by-case basis from a list of available attorneys. In **contract attorney** programs, private attorneys, firms, or local bar associations provide legal representation to indigents for a specific period contracted with the county. **Public defender** programs are usually public nonprofit organizations with salaried attorneys paid by the government. About half of all counties in the United

States have assigned counsel systems, and contract programs are found in about 11 percent of counties. Public defenders exist in 37 percent of all counties, which include most of the largest jurisdictions, serving two thirds of the U.S. population.[26] Table 12.2 illustrates the distribution of representation systems in the nation's seventy-five largest counties. As the table shows, 81 percent of all felony defendants receive appointed counsel (either public defenders or assigned counsel). Only 18 percent can afford to hire their own lawyer.

More than $1.3 billion is spent on indigent defense services annually in nearly five million cases. This represents an increase of 100 percent in eleven years. The average cost per case is $223.[27] Nevertheless, this cost is quite low compared to what is spent by the prosecution in pressing charges, because prosecutors typically have more investigators and staff support than do criminal defense attorneys. This difference in cost has led to criticisms of the way indigent defense works in practice. Critics believe that the government does not take the defense of indigents seriously, with low reimbursement for assigned counsel leading to poor-quality representation and inadequate defense investigations of the charges against their clients.[28]

The states vary in how they pay for indigent defense. In twenty states, the state government funds the defense of indigents; in ten states, it is funded by the county; and in twenty jurisdictions the funding is shared by the county and the state. Most counties (75 percent) require the defendant to repay a portion of his or her defense costs, but it is difficult to collect this money.[29]

There is a marked difference between the use of appointed counsel by federal defendants and by defendants in state courts. This difference is illustrated in Table 12.3, which shows that twice as many federal as state prison inmates hired their own lawyers (43 percent and 22 percent, respectively). It should be remembered that 95 percent of all criminal cases are adjudicated in state courts because most criminal law is defined and enforced by the states; comparatively few crimes are violations of federal law. Federal crimes include many "white collar" and "organized" crimes that involve wealthy or well-connected defendants who are able to hire their own lawyers. Conversely, most "street" crimes are committed by poor people who are unable to hire legal counsel. This accounts for much of the difference in the use of appointed legal counsel in state and federal cases.

Many people believe that public defenders provide better representation than do assigned counsel because they are salaried employees of the state and have nothing to lose by going to trial rather than accepting a plea agreement. This system has been criticized, however, because public defenders constantly deal with the same prosecutors and judges and may not wish to jeopardize these working relationships by pushing too hard in a particular case. In many ways, prosecutors, defense counsel, and judges form a **courtroom work group.** They represent distinct interests but share the goal of shepherding large numbers of cases through the adjudication process. As one observer put it, "The client, then, is a secondary figure in the court system. . . . He becomes a means to other ends of the organization's incumbents."[30] Defense attorneys who are perceived as pushing too hard in a case may be informally "punished" by such means as inconvenient scheduling or contrary rulings from judges and reluctance on the

TABLE 12.2

Type of Counsel at Adjudication for Felony Defendants in the Nation's Seventy-five Largest Counties (33,017 Defendants)

TYPE OF LEGAL COUNSEL	PERCENT OF DEFENDANTS
Public defender	59
Assigned counsel	22
Hired counsel	18
Pro se	1
Other	1

SOURCE: Steven K. Smith and Carol J. DeFrances, *Indigent Defense* (Washington, D.C.: Bureau of Justice Statistics, 1996).

courtroom work group
The group of prosecutors, defense counsel, judges, and other courtroom personnel who represent distinct interests but share the goal of shepherding large numbers of cases through the adjudication process.

TABLE 12.3

Type of Legal Counsel Representing State and Federal Inmates

TYPE OF LEGAL COUNSEL	STATE INMATE	FEDERAL INMATE
Hired own counsel	22%	43%
Appointed counsel	76%	54%
Both hired and appointed counsel	2%	2%
Number of inmates	679,590	52,645

SOURCE: Allen Beck et al., *Survey of State Prison Inmates* and *Survey of Inmates in Federal Correctional Facilities* (Washington, D.C.: Bureau of Justice Statistics, 1993).

Defense attorney Gerry Spence established a reputation by representing high profile defendants including Imelda Marcos of the Philippines, and Randy Weaver, whose wife was slain by federal agents in a stand-off at Ruby Ridge, Idaho.

part of prosecutors to share reports or to plea bargain.[31] Defense attorneys also need to maintain good relations with all other court personnel in order to support and build their law practices.[32] Therefore, it is necessary for the actors in the courtroom work group to "get along," even if that occurs at the expense of some defendants.

In addition to prosecutors, defense attorneys, and judges, the courtroom work group includes sheriffs, court clerks, stenographers, and witnesses. Sheriffs or *bailiffs* are responsible for maintaining order in the courtroom. They ensure the appearance of defendants, and sometimes they also handle general court security tasks and deal with witnesses. The *court clerk* keeps track of the cases that are pending before the court. This is accomplished by preparing the court's calendar of cases, calling each case as scheduled, and maintaining court records of case status and judicial rulings. Many court clerks are attorneys. A court stenographer or *court reporter* makes a transcript of each court appearance. Witnesses are also an important part of the courtroom work group because they are involved in every case. Most witnesses are police officers, and therefore are seen on a regular basis. Lay witnesses who are victims or witnesses of crimes rely on the attorneys, court clerk, and sheriff's officers to understand the proceedings. The ability of a defense attorney to work successfully with all these players can improve the treatment of his or her client in court and in jail.

Another type of witness is the coroner or medical examiner. Coroners are appointed or elected officials who investigate the cause of all suspicious deaths in the jurisdiction. Over the years the position of coroner came to be filled by laypersons who were politically well connected, but who were often incompetent. Today the office of medical examiner has been established in many jurisdictions, taking the place of the coroner. Medical examiners must be physicians with training in forensic pathology. The role of the medical examiner and of forensic science in solving criminal cases of all types has grown dramatically. This growth is largely the result of the invention and increasing sophistication of DNA testing, which allows very small samples of body tissue or fluids to be matched against those of a suspect. Similarities in the genetic code between the two samples are used to include or exclude suspects in cases. Similar advances have been made in drug testing in recent years.

In 1997, the Office of the Inspector General in the U.S. Department of Justice released a five hundred–page report that charged the FBI's forensic laboratory with making errors in its forensic testing. It was widely believed that thousands of convictions might be overturned, but a year later only twenty defendants had tried to overturn their convictions. Some of this inaction is due to the lack of legal counsel for most prisoners to challenge their convictions and the fact that under federal law a prisoner has only one year in which to file a habeas corpus petition after new evidence is discovered.[33] Nevertheless, the procedures followed by the FBI and other forensic laboratories have improved greatly, due in part to a laboratory accreditation program of the American Society of Crime Laboratory Directors, which imposes minimum standards on laboratory equipment, conditions, and staffing.

Several studies have attempted to assess the quality of defense counsel. Each has focused on whether or not someone who retains his or her own counsel receives better legal representation than someone who is represented by assigned counsel or a public defender. It is clear that case loads are high and funding for indigent defense is relatively low, but there are no national data that compare public funding of prosecution versus defense in criminal cases. Overall spending is much higher for prosecutor's offices than for public defender's offices, and it is likely that expenditures per case (on investigations, witness interviews, expert opinions, and legal research) are also significantly higher. A study of legal representation in Chicago found that public defenders obtained more guilty pleas than did private or assigned counsel.[34] However, a subsequent study by David Neubauer discovered that this difference may be due to the types of cases that public defenders handle. He found that 90 percent of the public defender case load in one city consisted of burglary, forgery, robbery, and theft cases.[35] Only 66 percent of defendants with private counsel were charged with these crimes.

Because criminality is strongly related to opportunities to commit crime, it is not surprising that indigent offenders commit different types of offenses than do middle-class offenders. Perhaps it is this difference that accounts for variations in the frequency of guilty pleas.[36] On the basis of the available information, therefore, no definite conclusions can be drawn from this debate—except that perhaps the quality of defense counsel cannot be gauged by looking at the proportion of guilty pleas they obtain.

A related issue in evaluating the effectiveness of indigent defense is the nature of attorney–client relations. Defendants usually cannot choose their lawyers, and the feeling that "you get what you pay for" often leads to suspicion, lack of cooperation, and guarded exchanges of information.[37] These circumstances may have a significant but unmeasured impact on the quality of legal representation.

The courtroom work group includes prosecutors, defense attorneys, judges, bailiffs, court clerks, stenographers, and witnesses. They work together in a sometimes informal process of adversarial sparring, negotiation, and moving the court case load.

Common Defenses in Criminal Cases

general defenses
Justifications or excuses for criminal conduct that are applicable to all criminal offenses.

justification defenses
Defenses that admit that criminal conduct occurred but claim that it was justified by overwhelming circumstances, such as self-defense.

excuse defense
Defense that claims that criminal conduct should be excused because the defendant cannot be held responsible for it. Insanity and duress are examples.

Several **general defenses** are applicable to all criminal offenses. There are two types of general defenses: justification and excuse. **Justification defenses** claim that the act was committed, but that it was justified by overwhelming circumstances, such as self-defense. **Excuse defenses** also involve admission of the conduct in question, but they argue that it should be excused because the defendant cannot be held responsible for it. Insanity and duress are examples of excuse defenses. The key distinction between defenses involving justification or excuse is that the former looks to justify the offender's *conduct* while the later seeks to excuse the *offender* as an individual. These defenses are well defined in law and are discussed in more detail in Chapter 5.

Recently there has been a trend toward attempting to create new types of justifications or excuses. In the case of the Menendez brothers, for example, adult children killed their parents because of abuse they had suffered as children years earlier. In this case the defense attempted to extend the right of self-defense for a period of more than ten years. In the Oklahoma City bombing case, Timothy McVeigh's defense attorney argued at the sentencing stage that his client had committed the crime in reaction to the government's actions in Waco, Texas,

In the Oklahoma City bombing case, Timothy McVeigh's defense attorney argued at sentencing that his client had committed the crime in reaction to the government's actions in Waco, Texas, where eighty people were killed in a fire during a government raid.

where eighty people were killed in a fire during a government raid.[38] In a Texas case, a man had shot two unarmed black men in the head. His lawyers argued that the defendant suffered from "a rational fear of other blacks in violent urban neighborhoods."[39] This came to be called the "urban survival defense." In another case, sleep apnea was said to have caused a man to kill his wife.[40] Bad chromosomes and multiple personalities (one of which committed a rape) have been put forth as excuses.[41] As defense attorney Alan Dershowitz has remarked, "If you can make it sound like an illness, people are much more sympathetic."[42] This was the intention of the defense attorney in the homicide case summarized at the beginning of this chapter who claimed that criminal conduct was the result of job-related stress.

Sometimes lawyers themselves can become defendants, and their excuses are similar to those just described. In 1998, defense lawyer Gary Kleitman was sentenced to three to six years in prison for stealing more than $366,000 from his clients. He argued that his sentence was excessive because he was suffering from various physical disorders and his wife was scheduled to undergo surgery for cancer. These medical problems created "crushing financial problems" that Kleitman could not handle and resulted in his stealing money from his clients.[43]

These attempts to create new justifications and excuses for criminal conduct violate a fundamental assumption of criminal law: individual responsibility. If individuals cannot be held responsible for their conduct, but instead are said to be victims of circumstances, the punitive and deterrent purposes of the criminal law are undermined. The ideas of individual volition and personal accountability for one's actions are necessary if punishment is to be meaningful. Historically, juveniles and the mentally ill have been treated as exceptions under the criminal law, because it cannot be assumed that they have the rationality required to understand the consequences of their actions. Apart from these exceptions, all people are held to a "reasonableness" standard in their conduct. Very few justifications and excuses for criminal conduct are recognized under law in order to maintain this standard. Efforts to add to this list of justifications and excuses attempt to broaden the category of exceptions, thereby turning offenders into "victims." It is clear that defenses such as these fall outside any recognized defense of justification or excuse. In fact, they have a very tenuous relationship with the act in question. Cases such as these are growing in number and have generated a great deal of attention, although they are usually unsuccessful when presented to a trial jury.[44] It remains to be seen whether these efforts will create a legal backlash and a return to more traditional claims of justification and excuse in criminal defense.

Another common defense strategy is to attack the government's case. This was accomplished most successfully in the criminal trial of O. J. Simpson, in which the defense was able to place the conduct of the police at the center of its case rather than focusing on the defendant's alibi. Carefully investigating the histories of government informants can be crucial, because juries are understandably reluctant to convict a defendant on the basis of testimony by a person with a questionable background.[45] Several acquittals in the organized crime trials of the 1980s and 1990s were the result of juries disregarding the testimony of informants. During its deliberations in one of the trials of the alleged "godfather" John Gotti, the jury asked to reexamine one of the charts produced by the defense, which displayed the backgrounds of seven witnesses for the prosecution. It listed sixty-nine crimes, including instances of murder and kidnapping.[46] The jury acquitted Gotti in this case, showing that close scrutiny of the government's case can be used successfully as a defense.

Issues for the Future

Two major issues that criminal defense must face in the future are the extent to which the defense will be permitted to consider the problems of the offender as well as the criminal act itself, and the larger question of what we expect the adjudication process to accomplish. In 1995, Colin Ferguson asked to represent himself in a trial in which he was accused of engaging in a shooting rampage on a Long Island Railroad train car in which six people were killed and nineteen others wounded. Legal and psychiatric experts argued that Ferguson was paranoid and delusional, but the judge ruled that he was competent to represent himself in court.[47] Ferguson later appealed his conviction, arguing that he was mentally incompetent to stand trial in the first place.[48] Such a series of events is evidence of confusion between granting defendants the legal right to represent themselves and the need to maintain the integrity of court proceedings.

Adjudicating the Offender or the Act?

In the Menendez case and others of a similar nature, the defense argued that the defendants should be excused because of abuse suffered as children.[49] Although some observers considered this argument outrageous, a number of states had already extended the excuse of self-defense to battered women who kill their husbands out of fear after a history of physical abuse, even though the husband might have been sleeping at the time of the murder.[50] It can be argued that the Menendez "child abuse" defense is simply an extension of the "battered woman syndrome" defense that was created in the 1980s. Both attempt to extend the principle of self-defense to situations that fall outside the traditional scope of this principle.[51] On one hand, self-defense is being expanded well beyond its logical limits when the defendant is successfully portrayed as a "victim." On the other hand, less sympathetic defendants, such as those convicted of assault and manslaughter for shooting trespassers, are treated according to the traditional rules of self-defense.

The same trend can be seen in the "urban survival defense," in which a defendant who took lives unlawfully is portrayed as a victim.[52] Even Timothy McVeigh's argument that the Oklahoma City bombing was necessary to retaliate against the government for its actions at Waco was an effort to stretch self-defense to new dimensions. Applying the logic of self-defense in these cases is a slippery slope, yet defendants and their attorneys are increasingly attempting to do so.

After the media onslaught that surrounded the O. J. Simpson trial, courts in Los Angeles proposed new rules to ban hallway interviews during trials.[53] Attorneys in that case often held impromptu news conferences after each day's proceedings in an effort to shape public opinion about the case. Such posturing can

contemporary issues

Getting a Fair Trial in Cases Involving Violence

Several recent cases have tested the ability of the criminal justice system to operate in a fair and neutral manner. The O. J. Simpson double-homicide case and the Oklahoma City bombing case illustrate opposite sides of the same issue: Is it more difficult for a well-liked celebrity or for a hated unknown person to receive a fair trial? Simpson was acquitted, while McVeigh was convicted at trial. Why?

As one scholar has suggested, major criminal cases have become political trials in which the victims, rather than the crime, are the focus of attention. We "think of these courtroom dramas by the names of the person shot or beaten."[A] If the crime is serious enough and there are no other likely suspects, the defendant is usually convicted. Yet this did not occur in the O. J. Simpson case, and it has not happened in other celebrated cases in the past.

The case of Lizzie Borden is one example. Lizzie and her sister were unmarried and lived with their father and stepmother in Fall River, Massachusetts, one hundred years ago. On one very hot morning someone savagely killed the stepmother with an axe. When the father returned home an hour later and lay down on the sofa, he was killed with the same axe. Since Lizzie's sister was out of town, Lizzie and the maid were the only people known to be around the house at the time of the murders. Lizzie was charged with the crime, but reporters did not believe that she was the murderer. As one historian put it, "She came to symbolize, in a way, American innocence. The jury chose to believe in the symbol. Such a person was simply incapable of violent crime. It must have been a stranger, or the maid, *or somebody*. . . anybody but the stiffly buttoned, silent woman sitting demurely in the courtroom."[B] Lizzie Borden was acquitted at trial, although some historians believe that she was the killer.[C]

It is easy to dismiss these types of cases as anomalies that were decided on the basis of race, sympathy, or outrage at the deaths of innocent victims, but there may be more to it than that. Why did so many observers believe that O. J. Simpson and Lizzie Borden were innocent but that Timothy McVeigh was guilty? In these cases there seemed to be a presumption of innocence or guilt before the facts were known. Were Simpson and Borden simply more innocent-looking? McVeigh was a military veteran without a prior criminal record, Borden was a reclusive spinster, and Simpson was a well-liked celebrity. Nothing about *who they are* tells us anything about their guilt or innocence. The only relevant information is *what they did*.

An 1890 photo of Lizzie Borden who was acquitted at trial of killing her father and stepmother with an axe in Fall River, Massachusetts.

Increasingly, more public and media attention is given to the nature of the *offender* than to the nature of the *offense*. This seems to occur most often in cases of violence, in which one often asks, Was the defendant capable of such a thing? This question misleads the public in its search for justice, which cannot be found in personality profiles but only in the facts and circumstances of the incident in question. In the same way that Lizzie Borden was prejudged one hundred years ago, this same phenomenon is occurring today. The only difference is that it appears to take place more often as crimes arise from a widening variety of motives, including hate, prejudice, political beliefs, perceived victimization by others or by the government, and an array of psychoses. As this list of motives grows longer, the propensity to prejudge cases on the basis of offenders' personalties instead of the facts will increase.

NOTES

[A]George P. Fletcher, *With Justice for Some* (Reading, MA: Addison-Wesley, 1996), p. 2.

[B]Lawrence M. Friedman, *Crime and Punishment in American History* (New York: Basic Books, 1993), p. 254.

[C]Robert Sullivan, *Goodbye Lizzie Borden* (Brattleboro, VT: S. Greene Press, 1974).

Defense attorney Stephen Jones' argument that his client's (Timothy McVeigh) role in the Oklahoma City bombing was necessary to retaliate against the government for its actions at Waco was an effort to stretch self-defense to new dimensions.

indirectly influence the jury, which may learn of these statements through the media. Similarly, guidelines have been proposed for lawyers who appear on television as legal commentators. Some lawyers who defend clients in criminal cases have accepted work as television commentators during subsequent civil cases such as that of O. J. Simpson. This can result in attorneys accidentally broadcasting client confidences, or not providing a candid assessment because of their prior involvement in a related case.[54] Here again it appears that the focus of defense attorneys is on building the image of the defendant rather than on responding to the crimes charged.

In a shocking example of this phenomenon, former assistant district attorney Steven Pagones was accused in 1987 of raping Tawana Brawley. The accusation was made by three prominent individuals from the New York City area, including the Reverend Al Sharpton. Pagones was cleared of the charge in 1988, and he then successfully sued his accusers on charges of defamation of character. This civil suit was tried in 1998 in a case that was marred by name-calling, contempt citations, and other disorderly behavior in the courtroom. A defense lawyer served a night in jail for contempt of court in refusing to obey a judge's order.[55] Although atypical, such behavior on the part of defense attorneys fuels the perception that they abuse the process in order to draw attention away from the facts of the case.

Crime Control or Due Process?

Among the most compelling questions for criminal defense in the future is, What do we want the criminal justice system to accomplish? The answer to this question is not straightforward and can represent quite different perspectives on the justice process.

Criminologist Herbert Packer described two ideal models of criminal justice operations that are useful in evaluating the system and its operations. According to the **crime control model,** repression of criminal conduct is the most important function to be performed by the criminal justice system. In order to accomplish this, it is necessary to achieve maximum speed, efficiency, and finality in criminal justice processing. Proponents of this model argue that deterrence is achieved when the penalty is imposed quickly and with certainty. This cannot occur when a prolonged series of pretrial hearings, continuances and other delays, and appeals distance the connection between the crime and the punishment. In contrast, the **due process model** considers preservation of individual liberties to be the most important function of the criminal justice system. Therefore, accuracy, fairness, and reliability in criminal procedure are keys to a properly functioning system according to this view.[56] Proponents of this model believe that careful attention to the rights of individuals when they are prosecuted by a much more powerful government is essential in order to ensure that only the guilty are convicted and that the public has a high level of confidence in the system. This cannot occur when so many cases are plea-bargained, defendants are encouraged to waive their constitutional rights, and the outcomes of cases are determined by negotiations behind closed doors rather than in court.

crime control model
A perspective that views repression of criminal conduct as the most important function to be performed by the criminal justice system, through speed, efficiency, and finality in criminal justice processing.

due process model
A perspective that considers preservation of individual liberties to be the most important function of the criminal justice system, through accuracy, fairness, and reliability in criminal procedure.

FUTURE ISSUES

School Violence by Children

In 1998, two boys, aged eleven and thirteen, skipped classes at their middle school in Arkansas. Armed with thirteen handguns and rifles and dressed in camouflage outfits, they waited outside the school and opened fire on their classmates as they left the building, shooting twenty-seven times from across the schoolyard. Four students and one teacher were killed.[A] Over the previous two years, similar shooting incidents had taken place in schools in Kentucky, Mississippi, Washington, Alaska, and Missouri.[B]

Although still rare, violence on school property appears to be occurring with increasing frequency, despite the fact that a majority of schools now control access to school buildings. A national survey found 4.2 percent of all 12- to 19-year-old students were victimized by a violent crime in 1995, compared to 3.4 percent six years earlier.[C] More than half of all juvenile victimizations occur in school or on school property, but only 23 percent of violent crimes against juveniles take place there. Violent crimes against juveniles are equally likely to occur at home.[D] Most offenses on school grounds are minor thefts, vandalism, and fights without weapons, and nearly half of elementary and secondary schools reported no crimes at all during 1996 to 1997.

Explanations for school violence vary considerably. The most cited causes include low self-esteem and rage combined with poor communication skills, inability to handle conflict appropriately, lack of adequate parental supervision, the presence of criminal adults in the families of violent juveniles, violent neighborhoods, violent films and television shows, and access to guns.[E] The diverse nature of these explanations makes it difficult to design prevention strategies, for it appears that a single strategy will not be adequate.

FUTURES QUESTION

Assuming that violence by juveniles in schools is a result of the causes just mentioned, propose strategies that might be effective in reducing it.

NOTES

[A]T. Trent Gegax, Jerry Adler, and Daniel Pederson, "The Boys Behind the Ambush," *Newsweek* (April 6, 1998), pp. 21–4; Jonah Blank, Jason Vest, and Suzie Parker, "The Children of Jonesboro," *U.S. News & World Report* (April 6, 1998), pp. 16–22.

[B]Gordon Witkin, "Anti-Violence Efforts Show Few Results," *U.S. News & World Report* (April 6, 1998), p. 22; Geoffrey Cowley, "Why Children Turn Violent," *Newsweek* (April 6, 1998), pp. 24–5; Thomas Toch, "Violence in Schools," *U.S. News & World Report* (November 8, 1993), pp. 30–46.

[C]Kathryn A. Chandler, Chris Chapman, Michael R. Rand, and Bruce M. Taylor, *Students' Reports of School Crime, 1989 and 1995* (Washington, D.C.: Bureau of Justice Statistics, 1998).

[D]Howard N. Snyder and Melissa Sickmund, *Juvenile Offenders and Victims: A National Report* (Washington, D.C.: Office of Juvenile Justice and Delinquency Prevention, 1995).

[E]Cowley, pp. 24–5; Melissa Sickmund, Howard N. Snyder, and Eileen Poe-Yamagata, *Juvenile Offenders and Victims: 1997 Update on Violence* (Washington, D.C.: Office of Juvenile Justice and Delinquency Prevention, 1997); Denise Gottfredson, Richard Rosenfeld, and Simon Singer, *Juvenile Crime: A Research Perspective* (Washington, D.C.: Consortium of Social Science Associations, 1997).

Although Packer recognizes that these models do not exist in their pure forms, they allow us to clarify the assumptions we make about criminal justice operations. For example, someone who claims that the largest problem in criminal justice is legal restrictions on the police in stopping, questioning, and searching suspicious individuals probably believes that extensive police powers are necessary to control crime. As a result, it is likely that this person subscribes to the crime control model and believes that repression of crime is the most important function of the criminal justice system. On the other hand, those who would argue that widespread use of plea-bargaining results in unfairness in the adjudication and sentencing process probably see accuracy and fairness as the primary objectives of the criminal justice system—and believe that the due process model best describes the ideals of criminal justice.

Although features of both models are valid and deserve attention, it is important to keep assumptions about the ultimate purpose of criminal justice in mind when considering specific issues.[57] Only in this way can ideological beliefs ("what ought to be") be separated from value-free evaluations of criminal justice operations and research ("what is"). For example, the federal government spent several million dollars on the defense of Timothy McVeigh in the Oklahoma City bombing case. Some observers considered this amount excessive. However, the underlying question is, Are speed and finality or accuracy and reliability more important in this case? Therefore, it is really not a question of money but, rather, a question about which model of justice should be paramount. Most people want both speed and accuracy, but it is difficult to achieve these goals simultaneously. Given the constraints imposed by limited resources, the emphasis placed on one or the other of these goals will depend on the philosophy of justice that dominates in a particular case or jurisdiction.

The balance between crime control and due process is complicated by perceptions. Many people believe that due process protections frustrate rather than advance justice. Two examples are the beliefs that defense lawyers lie in order to exculpate their clients and that they use legal technicalities to free defendants.[58] The facts generally do not support these beliefs, but the perception is aggravated when a prominent defense attorney states that "the vast majority of criminal defendants are in fact guilty of the crimes with which they are charged. Almost all of my own clients have been guilty."[59] Such statements can be used to question the relevance of the due process model. From a due process perspective, the guilt or innocence of the defendant is secondary to ensuring that the process is carried out with fairness and accuracy so as to reduce the *possibility* that an innocent person will be convicted unjustly. Thus, a primary difference between the two models lies in where errors are made. From the crime control perspective, the potential for wrongful conviction of a small number of innocent individuals is offset by the deterrent impact of more swift and certain punishment of offenders in general. From the due process perspective, it is worse to deny liberty to an innocent person than it is to let a small number of the guilty go free.

Critical Thinking EXERCISE

Should a Lawyer Defend a Guilty Person?

Many college students wish to go on to law school but do not want to become defense attorneys. Many argue that they do not want to represent guilty people. As one account put it, "What many people want to know is how defense attorneys can live with themselves after they help a guilty person escape punishment."[A] This view overlooks the fact that defense attorneys represent the legal rights of defendants, not their personality or speculations about their guilt or innocence. In fact, it is "not their job to decide who is guilty and not. Instead, it is the public defender's job to judge the quality of the case that the state has against the defendant."[B] According to the standards of the American Bar Association, "the defense lawyer is the professional representative of the accused, not the accused's alter ego."[C]

In a murder case that was appealed to the U.S. Supreme Court, a defense attorney did not permit his client to testify falsely about whether he had seen a gun in the hand of the victim. The defendant claimed that he was deprived of effective assistance of counsel because of the lawyer's refusal to permit him to perjure himself. The Supreme Court held that the defense lawyer's duty "is limited to legitimate, lawful conduct compatible with the very nature of a trial as a search for truth." As a result, "counsel is precluded from taking steps or in any way assisting the client in presenting false evidence or otherwise violating the law."[D] The proper role of a defense attorney is to represent a defendant in an honest way that seeks the truth in the case.

Nevertheless, there are those who claim that defense attorneys do not act honestly. It has been argued that the defense attorney is "more concerned with appearance and perceptions than with underlying facts [and] who puts greater reliance in 'personality' than in knowledge." Although the Code of Professional Responsibility prohibits false statements of fact or law in court, it is said that there is much "fiction weaving that customarily passes for argument to a jury."[E] As a result, there may be a gap between the principles and the actual practice of criminal defense.

Critical Thinking Questions

1. If a defense lawyer's role is not to represent "guilty people," why do many people belittle the importance of defense attorneys in criminal cases?
2. Identify a specific action or statement made by a defense attorney in a well-known case that leads you to believe that the attorney was acting inappropriately as the defendant's "alter ego."

Notes

[A]Lisa J. McIntyre, *The Public Defender: The Practice of Law in the Shadows of Repute* (Chicago: University of Chicago Press, 1987), p. 139.

[B]Ibid., p. 145; Charles M. Sevilla, "Criminal Defense Lawyers and the Search for Truth," *Harvard Journal of Law & Public Policy,* vol. 20 (Winter 1997) pp. 519–28.

[C]American Bar Association, *Standards for Criminal Justice,* number 4-1.1.

[D]*Nix v. Whiteside,* 475 U.S. 157 (1986).

[E]H. Richard Uviller, *Virtual Justice: The Flawed Prosecution of Crime in America* (New Haven: Yale University Press, 1996), pp. 153, 155.

Critical Thinking EXERCISE

Should the Right to Counsel Be Expanded?

The right to counsel under the Sixth Amendment has existed since the nation's founding. Nevertheless, it was not applied in a significant way in state courts until the 1960s, nearly two hundred years later. Through a series of decisions by the U.S. Supreme Court, the right to counsel has been extended to most stages of the criminal justice process, from police custody through sentencing. However, there are still some steps in the justice process in which legal counsel is not yet guaranteed.

If a police officer pulls an individual over on the highway and asks, "Have you been drinking?" or "Do you know how fast you were going?," his or her answers can be incriminating. If a person is in police custody, he or she must be informed of the right to remain silent and the right to have an attorney present during questioning. The Supreme Court has ruled that questions asked at a roadside stop do not constitute a custodial interrogation,[A,B] although it is probably not a good idea to pull away from a roadside stop without the officer's permission. The right to legal counsel when a suspect is booked, or brought before a grand jury, also has not been established by law.

Critical Thinking Questions

1. **Why do you believe that the right to legal counsel has not been extended to roadside interrogations or to bookings?**
2. **Why has the right to counsel not been extended to grand jury investigations?**
3. **Do you believe that the right to counsel should be extended to these stages of the justice process?**

Notes

[A]***Berkimer v. McCarty*, 104 S. Ct. 3138 (1984).**

[B]***Pennsylvania v. Bruder*, 109 S. Ct. 205 (1988).**

Summary

THE SIXTH AMENDMENT

- The Sixth Amendment to the U.S. Constitution guarantees the right of accused persons to have the assistance of counsel.
- The scope of the right to counsel has been expanded in a series of important Supreme Court cases, beginning with *Gideon v. Wainwright* in 1963.
- In 1970, the Supreme Court ruled that defendants are entitled to *effective* assistance of counsel, but it is difficult to demonstrate that the outcome of a case would have been different without counsel's errors.

THE NATURE OF CRIMINAL DEFENSE

- Comparatively few attorneys are involved in criminal law, primarily because most defendants are poor.
- To meet the representation requirement, most states use either assigned counsel, contract attorney programs, or public defenders. A large majority of felony defendants are represented by public defenders or assigned counsel.
- Prosecutors, defense counsel, and judges can be viewed as a courtroom work group. While they represent distinct interests, they share the goal of moving large numbers of cases through the adjudication process.
- Several general defenses are applicable to criminal offenses. Justification defenses claim that the act was justified by overwhelming circumstances, while excuse defenses argue that the defendant cannot be held responsible for the act.

ISSUES FOR THE FUTURE

- A major issue for criminal defense is the tendency to focus on the offender rather than on the criminal act. This has led to the creation of new defenses that attempt to go beyond the boundaries of concepts such as self-defense.

- Another issue is whether the crime control model (which emphasizes repression of criminal conduct) or the due process model (which emphasizes preservation of individual liberties) will dominate the justice process in a particular case or jurisdiction.

Key Terms

assigned counsel	courtroom work group	excuse defense
contract attorney	general defense	crime control model
public defender	justification defense	due process model

Questions for Review and Discussion

1. What important rights are guaranteed by the Sixth Amendment to the U.S. Constitution?
2. What was the significance of the Supreme Court case of *Gideon v. Wainwright*?
3. What is meant by "reasonably effective assistance of counsel"?
4. Why do most attorneys avoid the practice of criminal law?
5. What are the three types of systems used by states to provide counsel for indigent defendants?
6. Who are the participants in the courtroom work group?
7. Identify and describe the two basic types of defenses.
8. What are two key issues that must be faced by criminal defense in the future?

Notes

[1]Patricia Hurtado, "Lost Control and Snapped: Defense Cites Stress in Social-Club Killings," *Newsday* (May 5, 1998), p. 7.
[2]287 U.S. 45 (1932).
[3]304 U.S. 458 (1938).
[4]316 U.S. 455 (1942).
[5]Anthony Lewis, *Gideon's Trumpet* (New York: Vintage, 1966), p. 59.
[6]*Gideon v. Wainwright*, 83 S. Ct. 1340 (1963).
[7]*Powell v. Alabama*, 287 U.S. 45 (1932).
[8]*Escobedo v. Illinois*, 378 U.S. 478 (1963); *Miranda v. Arizona*, 384 U.S. 694 (1966).
[9]*Coleman v. Alabama*, 399 U.S. 1 (1970).
[10]*Douglas v. California*, 372 U.S. 353 (1963).
[11]*Gilbert v. California*, 388 U.S. (1967).
[12]*In re Gault*, 38 U.S. 1 (1967).
[13]See Jefferson Ingram, *Criminal Procedure: Cases and Materials* (Cincinnati: Anderson Publishing, 1995).
[14]*Argersinger v. Hamlin*, 407 U.S. 25 (1972).
[15]*McMann v. Richardson*, 397 U.S. 765 (1970).
[16]*Strickland v. Washington*, 104 S. Ct. 2052 (1984).
[17]104 S. Ct. 2060.
[18]104 S. Ct. at 2070.
[19]"More and More Lawyers," *USA Today* (May 18, 1992), p. 1.
[20]"Explosion in the Legal Field," *USA Today* (November 27, 1991), p.13A.
[21]Seymour Wishman, *Confessions of a Criminal Lawyer* (New York: Penguin, 1982), p. 231.

[22]Charles M. Sevilla, "Criminal Defense Lawyers and the Search for Truth," *Harvard Journal of Law & Public Policy,* vol. 20 (Winter 1997), pp. 519–28.

[23]Stephen Budiansky with Ted Gest, "How Lawyers Abuse the Law," *U.S. News & World Report* (January 30, 1995), pp. 50–6.

[24]92 S. Ct. 2006 (1972).

[25]Steven K. Smith and Carol J. DeFrances, *Indigent Defense* (Washington, D.C.: Bureau of Justice Statistics, 1996).

[26]Carla K. Gaskins, *Criminal Defense Systems* (Washington, D.C.: Bureau of Justice Statistics, 1984); Smith and DeFrances, p. 2.

[27]Robert L. Spangenberg, Judy Kapucinski, and Patricia A. Smith, *Criminal Defense for the Poor* (Washington, D.C.: Bureau of Justice Statistics, 1988); Smith and DeFrances, p. 2.

[28]Richard Klein, "The Emperor *Gideon* has No Clothes: The Empty Promise of the Constitutional Right to Effective Assistance of Counsel," *Hastings Constitutional Law Quarterly,* vol. 13 (1986), pp. 625–93.

[29]Ibid.

[30]Abraham S. Blumberg, "The Practice of Law as a Confidence Game," in George S. Bridges, Joseph G. Weis, and Robert D. Crutchfield, eds., *Criminal Justice* (Thousand Oaks, CA: Pine Forge Press, 1996), p. 269.

[31]James Eisenstein, Roy Fleming, and Peter Nardulli, *The Contours of Justice: Communities and Their Courts* (Boston: Little, Brown, 1988).

[32]Blumberg, p. 269.

[33]David E. Rovella, "Predictions of Big Effects from Ills in FBI Lab Prove False," *Fulton County Daily Report* (April 23, 1998), pp. 1–5.

[34]Dallin H. Oaks and Warren Lehman, *A Criminal Justice System and the Indigent* (Chicago: University of Chicago Press, 1968).

[35]David W. Neubauer, *Criminal Justice in Middle America* (Morristown, NJ: General Learning Press, 1974).

[36]Dean J. Champion, "Private Counsel and Public Defenders: A Look at Weak Cases, Prior Records, and Leniency in Plea-Bargaining," *Journal of Criminal Justice,* vol. 17 (1989), pp. 253–63.

[37]Roy B. Fleming, "Client Games: Defense Attorneys' Perspectives on Their Relations with Criminal Clients," in George S. Bridges, Joseph G. Weis, and Robert D. Crutchfield, eds., *Criminal Justice* (Thousand Oaks, CA: Pine Forge Press, 1996), pp. 276–82.

[38]Peter Annin, "McVeigh in the Dock," *Newsweek* (June 9, 1997), p. 41.

[39]Robert Davis, "We Live in an Age of Exotic Defenses," *USA Today* (November 22, 1994), p. 2

[40]Ibid., pp. 1–2.

[41]Alan Dershowitz, *The Abuse Excuse* (New York: Random House, 1994).

[42]Davis, p. 2.

[43]Margaret Gibbons, "Kleitman Granted Second Chance to Ask for Freedom," *The Legal Intelligencer* (May 6, 1998), p. 5.

[44]Tony Mauro, "Abuse Excuse Raises Public Outcry," *USA Today* (February 8, 1994), p. 1.

[45]Margaret Cronin Fisk, "In Drug Defense, Stress Constitution," *The National Law Journal,* vol. 20 (September 22, 1997), p. 6.

[46]Leonard Buder, "Gotti is Acquitted in Conspiracy Case Involving the Mob," *The New York Times* (March 14, 1987), p. 1.

[47]Bruce Frankel, "New York Shooting Victims on the Stand: You Did This," *USA Today* (February 9, 1995), p. 3.

[48]Kevin Johnson, "Train Gunman to Appeal, Use Incompetence Defense," *USA Today* (February 20, 1995), p. 2.

[49]Tony Mauro, "Child Abuse Becoming a Defense Trend," *USA Today* (September 24, 1993), p. 2.

[50]See Faith McNulty, *The Burning Bed* (New York: Dell, 1980).
[51]Robert Schwaneberg, "The Legal Risks of 'Self-Defense'," *Atlantic City Press* (March 15, 1981), p. 1.
[52]Steve Timko, "Murder Acquittal in 'Urban Fear' Trial," *USA Today* (April 12, 1995), p. 3.
[53]M. L. Stein, "L.A. Courts Restrict Press: Proposed Courthouse Rules Force Reporters to Wear Passes and Ban Hallway Interviews," *Editor & Publisher*, vol. 130 (November 8, 1997), p. 11.
[54]Christian Berthelsen, "Guidelines for Lawyers in Court of Television," *The New York Times* (April 20, 1998), p. 7.
[55]William Glaberson, "Calm Returns to Brawley Case, But Punished Lawyer Doesn't," *The New York Times* (May 1, 1998), p. 5.
[56]Herbert L. Packer, *The Limits of the Criminal Sanction* (Stanford, CA: Stanford University Press, 1968).
[57]John P. Conrad, "The Rights of Wrongdoers," *Criminal Justice Research Bulletin*, vol. 3 (1987); Walter B. Miller, "Ideology and Criminal Justice Policy," *Journal of Criminal Law and Criminology*, vol. 64 (1973).
[58]Sevilla, pp. 519–28.
[59]Alan M. Dershowitz, *The Best Defense* (New York: Vintage, 1983), p. xiv.

For Further Reading

F. Lee Bailey, *To Be a Trial Lawyer*, 2nd ed. (New York: Wiley, 1994).
Alan M. Dershowitz, *The Best Defense* (New York: Vintage Books, 1983).
Gerry Spence, *With Justice for None* (New York: Penguin, 1990).

chapter thirteen

Sentencing: Philosophy and Practice

The victim of too severe a law is considered as a martyr rather than a criminal.

CHARLES CALEB COLTON
(1780–1832)

In 1922, William McAlpin was convicted of bigamy in Santa Clara, California. At his sentencing the judge asked him, "Do you use liquor? Drugs? Do you ever gamble? Do you play any musical instruments?"[1] Were these questions legitimate or irrelevant? Should such factors be considered in deciding on a sentence?

Similar questions are asked at sentencing hearings today. "Do you use alcohol? Drugs? Are you employed? Is this your first offense?" Rather than relying on the offender's account, however, judges usually obtain the answers through drug tests, criminal record checks, and reports of probation

CHAPTER OUTLINE

TABLE 13.1

Arguments For and Against Consideration of Factors Not Related to the Offense

CONSIDER OR NOT FOR SENTENCING?	RELEVANT FOR SENTENCING	NOT RELEVANT FOR SENTENCING
Poor employment history	Failed to take advantage of legitimate job opportunities	Has not had legitimate opportunity to succeed
Drug or alcohol use	Crime is additional symptom of asocial behavior	Substance abuse may have clouded judgment
Prior offense	Did not learn lesson from previous sentences	Sentence received for prior offense is ended, and offender should not be punished again for it
Play musical instrument	Failed to capitalize on opportunities for success in legitimate society	Never had opportunity for constructive leisure activity

department investigators. Nevertheless, one can ask what relevance a prior offense has to the charge at hand. Why should use of drugs or alcohol be considered? Why should employment history be a factor? In each case a compelling argument can be made for or against the consideration of such factors, as is shown in Table 13.1. It is clear from this table that even the question of whether or not a person plays a musical instrument could conceivably be relevant for *either* increasing *or* reducing a sentence. Is there a point at which inquiries into an offender's background are not appropriate?

Although sentencing is the culmination of a criminal case that has proceeded from suspicion to probable cause to proof beyond a reasonable doubt, historically it has been the least certain stage of a criminal proceeding. The laws of criminal procedure that guide the earlier stages are less clear when it comes to sentencing because judges are given considerable latitude in imposing a sentence. This lack of clarity is due to uncertainty about the purpose of criminal sentences and about how any desired purpose can best be achieved through an actual criminal sentence.

Purposes of Sentencing

Sentencing is subject to much criticism: Sentences are seen either as too lenient or as too severe. It is rare for a sentence to be viewed as appropriate in a given case. However, judges do not decide on sentences in an arbitrary fashion. The degree of latitude given to judges is established by law. In most states, for example, a petty larceny (a misdemeanor) is punishable by up to one year in jail. A judge can choose any sentence, ranging from a fine (up to $1,000 in this kind of case) to probation or as much as a year in jail. The judge cannot sentence an offender to two years in jail or a fine of $10,000, for these sentences would fall outside the allowable range established by the legislature. This leeway is given to judges in an effort to individualize sentences on the basis of the nature of the offender and the circumstances of the offense.

How Do Judges Decide on a Sentence?

In 1995 in South Carolina, a young mother, Susan Smith, killed her two children by leaving them in a car that rolled into a lake. Smith could have been convicted of involuntary manslaughter or murder and received a death sentence, or she could have been found guilty but mentally ill. In the trial, the defense pointed out that she came from a troubled background. Her parents had divorced and her father had committed suicide when she was six. She had been molested by her stepfather at age fifteen and also later, even after she was married; the molestation was covered up by her mother. After Smith's divorce she was rejected by her new boyfriend because she had two children. She had a long history of depression. The defense also noted that she had confessed to her crime and showed deep remorse.[2]

Which of these factors should be considered in deciding on a sentence? And how should an appropriate sentence be determined? In the actual case, Smith was convicted of murder and sentenced to thirty years in prison. It is easy to see that other sentencing choices were available to the judge, and that other sentences could have been imposed and defended rationally. This case illustrates why it is important to understand the underlying rationale or philosophy of sentencing.

When a judge decides on a sentence, he or she first considers what the sentence should accomplish. The purposes of a sentence always consist of one or more of the following objectives: retribution, incapacitation, deterrence, or rehabilitation.

When a judge sentences for purposes of **retribution**, punishment is applied simply in proportion to the seriousness of the offense. The "eye for an eye" system of justice described in the Old Testament is an early form of retribution.[3] According to this concept, the more serious the crime, the more serious the punishment should be. The problem arises when one asks what the goal of retribution is. As an objective of sentencing, retribution makes no effort to change the offender and provides nothing for society except a form of revenge. Nevertheless, in recent years the use of retribution as a justification for punishment has become more popular as states have abandoned social reform as a purpose of sentencing.

retribution
Punishment is applied simply in proportion to the seriousness of the offense.

One version of the philosophy of retribution is known as *just deserts*. In this approach, punishment is based on the culpability of the offender and the seriousness of the crime. The future-oriented focus of rehabilitation and deterrence is rejected, and the punishment is based solely on the crime that brought the offender into court. Using the sentencing process as a way to reform or deter an offender in the future is seen as inappropriate, for it moves attention away from culpability for the past crime for which the offender was convicted.[4]

Sentences based on the concept of **incapacitation** are intended to prevent further criminal behavior by physically restraining the offender from engaging in future misconduct. The primary method of incapacitation in the United States is incarceration, although other methods are also used, such as suspending a license to practice law or medicine in cases of crimes committed by lawyers or physicians. Unfortunately, the use of incapacitation as a justification for punishment provides no clue as to how long it is necessary to incarcerate someone be-

incapacitation
Prevention of further criminal behavior by physically restraining the offender from engaging in future misconduct (usually through incarceration).

fore he or she poses no further threat to society. It is not economical to lock up large numbers of offenders for long periods because the burden on society is increased rather than lessened. Higher prison costs, the need to support families on welfare, and the inability to predict future criminal behavior make such a policy both expensive and unfair over the long term. Moreover, this rationale can be used to justify incarceration for both trivial and serious offenses. Using the rationale of incapacitation, a petty thief who steals many times conceivably could be incarcerated for as long as a one-time rapist.

It has been claimed that if "high-rate offenders" could be identified and incarcerated for long periods, a noticeable drop in crime rates would occur.[5] A major problem with this approach is that some individuals might be mistakenly identified as probable high-rate offenders. In addition, such a policy, termed **selective incapacitation,** would greatly increase prison populations. It also has been seen as violating due process by punishing offenders for *predicted* future behavior rather than for criminal acts that they have actually committed.[6]

selective incapacitation
Identification of potential high-rate offenders for incarceration for longer periods as a means of reducing crime.

Many states have **habitual offender laws** that are based on the notion of incapacitation. These laws can be applied to certain offenders who have committed two or more offenses within a certain period (usually ten years). Multiple offenders are subject to periods of incarceration ranging up to life imprisonment on the ground that they must be physically separated from society in order to prevent crime. In Buffalo, New York, a man who robbed a store of less than ninety dollars received a nine- to eighteen-year prison sentence because the robbery was his second felony. Under New York State law he could have received life in prison as a "persistent" felony offender.[7] Under California's "three strikes" law, Jerry Williams faced a prison term of twenty-five years to life if he was convicted of taking pizza from children at a California beach. He had two prior robbery convictions, making him a habitual offender and therefore subject to an extended sentence on grounds of incapacitation.[8] The rationale behind these laws is that multiple offenders, who apparently have not been deterred or reformed by past convictions, cannot be trusted to refrain from violating the law and must be separated from society. The popularity of incapacitation as a purpose of sentencing, despite its significant incarceration costs, remains high.

habitual offender laws
Subject multiple offenders to periods of incarceration ranging up to life imprisonment on the ground that they must be physically separated from society in order to protect fellow citizens from their criminal conduct.

Deterrence is another common purpose of sentencing. It aims to prevent crime through the example of offenders being punished. *General deterrence* is directed at preventing crime among the general population, while *special deterrence* is aimed at preventing future crimes by a particular offender. Unfortunately, the objectives of general and special deterrence are not always compatible. For example, a drunk driver who hits and kills a pedestrian may best be deterred through participation in an alcohol treatment program. Such a disposition may not serve the purposes of general deterrence, however, if the penalty is not perceived as adequate to deter the general public from engaging in such behavior. An even greater problem with the use of deterrence as a justification for punishment is that it is very difficult to prove its effectiveness because only those individuals who are *not* deterred come to the attention of the criminal justice system. To date, there is virtually no reliable evidence to suggest that criminal sanctions can deter crime.[9]

deterrence
Prevention of crime through the example of offenders being punished.

One important reason deterrence is ineffective is that it relies on certainty and speed of punishment.[10] That is, if penalties are high but the chances of being caught are low, it is doubtful that potential offenders will be deterred. The very low clearance rates for serious crimes illustrate the low probability that offenders will be caught. Nevertheless, if in the mind of the offender the perceived *risk of apprehension* is high, it is possible to achieve a deterrent effect.[11] For example, one study found that mailing warning letters to illegal cable users proved to be a deterrent to future cable tampering.[12]

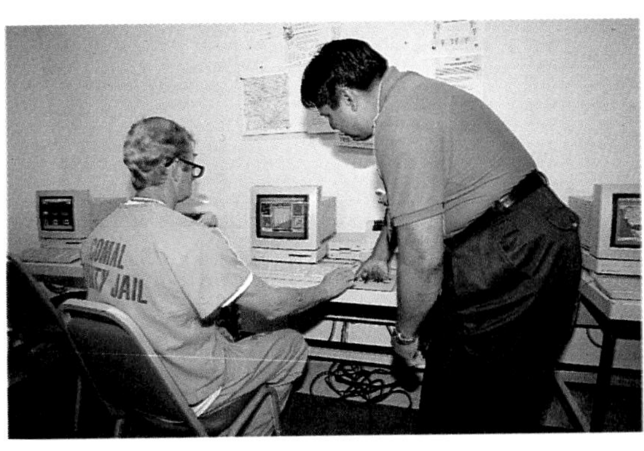

Rehabilitation or reformation sees criminal behavior as stemming from social or psychological shortcomings. The purpose of the sentence is to correct or treat these shortcomings in order to prevent future crimes.

In another approach, **rehabilitation,** or "reformation," sees criminal behavior as stemming from social or psychological shortcomings. The purpose of the sentence is to correct or treat these shortcomings in order to prevent future crimes. However, it is assumed that these shortcomings can be identified and treated effectively. Also, it presumes that it is proper to sentence an offender based on the likelihood of reform in the future rather than for criminal conduct already committed. The results of rehabilitation efforts thus far have been discouraging with failures outnumbering successes. Nevertheless, some rehabilitation programs have been shown to work when treatment strategies and offender needs are matched effectively.[13] In cases in which screening of offender needs has been conducted carefully and treatments are used that respond directly to these needs, some successes have been achieved, although valid evaluations of rehabilitation programs have been few.[14]

rehabilitation
The view that sees criminal behavior as stemming from social or psychological shortcomings; the purpose of sentencing is to correct or treat these shortcomings in order to prevent future crimes.

The lack of empirical evidence to support the four basic purposes of sentencing has contributed to concern about disparity in sentences. Disparity occurs when offenders with similar backgrounds who commit similar crimes receive different sentences. Disparity is to be expected, of course, when there is little agreement regarding what a sentence should accomplish. The result has been a trend toward mandatory and fixed sentences. This move toward uniformity in sentencing can be attributed to the widespread adoption of retribution and incapacitation as guiding philosophies in most jurisdictions.

Sentencing Choices

In addition to considering the various possible purposes of the sentence, the judge usually may choose among a number of sentencing options. As noted earlier, depending on the range of alternatives provided by law, a judge usually can fine an offender or impose a sentence of probation, incarceration, or restitution.

Fines can be used as punishment upon conviction for any offense. Statutes usually provide a maximum fine but allow the judge to impose any fine up to the maximum. Fines are also provided by law for serious crimes, and they may be imposed as an adjunct to a sentence of probation or incarceration. Fines obviously place a greater burden on the poor than on the wealthy and in 1970 the U.S. Supreme Court ruled in *Williams v. Illinois* that offenders cannot be held in jail beyond the maximum sentence allowed by law merely because they are unable to pay the fine.[15] In 1971, the Court ruled in *Tate v. Short* that it is unconstitutional to imprison an offender who cannot pay a fine while not imprisoning offenders with the means to pay fines.[16] Several jurisdictions are now experimenting with *day fines* that impose fines according to the daily income of the offender. This system is designed to make the imposition of fines more equitable.

A probation sentence places the offender under the supervision of the court, allowing him or her to remain in the community. Probation is the most widely used form of criminal sentence because most crimes are not violent and most offenders are not dangerous. Also, probation is much less expensive than incarceration and does not permit the offender to associate with more serious offenders, as often occurs in prison. (Probation is discussed further in Chapter 15.)

Sometimes a judge orders an offender to make restitution as a condition of probation. This means that the offender must make compensation to the victim for any losses caused by the offense. A number of states have laws that encourage restitution, but this approach is not utilized on a large scale. Most offenders are never caught, and those who are caught and convicted are often poor; restitution therefore is not feasible in many cases. This has led many states, as well as the federal government, to establish victim compensation programs in which the government reimburses victims for the costs of certain types of loss or injury due to crime. Although victim compensation is popular, in many states the programs are underfunded and been accompanied by burdensome paperwork requirements that discourage legitimate claims.

When an offender is sentenced to incarceration, he or she is physically separated from the community in a jail or a prison. Sentences of up to one year are served in county jails, while those of one year or more are served in state or federal prisons. Occasionally a judge delays—or suspends—the execution of a prison sentence and requires the offender to participate in an alcohol, drug, or gambling treatment program, or to pay restitution. This is called a **suspended sentence.** An offender who fails to fulfill the prescribed conditions can be incarcerated immediately (through imposition of the suspended sentence). On the other hand, an offender who satisfactorily fulfills the conditions avoids incarceration.

suspended sentence
A delayed imposition of a prison sentence that requires the offender to fulfill special conditions such as alcohol, drug, or gambling treatment or payment of restitution.

The Presentence Report

The presentence report is designed to help the judge decide on an appropriate sentence within the limits established by law. This report is written by a probation officer after an investigation of the offender's background. A typical presentence report includes the following information:

1. Personal information about the offender and his or her background
2. Detailed description of the offense and its circumstances
3. A description of the offender's criminal record
4. Family information and current family status
5. Education history
6. Employment and military history
7. Health history and status (including drug history)
8. Financial status
9. Mental health status
10. Sentencing recommendation made by the probation officer

A presentence investigation is carried out in virtually all felony cases and in some misdemeanor cases, since in such instances the sentence will have a significant impact on the offender. If there is any doubt about facts contained in the presentence report, the U.S. Supreme Court has ruled that an offender must be given an opportunity to refute or explain information contained in the report because his or her sentence will be based, in part, on that information.[17]

The probation officer's independent role in sentencing is sometimes impeded by the prosecution or defense withholding information and the fact that plea agreements do not always accurately reflect the facts of the case. It is crucial that the probation officer obtain objective information on which the sentencing decision will be made.[18]

In most states the probation officer ends the report with a sentencing recommendation. Studies have found a high correspondence between the recommendations contained in presentence reports and the actual sentences imposed by judges.[19] This is probably due to the shared experiences of prosecutors and judges with respect to offenders, as well as their individual reputations for leniency or severity in certain types of cases.

The Role of Victims

The prosecutor represents the jurisdiction in which the crime was committed, the defense counsel represents the legal rights of the accused, and the judge acts as a neutral arbiter. This system has led to widespread criticism because no one specifically represents the concerns of victims. The criticism peaked during the 1980s, when the presidential Task Force on Victims of Crime recommended a more formal role for crime victims in criminal proceedings.[20] In 1991, the U.S. Supreme Court permitted judges and juries to consider "victim-impact statements" in arriving at sentencing decisions. Before that time statements made by victims after the trial were considered inflammatory and prejudicial, and were not considered in sentencing hearings. A majority of states have now made victim-impact statements a mandatory part of criminal procedure, and most have also enacted a "Victim's Bill of Rights" that formally recognizes the role of victims in the justice process.

The effect of victim-impact statements on actual sentences is not clear. Several studies have found these statements to have little impact.[21] Other analyses indicate that victim-impact statements risk imposing sentences based on perceptions of the victim's worth rather than the seriousness of the crime.[22] Nevertheless, the inclusion of these statements in the criminal justice process is relatively new and changes in sentencing laws to accommodate the requests of victims are still occurring. It is therefore too early to determine the full impact of victim-impact statements.

Variations in Sentencing Systems

There are two general types of sentencing systems: indeterminate and determinate. Indeterminate sentencing systems are based on the philosophy that a wide sentencing range gives an offender an incentive to reform and allows a parole board to determine whether the offender is ready for release before he or she has served the maximum sentence. Determinate sentencing systems impose "fixed" sentences that provide little or no flexibility. This kind of sentencing rejects the notion of rehabilitation and replaces it with the philosophy of retribution, focusing on the seriousness of the crime and basing the sentence on the nature of the offense and the offender's prior record.

Indeterminate Sentencing

indeterminate sentencing
A system of sentencing that empowers the judge to set a maximum sentence (up to the limit set by the legislature), and sometimes a minimum sentence, for the offender to serve in prison.

Indeterminate sentencing systems empower the judge to set a maximum sentence (up to the limit set by the legislature), and sometimes a minimum sentence, for the offender to serve in prison. Throughout the sentence a parole board reviews the offender's progress toward rehabilitation in order to determine whether early release is justified. Therefore, the actual time to be served is set by the parole board. Indeterminate sentencing systems existed in most states until the 1970s, when growing criticism of criminal sentences became widespread. Consider the following points:

- Prison uprisings were found to result in part from disparity in sentences; offenders from similar backgrounds who had committed similar offenses received widely different sentences.
- There were few serious rehabilitation efforts and programs in prisons. Reform of offenders took a back seat to concerns of custody and security.
- Parole boards could not tell whether an offender had actually been rehabilitated. They had to rely on the offender's word, which sometimes did not correspond with his or her actual behavior when released back into the community.
- Several cases were widely publicized in which offenders who had been released early from prison assaulted or killed again.

This series of incidents and events led to a dramatic shift in the philosophy of sentencing. Beginning in 1975, states began to change from indeterminate to determinate sentencing.

Parole boards have been criticized for releasing offenders who commit new crimes. A problem has been in determining whether or not an offender has actually changed or been rehabilitated.

Determinate Sentencing

Determinate sentencing systems permit the judge to impose fixed sentences that cannot be altered by a parole board. In some states parole has been abolished. In others, allowable sentence ranges have been narrowed considerably, giving the judge little room for discretion.[23] This has had the effect of treating offenders similarly, as long as the offense is similar. The needs, problems, and backgrounds of offenders are much less important in a determinate sentencing system because the focus is on the crime that was committed rather than on the type of offender who committed it.

determinate sentencing
A sentencing system that permits judges to impose fixed sentences that cannot be altered by a parole board.

In practice, determinate sentencing has had a significant impact on sentence lengths and on the proportion of the sentence that is actually served in prison. In 1977, for example, 72 percent of offenders released from a state prison had served an indeterminate sentence and were released by a parole board. By 1992, fewer than 40 percent of prison releases were determined by a parole board.[24] In addition, the proportion of sentences served in prison before release is increasing. Between 1992 and 1994 alone, the proportion of a sentence served by prisoners convicted of violent crimes (i.e., homicide, sexual assault, robbery, or assault) rose from 44 to 48 percent of the sentence imposed.[25] This percentage will continue to rise as political and public concern regarding truth-in-sentencing escalates.[26] **Truth-in-sentencing** refers to the establishment of a closer relationship between the sentence imposed and the actual time served in prison prior to release. The Violent Crime Control and Law Enforcement Act of 1994 requires states that wish to qualify for federal financial aid to change their laws so that offenders serve at least 85 percent of their sentences.

truth-in-sentencing
A sentencing provision that requires offenders to serve the bulk of their sentence (usually 85 percent) before they can be released.

The impact of the trend toward determinacy and longer sentences is apparent when one examines data on correctional populations. As can be seen in Figure 13.1, the number of offenders sent to state prisons more than doubled from 1985 to 1995, reaching a record level of nearly one million inmates. Added to this

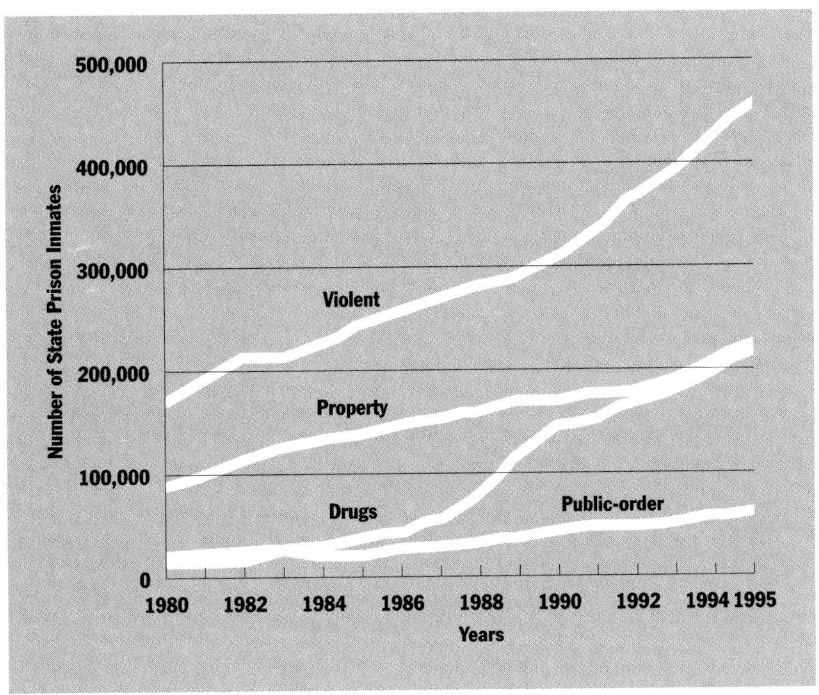

FIGURE 13.1
Number of state prison inmates, 1980 to 1995

SOURCE: Allen J. Beck et al., *Correctional Populations in the United States* (Washington, D.C.: U.S. Bureau of Justice Statistics, 1997).

FUTURE ISSUES

The Two Sides of Truth-in-Sentencing

There is frustration over the early release of offenders from prison. Early release decisions reflect time off for good behavior, evidence that the offender has reformed, or prison overcrowding and the need to create more bed space for newly sentenced offenders. Among the provisions of the federal Violent Crime Control and Law Enforcement Act of 1994 is an incentive for states to enact "truth-in-sentencing" laws.

Truth-in-sentencing laws require offenders to serve at least 85 percent of their imposed sentences no matter how well they behave in prison. The federal government offers large grants to states that adopt truth-in-sentencing laws. By 1998, twenty-seven states had truth-in-sentencing laws that met the federal government's guidelines. These states received more than four hundred million dollars in federal grants during 1996 and 1997. A survey by the U.S. General Accounting Office found that the availability of the federal grants was a factor for fifteen of the states that adopted truth-in-sentencing provisions.[A]

There are three major concerns associated with truth-in-sentencing laws and the federal government's push to have them implemented. These include (1) the cost of truth-in-sentencing, (2) the expansion of truth-in-sentencing, and (3) federal involvement in a state prerogative. All these issues have significant impact for the future.

The cost to implement truth-in-sentencing is extremely high because new prison construction is needed to house offenders for longer periods. The original plan in Virginia to abolish parole and implement truth-in-sentencing called for construction of twenty-five new prisons at a cost of two billion dollars.[B] Indeed, most of the twenty-three states that did not adopt truth-in-sentencing and did not receive federal funds during 1997 cited the high cost of prison construction, even with the federal grant money.[C]

A second concern is the expansion of truth-in-sentencing beyond violent crimes. In some states these new sentencing provisions do not exclude property or drug offenders. In Virginia, the governor's plan projected that almost four times more nonviolent offenders would be caught than violent offenders. This greatly increases the length of sentences and the costs of imprisonment without any offsetting benefit in protecting the public from violent offenders.

The third concern is the federal government's role in state lawmaking. Federal intervention in rewarding or penalizing states for adopting policies that the federal government likes or dislikes can be viewed as a way of extorting rather than encouraging compliance. Such methods represent "a significant shift in the traditional balance between the state and federal governments and a significant federalization of a traditionally local issue."[D]

FUTURES QUESTION

If you were a state official, how would you propose to achieve the goal of truth-in-sentencing laws without significantly increasing the costs of imprisonment in your state?

NOTES

[A]U.S. Comptroller General, *Truth in Sentencing: Availability of Federal Grants Influenced Laws in Some States* (Washington, D.C.: U.S. General Accounting Office, 1998).

[B]Virginia House Appropriations Committee Staff Report, *Analysis of Potential Costs under the Governor's Sentencing Reform Plan* (Richmond: Office of the Governor, 1994); Marc Mauer, "The Truth About Truth in Sentencing," *Corrections Today,* vol. 58 (February, 1996), pp. 1–9.

[C]U.S. Comptroller General, pp. 7–8; Lisa Stansky, "Breaking Up Prison Gridlock," *ABA Journal,* vol. 82 (May 1996), pp. 70–6.

[D]Steven R. Donziger, ed., *The Real War on Crime: The Report of the National Criminal Justice Commission* (New York: HarperPerennial, 1996), p. 24.

is another 88,000 federal inmates, triple the figure of ten years earlier. The fastest-growing segment of this population consisted of drug offenders, whose numbers increased more than fivefold.

These increases in prison populations are outpacing increases in the general U.S. population. As Table 13.2 indicates, the incarceration rate has doubled in a decade as the number of adults in prison or jail has mushroomed to 1.58 million, a rate of 598 per 100,000 population. If one adds to the total those on probation

TABLE 13.2

Trends in Numbers of Adults Under Correctional Supervision
(in Prison or Jail or on Probation or Parole)

YEAR	TOTAL ADULTS IN JAIL OR PRISON	INCARCERATION RATE PER 100,000 U.S. POPULATION	TOTAL UNDER CORRECTIONAL SUPERVISION	PERCENT OF U.S. ADULT POPULATION UNDER SUPERVISION
1985	0.74 million	312	3.01 million	1.7
1990	1.15 million	460	4.35 million	2.3
1995	1.58 million	598	5.37 million	2.8

SOURCE: Compiled from Allen J. Beck et al., *Correctional Populations in the United States* (Washington, D.C.: U.S. Bureau of Justice Statistics, 1997).

or parole, the number of adults under correctional supervision in the United States is 5.4 million, or 2.8 percent of the adult population. This is almost double the rate of a decade earlier.

The increase in prison populations is a direct result of an increase in the likelihood of offenders being sent to prison. These new incarcerations are occurring faster than are releases from state prison. In 1995, the rate of admissions into prisons (per one hundred state prisoners) was 55.5 percent; the release rate was 31.2 percent.[27] This difference of nearly 25 percent is the cause of prison crowding and new prison construction in many jurisdictions. The role of determinate and mandatory sentencing is evident when one compares the percentage of releases by parole boards with the percentage of releases required by those serving fixed sentences. In 1985, 42 percent of all inmates released from prison were released by a parole board; ten years later, only 32 percent were released by parole boards. Conversely, in 1985, 30 percent of inmates were mandatorily released at the end of their sentences. Ten years later, 39 percent were mandatorily released. This change reflects the decline of indeterminate sentencing and the role of parole boards in setting actual sentence lengths, and the corresponding rise in determinate sentencing and the use of fixed sentences.

Mandatory Sentencing

Mandatory sentences are a form of determinate sentencing. They impose fixed sentences on individuals convicted of certain types of crimes. Most crimes that are subject to mandatory sentences are gun-related crimes, drug offenses, and drunk-driving offenses. Mandatory sentences for certain crimes have been adopted in every state and by the federal government on the basis of their presumed deterrent and incapacitating effects. As noted in Chapter 11, mandatory sentences often shift decision-making discretion to the police and the prosecutor rather than eliminating discretion altogether. Mandatory sentencing disregards the fact that not all offenders are alike, even though they may commit the same crimes.[28] For example, a study in Massachusetts found that drug offenders were sentenced to mandatory prison terms, even though nearly half of them had no prior record of violent crimes.[29] In New York State the governor reduced the sentences of three drug offenders because he believed that their mandatory sentences were too long for the commission of nonviolent crimes.[30]

mandatory sentence
Fixed sentence for offenders convicted of certain types of crimes such as gun-related crimes, drug offenses, and drunk-driving offenses.

Moving discretion from sentencing to earlier stages of criminal procedure can be seen as an attempt to "correct" injustices that may arise in applying the same sentence to offenders from widely different backgrounds and crimes of differing seriousness.[31] At the same time mandatory sentences reduce the visibility of discretionary decisions at sentencing to the less visible arrest and charging stages of criminal procedure. Nevertheless, mandatory sentences remain popular as a mechanism to achieve "truth-in-sentencing," although at a high cost. These policies increase the number of inmates serving longer sentences and slow prison population turnover.[32] Extremely long mandatory sentences can be counterproductive because they incarcerate offenders for long periods (at great expense) well past their late teens and early twenties, the age when most violent crimes are committed.[33]

"Three strikes and you're out" laws impose long, mandatory sentences of up to life in prison for repeat offenders. They are a form of habitual offender law. A study of these laws in California found that they did not reduce crime rates below preexisting levels, concluding that the "three-strikes law was of no consequence in nine of the 10 cities examined."[34] Nevertheless, concern over a perceived decline in morality in society and deteriorating social conditions have been found to underlie public support for these laws.[35]

Sentencing Guidelines

Sentencing guidelines are a middle ground between indeterminate and determinate sentencing. They reduce disparity in sentencing by recommending a "guideline sentence" based on the seriousness of the crime and the offender's prior record. The guidelines are developed by examining averages of past sentences imposed on various combinations of offenders and offenses. This achieves the goals of proportionality and uniformity without mandating specific sentences for certain crimes or offenders. Judges may deviate from the "guideline" sentence only if they provide written reasons for doing so. For example, if a sentence of five to seven years is typical for past robbery offenders, judges may sentence outside this range only if they state their reasons for doing so. These reasons might include a particularly serious prior record or severe injury to the victim.

The U.S. Sentencing Commission was created in 1984 to implement changes in the federal sentencing system. The primary thrust was to emphasize the offense, rather than the offender, in criminal sentencing.[36] The Commission implemented federal sentencing guidelines in 1987 that apply to all federal offenses. By 1996, nine states also had adopted presumptive sentencing guidelines and four additional states had voluntary sentencing guidelines. Voluntary sentencing guidelines are created by a panel of judges, but no mechanism exists for dealing with judges who ignore the guidelines. Nonvoluntary or presumptive sentencing guidelines are developed by sentencing commissions created by legislatures. These commissions often *prescribe* a sentencing policy, rather than merely summarizing past practice, as is done with voluntary guidelines. Presumptive guidelines require the judge to hold a hearing and to provide written reasons for any departure from the sentencing guidelines.

Sentencing guidelines have several advantages and disadvantages. These are summarized in Table 13.3. The primary advantage of sentencing guidelines

TABLE 13.3

Advantages and Disadvantages of Sentencing Guidelines

ADVANTAGES	DISADVANTAGES
1. Promotes uniformity and proportionality in sentencing without the problems of mandatory sentences	1. Sentence uniformity appears to deteriorate after a few years' experience with sentencing guidelines
2. Allows for accurate projection and control of prison populations by the nature and length of the guideline sentences	2. The purpose of sentencing should revolve around considerations of justice, not managing the prison population
3. Allows for departures from guidelines where necessary	3. Violates constitutional separation of powers by permitting legislatures to set sentences, which is a judicial prerogative

is that they control disparity in sentencing while allowing greater flexibility than mandatory sentencing schemes. Disparity is considered to be unwarranted differences in sentences that cannot be accounted for by the nature of the crime or the background of the offender. On the other hand, there is concern that sentencing guidelines established by legislatures violate the constitutional doctrine of separation of powers by giving the legislature control over a judicial function (sentencing). For example, extremely high sentence guidelines have been established for federal drug offenses, and as a result a number of federal judges have refused to impose the guideline sentences; about fifty judges have refused to take new drug cases. As one federal judge observed, "We're building prisons faster than we're building classrooms. . . . The whole thing doesn't seem to be very effective."[37]

In addition, guideline sentences that punish crack cocaine much more severely than powdered cocaine have been found to disproportionately punish black offenders over whites. First-time offenders caught with five grams of crack cocaine receive a mandatory minimum term of five years in prison, whereas a first-time powdered cocaine offender must possess five hundred grams of the drug to receive the same sentence. This 100-to-1 ratio has been called excessive and discriminatory in light of the fact that crack cocaine is used more often by blacks while powdered cocaine is used more frequently by whites.[38]

Although sentencing guidelines have been found to increase uniformity in sentencing in many jurisdictions, this is not the case everywhere. After the first few years, uniformity tends to deteriorate.[39] Nevertheless, sentencing guidelines have been shown to reduce discrimination on the basis of race or gender.[40] Sentencing guidelines also make possible more accurate predictions of prison populations, and prison populations can be controlled by modifying the guidelines.[41]

It can be argued that the size of prison populations should not be a factor in sentencing guidelines because it is unrelated to any particular crime. Nevertheless, the public's fear of crime and willingness to support longer prison sentences have resulted in high prison expenses and new construction when, at the same time, there is pressure to reduce government spending. Sentencing guidelines may be able to limit the use of imprisonment so that available prison space is restricted to serious and habitual offenders, rather than being used for nonserious offenses.[42]

Efforts to Reform Sentencing Systems

Objections to the broad range of discretion exercised by judges are not new. More than two hundred years ago, in 1764, Cesare Beccaria argued that punishments should be set by legislatures rather than by judges.[43] Not until the 1900s, however, was empirical evidence gathered to demonstrate the dramatic variation in sentences imposed in apparently similar classes of cases.[44] The interest in sentencing reform that emerged during the 1930s and 1940s can be traced to two trends: studies that documented wide and unexplainable variations in criminal sentences, and dissatisfaction with sentences that did not account for the potential of offenders to be rehabilitated.[45]

As a result of these trends, three fourths of the states adopted some form of indeterminate sentencing by 1941. Under the new rule a parole board would determine the actual sentence within a broad range set by the judge. This would take into account the offender's potential for reform as well as providing a way to monitor disparity in sentences. As one observer stated, a parole board would "determine the length of incarceration to which every prisoner would be subjected. In other words, all cases clear through the same channel."[46] Indeed, at the federal level indeterminate sentencing was seen primarily as a way to reduce unwarranted variation among judges in sentencing decisions.[47]

In the late 1950s and early 1960s, questions arose as to whether the indeterminate sentencing system was achieving its goals. A growing body of evidence revealed that sentence disparity still prevailed under the indeterminate sentencing system and that methods designed to reduce this disparity (e.g., appellate review and sentencing councils) did not appear to work.[48] The ultimate result was a return to determinate sentencing, which began during the mid-1970s and continues today. Although the shift back toward determinate sentencing was due in part to dissatisfaction with the concept of rehabilitation, the effectiveness of efforts to curb unwarranted variation in sentences generated greater concern. This concern was an echo of the criticism that was expressed during the 1930s and 1940s with respect to determinate sentencing. Viewed in this way, the philosophical shifts from retribution to rehabilitation and back to retribution may simply be a manifestation of the inability of the criminal justice system to deal effectively with unwarranted disparity in criminal sentences, regardless of changes in the underlying philosophy of sentencing.[49] Concern about disparity in sentencing continues today as questions remain regarding the use of inappropriate nonlegal factors, such as age, race, and education of the offender and political conservatism of the court, in sentencing decisions.[50] This variation in the imposition of criminal penalties has had legal consequences as well.

The Eighth Amendment and Capital Punishment

The Eighth Amendment to the U.S. Constitution deals largely with the final stages of the criminal justice process. It is also one of the shortest amendments. It reads as follows: "Excessive bail shall not be required, nor excessive fines imposed, nor cruel and unusual punishment inflicted." The purpose of bail is to ensure that a

contemporary issues

Victim's Race and Death Penalty Decisions

It has long been debated whether the death penalty can be imposed justly and also blindly with regard to race. Of the more than 3,000 prisoners under a sentence of death in the United States, 42 percent are black. Of the 313 persons executed during the twenty years since the U.S. Supreme Court approved the death penalty in 1976, 38 percent have been black.[A] In both cases, the percentage of blacks is far above their proportion in the general population, leading to speculation that black defendants are discriminated against in death penalty cases. Less attention has been given to the impact of the race of the victim in murder cases.

In 1990, the investigative arm of Congress, the U.S. General Accounting Office (GAO), undertook an examination of the role of race in death penalty decisions. The researchers identified twenty-eight studies of the death penalty that included race as a variable. Each study was analyzed to determine whether race was a significant factor in death penalty cases. Their findings were remarkable, showing "a pattern of evidence indicating racial disparities in the charging, sentencing, and imposition of the death penalty."[B] In twenty-three of the twenty-eight studies the race of the *victim* was associated with the decision to charge the offender with murder or impose the death penalty. Legally relevant factors, such as the offender's prior criminal record, did not fully account for the racial disparities.

Interestingly, there was mixed evidence regarding the impact of the *defendant's* race. A slight majority of the studies found the race of the defendant to be significant, but in some studies white defendants were more likely to be sentenced to death; in others it depended on urban–rural differences or on other factors.[C] The GAO researchers concluded that "the results show a strong rate of victim influence: the death penalty sentence was more likely to be sought and imposed for an offender if the victim was white."[D] In contrast, the impact of the race of the defendant was not clear or uniform across the studies considered.

NOTES

[A]Tracy L. Snell, *Capital Punishment 1995* (Washington, D.C.: U.S. Bureau of Justice Statistics, 1996).

[B]Lowell Dodge, Testimony before the Subcommittee on Civil and Constitutional Rights Committee on the Judiciary, U.S. House of Representatives, May 3, 1990, p. 4.

[C]U.S. Comptroller General, *Death Penalty Sentencing: Research Indicates Pattern of Racial Disparity* (Washington, D.C.: U.S. General Accounting Office, 1990).

[D]Dodge, p. 6; David E. Rovella, "Race Pervades Death Penalty," *The National Law Journal*, vol. 20 (June 8, 1998).

defendant will appear for trial. If the suspect cannot afford bail, he or she must stay in jail until the trial. It is important to note that the Eighth Amendment does not require bail; it only states that the amount cannot be excessive. In many states, release on bail is not permitted in capital cases (i.e., those for which the death penalty applies). Otherwise, there are few restrictions on the amount of bail a judge may require. In a controversial decision, the U.S. Supreme Court held in *U.S. v. Salerno* that preventive detention without bail on grounds of predicted future dangerousness does not violate the Eighth Amendment. The Court did not consider such detention to be "punishment without trial."[51] This decision reflects the currently popular view that potentially dangerous criminals should be confined, even though our ability to predict future criminality accurately is poor, raising the question that offenders are being held for crimes they *might* commit in the future, rather than on the basis of the current charge.

The Eighth Amendment also states that fines cannot be excessive. The Supreme Court has not specified an amount that would constitute an excessive fine, but it has ruled that prison sentences imposed when offenders cannot pay fines discriminate against the poor and therefore are unconstitutional.[52] Other than this restriction, few conditions are placed on the imposition of fines. Maximum fines are, of course, fixed by the legislature and may vary, depending on the seriousness of the crime.

The portion of the Eighth Amendment that has been most rigorously scrutinized is the prohibition of cruel and unusual punishment. The courts have referred to it in cases of solitary confinement, corporal punishment, double-celling of inmates, mechanical restraints, and poor medical and sanitary conditions for prisoners,[53] but no penalty has received more attention than capital punishment—that is, the death penalty.

The Legal Status of the Death Penalty

In 1977, the U.S. Supreme Court ruled that the death penalty is excessive and disproportionate for the crime of rape and therefore is unconstitutional.[54] Since then, capital punishment has been applied primarily to murder cases.

During the 1930s, close to two hundred executions were carried out in the United States each year. By the 1960s, the number of offenders who received the death penalty dropped to fewer than fifty per year. Because of growing uncertainty about the constitutionality of capital punishment, executions were virtually halted in the mid-1960s. However, in two decisions during the 1970s the U.S. Supreme Court clarified the constitutionality of death sentences.

In 1972, the Court ruled in *Furman v. Georgia* that the administration of the death penalty in Georgia constituted cruel and unusual punishment. It was argued to the Court that death sentences were imposed in an arbitrary and discriminatory manner. In this case, Furman had been convicted of a murder that occurred during the course of a burglary attempt. The decision as to whether he would receive a sentence of life imprisonment or death was left entirely up to the jury, who had no guidance in making that decision.

The Supreme Court's lack of consensus on this issue was apparent when each of the nine Justices wrote a separate opinion in the case. The majority agreed, however, that Georgia's death penalty law provided for execution "without guidance or direction" as to whether life imprisonment, the death penalty, or other punishment was most appropriate in a given case of murder. The Supreme Court found the law to be unconstitutional because offenders who receive the death penalty

> **. . . are among a capriciously selected handful upon whom the sentence of death has in fact been imposed. . . . The Eighth and Fourteenth Amendments cannot tolerate the infliction of a sentence of death under legal systems that permit this unique penalty to be so wantonly and freakishly imposed.[55]**

The lack of guidance to judges and juries in determining when the death penalty should be imposed allowed for it to be imposed arbitrarily, and often selectively, against minorities. Therefore, it constituted cruel and unusual punishment and could not stand. The effect of this decision was to invalidate the death penalty laws of thirty-nine states.

By 1976, however, thirty-four states had enacted new death penalty statutes designed to meet the requirements of the *Furman* decision. These laws took one of two forms. They either removed all judicial discretion by mandating capital punishment upon conviction for certain offenses, or they established specific guidelines for judges to use in deciding whether death was an appropriate sentence in a given case.

The Supreme Court assessed the validity of the new laws in 1976 in the case of *Gregg v. Georgia*. Two hitchhikers, Troy Gregg and Floyd Allen, had been picked up in Florida by Fred Simmons and Bob Moore. A third hitchhiker, Dennis Weaver, rode with them to Atlanta, where he got out of the car at about 11 P.M. The four men who remained in the car later stopped to rest beside the highway. After Simmons and Moore left the car, Gregg told Allen that he was going to rob them. As Simmons and Moore came back toward the car, Gregg fired three shots at them and they fell to the ground; he next fired a shot into the head of each man at close range. Then he robbed them and drove away with Allen. The bodies of Simmons and Moore were discovered the next morning.

Upon reading about the shootings in an Atlanta newspaper, Weaver (the third hitchhiker) contacted the police and described his journey with the victims, including a description of the car. The next afternoon Gregg and Allen (still in Simmons's car) were arrested in Asheville, North Carolina. In the search incident to the arrest a .25-caliber pistol, later shown to be that used to kill Simmons and Moore, was found in Gregg's pocket. After receiving the warnings required by *Miranda v. Arizona* and signing a written waiver of his rights, Gregg signed a statement in which he admitted that he had shot and robbed Simmons and Moore but claimed that he had done so in self-defense. The next day, while being transferred to Lawrenceville, Georgia, Gregg and Allen were taken to the scene of the shootings, where Allen recounted the circumstances surrounding the killings.

The jury found Gregg guilty of two counts of armed robbery and two counts of murder. The judge instructed the jury that it could recommend either a death sentence or a life prison sentence on each count. The jury was free to consider any mitigating or aggravating facts and circumstances in recommending whether a death sentence or life imprisonment was most appropriate. The jury returned verdicts of death on each count. The Supreme Court of Georgia affirmed the convictions and the death sentences, but the U.S. Supreme Court decided to hear Gregg's arguments that the new Georgia death penalty statute still constituted "cruel and unusual punishment" in violation of the Eighth Amendment.

The Supreme Court upheld the Georgia law as constitutional because it requires the jury (which also has sentencing responsibility in some states) to focus

> **. . . on the particularized nature of the crime and the particularized characteristics of the individual defendant. While the jury is permitted to consider any aggravating or mitigating circumstances, it must find and identify at least one statutory aggravating factor before it may impose a penalty of death. In this way the jury's discretion is channeled. No longer can a jury wantonly and freakishly impose a death sentence; it is always circumscribed by the legislative guidelines.[56]**

As a result, Gregg's death sentence was upheld. Nevertheless, this decision, together with two other death penalty cases decided the same day, struck down some state statutes because they provided for mandatory death sentences in certain cases.[57] The Court believed that the standard of adequately guided discretion was not met when no discretion whatsoever was permitted. In addition, it held for the first time that as a form of punishment the death penalty is not inherently cruel and unusual.

The Supreme Court further refined its decision two years later when it struck down the Ohio death penalty statute, which did not permit a judge to consider mitigating factors such as age, no prior record, or the defendant's role in the crime. The Supreme Court concluded:

> **The Eighth and Fourteenth Amendments require that the sentencer, in all but the rarest kind of capital case, not be precluded from considering as a mitigating factor any aspect of a defendant's character or record and any of the circumstances of the offense that the defendant proffers as a basis for a sentence less than death. . . . The considerations that account for the wide acceptance of individualization of sentences in noncapital cases surely cannot be thought less important in capital cases.**[58]

Therefore, both mitigating *and* aggravating factors must be considered in determining the appropriateness of a particular sentence.

The death penalty was again called into question in 1987. The case of *McCleskey v. Kemp*[59] made it clear that claims of alleged discrimination in death sentences had not been resolved. Warren McCleskey, a black man, was charged with armed robbery and murder for killing a white police officer who was answering a silent alarm during a store robbery in Georgia. After consideration of both aggravating and mitigating circumstances, McCleskey was convicted and sentenced to death. He appealed the sentence on the ground that it was imposed in a racially discriminatory manner, presenting as evidence the findings of a statistical study that had examined more than 2,000 murder cases in Georgia during the 1970s. The investigators looked at 230 factors that may have accounted for differences in sentences imposed in these cases. They found that the racial combination of black defendants killing white victims was most likely to result in the death sentence. The Supreme Court denied McCleskey's appeal on two grounds. First, the majority held that "to prevail under the equal protection clause [of the Fourteenth Amendment], McCleskey must prove that the decision-makers in his case acted with discriminatory purpose." On this basis, the statistical study was "insufficient" to prove discrimination in McCleskey's particular case.

Second, the majority held that McCleskey's treatment did not violate the Eighth Amendment prohibition of cruel and unusual punishment. It held that the statistical study "indicates a discrepancy that appears to correlate with race" but is "a far cry from the major systemic defects identified in *Furman*." The majority found that despite the imperfections identified by the study, "our consistent rule has been that constitutional guarantees are met when the mode for determining guilt or punishment has been surrounded with safeguards to make it as fair as possible."[60]

In a sharply worded dissent, four Justices argued that proving discrimination in a particular case is irrelevant because the Court "since *Furman* has been concerned with the risk of the imposition of an arbitrary sentence, rather than the proven fact of one." The dissenters believed that the Court's decision should address reduction of the risk of arbitrary sentences and not wait for unfair results

Media and Criminal Justice

DEAD MAN WALKING

Perhaps no other sentencing issue is as controversial as the death penalty. As more and more Americans favor capital punishment for convicted murderers, opponents continue to point out that executions have not been proven to have a deterrent effect on crime. Yet many supporters of capital punishment counter that if nothing else, executions provide closure for the surviving families of the murder victims.

The 1995 film *Dead Man Walking* embraced all of these controversies in its story of a death row inmate who elicits the help of a nun as he faces the ultimate penalty for murder. Sister Helen Prejean befriends this inmate, Matthew Poncelet, assisting him in filing a last-minute appeal that might bring him a reprieve. As Sister Prejean and Matthew continue their discussion of his plight in light of the impending execution, however, she becomes a spiritual counselor who is troubled by Matthew's lack of remorse for his crimes. She does not believe that Matthew should die for the brutal rapes and murders that he surely committed, but she hopes that the threat of death will cause him to take responsibility for his actions.

The great worth of *Dead Man Walking* is that it takes no position on the death penalty. Sister Prejean hopes to save Matthew from execution, but she also seeks to understand the ramifications of his crimes. She visits the families of Matthew's murder victims and is faced with the unrelenting heartache of each parent. They remind her that their grief is compounded in knowing that their children, young people with such promising futures, suffered horribly in their final moments before death. The families insist that the depth of their tragedy is insulted by Matthew's very existence: It is unfair that the innocent victims are dead and that the murderer continues to live. Sister Prejean's understanding of their loss is made more acute by a visit with Matthew's family; his mother clearly doesn't see the sense in taking another life by executing her son. Do two wrongs make a right?

Dead Man Walking is a careful examination of the emotions and arguments claimed by all sides. The most important message of the movie is dramatized when Matthew is guided to the truth by Sister Prejean, and actually breaks down and faces the ramifications of his murderous behavior. His remorse is painful, and very genuine, but it comes too late. As he is strapped down for execution, the illogic and wastefulness in executing a truly remorseful person is made evident. Yet even as the lethal injection begins, the poignant scene of execution is interspersed with shocking scenes of the actual rapes and murders of Matthew's innocent victims. The viewer is not allowed to forget the senseless, heinous crimes for which Matthew is dying. Retribution, not revenge or incapacitation, is communicated in his final moments.

The film brings a great deal of integrity to the discussion of America's death penalty, but does not attempt to convince the viewer of any particular stance. The theme of *Dead Man Walking* is one of careful contemplation, ensuring that both advocates and opponents of capital punishment understand each other's position.

MEDIA AND CRIMINAL JUSTICE QUESTION

Are there ways to recognize the victim's loss and hold the offender accountable in murder cases without killing the offender?

to occur before intervening. Besides, it would be extremely difficult to obtain objective evidence to demonstrate discrimination in one's own case absent blatantly discriminatory actions or statements during the case. Second, the statistical study has "produced striking evidence that the odds of being sentenced to death are significantly greater than average if a defendant is black or his or her victim is white." According to the dissent, such evidence calls into question the effectiveness of the legal standards established in *Furman* and *Gregg*.[61]

Under current law, therefore, the death penalty can be imposed as long as both aggravating and mitigating circumstances are considered by the judge or jury in a nonarbitrary manner.[62] Clearly, it is difficult to establish whether or not a sentence was imposed fairly in any given case, although there is evidence to suggest that sentences are imposed unfairly based on such factors as conduct of the prosecutor or defense attorney, juror comprehension, and race.[63]

FIGURE 13.2

Persons under a sentence of death, 1955 to 1995

SOURCE: Tracy L. Snell, *Capital Punishment 1995* (Washington, D.C.: U.S. Bureau of Justice Statistics, 1996).

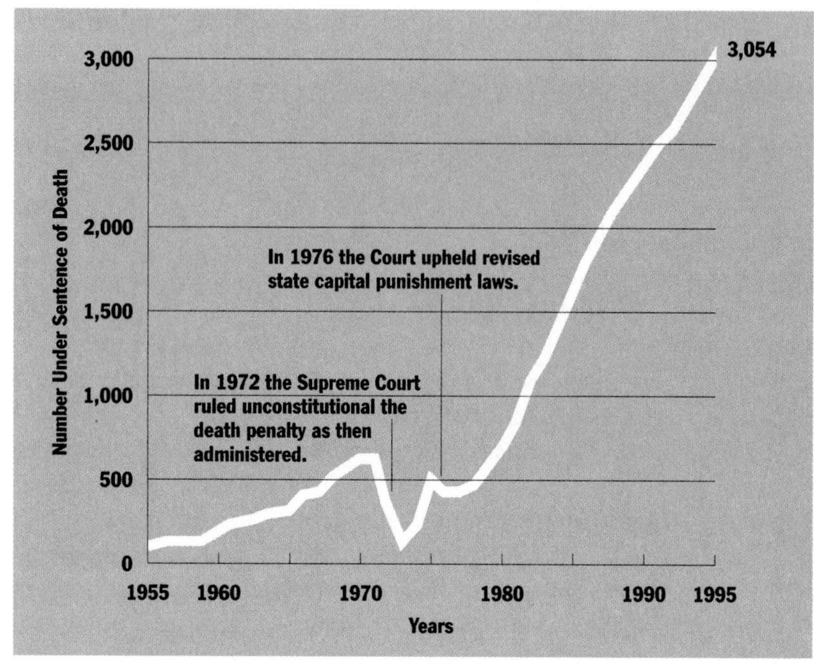

By 1997, a total of thirty-eight states, as well as the federal government, had enacted capital punishment laws in accordance with the guidelines set forth by the U.S. Supreme Court. As of 1996, a record 3,054 people were under sentence of death and awaiting execution. This continues an upward trend that began in 1977 after the Supreme Court's ruling in *Gregg v. Georgia,* which specifically stated that capital punishment was not inherently cruel and unusual. Figure 13.2 graphically illustrates the rise in the number of persons sentenced to death from 1955 to 1995. More people are now awaiting execution than at any time since 1930, when national statistics were first collected. Nearly 40 percent of the prisoners on death row are in only three states: Texas, California, and Florida.[64]

The Death Penalty Debate

Support for the death penalty remains high, although there is some reluctance to carry out executions once a sentence of death has been pronounced.[65] Since 1976, fewer than four hundred official executions have taken place, although the number is increasing. In 1997, seventy-four executions were performed, the highest number in more than forty years.[66] Since 1930, nearly 4,500 executions have been carried out.

The methods most commonly used to carry out executions are lethal injection (thirty-two states) and electrocution (eleven states). Seven states carry out death sentences with lethal gas, four by hanging, and three by firing squad. Sixteen states authorize the use of more than one method (lethal injection and an alternative method).[67] Federal offenders are executed using the method authorized in the state in which the execution takes place. Several states have provided an alternative to lethal injection because of concern that it may be found unconstitutional in a court challenge (i.e., does it constitute cruel and unusual punishment in the manner in which it causes death?). Each of the other four methods has been held not to violate the Eighth Amendment prohibition of cruel and unusual punishment.

Those who support the death penalty usually base their argument on one of four grounds: (1) The death penalty is a necessary punishment as retribution for the life unlawfully taken, (2) the death penalty will deter others from committing murder, (3) the death penalty is less expensive to administer than life imprisonment, and (4) errors in executing innocent persons are rare. Let us examine the evidence that exists to support these claims.

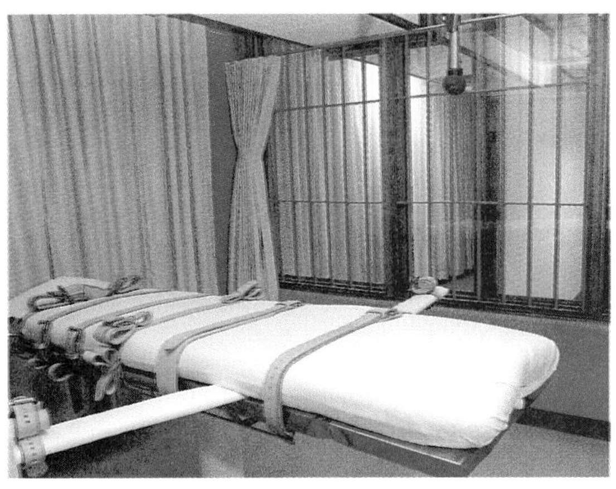

A gurney in the death chamber of the prison at Huntsville, Texas, where death row prisoners are strapped down for lethal injection. On the far side are viewing rooms for witnesses.

CAPITAL PUNISHMENT AS RETRIBUTION The retributionist argument is perhaps the oldest of all justifications for punishment. It can be traced at least as far back as the Old Testament. The books of Exodus [21:12–25], Leviticus [24:17–21], Numbers [35:30–1], and Deuteronomy [19:11–12] all warn that

> **. . . in case a man strikes any soul of mankind fatally, he should be put to death without fail. . . . And in case a man should cause a defect in his associate, then just as he has done, so it should be done to him. Fracture for fracture, eye for eye, tooth for tooth; the same sort of defect he may cause in the man that is what should be caused in him. And the fatal striker of a heart should make compensation for it, but the fatal striker of a man should be put to death.**

Although modern Israel, established in 1948, quickly abandoned the Mosaic law of "life for life" (except in cases of wartime treason or Nazi collaboration), many people continue to apply this notion of retribution in support of the death penalty.

Somewhat more puzzling is the fact that Christians sometimes use this justification for capital punishment despite Christ's teachings to the contrary. For example, the Gospel according to Matthew [5:38–9] recounts Jesus stating, "You heard that it was said, 'Eye for eye and tooth for tooth.' However, I say to you: Do not resist him that is wicked; but whoever slaps you on the right cheek, turn the other also to him." Such teachings prompted the disciples of early Christianity to oppose capital punishment. Adherence to this principle wavered, however, when non-Christians came to be seen as heretics and deserving of death. This change of heart relied heavily on Paul's declaration to the Romans [13:1–2]:

> **Let every soul be in subjection to the superior authorities, for there is no authority except by God; the existing authorities stand placed in their relative positions by God. Therefore he who opposes the authority has taken a stand against the arrangement of God.**

Some believed that Paul's statements meant that if the state permitted capital punishment, it must be God's will because government exists only by God's will. This line of reasoning continues to be employed today by those who defend the death penalty on the basis of biblical interpretation.

Regardless of the basis of the argument, little evidence has been demonstrated that capital punishment is effective as a form of retribution. Examinations of willful homicides in the United States have shown that fewer than half are murders (which involve premeditation or homicides committed during the course of a felony). Further, fewer than half of these (that is, 25 percent of the total) are prosecuted as capital cases. In these cases men and blacks have been executed much more often than have women and whites who were convicted of the same crimes. Even when a person is prosecuted for murder, the odds of actually receiving "just" retribution are extremely small.[68] For example, in Massachusetts between 1931 and 1950 a murder defendant faced a 29 percent chance of being convicted and a 4 percent chance of being put to death. In California, only 29 percent of all homicide convictions between 1950 and 1975 were capital cases. Six percent of defendants were sentenced to death and fewer than 2 percent were executed. In fact, the death penalty has never been imposed on any but a small minority of offenders convicted of homicide. During its greatest usage in the 1930s, death sentences resulted in only one of fifty homicide convictions. As criminologist Thorsten Sellin has pointed out, these examples actually *overestimate* the use of the death penalty as retribution.

> **Considering that these adjudicated murderers were only a part of a group that included the never-discovered offenders and those arrested but not prosecuted or convicted for lack of sufficient evidence, it is obvious that if retribution by death could be measured in relation to the number of actual murders, its failure would be even more evident.[69]**

Although in recent years supporters of retribution have succeeded in passing death penalty laws, it can be seen that only a small proportion of criminal homicides are actually subject to the death penalty. Moreover, the penalty is rarely imposed even in cases in which it is applicable. When it is applied, men and blacks receive a disproportionate share of the death sentences imposed.

It appears, therefore, that the goal of the retributionists has yet to be achieved. Even if the number of executions were to rise dramatically, it is unlikely that more than 2 percent of all homicide offenders sentenced would ever be executed, as was the case during the 1930s, when executions numbered more than two hundred per year. Nevertheless, limits on appellate review of sentences in death penalty cases have resulted in more executions in recent years, although the numbers are quite small compared to the 1930s. Trends in the number of people executed in the United States from 1930 to 1995 are illustrated in Figure 13.3. It is clear that the increase in executions during the 1990s is dwarfed by the number of executions that took place each year from 1930 to 1950.

THE DEATH PENALTY AND DETERRENCE The belief that the death penalty will prevent crime by deterring future murders is another common argument in support of capital punishment.[70] One aspect of this argument suggests that police officers in states without the death penalty are more likely to be killed than officers in states that provide for capital punishment for murder (at least murder of police officers). Studies have consistently found, however, that the numbers of police officers killed do not differ in death penalty and non–death penalty states.[71]

The deterrence argument also holds that capital punishment prevents the offender from committing another murder if released on parole. In the four-year period from 1969 to 1973, 6,835 male offenders serving sentences for murder were released on parole from state prisons. Fewer than 5 percent of those released were returned to prison for additional crimes; fewer than one-half of 1 percent committed willful homicides. From 1930 to 1962, only sixty-three offenders convicted of first-degree murder in New York State were released on parole, and one was returned to prison for committing an additional crime (a burglary). Other

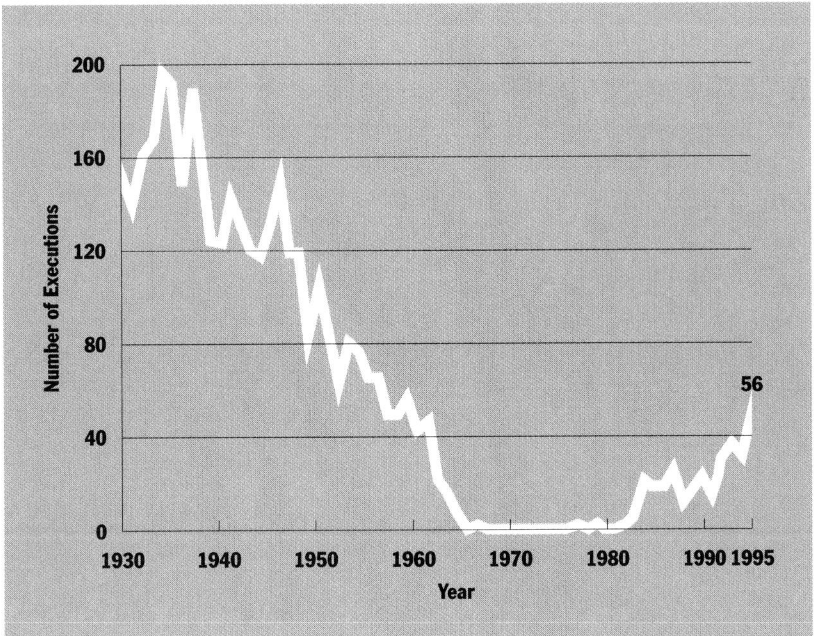

FIGURE 13.3

Persons executed, 1930 to 1995

SOURCE: Tracy L. Snell, *Capital Punishment 1995* (Washington, D.C.: U.S. Bureau of Justice Statistics, 1996).

follow-up studies have had similar results.[72] It is clear that murderers are very rarely released on parole and that when they are, it is extremely uncommon for them to be involved in another homicide.

Another way to assess the deterrent effect of capital punishment is to determine whether homicide rates increase when states abolish capital punishment, or to examine the homicide rates in neighboring states, one of which has a death penalty while the other does not. Obviously, if capital punishment prevents murders, states without a death penalty law should have higher homicide rates than neighboring states that employ the death penalty. A comparison of homicide rates and use of the death penalty in Maryland, Delaware, and New Jersey from 1920 to 1974 found no difference in homicide rates, even though each of these states retained, abolished, and sometimes reinstituted capital punishment during this fifty-five-year period. The number of executions in these states varied from none to a high of twenty-six per year, but in no case was a higher number of executions accompanied by a lower homicide rate. In fact, there was some evidence that homicide rates increased after the number of executions rose. Comparable findings were uncovered in tristate comparisons of Arizona, California, and New Mexico, and in Indiana, Ohio, and Michigan. Exhaustive studies have consistently shown the same results.[73] As Brian Forst has concluded, "The results of this analysis suggest . . . that it is erroneous to view capital punishment as a means of reducing the homicide rate."[74] Likewise, Scott Decker and Carol Kohlfeld found that "several different methods of examining the deterrent effect of executions resulted in the same finding; there is no evidence of a deterrent effect of executions in the state of Texas."[75] These findings mirror the conclusions of other criminologists.[76]

Police investigate the scene of a 1996 shootout in Philadelphia, which left an FBI agent and a suspect dead. Many argue that the death penalty helps to deter homicides, although the circumstances of most homicides work against this goal.

Studies that appear to show a deterrent effect have been repudiated on methodological grounds.[77] In fact, two studies present evidence that the number of homicides may be slightly increased following a legal execution. These studies found a few more homicides after executions than one would normally expect to occur. The "brutalization" hypothesis holds that a legal execution may "provoke" homicides by conveying the message that vengeance by means of killing is justified.[78]

There are several important reasons why the death penalty has not been shown to be a deterrent to criminal homicide. Most significantly, the offender must consider the consequences of his or her actions if deterrence is to take place. If one does not consider the possibility of being penalized for one's actions, no penalty, no matter how severe, will act as a deterrent. The crime of murder is rarely carried out in such a rational fashion. First, those who commit murder rarely set out to do so; rather most homicides occur as an unplanned act during the commission of a robbery or other felony. Thus, the death penalty is not considered as a possible outcome because murder was not an anticipated part of the crime. Second, offenders rarely believe that they will be caught. Because police solve only a small percentage of all serious crimes, the likelihood of punishment is very low. Certainty of punishment is extremely important if deterrence is to work. The lower the chances of being caught, the lower the deterrent effect of any penalty. Third, when criminal homicides occur, they are usually committed during a moment of intense anger or emotion in which reason is distorted. Police estimate that about half of all homicides occur during arguments between an offender and victim who know each other. Also, it is not unusual for the offender to be under the influence of alcohol or drugs, which certainly affects rational thinking. All of these circumstances work against the exercise of rational behavior, which is pivotal to the notion of deterrence.

ECONOMICS AND CAPITAL PUNISHMENT Some claim that carrying out the death penalty is more economical than housing an offender in prison for life. A study conducted in New York State during the 1980s found that the average cost of maintaining an inmate in prison was $16,214 per year. Therefore, it would cost $648,560 to incarcerate a thirty-year-old murderer if he lived to age seventy. On the other hand, the study revealed that the costs of the trials and multiple appeals usually involved in capital cases amount to more than $1.8 million.[79] In Florida, each execution costs the state $3.2 million—six times the cost of life imprisonment.[80] The high cost of capital punishment cases arises from the fact that virtually all death penalty states (thirty-seven of thirty-eight states) provide for automatic appellate review of death sentences. This review is usually conducted regardless of the offender's wishes in order to guard against the possibility of a mistake. Because of this time-consuming process, for all offenders executed since 1977 the average time between sentencing and execution was more than eight years.[81] Recent limitations on the right to appeal will reduce the time between sentencing and execution, but it remains to be seen whether the difference will be significant.[82]

The use of the death penalty for economic reasons thus does not hold up under scrutiny. It also overlooks the extremely small proportion of offenders who ever face the death penalty. As the New York State report concluded, "A criminal justice system with the death penalty is inordinately more expensive than a criminal justice system without the death penalty."[83]

ERRORS IN APPLYING THE DEATH PENALTY A major criticism of capital punishment is its finality. In a criminal justice system based on inexact legal standards such as "probable cause" and "proof beyond a reasonable doubt," there is always room for error.[84] There have been cases in which offenders who were executed have later been found to be innocent. In New York State, for example, at least eight offenders who were convicted of murder and executed have later been found to be innocent.[85] A systematic nationwide study found four hundred erroneous convictions in death penalty cases.[86] In 1995 alone, ninety-two persons on death row in twenty-one states had their sentences either overturned or removed; thirty of these had both their convictions and sentences overturned.[87] The 1996 Anti-Terrorism and Effective Death Penalty Act places restrictions on the appeals available to offenders sentenced to death. Some fear that these new limits will result in more erroneous convictions in murder cases.[88]

From 1977, the year after the U.S. Supreme Court reinstated the death penalty in *Gregg v. Georgia,* through 1996, nearly 5,000 offenders were sentenced to death. A total of 350 persons were executed during these twenty years, but another 1,870 had their convictions or sentences, or both, overturned or commuted, or died of natural causes or suicide while on death row. The large number of prisoners whose sentences are reduced or overturned has caused many to question the use of so final a penalty as capital punishment in so uncertain a process as the American criminal justice system.

Critical Thinking EXERCISE

Is Life Imprisonment a More Severe Punishment than the Death Penalty?

During the 1960s, a majority of Americans opposed the death penalty, but today public opinion polls show widespread support for capital punishment. This support is manifested in the death penalty laws of thirty-eight states and the federal government. The current support continues despite concerns about the deterrent effect of capital punishment and the fact that most other nations have abolished it. Even South Africa did away with capital punishment in 1995, after it had been in effect for 350 years.[A] This leaves the United States among the few Western democracies that still carry out death sentences.

In death penalty cases a judge or jury usually may choose between the death penalty and life imprisonment. Supporters of capital punishment argue that life imprisonment is a less severe penalty than life imprisonment. An argument can be made, however, that life imprisonment is actually a *more* severe sentence than the death penalty. This argument was made most persuasively by Cesare Beccaria in his 1764 *Essay on Crimes and Punishments.* Beccaria argued that "it is not the terrible yet momentary spectacle of the death of a wretch, but the long and painful example of a man deprived of liberty . . . which is the strongest curb against crimes." He believed that the impression left by an execution is mitigated by a tendency to forget the event because of its brevity. In addition, some offenders may desire death because they are vain or fanatic, or because they wish to escape their misery. Beccaria goes on to argue that life imprisonment is a better deterrent to crime than the death penalty. An execution provides only a single deterrent example, whereas "the penalty of a lifetime of servitude for a single crime supplies frequent and lasting examples" to others. "Adding up all the moments of unhappiness and servitude,"

Beccaria concludes, life imprisonment "may well be even more cruel; but [it is] drawn out over an entire lifetime, while the pain of death exerts its whole force in a moment."[B]

Beccaria also states that the death penalty is not useful "because of the example of barbarity it gives men." He notes, "It seems to me absurd that the laws, which are an expression of the public will, which detest and punish homicide, should themselves commit it, and that to deter citizens from murder, they order a public one."

Former New York State Governor Mario Cuomo opposed capital punishment on grounds similar to those set forth by Beccaria. His opposition to the death penalty was seen by many as a major cause of his failure to win reelection in 1994. During the previous year, Cuomo refused to send an inmate serving a life sentence from New York State to Oklahoma, where the inmate faced the death penalty, despite the inmate's stated wish to die. In 1994, the new governor sent the inmate to Oklahoma to be executed. Ironically, before execution the inmate wrote a statement that said, "Let there be no mistake, Mario Cuomo is wright [sic] . . . All jurors should remember this. Attica and Oklahoma State Penitentiary are living hells." Cuomo later remarked about the inmate, "He admitted that being allowed to die was an act of clemency for a double murderer, relieving him of the relentless confinement he dreaded more than death."[C]

Critical Thinking Questions

1. Do you agree or disagree with Beccaria's argument about the severity of life imprisonment versus the death penalty? What are your reasons for doing so?
2. How would you respond to Beccaria's comment that it appears absurd to express condemnation of homicide by committing it?

Notes

[A]Chris Eramus, "Death Penalty is Abolished in South Africa," *USA Today* (June 7, 1995), p. 4.

[B]Cesare Beccaria, *Essay on Crimes and Punishments* (1764) (Indianapolis: Bobbs-Merrill, 1984), Chap. 16.

[C]Doug Ferguson, "Grasso, Just Before Dying, Says Cuomo is Right: Life in Prison Would Be Worse," *The Buffalo News* (March 21, 1995), p. 14.

Is Castration a Reasonable Punishment for Sex Offenders?

It has been estimated that a rapist commits an average of seven rapes and that a child molester abuses an average of seventy-five children.[A] Nearly 28 percent of rapists released from prison are rearrested for another violent crime within three years.[B] Frustration over the apparent impossibility of preventing sex offenses has led to many desperate proposals. In the State of Washington, for example, the state senate passed a law that gives male sex offenders the option of undergoing castration in exchange for a 75 percent reduction in prison time.[C]

There appears to be some kind of compulsion among some sex offenders to seek out victims repeatedly despite prior punishment for sex crimes. This has led researchers to examine the biological makeup of "compulsive" sex offenders to determine whether organic factors can help explain their behavior. Some researchers have concluded that there are rapists who suffer from an abnormally high level of testosterone, the male sex hormone. Such individuals seek physical "release" and indeed appear to have an "uncontrollable" urge to rape. A possible example is the case of Alcides Quiles, who escaped from a Connecticut prison where he was serving time for raping a six-year-old boy, only to be caught after raping a two-year-old girl.[D]

The findings of research on rapists have led to use of the drug Depo-Provera, which brings about impotence. Although it is sometimes referred to as "medical castration," Depo-Provera relieves the biological urge in offenders who are believed to have a biological compulsion to rape.[E] Nevertheless, such drug treatments are controversial. Richard Seeley, director of Minnesota's Intensive Treatment Program for Sexual Aggressiveness, argues that "what's wrong with a sex offender is what's between his ears, not his legs." He claims that "rapists are who they learn to be—it's not a product of their hormones."[F]

In a Houston case, a defendant who was on probation for molesting a seven-year-old girl was charged with raping a thirteen-year-old girl. He offered to undergo surgical castration (removal of his testicles). The defendant faced life imprisonment if convicted, but the judge would put him on probation for ten years if he agreed to be castrated. The defense attorney stated that the castration penalty was "devised by eccentric right-wing lunatics and intentionally aimed at African-American males." Two physicians who had initially agreed to perform the surgery withdrew because of the controversy in the case.[G]

Abnormal hormone levels may help explain some sex offenses, but the number is probably a small proportion of all such offenses. Drug treatment and castration therefore remain controversial. Nevertheless, frustration about what to do with repeat sex offenders ultimately may lead to more serious consideration of the castration penalty in those cases.

Critical Thinking Questions

1. Do you believe that castration constitutes cruel and unusual punishment?
2. If you were a prosecutor, on what grounds would you argue in favor of drug treatment or surgical castration of a repeat sex offender? As defense counsel, how would you respond?
3. Would *you* opt for castration instead of life imprisonment if you had to make the choice?

Notes

[A]"Debate: Give Sex Offenders Longer Prison Terms," *USA Today* (March 7, 1990), p. 10.

[B]Lawrence A. Greenfeld, *Sex Offenses and Offenders* (Washington, D.C.: U.S. Bureau of Justice Statistics, 1997), p. 26.

[C]"Castration Bill," *USA Today* (February 13, 1990), p. 3.

[D]"Tot Killing," *USA Today* (October 20, 1990), p. 3.

[E]David Gelman, "The Mind of the Rapist," *Newsweek* (July 23, 1990), pp. 46–53; Craig Turk, "Kinder Cut: A Limited Defense of Chemical Castration," The New Republic, (August 27, 1997), p. 12.

[F]Ibid; Stacy Russell, "Castration of Repeat Sexual Offenders: An International Comparative Analysis," *Houston Journal of International Law,* vol. 19 (Winter 1997), pp. 425–59.

[G]Paul Leavitt, "Castration Case," *USA Today* (March 13, 16, 17, 1992), p. 3.

Summary

PURPOSES OF SENTENCING

- Judges may choose sentences within a range established by law in order to individualize sentences on the basis of the nature of the offender and the circumstances of the offense.
- When a judge sentences for purposes of retribution, punishment is applied simply in proportion to the seriousness of the offense.
- Sentences based on the concept of incapacitation are intended to prevent further criminal behavior by the offender.
- Habitual offender laws apply to offenders who have committed two or more offenses within a certain period.
- Deterrence aims to prevent crime through the example of offenders being punished.
- Rehabilitation sees criminal behavior as stemming from social or psychological shortcomings. The purpose of the sentence is to correct or treat these shortcomings.

SENTENCING CHOICES

- Depending on the range of alternatives provided by law, a judge usually can fine an offender or impose a sentence of probation, incarceration, or restitution.
- Occasionally a judge delays execution of a prison sentence and requires the offender to participate in an alcohol, drug, or gambling treatment program, or to pay restitution.
- A presentence report is written by a probation officer after an investigation of the offender's background and is designed to help the judge decide on an appropriate sentence.

THE ROLE OF VICTIMS

- A majority of states have made victim-impact statements a mandatory part of criminal procedure.

VARIATIONS IN SENTENCING SYSTEMS

- Indeterminate sentencing systems empower the judge to set a maximum sentence; throughout the sentence a parole board reviews the offender's progress in order to determine whether early release is justified.
- Determinate sentencing systems permit the judge to impose fixed sentences that cannot be altered by a parole board.
- The trend toward determinate sentencing has produced significant increases in prison populations.
- Mandatory sentences are fixed sentences imposed on individuals convicted of certain types of crimes.
- Sentencing guidelines recommend a "guideline sentence" based on the seriousness of the crime and the offender's prior record.
- Efforts to reform sentencing systems produced a shift toward indeterminate sentencing in the 1930s, followed by a return to determinate sentencing beginning in the 1970s.

THE EIGHTH AMENDMENT AND CAPITAL PUNISHMENT

- The Eighth Amendment bars excessive bail, excessive fines, and cruel and unusual punishment.
- The Supreme Court has ruled that the death penalty is cruel and unusual punishment except in cases of murder.
- There has been considerable controversy over how the death penalty is applied, with some critics claiming that it is imposed arbitrarily against minorities.
- Recent Supreme Court rulings require that both mitigating and aggravating factors be considered in determining the appropriateness of a particular sentence, including the death sentence.

THE DEATH PENALTY DEBATE

- Some supporters of the death penalty believe that it is a necessary punishment as retribution for the life unlawfully taken. There is little evidence that the death sentence has been effective as a form of retribution.
- Another common argument in support of capital punishment is that the death penalty will prevent crime by deterring future murders. Studies have found that there is no difference in homicide rates in states that have retained, abolished, and reinstituted capital punishment.
- A major criticism of capital punishment is its finality. Studies have found numerous cases of erroneous convictions in death penalty cases.

Key Terms

retribution
incapacitation
selective incapacitation
habitual offender law
deterrence
rehabilitation
suspended sentence
indeterminate sentencing
determinate sentencing
truth-in-sentencing
mandatory sentence

Questions for Review and Discussion

1. What are some arguments for and against considering factors other than the crime in deciding on an appropriate sentence for a convicted offender?
2. Name and describe the four main purposes of sentencing.
3. What is a suspended sentence?
4. Distinguish between indeterminate and determinate sentencing systems.
5. What are sentencing guidelines? What effect have they had in the states where they have been adopted?
6. What protections are provided by the Eighth Amendment to the U.S. Constitution?
7. What is the current legal status of the death penalty?
8. Describe the two main arguments in support of the death penalty.

Notes

[1]Lawrence W. Friedman, *Crime and Punishment in American History* (New York: Basic Books, 1993), p. 409.

[2]Susan Estrich, "A Just Sentence for Susan Smith," *USA Today* (August 3, 1995), p. 11.

[3]Exodus 21:12–25; Leviticus 24:17–21; Numbers 35:30–1; Deuteronomy 19:11–12.

[4]Andrew von Hirsch, *Doing Justice: The Choice of Punishments* (New York: Hill and Wang, 1976); Andrew von Hirsch, *Past or Future Crimes: Deservedness and Dangerousness in the Sentencing of Criminals* (New Brunswick, NJ: Rutgers University Press, 1985).

[5]Reuel Shinnar and Shlomo Shinnar, "The Effects of the Criminal Justice System on the Control of Crime: A Quantitative Analysis," *Law and Society Review,* vol. 9 (1975), pp. 581–611; Peter W. Greenwood, *Selective Incapacitation* (Santa Monica, CA: Rand Corporation, 1978).

[6]Stephen D. Gottfredson and Don M. Gottfredson, "Selective Incapacitation?," *Annals,* vol. 478 (1985), pp. 135–49; Andrew von Hirsch, "Selective Incapacitation Reexamined," *Criminal Justice Ethics,* vol. 7 (1988), pp. 19–35.

[7]"$79 Store Holdup Nets Man 18-Year Prison Sentence," *Buffalo Courier-Express* (September 15, 1981), p. 5.

[8]"Costly Pizza," *USA Today* (August 4, 1994), p. 3.

[9]See Alfred Blumstein, Jacqueline Cohen, and Daniel Nagin, eds., *Deterrence and Incapacitation: Estimating the Effects of Criminal Sanctions on Crime Rates* (Washington,

D.C.: National Academy of Sciences, 1978); Michael L. Radelet and Ronald L. Akers, "Deterrence and the Death Penalty: The Views of the Experts," *Journal of Criminal Law and Criminology*, vol. 87 (Fall 1996), pp. 1–16; Neal Kumar Katyal, "Deterrence's Difficulty," *Michigan Law Review*, vol. 95 (August 1997), pp. 2385–476.

[10]Scott H. Decker and Carol W. Kohlfeld, "Certainty, Severity, and the Probability of Crime," *Policy Studies Journal*, vol. 19 (1990), pp. 2–21.

[11]Daniel S. Nagin and Raymond Paternoster, "The Preventive Effects of the Perceived Risk of Arrest," *Criminology*, vol. 29 (1991), pp. 561–85.

[12]Gary S. Green, "General Deterrence and Television Cable Crime," *Criminology*, vol. 23 (1985), pp. 629–45.

[13]D. A. Andrews, et al., "Does Correctional Treatment Work?," *Criminology*, vol. 28 (1990), pp. 393–404.

[14]Lee Sechrest, Susan O. White, and Elizabeth D. Brown, eds., *The Rehabilitation of Criminal Offenders* (Washington, D.C.: National Academy of Sciences, 1979).

[15]399 U.S. 235 (1970).

[16]401 U.S. 395 (1971).

[17]*Gardner v. Florida*, 430 U.S. 349 (1977).

[18]Catharine M. Goodwin, "The Independent Role of the Probation Officer at Sentencing and in Applying *Koon v. United States*," *Federal Probation*, vol. 60 (September 1996), pp. 71–9.

[19]Robert M. Carter and Leslie T. Wilkins, "Some Factors in Sentencing Policy," *Journal of Criminal Law, Criminology, and Police Science*, vol. 58 (1967), pp. 503–14; Curtis Campbell, Candace McCoy, and Chimezie Osigweh, "The Influence of Probation Recommendations on Sentencing Decisions and Their Predictive Accuracy," *Federal Probation*, vol. 54 (1990), pp. 13–21.

[20]President's Task Force on Victims of Crime, *Final Report* (Washington, D.C.: U.S. Government Printing Office, 1982).

[21]Robert C. Davis and Barbara E. Smith, "The Effects of Victim Impact Statements on Sentencing Decisions: A Test in an Urban Setting," *Justice Quarterly*, vol. 11 (September 1994), pp. 453–69; Edna Erez and Pamela Tontodonato, "The Effect of Victim Participation in Sentencing on Sentence Outcome," *Criminology*, vol. 28 (1990), pp. 451–74.

[22]Amy K. Phillips, "Thou Shalt Not Kill Any Nice People: The Problem of Victim Impact Statements in Capital Sentencing," *American Criminal Law Review*, vol. 35 (Fall 1997), pp. 93–118.

[23]Andrew von Hirsch and Kathleen Hanrahan, "Determinate Penalty Systems in America: An Overview," *Crime & Delinquency*, vol. 27 (1981), pp. 289–316.

[24]Lawrence A. Greenfeld, *Prison Sentences and Time Served for Violence* (Washington, D.C.: U.S. Bureau of Justice Statistics, 1995).

[25]Lawrence A. Greenfeld, *Violent Offenders in State Prison: Sentences and Time Served* (Washington, D.C.: U.S. Bureau of Justice Statistics, 1995).

[26]Pamela L. Griset, "Determinate Sentencing and Agenda Building: A Case Study of the Failure of a Reform," *Journal of Criminal Justice*, vol. 23 (July–August 1995), pp. 349–62.

[27]Allen J. Beck et al., *Correctional Populations in the United States* (Washington, D.C.: U.S. Bureau of Justice Statistics, 1997), p. 13.

[28]Paul Simon and Dave Kopel, "Restore Flexibility to U.S. Sentences," *The National Law Journal*, vol. 19 (December 16, 1996), p. 15.

[29]Carey Goldberg, "Study Casts Doubt on Wisdom of Mandatory Terms for Drugs," *The New York Times* (November 25, 1997), p. 11.

[30]Raymond Hernandez, "Governor Commutes Sentences of 3 Convicted on Drug Charges: Clemencies are Seen as Protest to Sentencing Laws," *The New York Times* (December 25, 1997), p. B1.

[31]Michael Tonry, *Sentencing Reform Impacts* (Washington, D.C.: National Institute of Justice, 1987).

[32]John Wooldredge, "Research Notes: A State-Level Analysis of Sentencing Policies and Inmate Crowding in State Prisons," *Crime & Delinquency*, vol. 42 (July 1996), pp. 456–66.

[33]Dale Parent, Terence Dunworth, Douglas McDonald, and William Rhodes, *Mandatory Sentencing* (Washington, D.C.: National Institute of Justice, 1997).

[34]Lisa Stolzenberg and Stewart J. D'Alessio, "Three Strikes and You're Out": The Impact of California's New Mandatory Sentencing Law on Serious Crime Rates," *Crime & Delinquency*, vol. 43 (October 1997), pp. 457–69.

[35]Tom R. Tyler and Robert J. Boeckmann, "Three Strikes and You Are Out, But Why?: The Psychology of Public Support for Punishing Rule Breakers," *Law & Society Review*, vol. 31 (June 1997), pp. 237–65; David Shichor, "Three Strikes as a Public Policy: The Convergence of the New Penology and the McDonaldization of Punishment," *Crime & Delinquency*, vol. 43 (October 1997), pp. 470–93.

[36]Richard P. Conaboy, "The United States Sentencing Commission: A New Component in the Federal Criminal Justice System," *Federal Probation*, vol. 61 (March 1997), pp. 58–62.

[37]Bruce Frankel and Dennis Cauchon, "Judicial Revolt Over Sentencing Picks Up Steam," *USA Today* (May 3, 1993), p. 9; "Hands Tied," *The National Law Journal*, vol. 18 (January 15, 1996), p. 18.

[38]Dorothy K. Hatsukami and Marian W. Fischman, "Crack Cocaine and Cocaine Hydrochloride: Are the Differences Myth or Reality?," *Journal of the American Medical Association*, vol. 276 (1996), p. 1580; Kelly McMurry, "Researchers Criticize Cocaine Sentencing Guidelines," *Trial*, vol. 33 (April 1997), p. 17; Jeffrey L. Fisher, "When Discretion Leads to Distortion: Recognizing Pre-Arrest Sentence-Manipulation Claims Under the Federal Sentencing Guidelines," *Michigan Law Review*, vol. 94 (June 1996), pp. 2385–421.

[39]Michael Tonry, *Sentencing Matters* (New York: Oxford University Press, 1996); David Weisburd, "Sentencing Disparity and the Guidelines: Taking a Closer Look: *Federal Sentencing Reporter*, vol. 5 (1992), pp. 149–52; T. D. Miethe and C. A. Moore, "Socioeconomic Disparities under Determinate Sentencing Systems: A Comparison of Preguideline and Postguideline Practices in Minnesota," *Criminology*, vol. 23 (1985), pp. 337–63.

[40]Dale Parent, Terence Dunworth, Douglas McDonald, and William Rhodes, *The Impact of Sentencing Guidelines* (Washington, D.C.: National Institute of Justice, 1996).

[41]J. Garry, "Why Me? Application and Misapplication of Section 3A1.1, the Vulnerable Victim Enhancement of the Federal Sentencing Guidelines," *Cornell Law Review*, vol. 79 (November 1993), pp. 143–82.

[42]Parent, Dunworth, McDonald, and Rhodes, p. 5.

[43]Cesare Beccaria, *On Crimes and Punishments* (1764) (Indianapolis: Bobbs-Merrill, 1963), p. 13.

[44]T. Everson, "The Human Element in Justice," *Journal of the American Institute of Criminal Law and Criminology*, vol. 10 (1919), p. 90; Frederick J. Gaudet, George S. Harris, and Charles W. St. John, "Individual Differences in the Sentencing Tendencies of Judges," *Journal of the American Institute of Criminal Law and Criminology*, vol. 23 (1933), p. 811; Emil Frankel, "The Offender and the Court: a Statistical Analysis of the Sentencing of Delinquents," *Journal of Criminal Law and Criminology*, vol. 31 (1940), p. 448.

[45]Enrico Ferri, "The Nomination of a Commission for the Positivist Reform of the Italian Penal Code," *Journal of the American Institute of Criminal Law and Criminology*, vol. 11 (1920), p. 67; Sheldon Glueck, "Principles of a Rational Penal Code," *Harvard Law Review*, vol. 41 (1928), p. 453.

[46]Alexander Holtzoff, "The Indeterminate Sentence: Its Social and Legal Implications," *Federal Probation*, vol. 5 (1941), p. 5.

[47]Gunnar H. Nordbye, "The Indeterminate Sentence As a Method of Adjusting Inequality in Sentencing," *Federal Probation*, vol. 5 (1941), p. 23; Wayne Morse, Harold

Kennedy, and William Ellis, "Comments on the Federal Indeterminate Sentence Bill," *Federal Probation*, vol. 5 (1941), pp. 24–42.

[48]F. DeCosta, "Disparity and Equality of Criminal Sentences," *Howard Law Journal*, vol. 14 (1968), p. 29; Louis J. Sharp, "The Pilot Institute on Sentencing," *Federal Probation*, vol. 23 (1959), p. 9; Comment, "Criminal Procedure, Appealability of a Criminal Sentence—Sentence Modified on Appeal," *Rutgers Law Review*, vol. 16 (1961), p. 186.

[49]Jay S. Albanese, "Concern About Variation in Criminal Sentences: A Cyclical History of Reform," *Journal of Criminal Law and Criminology*, vol. 74 (1984), pp. 260–71; Pamela L. Griset, "Determinate Sentencing and Administrative Discretion Over Time Served in Prison: A Case Study of Florida," *Crime & Delinquency*, vol. 42 (January 1996), pp. 127–43.

[50]Joseph L. Gastworth and Tapan K. Nayak, "Statistical Aspects of Cases Concerning Racial Discrimination in Drug Sentencing: *Stephens v. State* and *U.S. v. Armstrong*," *Journal of Criminal Law and Criminology*, vol. 87 (Winter 1997), pp. 583–603; W. S. Wilson Huang, Mary A. Finn, R. Barry Ruback, and Robert R. Friedman, "Individual and Contextual Influences on Sentence Lengths: Examining Political Conservatism," *Prison Journal*, vol. 76 (December 1996), pp. 398–420.

[51]107 S. Ct. 2095 (1987).

[52]*Tate v. Short*, 91 S. Ct. 668 (1971).

[53]See *French v. Owens*, 777 F. 2d 1250 (7th Cir. 1985).

[54]*Coker v. Georgia*, 97 S. Ct. 2861 (1977).

[55]*Furman v. Georgia*, 92 S. Ct. 2726 (1972).

[56]*Gregg v. Georgia*, 96 S. Ct. 2909 (1976).

[57]*Roberts v. Louisiana* and *Woodson v. North Carolina*, 96 S. Ct. 3207 (1976).

[58]*Lockett v. Ohio*, 98 S. Ct. 2954 (1978).

[59]107 S. Ct. 1756 (1987).

[60]Ibid. at 1765.

[61]Ibid. at 1770.

[62]Jordan M. Steker, "The Limits of Legal Language: Decisionmaking in Capital Cases," *Michigan Law Review*, vol. 94 (August 1996), pp. 2590–624.

[63]Benjamin P. Cooper, "Truth in Sentencing: The Prospective and Retroactive Application of *Simmons v. South Carolina*," *University of Chicago Law Review*, vol. 63 (Fall 1996), pp. 1573–605; Ted Gest, "A House Without a Blueprint: After 20 Years, The Death Penalty is Still Being Meted Out Unevenly," *U.S. News & World Report* (July 8, 1996), pp. 41–5; Marvin D. Free, Jr. "The Impact of Federal Sentencing Reforms on African Americans," *Journal of Black Studies*, vol. 28 (November 1997), pp. 268–86; Linda A. Foley, Afesa M. Adams, and James L. Goodson, Jr., "The Effect of Race on Decisions by Judges and Other Officers of the Court," *Journal of Applied Social Psychology*, vol. 26 (July 1996), pp. 1190–2113; Scott Burgins, "Jurors Ignore, Misunderstand Instructions," *ABA Journal*, vol. 81 (May 1995), pp. 30–2; Leigh B. Bienen, "The Proportionality Review of Capital Cases by State High Courts After *Gregg*: Only 'The Appearance of Justice'," *Journal of Criminal Law and Criminology*, vol. 87 (Fall 1996), pp. 130–314.

[64]Tracy L. Snell, *Capital Punishment 1995* (Washington, D.C.: U.S. Bureau of Justice Statistics, 1996), p. 6.

[65]Marian J. Borg, "The Southern Subculture of Punitiveness?: Regional Variation in Support for Capital Punishment," *Journal of Research in Crime and Delinquency*, vol. 34 (February 1997), pp. 25–46; David A. Kaplan, "Life and Death Decisions," *Newsweek* (June 16, 1997), pp. 28–30.

[66]Ted Gest, "Texas Leads All States in Executions," *U.S. News & World Report* (February 2, 1998), p. 4.

[67]Ibid. at 4.

[68]David A. Kaplan, "Life and Death Decisions," *Newsweek* (June 16, 1997), pp. 28–31.

[69]Thorsten Sellin, *The Penalty of Death* (Beverly Hills, CA: Sage Publications, 1980), p. 72.

[70]"Death Penalty Debates Continue," *America*, vol. 176 (May 10, 1997), p. 3; George E. Pataki, "Death Penalty is a Deterrent," *USA Today Magazine* (March 1997), pp. 52–4.

[71]William C. Bailey, "Capital Punishment and Lethal Assaults Against Police," *Criminology*, vol. 19 (February 1992).

[72]Sellin, *The Penalty of Death*; Brian Forst, "The Deterrent Effect of Capital Punishment: A Cross-State Analysis of the 1960s," *Minnesota Law Review*, vol. 61 (1977); Richard Lempert, "The Effect of Executions on Homicides: A New Look in an Old Light," *Crime & Delinquency*, vol. 29 (January 1983); Hans Zeisel, "The Deterrent Effect of the Death Penalty: Facts v. Faith," in P. B. Kirkland, ed., *The Supreme Court Review, 1976* (Chicago: University of Chicago Press, 1977).

[73]See Charles L. Black, Jr., *Capital Punishment: The Inevitability of Caprice and Mistake* 2nd ed. (New York: Norton, 1981); Hugo A. Bedau, ed., *Capital Punishment in the United States*, 3rd ed. (New York: Oxford University Press, 1982); Sellin, *The Penalty of Death*; Dane Archer, Rosemary Gartner, and Marc Beittel, "Homicide and the Death Penalty: A Cross-National Test of a Deterrence Hypothesis," *Journal of Criminal Law and Criminology*, vol. 74 (1983), pp. 991–1013.

[74]Forst, "The Deterrent Effect of Capital Punishment: A Cross-State Analysis of the 1960s."

[75]Scott H. Decker and Carol W. Kohlfeld, "Capital Punishment and Executions in the Lone Star State: A Deterrence Study," *Criminal Justice Research Bulletin*, vol. 3 (1988).

[76]Michael L. Radelet and Ronald L. Akers, "Deterrence and the Death Penalty: The Views of the Experts," *Journal of Criminal Law and Criminology*, vol. 87 (Fall 1996), pp. 1–16.

[77]Decker and Kohlfeld, "Capital Punishment and Executions in the Lone Star State: A Deterrence Study"; Samuel Walker, *Sense and Nonsense About Crime*, 3rd ed. (Pacific Grove, CA: Wadsworth, 1993).

[78]William J. Bowers and Glenn L. Pierce, "Deterrence or Brutalization: What Is the Effect of Executions?," *Crime & Delinquency*, vol. 26 (October 1980); Brian Forst, "Capital Punishment and Deterrence: Conflicting Evidence?," *Journal of Criminal Law and Criminology*, vol. 74 (Fall 1983).

[79]New York State Defender's Association, *Capital Losses: The Price of the Death Penalty for New York State* (Albany, NY, 1982).

[80]Eric M. Freedman, "The Case Against the Death Penalty," *USA Today* (March 1997), pp. 48–50.

[81]Snell, p. 10.

[82]Marcia Coyle, "Innocent Dead Men Walking?," *The National Law Journal*, vol. 18 (May 20, 1996), p. 1.

[83]New York State Defender's Association, p. 50.

[84]David Stout, "Conviction for Child Abuse Overturned 10 Years Later," *The New York Times* (September 30, 1997), p. B3.

[85]Tony Mauro and Richard Benedetto, "Topic: The Death Penalty," *USA Today* (May 31, 1989), p. 8.

[86]Hugo A. Bedau and Michael L. Radelet, *Conviction of the Innocent* (Boston: Northeastern University Press, 1992); David E. Rovella, "Danger of Executing the Innocent on the Rise," *The National Law Journal*, vol. 19 (August 4, 1997), p. 7.

[87]Snell, p. 9.

[88]Coyle, p. 1.

For Further Reading

Lois G. Forer, *A Rage to Punish: The Unintended Consequences of Mandatory Sentencing* (New York: Norton, 1994).

Jon A. Meyer and Paul Jesilow, *Doing Justice in the People's Court: Sentencing by Municipal Court Judges* (Albany, NY: State University of New York Press, 1996).

Michael Tonry, *Sentencing Matters* (New York: Oxford University Press, 1996).

chapter fourteen

Prisons

The most anxious man in prison is the governor.

GEORGE BERNARD SHAW
(1856–1950)

The Virginia State Penitentiary was built in the shape of a horseshoe three stories high and housed men, women, and children. It opened in the year 1800. The cells had no heat, no light, and no plumbing. Solid oak doors made it impossible to see what was going on inside the cells. Sewage runoff ended in a ditch next to the James River, where a fierce odor lingered until the rains came and gave temporary relief. For the first thirty-eight years of the prison's existence, it was required by law that from 8 to 50 percent of a prisoner's sentence be served in solitary confinement. To meet this requirement, each prisoner was placed in a basement cell that was damp, unheated, and dark both day and night.[1]

In 1876, a Virginia prison report listed an inmate's death as resulting from a fall into a tub of boiling coffee. The inmate was ten years old. According to an 1880 report, 116 prisoners were eleven to seventeen years

CHAPTER OUTLINE

of age.[2] The prison was refurbished several times during the twentieth century before being closed in 1990. The purpose of prisons and their operating conditions have drawn concern from the very beginning.

Correctional Institutions in the United States

Although many aspects of American criminal justice originated in England, the use of prisons as a method of dealing with law violators is largely an American invention. During the Middle Ages confinement of criminals was considered wasteful, and instead corporal punishment of criminals was common. During the sixteenth century workhouses were used in Europe as a way to instill a work ethic into the poor (who were considered lazy).[3] These inmates made furniture and other items, and although workhouses were never used to house criminal offenders, they were a precursor of prisons. Interestingly, the establishment of prisons was brought about in response to concern for the humanitarian treatment of criminals.

Before the invention of the prison, corporal punishment was the primary method of punishment of criminals. This punishment often took the form of whipping and mutilation. Fines evolved as an alternative to corporal punishment, but poor offenders (the majority of criminals) could not afford them. In Colonial America laborers were scarce, and therefore minor offenders were often sentenced to work for their victims for a specified period.[4] Also, government structure and funding were weak, making long-term custody of offenders impractical. Jails were used for debtors and for those awaiting trial, as they were in Europe. Obviously, jail debtors were unable to earn money to repay their debts. It was not until the 1840s, however, that imprisonment of debtors was abolished in the United States.[5]

Incarceration became the primary form of sentence for poor offenders who could not afford to pay fines but whose offenses were not serious enough to deserve corporal punishment. Indeed, incarceration was seen as a humane alternative to corporal punishment. Physical punishment was associated with the Puritans, who believed that the doctrine of predestination made any attempt to rehabilitate offenders useless. The philosophers of the Enlightenment, however, advanced a more optimistic view. As stated in the Declaration of Independence, "We hold these truths to be self-evident, that all men are created equal, that they are endowed by their Creator with certain unalienable rights, that among these are life, liberty, and the pursuit of happiness." Rather than simply being part of human nature, crime and deviance were believed to result from negative environmental influences. As a result, many humanitarian groups called for reform of the penal system. The first of these groups was the Philadelphia Society for Alleviating the Miseries of Public Prisons, which was formed in 1787 by Dr. Benjamin Rush. He urged that capital and corporal punishment be replaced with incarceration. The Philadelphia Society (comprised mostly of Quakers) believed that criminals could be reformed if they were placed in solitary confinement, where they could reconsider their deviant acts and repent. This is where the term *penitentiary* originated.

In 1790, the Pennsylvania legislature was persuaded to convert the Walnut Street Jail in Philadelphia into an institution for the solitary confinement of "hardened and atrocious offenders." Each cell was small and dark, with a small high window so that the offender "could perceive neither heaven nor earth." No communication with the offender was allowed. Later, additional institutions were built, beginning with the Eastern Penitentiary in 1829. This system of incarceration became known as the **Pennsylvania system.** It promoted repentance through solitary confinement, was economical because it did not require long periods of confinement, and prevented offenders from being corrupted by mixing with other offenders. These principles soon fell prey to political and pragmatic considerations, however. The institutions quickly became overcrowded and offenders were incarcerated for longer periods. As the Frenchmen Gustave de Beaumont and Alexis de Tocqueville remarked after visiting a number of U.S. prisons:

Pennsylvania system
A philosophy of imprisonment that promoted repentance through solitary confinement and prevented offenders from being corrupted by mixing with other offenders.

> **Nowhere was this system of imprisonment crowned with the hoped-for success. In general it was ruinous to the public treasury; it never effected the reformation of prisoners. Every year the legislature of each state voted considerable funds toward the support of the penitentiaries, and the continued return of the same individuals into the prisons proved the inefficiency of the system to which they were submitted.[6]**

In addition, most early prisons were "impersonal institutions marked by brutality and neglect" that defeated the underlying purpose of the confinement.[7]

In 1819, a somewhat different system of incarceration was initiated in New York State. The **Auburn system** anticipated the industrial revolution with its emphasis on labor and meditation. Offenders worked every day, but they did so in complete silence. The Auburn system spread throughout the country and was seen as a significant advance in the treatment of offenders.

Auburn system
A philosophy of imprisonment that emphasized labor and meditation. Offenders worked every day, but they did so in complete silence.

During the second half of the nineteenth century, there was disillusionment with both the Auburn and Pennsylvania systems. Neither system effectively reformed prisoners, and neither appeared to have a deterrent effect on crime. As Beaumont and de Tocqueville observed in 1833, the silence and isolation of prisoners resulted in depression and death among both inmates and guards. They noted that in New York State twenty-six inmates in solitary confinement were pardoned by the governor, but fourteen of them were returned to prison a short time later for new offenses.[8]

In 1877, believing that education was the key to rehabilitation, Zebulon Brockway developed a new approach to incarceration at the Elmira Reformatory in New York State. Brockway changed the purpose of incarceration from custody to education. The Elmira Reformatory attempted to promote a school-like atmosphere in which inmates could progress at their own pace. The New York State legislature demonstrated its support for the program when it passed an indeterminate sentencing law that allowed for offenders to be released on parole when they showed signs of progress in the reformatory programs. By 1900, the reformatory movement had been adopted by a number of states.[9]

Disenchantment also arose with these education-based systems, however. Many prison administrators were reluctant to adopt the reform strategies and continued to emphasize discipline and control. Educational efforts often took a back seat to the more custodial demands of incarceration as punishment. Moreover, it was more difficult than expected to distinguish truly reformed prisoners from those who pretended to show signs of reform. As a result, parole policies were often based on superficial indications of reform. Also working against prison reform were overcrowding and poor management.[10]

Today prisons lack a clear philosophical purpose. Most try to do a little of everything: punishment, work, and education. The results are equally mixed. The expectations of prisons and prisoners vary widely from one institution to another, leaving few people satisfied with the outcome. Meditation, labor, and education have not been effective in deterring criminal behavior. This has caused some critics to argue that prisons should exist solely for purposes of punishment and not make any effort at reformation.[11] Such a view overlooks the fact that the vast majority of inmates will someday return to society and that prisons can serve an important function in preparing inmates for release.

Types of Prisons

One of the newest prisons in the United States is the ultra–maximum security federal prison in Florence, Colorado. It holds more than four hundred prisoners and it cost sixty million dollars to build. Dangerous inmates are confined in their cells twenty-three hours a day. When outside their cells, they wear leg irons and handcuffs and are accompanied by guards. The prison has been called the "Alcatraz of the Rockies" after the prison on the island of Alcatraz in San Francisco Bay, considered the toughest prison when it opened in the 1930s. Alcatraz was closed in 1963 because of the high cost of maintaining an island prison and a national shift toward rehabilitation as a model of punishment. The prison in Marion, Illinois, became the "end of the road" when it placed its violent inmates in a permanent lock-down status in the mid-1980s, after several assaults and deaths of staff and inmates.[12] The new prison in Colorado, designed exclusively for violent prisoners, opened in 1994. The inmates in the new prison are serving sentences that average forty years. All are men, and most will die in prison. The Florence prison also has its version of solitary confinement, a unit that holds 184 prisoners who never come into physical contact with another human.[13]

These "ultra-secure" prisons are reserved for the most violent inmates, especially those who have committed assaults while in other prisons or have records of escape or extreme violence. There are numerous other types of prisons, however, distinguished by level of custody. **Maximum security** institutions often have a wall surrounding the entire facility (eighteen to twenty-five feet high) and are designed to house dangerous felons who have committed violent crimes or who have a history of escape attempts. About 26 percent of all inmates are incarcerated in such institutions. **Medium security** institutions often have some facilities outside the main enclosure. Usually there are two rows of chain-link fence, topped with barbed wire, around the main enclosure. This type of prison holds felony offenders who have not committed violent crimes or whose prior record and institutional conduct are deemed not to require a maximum security setting. About 49 percent of all inmates are serving time in these institutions. **Minimum security** facilities usually have no fences but have locking outside doors and electronic surveillance devices around the perimeter of the institution. Inmates in these facilities are serving short sentences for nonviolent crimes, or are near the

maximum security
Prisons with a wall surrounding the entire facility that house dangerous felons (about 26 percent of all inmates are incarcerated in such institutions).

medium security
Prisons that have some facilities outside the main enclosure surrounded by two rows of chain-link fence, topped with barbed wire (half of all inmates are serving time in these institutions).

minimum security
Prison facilities that usually have no fences but have locking outside doors and electronic surveillance devices around the perimeter of the institution (about 23 percent of all inmates are in these institutions).

FUTURE ISSUES

Supermax Prisons

Prisons are using long-term solitary confinement to control violent prisoners with increasing frequency. The cost–benefit of these procedures is not well established. The prison building boom of the 1990s saw a number of states build high security "supermax" prisons, or high security units within prisons, to deal with unmanageable offenders. In Walpole, Massachusetts, the disciplinary unit does not permit convicts to have contact with any other inmates. They eat alone, cannot participate in work or education programs, and are allowed five hours of solitary per week in a six-by-thirty foot outdoor fenced area. When the weather is bad, they have no opportunity for exercise.

These conditions have been criticized as inhumane and have provoked a number of lawsuits alleging violations of the prohibition against cruel and unusual punishment. A Boston psychiatrist likens it to taking a dog that has bitten someone and kicking and abusing it in a cage for a year or more.[A] On the other hand, supermax facilities provide prison wardens with a way to manage violent offenders more efficiently. The new federal supermax prison in Florence, Colorado, holds four hundred inmates, two-thirds of whom are there for murder or attempted murder of another inmate, serious assault of a staff member, or a serious escape attempt. Some prison administrators believe it is easier to handle these violent inmates at a single location because it makes possible uniform staff training and high security procedures. Others believe that the supermax approach requires additional staff and expensive modifications to existing prison security. Also it may be easier to manage small groups of violent inmates than an entire institution of this type.[B]

Many inmates in supermax units have lost all time off for good behavior and will serve their maximum sentence. These inmates can be released directly into the community once their sentence is completed. Robert Verdeyen of the American Correction Association states that "I have not only seen inmates who were aggressive and hostile but actually psychotic released into the streets."[C]

During the 1990s a number of "supermax" prisons were built to deal with unmanageable offenders, escapees, and those serving life sentences.

FUTURES QUESTION

How would you propose to balance the need for security from violent inmates with the requirements of humane treatment and their pending release at the end of the maximum sentence?

NOTES

[A]Spencer P. M. Harrington, "Caging the Crazy: 'Supermax' Confinement Under Attack," *The Humanist*, vol. 57 (January–February 1997), pp. 14–20.

[B]Gregory L. Hershberger, "To the Max: Supermax Facilities Provide Prison Administrators with More Security Options," *Corrections Today*, vol. 60 (February 1998), pp. 54–8; Beverly Wolfus and Eugene Stasiak, "Measuring Conflict Tactics in Offender and Nonoffender Populations," *International Journal of Offender Therapy & Comparative Criminology*, vol. 41 (December 1997), pp. 325–40.

[C]Harrington, p. 15.

end of longer sentences and are therefore at low risk for escape. About 23 percent of all inmates are in minimum security institutions.

State and federal prisons differ in number, size, and capacity. Table 14.1 summarizes some important differences in the numbers of prisons and their populations. There were a total of 1,196 state and federal prisons in 1995, a number that had risen 15 percent in five years. State and federal prisons had a combined capacity of approximately 976,000 but held 1,023,572 inmates for an occupancy rate of 105 percent. A total of sixty-six new maximum security prisons were added in only five years, as were fifty-eight medium security and ninety-one minimum security prisons.[14] These figures make it clear that new prison construc-

TABLE 14.1

State and Federal Prisons

PRISON CHARACTERISTIC	STATE	FEDERAL
Number of prisons	1,084	112
Rated capacity	909,908	65,811
Inmates in custody	941,642	81,930
Percent capacity occupied	103%	124%
Maximum security	289	9
Medium security	438	25
Minimum security	648	91

SOURCE: James J. Stephan, *Census of State and Federal Correctional Facilities, 1995* (Washington, D.C.: Bureau of Justice Statistics, 1997).

tion has characterized the 1990s and that despite these new prisons, inmate populations still exceed prison capacity. About half of all state correctional facilities are located in the South, with the remainder equally distributed among the other regions of the country.[15]

The federal correctional system is similar to the state systems, but it houses only federal offenders whose cases have been tried in federal courts. Maximum security federal institutions are called **penitentiaries;** medium security facilities are **correctional institutions;** and federal facilities for pretrial detention and for those serving short sentences are called **metropolitan correctional centers** or **detention centers.** The federal corrections system also includes prison camps and community treatment centers.

penitentiaries
Maximum security federal correctional institutions.

correctional institutions
Medium security federal correctional institutions.

metropolitan correctional centers (detention centers)
Federal jail facilities for pretrial detention and for those serving short sentences.

The assignment of an offender to an institution at a particular custody level depends largely on whether or not the conviction was for a violent crime. For example, 62 percent of inmates in maximum security prisons were sentenced for a violent crime, compared to 45 percent in medium security and 34 percent in minimum security institutions. Conversely, more property and drug offenders are incarcerated in medium security prisons (47 percent of inmates) and minimum security prisons (60 percent of inmates) than in maximum security facilities (33 percent of inmates). Approximately 80 percent of all state prison inmates have a prior conviction and a record of probation or incarceration, but those with a prior record *and* current conviction for a violent crime are most likely to be assigned to maximum security prisons.[16]

The fact that only 62 percent of offenders in maximum security prisons were sentenced for a violent crime indicates that 38 percent of inmates in these facilities committed nonviolent crimes. Although many of these are repeat offenders, scarce and expensive prison space is at a premium. The number of criminals being sent to prison two or more times increased steadily from 18 percent of prison admissions in 1980 to 35 percent in 1995.[17] This suggests that prisons are ineffective and may be losing their deterrent force. As criminal justice researcher Al Blumstein has concluded, "we have now locked up so many people that we have lost the stigmatizing effect" of prisons.[18]

Who Is in Prison?

Many people believe that the sentences offenders currently receive are more lenient than ever before, but nothing could be further from the truth. In fact, the number of offenders in state or federal prisons increased by more than 130 percent from 1985 to 1997. There are now more than 1.2 million inmates in state and federal institutions, more than at any other time in the nation's history.[19] The reason for this increase is simple: More people are being sent to prison than are being released. In 1995, 957,439 male prisoners were admitted to state or federal prisons, while only 491,858 were released.[20] The rate at which they are released has also dropped, reflecting a general increase in the length of time served in prison by inmates.[21] As is discussed in Chapter 13, admissions to U.S. prisons have increased as states have shifted to determinate and mandatory sentencing systems and parole board release has been restricted or abolished. This trend is

contemporary issues

Private Prisons and Liability

The failure of correctional institutions to deter offenders from committing additional crime has plagued the system throughout its history. This failure, combined with efforts to reduce the size of government during the 1980s, led to proposals to allow entire prisons to be operated by private contractors. To date, more than fifty private correctional facilities housing adult prisoners have been established. Most are medium or minimum security facilities, and the vast majority are located in three states—Texas, Florida, and California—which are also the three states with the largest inmate populations.

Corrections Corporation of America is the largest private contractor in this field, followed by Wackenhut. These corporations have offered competitive bids to build or remodel prisons and to manage and operate them. Proponents of this approach contend that private contractors can operate prisons less expensively than the government while maintaining the same level of custody and quality of service. Opponents argue that it is improper for private contractors to supervise offenders sentenced by the state and that costs cannot be reduced significantly over the long term.[A]

Despite this debate, many states are currently under court order to reduce overcrowding or to improve conditions inside prisons. They are building new prisons to handle the exploding prison population and seeking ways to pay for them without raising taxes. Private contractors offer construction and supervision costs that, at least initially, appear lower than those the state has borne in the past.[B]

Recently, the investigative arm of Congress, the U.S. General Accounting Office (GAO), reviewed a series of studies that compared public and private correctional facilities in terms of cost of operation and quality of service. The results were mixed. Some of the studies found that private facilities were cheaper while providing similar levels of service. One found private facilities to be more costly, whereas still others found no difference. The GAO concluded that the studies provided little guidance for jurisdictions seeking to reduce costs.[C] Privatization of prisons is likely to continue, however, because it relieves states of the immediate burden of financing prisons on their own, which can cost $75,000 per bed. The long-term outlook is less clear.

Liability issues may ultimately play a central role in determining the future of private prisons. In its 1996 budget the Federal Bureau of Prisons had proposed to contract with private companies for the majority of its future minimum security and pretrial detention facilities. However, this decision was reversed when the Justice Department found that it was unable to reduce the risk of a strike or walkout by private corrections officers.[D] If corrections officers failed to appear for work, the result could be chaos in an unsupervised prison. Concerns about liability for any disorder that might occur if private prison guards ever went on strike nixed the federal government's privatization plans, at least for now.

In 1997, the U.S. Supreme Court ruled that, unlike publicly employed corrections officers, private prison guards are not immune from allegations of civil rights violations. In the case in question, an inmate alleged that corrections officers at South Central Correctional Center in Tennessee, which is operated by Corrections Corporation of America, violated his Eighth Amendment rights by placing restraints on him that were too tight and caused serious injury requiring hospitalization. The Supreme Court held the privately employed corrections officers responsible, stating that "mere performance of a governmental function does not support immunity for a private person, especially one who performs a job without government supervision or direction."[E]

The Court denied immunity protection to private prison guards in a narrow way, leaving the door open for a "special good faith defense" for private prison operators in future cases. The Court did not indicate what that defense might be. It will be interesting to see how the growth of private prisons is affected by the liability issues it has just begun to face.

NOTES

[A]Matt Bai, "On the Block," *Newsweek* (August 4, 1997), pp. 60–1; Norman Seabrook and Katherine Lapp, "Should Corporations Run the Jails?," *The Daily News* (August 23, 1995), p. 7.

[B]Sam Vincent Meddis and Deborah Sharp, "Prison Business in a Blockbuster," *USA Today* (December 13, 1994), p. 10.

[C]U.S. Comptroller General, *Private and Public Prisons* (Washington, D.C.: U.S. General Accounting Office, 1996), p. 3.

[D]Ibid., p. 1; Barbara Ann Stolz, "Privatizing Corrections: Changing the Corrections Policy-Making Subgovernment," *Prison Journal*, vol. 77 (March 1997), p. 92.

[E]*Richardson v. McKnight*, 117 S. Ct. 2100 (1997).

merely an extension of the overall trend since 1925. Despite some fluctuations during the Great Depression (up), World War II (down), and the early 1960s (up), the rate of incarceration has been increasing steadily. In 1925, there were 91,699 state and federal prisoners, an incarceration rate of 79 per 100,000 U.S. popula-

FIGURE 14.1

Number of state and federal prisoners sentenced, 1925 to 1997

SOURCE: Compiled from Stephanie-Minor Harper, *State and Federal Prisoners, 1925–1985* (Washington, D.C.: Bureau of Justice Statistics, 1986); Allen J. Beck et al., *Correctional Populations in the United States* (Washington, D.C.: Bureau of Justice Statistics, 1997); Darrell K. Gilliard and Allen J. Beck, *Prisoners in 1997* (Washington, D.C.: Bureau of Justice Statistics, 1998).

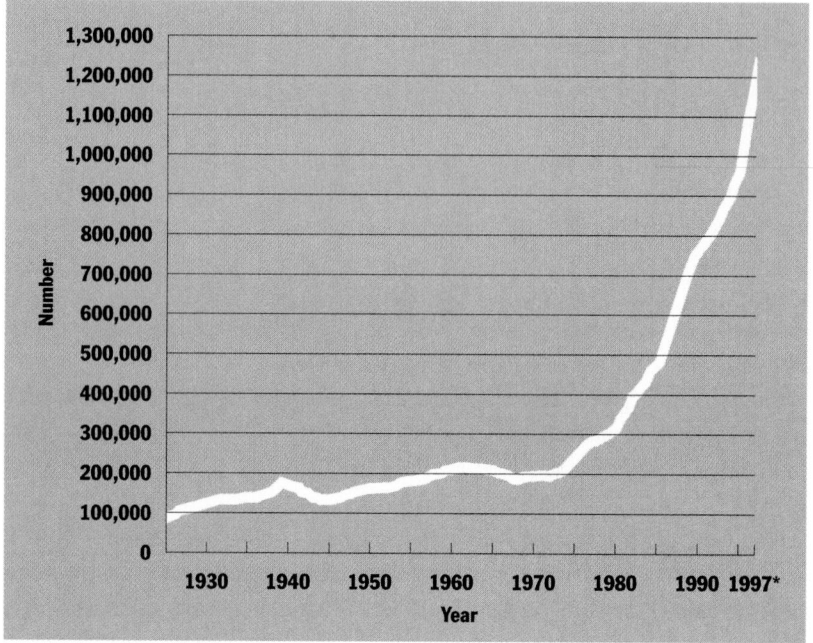

tion.[22] Seventy years later, in 1997, a record high was reached with 1,725,842 prisoners and an incarceration rate of 445 per 100,000 population. This trend is illustrated in Figure 14.1.

The result of this explosion of the prison population is overcrowding and new construction. As of 1995, state correctional facilities were operating at an average of 103 percent capacity. A total of 378 state correctional facilities (27 percent) are under court order to reduce overcrowding or correct conditions that violate the law (usually involving health or safety). New construction has increased total prison capacity by 40 percent since 1990, but the number of inmates has increased by 43 percent. One third of correctional facilities in the United States are less than ten years old, although nearly a quarter of correctional institutions are at least fifty years old.[23]

Although the average felony sentence of six years in prison has not changed significantly since 1990, truth-in-sentencing laws and parole restrictions have substantially increased the length of time served. For example, newly sentenced federal offenders will serve at least 85 percent of their sentences, as will violent felons in nearly half the states.[24] This change in sentencing laws has had a dramatic impact on the average daily population of prisons.

GENDER In the last decade the number of women incarcerated in state, federal, or local jails or prisons in the United States has more than doubled. The rate of incarceration has increased from 27 per 100,000 women in 1985 to 68 per 100,000, a growth rate of 250 percent. Men still outnumber women in the inmate population by a factor of about thirteen to one, but the gap is narrowing—it was eighteen to one a decade ago.[25] This rapid growth can also be seen in the fact that women constituted 4 percent of the total prison and jail population in the United States in 1980 and more than 6 percent in 1997.[26] This suggests that women are committing more offenses and are more likely to receive jail or prison sentences upon conviction for these crimes than they were in the past. The special concerns posed by growing numbers of women in prison are discussed later in the chapter.

INMATE BACKGROUNDS The backgrounds of inmates reveal many factors that have been found to be associated with crime. Education, family background, and drug use are among the most revealing of these.

Most people who commit felonies and are sentenced to state prisons are not highly educated. Approximately 20 percent have less than a ninth grade education and another 50 percent did not graduate from high school. Therefore, 70 percent of prison inmates in the United States lack a high school education. Two thirds of inmates in state prison are under age thirty-five. Approximately 35 percent are white, 50 percent black, and 17 percent Hispanic.[27] Approximately 47 percent were sentenced to prison for a crime of violence, 25 percent for a property crime, and 21 percent for a drug offense. About 4 percent of state prison inmates are not U.S. citizens.

The family background of adult inmates is revealing. A large proportion (43 percent) were raised in a single-parent household, and 17 percent lived in a foster home or other institution at some time. Thirty percent of inmates report that their parents abused either alcohol or drugs, and 50 percent of inmates were under the influence of alcohol or drugs at the time of their current offense. A total of 43 percent of female inmates and 12 percent of males report that they were physically or sexually abused in the past. Thirty-seven percent have an immediate family member who has been incarcerated, and 94 percent have been convicted for a violent crime *or* have a prior record of probation or incarceration.[28] The high incidence of troubled backgrounds far exceeds national averages.

A significant problem in breaking the cycle of crime and imprisonment is the fact that 42 percent of incarcerated women and 32 percent of male inmates have two or more children under age eighteen. These children usually live with the other parent or with grandparents, although 12 percent live in foster homes or other institutions. In addition, 6 percent of female inmates are pregnant when they enter prison, and 32 percent of inmates sentenced for violent crimes victimized a relative, intimate, or person whom they knew well.[29]

This combination of family and substance abuse, lack of education and long criminal history, and incarcerated parents of new children does not bode well for efforts to break the cycle of high-risk persons who are likely to engage in criminal behavior. Even if effective measures could be implemented to improve education, provide substance abuse treatment, and maintain family integrity, there is an entire generation of parents in prison who are unlikely to provide effective supervision for their children, who are at risk for becoming offenders themselves.

The Operation of Prisons: Custody or Reform?

It is generally agreed that the purpose of prison is to serve as punishment for a crime. There is less agreement as to what should occur *inside* prisons. The prevailing legal view is that deprivation of liberty through imprisonment *is* the punishment and that prison should not inflict additional punishment on offenders. For example, a prisoner in the Southern Ohio Correctional Facility sued the state, arguing that housing two inmates in a single cell ("double-celling") violates the

Prison crowding has been a continuing problem, resulting in make-shift prison housing arrangements and ongoing debates about whether custody or reform is the primary focus of confinement.

Eighth Amendment prohibition against cruel and unusual punishment. Studies had recommended approximately six by nine feet of space for each inmate in a cell, but the double-celling had cut that space by 40 percent. Lower courts ruled in favor of the inmates, but the U.S. Supreme Court reversed the decision in *Rhodes v. Chapman,* holding that double-celling is not by itself cruel and unusual punishment. The Court stated that "such conditions are restrictive and even harsh, [but] they are part of the penalty that criminal offenders pay for offenses against society."[30] Therefore, "restrictive and even harsh" conditions in prison are permissible, although the Court indicated that the deprivation of essential food, medical care, or sanitation is not permissible.

Numerous other challenges have been made to the conditions of confinement in recent years. Each case involved interpretation of the Eighth Amendment prohibition against cruel and unusual punishment. Stated another way: If punishment is permitted, under what conditions does it become cruel and unusual? In a landmark case, *Estelle v. Gamble,* the Supreme Court held that "deliberate indifference to serious medical needs of prisoners" violates the Eighth Amendment because it permits "unnecessary and wanton infliction of pain" and offends "evolving standards of decency."[31] These phrases have become benchmarks in determining whether specific prison conditions, though harsh, exceed the limits imposed by the Constitution.

In a 1991 case, *Wilson v. Seiter,* an inmate at the Hocking Correctional Facility in Ohio filed suit, claiming that the conditions of his confinement violated the Eighth Amendment. Those conditions included excessive noise, overcrowding, inadequate heating and cooling, improper ventilation, unclean restrooms, unsanitary food preparation, and housing among mentally and physically ill inmates. As in previous cases, the U.S. Supreme Court agreed that prison officials had shown "deliberate indifference." The Court also held, however, that inmates must show that prison officials had "intent" or a "culpable state of mind" in allowing these conditions to exist.[32] Therefore, it is not enough simply to demonstrate the existence of the deplorable conditions. Prison officials must have known about the conditions and failed to act. This is a difficult burden of proof and will make it harder for claims regarding conditions of confinement to stand up in court.

Many people believe that prisons should not only punish offenders but also control crime. Some argue that crime is controlled merely by keeping the offender off the streets for a specified period. More often, it is hoped that prison will have a deterrent or reformative effect on the offender. That is to say, the unpleasant experience of imprisonment might deter new criminal activity upon re-

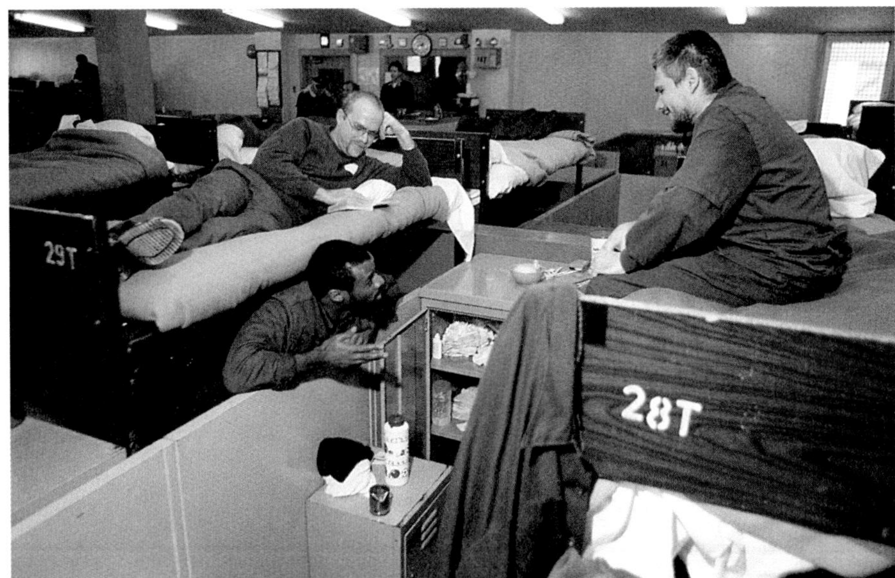

A recent national survey of wardens and state corrections commissioners identified three significant problems they face: prison overcrowding, gang-affiliated inmates, and understaffed treatment programs.

lease, or the offender might come to see the error of his or her ways during imprisonment and make a genuine effort to reform.

The statistical evidence shows quite clearly that the experience of imprisonment does not deter *recidivism* upon release. Recidivism refers to re-offending by criminals. Over 60 percent of inmates in state prisons have been incarcerated before. Counting those who were on probation, 94 percent of all inmates have been under some form of correctional supervision before their current incarceration.[33] Criminal justice researcher Don Gottfredson concludes that current incarceration policies are expensive, do not contribute to public safety, and add to the burden shouldered by taxpayers.[34] *The Economist* magazine in London draws the same conclusion.[35] Nevertheless, prison administrators must find ways to handle the growing number of offenders sentenced to their facilities.

Prison administrators attempt to manage inmates in a way that creates the fewest problems for staff and other inmates during their term. Three major managerial approaches identified by John DiIulio are the control model, responsibility model, and consensus model.[36] DiIulio sees the *control model* characterized by strict enforcement of prison rules and few privileges for prisoners. This approach produces large numbers of rule violations and can increase the level of tension within a prison. Studies have found that such a formal management is not the most effective way to prevent prison disorder.[37] The *responsibility model* gives inmates more autonomy and the staff guides their decision-making rather than making all decisions for them. This approach employs minimal restraint except in cases requiring the protection of staff or other inmates. The *consensual model* maintains order by agreement on the validity of rules between inmates and staff. Inmates are placed in a position of participating in the operation of the prison, although DiIulio believes that such a model is not effective because the inmates' self-interest leads them to attempt to manipulate the system. There continues to be debate over the impact of prison administration on inmate conduct.[38] Nevertheless, each of these models could be applied in a prison environment, depending on the security level of the institution, the types of offenders involved, and the willingness of staff to support the management model employed.

A recent national survey of wardens and state corrections commissioners identified three significant problems they face: prison overcrowding, gang-affiliated inmates, and understaffed treatment programs. The majority reported that their prisons were at or over capacity, making it difficult to maintain inmate and staff security and appropriate conditions of confinement. More than 70 percent indicated that improvement is needed in the identification of gang-affiliated inmates and in staff training programs designed to control gang activities. (Prison gangs are discussed further later in the chapter.) Three fourths of the wardens indicated a need for more staff to provide treatment for alcohol and substance abuse, mental health, parenting, and vocational education.[39] This suggests that it is often difficult for even motivated inmates to obtain access to education or treatment to address their problems.

Jails

In August 1992, a black Mississippi teenager was discovered hanging by his shoelace in the Simpson County jail. In a period of only five years, forty-one other suicides were committed by inmates in Mississippi jails. The U.S. Civil Rights Commission requested a federal investigation into this situation. Questions were raised not only about why so many suicides were occurring, but also about whether some inmates had been murdered and then hanged to make their deaths look like suicide.[40] Although prisons attract more attention from the media and policymakers than do jails, the deplorable conditions in many jails have been highlighted in cases such as these.

Jails are operated by counties and municipalities. They hold two main categories of inmates: those awaiting trial and those serving sentences of one year or less. Jails also perform other functions, as outlined in Table 14.2.

TABLE 14.2

Functions of Jails*

- Receive individuals pending arraignment and hold them awaiting trial, conviction, or sentencing
- Readmit probation, parole, and bail-bond violators and absconders
- Temporarily detain juveniles pending transfer to juvenile authorities
- Hold mentally ill persons pending their movement to appropriate health facilities
- Hold individuals for the military, for protective custody, for contempt, and for the courts as witnesses
- Release convicted inmates to the community upon completion of sentence
- Transfer inmates to federal, state, or other authorities
- House inmates for federal, state, or other authorities because of crowding of their facilities
- Relinquish custody of temporary detainees to juvenile and medical authorities
- Sometimes operate community-based programs with electronic monitoring or other types of supervision

*In addition to confining persons before and after adjudication.

SOURCE: Craig A. Perkins, James J. Stephan, and Allen J. Beck, *Jails and Jail Inmates* (Washington, D.C.: Bureau of Justice Statistics, 1995).

Jails hold probation and parole violators and bail absconders. They may hold mentally ill persons on a temporary basis. They often serve as transfer points between prisons and house offenders who cannot be admitted to state or federal prisons because of overcrowding. Such a "mixed bag" of suspects, defendants, and offenders makes for a crowded, and sometimes confusing, jail environment.

The number of jail inmates has more than doubled over the last decade, although the total number of jails remains about the same at 3,300. Jail space also nearly doubled over the decade, however, owing to new construction and renovation. Five states—California, Texas, Florida, New York, and Georgia—account for about half the total jail population of more than 500,000 inmates. Similarly, about 6 percent of all jails house more than half of all jail inmates. Seventy-six jails hold 1,000 or more inmates each. They are counterbalanced by 1,874 jails that hold fewer than fifty inmates each.[41]

Local jails employ more than 165,000 persons, more than 70 percent of whom are corrections officers who provide security services and inmate supervision. Because of rapid hiring, staff–inmate ratios have improved despite the dramatic growth in jail populations. There are approximately four inmates per corrections officer. It costs just under $10,000 per year to house an inmate in jail.[42]

A total of 647 inmates died in jail during 1993, the date of the last complete count. Illness was the leading cause of death (43 percent), followed by suicide (36 percent) and acquired immune deficiency syndrome (AIDS; 10 percent). Homicides accounted for 3 percent of deaths in jail. The death rate per 100,000 jail inmates has declined by more than 35 percent in ten years, as illustrated in Table 14.3. This is due primarily to the huge increase in new jail construction, which has eliminated bars that made it easy for inmates to commit suicide. New jails have also reduced reliance on cells holding more than one inmate, which are conducive to confrontations between inmates.

The reasons for the doubling of the jail population in ten years are similar to those for the increase in prison populations. The total number of arrests increased 20 percent over the same period, to fourteen million per year. This has had the effect of increasing the numbers of offenders who receive jail sentences. As with prisons, the largest source of growth was drug offenders. One consequence of overcrowding in both state and federal prisons is that nearly 12 percent of all jail inmates are waiting for state or federal authorities to make room for them in prisons, more than triple the number a decade earlier.[43]

TABLE 14.3

Deaths Per 100,000 Inmates in Jail

	NO. OF DEATHS PER 100,000 JAIL INMATES*		
CAUSE	**1983**	**1988**	**1993****
Total	232	199	149
Illness/natural cause (excluding AIDS)	88	82	67
Acquired immune deficiency syndrome	—	20	15
Suicide	129	85	54
Homicide	5	3	4
Other	9	10	9

—Not available.

*To compare years, the number of deaths during each annual period ending June 30 was divided by the average daily population and then multiplied by 100,000.

**Based on the average daily population of jails that reported data on deaths (434,145).

SOURCE: Craig A. Perkins, James J. Stephan, and Allen J. Beck, *Jails and Jail Inmates* (Washington, D.C.: Bureau of Justice Statistics, 1995).

A national survey of jail administrators identified two primary problems: overcrowding and gangs. Despite aggressive jail construction in recent years, many jails are still overcrowded. This is due in part to growing numbers of offenders held in local jails who should be serving their sentences in state or federal prisons. These temporary inmates have taken up the additional cell space gained through new construction. Crowding also makes it difficult to classify inmates appropriately. Like prison administrators, jail administrators stated that improvement is needed in identifying gang members and also in staff training programs on gang control.[44] In response to jail crowding, many states have developed alternatives designed to keep more suspects, defendants, and offenders out of jail. These include electronic monitoring and day reporting centers, which are discussed further in Chapter 15.

Inmate Life

Whether one believes that inmates should be treated harshly or humanely, no one argues that they should be idle or bored. Nevertheless, that is perhaps the most typical condition of inmates in jails and prisons today. They spend most of the day and night in their cells; depending on security level, they may leave the cell to eat (although most jail inmates eat in their cell). Most inmates are allowed to exercise outside their cells for several hours each day. The exercise consists largely of walking, lifting weights, or playing basketball. Most prisoners are assigned a job to do each day, but in most cases the job is menial in nature and lasts for only a few hours. Typical jobs include sweeping and polishing floors, washing dishes, and preparing food. Prisons usually have small libraries, but many prisoners cannot read. Prisoners who seek education or drug or alcohol treatment usually do not have access to it or must wait for long periods before being admitted to programs. Often the progress that inmates make in these programs is

Whether one believes that inmates should be treated harshly or humanely, no one argues that inmates should be idle or bored. There has been criticism of the availability of weight-lifting for inmates because it increases their strength and might be used criminally.

quickly undone. For example, education in conflict resolution skills is undermined when the inmate returns to the general inmate population, where threats and violence are common and there is no inmate or staff support for the educational efforts being made.

Major issues of inmate life can be grouped into eight categories: drugs and treatment, women in prison, AIDs, prisoners' rights, work in prison, prison rule violations, prison gangs, and riots. In the rest of this chapter we will consider each of these issues in turn.

Drug Use and Treatment

An inmate at the Marcy Correctional Facility in New York State relied on visitors to supply him with drugs. Some smuggled drugs into prison in the heels of sneakers. Female friends passed small balloons filled with heroin from their mouths to his when they kissed in the visiting room. He then swallowed the balloons or hid them on his body. Sometimes corrupt prison employees would provide drugs.

There is considerable evidence that drug use is rampant in prisons and jails. Since 1990, twenty-six corrections officers have been charged with smuggling drugs into Rikers Island Jail in New York City. In 1994, a convicted murderer was found dead of a cocaine overdose in his cell at the Great Meadow Correctional Facility in New York. A hypodermic needle was found in his hand. Reports from Mississippi, the District of Columbia, Georgia, and other jurisdictions have found significant drug use in prisons, although such use is clearly prohibited.[45]

Most state departments of corrections deny that drugs are readily available in prison, although they admit that drugs are present. As one corrections official explains, "Unless you searched everyone going in and out, kept all packages out and locked all inmates in their cells for 24 hours a day, you're going to have contraband."[46]

The effort to prevent drug use in prison has been called a "cat-and-mouse" game in which corrections officers resort to strip-searches and unannounced cell searches while prisoners become more inventive at smuggling drugs, using sophisticated techniques such as obtaining liquefied LSD painted on the back of postage stamps. To combat the problem, most states and the federal prisons now use random drug (urine) testing of inmates. Those found using drugs have privileges taken away or are placed in solitary confinement. Because of overcrowding, however, most inmates are tested less than once a year, and therefore little deterrent effect is achieved. Prison officials point to their drug-testing findings to show that fewer than 10 percent of all inmates test positive for drugs.[47] On the other hand, because of the limited scope of this testing a great deal of drug usage is probably missed.

There has always been a high demand for drugs among prisoners. In fact, there are anecdotes of prisoners making a form of wine from fruit juice and other substances long before drugs became widely popular. The increase in very long sentences adds to the feeling of hopelessness, aggravated by the constant fear of forced sex and unprovoked fights in a population of desperate, angry, and frustrated prisoners. This in turn increases the tendency to seek temporary "escape" or relief from the prison environment through drug use.

A large number of inmates exhibit high levels of anger, fear, and frustration *before* their crime and incarceration. This accounts for the high rates of drug use among offenders as well as the fact that drug offenders are the fastest-growing segment of the prison population. More than 60 percent of inmates report regular drug use at some point during their lives, and about a third committed their offense while under the influence of drugs. In fact, 17 percent of inmates committed their offense in order to obtain money to buy drugs.[48]

Effective drug treatment would reduce the demand for drugs among inmates and released prisoners and have long-term impacts on prison drug smuggling and rates of re-offending. Few efforts to accomplish this goal have been effective, however. A review of a small number of successful prison-based drug treatment programs found that they shared several features. Each program had a special source of funds earmarked for drug treatment that could not be put to other uses. This prevented the continual start-up and stoppage of programs that are common in prison settings. All of the successful programs were "guests" of the correctional institution and were not operated by the institution itself. Therefore they could focus on the program and not be concerned with custodial issues. In Delaware, a self-contained treatment environment was established inside a men's maximum security prison for drug-involved offenders. Such a *therapeutic community* model is based on the notion that a person's attitudes, values, and self-esteem must change together with the targeted drug use behavior in order to create lasting change. The self-contained therapeutic community separates the inmates in the program from the drugs and violence that exist elsewhere in the prison. An evaluation of this program found that inmates who completed it were nearly half as likely to remain drug-free and arrest-free after six months than a comparison group of nonparticipating offenders.[49] Other successful programs used a variety of treatment strategies, employed trained social workers and counselors rather than corrections officers, and included training-in-life skills. Contact was maintained with participants after the program ended. Traditional prison-based drug treatment programs were much less likely to have these features.[50]

Four barriers to the success of drug treatment programs for inmates have been identified. They are changes in priorities, limited resources, staff resistance, and prisoner reluctance.[51] Since new administrations often change priorities and spending within prisons, continuity or long-term commitment is never achieved. When funding becomes tight, programs for inmates are often the first thing to disappear from prisons. Resistance by prison staff who do not believe that inmate drug treatment is important can undercut treatment programs through prejudicial treatment of participating inmates and drug treatment staff. Finally, drug-using offenders are often resistant to change, and it takes time to convince them of the benefits of treatment.

Women in Prison

As was noted earlier, the number of women in prison has more than doubled in the past decade. This increase is due to the more severe sentences now available for many crimes and to increased willingness on the part of judges to send women to prison. This situation has far-reaching consequences for prison life. Female inmates closely resemble male inmates in terms of age, race, marital status, and education, but they are much more likely to be serving time for a drug offense (33 percent versus 21 percent for men) and much less likely to be incarcerated for a violent crime (32 percent versus 47 percent for men). Women are also far less likely to have a prior criminal record than their male counterparts.[52]

The growing numbers of women in prison pose some unique challenges. Among these are dealing with the nature of their crimes, their family histories, and child care issues. Women serving a sentence for a violent crime are twice as likely as men to have committed the crime against an intimate or relative. Conversely, half of all victims of male offenders were strangers, whereas only 35 percent of victims of females were strangers. This corresponds with the fact that female inmates are far less likely to have criminal histories than are males. These differences call for different approaches to treatment and custody of female inmates.[53]

Like male inmates, female inmates often grew up in single-parent homes (42 percent) or lived in a foster home or institution (17 percent). Unlike the men, however, the women are more likely to have a family member who has been incarcerated (47 percent versus 37 percent for men) and a parent or guardian who abused alcohol or drugs (34 percent versus 26 percent for men). Most significantly, 43 percent of women inmates were physically or sexually abused in the past (compared to 12 percent of men). For 32 percent of the women inmates, this abuse took place before age eighteen. These data are summarized in Table 14.4. Table 14.4 also indicates that the abuse suffered was evenly divided between physical and sexual abuse. Half of female inmates

TABLE 14.4

Prior Physical or Sexual Abuse* of State Prison Inmates

	PERCENT OF STATE PRISON INMATES		
	TOTAL	FEMALE	MALE
Ever physically or sexually abused before current incarceration			
No	86.1%	56.8%	87.8%
Yes	13.9	43.2	12.2
Before age 18	11.9	31.7	10.7
After age 18	4.2	24.5	3.0
Physically abused	11.3	33.5	10.0
Sexually abused	6.8	33.9	5.3
Number of inmates	700,475	38,109	662,367
Relationship of abuser to inmate**			
Intimate	11.2%	49.8%	3.0%
Spouse/exspouse	6.1	30.5	1.0
Boyfriend/girlfriend	6.6	27.6	2.2
Relative	68.1	56.1	70.6
Parent/guardian	53.7	37.7	57.1
Other relative	22.6	26.5	21.7
Friend/acquaintance	22.8	20.1	23.4
Someone else	21.2	19.6	21.6
Refusal	1.1	1.3	1.1

*Sexual abuse includes fondling, incest, molestation, sodomy, rape, and other types of sexual assault. Detail adds to more than total because some inmates were abused both before and after age 18, or were both sexually and physically abused; inmates may also have reported more than one abuser.

**Based on those inmates who were abused and knew their abuser.

SOURCE: Tracy L. Snell and Danielle C. Morton, *Women in Prison* (Washington, D.C.: Bureau of Justice Statistics, 1994).

The number of women in prison has doubled during the last decade. They are much more likely to be serving time in prison for drug offenses and property crimes than are men.

reported abuse inflicted by an intimate, and 56 percent reported abuse by a relative.[54] The anger and frustration caused by such abuse and neglect are often a factor in assaults that occur within intimate relationships.

A third challenge posed by the increase in numbers of female prisoners is child care issues. More than three-fourths of women in prison have children, two-thirds of whom are under age eighteen. That translates into 56,000 children under age eighteen with mothers in prison. Half of female inmates' children are living with a grandparent, 25 percent live with the other parent, and 10 percent are in foster homes or institutions. Most female inmates have some contact with their children, but 52 percent are never visited by their children, 21 percent never receive mail from them, and 28 percent never receive a telephone call. Contact with their children, if it occurs, is not very frequent.[55]

Efforts to help maintain family contact and supervision of children of inmates might include pre- and postnatal training and care (25 percent of female inmates either are pregnant when they enter prison or have recently given birth). Travel to prison could be provided for inmates' children, and prison visiting areas could be made less inhospitable for children. More prisons could allow very young children to stay with their mothers for a specified period and encourage fathers to take greater responsibility in the lives of both the mothers and their children. According to the superintendent of the Bedford Hills Correctional Facility for women in New York State, we "would do well to invest in programs for drug abusers, for battered women, for incest survivors and for the children of inmates."[56]

AIDS in Prison

Approximately 2.5 percent (about 22,000) of inmates in state and federal prisons are known to be infected with human immune deficiency virus (HIV), which causes AIDS. About 1 percent of inmates have actually contracted AIDS. Another 7,000 jail inmates have HIV, with about 20 percent of them manifesting AIDS symptoms.[57] These figures understate the severity of the problem because testing policies vary in different jurisdictions. The Federal Bureau of Prisons and fifteen states test all inmates for HIV upon admission or release. In most jurisdictions, however, inmates are tested only if they exhibit HIV-related symptoms or if the inmate requests a test. Such requests are uncommon because inmates who test positive for HIV often face discrimination. In Georgia, for example, a 34-year-old inmate was placed in isolation in a city jail. He wanted to mop floors so that his six-month sentence for drunk driving would be reduced one day for each day of work. He was denied this opportunity because he had HIV, and as a result he had to serve two extra months in jail. In Mississippi and Alabama, inmates with HIV are separated from all other prisoners and denied equal access to prison jobs, early release, education, the chapel, and the library. As one inmate stated, "the stress, the depression, the boredom, the hopelessness—it's overwhelming."[58]

Nearly 1,000 prisoners die of AIDS-related diseases each year, accounting for a third of all prison deaths. HIV and AIDS cases in prison have been in the range of 2 to 3 percent throughout the 1990s. Many inmates and staff are afraid that they may contract HIV through fights, sexual contact, or other involuntary exposure to blood or body fluids. The segregation of inmates with HIV reduces these fears. Nevertheless, prison administrators continue to worry that the disease will spread throughout a captive population.

There are three competing perspectives that need to be accounted for in addressing the issue of HIV in prison: those of administrators, inmates, and correctional staff. Administrators must ensure that both staff and inmates are educated about HIV in order to show how the spread of AIDS can be halted through reasonable protective measures. Prison administrators must also provide adequate protection against rape and other assaults within the prison; prisons can be held liable for failures to provide such protection.[59] Mandatory testing of all inmates may be the only way to assess the true extent of the problem and the effectiveness of prevention strategies.

Inmates have a right to medical treatment for AIDS-related illnesses. Treatment is expensive, however, and a number of lawsuits have been filed by inmates claiming inadequate treatment of their medical conditions. The extent of treatment that prisons must provide in these cases remains unclear, although courts have generally upheld special restrictions on inmates with HIV that may interfere with medical treatment when they are based on legitimate health, safety, and security considerations.

It is necessary that the staff be equipped with the information, training, equipment, and security measures required for working with inmates who have HIV. The courts require a "reasonable standard of care" in this regard. On occasion, prison staff refuses assignments that involve HIV or AIDS inmates.[60] This can be prevented with the proper training and equipment.

The fastest-growing segment of the prison population consists of drug offenders. The widespread sharing of hypodermic needles and other unsanitary practices promote the spread of HIV among these inmates. All disease spreads more quickly in a closed environment, but with education and reasonable precautions the spread of HIV within prisons can be controlled.

Prisoners' Rights

An inmate in a Texas prison was a Buddhist, but he was not permitted to use the prison chapel or correspond with his Buddhist religious advisor. When he shared Buddhist religious material with other inmates, he was placed in solitary confinement on a diet of bread and water for two weeks for violating prison rules. The inmate alleged that his First Amendment right to freedom of religion had been violated.

The scope of prisoners' legal rights has been carved out by the courts in a large number of cases. Most of these cases involve alleged violations of the Eighth Amendment prohibition against cruel and unusual punishment. In this section important rights of prisoners under the First and Fourth Amendments are summarized. In every case the issues are the same: What rights does a prisoner surrender as a condition of his or her confinement, and what rights do all individuals have regardless of whether or not they are incarcerated?

In the case of the Buddhist inmate, the Texas Department of Corrections argued that inmates with unconventional religious beliefs should not be guaranteed the right to practice their religion in prison. The U.S. Supreme Court disagreed, noting that although Buddhism may be unconventional in the United States, it was established in 600 B.C., long before Christianity. The Court held that the inmate's First Amendment protection of free exercise of religion was violated.[61] The prison system provided chaplains for the Jewish and Christian faiths, as well as Bibles. By refusing to allow the inmate to practice Buddhism, the Texas Department of Corrections discriminated unfairly against the inmate and violated his First Amendment guarantee of freedom of religion.

In a subsequent case the Court made it clear that there are limits on the freedom to practice religion in prison. Islamic inmates in a New Jersey prison were not permitted to attend a religious service on Friday afternoons. The prison did not permit inmates to attend services or meetings in buildings outside their housing unit unless they had "minimum" security status. Inmates who worked outside the prison were not allowed to return to buildings during the day for security reasons. The U.S. Supreme Court ruled against the inmates stating that because there was a "rational connection to the legitimate governmental interest in institutional order and security," the decision by prison officials was seen as reasonable and did not violate the First Amendment.[62] These cases are typical of court holdings in this area, recognizing the right to express religious belief within the limits imposed by a prison setting.[63]

The Fourth Amendment protects individuals from intrusions by the government without probable cause linking them to a crime. The extent to which inmates continue to enjoy the right to privacy was not clear or uniform until the 1980s. A landmark case began at Bland Correctional Center in Virginia, where two corrections officers conducted a warrantless search of an inmate's cell. The officers discovered a ripped pillow case in the trash basket and charged the inmate with destroying state property. The inmate filed suit, contending that the search of his cell violated the Fourth Amendment and had no purpose other than harassment.

The Supreme Court held in *Hudson v. Palmer* that "society is not prepared to recognize any subjective expectation of privacy that a prisoner might have in his prison cell . . . and the Fourth Amendment . . . does not apply within the confines of the prison cell." If inmates had such constitutional protection in their cells, it would contradict "the concept of incarceration and the needs and objectives of penal institutions" in maintaining custody and security.[64] This ruling makes clear that inmates have no reasonable expectation of privacy in their cells. Therefore, no warrant or probable cause is required for such searches.

These cases illustrate how the Supreme Court has weighed constitutional rights against the demands of running a prison in two important legal areas. It can be seen that the Court is sensitive to the requirements for operating a secure prison, while also attempting to address the appropriate scope of individual protections in the prison environment.

Work in Prison

In a 1981 speech Chief Justice Burger asked corrections agencies to establish "factories with fences" in order to provide inmates with the job skills they would need upon release.[65] This proposal is similar to the Auburn system described earlier, in which prisoners worked in a workshop during the day and slept alone at night. The primary difference is that the Auburn system forbade any conversation among inmates for the duration of their sentence.[66]

Nearly all observers have viewed inmate work favorably. Work can help inmates learn discipline, accountability, and job skills, and can sometimes enable them to earn compensation for victims. Nevertheless, starting in the 1930s and 1940s prison-made products were banned from the open market in response to protests by businesses and labor unions regarding unfair (low wage) competition from inmate labor. In 1979, legislation was passed to restore the relationship between outside businesses and prison labor. Since then, a large number of successful inmate work programs have been created. In Kansas, for example, female inmates from the Topeka Correctional Facility perform housing renovation work in low-income homes. Operation Outward Reach is a nonprofit organization that contracts with five Pennsylvania prisons to provide vocational training in carpentry and masonry. Inmates also perform low-cost construction work for senior citizens and the poor. The Wisconsin Department of Corrections is engaged in the Recycled Mobile Home Project, which rehabilitates homes for the rural homeless and low-income families.[67] There are many other examples of prison and jail work programs that reduce the cost of operating correctional facilities and produce useful products or services.[68]

TABLE 14.5

Work Assignments for Prison Inmates

	PERCENT OF INMATES
Work Assignments*	69
General janitorial	13
Food preparation	13
Maintenance, repair, or construction	9
Grounds and road maintenance	8
Library, barbershop, office, or other service	8
Goods production	4
Farming, forestry, or ranching	4
Laundry	3
Hospital or medical	1
Other	12
No work assignment	31

*Inmates could report more than one work assignment.

SOURCE: Allen Beck et al., *Survey of State Prison Inmates* (Washington, D.C.: Bureau of Justice Statistics, 1993).

Table 14.5 shows that nearly 70 percent of all inmates perform work assignments in prison. Most tasks performed by inmates involve maintenance of the correctional facility itself. These tasks produce savings for the state because it does not have to contract outside firms for services. Only about two thirds of inmates are paid for their work; the average wage is fifty-six cents per hour. Work that involves farming, manufacturing, or other skills accounts for only a small percentage of inmate work assignments. This is due in part to the fact that there are many inmates but comparatively few meaningful work opportunities.

Many businesspeople fear that cheap prison labor will drive down prices and force companies out of business. A Connecticut manufacturer of draperies complained that his sales to the government dropped by 50 percent because of competition from Federal Prison Industries.[69] Federal Prison Industries may bid on any government contract it can fulfill, and it can fulfill contracts more cheaply than most private companies because inmate labor is very cheap. As a result, labor unions are strongly opposed to inmate labor.

Since most states permit inmate labor only to supply government agencies, prisons do not compete against other businesses in the open market. Prison industry produces office furniture, clothing, textiles, bedding, electronic equipment, gloves, and optics.[70] Nevertheless, companies that do a great deal of business with the government, supplying products or services that Prison Industries can also provide, have difficulty competing. On the other hand, federal inmates who are employed in joint ventures with private firms have paid nearly two million dollars in victim compensation, two million dollars in family support payments, more than three million dollars in taxes, and five million dollars toward payment of the cost of their incarceration.[71] An appropriate balance among preparing inmates for release, having inmates offset the costs of their incarceration, and competing fairly with the private sector has yet to be achieved.

Violations of Prison Rules

A national survey of state prisons found that 53 percent of inmates have been charged with violating prison rules at least once. Examples of prison rules include maintaining a neat cell; rules for dress; restrictions on noise, foul language, and littering; and appropriate response to commands, among many others. Rule violations in prison have not changed significantly over the course of a decade.[72] This translates into an average of 1.5 rule violations per year per inmate.

Such a high rate of violations has led to questions regarding the appropriateness of prison rules, which are designed to maintain order and security. Prison administrators point to the fact that inmates outnumber corrections staff by a ratio of three to one and that numerous assaults on corrections officers have occurred.[73] Detailed rules, such as those that prohibit extortion and assault, are also needed to protect inmates from one another. Inmates argue that some prison rules are petty or not widely known and serve as a means for harassing inmates. Rules that prohibit horseplay and failing to follow sanitary regulations are examples.

The Supreme Court has held that inmates are entitled to due process (i.e., a hearing) and that some evidence of violation must be presented in cases in which penalties, such as solitary confinement, are possible.[74] Inmates do not have the right to counsel or to cross-examination of witnesses against them in prison disciplinary hearings.[75] More than 90 percent of inmates charged with prison rule violations are found guilty.

Disciplinary procedures vary from one state to another. Penalties range from a notation of the violation in the inmate's file to a disciplinary hearing within the prison. The warden usually serves as the final avenue of appeal in these matters. If the rule violation is also a crime, the offense may be referred for prosecution. This is usually reserved for the most serious violations. As Table 14.6 indicates, 31 percent of prison rule violators were placed in solitary confinement or otherwise separated from other prisoners. This was the most commonly imposed penalty for prison rule violations. The second most common penalty was loss of "good time," or credit toward early

TABLE 14.6

Sanctions Imposed on Prison Rule Violators

	INMATES WHO RECEIVED PUNISHMENT (%)*	
PUNISHMENT	**ALL RULE VIOLATORS**	**TOTAL INMATE POPULATION**
Solitary confinement or segregation	30.9	14.8
Loss of good time	25.0	12.0
Confinement to own cell or quarters	15.8	7.6
Loss of entertainment or recreational privileges	15.4	7.4
Loss of commissary or store privileges	13.1	6.3
Reprimand	9.4	4.5
Extra work	8.5	4.0
Loss of job assignment	7.0	3.4
Loss of visiting privileges	6.3	3.0
Higher custody level within facility	5.8	2.8
Transfer to another facility	5.6	2.7
No punishment or punishment suspended	6.7	3.2

*The percent of inmates who received each type of punishment sums to more than 100 percent because some inmates received more than one punishment for an infraction. The table excludes approximately 3 percent of all inmates who received punishment in the form of fines, fees, or restitution requirements or who lost rights to participate in drug, alcohol, vocational, or educational programs and 1 percent for whom type of punishment was not reported.

SOURCE: James Stephan, *Prison Rule Violators* (Washington, D.C.: Bureau of Justice Statistics, 1989).

Media and Criminal Justice

AMERICAN ME

The 1992 film *American Me* encompasses thirty years of Chicano gang life in eastern Los Angeles, but the core of its story is actually about a prison where the inmates simply continue gang activities as an offshoot of the outside world. The plot revolves around a young man named Santana, who as a teenager becomes involved in a street gang. A first break-in results in an arrest that lands Santana in reform school, where he gets into trouble again and is sent directly to Folsom Prison.

The movie covers Santana's eighteen years in prison, sparing the viewer no detail of the horrific realities of life behind bars. There, Santana soon finds himself the leader of the Latino gang, a position that enables him to run a drug operation on the outside. The movie presents this as a norm, indicating that prisoners can actually control drug traffic and that prison officials ignore such truths. The specific methods of the smuggling operation are graphically presented, as are the gang rapes and other violent necessities of prison life—such as burning prisoners alive or strangling relatives. The scenes are rife with the wretched energy of desperate prisoners, who have nothing to lose by committing crime while serving their sentences.

Santana creates a gang culture that is predictably at war with other groups such as the Italian Mafia and the black street gangs. He is a "big" man in the prison, well known and respected by Latinos on the outside, and yet in his Chicano pride he understands the hopelessness of the cyclical nature of gang activity. Santana realizes that an entire Latino generation is being lost to drugs, guns, and crime, but believes this is a result of a crumbling society, not racism. He notices that prison killings that were once carefully planned retaliations have become mundane murders for the sake of a quick adrenaline rush. He had entered the Chicano gang life on principle, a product of the Zoot Suit riots of the 1940s. As he nears his release date, however, Santana sees that young Chicanos are being recruited and used by gangs as a means of criminal warfare, not ethnic pride. As older gang members perish in prison as the result of such gang violence, new Chicano youth are constantly being incarcerated, leaving Santana to wonder at the worth of it all.

Upon release, Santana finds that life on the outside is so foreign that the viewer wonders if society will allow him to live a reformed life. He returns to the barrio to find his younger brother and neighbor's sons being destroyed by the same gang culture he helped to create.

The movie is disturbing in its success at conveying the institutionalized mentality of inmates: Prison is a place that creates, not cures, criminality. Based on true events, *American Me* is a stomach-wrenching depiction of prison life and gang violence. Its graphic realities of prison life will cause viewers to reassess the correctional settings that incarcerate people in a violent and drug-infested world where only the most hardened criminals survive their sentences.

MEDIA AND CRIMINAL JUSTICE QUESTION

If prisons do not rehabilitate offenders and may make them worse, what would you recommend that the prison system do to change this situation?

release for good behavior, followed by lost recreational privileges or confinement to one's cell for some period of time.

Most rule violations are committed by inmates who have been in prison from one to two years. Inmates who had served five years or more had the lowest incidence of violations. This is associated with age; young inmates (ages eighteen to twenty-four) were charged with violations far more than inmates in any other age group. Inmates with a history of drug use and more extensive criminal histories also were more likely to be charged with rule violations.[76] In sum, younger inmates with a long criminal history and a history of drug use are most likely to violate prison rules. This does not bode well for the future, as increasing numbers of young drug offenders are being sentenced to long prison terms with little possibility for early release (as discussed in Chapter 13). It remains to be seen whether the combination of long sentences, large numbers of drug-involved offenders, and prison overcrowding combine to create prison unrest on a large scale.

Prison Gangs

As was noted earlier, surveys of jail and prison administrators have found that identifying gang members and training staff how to handle gangs are among their most pressing concerns. This issue of gangs in prisons first arose during the late 1980s, when cocaine and crack use became widespread and gangs formed to engage in narcotics trafficking.[77] Twenty percent of all male inmates are believed to be gang members, compared to only 3 percent of female inmates.[78] More than half of all adult state correctional facilities report that racial conflicts are a problem and that these conflicts are aggravated by gang affiliations. Institutions with a high level of racial disturbances have been found to have a high rate of gang-related disturbances as well.[79]

Table 14.7 lists the gangs that are among the most common in prisons. Members of the Crips, Black Gangster Disciples, and Bloods/Piru gangs are among the inmates in more than 40 percent of state correctional institutions.

Many gangs listed in Table 14.7 are primarily drug-trafficking organizations, and their members are part of the fastest-growing segment of the prison population, those incarcerated for drug-related crimes. These inmates, not surprisingly, often engage in drug trafficking within the prison. Many are also involved in gambling, protection, and extortion rackets.

Current methods for dealing with prison gangs include formal staff training, but this training is not very extensive. A majority of jails and prisons have rules that prohibit gang recruitment, but as noted earlier, it is difficult to identify gang members upon admission to prison. Better communication among police, prosecutors, and corrections officials and improved screening would help to solve this problem. Many state prisons do not take gang membership into account as part of their inmate classification system,[80] although some states have enacted policies that segregate known gang members to high security "supermax" prisons. These high security prisons are generally reserved for those who have committed a serious assault while confined. Placement in one of these supermax facilities based on the status of gang affiliation rather than because of an actual assault has been criticized on grounds of unfairness.[81]

When it comes to dealing with existing gangs in prisons, most wardens do not believe that solitary confinement or segregation is effective in controlling gang members. Many wardens believe that a central federal facility could handle the gang problem more effectively. Currently they rely on transfers of gang members within the state prison system in an attempt to control the proliferation of gangs behind bars. Most troubling is the fact that 80 percent of prison administrators report that "gang members generally have a stronger affiliation with their gang after serving time."[82] The reason for the strengthening of gang ties in prison is that inmates have more opportunities to meet gang leaders and advance in the gang hierarchy there than on the street, where competition is greater. It appears that as long as drug trafficking is controlled by gangs, imprisoning gang members disrupts but does not end gang activity.

TABLE 14.7

Gangs Most Frequently Cited by Prison Officials as among the Top Three in State Correctional Facilities

GANG	PERCENT
Crips (various factions)	15.4
Black Gangster Disciples	13.9
Bloods/Piru factions	11.7
Vice Lord factions	7.1
Aryan Brotherhood	6.8
Latin King factions	4.5

SOURCE: George W. Knox et al., "Preliminary Results of the 1995 Adult Corrections Survey," *Journal of Gang Research*, vol. 3 (Winter 1996), pp. 27–63.

Prison Violence

The number of violent incidents in prison has increased sharply in recent years. At the Atlanta Federal Penitentiary, for example, five inmate murders were com-

TABLE 14.8

Key Factors in Eight Prison Riots

INSTITUTION	DURATION	NO. OF HOSTAGES	METHOD OF RESOLUTION
Kirkland Correctional Institution	6 hours	22	Ultimatum and riot squad
U.S. Penitentiary, Atlanta, Georgia	11 days	More than 100	Negotiations
Mack Alford Correctional Center	3 days	8	Negotiations and "waiting" strategy
Coxsackie Correctional Facility	14 hours	5	Negotiations
Idaho State Correctional Institution	1 day	None	Ultimatum and riot squad
Pennsylvania State Correctional Institution at Camp Hill	3 days (two riots)	First riot: 8 Second riot: 18	First riot: negotiations Second riot: State Police Force
Arizona Sate Prison Complex (Cimarron Unit)	About 1 hour	None	Immediate force by riot squad
Federal Correctional Institution, Talladega	10 days	11	Negotiations used and abandoned in favor of planned tactical strike

SOURCE: Bert Useem et al., *Resolution of Prison Riots* (Washington, D.C.: National Institute of Justice, 1995).

mitted in only sixteen months during the mid-1990s. The numbers of assaults on federal corrections officers have increased throughout the prison system. Prison officials blame overcrowding and mandatory sentences that leave inmates with the feeling that they have nothing to lose because their sentences are so long to begin with. As the president of the Southern Christian Leadership Conference put it, "These prisons are powder kegs waiting to blow. Anytime you take away hope, that leads to despair and desperate people will do desperate things."[83] Prisons are susceptible to uprisings because inmates outnumber staff by a three-to-one margin, as was noted earlier. In addition, many prisons are old and inmates often move throughout the facility during the day, so that the ability to lock an entire cellblock of inmates away from staff is not always available when trouble arises.

During the 1980s, at least eight prison riots occurred. These are summarized in Table 14.8. The riots lasted from one hour to eleven days, and most involved hostage-taking. At Kirkland Correctional Institution in South Carolina, inmates seized control of the unit holding the most violent inmates. They climbed the fence around it and used construction tools left on the grounds to release seven hundred inmates. A riot squad responded and was able to end the disturbance in six hours. On the other hand, the Atlanta Federal Penitentiary had an uprising that lasted eleven days and involved more than one hundred hostages. This riot, which began when the government announced that 2,500 Cubans being held there would be sent back to Cuba, was resolved through extensive negotiations.

A study sponsored by the National Institute of Justice analyzed these eight riots and made a set of recommendations regarding prison riot plans and prevention strategies. These are summarized in Table 14.9. Clearly defined lines of authority in the command structure, clear guidelines on the use of force, interagency cooperation, and training programs were seen as the

TABLE 14.9

Elements in Handling Prison Riots

Findings: On the basis of an in-depth examination of eight disturbances, the study concluded that proactive planning and preparation along with reactive problem solving is the most effective approach to prison riot resolution. A prison's riot plan should include:

- A command structure with well-defined lines of authority
- Clear guidelines on the use of force, including staff and weapons assignments
- Interagency cooperation terms that specify the roles of such units as the State Police and the local fire department
- Training programs that address tactical strategies and mental readiness for emergencies

Strategies to prevent and deal with riots must address many factors including:

- Maintaining supervision of experienced staff members who follow sound security practices
- Ensuring the security of the physical plant and equipment
- Discerning the signs of a probable riot from false clues and relaying reliable information up the chain of command
- Selecting the most appropriate means of resolving a riot: use of force, negotiations, or a combination of tactics
- Using strategies that range from immediate use of force to waiting until inmate leaders are ready to negotiate
- Addressing issues of staff morale and emotional support after a riot ends
- Incorporating the lessons learned from experiences with disturbances into revised riot plans

SOURCE: Bert Useem et al., *Resolution of Prison Riots* (Washington, D.C.: National Institute of Justice, 1995).

most important elements in responding to a riot situation. Long-term prevention strategies include supervision by experienced staff, sound security practices, intelligence information, selection of appropriate strategies (i.e., negotiation versus force), and addressing staff morale after a riot has occurred.[84]

The frequency of prison riots continued to increase in the 1990s.[85] In 1993, riots occurred in three federal prisons over the crack cocaine law that imposes mandatory ten-year, no-parole sentences for possession of only fifty grams of crack. In 1995, there were uprisings in prisons in Alabama, Illinois, Pennsylvania, and Tennessee in which twelve corrections officers were injured and millions of dollars in damage was done.[86] Twenty-one percent of state prison administrators reported that a riot occurred in their facility during 1995.[87] The need for greater preparedness and appropriate responses to prison riots is apparent. The U.S. Supreme Court has held that the shooting of a prisoner without warning in an effort to suppress a prison riot is not cruel and unusual.[88] Riot situations that are handled badly, such as the one in Attica in 1971 that resulted in the death of ten corrections officers and twenty-nine convicts, usually involve immediate forceful intervention. Most prison disturbances today are handled with more patience because the inmates remain locked inside and a quick resolution is not needed. Negotiations defuse anger over a period of hours and days, resulting in both inmates and staff being less likely to engage in further violence. Also, recriminations and lawsuits emanating from violent responses to inmate uprisings last for many years after the incident, making it difficult to implement new prison procedures without constant reminders of the past.[89]

Critical Thinking EXERCISE

A Case of HIV Discrimination?

Shannon Weatherford served about two years in prison for a burglary she committed in Texas. Before being released she was transferred to a prerelease center, where she dressed in street clothes, took a computer course, worked in the warden's office, and was several weeks away from completing a drug rehabilitation program. She had unlimited access to a pay phone. Then she tested positive for HIV.

Weatherford was immediately placed with other HIV inmates and transferred back to a regular prison. There she wore prison clothes, worked on a prison hog farm, and was ordered to complete another drug rehabilitation program that would last ten months but would not begin for another six months. Telephone contact with the outside was limited to one five-minute call every three months. Her family visits were reduced in length by half, and she was no longer permitted to wear makeup. Prison officials claimed that all females demonstrating symptoms of HIV are transferred to that prison.

When Weatherford went up for parole, it was denied because she had been moved to a new correctional institution. Weatherford claims that she is "the picture of health," and has not seen a doctor since she arrived at the new prison.

Critical Thinking Questions

1. Is Weatherford being punished for being HIV positive?
2. What would your opinion be if you were a prison administrator?
3. Does the inmate have any valid legal claim for unfair treatment?

SOURCE: Dennis Cauchon, "AIDS in Prison: Locked Up and Locked Out," *USA Today* (March 31, 1995), p. 6.

Critical Thinking EXERCISE

The Elderly Inmate

Willie Coleman has been in prison in South Carolina for nearly fifty years for killing his wife. At eighty years of age, he has heart problems and high blood pressure. He has not had a visitor since 1965. There are more than 10,000 prisoners aged sixty-five or older in the United States, a number that has doubled in a decade as a result of changes in sentencing and release policy.[A]

The average maximum federal prison sentence has increased by more than five years over the last decade. The average prison sentence for drug offenses has more than doubled over that period.[B] The percentage of their sentences served by inmates before release has also increased steadily in recent years as states and the federal government have shifted to determinate sentencing systems and the abolition of parole release.[C] It is predicted that by the year 2010 one third of prison inmates will be fifty-one years of age or older.[D]

As the inmate population ages, there is concern about the higher health care costs that older people incur. Some have suggested releasing elderly offenders early, but victims oppose early release; moreover, long-term elderly inmates often have no place to go upon release. They have no family members who would be willing to take care of them, and they are too old to compete in the work force. In essence, they have aged out of their crime-prone years, passed middle age, and entered their retirement years, yet are still in prison. Prisons are having difficulty in finding private care facilities that will take these inmates when they are eligible for parole. The result is a large number of elderly inmates who have been in prison for much of their lives, whose sentences are ending, but who have no place to go.

Critical Thinking Questions

1. A person is incarcerated for twenty or thirty years and paroled at age sixty-five. The inmate has no money and no one to take him or her in. What would you do as a corrections administrator?
2. Who should pay for medical care for inmates who require heart surgery, expensive medication, or help with physical or mental disabilities during their prison terms?
3. What is a possible long-term solution to these problems?

Notes

[A]Tom Watson, "Prisons' Graying Inmates Exact a Price," *USA Today* (March 17, 1995), p. 12.

[B]Allen J. Beck and Darrell K. Gilliard, *Prisoners in 1994* (Washington, D.C.: Bureau of Justice Statistics, 1995).

[C]Lawrence A. Greenfield, *Prison Sentences and Time Served for Violence* (Washington, D.C.: Bureau of Justice Statistics, 1995).

[D]Connie L. Neeley, Laura Addison, and Delores Craig-Moreland, "Addressing the Needs of Elderly Offenders," *Corrections Today,* vol. 59 (August 1997), pp. 120–4.

Summary

CORRECTIONAL INSTITUTIONS IN THE UNITED STATES

- Before the invention of the prison, corporal punishment was the primary method of punishment of criminals.
- Incarceration was used for poor offenders who could not afford to pay fines but whose offenses were not serious enough to deserve corporal punishment.
- The Pennsylvania system of incarceration promoted repentance through solitary confinement.
- The Auburn system emphasized labor and meditation.
- Various attempts to encourage education within prisons have been unsuccessful, and today prisons lack a clear philosophical purpose.

TYPES OF PRISONS

- Prisons are classified according to level of custody: maximum security, medium security, and minimum security.
- The assignment of an offender to an institution at a particular level of custody depends largely on whether the conviction was for a violent crime.

WHO IS IN PRISON?

- The number of people in prisons has grown dramatically in recent decades, resulting in overcrowding.
- The proportion of prisoners who are women is growing rapidly.
- Prisoners tend to be poorly educated and to come from single-parent households where alcohol or drugs were used. Many were physically or sexually abused and have family members who have been incarcerated.

THE OPERATION OF PRISONS: CUSTODY OR REFORM?

- A number of court cases have been brought by prisoners who allege that certain conditions of imprisonment constitute cruel and unusual punishment.
- Although many people believe that prisons should not only punish offenders but also deter crime, the evidence shows that imprisonment does not deter offenders from committing further crimes upon release.

JAILS

- Jails are operated by counties and municipalities. They hold inmates awaiting trial and those serving sentences of one year or less.
- The jail population has doubled in the last ten years.

INMATE LIFE

- Drug use is prohibited in prisons yet is widespread.
- Many offenders who use drugs in prison were convicted of drug law violations or used drugs before being convicted on some other charge.
- Drug treatment programs in prisons have had little success.

- The growing numbers of women in prison pose challenges related to the nature of their crimes, their family histories, and child care issues.
- All inmates are tested for HIV. Those who test positive often face discrimination.
- The Supreme Court has heard cases involving prisoners' rights in the areas of free exercise of religion and the right to privacy.
- Nearly all observers have viewed inmate work favorably, but many businesspeople fear that cheap prison labor will drive down prices and force companies out of business.
- The Supreme Court has held that inmates are entitled to due process in cases of violation of prison rules.
- Most rule violations are committed by younger inmates who have been in prison from one to two years, have a history of drug use, and have a long criminal history.
- Twenty percent of all male inmates are believed to be gang members. However, it is difficult to identify gang members upon admission to prison.

PRISON VIOLENCE

- The number of violent incidents in prison has increased sharply in recent years.
- The National Institute of Justice has made several recommendations regarding prison riot plans and prevention strategies. They include clearly defined lines of authority in the command structure, clear guidelines on the use of force, interagency cooperation, and training programs.

Key Terms

Pennsylvania system
Auburn system
maximum security
medium security
minimum security
penitentiaries
correctional institutions
metropolitan correctional centers (detention centers)

Questions for Review and Discussion

1. What were the origins of the concept of incarceration?
2. What are the three main types of prisons?
3. What are the most typical characteristics of prison inmates?
4. What functions are performed by jails?
5. Why is drug use pervasive in prisons, and what factors interfere with efforts to prevent it?
6. What are the unique challenges associated with the growing numbers of women in prison?
7. What issues are raised by the presence of HIV and AIDS in prisons?
8. How has the Supreme Court ruled in major cases involving prisoners' rights?
9. What are the advantages and disadvantages of prison labor?
10. What are the implications of the presence of gang members in prisons?
11. What actions could be taken to prevent prison riots?

Notes

[1]Paul W. Keve, "Old Story," *Richmond Times-Dispatch*, July 6, 1986, pp. F1–2.
[2]Ibid.
[3]Luke Owen Pike, *A History of Crime in England* (Montclair, NJ: Patterson Smith, 1968); Harry Elmer Barnes, *The Story of Punishment* (Montclair, NJ: Patterson Smith, 1972).

[4]Herbert A. Johnson and Nancy Travis Wolfe, *History of Criminal Justice,* 2nd ed. (Cincinnati: Anderson Publishing, 1996), p. 127.
[5]Ibid., p. 128.
[6]Gustave de Beaumont and Alexis de Tocqueville, *On the Penitentiary System in the United States and Its Application in France* (1833) (Carbondale: Southern Illinois University Press, 1979), pp. 39–40.
[7]Robert Johnson, *Hard Time: Understanding and Reforming the Prison,* 2nd ed. (Belmont, CA: Wadsworth, 1996), p. 29.
[8]Ibid., p. 41.
[9]Lawrence M. Friedman, *Crime and Punishment in American History* (New York: Basic Books, 1993), pp. 160–1.
[10]David J. Rothman, *The Discovery of the Asylum* (Boston: Little, Brown, 1971).
[11]Ernest van den Haag, *Punishing Criminals* (New York: Basic Books, 1975).
[12]Gregory L. Hershberger, "To the Max: Supermax Facilities Provide Prison Administrators with More Security Options," *Corrections Today,* vol. 60 (February 1998), pp. 54–8.
[13]Dennis Cauchon, "The Alcatraz of the Rockies," *USA Today* (November 16, 1994), p. 6.
[14]James J. Stephan, *Census of State and Federal Correctional Facilities, 1995* (Washington, D.C.: Bureau of Justice Statistics, 1997).
[15]Darrell K. Gilliard and Allen J. Beck, *Prison and Jail Inmates at Midyear 1997* (Washington, D.C.: Bureau of Justice Statistics, 1998); Allen Beck et al., *Survey of State Prison Inmates* (Washington, D.C.: Bureau of Justice Statistics, 1993), p. 28.
[16]Ibid.
[17]Fox Butterfield, "Punitive Damages; Crime Keeps on Falling, But Prisons Keep on Filling," *The New York Times* (September 28, 1997), p. 1.
[18]Ibid.
[19]Allen J. Beck et al., *Correctional Populations in the United States* (Washington, D.C.: Bureau of Justice Statistics, 1997), p. 6.
[20]Ibid., p. 96.
[21]Christopher J. Mumola and Allen J. Beck, *Prisoners in 1996* (Washington, D.C.: Bureau of Justice Statistics, 1997), p. 12.
[22]Stephanie Minor-Harper, *State and Federal Prisoners, 1925–85* (Washington, D.C.: Bureau of Justice Statistics, 1986).
[23]Beck, *Correctional Populations in the United States,* p. v.
[24]Patrick A. Langan and Jodi M. Brown, *Felony Sentences in the United States* (Washington, D.C.: Bureau of Justice Statistics, 1997).
[25]Ibid., p. 7.
[26]Gilliard and Beck, p. 4.
[27]Beck et al., *Survey of State Prison Inmates.*
[28]Ibid., pp. 7–9.
[29]Ibid., p. 16.
[30]*Rhodes v. Chapman,* 452 U.S. 337 (1981).
[31]429 U.S. 97 (1976).
[32]*Wilson v. Seiter,* 59 U.S. 4671 (1991).
[33]Beck et al., *Survey of State Prison Inmates,* p. 11.
[34]Don M. Gottfredson, "Prison is Not Enough," *Corrections Today,* vol. 57 (August 1995), pp. 16–20.
[35]"Just Deserts: Prisons in America," *The Economist,* vol. 342 (March 15, 1997), p. 33.
[36]John Dilulio, *Governing Prisons: A Comparative Study of Correctional Management* (New York: The Free Press, 1987).
[37]Michael D. Reisig, "Rates of Disorder in Higher-Custody State Prisons: A Comparative Analysis of Managerial Practices," *Crime & Delinquency,* vol. 44 (April 1998), pp. 229–45.
[38]M. Colvin, *The Penitentiary in Crisis: From Accommodation to Riot in New Mexico* (Albany: SUNY Press, 1992).

[39]Tom McEwen, *National Assessment Program: Wardens and State Commissioners of Corrections* (Washington, D.C.: National Institute of Justice, 1995).

[40]Mark Mayfield and Tom Watson, "Jail Deaths Spark Call for Probe," *USA Today* (February 19, 1993), p. 3.

[41]Craig A. Perkins, James J. Stephan, and Allen J. Beck, *Jails and Jail Inmates* (Washington, D.C.: Bureau of Justice Statistics, 1995), p. 4; Darrell K. Gilliard and Allen J. Beck, *Prison and Jail Inmates, 1995* (Washington, D.C.: Bureau of Justice Statistics, 1996).

[42]Ibid., p. 10.

[43]Ibid., p. 14.

[44]Tom McEwen, *National Assessment Program: Survey of Jail Administrators* (Washington, D.C.: National Institute of Justice, 1995).

[45]Matthew Purdy, "Bars Don't Stop Flow of Drugs into the Prisons," *The New York Times* (July 2, 1995), p. 1.

[46]Ibid., p. 28.

[47]Ibid.

[48]Beck et al., *Survey of State Prison Inmates,* pp. 21–2.

[49]James A. Inciardi, *A Corrections-Based Continuum of Effective Drug Abuse Treatment* (Washington, D.C.: National Institute of Justice, 1996).

[50]Marcia R. Chaiken, *Prison Programs for Drug-Involved Offenders* (Washington, D.C.: National Institute of Justice, 1989).

[51]Ibid., pp. 3–4.

[52]Tracy L. Snell and Danielle C. Morton, *Women in Prison* (Washington, D.C.: Bureau of Justice Statistics, 1994).

[53]Barbara A. Koons, John D. Burrow, Merry Morash, and Tim Bynum, "Expert and Offender Perceptions of Program Elements Linked to Successful Outcomes for Incarcerated Women," *Crime & Delinquency,* vol. 43 (October 1997), pp. 512–42.

[54]Ibid., p. 5.

[55]Ibid., p. 7.

[56]George J. Church, "The View from Behind Bars," *Time* (Fall 1990), pp. 20–2.

[57]Peter M. Brien and Caroline Wolf Harlow, *HIV in Prisons and Jails* (Washington, D.C.: Bureau of Justice Statistics, 1995).

[58]Dennis Cauchon, "AIDS in Prison: Locked Up and Locked Out," *USA Today* (March 31, 1995), p. 6.

[59]Marianne Takas and Theodore M. Hammett, *Legal Issues Affecting Offenders and Staff* (Washington, D.C.: National Institute of Justice, 1989).

[60]Ibid., p. 5.

[61]*Cruz v. Beto,* 405 U.S. 319 (1972).

[62]*O'Lone v. Estate of Shabazz,* 107 S. Ct. 2400 (1987).

[63]See *Howard v. Smith,* 365 F. 2d 28 (4th Cir. 1966); *Hill v. Blackwell,* 774 F. 2d 338 (8th Cir. 1985).

[64]*Hudson v. Palmer,* 468 U.S. 517 (1984).

[65]Warren E. Burger, "More Warehouses or Factories with Fences?," *New England Journal of Prison Law,* vol. 8 (Winter 1982), pp. 111–20.

[66]David J. Rothman, *The Discovery of the Asylum* (Boston: Little, Brown, 1971), p. 82.

[67]Lee Roy Black, "Exemplary Programs Make All Participants Winners," *Corrections Today* (August 1996), pp. 84–7.

[68]George E. Sexton, *Work in American Prisons: Joint Ventures with the Private Sector* (Washington, D.C.: National Institute of Justice, 1995); Rod Miller, George E. Sexton, and Victor J. Jacobsen, *Making Jails Productive* (Washington, D.C.: National Institute of Justice, 1991).

[69]Harry Maier, "Some Businesses Fear Prison Labor," *USA Today* (January 10, 1991), p. 12B.

[70]Aaron Epstein, "Study Shows Benefits of Prison Work Programs," *The Buffalo News* (December 26, 1991), p. 8.

[71]Sexton, p. 13.
[72]James Stephan, *Prison Rule Violators* (Washington, D.C.: Bureau of Justice Statistics, 1989).
[73]Frank Green, "Guards Say Reform Endangers Lives," *Richmond Times-Dispatch* (March 27, 1997), p. 1.
[74]*Wolff v. McDonnell*, 418 U.S. 539 (1974); *Superintendent, Massachusetts Correctional Institution, Walpole v. Hill*, 37 Cr. L. 3107 (1985).
[75]*Baxter v. Palmigiano*, 425 U.S. 308 (1976).
[76]Stephan, *Prison Rule Violators*, pp. 3–4.
[77]Jay S. Albanese and Robert D. Pursley, *Crime in America: Some Existing and Emerging Issues* (Upper Saddle River, NJ: Prentice Hall, 1993), pp. 200–23.
[78]George W. Knox et al., "Preliminary Results of the 1995 Adult Corrections Survey," *Journal of Gang Research*, vol. 3 (Winter 1996), pp. 27–63.
[79]Ibid., p. 39.
[80]Ibid., p. 47.
[81]Scott N. Tachiki, "Indeterminate Sentences in Supermax Prisons Based Upon Gang Affiliations," *California Law Review*, vol. 83 (July 1995), pp. 1115–49.
[82]Ibid., p. 37; George W. Knox, *An Introduction to Gangs* (Bristol, IN: Wyndham Hall Press, 1994).
[83]Tom Watson, "High-Security Prisons are 'Waiting to Blow'," *USA Today* (January 26, 1995), p. 4.
[84]Bert Useem, Camille Graham Camp, George M. Camp, and Renie Dugan, *Resolution of Prison Riots* (Washington, D.C.: National Institute of Justice, 1995).
[85]Steve Marshall, "Nine Guards Injured in Ohio Prison Riot," *USA Today* (April 12, 1993), p. 10; Paul Leavitt, "Five Montana Inmates Killed in Uprising," *USA Today* (September 23, 1991), p. 3; Dianne Barth and Roger Neumann, "New York Inmates Hold Three Hostages," *USA Today* (May 29, 1991), p. 3.
[86]Kevin Johnson, "Rioting Inmates Locked Away," *USA Today* (October 23, 1995), p. 2.
[87]Knox, "Preliminary Results of the 1995 Adult Corrections Survey," p. 42.
[88]*Whitley v. Albers*, 106 S. Ct. 1078 (1986).
[89]Bruce Porter, "Terror on an Eight-Hour Shift," *The New York Times Magazine* (November 26, 1995), p. 42; Bruce Frankel, "Attica Inmates' Suit to Begin," *USA Today* (September 9, 1991), p. 3.

For Further Reading

Charles P. Cozic, ed., *America's Prisons: Opposing Viewpoints* (San Diego, CA: Greenhaven Press, 1997).

John Irwin and James Austin, *It's About Time: America's Imprisonment Binge*, 2nd ed. (Belmont, CA: Wadsworth, 1997).

Jerome Miller, *Last One Over the Wall: The Massachusetts Experiment in Closing Reform Schools* (Columbus: Ohio State University Press, 1993).

chapter fifteen

Corrections in the Community

To punish and not prevent, is to labour at the pump, and leave open the leak.

THOMAS FULLER
(1654–1734)

What should be done with a misdemeanor offender who commits a nonviolent offense? Vandalism, public drunkenness, disorderly conduct, and all the other lesser crimes against public order and property certainly deserve attention, but *how much* attention should they be given by the criminal justice system? Should the punishment be jail time? A fine? Something else?

These questions are not new. In 1841, a Boston bootmaker named John Augustus raised the same issues. A public drunk was sentenced to jail, but Augustus intervened by posting the man's bail on the promise he would stop drinking. From that point on, Augustus acted as a "private angel and guardian of men convicted of crime." By the time of his death in 1859, he

CHAPTER OUTLINE

had posted bail for 2,000 convicts.[1] His idea that a middle ground should exist between jail and freedom formed the basis for the invention of probation in the late 1800s. Today this idea seems little more than common sense and has been adopted by every state.

community corrections
Sanctions that are *alternatives to incarceration* in jail or prison (such as monetary penalties, probation, intensive supervision, and home confinement and electronic monitoring), or supervision in the community *after a sentence of incarceration* has been served (such as parole, work release, furloughs, and halfway houses).

This middle ground, known as **community corrections,** has since grown to encompass two different types of sanctions:

1. Sanctions that are *alternatives to incarceration* in jail or prison, such as monetary penalties, probation, intensive supervision, and home confinement and electronic monitoring.
2. Supervision in the community *after a sentence of incarceration* has been served. Here the goal is to promote a smooth transition from confinement to freedom. Parole, work release, furloughs, and halfway houses fall into this category.

This chapter examines each of these forms of community corrections from the perspective of the offender, potential victims, and the goals of the criminal justice system. While everyone agrees that prisons are expensive, do these other forms of criminal sanction work effectively in protecting the community and holding offenders accountable?

Sanctions in Lieu of Incarceration

It can be argued that *community corrections* is a contradiction in terms. The argument goes like this: The two primary purposes of corrections are to punish offenders and to protect the public. Allowing offenders to serve their sentences in the community violates both of these purposes because nonprison sentences do not provide "enough" punishment and create the risk of further offenses by criminals who are not incarcerated. Responses to this argument focus on either economics or rehabilitation:

1. Imprisonment is the most severe and expensive type of criminal sanction, and therefore should be reserved for offenders who commit the most serious crimes.
2. The vast majority of offenders commit nonviolent crimes and will eventually be released from prison. Imprisonment does little to change offenders for the better, so in the long run public protection is best assured by reforming criminals. Community-based alternatives to imprisonment are the best way to accomplish this.

Both arguments are correct, but are not generally accepted by the public, which believes that imprisonment is necessary if society is to be protected.[2] The factor most responsible for the dramatic growth in community corrections in recent years has not been a change of heart on the part of the public. If anything, public views on crime, criminals, and punishment have hardened. Instead, the dramatic growth in arrests and prison populations, combined with the soaring costs of building new prisons and operating them, has led to more careful consideration of community corrections.[3] One survey asked several hundred residents how they would sentence twenty convicted offenders, and virtually all thought that prison was appropriate. After the costs of incarceration and available alternatives to prison were explained, however, many offenders were "resentenced" to community sanctions.[4]

Alternatives to incarceration take several forms. Among these are monetary penalties, probation, intensive supervision, and home confinement and electronic monitoring.

Monetary Penalties

In Massachusetts in 1736, a thief was to be fined or whipped upon a first conviction. The next time he would pay triple damages, sit for an hour on the gallows platform with a noose around his neck, and then be taken to the whipping post for thirty lashes. A third conviction resulted in death by hanging. Likewise, a burglar would first be branded with the letter B on his forehead. If convicted a second time, he would sit on the gallows platform with a noose around his neck for an hour and then be whipped. Upon a third conviction, he was deemed "incorrigible" and hanged. The rationale of the Colonists was apparent: "Anyone impervious to the fine and the whip, who did not mend his ways after an hour with a noose about him, was uncontrollable and therefore had to be executed."[5] This progression of penalties continued well into the eighteenth century, and incarceration was rarely part of this sequence. Jail was reserved for suspects awaiting trial and for debtors.[6]

Fines and whippings were the two most commonly employed penalties during the eighteenth century. Fines were effective when the offender had some wealth, whereas whipping could be applied more generally. There was no clear-cut division by type of crime that distinguished offenders who were fined from those who were whipped. The choice of punishment depended on the circumstances of the offender rather than on those of the offense.[7] Today criminal punishment has become more "civilized"; whipping is seen as barbaric and incarceration is viewed as providing more punishment and better protection of the public.

Fines continue to be the most common form of criminal sanction in the United States, although they are used primarily in cases involving minor crimes or as an adjunct to incarceration for more serious offenses. This differs from the way fines are used in other parts of the world. In England, more than a third of violent felonies are punished solely by fines. In Germany, the proportion is even higher.[8] In the United States, the public does not see fines as a serious enough penalty for most felonies, although judges often use them in cases that involve nonviolent crimes by first offenders who have the ability to pay.[9]

There are at least two problems in the current use of fines as a form of criminal sanction: proportionality and collection. In most states the maximum fine for an offense is set by law without regard for the wealth of the offender. As a result, fines often lack meaning for wealthy offenders, while poor offenders (the largest offender group) often cannot pay even a moderate fine. Second, many fines go uncollected because of the lack of effective enforcement and collection systems in most states.[10]

Day fines, which are commonly used in Europe, offer a solution to the problem of proportionality. They are called "day fines" because the amount of the fine is based on some percentage of an offender's daily earnings. Simply stated, day fines attach "unit value" to the seriousness of the offense (usually between 5 and 120 units). The fine is then calculated by multiplying these units of seriousness

Media and Criminal Justice

SCARED STRAIGHT!

The documentary *Scared Straight!* was released in 1978 amidst great controversy about the method of community-based corrections depicted in the film. The controversy continued after the movie won an Academy Award, and reviewers won their fight to have the film shown on public television in spite of unprecedented profanity.

Among corrections and criminal justice practitioners, *Scared Straight!* remains a classic to this day. The movie presents a radical program begun in the 1970s to deter juvenile delinquents from committing more crime. The concept is simple: Take young offenders who show no sign of desisting from their criminal ways, and let them see the realities of life in state prison. After a tour of the disgusting facilities, where prisoners shout sexually charged taunts from their cells and the offenders are briefly locked in cells for effect, the group is put in a room with a group of hard-core convicts. The convicts, all of them violent and most of them "lifers," are permitted to use every nonphysical method available to literally scare the crime right out of the teenagers.

The camera is merciless in its observations of the teens, covering their attitudes and experiences before, during, and after the encounter with the inmates. Before entering the prison, the teens bragged about their crimes: "If you got something I want, I'll take it from you!" and "I never killed anyone yet, but I sliced a few people." One teen announced that his goal was to go to security school, where he could learn the technical side of locks and alarms so as to better prepare himself for a life of crime.

The heart of the documentary centers on the encounter with the convicts, who are clearly *not* acting as they use in-your-face profanity, vulgarity, and threats of violence to communicate their message. One double-lifer explains to a tough-acting youth that he could rip the boy's eye out of his head and destroy it long before a guard could come to his rescue. Tears of terror well up in the boy's eyes as the convict points out the obvious: They can't give a double-lifer any more time than that which he already has, so he has nothing to lose by being violent.

The end results are astonishing. After several hours of being terrorized by the inmates, the juvenile delinquents exhibit a complete change of attitude. The youth who bragged of planning to be a professional thief now suddenly insists that he has changed his mind, and now wants to get a real job. Only one of the seventeen delinquents in the group recidivated during the three months following the Scared Straight program. As the Rahway Prison warden points out in the end, it doesn't cost the taxpayer anything, the inmates consider the program a worthy use of their otherwise wasted time, and it actually seems to have a lasting impact on the teens.

Follow-up studies indicate that the long-term recidivism rate of Scared Straight teens was not nearly as low as initial statistics indicated, but supporters argue that if even one delinquent is permanently deterred by the experience, the program is a success. The Scared Straight program still exists today, made popular by the *Scared Straight!* film, and is now often extended to even younger "at risk" youth.

MEDIA AND CRIMINAL JUSTICE QUESTION

Why do you believe that Scared Straight programs do not affect long-term recidivism rates of the juveniles who participate?

by a percentage of the offender's daily income. For example, an offender who takes home $40 per day is able to keep 40 percent ($16) for housing, 20 percent ($8) for food and clothing, and up to 40 percent of the remainder ($6.40) to support dependents. In this case the fine (gauged to the seriousness of the offense) could range up to nearly $10 per day, or 25 percent of the offender's daily income. Therefore, the amount of the fine is proportional both to the offense and to the offender's ability to pay.

A test of day fines in Staten Island, New York,[11] found that average fine amounts were higher under the day fine system, but that collection rates were not affected. Significantly, fewer arrest warrants were issued for failure to appear at postsentencing hearings, suggesting a higher compliance rate among offenders. Also, judges were more comfortable imposing monetary penalties under such an income-based system. Day fine programs have now been implemented in Phoenix and in Connecticut, Iowa, and Oregon.[12]

Despite their advantages, day fine systems are still uncommon in the United States, where traditional offense-based fines are still used in most jurisdictions. There is some concern that day fines are unconstitutional in that they allow different fines for the same offense, thus violating the Fourteenth Amendment guarantee of equal protection of the laws. Nevertheless, there have not yet been court challenges to day fines.

The Justice Department keeps track of fines received by U.S. Attorney's Offices, but fines are also collected through courts by probation departments, or in the form of payments to the victim.[13] The U.S. Courts National Fine Center was established to centralize and better organize the fine-collection process in the federal courts and to improve coordination among agencies. There is no analogous agency at the state or local level, and the federal system has not yet adopted a day fine system, although the successful experiences in Europe and in several locations in the United States suggest that day fines will become more common in the future.

Probation

probation
A criminal sentence of community supervision of the offender that is conducted by a probation officer.

Probation is a criminal sentence of community supervision of the offender that is conducted by a probation officer. The term *probation* was first used by John Augustus to describe his efforts to bail offenders out of jail and allow them to live under supervision in the community. Augustus worked without pay, and he often placed those he bailed out of jail in his own home. He was careful in whom he selected, accounting for "the previous character of the person, his age and the influences by which in the future he would likely be surrounded."[14] He helped offenders of all kinds, and reported only ten absconders among the 2,000 cases he handled. Augustus worked as a volunteer for eighteen years. Massachusetts did not use paid probation officers until 1878, when it enacted the first probation statute. Other states soon copied Massachusetts's provisions for providing probation officers to investigate cases and recommend sentences. This growth in probation was aided by the invention of the juvenile court at the turn of the century. This step formally recognized that juveniles should be handled differently than adults, and probation supervision seemed appropriate in a large number of juvenile cases. The first directory of probation officers, published in 1907, identified 795 probation officers, who worked primarily in juvenile courts.[15] By 1920, every state had adopted probation for juveniles, and thirty-three states had provisions for adult probation.[16]

Today probation is administered in a variety of ways. In thirty-four states, adult probation is part of the executive branch of government, while in nineteen others it is part of the judicial branch at the state or local level. In half the states a central probation system operates throughout the state; in others probation is operated by the county government, and in the remainder it is administered by the municipality. This variation is similar to that among police agencies, which also exist at all levels of government. There is debate over whether probation is best administered at the state or local level and whether it is best administered by the executive or judicial branch of government. A national commission concluded that probation is administered best at the state level by the executive branch of government.[17] There appears to be a trend in this direction, as several states have changed the way they administer probation during the last twenty years.[18]

The case loads of probation officers vary widely, ranging from 13 to 400 offenders per officer with an average of 188.[19] It is widely recognized that the number of offenders per probation officer is not directly correlated with rates of re-offending. Classification of offenders is used in most jurisdictions to predict the likelihood of successful probation and the amount of supervision required. Classification or "risk prediction" scales summarize the outcomes in similar, past cases and can be compared with a current case. These classification techniques have been used successfully to distinguish among high-, medium-, and low-risk offenders.[20] For example, offenders with substance abuse problems and prior felony records are much more likely to violate the conditions of probation and re-offend. Classification systems identify these and other high-risk factors so that these offenders will receive more intensive supervision in order to reduce the risk of probation violations.

Probation is the most widely used form of correctional supervision in the United States. As Figure 15.1 illustrates, of the more than 5.3 million adults under correctional supervision in the United States (2.8 percent of the adult population), 3 million are on probation.[21] Only five years earlier, 4.3 million adult offenders were under some form of correctional supervision, including 2.67 on probation.[22] This represents an increase of 23 percent. Of offenders serving probation sentences, 60 percent had been convicted for felonies, one fourth had committed misdemeanors, and 15 percent had been convicted for driving under the influence of alcohol.[23]

Offenders who are sentenced to probation usually have conditions attached to their sentences. These conditions are designed to control the offender's present behavior and to change it in the future. Conditions of control might include

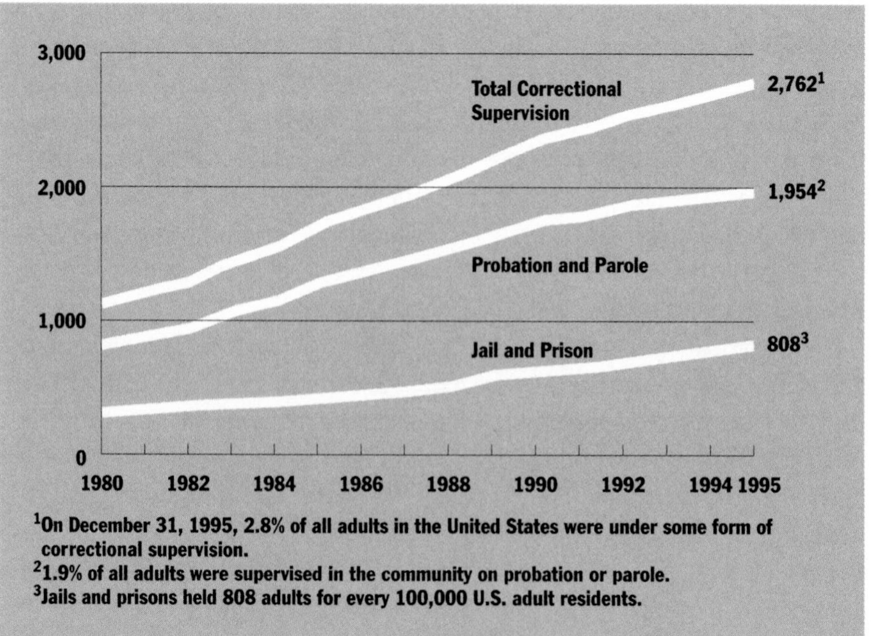

FIGURE 15.1

Adults under correctional supervision per 100,000 residents

SOURCE: Allen J. Beck, Jodi M. Brown, and Darrell K. Gilliard, *Probation and Parole 1995* (Washington, D.C.: Bureau of Justice Statistics, 1996).

the following: no association permitted with known criminals, no possession of weapons allowed, no use of alcohol or drugs, and no leaving the jurisdiction. Conditions designed to change behavior include mandatory drug/alcohol testing or treatment, education or employment requirements, community service, payment of fines, and restitution to the victim. The conditions of control are designed to reduce the risk to the community while the offender is under supervision. The conditions seeking change are designed to produce conforming behavior once the probation sentence has ended. These changes are expected to result from treatment of addiction, steady employment, and greater understanding of the consequences of criminal behavior. One survey of felony probationers found that among those who completed their term, 69 percent satisfied all conditions and 47 percent of those with financial penalties paid them in full.[24]

A national survey of probation directors reported that staff shortages are their most significant problem. Those shortages are a result of the rapid growth in the use of probation as a sentencing option in recent years. Jail and prison crowding has created pressure to employ probation supervision in a growing number of cases. Another problem is lack of coordination. Probation officers are required to work with judges, police, victims, and jail officials, and coordination among these various actors is often difficult because of differing interests and needs. For example, expanded police hiring has contributed to more arrests and adjudications, but there has not been a corresponding increase in probation resources to supervise those sentenced to probation. Finally, probation directors feel that the public does not understand their mission and operation, contributing to a lack of respect for probation as a correctional alternative.[25]

Supervision of offenders in the community poses a risk that prisons do not: People under correctional supervision might commit further crimes. This is the primary reason for negative public attitudes toward probation. Although probation is less expensive than incarceration, the huge prison construction programs in many states provide evidence that the public is willing to spend tax dollars in order to guarantee public safety. Indeed, the public's misgivings about probation are supported by research evidence. A major study of felony offenders on probation found that 46 percent of all probationers had been sent to jail or prison or had absconded (their whereabouts unknown) within three years of sentencing. In addition, 62 percent of probationers were arrested for another felony or were brought to a disciplinary hearing for violating a condition of their probation. These findings are summarized in Figure 15.2.

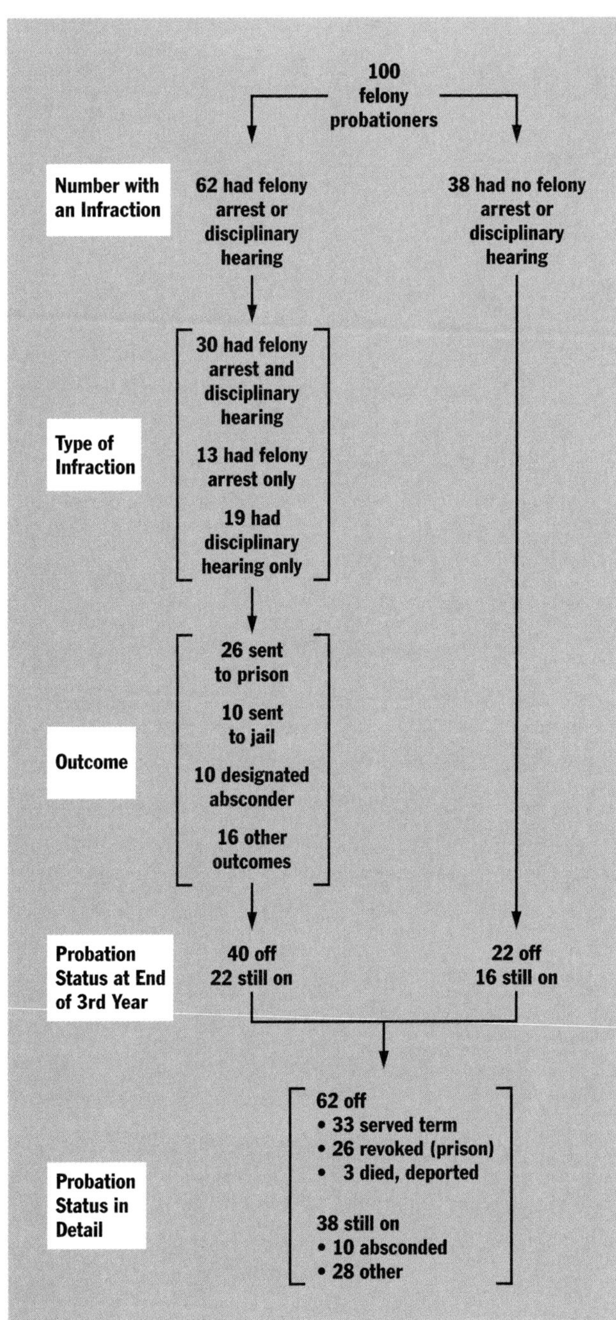

FIGURE 15.2

Findings of a study that tracked one hundred felons through their first three years of probation

SOURCE: Patrick A. Langan and Mark A. Cuniff, *Recidivism of Felons on Probation* (Washington, D.C.: Bureau of Justice Statistics, 1992).

While these statistics are discouraging, critics have noted that there were some methodological problems in this national survey. One is that the survey did not include misdemeanor offenders, who are much more likely to complete probation successfully. Another problem is that 21 percent of the felons on probation had *not* been recommended for probation in the presentence report, a finding that holds true for all probationers nationwide. These offenders were nearly twice as likely to have their sentence revoked as those recommended for probation.[26] This suggests that had judges followed the sentence recommendation in the presentence report, overall success rates on probation would be considerably higher.

Therefore, it appears that probation works best for misdemeanor offenders and for felons who are recommended for probation at sentencing. Felons who are not recommended for probation are significantly less likely to complete probation successfully, and this affects the findings of statistical studies of probation.

Intensive Supervision

intermediate sanctions
A sentence designed to provide more rigorous supervision than normal probation, yet something less expensive than incarceration.

intensive supervision
Maintaining small case loads, frequent contact with offenders under supervision, and special conditions such as random drug tests, curfews, restitution to victims, electronic monitoring, or house arrest.

Dissatisfaction with probation, combined with the need to use prison space more efficiently, has produced a movement toward **intermediate sanctions.** Intermediate sanctions are designed to provide more rigorous supervision than normal probation, yet something less expensive than incarceration. These sanctions attempt to result in more punishment at less cost. However, they raise three questions: (1) Are costs actually reduced?, (2) are these sanctions effective in controlling prison populations?, and (3) do they protect the community?[27]

The oldest and most common form of intermediate sanction is intensive supervision programs for probationers and parolees. **Intensive supervision** is achieved by maintaining small case loads, frequent contact with offenders under supervision, and special conditions such as random drug tests, curfews, restitution to victims, electronic monitoring, or house arrest. Georgia was the first state to evaluate its intensive supervision program, and reported both reduced costs and lower recidivism.[28] Between 1980 and 1990, some form of intensive supervision was adopted in every state. Today more than 3 percent of all probationers and 5 percent of parolees are in an intensive supervision program.[29]

Evaluations of intensive supervision programs have shown mixed results. An evaluation of fourteen programs in nine states found that they provided effective surveillance of offenders but were costly and failed to reduce recidivism.[30] A study in England found a high rate of recidivism for offenders on intensive probation, but the rate was no higher than for those offenders serving prison sentences.[31]

It has been suggested that greater emphasis on treatment would lead to behavioral changes that would result in lower recidivism. In California and Texas, offenders under intensive supervision who received substance abuse counseling, held jobs, paid restitution, and performed community service re-offended at a rate that was 10 to 20 percent lower than that of offenders who did not receive such treatment.[32] However, an evaluation published in 1997 concluded that there is little evidence that intensive supervision programs either rehabilitated or deterred offenders from committing additional crimes more effectively than the sentencing options they replaced.[33] Thus, while intensive supervision

contemporary issues

The Return of Chain Gangs

In 1995, Alabama and Florida became the first states to reintroduce chain gangs as a correctional technique. Chain gangs are groups of offenders, sometimes chained together at the ankle, who are taken out of prison to perform roadside cleanup tasks under the supervision of an armed guard. The inmates are returned to the prison at dusk.

On one hand, it can be argued that chain gangs are a part of community corrections. Inmates are on a form of "work release" (albeit under strict supervision), forced to perform work, and returned to prison at the end of the day. Prison officials point out that one corrections officer can supervise up to forty chained prisoners, making chain gangs a cost-effective form of supervision. Likewise, chain gangs serve as a visible deterrent to passersby, unlike inmates in prisons out of public view. The wearing of leg irons has also been said to instill discipline and shame.

On the other hand, chaining criminals together is a throwback to the past; one politician has called it "a return to slavery." Chain gangs were used to control African Americans in the South after the Civil War, and some believe they symbolize a legacy of racial injustice. Chain gangs are humiliating and can make an inmate "feel like an animal." The resulting anger may cause greater frustration and possibly more violence or vengeance by offenders upon release. Furthermore, there is no empirical evidence to show that chain gangs deter future criminal activity.

Is there a way to balance the public demand for more severe penalties with the resurgence of chain gangs and their historical connection with racial oppression?

The reintroduction of chain gangs as a way to deal with offenders has been controversial. Some believe it is a cost-effective deterrent while others see it as a dehumanizing way to instill anger.

SOURCES

Adam Cohen, "Back on the Chain Gang," *Time* (May 15, 1995), p. 26.

"Florida Reintroduces Chain Gangs," *Harvard Law Review,* vol. 109 (February 1996), pp. 876–81.

Tessa M. Gorman, "Back on the Chain Gang: Why the Eighth Amendment and the History of Slavery Proscribe the Resurgence of Chain Gangs," *California Law Review,* vol. 85 (March 1997), pp. 441–78.

Paul Leavitt, "Chain Gangs," *USA Today* (May 6, 1996), p. 3.

Marylee N. Reynolds, "Back on the Chain Gang," *Corrections Today,* vol. 58 (April 1996), pp. 108–15.

Emily S. Sanford, "The Propriety and Constitutionality of Chain Gangs," *Georgia State University Law Review,* vol. 13 (July 1997), pp. 1155–86.

Lori Sharn, "Chain Gangs Back in Alabama," *USA Today* (May 4, 1995), p. 3.

programs have an intuitive appeal, they have not generally produced the anticipated outcomes. There are at least two reasons for this lack of success: (1) the offenders chosen for intensive supervision are inappropriate, or (2) intensive supervision discovers more criminal activity. It is possible that a higher success rate can be achieved if offenders are more carefully screened before being assigned to intensive supervision programs. For example, substance abuse counseling works best for those motivated to kick the habit. Offenders not motivated in this way may be poor risks regardless of the level of supervision imposed. Second, closer supervision of offenders in the community may result in discovery of more recidivism. Therefore, offenders on intensive supervision may not be committing any more crimes than they had in the past, but probation officers are now aware of the crimes because of more frequent contact with the offenders.

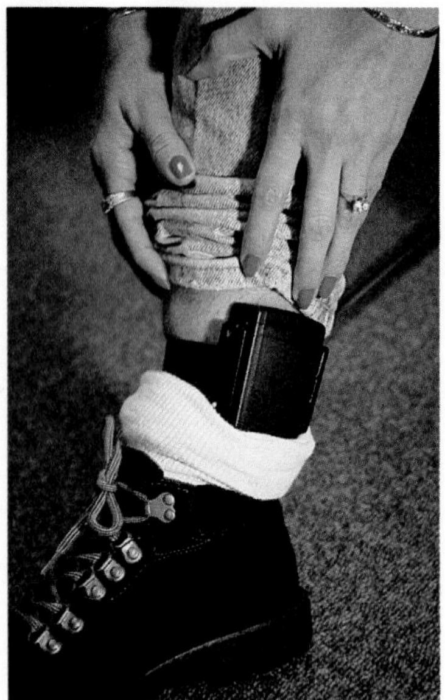

Ankle bracelets are a type of electronic monitoring which permits remote surveillance of an offender in the community. The device cannot be removed without setting off an alarm.

house arrest
A condition of probation or parole in which an offender is not permitted to leave his or her residence for purposes other than work, school, treatment, or other approved reasons.

net-widening
The process by which more offenders are placed under supervision of the criminal justice system even though the intent of the intervention was to divert offenders out of the system.

Home Confinement and Electronic Monitoring

An offender under home confinement is not permitted to leave his or her residence for purposes other than work, school, treatment, or other approved reasons. This form of punishment, sometimes called **house arrest,** can be a condition of probation or parole and is employed to varying degrees in every state.

A primary issue in home confinement is ensuring compliance with the order to stay at home. Increasingly this is being accomplished through electronic monitoring. Such monitoring takes one of two forms: programmed or continuous contact. In programmed contact, the offender is called at home at random intervals and is required to verify his or her presence by voice or a code, or electronically through a device strapped to his or her wrist. In continuous contact, the offender wears an ankle bracelet that cannot be removed without setting off an electronic alarm. If the offender moves out of range of a receiver located in his or her telephone, the supervision office is notified electronically. In recent years, electronic monitoring has become synonymous with house arrest because manual monitoring requires more direct checks of offenders' whereabouts. The lower cost of electronic monitoring, combined with its more efficient surveillance of offenders in the community, has led to its widespread adoption during the last decade.

The primary cost savings offered by home confinement is reduced jail or prison costs. If an offender can be supervised effectively in the community, the state does not have to pay for room, board, and round-the-clock supervision in jail or prison. In a 1998 study, Virginia reported a total cost per day of $5.67 for an offender on home confinement with electronic monitoring compared to an average jail cost of $47 per day.[34] On the other hand, if offenders under house arrest would normally have been released or placed on simple probation, costs are increased, because more resources are being devoted to surveillance of offenders in the community. This phenomenon is referred to as **net-widening.** It refers to the process by which more offenders are placed under supervision of the criminal justice system even though the intent of the intervention was to divert offenders out of the system.

The effectiveness of home confinement has not been evaluated in a systematic way, although evidence from a growing number of jurisdictions has shown some of its strengths and weaknesses as an intermediate sanction. Since its founding in 1983, Florida's home confinement program, the Community Control Program, has placed more than 50,000 offenders under house arrest, mostly using manual monitoring. Each offender has a minimum of twenty-eight contacts a month with probation or parole officers. An evaluation found that about half of the offenders sentenced to house arrest would otherwise have been placed on probation, suggesting a net-widening effect.[35] The other half would otherwise have been sentenced to prison, suggesting a positive effect on prison overcrowding. A follow-up study compared two groups of offenders matched by age, gender, type, and severity of offense, and prior felony convictions. One group had been sentenced to house arrest, the other to prison. The results are summarized in Table 15.1.

The study found that reconviction rates for new offenses were somewhat lower for Florida Community Control Program offenders (19.7 percent) than for those who had been sentenced to prison and then released (24.3 percent). The Florida evaluation found that drug offenders performed best, with a recidivism

TABLE 15.1

Recidivism of Offenders Sent to Prison and Placed under House Arrest in Florida

	PRISON		HOUSE ARREST	
RECIDIVISM	**NO.**	**PERCENT**	**NO.**	**PERCENT**
None	477	75.7	445	70.6
Finding of technical violation*	N/A	N/A	61	9.7
Conviction for new offense	153	24.3	124	19.7
Total	630	100.0	630	100.0

*Since offenders discharged from prison in Florida do not receive parole supervision, no technical violations are possible.

SOURCE: Dennis Wagner and Christopher Baird, *Evaluation of the Florida Community Control Program* (Washington, D.C.: National Institute of Justice, 1993).

rate of 11 percent for those sentenced to house arrest compared to 27 percent for those sentenced to prison.

A seven-year study of offenders convicted of drunk driving or driving with a suspended license found that 97 percent successfully completed the electronic monitoring phase of their house arrest sentence. However, a third of these offenders committed a new offense or technical violation while on regular probation.[36] This suggests that electronic monitoring may have only a temporary effect. In many jurisdictions house arrest lasts no more than three months, followed by regular probation. House arrest may be effective for offenders with family members who do not mind the inconvenience of a home-bound person who receives telephone monitoring calls or signals at all hours. However, offenders usually become bored and frustrated by their inability to engage in most behaviors, from doing the laundry to going for a walk. As a result, house arrest is more punitive than rehabilitative in nature, and offenders view electronic monitoring as punitive, but better than jail.[37] The building frustration with the limitations of life under house arrest may ultimately lead to violations of the supervision.

Another significant problem with electronic monitoring has to do with technology, as the technology of surveillance is not perfect. Radio interference with electronic transmitters and receivers, mountainous terrain, and even cast-iron bathtubs have caused false alarms and nonalarms.[38] In one case, a convict under house arrest was able to sell heroin from his apartment.[39] In another an offender was able to remove his bracelet and commit a homicide. (After the latter case New Jersey dropped its use of electronic monitoring for early parolees for three years.[40]) Incidents such as these give rise to concern over adequate protection of the community.[41] In response, electronics vendors are now marketing new, improved electronic monitoring equipment that overcomes some of the flaws of earlier versions. There has also been some improvement in technology, which is as important as improvement in the response capabilities of probation and parole agencies that oversee home confinement programs. A study of seventy-eight offenders who successfully completed house arrest programs found that nearly half had violated the conditions of their house arrest. Also, many offenders do not make it through the program without the agency having made several unsuccessful attempts to contact them.[42] It seems clear that the effectiveness of surveillance, as measured by prevention and timely response to violations of conditions, must improve if the public is to view home confinement as an acceptable alternative to imprisonment.

FUTURE ISSUES

The Spiderman Solution and A Clockwork Orange

"Electronic bracelets" for monitoring offenders were first used in the 1980s. This innovative technology was inspired by a *Spiderman* comic that featured a similar device.[A] As is explained in this chapter, electronic monitoring use of technology has since become common throughout the United States.

Similar ideas on the borderline of technology and behavior have existed for some time. Ralph Schwitzgebel proposed an "electronic alternative to imprisonment" in 1968. In his scenario, a monitoring unit worn by the offender would send and receive signals from repeater stations throughout the neighborhood.[B] However, are there limits to such efforts to control the behavior of offenders and ex-offenders?

A study of chronic alcoholics conducted more than thirty years ago involved placing a small amount of the alcoholic's favorite liquor in a glass in front of him. A few seconds after tasting the alcohol, the alcoholic was injected with a drug that simulated suffocation. To recover, the alcoholics had to be given air. This procedure was repeated in an attempt to extinguish the drinking behavior by associating it with violent illness.[C] Many experiments of this type (called aversive suppression) have been carried out, using drugs such as the one just described. Drug use, fetishes, sexual deviancy, and shoplifting are among the undesirable behaviors that have been treated in this way.[D] These techniques have also been used within prisons where "convicted bank robbers are shown films of crimes much like their own and are then shocked and injected with nauseous drugs in the hope that they will become sick at even the thought of such capers when released."[E]

This appears to be another case of science imitating fiction. In 1963, Anthony Burgess's futuristic novel *A Clockwork Orange* described a remarkably similar treatment in which a violent sex offender was strapped to a chair and forced to watch films depicting extremely violent assaults and sexual abuse. The offender was injected with a drug that made him quite nauseous in the hope that he would associate these acts with nausea and thereby be deterred from committing additional crimes in the future.

Attempts to change behavior through aversive suppression have not proved to be effective. Several reviews of the research literature have found inconclusive support for the ability of these programs to change behavior over an extended period. As Eugene Burnstein explains, "Punishment controls by suppressing performance; it does nothing to diminish the tendency to engage in the performance, and under the threat of punishment persons are likely to suppress an action only while being monitored. Indeed, when punishment is discontinued, the suppressed act reappears in even more vigorous form."[F] In the case of *A Clockwork Orange,* this is precisely what occurred. The effects of the drug soon wore off, and the suppressed behavior reemerged. It appears the lessons of fiction have not always been heeded in our search for ways to control crime more effectively.

After Prison

As we have seen in earlier chapters, fewer than 2 percent of all felony convictions are for murder, and fewer than 18 percent are for violent crimes.[43] Violent offenders served the longest sentences and on average the majority of offenders are released from prison after serving a sentence of seventy-nine months. To ensure that public safety is maintained, measures must be taken to reduce the incidence of repeat offenses. For this reason, various kinds of programs have been developed to foster successful entry of offenders back into the community.

parole
A sentence consisting of supervision of offenders in the community who were dangerous enough to have been sent to prison but are near the end of their sentences.

Parole

Parole is perhaps the least popular component of the criminal justice system. It consists of supervision of offenders in the community who were dangerous enough to have been sent to prison but are near the end of their sentences. Parole officers supervise the highest-risk offenders, who sometimes commit new

FUTURES QUESTION

Why do you think that behavior modification efforts of the kind described here do not have lasting effects even when they have been reinforced many times?

NOTES

[A]"Probation 'Bracelets': The Spiderman Solution," *Corrections Magazine,* vol. 9 (June 1983), p. 4.

[B]Ralph K. Schwitzgebel, "Electronic Alternatives to Imprisonment," *Lex et Scientia,* vol. 5 (1968), pp. 99–104.

[C]J. Clancy, E. Vanderhoff, and P. Campbell, "Evaluation of an Aversive Technique as a Treatment for Alcoholism," *Quarterly Journal of Studies on Alcohol,* vol. 28 (1967), pp. 476–85.

[D]William T. Query, "Field Dependency, Power and Locus of Control, Variables in Alcohol Aversion," *Journal of Clinical Psychology,* vol. 39 (March 1983), pp. 279–83; M. J. Raymond, "Case of Fetishism Treated by Aversion Therapy," *British Medical Journal,* vol. 2 (1965), pp. 854–7; R. Liberman, "Aversive Conditioning of Drug Addicts: A Pilot Study," *Behavior Research and Therapy,* vol. 6 (1968), pp. 229–31; C. H. Farrar, B. J. Powell, and L. K. Martin, "Punishment of Alcohol Consumption by Apneic Paralysis," *Behavior Research and Therapy,* vol. 6 (1968), pp. 13–16; G. S. Alford, D. Wedding, and S. Jones "Faking 'Turn-ons' and 'Turn-offs': The Effects of Competitory Covert Imagery on Penile Tumescence Responses to Diverse Sexual Stimulus Materials," *Behavior Modification* (January 1983), pp. 112–25; J. H. J. Bancroft, H. G. Jones, and B. R. Pullan, "A Simple Transducer for Measuring Penile Erection, with Comments on its Use in the Treatment of Sexual Disorders," *Behavior Research and Therapy,* vol. 4 (1966), pp. 239–41; Adrian Raine, Peter H. Venables, and Mark Williams, "High Autonomic Arousal and Electrodermal Orienting at Age 15 Years as Protective Factors Against Criminal Behavior at Age 29 Years," *American Journal of Psychiatry,* vol. 152 (November 1995), pp. 1595–601; Peter B. Wood et al., "Nonsocial Reinforcement and Habitual Criminal Conduct: An Extension of Learning Theory," *Criminology,* vol. 35 (May 1997), pp. 335–67.

[E]Wayne Sage, "Crime and the Clockwork Lemon," *Human Behavior* (September 1974), p. 17.

[F]Eugene Burnstein, "The Notion of Control in Psychological Theory," in J. P. Gibbs, ed., *Social Control: Views from the Social Sciences* (Thousand Oaks, CA: Sage, 1982), p. 28. See also R. M. Church, "The Varied Effects of Punishment on Behavior," *Psychological Review,* vol. 70 (1963), pp. 369–402; Robert Emery and David Marholin, "An Applied Behavior Analysis of Delinquency," *American Psychologist* (October 1977); Robert Ross and Brian McKay, "Behavioral Approaches to Treatment in Corrections: Requiem for a Panacea," *Canadian Journal of Criminology,* vol. 20 (July 1978).

crimes. The public is outraged when crimes are committed by parolees. Many people cannot understand why dangerous offenders are allowed to go back into the community in the first place.

The logic behind parole is simple: It provides a way for inmates to serve the last part of their sentence in the community under supervision in order to make a successful readjustment to freedom. Parole is one of three ways in which inmates are released. A second method is based on the accumulation of "good-time" credits, which are awarded to inmates for each day on which they obey prison rules. The third type of release is called "maxing-out." This occurs when the offender has served the entire sentence and has not been granted parole or accumulated enough good-time credits to justify early release. Parole is generally available only to prison inmates, not to jail inmates, who must serve their entire sentences, even though jail inmates have committed less serious crimes and presumably would be better candidates for parole.

In the United States parole is associated with indeterminate sentencing. Zebulon Brockway included indeterminate sentencing and parole in his innovative program for youthful offenders. He persuaded the New York State legislature to adopt indeterminate sentencing and shift the authority for prisoner release from the courts to corrections officials.[44] Parole release is decided by a parole board consisting of corrections officials or political appointees, or both, who evaluate the inmate's record and behavior inside the prison. Using their discretion, they may release the inmate to serve the remainder of the sentence under community supervision. Parole thus is designed to provide supervised transition from prison to life in the community.

Offenders who are not released by the parole board can be granted supervised mandatory release if they accumulate enough good-time credits. These offenders are also supervised by parole officers. Inmates who "max out" and complete their sentences in prison are released, but because their sentence has ended they are not supervised in the community.

Dissatisfaction with parole has led to changes in both law and policy in recent years. Some states now require offenders to serve a greater proportion of their sentence before they are eligible for release. The federal government has passed a "truth-in-sentencing" law that requires federal offenders to serve at least 85 percent of their sentence before release. This law also abolished parole release for federal offenders, making good-time credit the only way to obtain early release (with 15 percent the greatest reduction of sentence allowable). A growing number of states are following suit by abolishing or severely restricting parole release and cutting back on good-time credit. By 1995, eleven states had abolished parole.[45] In addition, nineteen states have abolished mandatory release based on good-time credits.[46]

These restrictions on release have increased prison overcrowding, since more offenders are serving a larger proportion of their sentence. Combined with growing numbers of inmates being sent to prison, they have caused prison populations to mushroom. This has contributed to a record number of offenders under parole supervision, despite the greater difficulty of obtaining release on parole. In 1990, there were 456,803 adults on parole. By 1995, the number had reached 690,371, an increase of 51 percent in only five years.[47] More than 80 percent of offenders released from prison are under some form of parole supervision, and the number of parolees is likely to increase further in coming years.

As with probation, it is not clear whether parole has failed or whether the society's expectations have exceeded its commitment to the idea behind parole. Managing high-risk offenders in the community is a difficult task under the best of circumstances. High case loads, poorly trained and educated parole officers in some states, and few resources for helping offenders make the transition into the community are major issues. In many jurisdictions the case loads of parole officers are too high for meaningful supervision, suggesting a lack of commitment to parole as a correctional strategy. Moreover, parole officers are not uniformly educated or trained. In some states, a Bachelor's degree and minimum training are required; in others, there is no such standard. As a result, the quality of parole officers varies greatly. Also, in many jurisdictions, parole officers lack the tools or resources necessary to help offenders adjust to life in the community. Job training opportunities, job placement, training in basic skills, and substance abuse treatment are examples of the types of resources that parole officers need if they are to intervene successfully in the lives of parolees. Despite these shortcomings, however, approximately 60 percent of parolees have not returned to prison after three years. About half of those who do are sent back for technical violations (e.g., drug test failure, curfew violations, nonparticipation in required programs) rather than for new crimes.[48]

A great deal of attention has been given to the parole release decision during the last twenty years. Some claim that unsuitable candidates have been released from prison and placed on parole, reducing the effectiveness of parole and affecting public safety. Parole guidelines have been adopted in many states and have contributed to more appropriate and consistent parole decisions.[49] These guidelines attempt to make parole release decisions more uniform by employing standardized criteria. The two primary criteria used are the seriousness of the offense and the prior criminal record of the offender. Other factors included in parole guidelines are behavior inside the prison, participation in rehabilitation programs, and employment plans upon release. Nevertheless, public confidence in parole continues to erode, and eleven states have abolished parole release altogether.

Work Release and Furloughs

Prolonged incarceration can lead to a serious decline in inmates' capacity to function outside of prison. This decline is seen in several areas, including vocational and social skills, independence and self-esteem, and family and community support.[50] Temporary release programs are designed to reduce these effects by permitting inmates to enter the community on certain days for work, study, treatment programs, or family visitation. Given the increase in average sentence lengths in recent years, it is likely that temporary release will become even more important in the future.

Work release first began as a way to encourage inmate discipline and the work ethic. It was a response to complaints that offenders in prison were idle while free citizens had to work to support themselves. Today the reverse argument is employed. Paid employment for inmates is criticized when there is not always enough work available for law-abiding citizens.[51] Depending on one's view, therefore, work release can be seen as a punitive consequence of incarceration or as a rehabilitative benefit.

work release
A program that permits eligible inmates to work during the day at regular jobs outside the jail or prison, returning to the prison at night.

Work release programs permit eligible inmates to work during the day at regular jobs outside the jail or prison, returning to the prison at night. It is generally not available in maximum security institutions. For inmates in medium or minimum security institutions, the ability to work is often affected by the location of the prison. Many prisons are located in rural areas, where there are fewer opportunities for employment.

The work release experience is designed to instill discipline, a routine, and work habits that closely resemble those found outside of prison. Inmates are paid the prevailing wage, although they are required to submit their earnings to the corrections authorities, who deduct 5 or 10 percent for room and board in the prison and payment of welfare agencies that may be supporting the inmate's family. The remainder of the inmate's earnings is placed in forced savings until the inmate is released. Approximately 65,000 inmates, or fewer than 5 percent of the total inmate population, are involved in work release programs.

study release
A program similar to work release where an inmate attends school by day and returns to the jail or prison at night.

Study release is similar to work release, except that the inmate attends school by day and returns to the jail or prison at night. The study might consist of high school equivalency, vocational training, or college education. The inmate must meet the same entrance requirements as any other student, apply for admission, be accepted, and obtain permission from correctional authorities to attend the educational institution. Like work release, study release is feasible only for inmates in correctional institutions near educational institutions. This is not true of most prisons.

Two factors are most responsible for the limited use of study release: funding and public pressure. Unlike work release, study release costs money. Therefore, like any other student, an inmate must apply for financial aid to cover the cost of education. Funding is not always available, so most prison education is limited to that which takes place within prison walls. Public pressure also limits the use of study release. Concerns over public safety, along with complaints that inmates are being allowed to attend schools that many free citizens cannot afford, deter many corrections officials from allowing inmates to participate in study release. As a result, only 355 inmates are currently participating in study release programs.[52]

furlough
Unsupervised leave from prison that is granted for only a few hours to permit an eligible inmate to attend a relative's funeral, visit loved ones, attend a job interview in preparation for release, or otherwise attend to personal or family matters.

Furloughs are unsupervised leaves from prison that are granted for only a few hours. Their purpose is to permit an eligible inmate to attend a relative's funeral, visit loved ones, attend a job interview in preparation for release, or otherwise attend to personal or family matters. Similar to work and study release, furloughs are designed to prepare the inmate for a successful transition into free society. This goal must be balanced against the risk that the inmate might commit new crimes.

The most infamous case of a furlough violation is that of Willie Horton. Horton was convicted of murder in Massachusetts and sentenced to life imprisonment. He was released on a furlough and did not return. He then kidnapped and raped a Maryland woman and assaulted her fiancé, and was arrested and tried for his new crimes. Shortly thereafter, the governor of Massachusetts, Michael Dukakis, ran against George Bush in the 1988 presidential election. The Bush campaign used the Horton case in commercials criticizing Dukakis for permitting furloughs for dangerous offenders. These advertisements hurt Dukakis's presidential ambitions, but more importantly, they undoubtedly had an impact on the use of furloughs around the United States. Since furlough programs are permitted by state corrections policy or by state law, Dukakis received criticism for a policy he did not implement.

The available data suggest that furloughs are uncommon; fewer than 42,000 inmates (or fewer than 3 percent of all inmates) are granted furloughs each year. In one year a total of 2,084 crimes were committed by inmates on furloughs and 3,960 offenders absconded or returned late.[53] This is a failure rate of only 2 percent. Nevertheless, one sensational crime or violation can produce enough public and political outrage to kill a program, regardless of its merits.

halfway house
Residential center for ex-offenders in the community. Most halfway house residents are parolees or similar inmates near the end of their sentence.

Halfway Houses

Halfway houses are residential centers for ex-offenders in the community. Residents of halfway houses can be categorized as either halfway in or halfway out. Those who are "halfway in" have been sentenced to probation or diverted from the criminal justice system and are serving time in a halfway house as an alternative to incarceration. Those who are "halfway out" are near the end of their prison sentences or are on parole.[54] Most halfway house residents are parolees or similar inmates near the end of their sentence.

The more than nine hundred halfway houses in the United States have an average of twenty-five residents each. These facilities are located in multiple-family homes or apartment buildings, and residents spend from eight to sixteen weeks there.[55] At present 31,000 inmates, or fewer than 5 percent of the total on parole, are living in halfway houses.

Halfway houses are considered a minimum custody correctional facility, and only offenders with that security status are eligible. The financial distinction between a halfway house and a minimum security prison is significant. A minimum security prison bed costs an average of $32,000 to build, whereas a maximum security bed costs $80,000.[56] Although there is no reliable estimate of the cost of halfway houses, they are considerably less expensive than prisons because of their lower security requirements. More than 90 percent of halfway houses are operated by private agencies that contract with the government to provide services for inmates.

Halfway houses refer residents for counseling, treatment, and employment services, and some provide these services themselves. Thus, halfway houses provide extra custody and services for offenders on probation, or less secure custody and services for offenders after prison. Offenders serving time in halfway houses often have no residence of their own and no family members who are willing to take them. The halfway house provides food and shelter for a short period, enabling the offender to obtain a stable job and enough income to become self-sufficient.

Day reporting centers provide intensive supervision and treatment for offenders. They combine high levels of surveillance with services that include job-seeking skills, life skills, drug abuse education and treatment, and education. Day reporting centers provide services often needed by halfway house residents, but they operate independently of them. In 1990, there were only thirteen day reporting centers in the United States, but by 1994, 114 centers had been established in twenty-two states.[57]

Halfway houses originated with private efforts to help the homeless. Houses established by the Quakers, the Salvation Army, and other religious and civic organizations to help the destitute and homeless emerged during the 1800s, and many of them are still in operation.[58] As the treatment model of corrections became popular during the 1960s, government support and funding became available to sponsor ex-offenders in the community.[59] It was logical for existing private establishments to contract with the government to provide similar services for offenders.

There are no national data on the effectiveness of halfway houses, but individual reports have shown that they provide a useful, relatively low-cost transition for inmates returning to the community.[60] Their impact on recidivism has not been studied systematically, although it appears that recidivism rates for halfway house residents are comparable to those for offenders on parole.[61] This is significant because offenders in halfway houses are probably at higher risk of re-offending because of their lack of supportive family ties.

A continuing problem with halfway houses is public acceptance. Most people are reluctant to have ex-offenders living in their neighborhoods. Communities are more receptive, however, when they are given a voice in the usage and operation of the halfway house, when some space in the halfway house is available to community organizations, and when efforts are made to show how the residents might make a positive contribution to the neighborhood.[62] For example, halfway houses can help to stabilize a deteriorating neighborhood by establishing a visible presence of residents in a well-kept building that is open for community use.

Pardons

pardon
A reprieve from a governor or the President that excuses a convicted offender and allows him or her to be released from prison without any supervision.

Pardons are not actually a form of sentence, but they do allow a convicted offender to be released from prison without any supervision. Historically, pardons have been used as a form of parole to reward "reformed" offenders or those who in hindsight were deemed to have been given too severe a sentence. For example, from the late 1700s to the late 1800s England sent its prisoners to Australia. The governor could release convicts from their sentences by granting an *absolute pardon,* which restored all rights, including the right to return to England. A *conditional pardon* gave the convict Australian citizenship but not the right to return to England. A *ticket of leave* freed convicts from their obligation to work for the government or a master so that they were free to work elsewhere.[63] The power to pardon resided in the King.

When the U.S. Constitution was drafted, the President was given the power to pardon. Article II states that "he shall have Power to grant Reprieves and Pardons for Offenses against the United States, except in Cases of Impeachment."

There is considerable evidence that pardons were once used as a form of parole. During the mid-1800s, more than 40 percent of offenders released from prisons were pardoned. In Ohio, pardons were granted to inmates to make room for new prisoners. Similar circumstances existed in other states until parole was adopted to make the release process more standardized and objective.[64]

Today pardons are acts of clemency rather than parole. They are entrusted to the chief executive: the governor in the case of state offenses, the President in the case of federal crimes. A pardon excuses the offender from criminal penalties. Pardons are rare, and in most cases they are granted in order to remedy a miscarriage of justice. In a number of cases people serving prison sentences for murder have been pardoned when it was discovered that someone else committed the crime. On a less dramatic level, first offenders' criminal records are expunged if they complete special conditions and are not rearrested within a specified period; technically, this constitutes a pardon.

commutation
A modification or reduction of a sentence imposed on an offender.

Pardons are distinguished from **commutations,** which modify or reduce a sentence imposed on an offender. Commutations of death sentences to life imprisonment occur occasionally, especially during the holiday season. It is common for a governor to reduce the sentence of a death row inmate as a sign of humane concern, a gesture that is often done at the end of the governor's term and therefore cannot harm him or her politically.

Legal Issues

The freedom of an offender on probation or parole is tenuous. It depends on the offender's conduct in conforming to the law and to the conditions of supervision, and on the discretion of the supervising officer in assessing the seriousness of the offender's conduct. In a Georgia case, a first-time offender on probation for a burglary and theft had to repay $750 in fines and restitution according to a specified payment plan. The probationer was laid off from his job and could not pay the amount due on time; his probation was revoked and he was sent to prison. The case reached the Supreme Court, which held that failure to pay because of indigence is unlawful because it punishes a person for being poor and thus violates the equal protection clause of the Constitution. [65]

When probation or parole is revoked, due process of law must be observed because the offender's freedom is at stake. For this reason, the offender has many of the same rights as defendants at criminal trials, including written notice of the charges, the opportunity to refute them, the right to cross-examine witnesses, a "neutral and detached" body hearing the case, and written reasons for the decision.[66] There are no such due process guarantees in parole release decisions, unless the state specifically provides them. The Supreme Court has held that discretionary parole release does not carry due process rights under the Fourteenth Amendment because there is no presumption that an inmate has a right to be released before the end of the prison sentence.[67] However, if a state writes its parole law in a way that demonstrates a presumption that the inmate *will* be released on parole, due process protections apply.[68] In recent years states have moved away from the presumption of parole release. Therefore, most parole release decisions are administrative decisions that lack procedural safeguards.

The question of the proper role of a probation officer as a government agent arises when an offender makes incriminating statements while under supervision. In a landmark case, *Minnesota v. Murphy,* a probationer admitted to his probation officer that he was responsible for a rape and murder for which he had never been charged. The probation officer used these admissions as the basis for new charges against the probationer. The probationer argued at trial that his confession should be suppressed because he had not been informed of his *Miranda* rights when speaking to his probation officer. The Supreme Court held that the *Miranda* warning was not required because the probationer was not "in custody" when he confessed, and therefore his admission was voluntary.[69]

Questions also arise when a probationer's home is searched to determine whether a law has been violated. This might involve illicit drugs, guns, or other evidence of wrongdoing. The Supreme Court has held that a probation officer may search the home of a probationer without probable case as long as there are at least "reasonable grounds" related to the "special needs" of probation supervision.[70] The Court compared probation to the operation of government schools, prisons, or other government-regulated industry. There are "special needs" in these environments to provide supervision and security that do not apply in society at large. Because they have been convicted of a crime, probationers enjoy somewhat reduced constitutional protections. Therefore, probable cause and a warrant are not required for searches by probation officers. It is apparent from these legal decisions that offenders on probation and parole have limited legal protections compared to those enjoyed by suspects and defendants at earlier stages of the criminal justice system.

Alternative Sentences

In California an 18-year-old boy pleaded guilty to burning a cross on the lawn of a black family's home. No one was hurt, but a crime was committed.

What is an appropriate sentence? Jail? Probation? A fine?

The judge ordered the offender to read *The Diary of Anne Frank,* an autobiographical account of a young girl in hiding during the Nazi Holocaust. The offender had to submit a book report to the court.[71] In a Maryland case, a teenager convicted of a drive-by shooting was required to read *The Ox Bow Incident* and write a report on it while serving his jail sentence. The book describes people who take the law into their own hands and end up injuring the innocent.[72] In Jacksonville, Florida, a 17-year-old girl pleaded guilty to manslaughter after she suffocated her newborn child and left the infant in a trash can. In addition to two years in prison, the judge imposed ten years of birth control as part of the plea agreement.[73]

In each of these cases the judge, believing that no existing sanction was appropriate, invented an alternative sentence that fit the nature of the crime and the offender. The invention of new criminal sanctions has become more common in the late twentieth century and has interesting implications both for society and for the criminal justice system.

"Alternative sentences" are of two general types: those that center on justice for the victim ("restorative") and those that attempt to punish the offender in accordance with the nature of the offense ("authentic"). In **restorative justice** the criminal justice process is directed primarily at repairing the injury to the victim rather than focusing on the adversarial relationship between the government and the offender. **Authentic justice** is based on the idea that sanctions should be more closely related to the crime and that offenders should be punished in ways that neutralize their gain.

restorative justice
Sanctions should be directed primarily at repairing the injury to the victim rather than focusing on the adversarial relationship between the government and the offender.

authentic justice
Sanctions should be more closely related to the crime and offenders should be punished in ways that neutralize their gain.

The sections that follow examine several forms of restorative and authentic justice. Examples of restorative justice include restitution to the victim, mediation programs, and repairing harm to victims. Examples of authentic justice include shock incarceration, corporal punishment, public humiliation, and forced medical interventions.

Alternative sentences to either repair the injury to the victim or more closely mirror the nature of the crime are becoming more common. These sentences can also include service to the community at large.

Restorative Justice

Today cases are often selected for prosecution on the basis of a prosecutor's judgments as to whether proof of guilt can be established beyond a reasonable doubt. Key factors are the availability of evidence and the likelihood of conviction. Supporters of restorative justice believe that the impact of the crime on the victim is more important. They seek ways to "make the victim whole." In their view, the focus on "winning" cases begs the question: Who are we winning the case *for*? As we have seen, most prosecutors are elected, and winning cases may attract votes from a public that is gratified when offenders are convicted and sentenced to prison. However, this does not help those who were victimized by the offense. The restorative model aims to correct this imbalance in emphasis. An example is a program in Vermont where nonviolent offenders can choose to be sentenced by a judge or meet with members of the community in which the crime was committed.[74] This process allows for the community to more directly influence the justice process to address the harm caused by the offense. Based on a tradition that sees crime breaking the peace among citizens in a community, a similar program in upstate New York attempts to make offenders accountable to their victims and communities.[75]

Restitution to the Victim

In the most common form of restorative justice, the offender provides restitution to the victim. The restitution usually takes the form of money, but it can also include returning property or performing services for the victim. In cases of juvenile delinquency, for example, an offender may be required to remove graffiti from a building or earn money to replace stolen or damaged property. In such cases, the victim is compensated for the loss either directly or indirectly. Restitution serves both as a way to restore the victim to his or her previous condition and as a way to punish the offender.

While there is widespread support for the concept of restitution to the victim, this approach is not used often in the criminal justice process. Most offenders are poor and have spent or lost any gain they received from the crime. They often possess few job skills and little education. Under the restorative model the offender is provided an opportunity to work to earn money or to provide services to compensate the victim. Under this model fines would be gauged to the victim's loss and be paid to the victim.

Community service is a way that offenders can be held accountable when direct restitution is not possible. As a condition of release, an offender can be required to work without pay for a civic, nonprofit, or government organization. Restoration of the grounds of public buildings and schools, conservation projects, and maintenance are among the community service tasks that have been performed by offenders. This form of restitution offers offenders the opportunity to make amends with dignity while providing needed services to the community.[76]

Criminal offenses can have many victims. A homicide has an obvious direct victim, but it also has indirect victims such as surviving family members, the neighborhood where the crime occurred, employers and insurance companies, and the general public. These indirect victims reflect the fact that crimes are violations of the social order: The balance of justice within the community is upset when a crime is committed. Restitution has generally been limited to direct victims of crimes, but it is clear that the families of homicide victims, people who are seriously injured by violent crimes, and people who are financially ruined by theft or fraud suffer a long-term impact that often is not addressed by the criminal justice process. Some observers therefore believe that efforts should be made to make the justice system more responsive to the needs of victims.

Mediation

After a crime has been committed, it is rare that the offender and the victim ever speak to each other again. They may not even see each other, except in court. The prosecutor speaks on behalf of the jurisdiction (which includes the victim), while the defense attorney represents the accused person. This arrangement further distances the offender from the victim and promotes an adversarial relationship.

Mediation programs provide a forum in which the offender and the victim meet in a neutral setting in an "atmosphere of structured informality."[77] At these meetings both the victim and the offender relate their versions of what happened and how it affected them. They can ask each other questions and communicate their feelings, anger, and remorse. They discuss ways in which the balance of justice could be restored in a fair and equitable manner. This may involve an apology, restitution, community service, or other alternative. Once an agreement has been reached, it is put in writing and the victim and offender discuss a restitution schedule, whatever monitoring may be involved, and follow-up procedures.[78]

Four benefits of such a program have been identified. First, mediation gives victims direct input into the justice process. Second, it enables victims and offenders to communicate on a personal level, rather than through attorneys or not at all. Third, it allows victims to obtain closure on the trauma caused by the criminal event by exercising some control over its ultimate outcome. Fourth, it forces offenders to see victims as people with hopes, fears, and dreams similar to theirs. It thus leads offenders to understand and feel empathy for others. Studies have found that some victim–offender mediation programs do have these results. Victims are more likely to feel that justice has been done in mediated cases; in addition, higher rates of successful restitution and lower recidivism rates have been reported.[79]

Repairing Harm to the Victim

Restitution most often takes the form of monetary compensation. However, in many cases the harm caused to victims is physical, psychological, and emotional in nature. Victims of violent crimes are often made to feel partially responsible for the victimization because of the bad neighborhood they were in, the lateness of the hour, the company they kept, the words they used, or the clothes they wore. Although none of these factors has any bearing on the offender's liability, defense attorneys often attempt to project at least partial responsibility on the victim in order to reduce the amount of blame placed on the offender. The result is a process in which attempts are constantly made to shift blame between the offender and the victim while little effort is made to repair the harm caused by the offense, regardless of the outcome of the case.

TABLE 15.2

Characteristics of the Retributive and Restorative Models of Justice

RETRIBUTIVE JUSTICE	RESTORATIVE JUSTICE
Crimes are acts against the state	Crimes are acts against another individual or the community
Crime is controlled by the criminal justice system	Crime control comes from the community
Punishment holds offenders accountable	Assuming responsibility and taking action to remedy harm results in accountability
Victims are part of the community protected by the criminal justice system	Victims are harmed by crime and are central in determining accountability
Justice is pursued through the adversarial system	Justice is pursued using dialogue and reconciliation, negotiation, and reparation
The focus is on punishing the crime that occurred in the past	The focus is on the consequences of the crime and how to make the victim and community whole again in the future
Punishment changes behavior through retribution and deterrence	Punishment alone is not effective because it disrupts possibilities for harmony within the community

In an Alabama case a pregnant woman was killed, but her baby survived. The focus of the criminal case was exclusively on the culpability of the accused person.[80] Very little attention was given to the orphaned infant, and the long-term impact of custody decisions. Similarly, there is a growing movement for police to make arrests in domestic violence cases, but less effort has been devoted to supporting the victims of such violence. In Georgia, for example, as many as half the women and children who seek shelter from abusive family members are turned away because of lack of space.[81] The restorative approach seeks to shift the focus of the justice process toward repairing the harm done to the victim. This is accomplished by direct involvement of victims and the community at large in the justice process through reliance on dialogue, negotiation, accountability, and reparation in achieving justice.

Table 15.2 illustrates the differences between the elements of the restorative justice model and the traditional retributive model of justice. The role of the community, the accountability of the offender, and the centrality of victims to case resolution distinguish the restorative model, whereas the role of government, the adversarial relationship between the government and the offender, and punishment are featured in the retributive model, which underlies much of contemporary criminal justice.

Authentic Justice

As we have seen, fines (paid to the government), probation, and incarceration are the traditional methods used to punish offenders. They are "virtual" sanctions in the sense that they bear no direct relationship to the offense committed. For example, a robbery or assault has nothing in common with a prison or probation sentence in terms of behavior or impact. We simply equate certain sentences with certain crimes. On the other hand, locking someone up in prison for a period of years might be an "authentic" punishment for an offender who kidnapped a person and held him or her captive for an extended period. In the same way, an offender who stole several thousand dollars would receive an authentic sentence if he or she were forced to pay back at least that amount to the victim.

Authentic justice attempts to link the nature of the penalty with the nature of the offense in a more explicit way than has traditionally been the case. This is usually accomplished by having the penalty mimic the crime to the extent possible. Examples of authentic justice include shock incarceration, corporal punishment, public humiliation, and medical interventions for sex offenders.

Shock Incarceration

At a "boot camp" for inmates in Florida, the regimen is not easy: "Heads shaved. No phone calls for 44 days, then just to family. No TV, no recreation room. Marching in cadence. Obstacle courses. Spartan barracks. Psychological and substance abuse counseling. Five hours of classes. Homework. And a parade of victims, who tell the boys what it feels like on the other side of a gun."[82] This routine is much more severe and demanding than that experienced by most prisoners.

shock incarceration
Short-term military-style "boot camps" designed primarily for nonviolent young offenders and featuring a military atmosphere and strict discipline.

Many such **shock incarceration** programs were developed during the 1980s. They are short-term (three to six months) military-style boot camps designed primarily for nonviolent offenders. Although there is some variation in how boot camp programs are run, they all maintain a military atmosphere and strict discipline, and are populated by young offenders for short terms. The extent of the camps' military atmosphere is manifested by the fact that the U.S. Army and Marine Corps train corrections officers to serve as drill sergeants in boot camps.[83]

Shock incarceration programs are examples of authentic justice because they attempt to mirror the nature of the crimes committed more closely than does traditional incarceration. They try to recreate the shock of being victimized through a complete change in routine, attitude, behavior, and discipline. Boot camps are considered a better alternative to long-term imprisonment, in which inmates are generally inactive. Shock incarceration forces inmates to engage in physical ac-

Shock incarceration programs are short-term military-style "boot camps" designed primarily for non-violent offenders who are subject to a strict and demanding routine.

TABLE 15.3

Characteristics of Boot Camp Programs

CHARACTERISTICS	FEDERAL AND STATE* (n = 35)	LOCAL (n = 8)	JUVENILE (n = 9)
Year opened			
Before 1988	7	0	0
1988–1990	13	2	0
1991–1993	14	6	6
1994	1	0	3
Capacity			
Male	8,678	806	455
Female	626	102	0
Total capacity	9,304	908	455
Minimum length of residential boot camp			
< 3 months	2	4	1
3 months	15	2	2
4 months	9	0	5
6 months	9	2	1

*There were 32 states known to operate boot camps at the time of the study.

SOURCE: Blair B. Bourque, Mei Han, and Sarah M. Hill, *A National Survey of Aftercare Provisions for Boot Camp Graduates* (Washington, D.C.: National Institute of Justice, 1996).

tivity, drills, work, education, and counseling in order to change their attitudes and behavior patterns. The main characteristics of boot camp programs are summarized in Table 15.3.

Because of the rigorous physical activity they require, shock incarceration programs are designed for younger offenders. Most programs are planned for inmates who are serving sentences of less than five years or who are in the second half of a longer sentence and have good records. Although originally designed for first offenders, a growing number of boot camp programs accept offenders with prior records of incarceration and convictions for violent crimes (Table 15.4).

Shock incarceration programs for jail inmates also emerged during the last decade. As was noted earlier, a growing number of jail inmates have been sentenced to state prison but are being held in local jails because of a lack of space in prisons. Jails also hold a number of parole violators for whom there is no room in state prisons. There are now more than twenty-five jail boot camps where inmates stay for two to four months, a shorter stay than is typical in prison boot camps.[84]

Usually offenders volunteer to participate in boot camps in place of a longer sentence in a traditional prison. An underlying premise is that prisons have not been successful in deterring further crimes by offenders after release. The "shock" portion of shock incarceration is designed to alter the offender's attitude, self-control, and lifestyle, like basic training in the military. Many inmates are not well prepared for shock incarceration. It is difficult to change a lifestyle that has developed over a period of years and is characterized by poor school attendance, drug use, lack of employment, and low levels of physical activity. Nevertheless, shock incarceration attempts to address these lifestyle issues, whereas traditional incarceration tends to reinforce lethargic, unproductive behaviors, which continue after release.

TABLE 15.4

Eligibility Criteria for Boot Camps

ELIGIBILITY REQUIREMENTS	FEDERAL AND STATE (n = 35)	LOCAL (n = 8)	JUVENILE (n = 9)
Maximum age			NA
25 or under	7	3	
26–30	8	1	
31–35	7	0	
36–40	3	0	
No limit	10	4	
Maximum sentence			NA
Between 1 and 4 years	9	1	
Between 5 and 10 years	15	1	
Other	11	6	
Requirement that enrollment be voluntary	27	6	3
Exclude those with			
Prior incarceration	23	1	0
Violent crimes	33	6	3

SOURCE: Blair B. Bourque, Mei Han, and Sarah M. Hill, *A National Survey of Aftercare Provisions for Boot Camp Graduates* (Washington, D.C.: National Institute of Justice, 1996).

Evaluations of the impact of shock incarceration programs have had mixed results. These programs generally have not reduced recidivism compared to traditional incarceration. At the same time, offenders report that shock incarceration was a constructive experience.[85] In contrast, inmates who serve their sentences in prison do not view their experience as constructive. Part of the reason why boot camps have not had a stronger impact on recidivism is variation in the amount of time devoted to rehabilitative activities such as education, as well as lack of supervision or follow-up in the community after release. A national survey of fifty-two boot camp programs found that only thirteen had aftercare programs targeted at boot camp "graduates."[86] Therefore, most offenders completing boot camp programs are released to traditional probation or parole supervision, and the behaviors instilled in the boot camp program are not reinforced after release. Thus, offenders are, in essence, starting over when they reach the community.[87] Boot camp graduates who are placed on intensive probation or parole supervision are under greater surveillance than traditional probationers and parolees, but more intensive services such as employment assistance and family counseling are not provided.

The possibility for long-term behavioral change through a short boot camp program has led to the development of similar programs for juveniles. Three demonstration programs were established in Cleveland, Denver, and Mobile, Alabama. An evaluation of these programs found offender completion rates to be high (between 80 and 94 percent). Committed youths also improved in educational skills, physical fitness, and behavior. Attitude surveys completed by youths also showed improvements in respect for authority, self-discipline, teamwork, and personal appearance after completion of the program. The costs of shock incarceration per offender were lower than those of incarceration in traditional state or local corrections facilities.[88]

TABLE 15.5

Family Characteristics of Inmates in Three Boot Camp Programs

FAMILY CHARACTERISTICS	CLEVELAND (n = 118)*	DENVER (n = 76)*	MOBILE (n = 120)*
Percentage of youths residing with			
Both parents	11.9	15.8	15.0
Parent and stepparent	13.5	14.5	15.0
Single parent	60.2	31.6	51.7
Other relatives	11.8	11.7	10.8
Other**	2.5	26.2	7.5
Percentage of families receiving public assistance	57.7 (n = 104)	—	45.9 (n = 109)
Percentage of youths with one or more delinquent siblings	43.0 (n = 114)	32.3 (n = 68)	33.0 (n = 109)
Percentage of youths with a parent or guardian who			
Has been referred for child neglect or abuse	36.4 (n = 110)	30.3 (n = 66)	11.2 (n = 107)
Is known to have a criminal record	47.7 (n = 109)	28.6 (n = 63)	17.3 (n = 104)

*Numbers in parentheses indicate cases with complete data.
**Includes foster home, group home, runaway.

SOURCE: Blair B. Bourque et al., *Boot Camps for Juvenile Offenders: An Implementation Evaluation of Three Demonstration Programs* (Washington, D.C.: National Institute of Justice, 1996).

A continuing problem is how to keep offenders in aftercare services once the boot camp regimen is completed. Juveniles who remained in aftercare for at least five months reported positive changes in attitudes and behavior, but nearly half of the juveniles dropped out of aftercare, were arrested for new offenses, or were removed from the program for rule violation.[89] There are many reasons for these failures in follow-up, but the major one is troubled home environments after release.

As Table 15.5 illustrates, the majority of youths in boot camp programs are from single-parent homes; about half come from families receiving public assistance and more than a third have one or more delinquent siblings. Even more significant is that about 30 percent of juveniles in boot camps have a parent or guardian who has been sent to court for child neglect or abuse, and more than a third of the parents have a criminal record. These factors make it difficult for a boot camp graduate to be successful in the community.

Another factor in ineffective boot camp programs is high staff turnover. In addition, staff members find it difficult to achieve a healthy balance between military discipline and remedial education and counseling.[90] The military discipline in boot camps is designed to build esteem, not simply to punish, but strict discipline and a hard physical regimen do not mix easily with education, counseling, and other rehabilitative services.[91]

Corporal Punishment

In 1994, an Ohio teenager, Michael Fay, committed acts of vandalism while visiting Singapore. Along with some friends, he spray-painted and threw eggs and bricks at eighteen cars over a ten-day period. Singapore police also found stolen flags and signs in Fay's Singapore apartment. Fay was sentenced to four months in prison, a $2,320 fine, and six lashes with a wet rattan cane. This kind of caning, administered by an expert in martial arts, breaks the skin and leaves permanent scars on the buttocks.[92] The sentence caused an uproar in the United States, with some people defending it and others vehemently opposing it.

corporal punishment Physical punishment for a commission of a crime.

Corporal punishment is defined as physical punishment short of the death penalty. It has often been associated with torture and mutilation. Most forms of corporal punishment are illegal in the United States under the Eighth Amendment's prohibition against cruel and unusual punishment. In 1990, however, legislation was introduced in Texas that would result in a finger being amputated for each conviction of a drug dealer.[93] This was an effort to imitate the penalty for theft in some Islamic countries, which is amputation of the offender's right hand.[94] Although such a penalty would seem to constitute a violation of the Eighth Amendment, courts may decide whether it is within the "limits of civilized standards" or "totally without penological justification."[95]

The history of public attitudes toward various forms of punishment suggests that mutilation has not always been considered cruel and unusual punishment and may not be considered as such in the future. In the Colonial era, for example, offenders were sometimes placed in stocks (hands and feet locked into a wooden wall while they sat), the pillory (head and hands locked into a wooden wall while they stood), and ducking stools (tied to a lever and submerged under water until they were breathless). Today these forms of corporal punishment may be considered uncivilized, but they continued to be used into the 1800s. The question remains as to whether forms of corporal punishment exist that are not cruel and unusual and may be effective in preventing future crimes.

The U.S. State Department protested Michael Fay's punishment in Singapore, claiming that it was too severe. President Clinton called the punishment extreme and asked that it be reconsidered. This reaction is interesting in view of the long history of whipping as a form of punishment in the United States and elsewhere. It was used to punish offenders as far back as the time of ancient Egypt, when Hebrew slaves were whipped by their Egyptian masters if they failed to produce enough bricks.[96] The Romans, and later the English, used whipping to punish slaves and vagrants. Whipping was used extensively between 1600 and 1900 for a variety of crimes both major and minor, in England, Holland, Russia, and many other countries. During the early 1800s, England prohibited the whipping of women, but it was not until 1948 that whipping was abolished altogether as a form of punishment.[97]

Whipping was employed more often in the American Colonies than it was in England. Lying, swearing, failure to attend church services, stealing, selling rum to Indians, adultery (for women), and drunkenness were among the offenses for which people could be whipped. After the American Revolution, incarceration came into use as an alternative to whipping. By 1900, all states except Maryland and Delaware had abolished whipping. The last known "floggings" occurred around 1950 in those two states, and the Delaware law was not repealed until 1972.[98]

Despite the American protests of the whipping in Singapore, the penalty is still used in many countries. A bill to permit whipping of drug dealers was introduced in the Delaware legislature in 1990 but was not passed. Similar legislation was introduced in California, St. Louis, and Sacramento to punish vandals.[99] Amnesty International has reported that whipping is still legal in at least thirteen countries, including some in the Middle East, Africa, the Caribbean, and the Far East.[100]

Singapore responded to criticism of its use of corporal punishment by stating that "it is because of our tough laws against anti-social crime . . . that we do not have a situation like, say New York, where even police cars are not spared by vandals."[101] This leads to the question of whether whipping is effective as a deterrent to crime. An evaluation of the impact of whipping on subsequent criminal behavior of offenders in the United States found that 62 percent of offenders who were whipped were later convicted of another offense. Further, 65 percent of those who were whipped twice were convicted a third time.[102] Despite their failure as a deterrent, whipping and other forms of corporal punishment, such as paddling of schoolchildren, continue to attract attention from the public and some policymakers.[103] There are two reasons for this: Corporal punishment more directly imitates the pain suffered by the victim, and it is of short duration and therefore much less expensive to administer than traditional incarceration (which also has not been shown to deter subsequent offending).

Public Humiliation

A judge in Pensacola, Florida, has given people convicted of minor crimes a choice: Serve jail time or buy an advertisement in the local newspaper that shows their photo and details of the crime.[104] A judge in Albany, New York, ordered a six-time drunken-driving offender to place a fluorescent sign saying "Convicted DWI" on his license plates.[105] This newly popular type of "sentencing by public humiliation" has a long history.

Public humiliation has taken many different forms. In ancient Greece, deserters from the army were displayed in public wearing women's clothes. In England, public drunkards were walked through the streets wearing only a barrel.[106] Bridles were used on certain offenders in England and Colonial America. These devices looked like cages that fit over the head with a metal plate that fit into the

The stocks were used as a means of public humiliation and punishment of offenders in America until the early 1800s.

mouth. Any movement of the tongue was painful. Bridles were used primarily on "Scolds," women who habitually lied or found fault with others.[107] Use of stocks, pillories, and the ducking stool continued in England, France, and America until the early 1800s. These devices held the offender in public view in extremely uncomfortable positions for the purpose of ridicule and punishment. Although the punishment itself was not painful, it was humiliating and exposed the offender to abusive remarks and to objects thrown by passersby. Offenders were sometimes seriously injured or killed when exposed in this manner.[108]

Branding of offenders through permanent scarring dates back to the beginnings of Western civilization. It was used in ancient Greece, and in fourth century England offenders were branded on their thumbs (e.g., "M" for murderer) so that a judge could determine whether a person had a prior record. Branding was employed in the United States until the 1800s, and offenders were usually banished from the country.[109] Nathaniel Hawthorne's classic book, *The Scarlet Letter,* written in 1850, described the practice of forcing offenders to sew letters on their clothing to represent the crimes they had committed. The letters (and sometimes complete descriptions of offenses, worn around the neck) were often used in the American Colonies as punishments for blasphemy and public drunkenness.[110]

These sentences have been mimicked in recent years, although not duplicated. As was noted earlier, judges in some localities have required convicted drunk drivers to put bumper stickers on their cars that identify themselves as such. Other judges have required men caught soliciting prostitutes and those convicted of other minor crimes to pay to have their names, photos, and descriptions of their crimes printed in local newspapers. In one case, Regency Cruises agreed to pay a $250,000 fine for dumping twenty plastic bags of garbage into the Gulf of Mexico, and the company was forced to run full-page advertisements in area newspapers stating that it had been convicted of the offense.[111]

Are these authentic sanctions, or does public humiliation accomplish no other purpose than shaming? It has been argued that shaming is a useful form of punishment because it goes beyond mere punishment and instills feelings of guilt.[112] John Braithwaite claims that the criminal law is "too clumsy and costly a device to be a front-line assault weapon" in sanctioning and preventing crime.[113] He argues that consumer and professional groups, along with self-regulation, are better ways to deter corporate crime, and the analogy may hold for the crimes of individuals as well. Just as media exposure of misdeeds and consumer distrust can do much to prevent repeat offenses by corporations, exposure of individual misdeeds to the media and to neighbors may have a similar impact outside the traditional sentencing process. In this way, public humiliation may exact a deterrent and preventive effect that traditional prison and probation criminal sentences have been unable to achieve with any consistency.

Since these sentences are often linked to reduced sentences and no jail time, they are rarely challenged in court. When they have been challenged, they have been found to be constitutional under most circumstances.[114] Public humiliation sentences are still rare, and no evaluation of their impact has been conducted. It will be interesting to see if public shaming has any greater effect than other forms of sentencing. Nevertheless, the line must be carefully drawn between sanctions that attempt to be more authentic in relation to the crime committed and those that are simply cruel or vindictive.

Media and Criminal Justice

A CLOCKWORK ORANGE

Stanley Kubrick's 1971 film *A Clockwork Orange* (based on the novel by Anthony Burgess) is considered by many critics to be a cult classic, offering a timeless and disturbing prediction of crime and corrections in a futuristic society. Through first-person narrative, the film traces the criminal adventures of its teenaged hero, Alex DeLarge, and his gang of juvenile cohorts, The Droogs. While written nearly thirty years ago, *A Clockwork Orange* has possibly gained impact over the years, as its "sci-fi" depiction of a disintegrated society where the streets are overrun with teenaged gangs strikes a chord of reality as we enter the twenty-first century.

A typical night for Alex's gang starts off in the Korova milk bar, where the youths drink drug-laced milk that "sharpens them up for a bit of the old ultraviolence." Once happily under the influence, the gang embarks on a night of what we now consider "wilding": They ridicule and beat a beggar, and later begin a fight with a rival gang that is in the midst of raping a woman. They steal a car, break into a home, physically and sexually assault the inhabitants, and then return to the milk bar for a few more drinks before going home and sleeping through the school day.

Alex's carefree attitude and empowering violence are what is most disturbing; he is morally repugnant and without a conscience, the epitome of a sociopath. The controversy of *A Clockwork Orange,* however, is not so much Alex's violence as Alex's "rehabilitation." Once caught and incarcerated, Alex is given the option of participating in an experimental "aversion" therapy. Thinking only of early release, Alex agrees. He is then placed in restraints, his head locked in a vise with his eyes held open with "lidlocks." While eyedrops are dripped into his unblinking eyes, Alex is administered an intravenous drug that causes him to experience a paralyzing nausea, an indescribable sensation of pain and dying from which he cannot escape. As the drug takes its effect, Alex must watch films of horrific violence featuring graphic wartime slaughter, decapitations, rape, and maiming of humans. The purpose of this technique is evident; after a while, Alex has been psychologically "operantly conditioned" to associate all sex and violence with the drug-induced sickness.

The film actually serves to show the perceived benefits of such aversion therapy as well as the unanticipated dangers. After his release, Alex is unable to engage in any sort of sexual or violent activity without falling down in physical agony as the association with pain sets in. This becomes problematic when the rehabilitated Alex cannot even defend himself against violent aggressors. In the end, the experiment comes full circle when it is suggested that the effect of the treatment is short-lived.

In an era in which sexual predators are now offered (or required, in some states) rehabilitative therapy meant to "reprogram" their improper sexual and violent fantasies, *A Clockwork Orange* is no longer regarded as futuristic. As sentences increasingly include drug therapies and behavior-modification treatments, the role of aversion therapy is likely to expand in meeting correctional objectives.

MEDIA AND CRIMINAL JUSTICE QUESTION

If aversion therapy was shown to be effective, what constitutional questions might be raised in its use on offenders?

Forced Birth Control

Darlene Johnson, a mother of four children and pregnant with a fifth, was convicted of three counts of child abuse. The Visalia, California, judge sentenced her to a year in jail, to be followed by implantation of a birth-control device that would prevent her from conceiving any more children. According to the judge, "It is not safe for her to have children."[115] Is such a sentence cruel and unusual, or is it authentic justice?

The contraceptive Norplant was approved by the U.S. Food and Drug Administration in 1990 for public use. Norplant prevents conception when six small rods containing hormones are placed under the skin in a woman's arm. The rods can be implanted for up to five years.[116] The question for criminal justice is whether such a device can or should be used as a condition of sentencing in cases involving mistreatment of children. From the perspective of restorative justice, the use of Norplant may prevent abuse of new victims, but it does not address the current or future harm done to present victims. Those who advocate authentic justice believe that use of Norplant is justified because it forces the offender to suffer the consequences of misconduct in the parental role and prevents the offender from continuing in that role in the future. Once again, however, *existing* victims are not protected, only *future* victims.

Norplant has been made available in school clinics in Baltimore in response to the city's high teenage pregnancy rate. A similar program was initiated in Washington, D.C., where teenage mothers accounted for 18 percent of all births.[117] This use of Norplant outside the criminal justice system points to growing acceptance of this form of contraception, although the coercion inherent in criminal sentencing poses important legal and social issues. Is forced birth control a weak technological attempt to solve a problem that is educational, social, and cultural in nature? Does the use of Norplant discriminate against women inasmuch as it holds them entirely responsible for parenting and abuse, even though men also play a significant role in this process? Is it used in discriminatory fashion against minorities and the poor? Can the use of Norplant be extended beyond the length of a normal jail or probation sentence? These questions have yet to be addressed by the criminal justice system as it looks for sentences that more directly mirror the nature of the harm inflicted by offenders.

Depo-Provera for Sex Offenders

It has been estimated that rapists commit an average of seven rapes and that a child molester abuses seventy-five children.[118] Frustration over the difficulty of preventing sex offenses has led to proposals such as one enacted by the State of Washington state legislature that requires male sex offenders to be given the option of castration in return for a 75 percent reduction in prison time.[119] In 1997, California enacted a law that requires chemical castration of parolees with more than one conviction for child molestation.[120] More common, however, are efforts to treat sex offenders with drugs that reduce their sex drive.

The compulsion of some sex offenders to seek out victims repeatedly, despite prior punishment for sex crimes, has led researchers to examine possible biological factors in this type of crime. Some researchers have concluded that there are rapists who suffer from an abnormally high level of the male sex hormone testosterone. As a result, these offenders have an "uncontrollable" urge to seek physical "release." (As an example, consider the case of Alcides Quiles, who escaped from a Connecticut prison while serving time for raping a six-year-old boy, only to be caught after raping a two-year-old girl.[121]) This condition has led to the use of the drug Depo-Provera, which causes impotence. Sometimes referred to as "chemical castration," Depo-Provera relieves the biological urge in sex offenders.[122] It does this through its active ingredient, which is a synthetic hormone similar to progesterone. (Depo-Provera is also used as a contraceptive, as one injection protects a woman against pregnancy for three months.[123])

Such drug treatments remain controversial. Richard Seeley, director of Minnesota's Intensive Treatment Program for Sexual Aggressiveness, argues that "what's wrong with a sex offender is what's between his ears, not his legs." He claims that it is the rapist's thinking that is dysfunctional, not his sexuality: "Rapists are who they learn to be—it's not a product of their hormones."[124] Rape is often the result of anger and rage in which the offender seeks domination or control over the victim. This anger is not affected by Depo-Provera. This debate continues today. A Texas judge offered a sex offender the opportunity for physical castration (removal of the testicles) in exchange for his freedom. The possibility was abandoned when no physician would come forward to perform the procedure. This will not always be the case, however. A Texas gubernatorial candidate supported chemical castration for sex offenders seeking parole.[125]

As with Norplant, the use of Depo-Provera as a sentencing option is an outgrowth of frustration over the ineffectiveness of traditional sentencing alternatives. The social and legal issues posed by Depo-Provera mirror those posed by Norplant, with the added concern that physical castration is a permanent condition. Chemical castration can be reversed, however, by discontinuation of the drug. Chemical castration through Depo-Provera has drawn support not because it is likely to be more effective than traditional sentencing (remember that it is unclear what proportion of rapes have hormonal versus social causes), but because such a sentence more authentically reflects the nature of the crime committed.

Forfeiture of Assets

The war on drugs reflected growing frustration over drug abuse and drug-related crime. However, long prison sentences for drug offenders appear to have had a minimal impact on the drug trade. The result is an increased emphasis on a more authentic and restorative sanction: taking the profit out of the highly profitable drug trade.[126]

In response to the perception that drug offenders often consider prison sentences merely a price to be paid for conducting their illicit business, the Organized Crime Drug Enforcement Task Force (OCDETF) Program was established in 1983 to prosecute high-level drug traffickers. Consisting of members from all the major federal law enforcement agencies, OCDETF has attempted to seize the illicit assets of drug traffickers. This involves a civil or criminal forfeiture of property if the government can prove that the property was acquired or used illegally. A criminal forfeiture occurs when property is seized after the owner has been convicted of certain crimes, such as drug trafficking or racketeering. A civil forfeiture requires only that the government show probable cause that the property was involved in criminal activity. The burden shifts to the property owner, who must show that such probable cause does not exist.[127] For example, when organized crime boss John Gotti was convicted of racketeering, the government filed a civil forfeiture suit against seven buildings and three businesses that it believed were involved in Gotti's illegal activities. These businesses included a social club, a bar, a restaurant, and a clothing manufacturer, among others.[128] Similarly, in a North Carolina case drug traffickers used their illicit profits to buy property within the state; they then sold that property and bought property in Florida. Using asset forfeiture, the government was able to seize the Florida property as "derivative proceeds" of crime.[129]

Cash, cars, boats, planes, jewelry, and weapons constitute 95 percent of all seized assets, although real estate has higher monetary value.[130] Seized property is appraised, and each month the government lists forfeited property in *USA Today* to notify anyone who may hold a claim or lien on the property that it will be put up for auction. In some jurisdictions the seized property can be used by law enforcement agencies in combatting crime by using seized cars as surveillance vehicles and cash for undercover drug purchases. In this way, the proceeds of crime, especially high-profit drug crimes, can be seized to wipe out any financial gain achieved through illicit activities. From 1979 to 1994, the value of property seized by the federal government in asset forfeiture cases rose from thirty-three million to two billion dollars.[131]

In 1996, the Supreme Court held that civil forfeitures are not excessive under the Eighth Amendment but did not explain when a forfeiture is considered excessive.[132] For example, a drug dealer who is found to have packaged drugs in his house, transported them in his car, and held drug-related telephone conversations from his boat can have his house, car, and boat seized under forfeiture provisions in addition to any criminal penalties he may face. In 1997, the Supreme Court ruled that civil forfeitures that occur together with criminal punishment do not violate the constitutional protection against double jeopardy.[133] Therefore, it is not considered double punishment to be convicted of a crime and incarcerated and then to have the government pursue a civil forfeiture. Several instances in which innocent persons lost property and were injured in civil seizures based on false informant tips have resulted in closer scrutiny of the forfeiture process.[134] Nevertheless, asset forfeiture thus is an alternative sanction that attempts to address the motives behind profit-driven crimes and restore the balance of justice.

Offender Fees

The rising cost of corrections has led many jurisdictions to impose offender fees. These fees are assessed to help pay for the cost of probation, parole, prison, or other forms of correctional supervision. Offender fees are now imposed in forty states, although not all states impose fees on all offenders. Some states restrict fees to probationers or jail inmates, or base the fee on the type of offense, type of offender, or ability to pay.

Offender fee programs are based on the recognition that most offenders under community supervision are employed and can afford reasonable fees, and that the costs of operating state and local corrections systems are skyrocketing as correctional populations grow. In 1990, more than 2.6 million people were on probation. An offender fee of twenty dollars per month for six months would generate more than three hundred million dollars per year. In Texas, one-half the total cost of probation supervision is paid by offender fees.[135] To be effective, such a program must be systematic, and collections must be closely monitored to ensure compliance.[136]

Offender fee programs can be seen as a way to hold offenders accountable for their conduct and its long-term consequences. The fees offset the impact the offender has on the criminal justice system by providing compensation to the state for it. They attempt to reestablish the balance of justice in the community by helping to return the justice system to its previous status before the crime was committed.

Changing the Physical Environment

As with explanations of the causes of crime, the sanctioning of criminals vacillates between consideration of individual and social factors. A sanction such as Depo-Provera emphasizes that the causes and prevention of crime lie at the level of the individual, whereas public humiliation places value on shaming and the social aspects of crime causation and prevention. Changing the physical environment is another alternative sanction that emphasizes the social aspects of crime prevention.

In a 1972 book entitled *Defensible Space,* Oscar Newman argued that properly designed physical features in a neighborhood (e.g., building design, lighting, bushes, traffic patterns) will reduce crime.[137] A subsequent study of sixty-three public housing sites found that in sites with more defensible space residents exercised more control over exterior spaces and were less fearful and less victimized by crime. Such sites had fewer apartments per entrance, fewer floors per building, and more open views of the outside.[138] In a North Miami, Florida, neighborhood, street barriers and altered traffic patterns were shown to reduce drug dealing and crime in the area.[139] Fewer through streets and more dead ends reduce traffic flow and make it easier to know when strangers are in the neighborhood. In Seattle, removal of overgrown trees and bushes and better lighting were found to reduce the incidence of drug dealing, vandalism, and loitering.[140] These are among a variety of ways in which communities can be made safer by changing the physical environment.[141]

When offenders are enlisted to help in making neighborhoods safer, the goals of both restorative and authentic justice are served. Refurbishing of parks, installation of exterior lights, repair or demolition of deteriorated buildings, and community block watch patrols are examples of ways in which offenders can participate in constructive efforts to prevent crime. At present, very few such programs make use of offenders. Rather than limiting crime prevention to the police and community residents, however, it would be desirable to involve offenders themselves in efforts to create safer communities.

Critical Thinking EXERCISE

Registering Former Sex Offenders

The public has grave doubts about the ability of community corrections to control the conduct of ex-offenders. Nowhere is this more evident than in the case of sex offenders. Public concern reached a crescendo in 1994, when a seven-year-old New Jersey girl, Megan Kanka, was raped and murdered by a twice-convicted sex offender who was living across the street. Within six months of the incident, New Jersey passed a law that requires ex–sex offenders to register with police and for the community in which such an offender is living to be notified. The law also re-

quires offenders to notify police of their location every ninety days, with penalties of seven months in jail and a fine if they do not comply.

A majority of the states followed New Jersey's lead. However, the New Jersey law was struck down in lower courts. Once an offender has served his or her sentence, it was argued, the punishment has ended. Notification laws allow a criminal sentence to continue as long as the offender lives, thereby punishing the offender again and again.

Despite these arguments, the Supreme Court held in 1995 that it is constitutional to notify a community when a former sex offender lives there or moves into the area.[A] In 1998, the Court again rejected a challenge to New Jersey's Megan's Law. The Court left intact the provisions of the law, now adopted by thirty-seven states.[B] The Court also ruled that judges must hold a hearing to determine whether an individual sex offender is subject to the notification law and the extent of the warning to be given to the community. This due process provision is unlikely to make a great difference, as a CD-ROM has been released that lists the zip codes of California's 64,000 registered sex offenders. Four days after one offender's name was listed, a paroled child molester's car was fire-bombed; the crime was allegedly carried out by his neighbors.[C] A New Jersey man was attacked and beaten up by two men and his son, who mistakenly believed that he was a child molester.[D] Notification of the community regarding the release of sex offenders appears to produce panic rather than providing useful information. Since the notification itself implies that the state has some belief that the ex-offender may still be dangerous, it is not surprising that some individuals have had extreme reactions.

Even though fewer than 10 percent of all offenders are sex offenders, these cases are highly publicized, and public concern is quite high.[E] Nevertheless, few incarcerated sex offenders receive treatment, and the treatment they do receive appears to be ineffective in many cases. Until more effective treatment of sex offenders occurs, notification may frustrate and aggravate the public rather than help it.

Notes

[A]Steve Marshall, "Megan's Law Upheld," *USA Today* (July 26, 1995), p. 2; *Doe v. Poritz,* 116 S. Ct. 512 (1995).

[B]"New Jersey's Megan's Law on Sex Offenders Left Intact by Nation's Highest Court," *The Buffalo News* (February 23, 1998), p. 4.

[C]Arlyn Tobias Gajilan and Beth Glenn, "Sex-Crime Database," *Newsweek* (August 11, 1997), p. 12.

[D]Paul Leavitt, "Sexual Predators," *USA Today* (August 28, 1993), p. 3.

[E]Peter Finn, *Sex Offender Community Notification* (Washington, D.C.: National Institute of Justice, 1997).

Critical Thinking Questions

1. Why do you believe ex–sex offenders have been singled out for attention, rather than offenders who have committed murder, aggravated assault, or other serious crimes?
2. Under the guidelines set forth by the Supreme Court, in what way could a court hearing shed light on the necessity of notifying a community about the release or move of a former sex offender?

Critical Thinking EXERCISE

House Arrest in a Nice House?

In 1990, actor Kelsey Grammar was sentenced to house arrest after pleading no contest to a felony cocaine possession charge. He had to wear an electronic bracelet on his wrist for ninety days, serve three years' probation, pay a five hundred dollar fine, perform three hundred hours of community service, and complete a drug abuse treatment program.

Grammar was stopped by police for driving with expired license plates. A radio check indicated that he had missed a court appearance on a prior drunk-driving conviction, so a warrant for his arrest was outstanding. While he was in the police car, a packet of cocaine fell from his pocket.

Two years earlier, John Zaccaro, Jr., son of politician Geraldine Ferraro, had been sentenced to four months of house arrest for selling cocaine. His house was a $1,500 per month luxury apartment with maid service and cable television.

House arrest has been proposed as an intermediate sanction between probation and imprisonment. If the house is luxurious, however, the punitive aspects of the confinement may be lost. This brings up questions parallel to those raised by the confinement of an offender in minimum versus maximum security prisons. Are there certain kinds of offenders and offenses that deserve different levels of deprivation within a home?

Critical Thinking Questions

1. **Is house arrest appropriate for these offenders? Why or why not?**
2. **Knowing that prisons are overcrowded and that efforts should be made to keep nonviolent offenders out of prison, what alternative sentences would you propose in the cases just described?**

Summary

SANCTIONS IN LIEU OF INCARCERATION

- Monetary fines are the most common form of criminal sanction in the United States. They are used primarily in cases involving minor crimes or as an adjunct to incarceration for more serious offenses.
- Fines have problems of proportionality and collection, which can be overcome by the use of "day fines" based on offenders' daily earnings.
- Probation is a system in which offenders are allowed to live in the community under supervision. Offenders who are sentenced to probation usually have conditions attached to their sentences.
- Supervision in the community poses the risk that people under correctional supervision might commit further crimes.
- Dissatisfaction with probation, combined with the need to use prison space more efficiently, has produced a movement toward intermediate sanctions, which provide more rigorous supervision than normal probation yet are less expensive than incarceration.
- Intensive supervision is achieved by maintaining small case loads, frequent contact with offenders under supervision, and special conditions such as random drug tests.

- An offender under home confinement or house arrest may leave his or her residence only for approved reasons. Compliance is increasingly accomplished through electronic monitoring.

AFTER PRISON

- The purpose of parole is to allow inmates to serve the last part of their sentence in the community under supervision in order to make a successful readjustment to freedom.
- Parole is associated with indeterminate sentencing. Parole release is decided by a parole board consisting of corrections officers.
- Offenders who are not released by a parole board can be granted supervised mandatory release if they accumulate enough good-time credits.
- Because prolonged incarceration can reduce inmates' capacity to function outside of prison, some states have temporary release programs that allow inmates to enter the community for work, study, or other purposes.
- Work release programs permit eligible inmates to work during the day at regular jobs and return to the prison at night. Furloughs are unsupervised leaves from prison that are granted for only a few hours.
- Halfway houses are residential centers for ex-offenders in the community. They refer residents for counseling, treatment, and employment services.
- Pardons allow a convicted offender to be released from prison without any supervision. They excuse the offender from criminal penalties—unlike commutations, which modify or reduce a sentence.

LEGAL ISSUES

- When probation or parole is revoked, due process of law must be observed because the offender's freedom is at stake.
- Questions of legality arise when an offender makes incriminating statements while under supervision and when a probationer's home is searched to determine whether a law has been violated.

RESTORATIVE JUSTICE

- Advocates of restorative justice believe that who wins the case is less important than "making the victim whole."
- In the most common form of restorative justice, the offender provides restitution to the victim.
- Mediation programs provide a neutral setting in which offenders and victims can ask each other questions and communicate their feelings about the offense.
- Some forms of restorative justice are designed to repair the physical or psychological harm done to the victim.

AUTHENTIC JUSTICE

- Authentic justice seeks to link the nature of the penalty with the nature of the offense in an authentic way.
- Shock incarceration creates a military-style "boot camp" atmosphere in which inmates are forced to engage in physical activity, drills, work, education, and counseling. Usually offenders volunteer to participate in boot camps in place of a longer sentence in a traditional prison.
- Corporal punishment is physical punishment short of the death penalty. It has a long history in the United States and is supported by some advocates of authentic justice because it imitates the pain suffered by the victim.
- Public humiliation also has a long history and can take many different forms. Although there is renewed interest in this approach, public humiliation sentences are still rare.
- Forced birth control has been used as a punishment in cases involving child abuse.
- Some jurisdictions have attempted to treat sex offenders with drugs that reduce their sex drive. These treatments are controversial because some experts believe

that the behavior of sex offenders is psychologically rather than biologically motivated.

- Forfeiture of assets is increasingly being used in cases involving drug trafficking.
- Some jurisdictions impose offender fees on offenders under community supervision who are employed and can afford reasonable fees.

CHANGING THE PHYSICAL ENVIRONMENT

- Some experts believe that properly designed physical features in a neighborhood will lead to less crime.

Key Terms

community corrections
probation
intermediate sanctions
intensive supervision
house arrest
net-widening
parole
work release
study release
furlough
halfway house
pardon
commutation
restorative justice
authentic justice
shock incarceration
corporal punishment

Questions for Review

1. Why could it be said that *community corrections* is a contradiction in terms?
2. What do we mean when we say that there is a problem of proportionality in the use of fines as a criminal sanction?
3. What kinds of conditions are usually attached to the sentences of offenders on probation?
4. In what circumstances does probation appear to work best?
5. What are the advantages and disadvantages of house arrest?
6. What is parole, and why is it unpopular with the public?
7. What is meant by "truth-in-sentencing"?
8. Why are inmates sometimes permitted to participate in work release programs?
9. What is a halfway house?
10. What is the difference between a pardon and a commutation?
11. What legal issues are associated with probation and parole?
12. What is the philosophy underlying restorative justice?
13. What are the major forms of restorative justice?
14. What is meant by authentic justice?
15. What are the main features of shock incarceration, and what is their purpose?
16. What are some drawbacks of boot camp programs?
17. Briefly describe the history of corporal punishment in the United States.
18. Give an example of public humiliation as a criminal sanction.
19. What are some arguments against the use of forced birth control for child abusers?
20. Why is the use of drug treatments for sex offenders controversial?
21. What is the purpose of forfeiture of assets in drug trafficking cases?
22. What are offender fees?

Notes

[1]Lawrence M. Friedman, *A History of American Law,* 2nd ed. (New York: Basic Books, 1985), p. 596.

[2]Michael N. Castle, *Alternative Sentencing: Selling It to the Public* (Washington, D.C.: National Institute of Justice, 1991), p. 1; Dan M. Kahan, "What Do Alter-

native Sanctions Mean?," *University of Chicago Law Review,* vol. 63 (Spring 1996), pp. 591–653.

[3]"If Not Jail, What?," *The Economist,* vol. 337 (December 9, 1995), p. 26.

[4]Cited in *Alternative Sentencing,* p. 2; Laura A. Winterfield and Sally T. Hillsman, *The Staten Island Day-Fine Project* (Washington, D.C.: National Institute of Justice, 1993), p. 1.

[5]David J. Rothman, *The Discovery of the Asylum* (Boston: Little, Brown, 1971), p. 52.

[6]Ibid., p. 48.

[7]Ibid., p. 49.

[8]Sally T. Hillsman, Barry Mahoney, George Cole, and Bernard Auchter, *Fines as Criminal Sanctions* (Washington, D.C.: National Institute of Justice, 1987); Floyd Feeney, *German and American Prosecutions* (Washington D.C.: Bureau of Justice Statistics, 1998).

[9]Ibid.

[10]George F. Cole, *Innovations in Collecting and Enforcing Fines* (Washington, D.C.: National Institute of Justice, 1989).

[11]Winterfield and Hillsman, *The Staten Island Day-Fine Project.*

[12]Vera Institute of Justice, *How to Use Structured Fines (Day Fines) as an Intermediate Sanction* (Washington, D.C.: Bureau of Justice Assistance, 1996).

[13]U.S. Comptroller General, *National Fine Center* (Washington, D.C.: U.S. General Accounting Office, 1993).

[14]John Augustus, *John Augustus, First Probation Officer* (Montclair, NJ: Patterson Smith, 1972), p. 34.

[15]Howard Abadinsky, *Probation and Parole: Theory and Practice* (Upper Saddle River, NJ: Prentice Hall, 1997), p. 33.

[16]David Rothman, *Conscience and Convenience: The Asylum and Its Alternatives in Progressive America* (Boston: Little, Brown, 1980), p. 44.

[17]National Advisory Commission on Criminal Justice Standards and Goals, *Corrections* (Washington, D.C.: U.S. Government Printing Office, 1973), p. 316.

[18]National Institute of Corrections, *State and Local Probation Systems in the United States* (Washington, D.C.: U.S. Department of Justice, 1993).

[19]Thomas P. Bonczar, *Characteristics of Adults on Probation, 1995* (Washington, D.C.: Bureau of Justice Statistics, 1997); George M. Camp and Camille G. Camp, *The Corrections Yearbook 1994: Probation and Parole* (South Salem, NY: Criminal Justice Institute, 1994).

[20]Jay S. Albanese, Bernadette A. Fiore, Jerie H. Powell, and Janet R. Storti, *Is Probation Working?: A Guide for Managers and Methodologists* (Lanham, MD: University Press of America, 1981).

[21]Allen J. Beck, Jodi M. Brown, and Darrell K. Gilliard, *Probation and Parole 1995* (Washington, D.C.: Bureau of Justice Statistics, 1996).

[22]Louis Jankowski, *Probation and Parole 1990* (Washington, D.C.: Bureau of Justice Statistics, 1991).

[23]Patrick A. Langan, *Felony Sentences in the United States* (Washington, D.C.: Bureau of Justice Statistics, 1996), p. 2.

[24]Patrick A. Langan and Mark A. Cuniff, *Recidivism of Felons on Probation* (Washington, D.C.: Bureau of Justice Statistics, 1992).

[25]Randall Guynes, *Difficult Clients, Large Caseloads Plague Probation, Parole Agencies* (Washington, D.C.: National Institute of Justice, 1988).

[26]Langan and Cuniff, *Recidivism of Felons on Probation*; Bonczar, *Characteristics of Adults on Probation.*

[27]Todd R. Clear and Patricia Hardyman, "The New Intensive Supervision Movement," *Crime & Delinquency,* vol. 36 (1990), pp. 42–60; Rebecca D. Petersen and Dennis J. Palumbo, "The Social Construction of Intermediate Punishments," *Prison Journal* vol. 77 (March 1997), pp. 77–92.

[28]Billie S. Irwin and Lawrence A. Bennett, *New Dimensions in Probation: Georgia's Experience with Intensive Probation Supervision* (Washington, D.C.: National Institute

of Justice, 1987); Billie S. Irwin, "Turning Up the Heat on Probationers in Georgia," *Federal Probation*, vol. 50 (1986), p. 2.

[29]Allen J. Beck, *Correctional Populations in the United States* (Washington, D.C.: Bureau of Justice Statistics, 1997).

[30]Joan Petersilia and Susan Turner, *Evaluating Intensive Supervision Probation/Parole: Results of a Nationwide Experiment* (Washington, D.C.: National Institute of Justice, 1993).

[31]Ian D. Brownlee, "Intensive Probation with Young Adult Offenders: A Short Reconviction Study," *British Journal of Criminology*, vol. 35 (Autumn 1995), pp. 599–612.

[32]Ibid., p. 9.

[33]Dale Parent, Terence Dunworth, Douglas McDonald, and William Rhodes, *Intermediate Sanctions* (Washington, D.C.: National Institute of Justice, 1997), p. 4.

[34]Virginia State Crime Commission, *The Use of Home Electronic Incarceration in Virginia* (Richmond: Commonwealth of Virginia, 1998).

[35]Dennis Wagner and Christopher Baird, *Evaluation of the Florida Community Control Program* (Washington, D.C.: National Institute of Justice, 1993).

[36]J. Robert Lilly, Richard A. Ball, David Curry, and John McMullen, "Electronic Monitoring of the Drunk Driver: A Seven Year Study of the Home Confinement Alternative," *Crime & Delinquency*, vol. 39 (1993), pp. 462–84.

[37]Terry L. Baumer and Robert I. Mendelsohn, "Electronically Monitored Home Confinement: Does It Work?," in James M. Byrne, Arthur J. Lurigio, and Joan Petersilia, eds., *Smart Sentencing: The Emergence of Intermediate Sanctions* (Newbury Park, CA: Sage, 1995), pp. 54–67.

[38]Baumer and Mendelsohn, 1995.

[39]"Paterson," *USA Today* (June 1, 1992), p. 8.

[40]"Trenton," *USA Today* (October 9, 1992), p. 10; "Newark," *USA Today* (January 16, 1995), p. 6.

[41]Daniel Ford and Anneseley K. Schmidt, *Electronically Monitored Home Confinement* (Washington, D.C.: National Institute of Justice, 1985).

[42]Baumer and Mendelsohn, pp. 60–3.

[43]Patrick A. Langan, *Felony Sentences in the United States.*

[44]Belinda Rodgers McCarthy and Bernard J. McCarthy, Jr., *Community-Based Corrections*, 3rd ed. (Belmont, CA: Wadsworth, 1997), p. 270.

[45]Peggy B. Burke, *Abolishing Parole: Why the Emperor Has No Clothes* (Lexington, KY: American Probation and Parole Association, 1995); Garay Spencer, "Pataki Proposes Bill to End Parole for Violent Felons," *New York Law Journal* (March 12, 1998), p. 1.

[46]National Institute of Corrections, *Status Report on Parole, 1995* (Washington, D.C.: U.S. Department of Justice, 1995).

[47]Louis Jankowski, *Probation and Parole* (Washington, D.C.: Bureau of Justice Statistics, 1991); Beck, Brown, and Gilliard, *Probation and Parole 1995.*

[48]California and Oregon statistics cited in William M. DiMascio, *Seeking Justice: Crime and Punishment in America* (New York: Edna McConnell Clark Foundation, 1997), p. 23.

[49]Don M. Gottfredson, Leslie T. Wilkins, and Peter B. Hoffman, *Guidelines for Parole and Sentencing* (Lexington, MA: Lexington Books, 1978).

[50]Bernard McCarthy and Belinda McCarthy, *Community-Based Corrections*, 1997, p. 294.

[51]Linda Smith, "Intermediate Sanctions: Getting Tough in the Community," in Ira J. Silverman and Manuel Vega, eds., *Corrections: A Comprehensive View* (St. Paul: West Publishing, 1996), p. 520.

[52]Camille G. Camp and George Camp, *The Corrections Yearbook 1995* (South Salem, NY: Criminal Justice Institute, 1995).

[53]Ibid., p. 54.

[54]Donald J. Thalheimer, *Halfway Houses* (Washington, D.C.: U.S. Government Printing Office, 1975).

[55]Ibid., p. 64; Dale Parent, *Residential Community Corrections: Developing an Integrated Correction Policy* (Washington D.C.: National Institute of Corrections, 1990).

[56]Ibid., p. 47.

[57]Dale G. Parent, "Day Reporting Centers: An Evolving Intermediate Sanction," *Federal Probation,* vol. 60 (December 1996), pp. 51–4.

[58]Oliver J. Keller and Benedict S. Alper, *Halfway Houses: Community-Centered Correction and Treatment* (Lexington, MA: Lexington Books, 1970).

[59]President's Commission on Law Enforcement and Administration of Justice, *Task Force Report: Corrections* (Washington, D.C.: U.S. Government Printing Office, 1967).

[60]Edward Latessa and Harry Allen, "Halfway Houses and Parole: A National Assessment," *Journal of Criminal Justice,* vol. 10 (1982), p. 161.

[61]P.G. Connelly and B. R. Forschner, "Predictors of Success in a Co-Correctional Halfway House: A Discriminant Analysis," in T. Ellsworth, ed., *Contemporary Community Corrections* (Prospect Heights, IL: Waveland Press, 1992).

[62]Margot C. Lindsay, *A Matter of Principle: Public Involvement in Residential Community Corrections* (Washington, D.C.: National Institute of Corrections, 1990).

[63]Richard Hughes, *The Fatal Shore* (New York: Knopf, 1987).

[64]Christopher Hibbert, *The Roots of Evil: A Social History of Crime and Punishment* (Boston: Little, Brown, 1968).

[65]*Bearden v. Georgia,* 461 U.S. 660 (1983).

[66]*Morrissey v. Brewer,* 408 U.S. 471 (1972); *Gagnon v. Scarpelli,* 411 U.S. 788 (1973).

[67]*Greenholtz v. Nebraska Penal Inmates,* 442 U.S. 1 (1979); *Jago v. Van Curen,* 454 U.S. 14 (1981).

[68]*Board of Pardons v. Allen,* 482 U.S. 369 (1987).

[69]*Minnesota v. Murphy,* 465 U.S. 420 (1984).

[70]*Griffin v. Wisconsin,* 483 U.S. 868 (1987).

[71]Cited in Marilyn D. McShane and Wesley Krause, *Community Corrections* (New York: Macmillan, 1993), p. 4.

[72]"Judge Throws Book at Shooter," *The Buffalo News* (April 14, 1995), p. 3.

[73]Paul Leavitt, "Birth Control Sentence," *USA Today* (November 15, 1990), p. 3.

[74]Mark Hansen, "Repairing the Damage: Citizen Boards Tailor Sentences to Fit the Crimes in Vermont," *ABA Journal,* vol 83 (September 1997), p. 20.

[75]Joe Loconte, "Making Criminals Pay: A New York County's Bold Experiment in Biblical Justice," *Policy Review,* vol. 87 (January–February 1998), pp. 26–32.

[76]Richard J. Maher and Cheryl Holmes, "Community Service: A Way for Offenders to Make Amends," *Federal Probation,* vol. 61 (March 1997), pp. 26–8.

[77]Martin Wright and Burt Galawy, eds., *Mediation and Criminal Justice: Victims, Offenders, and Community* (Newbury Park, CA: Sage, 1989), p. 2.

[78]Robert Coates and John Gehm, "An Empirical Assessment," in M. Wright and B. Galawys, eds., *Mediation and Criminal Justice* (Newbury Park, CA: Sage, 1989), pp. 251–6.

[79]Mark Umbreit et al., *Victim Meets Offender: The Impact of Restorative Justice and Mediation* (Monsey, NY: Criminal Justice Press, 1994); Mark S. Umbreit and Mike Niemeyer, "Victim Offender Mediation: From the Margins Toward the Mainstream," *Perspectives* (Summer 1996), p. 28.

[80]Etta F. Morgan and Ida M. Johnson, "Kidnapping and Murder for Motherhood," paper presented at the Annual Meeting of the Southern Criminal Justice Association (Richmond, VA, 1997).

[81]Elizabeth H. McConnell, "Issues in Family Violence in Georgia," paper presented at the Annual Meeting of the Southern Criminal Justice Association (Richmond, VA, 1997).

[82]Deborah Sharp, "Boot Camps Try for Rehabilitation," *USA Today* (November 9, 1993), p. 3.

[83]Doris Layton MacKenzie, "Boot Camp Programs Grow in Number and Scope," *NIJ Reports* (November–December 1990), pp. 6–8; Jon R. Sorensen, "Shock Camps Get High Marks Despite Violent Incidents," *The Buffalo News* (April 15, 1996), p. 8.

[84]James Austin, Michael Jones, and Melissa Bolyard, *The Growing Use of Jail Boot Camps: The Current State of the Art* (Washington, D.C.: National Institute of Justice, 1993).

[85]Michael Peters, David Thomas, and Christopher Zamberlan, *Boot Camps for Juvenile Offenders* (Washington, D.C.: Office of Juvenile Justice and Delinquency Prevention, 1997).

[86]Blair B. Bourque, Mei Han, and Sarah M. Hill, *A National Survey of Aftercare Provisions for Boot Camp Graduates* (Washington, D.C.: National Institute of Justice, 1996).

[87]Ibid., p. 13.

[88]Blair B. Bourque et al., *Boot Camps for Juvenile Offenders: An Implementation Evaluation of Three Demonstration Programs* (Washington, D.C.: National Institute of Justice, 1996).

[89]Ibid.

[90]Ibid., p. 2.

[91]Cited in *NIJ Reports* (November–December 1990), p. 5.

[92]Andrea Stone, "Whipping Penalty Judged too Harsh—by Some," *USA Today* (March 10, 1994), p. 3.

[93]Tom Squitieri, "Proposals Seek More Drastic Punishments," *USA Today* (February 14, 1990), p. 3.

[94]Sam S. Souryal and Dennis W. Potts, "The Penalty of Hand Amputation for Theft in Islamic Justice," *Journal of Criminal Justice,* vol. 22 (1994), pp. 249–65.

[95]*Trop v. Dulles,* 356 U.S. 86, 1958; *Rhodes v. Chapman,* 452 U.S. 337, 1981.

[96]W. M. Cooper, *A History of the Rod in all Countries* (London: John Camden Hotten, 1870).

[97]L. A. Parry, *The History of Torture in England* (Montclair, NJ: Patterson Smith, 1934); Graham Newman, *The Punishment Response* (New York: Lippincott, 1978).

[98]S. Rubin, *The Law of Criminal Correction* (St. Paul: West Publishing, 1973).

[99]Paul Leavitt, "Calls for Caning Keep on Coming," *USA Today* (May 25, 1994), p. 3.

[100]Amnesty International, *1991 Report* (New York: Amnesty International, 1991).

[101]Cited in Stone, p. 3.

[102]R.G. Caldwell, *Criminology,* 2nd ed. (New York: Ronald Press, 1965).

[103]Tamara Henry, "Groups Seek to Lay Down Law on Corporal Discipline," *USA Today* (March 8, 1994), p. 6D; Newman, *The Punishment Response.*

[104]"Pensacola," *USA Today* (August 5, 1993), p. 9.

[105]"Albany," *USA Today* (June 14, 1995), p. 11.

[106]G. Ives, *A History of Penal Methods* (Montclair, NJ: Patterson Smith, 1914).

[107]Newman, *The Punishment Response;* W. Andrews, *Bygone Punishments* (London: William Andrews, 1899).

[108]A.M. Earle, *Curious Punishments of Bygone Days* (Montclair, NJ: Patterson Smith, 1896).

[109]H. Oppenheimer, *The Rationale of Punishment* (Montclair, NJ: Patterson Smith, 1913); Parry, *The History of Torture in England.*

[110]Earle, *Curious Punishments of Bygone Days.*

[111]Tony Mauro, "Judge Orders 'Humiliation' Ads: Papers Uneasy," *USA Today* (December 15, 1990), p. 3; "Albany," *USA Today*; "Pensacola," *USA Today;* "Tampa," *USA Today* (December 9, 1994), p. 6.

[112]James Q. Whitman, "What is Wrong with Inflicting Shame Sanctions?," *Yale Law Journal,* vol. 107 (January 1998), pp. 1055–92; Kelly McMurry, "For Shame," *Trial,* vol. 33 (May 1997), pp. 12–15.

[113]John Braithwaite, *Corporate Crime and the Pharmaceutical Industry* (London: Routledge & Kegan Paul, 1984); John Braithwaite, "Transnational Regulation of the Pharmaceutical Industry," *The Annals,* vol. 525 (January 1993).

[114]Henry J. Reske, "Scarlet Letter Sentences," *ABA Journal,* vol. 82 (January 1996), pp. 16–18; Darryl van Duch, "State High Court Rejects Ridicule as Unreasonable," *The National Law Journal,* vol. 19 (May 5, 1997), p. 6.

[115]Leavitt, p. 3.

[116]Kim Painter, "Norplant Gets a Shot in the Arm," *USA Today* (August 22, 1995), p. 4D.

[117]Paul Leavitt, "Baltimore Schools Offer Teens Norplant," *USA Today* (December 4, 1992), p. 3.

[118]"Debate: Give Sex Offenders Longer Prison Terms," *USA Today* (March 7, 1990), p. 10.

[119]"Castration Bill," *USA Today* (February 13, 1990), p. 3.

[120]Kay-Frances Brody, "A Constitutional Analysis of California's Chemical Castration Statute," *Temple Political & Civil Rights Law Review,* vol. 7 (Fall 1997), pp. 141–70.

[121]"Tot Killing," *USA Today* (October 20, 1990), p. 3.

[122]David Gelman, "The Mind of the Rapist," *Newsweek* (July 23, 1990), pp. 46–53.

[123]Dori Stehlin, "Depo-Provera: The Quarterly Contraceptive," *FDA Consumer* (March 1993).

[124]Gelman, p. 47.

[125]Squitieri, p. 3.

[126]U.S. Comptroller General, *Asset Forfeiture: Need for Stronger Marshals Service Oversight of Commercial Real Property* (Washington, D.C.: U.S. General Accounting Office, 1991).

[127]George N. Aylesworth, *Forfeiture of Real Property: An Overview* (Washington, D.C.: Bureau of Justice Assistance, 1991).

[128]Joseph P. Fried, "Government Sues to Seize Gotti's Ill-Gotten Assets," *The New York Times* (January 15, 1993), p. B1.

[129]*United States v. One Parcel of Real Estate,* 675 F. Supp. 645 (D. Fla. 1987).

[130]G. Patrick Gallagher, *The Management and Disposition of Seized Assets* (Washington, D.C.: Bureau of Justice Assistance, 1988), p. 2.

[131]Laurie E. Ekstrand, *Asset Forfeiture: Historical Perspective on Asset Forfeiture Issues* (Washington, D.C.: U.S. General Accounting Office, 1996).

[132]*Austin v. United States,* 116 S. Ct. 994 (1996); Jerome Spencer, "Auspices of Austin: Examining Excessiveness of Civil Forfeitures under the Eighth Amendment," *American Criminal Law Review,* vol. 35 (Fall 1997), pp. 163–89.

[133]Matthew Costigan, "Go Directly to Jail, Do Not Pass Go, Do Not Keep House," *Journal of Criminal Law and Criminology,* vol. 87 (Spring 1997), pp. 719–50; *U.S. v. Ursery,* 116 S. Ct. 2135 (1996).

[134]Robert E. Bauman, "Take It Away," *National Review,* vol. 47 (February 20, 1995), pp. 34–8.

[135]Peter Finn and Dale Parent, *Making the Offender Foot the Bill: A Texas Program* (Washington, D.C.: National Institute of Justice, 1992).

[136]Dale Parent, *Recovering Correctional Costs through Offender Fees* (Washington, D.C.: National Institute of Justice, 1990).

[137]Oscar Newman, *Defensible Space* (New York: Macmillan, 1972).

[138]Oscar Newman and Karen Franck, *Factors Influencing Crime and Instability in Urban Housing Developments* (Washington, D.C.: U.S. Government Printing Office, 1980); Oscar Newman and Karen Franck, "The Effects of Building Size on Personal Crime and Fear of Crime," *Population and Environment,* vol. 5 (1982), pp. 203–20.

[139]R. Atlas, "The Other Side of CPTED," *Security Management* (March 1991).

[140]D. L. Weisel, C. Gouvis, and A. V. Harrell, *Addressing Community Decay and Crime: Alternative Approaches and Explanations* (Washington, D.C.: The Urban Institute, 1994).

[141]See Ralph B. Taylor and Adele V. Harrell, *Physical Environment and Crime* (Washington, D.C.: National Institute of Justice, 1996); Dan Dleissner and Fred Heinzelmann, *Crime Prevention through Environmental Design and Community Policing* (Washington, D.C.: National Institute of Justice, 1996).

For Further Reading

Paul H. Hahn, *Emerging Criminal Justice: Three Pillars for a Proactive Justice System* (Sage Publications, 1998).

Mark S. Umbreit, *Victim Meets Offender: The Impact of Restorative Justice and Mediation* (Monsey, NY: Criminal Justice Press, 1994).

Daniel Van Ness and Karen Heetderks Strong, *Restoring Justice* (Cincinnati: Anderson Publishing, 1997).

chapter sixteen

International Criminal Justice

The truth is that a vast restructuring of society is needed if remedies are to become available to the average person. . . . Where there is a persistent sense of futility, there is violence; and that is where we are today.

JUSTICE WILLIAM O. DOUGLAS
(1898–1980)

On April 14, 1998, a 32-year-old Paraguayan, Angel Breard, was put to death by lethal injection in Virginia. He had been convicted of a murder in Virginia but had never been informed of his right to consult with the Paraguayan consulate during his adjudication. The omission violates a Vienna Convention signed by more than 130 countries, including the United States. The world court unanimously instructed the United States to delay the execution so it could consider a protest from Paraguay. U.S. Secretary of State, Madeleine Albright, also petitioned the governor of Virginia to delay the execution, but it was carried out anyway.[1]

CHAPTER OUTLINE

The governor commented that Americans needed to be protected and that the prisoner received all necessary protections in the criminal justice process. On the other hand, the Secretary of State is concerned that if the United States ignores the international convention, other nations will follow suit, thereby endangering Americans traveling abroad. This case illustrates how crime and justice can have direct international consequences as well as the impact of a single case globally. This chapter examines the extent of crime around the world and how it is becoming international in nature, and trends toward an international system of adjudication.

The Risk of Crime around the World

The United States is not the only nation with a violent crime problem. In Mexico a former governor was shot and killed at a busy intersection in broad daylight. The assailant wanted to steal his watch. Armed robberies in Mexico City are said to have risen by as much as 70 percent in recent years.[2] Crime "seems to be almost out of control in China these days."[3] A Chinese bank robber killed a cab driver and three female tellers, and a thief strangled a girl during a burglary attempt. In Rio de Janeiro, Brazil, a city of eleven million inhabitants, about twenty people are shot and killed each day.[4] In Japan, a nerve gas attack on a Tokyo subway injured 5,000 people and killed ten. A month later Japan's national police chief was shot on his way to work.[5] These acts of violence occur with alarming frequency all over the globe. Do these crimes accurately reflect the overall crime situation in these countries? How does the United States compare in its handling of crime and violence?

As is discussed in Chapter 3, in the United States major violent and property crimes are counted annually. The Uniform Crime Reports count eight serious crimes known to the police, and the national victimization survey counts six of those crimes (excluding murder and arson) to determine the level of crime that

Rates of violent crime are higher in the United States than in most other industrialized nations. This has resulted in international studies of the factors associated with low and high crime rates.

actually occurs, whether or not it is reported to police. Unfortunately, there is no international analogy to the Uniform Crime Reports or victimization surveys. Different nations use different methods to count crimes, and some approach the task more diligently than others. Some countries regard crime as a blot on their national image, and others do not see the significance of documenting it in statistical terms.[6]

A major problem in comparing crime rates in different nations is the way crimes are counted. In some nations, rape is rarely reported to the police because victims do not believe it will be taken seriously by police officials. In other nations, crimes are not reported because citizens fear the police. In still other countries, record-keeping is not uniform, and therefore not all crimes brought to the attention of police are included in official figures. The result of these methodological problems is that the number of crimes reported to the police is generally lower than the level of crime that is actually occurring. In the United States, victimization surveys have revealed that more than a third of all crime is not reported to police, and it is likely that this figure is higher in other nations.

Incidence of Major Crimes

Despite these problems, several efforts have been made to obtain some kind of international comparison of the incidence of major crimes. There are two reasons for these efforts: (1) Without periodically collected baseline data about the incidence of crime, it is impossible to distinguish long-term trends from year-to-year fluctuations, and (2) a comparison of crime rates in different nations might provide clues as to why some nations are more successful than others in controlling crime rates.

The two major multinational efforts to measure the extent of crime in different countries are Interpol and the United Nations crime surveys. Interpol is the International Police Organization, headquartered in Lyons, France. It provides a resource for crime data and intelligence information to member police agencies around the world. Every two years Interpol requests crime reports from each member nation for seven offense categories (murder, sex offenses, serious assault, theft, fraud, counterfeit currency, and drug offenses). Some of these offenses are difficult to compare; for example, the United States counts only rape in the category "sexual offenses," whereas most other nations count sex crimes of all types. Likewise, the nature of drug offenses varies widely by country, making cross-national comparisons problematic. Even murders can sometimes be counted incorrectly, because accidents, suicides, attempted homicides, and "questionable" deaths are either included or erroneously excluded in some countries. Therefore, it is important to be wary of crime "rankings" among nations when using crimes reported to police. Definitional and reporting problems make such rankings suspect.

A comparison of homicides as reported to Interpol, the United Nations, and the World Health Organization reveals differences within the same countries in the same years. Some countries, such as Ecuador, Ireland, Norway, and Thailand, reported fewer attempted and actual homicides than actual homicides, which of course is impossible.[7] Despite such anomalies, however, the homicide figures reported by most nations are more consistent than those for other offenses because of the presence of a deceased victim and the more intensive investigation that occurs in these cases.

The United Nations undertook its first world crime survey in 1978, and has conducted three additional surveys since then. These surveys have continually increased in scope, but participation has not been uniform. A quarter of the countries responding to the first U.N. survey did not respond to the second, and 30 percent of those who responded to the second did not respond to the first. In addition, many questions were asked in later surveys that were not asked in the first survey.[8]

Nevertheless, the surveys made several important findings. First, theft is the most commonly committed crime in all nations, and its rate goes up in industrialized nations (where there apparently is more to steal). Property crimes were ten times higher in Western developed countries (and in the Caribbean) than elsewhere. Second, assault is the most common crime of violence, although it occurs between four and ten times less often than do crimes of theft. Latin America and the Caribbean regions experience the highest rates of homicide, assault, and other violent crimes. Third, men commit reported crimes at a rate that is ten times higher than that of women.[9]

Dane Archer and Rosemary Gartner gathered police statistics for five crimes in 110 different nations and forty-four major cities for the period 1900 to 1970.[10] They focused on homicide because of the higher reliability of reporting and definition of the offense. They made three interesting findings regarding the nature and correlates of homicide:

1. *Postwar homicides:* Homicide rates increase consistently after wars, suggesting that wartime violence may "legitimize" violence in a free society.
2. *Cities and homicides:* Any area that was more urban had a higher homicide rate than the national average. This suggests that population density has an impact on criminality.
3. *Death penalty:* When the death penalty was abolished in a country, the homicide rate generally decreased, suggesting that the death penalty does not usually prevent murders.

These findings reveal long-term longitudinal trends across cultures. Related work by Richard Bennett and James Lynch is helping to build more comparable crime and criminal justice databases to allow for more meaningful and detailed analyses of trends around the world.[11]

Victimization

Victimization surveys have been conducted on the national or city level in a growing number of countries, including Canada, England, Finland, Germany, Israel, Mexico, and the Netherlands.[12] In a significant move forward, fourteen nations participated in a standardized victimization survey. Overall victimization rates were found to be highest in the United States (28.8 percent of the population), followed by Canada and Australia. The lowest incidence of crime victimization was reported in Northern Ireland, Switzerland, and Finland (about 15 percent of the population). The results for all the nations involved in the survey are summarized in Figure 16.1.

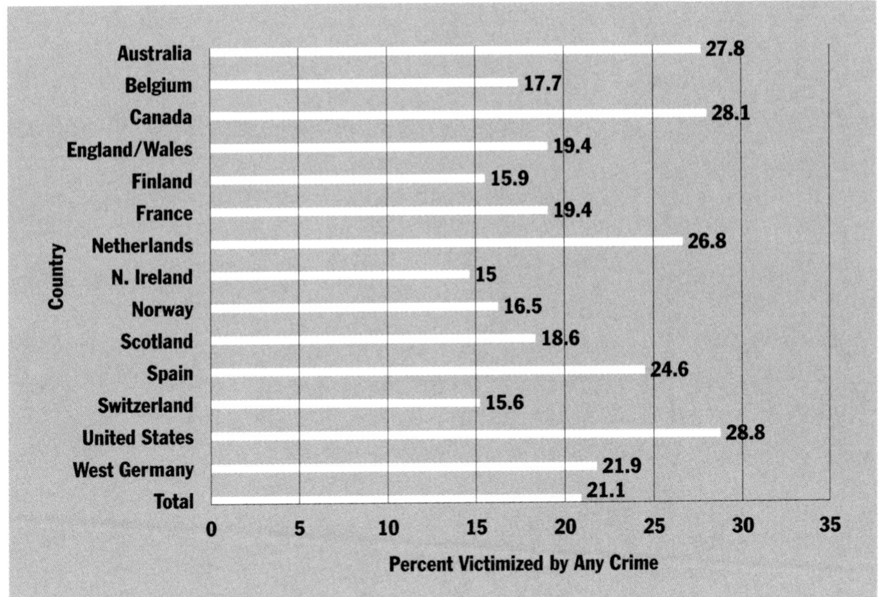

FIGURE 16.1

Overall crime victimization rates for selected countries

SOURCE: *Crime Across the World*, 1990, J. Van Dijk, P. Mahew, and M. Killias. With the kind permission of Kluwer Law International.

The survey found that theft is closely related to opportunities: Nations with the highest rates of car ownership had the highest rates of automobile thefts; those with the highest rates of bicycle ownership had the highest rates of bicycle theft. Similarly, the methods used to commit robberies closely resembled the tools available to offenders. In the United States, for example, 28 percent of robbers used a gun, a figure that mirrors the percent of Americans who own guns (29 percent). Conversely, only about 8 percent of robbers in other nations used guns, a proportion that reflects rates of gun ownership in other countries (6 percent).[13]

Rates of assaults and threats were much higher in the United States (5.4 percent), followed by Australia (5.2 percent) and Canada (4.0 percent), than they were in Europe, where the average was 2.5 percent (ranging from 0.5 percent in Switzerland to 3.4 percent in the Netherlands). The ability of some cultures to resolve disputes without resorting to assaultive behavior is an area that needs further cross-national study.

Victimization surveys in various countries have produced two common findings: (1) Crime is not often reported to police, and (2) victims and offenders share many of the same characteristics.[14] These findings are consistent with those of victimization surveys in the United States, and they suggest that criminals generally victimize people in the same socioeconomic class as themselves and that the number of crimes reported to police is significantly lower than the number actually committed.

In an effort to explain why low-crime countries avoid criminal behavior with greater success than other nations, Freda Adler examined ten countries that have low crime rates as measured by the U.N. world crime surveys: Switzerland, Ireland, Bulgaria, Germany, Costa Rica, Peru, Algeria, Saudi Arabia, Japan, and Nepal. She studied forty-seven different socioeconomic and cultural factors ranging from birth rates to literacy, and found that they explained little of the variation in crime rates in these nations. Also, in no country did the agencies of criminal justice appear to prevent crime (i.e., with different policies, laws, prac-

contemporary issues

Who Goes to Prison?: Comparing England and the United States

During the 1990s, jail and prison population figures for the United States were combined and compared with those for England and Wales for the first time. England and Wales share a common prison system, making possible a realistic comparison of incarceration rates and offenses.

Of great concern is the cost of imprisonment and the length of sentences imposed. In England and Wales there are approximately 119 jail and prison inmates per 100,000 adults. In the United States, the incarceration rate is 640 per 100,000, a rate five and one-half times higher. Interestingly, inmates in prison and jail in the two countries share many of the same characteristics:

- More than 90 percent are male.
- More than half have a prior record of imprisonment.
- About 80 percent are serving sentences (not awaiting trial or sentencing).
- About a third have a family member who served time in prison.
- They are less educated than the general adult population.
- A majority of female inmates report that someone other than a current or former spouse is caring for their children.

These similarities point to specific correlates of crime, including poor role models, poor education, and a prior history of crime. These correlates are similar in both countries.

Differences between the two groups of inmates include family status, race, and employment history:

- Seventy percent of U.S. inmates are single or divorced, compared to 55 percent in England and Wales.
- Forty-five percent of the U.S. inmate population is black (versus 11 percent of the general population), whereas 11 percent of the inmates in England and Wales are black (versus 2 percent of the general population).
- Sixty-six percent of U.S. inmates were employed before they were imprisoned, compared to 51 percent of inmates in England and Wales.

Despite these differences, in both countries single and divorced people account for the majority of prison and jail inmates. It is also true that the majority were employed in some kind of work before incarceration. Third, in both countries minorities are overrepresented in the jail and prison population.

Although the inmate profiles are similar, the rate of incarceration is dramatically higher in the United States. Part of the reason for this difference is longer average sentences. Thirty-four percent of U.S. inmates have sentences longer than ten years, compared to only 4 percent in England and Wales. This more punitive approach has not had an impact on crime, however. The rate of crimes known to police is twice as high in the United States as it is in England and Wales, while the number of police per capita is quite similar (240 per 100,000 in the United States compared to 256 in England and Wales). Closer study of the correlates and long-term impacts of high incarceration rates may result in the discovery of better ideas for preventing crime and dealing with offenders.

SOURCE: James P. Lynch, Steven K. Smith, Helen A. Graziadei, and Tanutda Pittayathikhun, *Profile of Inmates in the United States and in England and Wales* (Washington, D.C.: Bureau of Justice Statistics, 1994).

synnomie The sharing of values to the point of harmonious accommodation of divergent views.

anomie Normlessness, or lack of attachment to conventional social goals, or means for attaining them.

tices, and penalties). Adler concluded that all ten low-crime countries "appear to have developed some form of strong social control, outside and apart from the criminal justice system."[15]

Two key characteristics of low-crime nations are solid family systems and strong religious tradition, practice, and belief.[16] This suggests that crime may be an outgrowth of instability within families or religious communities, regardless of cultural differences in countries' location, history, or economics. Adler coined the term **synnomie** to indicate the sharing of values to the point of harmonious accommodation of divergent views. This is the opposite of **anomie,** a term that is often used to indicate the disharmony that is created by social disorganization

Two key characteristics of nations with low crime rates are strong family systems and strong religious tradition, practice, and belief.

and that pushes people toward deviant behaviors. As Adler observed, "The sharing of activities 'for the common good' accounts for apparently strong social solidarity" and low crime in these nations.[17] Investigations such as Adler's, together with efforts to measure crime rates in different cultures more accurately, represent the beginnings of a "global criminology" that will take the study of crime and criminal justice beyond individual cultures and countries to the world as a whole.[18] This will become increasingly important with the growing ease of international travel and the rise in international criminal activity.

International Crimes

Just as advances in technology and the fall of communism have made worldwide communication and travel much simpler in recent years, they have also made the commission of crime much easier. Passenger miles flown on international commercial flights have increased by twenty times over the last three decades, to more than six hundred billion miles per year. Global imports have increased by a factor of ten, to $3,500 billion over the same period.[19] International smuggling, drug distribution, alien smuggling, hijacking, and political crimes have grown in proportion to the growth of international communication and movement among countries. As criminal justice researcher Jonathan Winer has observed, "The very networks that legitimate businesses use to move goods so cheaply are the same networks that criminals use to move illicit goods just as easily."[20]

Importing Stolen Vehicles

One manifestation of the growth of international communication and movement is the growing international trade in stolen vehicles. Of the 1.5 million vehicles stolen each year in the United States, approximately 200,000 are shipped overseas for resale. Ten years ago that international market barely existed.[21] At the busiest seaport in the United States, Los Angeles–Long Beach, 225 vehicles, valued at ten million dollars, were seized during 1995. This number increased from only ninety stolen vehicles two years earlier. In order to hide stolen cars from investigators, thieves often conceal them behind false container walls or in large steel containers bound for overseas shipping. A single ship holds as many as 4,000 steel containers, each as large as a semitrailer. The United States has 130

TABLE 16.1

Overseas Destinations for Vehicles Stolen in the United States

Australia/Pacific Rim:
Porsches, Lexuses, Mercedes (luxury vehicles)

Central and South America:
Ford Explorers, Nissan Pathfinders, Chevrolet Suburbans, Jeep Grand Cherokees (rugged four-wheel drive vehicles)

Eastern Europe:
Harley-Davidson motorcycles, Mercedes, Jaguars, Oldsmobiles, BMWs (status vehicles)

The Middle East:
BMWs, Lincoln Town Cars, Cadillacs, Chevrolet Suburbans (luxury vehicles with powerful air conditioners)

SOURCE: National Insurance Crime Bureau.

seaports, and ten million containers leave the Los Angeles-Long Beach seaport alone each year. Criminals pay thieves to steal desired cars off the street, or the cars are bought or rented by using false identification and making a cash deposit; they are then driven away, never to return. Table 16.1 provides a list of popular overseas destinations of vehicles that are in high demand.

On the foreign end, ownership and registry of stolen vehicles are not very difficult. Some countries have no central registry of vehicles. In others, registration requirements can be overcome with cash payoffs from aspiring car owners. In still other nations, crimes of violence and political unrest are the focus of police attention, and police are not overly concerned with imports of stolen cars.

A major reason why people in other countries do not simply buy the cars outright is lack of availability in many places, and the huge import duties elsewhere. A $50,000 Lexus, for example, was selling in a Thailand showroom for $180,000.[22] The total cost of international vehicle smuggling is estimated at one to four billion dollars annually. A representative of the National Insurance Crime Bureau remarked, "It's getting to be of epidemic proportion."[23]

Drug Smuggling

The problem of international automobile smuggling is mirrored by the problems faced in international drug smuggling. Drug smuggling begins in a source country where coca or opium is grown, usually in Central or South America or in Asia. Next, the raw plant must be processed. This can be done in the source country or in a nation where smuggling is relatively easy. Once the product has been transformed into a consumable product, it must be smuggled to the consumer market. (North America and Europe are the largest consumer drug markets.) After the drug has been sold to the consumer, money must be "laundered" through a legitimate business and transferred overseas, or else large amounts of cash must be physically smuggled by couriers back to the manufacturing and source countries. The laundering consists of reporting the drug money as part of income from a legitimate business, such as a restaurant or other concern that has a large number of cash transactions. This makes the illicit money look as if it was lawfully earned as part of the legitimate business.

Here is an example of how this works in practice. Nigerian heroin smugglers recruited non-Nigerian residents of Dallas to serve as couriers, smuggling heroin into the United States. The recruiters provided airline tickets and expense money for the couriers, in addition to a salary of $5,000 to $10,000 per trip. The first courier was sent to Thailand, the heroin source, and took the heroin from there to an intermediate nonsource nation (such as the Philippines, Kenya, Poland, or western Europe), where it was delivered to a second courier. The second courier concealed the heroin in a suitcase, or strapped it to his or her body, and smuggled it into the United States. The strategy was designed to deceive U.S. authorities, who would not suspect a courier who had not been to the source country.[24] Such a scheme capitalizes on multiethnic cooperation among criminals, and points to the need for international cooperation and surveillance by law enforcement agencies.

The two primary opportunities for preventing drug smuggling occur at the courier stage, when the finished product is being smuggled to the market, or

Drug smuggling and illegal immigration often occur by boat. This has caused problems in trying to secure the extensive water borders to the United States.

when the illicit cash is being returned from the consuming country. In the United States, profiles have been established for drug couriers, and "high risk" and "source" nations and airports have been identified that lack effective controls on drug manufacturing or contraband. The profiles are descriptions of travelers who appear likely to be carrying drugs, such as those who are making short international trips, carrying little luggage, appearing in a hurry, and paying for their tickets in cash. To circumvent this strategy, drug manufacturers ship drugs by courier to a "safe" nation, where a second courier, who does not fit the profile and does not come from a source country, carries the drugs to the consuming nation (as in the case just described).[25]

Illegal Immigration

Illegal immigration is a third example of transnational crime. Many people throughout the world wish to come to the United States and other developed countries, but have little chance of lawful immigration. Chinese smuggling rings have transported illegal immigrants to New York City by boat for a charge of $30,000 or more per person. Sometimes the "cargo" is smuggled by boat to Canada or Mexico and then transported by land to the United States.[26] The huge smuggling fee often turns the new arrivals into virtual slaves to their transporters.[27] Because they are illegal aliens, it is difficult for them to obtain legitimate employment, and therefore they are often exploited by unscrupulous employers, become prostitutes or drug couriers, or become involved in criminal activity to raise the money to pay their smuggling fee.[28] The impacts are felt by the U.S. criminal justice system as well as by the illegal immigrants themselves. Nearly half of the non-U.S. citizens prosecuted in federal court are living in the United States illegally. Most have been charged with drug or immigration offenses, which have risen by more than 10 percent per year over the last decade. Nearly 20,000 noncitizens are now incarcerated in federal prisons.[29]

Immigrants also continue to be victimized by their smugglers. In Los Angeles, for example, eight Thai nationals were arrested for enslaving fifty-six illegal immigrants. Money was extorted from the immigrants in exchange for safe passage to the United States, where they were required to work seventeen-hour days.[30] As William McDonald has remarked, "The problems of organized crime involved in the fraud, corruption, smuggling, and victimization associated with illegal immigration represent a growing area of need for transnational police cooperation which threatens to eclipse international drug trafficking as a social problem in the global village."[31]

U.S. authorities are able to identify only 5 percent of the vessels carrying illegal immigrants.[32] Given the vast extent of the nation's borders and the inability of any nation to search every person, car, boat, and plane that crosses its borders, international cooperation and coordination of law enforcement efforts are clearly needed.

Terrorism and Hate Crimes

Terrorism and hate crimes are criminal acts committed for political or social purposes. They are distinguished from most other forms of crime in that the offenders usually have no personal financial motive. Instead, they attempt to make a larger "point" beyond their own self-interest. Their purpose may be overthrow of the government, or they may wish to publicize an unpopular opinion. Hate crimes always involve prejudice in some form, usually racial or ethnic in nature. Terrorism sometimes entails prejudice, but more often it stems from political motives or causes. The Federal Bureau of Investigation defines **terrorism** as "the unlawful use of force or violence against persons or property to intimidate or coerce a government, the civilian population, or any segment thereof, in furtherance of political or social objectives."[33] Hate crimes can also be defined in this way. The primary difference is the target: In the case of terrorism, the government is usually the target; with hate crimes, a particular minority is generally the target.

terrorism
Offenses designed to intimidate or coerce a government or civilians in furtherance of political or social objectives.

Both terrorism and hate crimes are relatively new concerns for the American criminal justice system. Before the 1980s, major acts of terrorism occurred almost exclusively in foreign countries, and hate crimes had not been defined as such and were not counted in any systematic way. This changed in 1993 with the bombing of the World Trade Center in New York City, which killed six people. The offenders were convicted and the mastermind was sentenced to 240 years in solitary confinement.[34] Nevertheless, this was followed by other terrorist events, culminating in the 1995 Oklahoma City bombing, which killed 168 people, making it the deadliest terrorist act ever committed in the United States. Acts of terrorism and hate crime now occur regularly in the United States as well as in other parts of the world. U.S. embassies have been bombed fifteen times in twelve countries since 1983.[34a] Aircraft bombings, plots against government agents, church burnings, periodic random killings of minorities, and actions by "hate" groups founded on a premise of racial inequality illustrate the extent of the problem in the United States.[35]

Trends in terrorist incidents in the United States are illustrated in Figure 16.2. There has been a general decline in the number of terrorist incidents since the 1980s, but those that are still being committed are becoming more deadly. In addition, law enforcement authorities are giving higher priority to terrorism inves-

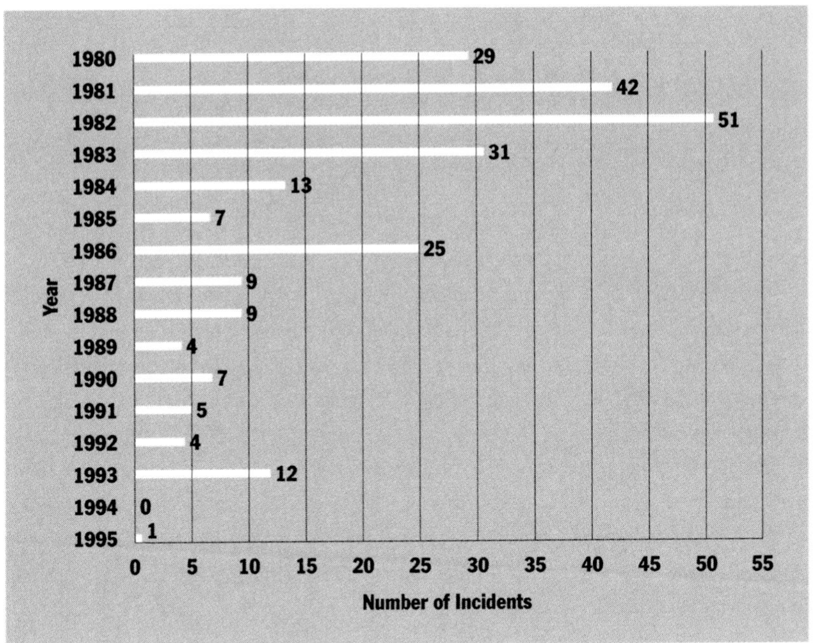

FIGURE 16.2

Terrorist incidents in the United States, 1980 to 1995

SOURCE: Federal Bureau of Investigation, *Terrorism in the United States* (Washington, D.C.: U.S. Government Printing Office, 1997).

tigations, with emphasis on the *prevention* of terrorist acts. Trends in the prevention of terrorism in the United States are illustrated in Figure 16.3.

Figures 16.2 and 16.3 indicate that a significant number of terrorist acts are prevented or interrupted. This points to the need for improved intelligence gathering on terrorist activities.

Statistics for **hate crimes** were not collected before the 1990s. In 1991, 4,755 incidents of hate crimes were reported in the United States. By 1994, the number had risen to 5,932, an increase of 25 percent. More than 70 percent of these incidents are racial or ethnic in nature, and 52 percent of these involve antiblack motives. Nearly 18 percent of all reported incidents are religious in nature; 86 per-

hate crimes
Offenses motivated by prejudice, usually against a particular race, religion, or sexual orientation.

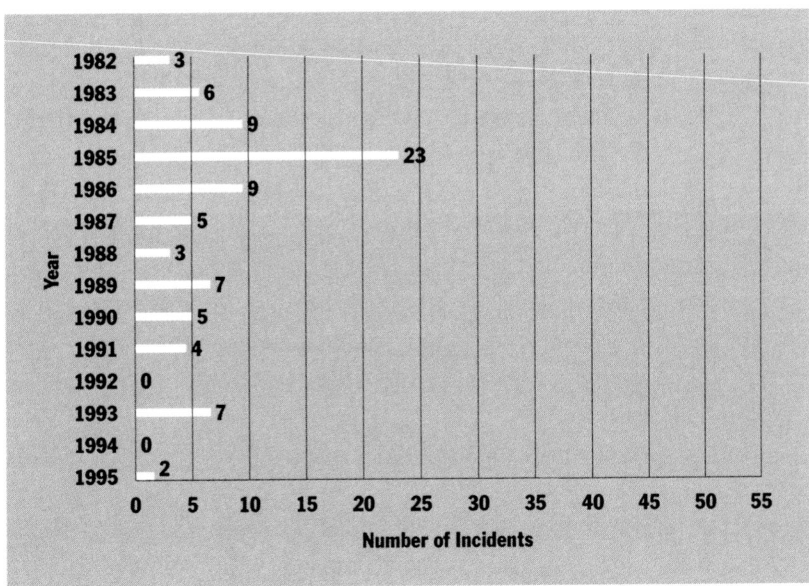

FIGURE 16.3

Terrorism preventions in the United States, 1982 to 1995

SOURCE: Federal Bureau of Investigation, *Terrorism in the United States* (Washington, D.C.: U.S. Government Printing Office, 1997).

FUTURE ISSUES

Penalty Enhancement for Hate Crimes?

Many states have passed statutes that make hate crimes separate offenses subject to enhanced penalties. The theory is that offenses motivated by bigotry are more serious than similar offenses committed without such motives. This leads to an important question: Is it fair to punish an offender solely on the basis of his or her motive? Remember that the criminal law punishes offenders for their *conduct*, not their motives. If an individual intentionally goes out and kills someone, the law does not care whether it was done for revenge, for money, or for the exercise. A judge can take the circumstances of the crime into account when deciding on a sentence, but he or she must stay within the sentencing range set by the legislature.

Can and should the legislature create a different penalty for a criminal who assaults a victim with the motive of robbery than for a criminal who attacks a victim with the motive of hatred based on racial or other bias? Arguments in favor of enhanced penalties for hate crimes include the fact that such crimes are more harmful than those not based on hate because they transmit a threatening message in addition to any physical or property harm they cause. They have a much greater destabilizing effect on the community than do other crimes. Also, the seriousness of crimes is commonly based on criminal intention. Enhancing penalties for hate crimes goes one step further and includes prejudice as an aggravating factor in the sentencing decision.

Arguments against enhanced penalties for hate crimes include the fact that they punish *thought* versus action and thereby exceed the allowable scope of the criminal law. These penalties may violate First Amendment protections of free speech and Fourteenth Amendment guarantees of equal protection of the law by treating offenders differently according to the beliefs they express. Also, some fear that hate crime statutes may ultimately be used against minorities holding unpopular views, rather than in their defense.

FUTURES QUESTION

Which position on penalty enhancement for hate crimes do you find most persuasive? Defend your view.

SOURCES

"Symposium: Penalty Enhancement for Hate Crimes," *Criminal Justice Ethics*, vol. 11 (Summer/Fall 1992), pp. 3–63.

Brent L. Smith and Kelly R. Damphousse, "Punishing Political Offenders: The Effect of Political Motive on Federal Sentencing Decisions," *Criminology*, vol. 34 (August 1996), pp. 289–321.

cent of these are anti-Jewish. Nearly 12 percent of all incidents involve sexual orientation; of these, 73 percent target homosexual men.[36] It is clear that minority groups are most likely to be the targets of hate crimes, and that prejudice against a particular race, religion, or sexual orientation motivates these offenders.

The following case illustrates how the problems of hate crime and terrorism merge. Two men who belonged to an organization known as the Aryan Nations traveled from Idaho to Seattle, Washington, with the intent of exploding a bomb inside a gay bar. They were arrested after they bought the parts required for the bomb, but before they had assembled it. The arrest was based on evidence gathered by an undercover informant, who had penetrated the Aryan Nations organization and had accompanied the two men on their trip to Seattle. The men were convicted of conspiracy involving interstate travel to kill or hurt human beings in violation of federal law.

The two men appealed their convictions arguing that there was insufficient evidence of a conspiracy. They claimed that the government had failed to prove beyond a reasonable doubt that there existed an agreement to engage in the crimes charged, that one or more overt acts were taken to carry out the alleged conspir-

Minority groups are most likely to be the targets of hate crimes. Prejudice against a particular race, religion, or sexual orientation motivates these offenders.

acy, and that they had the intent to commit the crimes charged.[37] The U.S. Court of Appeals found the testimony of the undercover informant, as well as tape-recorded statements of the conspirators, to be convincing evidence of a conspiracy. Before they had left for Seattle, the men had discussed obtaining a bomb from a third party. When he could not be found, the defendants "actively participated in purchasing the components necessary to build another pipe bomb." Once in Seattle, they contacted a friend and tried to borrow a drill to use in assembling the bomb. The testimony of the undercover informant revealed that they had discussed the effect an explosion from a similar bomb would have on a roomful of people. When the group discussed the number of homosexuals that would be killed by such a bomb, they concluded that "the gravel and nails inside it would be lethal." One defendant also told the other that it is best "to buy pipe and pipe caps for the bombs at various stores."[38] The court concluded that once a conspiracy has been shown to exist, evidence establishing a defendant's connection with it beyond a reasonable doubt "is sufficient to convict the defendant of knowing participation in the conspiracy," even though the connection may be slight.[39] It can be seen from this case that the concerns of criminal organization and conspiracy that arise in hate crimes are nearly identical to those posed by terrorism.

The most infamous recent case of a terrorist is that of Theodore Kaczynski. Called the "Unabomber," Kaczynski pleaded guilty to killing three people and injuring two others in five mail bombings. He also admitted responsibility for an additional eleven bombs that injured twenty-one other people. Kaczynski is a 55-year-old mathematician who believes he was waging a struggle for individual autonomy against the forces of technology. He lived alone in a remote cabin in the woods for twenty-five years. His targets were university professors and others he believed represented the growth of technology. Kaczynski's motives can be viewed both as terrorism and hate crimes. He had a political agenda and his choice of victims was based on a strong prejudice against people who advocated technological advancement. Kaczynski ultimately pleaded guilty and was sentenced to life in prison with no chance of parole.[40]

According to the FBI and others, leftist extremist groups have posed the predominant terrorist threat in the United States over the last thirty years. Arrests of key members during the 1980s, combined with the fall of the former Soviet Union, "deprived many leftist groups of a coherent ideology or spiritual patron. As a result, membership and support for these groups waned."[41] In their place, right-wing extremist groups seem to be attracting more supporters. These groups often adhere to an antigovernment or racist ideology. The FBI has found that recruits to these groups feel displaced by rapid cultural and economic changes and in some cases are "seeking some form of personal affirmation." As U.S. society continues to change, the FBI predicts that the potential for hate crimes by extremist right-wing groups will increase.[42]

In 1998, President Clinton proposed a record $6.7 billion to fight terrorism, including new coordination of multiagency efforts to detect explosives, gather intelligence, and respond more effectively to terrorist incidents. This initiative is designed to organize more efficiently antiterrorism efforts that have been splintered among different agencies.[43]

Transnational Law Enforcement

Interpol

The International Criminal Police Organization (Interpol) was begun in 1923 and took its current name in 1956. It is composed of 177 member nations. Interpol assists member law enforcement agencies that require information of a transnational nature about crimes or criminals.[44] It provides information in four languages: Arabic, English, French, and Spanish. The U.S. National Central Bureau (USNCB) is the point of contact between Interpol and police agencies in the United States. It is located within the U.S. Department of Justice and is jointly managed with the U.S. Department of Treasury. All requests from federal, state, or local police are transmitted to Interpol through the USNCB.[45]

The importance of Interpol will increase as internal and external security concerns merge. As Malcolm Anderson has observed,

> **The blurring of the distinction between internal and external security, resulting from the disintegration of the Soviet empire and the removal of the immediate threat of a military confrontation between the super-powers has altered the context in which police cooperation takes place. State security is now threatened by political violence which falls short of conventional military operations but which arises from complex criminal conspiracies—areas formerly considered squarely in the domain of policing.[46]**

Media and Criminal Justice

CITIZEN X

The American criminal justice system is often noted for its faults, but even critics agree that the United States's justice system is far more successful in securing justice than its international counterparts. Many films have depicted forms of justice within other nations: *Midnight Express* (1978) shows routine torture and prison life in Turkey, *In the Name of the Father* (1993) depicts a miscarriage of justice in England, *A Cry in the Dark* (1988) recounts the famous "dingo" murder case of Australia, *A World Apart* (1989) provides a look at justice in apartheid South Africa, and *Red Corner* (1997) portrays human rights violations in the court system of Red China.

While all of these movies are excellent for their portrayal of international systems of criminal justice, the 1994 HBO movie *Citizen X* offers viewers a rare perspective of the former Soviet Union. Based on the true story of a Russian serial killer, the film is presented from the vantage point of a forensic scientist who is appointed to the Soviet police "Killer Department." The forensic expert finds that he must become an amateur detective in a department in which police and military officers are one and the same, and all are subject to political whim. As more and more bodies are unearthed in the locale, he finds himself under constant pressure by the government committees to solve the mysterious murders—but only in keeping with the Soviet agenda. As one committee member puts it when faced with the suggestion that the murders are the work of one man: "There are no serial killers in the Soviet state. That is a decadent Western phenomenon."

Citizen X is a remarkable film in that it not only portrays one investigator's fight to profile and capture a prolific serial killer, but it spares no detail in showing the frustration of conducting a criminal investigation in a realm of uncooperative bureaucrats. The antiquated equipment, the unsophisticated investigatory procedures, and the tragic suicide of an innocent youth (the victim of a committee-ordered investigation of homosexuals) are all realities of the Soviet era. The killer, it is soon realized, will only be caught if the investigator proceeds to humor the committee with its political mandate, while also proceeding to use FBI-proven methods of psychological profiling to find and capture the killer.

The serial killer "Citizen X" is eventually apprehended using a profile worked up by a Russian psychiatrist with the help of the United States's FBI. The killer admits to the slaying of more than fifty young boys and girls, the psychopathic acts of a demoralized and powerless man. It is a small victory for the psychiatrist and forensic investigator, who wonder how many deaths could have been prevented if it were not for the obstruction and bureaucracy of the Soviet justice system.

The punishment for the serial killer is execution, but unlike the United States, in Russia death is quick and sure. The Soviet method of capital punishment is demonstrated in shooting the unsuspecting killer in the back of the head as he enters a small cell designed specifically for this purpose. It is a chilling ending to a true story, and one that raises questions about what changes, if any, have actually been instituted in post-Soviet Russia.

MEDIA AND CRIMINAL JUSTICE QUESTION

What measures are being undertaken to improve investigative procedures and the adjudication of offenders in the former Soviet republics?

Organized crime, drug trafficking, corruption, and other traditional concerns of law enforcement are becoming national security concerns in many nations. The demise of the Soviet Union has freed intelligence agencies and the military to focus on transnational crime rather than on military threats. Evidence that reliance on Interpol is increasing can be seen in the fact that the USNCB staff grew from six to eighty-one between 1979 and 1995. This reflects an increase in transnational criminal activity as well as greater attention to international criminal matters on the part of U.S. agencies.[47]

Another effort to combat transnational crimes is Europol, which was established in 1991 to share information about drug trafficking among member countries of the European Union. Europol emerged out of growing concern over drug trafficking and money laundering, as well as the need for better coordination among European police agencies and customs officials. The removal of many of the barriers to free trade and economic growth in Europe since the late 1980s has made it easier to communicate and travel among the European nations. This situation also makes it easier for criminals to smuggle stolen property and drugs across borders. Europol is seen as a mechanism for organizing international law enforcement activities.[48]

The need for shared information is paralleled by the need for trained law enforcement personnel. Efforts are being made to professionalize law enforcement agencies around the world. The Federal Bureau of Investigation now trains law enforcement officials from other nations in a program sponsored by the U.S. State Department. These officials come to the United States to be trained in modern law enforcement and prosecution techniques. In addition, the FBI opened an international police training academy in Budapest in 1995 and an office in Moscow in 1994. As FBI Director Louis Freeh observed, there is a need for "a centrally located school where we can develop a network of police partners in countries where we do not now have those relationships."[49]

More than 1,600 American law enforcement personnel are now working overseas. Nearly a third of these are agents with the Drug Enforcement Administration (DEA), which has agents in thirty nations. The U.S. Immigration and Naturalization Service, Customs Service, and Coast Guard each have law enforcement personnel in more than twenty countries. The FBI, Internal Revenue Service, Secret Service, and Bureau of Alcohol, Tobacco, and Firearms also have agents assigned overseas.[50] This high level of international law enforcement activity points to the growth in international crime and the need for coordination of law enforcement activities.

In June 1994, the United Nations held a conference on international money laundering in which forty-five countries participated.[51] A second U.N. gathering, the World Ministerial Conference on Organized Transnational Crime, was held in Naples in November 1994. The purpose of the meeting was to examine existing international standards, legislation, and models for cooperation in dealing with international organized crime. The conference was attended by representatives from 142 countries.[52] The high level of interest and concern about these problems is clear from the level of participation. These meetings permit open discussion of the problems posed by international criminal behavior, along with possible solutions.[53] This is extremely important when so many U.S. law enforcement agencies are working in other countries. Nations can feel threatened when consensus has not been reached about the seriousness of the problem and the appropriateness of the measures taken. It is through such efforts that international law enforcement trust, cooperation, and professionalism are improving. It also is a mechanism for placing pressure on nations that are not diligent in their efforts to thwart transnational crime.

International Justice

The idea of an international criminal court to prosecute genocide, crimes against humanity, and war crimes was first considered when the United Nations was established after World War II. Differences of opinion among nations stalled the process until 1992, when the General Assembly called for a draft statute for an international criminal court. Renewed interest was largely the result of alleged war crimes and genocide in Yugoslavia and Rwanda.[54] The United Nations Security Council established an ad hoc International Criminal Tribunal to investigate these incidents. In Rwanda, it was alleged that genocide occurred when 500,000 members of the Tutsi minority were killed and a million others fled the country. In Yugoslavia, responsibility was sought for mass murders in Bosnia, where soldiers went from house to house shooting Muslims and burning their houses in an attempt at "ethnic cleansing."[55] Since that time, the precise composition and jurisdiction of the proposed international court, process for appeals and reviews, and enforcement issues have been fleshed out.

One reason for the delay in the establishment of an international court is opposition by the United States, which fears that such a court would act as a barrier to the use of diplomatic pressure and diplomatic solutions to international problems.[56] Nevertheless, the ability of such a court to convict criminals for international crimes could do much to enhance the moral and political force against war crimes and other international offenses. The likelihood that such a court could succeed is suggested by the fact that seventy-seven indictments have been handed down and twenty suspects are in custody in the war crimes tribunal investigating incidents in the former Yugoslavia. Rwanda's former prime minister and defense minister are in custody, and three trials are under way in that tribunal. All this has been accomplished through a melding of different legal systems, rules of evidence, and even witness-protection programs without any help from police or military officials.[57] Nevertheless, resistance continues from powerful nations reluctant to accept rulings of the world court in specific cases. As described earlier, the United States did not delay the execution of the Paraguayan man in 1998, as requested by the court. Cases such as these cast doubt on the ability of an international court to enforce its rulings.[58]

International Corrections

There is no proposal for a "world prison" similar to the proposed world court. Individuals who are adjudicated in the world court will be sent to their own country or exiled to agreed-upon locations. The penalties to be imposed on those who commit international crimes might be difficult to establish because of wide variations in the punitiveness of sentences in different nations. Table 16.2 compares incarceration rates in different nations. As the table shows, the United States's per capita prison population is higher than that of any other country surveyed except Russia. In addition, the United States has more offenders in prison (1.6 million) than any other nation, by a wide margin. This has been a source of criticism in the United States, given the fact that its rate of violent crime is also among the world's highest. It cannot be said that the nation's incarceration policy has any direct impact on its crime rate.

The scope and limits of criminal punishment vary widely from one culture to another. Most nations, including all the Western industrialized countries, prohibit the death penalty or simply do not implement it. Nations that keep death

TABLE 16.2

International Incarceration Rates

NATION	NUMBER OF INMATES	RATE OF INCARCERATION (PER 100,000)	NATION	NUMBER OF INMATES	RATE OF INCARCERATION (PER 100,000)
Russia	1,017,372	690	Spain	40,157	105
United States	1,585,401	600	Malaysia	20,324	104
Belarus	52,033	505	China	1,236,534	103
Ukraine	203,988	390	England/Wales	51,265	100
Latvia	9,608	375	France	53,697	95
Lithuania	13,228	360	Germany	68,396	85
Singapore	8,500	287	Italy	47,323	85
Moldova	10,363	275	Austria	6,761	85
Estonia	4,034	270	Switzerland	5,655	80
South Africa*	110,120	265	Turkey	49,895	80
Cook Islands	45	225	Belgium	7,401	75
Hong Kong	12,741	207	Sweden	5,767	65
Romania	45,309	200	Netherlands	10,143	65
Czech Republic	19,508	190	Denmark	3,421	65
Thailand	106,676	181	Finland	3,018	60
Poland	65,819	170	Greece	5,897	55
Slovakia	7,979	150	Norway	2,398	55
South Korea	61,019	137	Ireland	2,032	55
Kiribati	91	130	Croatia	2,572	55
New Zealand	4,553	127	Malta	196	55
Portugal	12,150	125	Solomon Islands	150	46
Fiji	961	123	Iceland	113	40
Hungary	12,455	120	Bangladesh	44,111	37
Canada	33,882	115	Japan	46,622	37
Luxembourg	469	115	Cyprus	202	30
Brunei Darussalam	312	110	Slovenia	630	30
Bulgaria	9,684	110	Cambodia	2,490	26
Scotland	5,697	110	Philippines	17,843	26
Macau	439	107	India	216,402	24
Northern Ireland	1,740	105			

*Rate per 100,000 population.

SOURCE: Marc Mauer, *Americans Behind Bars: U.S. and International Use of Incarceration, 1995* (New York: The Sentencing Project, 1997).

penalty laws on the books usually reserve them for war crimes or cases of genocide.[59] There are exceptions, however, primarily in developing countries such as China, where it is alleged that more than 1,000 offenders are executed each year and their body organs harvested.[60] Nevertheless, despite these exceptions, the worldwide trend is clearly away from use of the death penalty.

In similar fashion, the use of corporal punishment has diminished. Instances of whipping, branding, maiming, and similar forms of punishment have declined steadily around the world.[61] As is noted in Chapter 15, however, there are notable exceptions, such as Singapore, where caning is still practiced.

Although international differences in the punishment of criminals are to be expected, there are "human rights" or baseline standards of humane treatment that should apply everywhere. In an effort to specify the precise nature and scope of human rights in criminal justice, the United Nations established the *Standard*

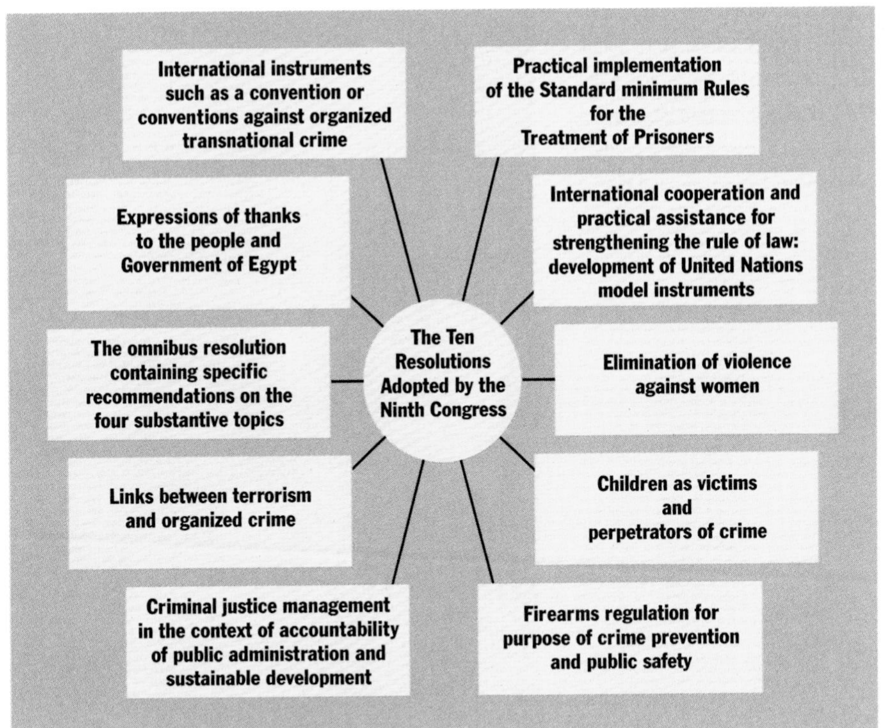

FIGURE 16.4
Resolutions from the Ninth United Nations Congress on the Prevention of Crime and the Treatment of Offenders

SOURCE: "Ninth United Nations Congress on the Prevention of Crime and the Treatment of Offenders," *United Nations Crime Prevention and Criminal Justice Newsletter*, nos. 28/29 (November 1995).

Minimum Rules for the Treatment of Prisoners. These rules were adopted at the first United Nations Congress on the Prevention of Crime and Treatment of Offenders, held in 1955. They represent a worldwide consensus on major issues such as torture, interrogation, and the living conditions of prisoners. These standards continue to be used in the training of law enforcement officers, corrections officers, and peacekeepers throughout the world.

Since 1955, the United Nations has held Congresses on the Prevention of Crime and the Treatment of Offenders every five years. The 1995 Congress was attended by a record 1,899 participants from 138 countries, fifteen intergovernmental organizations, and forty-eight nongovernmental organizations. This represents an overwhelming majority of the world's nations. The United Nations has since adopted a *Code of Conduct for Law Enforcement Officers, Declaration of Basic Principles of Justice for Victims of Crime and Abuse of Power*, and *Basic Principles on the Independence of the Judiciary*.[62] The multinational analysis and discussion of these important issues help promote consensus regarding the appropriate limits of the law and criminal justice. The level of dialogue among nations on issues of crime and justice has continued to expand, as have the topics discussed.

The ten resolutions adopted by the 1995 Congress are presented in Figure 16.4. They deal with issues ranging from the link between terrorism and organized crime to the elimination of violence against women.[63] Although United Nations resolutions do not have the force of law, they exert strong pressure on a growing number of nations. In addition, serious violations may ultimately come to the attention of the world court.

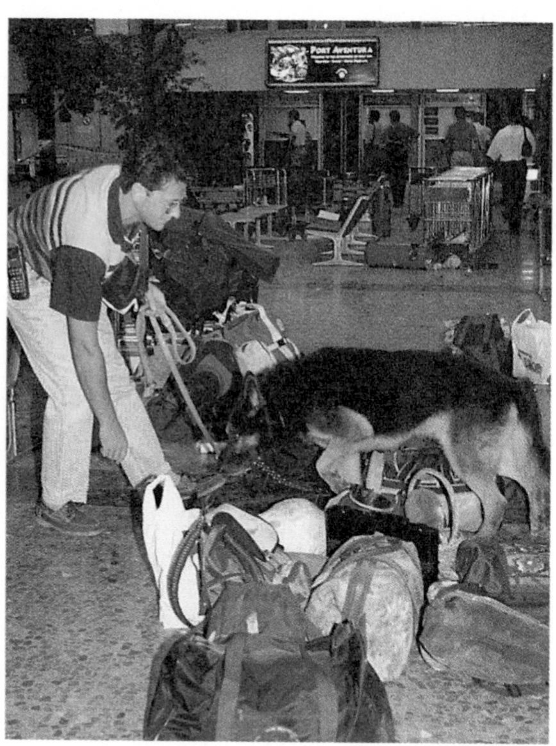

A plainclothes police officer and dog check bags after a 1996 bombing at an airport in Spain. Incidents like this have increased international pressure for better security screening at airports around the world.

Legal and Ethical Problems

During the 1980s, a narcotics cartel was responsible for transporting drugs from Mexico to the United States. The U.S. Drug Enforcement Administration was having some success in interrupting the drug flow with large seizures of drugs and cash. The cartel retaliated against DEA agents stationed in Mexico, killing DEA agent Enrique Camarena, various informants, and others mistakenly believed to be associated with the DEA.[64] The United States had a strong interest in apprehending those responsible and bringing them to trial. Because Mexican authorities seemed unable to bring the suspects to justice, U.S. agents forcibly abducted a suspect from Mexico for trial in the United States. Is such an action ethical or legal?

The forcible abduction of a fugitive from one country to be brought to justice in another can be seen as a violation of international law. This is because nations are generally bound to respect the laws of other nations when operating inside their territory. The DEA case just described was unusual, and it went all the way to the U.S. Supreme Court. The Court held that even the forcible abduction of a suspect from a foreign country does not preclude prosecution in the United States.[65] This ruling was made despite the fact that the abduction was illegal under Mexican law.

Situations such as these occur only rarely, usually in very serious cases such as mass murders, treason, or the killing of a public official. Nevertheless, such actions violate the national sovereignty of the foreign country. They can result in public protest and unrest, acts of retaliation, unrelated sanctions (e.g., economic), and tension in diplomatic relations that can last for years.

In a similar way, fugitives from justice are sometimes "lured" from nations without *extradition agreements,* or from nations that wish to protect their citizens from the justice systems of other nations. Extradition agreements are treaties between the United States and other countries that provide for the surrender of any fugitives accused or convicted of a crime in one country to be tried or punished, or both, in the home country. These fugitives are usually tricked by means of false drug deals or conspiratorial meetings in other countries. When such "lures" are discovered, the target nation is usually outraged by the presence of undercover operatives working within their nation without their knowledge. Sometimes even a telephone call to a fugitive living in their country is seen as objectionable.[66] As with the forcible abduction of fugitives from foreign countries, the luring of fugitives by means of deception raises both ethical and legal questions that, to date, are not guided by generally accepted principles of ethics or international law.

A third example of this problem has to do with *extraterritorial subpoenas.* For example, Swiss banks are known for their protection of the privacy of depositors. U.S. prosecutors have served extraterritorial subpoenas on U.S. branches of banks operating in nations with strong secrecy laws, such as Switzerland. If the banks do not produce the records requested, they may be fined. The problem is that foreign governments view this practice as an invasion of their national sovereignty.[67] Extraterritorial subpoenas have been resisted in court and through diplomatic channels, although U.S. courts have upheld the use of evidence obtained in this fashion.[68] Here again, the self-interest of the United States in obtaining evidence for a criminal prosecution is pitted against concerns for the legal rights and sovereignty of other nations. As international concerns regarding money laundering increase, it is likely that tensions will continue to rise until binding international agreements or laws can be established.

Is extraterritorial apprehension of a crime suspect, the luring of a foreign fugitive by trick, or an extraterritorial subpoena worth the threat to international relations and stability? Crimes that are considered serious in some nations are not seen as such in others. The "duty" to cooperate in criminal investigations is not always considered to be a duty by all nations involved. If there is no enforceable international law that prohibits such conduct, what will prevent powerful countries from forcing their will on less powerful ones? Such a debate has both legal and ethical dimensions related to the duty that nations have to assist one another when appropriate. The proposed world court may ultimately become an enforcement mechanism to ensure that international obligations are clearly spelled out and enforced, and that all nations have equal standing in cases of international justice.

Critical Thinking EXERCISE

Political Asylum in Genital Mutilation Cases?

Fauziya Kasinga came to the United States from Togo in 1994. Her female relatives had forced her into an arranged marriage there and were ready to subject her to genital mutilation. Female

genital mutilation is a centuries-old cultural practice that involves mutilation or removal of the clitoris to reduce sexual sensation. It is the equivalent of castration for males. In some countries, women mutilate their toddler daughters without anesthesia or sterilized instruments, sometimes causing infection, infertility, painful intercourse, or death.

Kasinga is asking for political asylum in the United States. Under U.S. law, individuals can be granted asylum only if they can demonstrate "credible" fear of persecution due to ethnicity, race, religion, political opinion, or membership in a social group or class. A lower hearing board of the Immigration and Naturalization Service turned down Kasinga's request, holding that female genital mutilation is not a form of persecution. She appealed to a higher board. If it grants her asylum, millions of women from more than twenty African and Middle Eastern countries could claim asylum for the same reasons.

Critical Thinking Questions

1. What is the balance that must be achieved in considering a request for political asylum in a case such as this?
2. How would you rule in this case, and why?

SOURCE: Maria Puente, "Togo Teen-ager Seeking Asylum from Mutilation," *USA Today* (May 3, 1996), p. 2; see also Peter Annin and Kandall Hamilton, "Marriage or Rape? Cultures Clash Over Arranged Nuptials," *Newsweek* (December 16, 1996), p. 78.

Critical Thinking EXERCISE

Judicial Attitudes and Sentencing Outcomes in Germany

In Germany, judges are appointed for life. A study attempted to determine whether there was any relationship between a judge's attitudes and the success of offenders in meeting the conditions of community service sentences. Judges were identified as either "authoritarian" or "liberal" based on the basis of an analysis of 2,000 actual cases. Liberal judges were more communicative, more positive in their expectations of offenders, and less punitive in their sentences. Authoritarian judges were less communicative, had negative expectations of offenders, and were more punitive in sentencing.

In Germany social workers are responsible for monitoring community service. They were also categorized as "authoritarian" or "liberal." The study found that in cases in which both the judge and the social worker were liberal, offenders successfully fulfilled the conditions of the sentence in 93.5 percent of the cases. In cases in which both judge and social worker were authoritarian, the success rate averaged only 72.7 percent. When one party was liberal and the other authoritarian, the success rate averaged 87 percent. The researchers concluded that outcomes appeared to be related to the expectations of the judges who sentenced the offenders and the social workers who supervised them.

Once they were made aware of these findings, judges in Munich arranged to have a psychologist observe and analyze their behavior. This resulted in some judges modifying their behavior or switching from criminal to civil cases.

Critical Thinking Questions

1. **What factors, other than the attitudes of the judge or social worker, might have affected the performance of the offenders under supervision?**
2. **Do you believe that the attitude of the judge or that of the social worker played a more important role in the outcome of any given case?**
3. **If this study were duplicated in the United States and researchers found that judges' and social workers' attitudes have a direct impact on offenders' behavior, do you believe the response would be similar to or different from that of judges in Germany?**

SOURCE: Christian Pfeiffer, *Alternative Sanctions in Germany* (Washington, D.C.: National Institute of Justice, 1996).

Summary

THE RISK OF CRIME AROUND THE WORLD

- It is difficult to compare crime rates in different nations because of various methodological problems.
- The world crime surveys conducted by the United Nations have found that theft is the most common crime. Assault is the most frequently committed violent crime.
- Victimization surveys have found that crime is not often reported to police and that victims and offenders share many of the same characteristics.
- Countries with low crime rates appear to have developed strong social control through family systems and religious tradition, practice, and belief.

INTERNATIONAL CRIMES

- Greater ease of travel and communication has made the commission of crime much easier.
- Among the most significant types of international crime are importation of stolen vehicles, drug smuggling, and illegal immigration.

TERRORISM AND HATE CRIMES

- Terrorism is the unlawful use of force or violence against persons or property to intimidate or coerce a government, the civilian population, or any segment thereof, in furtherance of political or social objectives.
- Hate crimes are similar to terrorist acts except that a particular minority is usually the target.
- A general decline in the number of terrorist incidents has been seen since the 1980s, but those that are still being committed are becoming more deadly.

TRANSNATIONAL LAW ENFORCEMENT

- The International Criminal Police Organization (Interpol) assists member law enforcement agencies requiring information about crimes or criminals of a transnational nature.
- Europol shares information about drug trafficking among member countries of the European Union.
- Efforts are being made to professionalize law enforcement agencies around the world.
- Efforts to establish an international criminal court have been hampered by differences of opinion among nations.
- Although there are international differences in the punishment of criminals, basic standards of treatment should apply everywhere. These have been codi-

fied by the United Nations in the *Standard Minimum Rules for the Treatment of Prisoners.*

- The forcible abduction of a fugitive from one country to be brought to justice in another raises legal and ethical problems. Similar problems arise when fugitives are lured to other countries.

Key Terms

synnomie	terrorism
anomie	hate crimes

Questions for Review and Discussion

1. What are some of the methodological problems faced in efforts to compare crime rates in different nations?
2. What factors appear to account for different rates of theft in different countries?
3. What characteristics did Adler identify in her study of countries with low crime rates?
4. What are some major types of international crime?
5. How is drug smuggling carried out?
6. What is the distinction between terrorism and hate crimes?
7. What is Interpol?
8. Why has the proposed international criminal court not been established?
9. What are some of the resolutions adopted by the 1995 U.N. Congress on the Prevention of Crime and Treatment of Offenders?
10. What problems are raised by the forcible abduction of a fugitive from one country to be brought to justice in another?

Notes

[1]"And We Are the Law," *The Economist*, vol. 347 (April 18, 1998), p. 27.

[2]Nick Anderson, "Mexico Racked by Crime Surge," *USA Today* (February 29, 1996), p. 3.

[3]George Wehrfritz, "Crime: 'You Dies, I Live'," *Newsweek* (July 22, 1996), p. 67.

[4]"Gun Violence Strikes at Heart of Safety in Southern America," *CJ the Americas* (December–January 1996), p. 4.

[5]"Crime, Terrorism, and Disorder Threaten Country's Confidence," *CJ International*, vol. 11 (May–June 1995), pp. 3–4; Nicola Wasson, "Japan's Top Cop Shot by Gunman," *USA Today* (March 30, 1995), p. 1.

[6]Badr-El-Din Ali, "Methodological Problems in International Criminal Justice Research," *International Journal of Comparative and Applied Criminal Justice*, vol. 10 (1986), pp. 167–76.

[7]Erika Fairchild, *Comparative Criminal Justice Systems* (Belmont, CA: Wadsworth, 1993), pp. 12–13.

[8]Graeme Newman and Bruce DiCristina, "Data Set of the First and Second United Nations World Crime Surveys," *United Nations Crime and Justice Information Network* (Vienna, Austria: United Nations Crime Prevention and Criminal Justice Branch, 1994).

[9]United Nations, *Third United Nations Survey of Crime Trends, Operations of Criminal Justice Systems and Crime Prevention Strategies* (Vienna, Austria: Crime Prevention and Criminal Justice Branch, 1990).

[10]Dane Archer and Rosemary Gartner, *Violence and Crime in Cross-National Perspective* (New Haven, CT: Yale University Press, 1984).

[11]James P. Lynch, "Building Data Systems for Cross-national Comparisons of Crime and Criminal Justice Policy: A Retrospective," *ICPSR Bulletin*, vol. 15 (February 1995), pp. 1–6; Richard Bennett and James P. Lynch, "Does a Difference Make a Difference?: Comparing Cross-National Crime Indicators," *Criminology*, vol. 28 (1990), pp. 152–81.

[12]See Ton Eijken, "Surveys Provide Insight into Crime," *CJ Europe*, vol. 5 (March–April 1995), pp. 1, 8–11.

[13]Jan van Dijk, Peter Mayhew, and Martin Killias, *Experiences of Crime across the World* (Boston: Kluwer, 1990).

[14]Jan van Dijk, Peter Mayhew, and Martin Killias, *Experiences of Crime across the World* (Boston: Kluwer, 1990); Wesley Skogan, "Reporting Crimes to the Police: The Status of World Research," *Journal of Research in Crime & Delinquency*, vol. 21 (1984), pp. 113–37.

[15]Freda Adler, *Nations Not Obsessed with Crime* (Littleton, CO: Fred B. Rothman, 1983), p. 130.

[16]Adler, *Nations Not Obsessed with Crime.*

[17]Ibid., p. 132.

[18]William F. McDonald, "Crime and Justice in the Global Village: Towards Global Criminology," in W. F. McDonald, ed., *Crime and Law Enforcement in the Global Village* (Cincinnati: Anderson, 1997), pp. 3–21.

[19]R. Barnet and J. Cavanagh, *Global Dreams* (New York: Simon and Schuster, 1994).

[20]Jonathan M. Winer, "International Crime in the New Geopolitics: A Core Threat of Democracy," in McDonald, p. 41.

[21]Carol J. Castaneda, "Car Thieves Wheeling and Dealing Overseas," *USA Today* (March 4, 1996), p. 3.

[22]Ibid.

[23]Ibid.

[24]"Worldwide Nigerian Heroin Smuggling Ring Smashed," *Organized Crime Digest* (May 27, 1992), p. 3; "New Breed of Smugglers," *USA Today* (September 23, 1991), p. 3.

[25]U.S. Comptroller General, *Drug Control: Interdiction Efforts in Central America Have Had Little Impact on the Flow of Drugs* (Washington, D.C.: U.S. General Accounting Office, 1994).

[26]"Alien Smuggling is the Dangerous New China Trade," *Organized Crime Digest*, vol. 14 (June 9, 1993), p. 10.

[27]Bruce Frankel, "INS Getting Cagey in Cat-and-Mouse Game," *USA Today* (August 6, 1993), p. 10; "Chinese Smuggling," *USA Today* (September 1, 1993), p. 3.

[28]William F. McDonald, "Illegal Immigration: Crime, Ramifications, and Control (The American Experience)," in McDonald, pp. 65–88.

[29]John Scalia, *Noncitizens in the Federal Justice System* (Washington, D.C.: Bureau of Justice Statistics, 1996); Norman J. Rabkin, *Criminal Aliens: INS' Efforts to Identify and Remove Imprisoned Aliens Need to be Improved* (Washington, D.C.: U.S. General Accounting Office, 1997).

[30]F. Swaboda, J. Webb, and M. Pressler, "U.S. Targets 'Slave Labor' Sweatshop," *Washington Post* (August 16, 1995), p. 1.

[31]William F. McDonald, "Illegal Immigration," in McDonald, p. 83.

[32]U.S. Comptroller General, *Immigration Enforcement: Problems in Controlling the Flow of Illegal Aliens* (Washington, D.C.: U.S. General Accounting Office, 1993).

[33]Federal Bureau of Investigation, *Terrorism in the United States, 1995* (Washington, D.C.: U.S. Government Printing Office, 1997), p. 2.

[34]Benjamin Weiser, "'Mastermind' and Driver Found Guilty in 1993 Plot to Blow Up Trade Center," *The New York Times* (November 13, 1997), p. 1; Gary Fields, "Yousef Sentenced to 240 Years in Solitary," *USA Today* (January 1, 1998), p. 4.

[34a]Alan Cooperman, "Terror Strikes Again," *U.S. News & World Report* (August 24, 1998), pp. 8–19.

[35]David E. Kaplan and Mike Tharp, "Terrorism Threats at Home: Two Years After Oklahoma City, Violent Sects Still Abound," *U.S. News & World Report* (January 5, 1998), pp. 22–7.

[36]Federal Bureau of Investigation, *Hate Crime Statistics* (Washington, D.C.: U.S. Government Printing Office, 1996); Kathleen Maguire and Ann L. Pastore, eds., *Sourcebook of Criminal Justice Statistics—1993* (Washington, D.C.: Bureau of Justice Statistics, 1994).

[37]*U.S. v. Winslow, Nelson, and Baker,* 962 F. 2d 845 (9th Cir. 1992) at 849.

[38]Ibid.

[39]Ibid; also *United States v. Stauffer,* 922 F. 2d 508 (9th Cir. 1990) at 514–15.

[40]Gordon Witkin and Ilan Greenberg, "End of the Line for the Unabomber," *U.S. News & World Report* (February 2, 1998), p. 34; Ted Gest, "End of the Line," *U.S. News & World Report* (May 18, 1998), p. 37.

[41]Ibid., p. 11; Brent L. Smith, *Terrorism in America: Pipe Bombs and Pipe Dreams* (Albany: State University of New York Press, 1994), pp. 198–9.

[42]Ibid.

[43]"The Real Battle," *U.S. News & World Report* (April 27, 1998), p. 7; U.S. Comptroller General, *Combatting Terrorism: Federal Agencies' Efforts to Implement National Policy and Strategy* (Washington, D.C.: U.S. General Accounting Office, 1997); U.S. Comptroller General, *Terrorism and Drug Trafficking: Responsibilities for Developing Explosives and Narcotics Detection Technologies* (Washington, D.C.: U.S. General Accounting Office, 1997).

[44]Fenton Bresler, *Interpol* (Toronto: Penguin Books, 1993); Michael Fooner, *Interpol* (New York: Plenum, 1989).

[45]Interpol web page.

[46]Malcolm Anderson, "Interpol and the Developing System of International Police Cooperation," in McDonald, p. 101.

[47]Ethan A. Nadelmann, "The Americanization of Global Law Enforcement: The Diffusion of American Tactics and Personnel," in McDonald, p. 124.

[48]John Benyon, "The Developing System of Police Cooperation in the European Union," in McDonald, p. 115.

[49]Ordway P. Burden, "Law Enforcement Agencies Working Overseas," *CJ International,* vol. 11 (November–December 1995), p. 17.

[50]Ibid.

[51]"International Conference on Preventing and Controlling Money-Laundering and the Use of the Proceeds of Crime: A Global Approach," *United Nations Crime Prevention and Criminal Justice Newsletter,* nos. 24/25 (January 1995).

[52]"The World Ministerial Conference on Organized Transnational Crime," *United Nations Crime Prevention and Criminal Justice Newsletter,* nos. 26/27 (November 1995).

[53]See Gary T. Marx, "Social Control Across Borders," in McDonald, pp. 23–39.

[54]"Preparatory Committee on Establishment of International Criminal Court to Meet at Headquarters," *United Nations Press Release,* August 1, 1997.

[55]Thomas Omestad, "Croats Wave White Flags," *U.S. News & World Report* (October 20, 1997), p. 42.

[56]Gerhard O. W. Mueller, "Enforcing International Criminal Justice," in McDonald, pp. 139–50.

[57]Thomas Omestad, "The Brief for a World Court," *U.S. News & World Report* (October 6, 1997), pp. 52–4; Omestad, "Croats Wave White Flags."

[58]"All Gum, No Teeth? World Criminal Court," *The Economist,* vol. 346 (March 14, 1998), pp. 50–1.

[59]Franklin Zimring and Gordon Hawkins, *Capital Punishment and the American Agenda* (New York: Cambridge University Press, 1986).

[60]Harry Wu Hongda, "A Grim Organ Harvest in China's Prisons," *World Press Review* (June 1995), pp. 22–3.

[61]Erika Fairchild, *Comparative Criminal Justice Systems* (Belmont, CA: Wadsworth, 1993), pp. 190–1.

[62]"Third and Fourth Sessions of the Commission on Crime Prevention and Criminal Justice," *United Nations Crime Prevention and Criminal Justice Newsletter*, nos. 30/31 (December 1995).

[63]"Ninth United Nations Congress on the Prevention of Crime and the Treatment of Offenders," *United Nations Crime Prevention and Criminal Justice Newsletter*, nos. 28/29 (November 1995).

[64]*United States v. Vasquez-Velaso*, 15 F. 3d 833 (9th Cir. 1994); *United States v. Lopez-Alvarez*, 970 F. 2d 583 (9th Cir.) *cert. denied* 113 S. Ct. 504 (1992).

[65]*United States v. Alvarez-Machain*, 112 S. Ct. 857 (1992).

[66]Thomas G. Snow, "Competing National and Ethical Interests in the Fight Against Transnational Crime: A U.S. Practitioner's Perspective," in McDonald, pp. 169–86.

[67]Ibid., p. 173.

[68]*In re Grand Jury Subpoena Directed to Marc Rich and Co.*, 707 F. 2d 663 (2nd Cir., 1983).

For Further Reading

Obi Ebbe, ed., *Comparative and International Criminal Justice Systems* (Boston: Butterworth-Heinemann, 1996).

William F. McDonald, ed., *Crime and Law Enforcement in the Global Village* (Cincinnati: Anderson Publishing, 1997).

Michael Tonry and Kathleen Hatlestad, eds., *Sentencing Reform in Overcrowded Times: A Comparative Perspective* (New York: Oxford University Press, 1997).

chapter seventeen

Dealing with Sophisticated Crimes

A criminal is a person with predatory instincts who has not sufficient capital to form a corporation.

HOWARD SCOTT
(1970)

CHAPTER OUTLINE

The last two decades have witnessed a series of crimes and questionable incidents characterized by escalating levels of seriousness, violence, and sophistication. Some examples:

- In 1997, the chief financial officer at Day-Lee Foods is convicted of stealing $100 million in the largest embezzlement case in U.S. history.[1]
- The space shuttle *Challenger* explodes soon after lift-off, promoting an investigation to determine whether suppliers may have known about defective parts.[2]
- Thousands of women wearing the Dalkon Shield birth control device contract pelvic inflammatory disease and some die.[3]

MARINE
05/76
SHELL

- More than one hundred "bosses," "underbosses," and "captains" of organized crime groups are convicted of racketeering and other crimes, receiving average sentences of twenty-five years each.[4]
- Three executives from Columbia/HCA Healthcare Corporation are indicted on charges of massive health care fraud.[5]
- Toxic dumping at Love Canal results in evacuation of 1,300 families and a cleanup that costs $250 million.[6]
- Drexel, Burnham, Lambert, Inc., a Wall Street brokerage firm, pleads guilty to securities fraud and is fined $650 million.[7]
- Insider trading scandals, in which stocks are traded illegally on the basis of information that is not available to the public, result in fines of $25 million. One insider trader, Ivan Boesky, is sentenced to three years in prison and a $300 million fine.[8]

Is there a pattern to these crimes? Do these unrelated incidents have any common threads?

Much of this book has addressed traditional "street" crimes of violence and property. This is because the U.S.'s concern about crime and criminal justice emanates largely from concern about murder, rape, robbery, assault, burglary, larceny, and theft. These crimes are serious, but they are not the *most* serious crimes occurring today.

The most important thread linking together the incidents just listed is *organization*. Whereas most street crimes are either random or involve very little planning, sophisticated crimes require planning or organization in order to succeed. Most street crimes take only a few minutes or even seconds to accomplish. Sophisticated crimes often take days, weeks, and sometimes months to plan and carry out. In the case of Day-Lee Foods in California, a meat-packing firm, the chief financial officer began writing checks to himself from company accounts and deposited them into his automatic teller machine (ATM). To circumvent company audits, he used handwritten checks rather than computer-generated checks, which were routinely audited. He used lines of credit to replace the missing cash, and then concealed the loans by manipulating other company accounts. These manipulations allowed him to pay his exwife $600,000 per year in family support payments, even though his annual salary was only $150,000! He was able to finance a lavish lifestyle for himself and his exwife until the Internal Revenue Service (IRS) arrested him in 1997. Ultimately, he embezzled $100 million; it took seven years to carry out this crime, the largest embezzlement in U.S. history.[9]

Consider the similarities between the Day-Lee Foods case and another crime that occurred more than a half-century earlier. The famous gangster Al Capone was widely believed to be involved in illegal gambling and bootlegging, but no one was able to prove it. Then the IRS examined his bank accounts and spending habits in Miami and Chicago and found that he had spent $7,000 for suits, $1,500 per week for hotel bills, $40,000 for a house on Palm Island, $39,000 on telephone calls, and $20,000 for silverware. This spending pattern suggested that he earned $165,000 per year. The IRS asked Capone to show how he lawfully earned this amount of money. Capone could not do so and was tried and convicted for failure to pay income taxes on $1 million of illegal income.[10]

In both cases it can be seen that planning and organization were central to the commission of the crimes, and that the crimes can be ongoing in nature. Sophisticated crimes are characterized by such planning. These are the most serious crimes occurring today, and they are the subject of this chapter. The following sections highlight several types of sophisticated crime, presenting definitions of these crimes, a typology for understanding their nature and extent, and possible future trends.

Conspiracy

The closest the criminal law comes to punishing the kind of criminal planning that underlies cases such as the two just described is through the crime of **conspiracy.** Conspiracy takes places when two or more persons agree to commit a crime, or to carry out a legal act in an illegal manner. Conspiracy, then, is essentially *preparation* or planning to commit a crime. It is characterized by the five elements summarized in Table 17.1.

conspiracy
Agreement of two or more persons to commit a crime or carry out a legal act in an illegal manner.

As Table 17.1 indicates, two or more people are needed to form a conspiracy, although the agreement between them can be tacit or otherwise inferred from the circumstances of the incident. The question that commonly arises in conspiracy cases is whether an offender truly acted alone or actually acted on behalf of, or in concert with, others. Consider the case of Beech-Nut Nutrition Corporation. The company's director of research told a vice president that apple juice concentrate purchased from a supplier was adulterated, containing sugars and syrups that did not come from apples. In fact, the concentrate was largely sugar syrup. The vice president took no action. Subsequently, a company plant manager in San Jose, California, informed the vice president that the apple concentrate he had received was "almost pure corn syrup." He recommended that Beech-Nut demand a refund from the supplier, but the vice president instructed the manager to use that syrup in the company's mixed juices, which were labeled "100% pure juice." Several other employees also informed the vice president of problems with the apple juice during the next few years. These employees were criticized for not being "team players," and one of them was threatened with dismissal.

Nearly four years after the original detection of adulterated concentrate, a detective hired by the Processed Apple Institute visited the vice president at the Beech-Nut manufacturing facility in Canajoharie, New York, and told him that the company was about to be sued for its use of adulterated concentrate. The vice president immediately severed Beech-Nut's contract with the supplier and returned whatever concentrate he could.

Unfortunately, Beech-Nut had an existing inventory worth millions of dollars. To avoid seizure of these products by New York State officials, the president of Beech-Nut had the juice transported to a warehouse in Secaucus, New Jersey, during the night. He offered distributors huge discounts to buy the juice so that it would not be seized, which would result in a large economic loss for the company. Ultimately, Beech-Nut negotiated with the government a national recall of apple juice. By the time of the recall, however, nearly all the adulterated apple juice had been sold. The president and vice president of Beech-Nut were eventually indicted

TABLE 17.1

Elements of Conspiracy: Legal Aspects

1. Two or more people are needed, although no formal agreement is required.
2. Participation need be only slight with reasonable knowledge of the conspiracy's existence, although mere presence by itself is insufficient for liability.
3. An overt act in furtherance of the conspiracy is usually required for liability.
4. Voluntary participation is required, and a person is liable for the acts of coconspirators.
5. Effective withdrawal from a conspiracy requires an act to either defeat or disavow the purposes of the conspiracy.

SOURCE: Jay Albanese, *Organized Crime in America*, 3rd ed. (Cincinnati: Anderson Publishing, 1996).

Adulterated food and other manufactured products can result in fraud, injury, or death to large numbers of people. This is the primary reason for the strict regulation of these industries.

and convicted, along with the suppliers of the tainted concentrate, for conspiracy to violate food and drug laws and introducing adulterated and misbranded apple juice into interstate commerce.[11]

The vice president argued on appeal that there was no agreement between him and the suppliers of the concentrate and that the elements of conspiracy therefore were not present. The U.S. Court of Appeals held that a defendant is part of a conspiracy if there is "some indication that [he] knew of and intended to further the illegal venture" or that he "encouraged the illegal use of the goods or had a stake in such use." The Court found the evidence "ample to permit the . . . jury to infer that the vice president and the concentrate suppliers were participants in a single scheme of passing off bogus substances as pure 100% fruit juice."[12] Thus, it can be seen that a formal agreement is not necessary for the crime of conspiracy. In this case no crime was "planned," but allowing unlawful conduct to continue in an organized fashion was sufficient to establish criminal liability.

For conspiracy to be established, it is also necessary that the offenders participated voluntarily and that withdrawal from the conspiracy would require more than simply walking away to avoid liability. Effective withdrawal from a conspiracy requires proof of an "affirmative action" by the defendant that works to defeat the conspiracy. The reason for this is that the goal of the conspiracy need not be achieved for a conviction to occur. Therefore, something more than merely walking away after being involved in the planning of a crime is needed to absolve one of responsibility for that crime. Otherwise, lower-level criminals who carried out conspiracies would be punished while those higher up, who were involved in the planning, could escape prosecution despite their significant role.

The importance of conspiracy can be seen in virtually every case of white-collar, computer, and organized crime. In every case, planning and organization are key parts of the criminal design. Making conspiracy a crime provides a means of punishing the *planning* activities of sophisticated criminals, thereby thwarting the criminal designs of these offenders.

Media and Criminal Justice

SE7EN

The plot of the 1995 psychological thriller *Se7en* revolves around two homicide detectives and their search for a perverse, psychopathic, and incredibly intelligent serial killer. The scenes of death in this movie are graphic, but not gratuitously so: Each scene of the crime is carefully displayed as homage to the killer's motivation, and the viewer is soon working with the two detectives to predict the killer's next move.

Se7en provides a dark and fascinating look into the mind of its serial killer, but also features some state-of-the-art techniques now used by investigators of such sophisticated crimes. In the movie, a veteran homicide detective named Somerset uses psychological introspection to get inside the killer's head, even though the newer detective believes that good old-fashioned beat work will catch the killer sooner. Somerset's determination to look at the "big picture" for clues as to the killer's psyche soon pays off, as the detectives come to realize that the killer is symbolically dispatching the Seven Deadly Sins with each murder.

The first victim is an obese man, found sitting at a table with his hands and feet tied to the chair, apparently forced to eat plates of spaghetti until suffering a heart attack. Somerset believes that there is significance in the fact that the overweight victim was forced to eat himself to death, and thus recognizes the first deadly sin: gluttony. The detective then conducts his background investigation at the public library, where he reads the classics of Milton, Chaucer, Aquinas, and Dante to determine who the killer might strike next. His research is a reflection of the popular practice of "profiling" criminal minds through behavioral science and forensic psychology. In the film, the detectives' research is affirmed as they recognize each of the Seven Deadly Sins in new homicides: A lawyer is killed by losing a pound of flesh (greed), a supermodel has her face disfigured and nose cut off (vanity), a welfare-dependent drug addict is kept prisoner and slowly starved to death with intravenously administered drugs (sloth), and so on.

By understanding the modus operandi, the detectives are able to predict the killer's next move, but only to a certain degree. It is a combination of profiling and some tried-and-true investigatory practices—such as getting the names of people who had previously checked out the Chaucer and Dante books from the library, and even breaking down the suspect's door without a warrant—that brings them closer to the killer.

The end of the movie is extremely disturbing, but perfectly in keeping with the chosen theme of the serial killer. As crime is in real life, the plot of the film is quite unpredictable. In a very symbolic way, the serial killer wins out over the detectives, proving that he is actually more sophisticated and intelligent than they had thought.

Should the detectives have been able to anticipate the killer's final crime? The movie depicts how the profiling of a sophisticated serial killer is a necessary means of catching such criminals, but also reveals the limitations of such techniques. *Se7en* shows that as crimes become more complex in both motivation and technique, police must now "get inside the mind" of the sophisticated offender if such crimes are to be solved.

MEDIA AND CRIMINAL JUSTICE QUESTION

If it were possible to predict the future crimes of offenders with a high degree of accuracy, explain why it should or should not be possible to detain or punish them for the crime that has not yet been committed?

White Collar Crime

White collar crime goes beyond the crimes committed by businesspeople who often wear jackets, ties, and white shirts. It is easy to distinguish a mugging from an embezzlement, but what about the difference between simple theft and fraud? Or between assault and an injury caused by a defective product? The distinctions between white collar and traditional street crimes are not always clear. These two categories of offenses are not distinguishable by the amount of harm they cause because frauds or unsafe products can cause much more injury and harm than any number of street crimes. Nor are they distinguishable by the level of violence involved. Many street crimes, such as larceny and burglary, involve no personal confrontation, but conspiracy, extortion, or food and drug manufacturing violations can involve threats, injury, and even death. The distinctions between white collar crime and more traditional forms of crime therefore do not lie in the nature of the victim, or violence, or injury. Instead, white collar crime is distinguishable by the manner in which it is carried out, given available opportunities. The opportunity to commit such crimes is often determined by one's position in society. One cannot embezzle funds without first holding a position of financial trust, and one cannot commit regulatory offenses without holding a particular position in business or industry. Thus, *access* to financial or governmental resources provides the *opportunity* to commit white collar offenses.

Street crimes are characterized by the use of force or stealth. *Force, stealth, or both* are required for homicide, rape, robbery, assault, burglary, larceny, or arson. In contrast, white collar crimes are characterized by *planning and deceit,* which are required to carry out a successful conspiracy, fraud, extortion, embezzlement, forgery, or regulatory offense. Thus, white collar crime can be defined as follows:

> **Planned illegal or unethical acts of deception committed by an individual or organization, usually during the course of legitimate occupational activity by persons of high or respectable social status, for personal or organizational gain that violates fiduciary responsibility or public trust.[13]**

This definition highlights several facts about white collar crime:

- It can be committed by an individual or by an organization or group of individuals.
- Deception, trickery, or fraud lies at the heart of white collar crime.
- Most white collar crimes emanate from otherwise legitimate occupational activity, in which access to money or information makes possible its misuse.
- White collar offenses sometimes lie on the border between illegal and unethical behavior, where what a company may do can cause harm or even death, but where the conduct may not violate the criminal law. Many such offenses are adjudicated in civil proceedings to determine compensation, rather than in criminal court to determine guilt.

embezzlement
The purposeful misappropriation of property entrusted to one's care, custody, or control, to which one is not entitled.

Given these general attributes, it is possible to create a typology of white collar crimes as shown in Table 17.2.

TABLE 17.2

A Typology of White Collar Crime

CRIMES OF THEFT	CRIMES AGAINST PUBLIC ADMINISTRATION	REGULATORY OFFENSES
Embezzlement	Bribery	Administrative violations
Extortion	Obstruction of justice	Environmental violations
Forgery	Official misconduct	Labor violations
Fraud	Perjury	Manufacturing violations
		Unfair trade practices

SOURCE: *WHITE COLLAR CRIME IN AMERICA* by ALBANESE, JAY, © 1995. Reprinted by permission of Prentice-Hall, Inc., Upper Saddle River, NJ.

White Collar Thefts

As the table illustrates, white collar crimes can be divided into three groups: theft, offenses against public administration, and regulatory offenses. White collar thefts include embezzlement, extortion, forgery, and fraud. **Embezzlement** is the purposeful misappropriation of property entrusted to one's care, custody, or control to which one is not entitled. In some states it is called "misapplication of property" and is included under theft as a type of larceny. The essential element of embezzlement is violation of financial trust. An example is the former police chief in

Rochester, New York, who was convicted of stealing $243,000 in police department funds over a three-year period.[14] Embezzlement is usually punished on the basis of how much money or property is misappropriated.

Extortion also involves theft, but it is accomplished in a different manner. It consists of purposely obtaining property from another person with his or her consent, induced through wrongful use of force or fear or under the guise of official authority. Many states classify extortion as a type of larceny or theft. Extortion is sometimes called blackmail, as in the case of Sol Wachtler, Chief Judge of the New York State Court of Appeals, who was charged with telling his former lover that he would sell sexually explicit photos of her and her new boyfriend if she did not give him money.[15]

extortion
Purposely obtaining property from another person with his or her consent, induced through wrongful use of force or fear or under the guise of official authority.

A person who falsely makes or alters an official document with intent to defraud commits the crime of **forgery.** The penalty for forgery is often based on the type of document that is forged. Forgery also includes other offenses that are sometimes defined separately under state law. Counterfeiting, criminal possession of forged instruments, unlawful use of slugs, and falsifying business records are all variations of the crime of forgery. In one large forgery case, police found 250,000 fake Social Security cards, green cards, and counterfeit twenty-dollar bills in a suspected eight million dollar operation at a Los Angeles print shop.[16]

forgery
Falsely making or altering an official document with the intent to defraud.

Still another type of white collar theft is **fraud,** or purposely obtaining the property of another person through deception. Fraud is at the heart of the concept of white collar crime. Together with conspiracy, it forms the basis for many organized illegal acts. In many states bankruptcy fraud, false advertising, issuing a bad check, fraudulent accosting, criminal impersonation, and theft of services are considered specific types of fraud. Fraud thus involves larceny-by-trick or deceit. A common form of fraud is the telemarketing scam. In a typical case, a New Jersey company used a 900 number to charge up to twenty-eight dollars per call for people who responded to mail announcing that they had won a prize, which turned out to be worthless jewelry.[17]

fraud
Purposely obtaining the property of another person through deception.

Offenses against Public Administration

The second category of white collar crimes can be called offenses against public administration. The crimes in this category include bribery, obstruction of justice, official misconduct, and perjury. **Bribery** involves the voluntary giving or receiving of anything of value with the intent of influencing the action of a public official. The more important, or serious, the official act to be performed, the more serious the penalty. Bribery law also works two ways: One can be convicted of bribery for either offering a corrupt payment or for receiving it. In South Carolina, for example, fifteen legislators and six lobbyists were among those convicted after the Federal Bureau of Investigation videotaped legislators taking cash from a lobbyist in exchange for their votes.[18] Seven Arizona legislators were charged in a similar bribery scandal.[19]

bribery
Voluntarily giving or receiving anything of value with the intent of influencing the action of a public official.

Intentionally preventing a public servant from lawfully performing an official function is **obstruction of justice.** In the Watergate scandal, for example, members of the White House staff refused to cooperate with investigations of alleged wrongdoing, and some were ultimately convicted of purposely concealing relevant information, which was obstruction of justice.[20]

obstruction of justice
Intentionally preventing a public servant from lawfully performing an official function.

official misconduct
The unauthorized exercise of an official function by a public official with intent to benefit or injure another.

Official misconduct is the unauthorized exercise of an official function by a public official with intent to benefit or injure another. A person who uses an elected office for personal gain is guilty of official misconduct. Such misconduct can result from an act of omission (failure to perform legal duties) or commission (exercising powers in an unauthorized manner). People who use their public office to "fix" tickets, obtain permits without payment, or solicit sex are committing official misconduct. A police officer was convicted of this crime when he tried to get the driving records of a woman he was accused of raping.[21]

perjury
Making a false statement under oath in an official proceeding.

When someone makes a false statement under oath in an official proceeding, he or she is guilty of **perjury** or false swearing. The punishment for perjury is usually based on the nature of the proceeding. Perjury during a trial or grand jury proceeding is considered more serious than false swearing on an affidavit. John Poindexter, former national security advisor to President Reagan, was convicted of perjury when he was shown to have lied to Congress as part of the cover-up in the Iran–Contra affair.[22]

Regulatory Offenses

regulatory offenses
Five categories of offenses designed to ensure fairness and safety in the conduct of business, including administrative, environmental, labor, and manufacturing violations, as well as unfair trade practices.

The third category of white collar crimes is **regulatory offenses.** These offenses are designed to ensure fairness and safety in the conduct of business. There are hundreds of types of regulatory offenses, but they can be grouped into five different categories: administrative, environmental, labor, and manufacturing violations, as well as unfair trade practices.

Administrative offenses involve the failure to comply with court orders or agency requirements. Failure to keep adequate records, submit compliance reports, acquire a valid permit, and the like are against the law where these procedures are required. For example, in 1992, Equifax, a leading credit-reporting agency, settled a case brought by eighteen states that alleged it was issuing inaccurate credit reports. The company agreed to make credit reports easier to read, explain to consumers how a credit rating is derived, and resolve disputed reports within thirty days. Another credit-reporting agency, TRW, settled a similar case brought by nineteen states.[23]

Environmental violations include emissions or dumping in violation of legal standards. Discharges into the air or water without a permit, failure to adequately treat waste before disposal, and deposit of hazardous waste in a landfill are examples of environmental violations. In 1992, Rockwell International pleaded guilty to felony charges that it had stored hazardous waste without a permit in containers that leaked the waste into reservoirs outside Denver, Colorado. The company agreed to pay an $18.5 million fine.[24]

Labor violations can take several forms, including discriminatory practices, unsafe exposure, and unfair treatment of employees. Examples include firing without cause and refusing employment, in addition to more serious offenses. One such case was that of Imperial Food Products. Company officials were charged with twenty-five counts of involuntary manslaughter for locked exits and other safety violations that resulted in the deaths of twenty-five workers in a fire at Imperial's chicken-processing plant in Hamlet, North Carolina.[25]

The manufacture of unsafe products is the essence of *manufacturing violations.* Electrical shock hazards, fire hazards, and lack of adequate labeling or directions are examples of such violations. In one case the Federal Trade Commission found that Kraft had falsely advertised its "Singles" cheese slice as containing the same amount of calcium as five ounces of milk when in fact the level was measurably lower than that.[26]

Unfair trade practices are those that prevent fair competition in the marketplace. Monopolization, price discrimination, price-fixing, and bid-rigging are examples of unfair trade practices. In one case, the State of Florida filed a lawsuit against three manufacturers of infant formula, claiming that they had conspired to raise the price of baby formula. It was pointed out that formula prices had risen 155 percent while the price of milk, the primary ingredient, had risen only 36 percent over the same period.[27]

As these offense categories illustrate, regulations are designed to protect the public from unscrupulous or dangerous practices of business and government. This category of white collar crime is very important because white collar crimes often involve deviations from legitimate business or governmental activity. The penalties for violation of regulations sometimes involve criminal sanctions; regulatory offenses therefore are part of the criminal law.

An important question is whether white collar crime is increasing or decreasing. An answer is not readily available because there are no regularly collected data for white collar crimes as there are for street crimes. Victimization surveys count only rape, robbery, assault, burglary, larceny, and motor vehicle theft. The Uniform Crime Report, however, includes forgery/counterfeiting, fraud, and embezzlement in its tallies of arrests (which represent only offenders who are caught). Arrest trends for these offenses over the last twenty-five years indicate that dramatic increases have occurred. As Table 17.3 indicates, arrest rates for all these offenses have risen over the last twenty-five years even when controlling for population growth. The rate of arrests for fraud has increased by 321 percent in twenty-five years.

Employment trends also indicate an increase in white collar crime. The proportion of the U.S. population employed in jobs that provide access to information and financial accounts is increasing, and as a result more people will have access to criminal opportunities involving misuse of authority and funds.[28] Demographic trends also suggest that white collar crime will increase. The average age of the U.S. population is rising. In 1970, the median age was 28, but by 2000 it will be 35.5 and by 2025 it will be about 38.[29] The aging of the U.S. population is due to a low birthrate combined with the fact that people are living longer than earlier generations. The net result is more people in the "white collar prone" over-25 age group. (The majority of those arrested for forgery, embezzlement, and fraud are over 25.)

TABLE 17.3

Arrests for White Collar Crimes*

OFFENSE	1970	1980	1995	PERCENT CHANGE IN RATE
Forgery/ counterfeiting	43,833 (28.9)	72,643 (34.9)	91,991 (46.8)	+62%
Fraud	76,861 (50.7)	261,787 (125.7)	320,046 (162.9)	+321%
Embezzlement	8,172 (5.4)	7,885 (3.8)	11,605 (5.9)	+9%

*Number and (rate) per 100,000 population.

SOURCE: Data compiled from Federal Bureau of Investigation, *Crime in the United States* (Washington, D.C.: U.S. Government Printing Office, published annually).

Computer Crime

In the same way that the invention of the automobile early in the twentieth century may have doubled the number of offenses in the criminal codes of the United States, the invention of the computer is likely to have the same impact in the twenty-

contemporary issues

Avoiding Cybertheft

A 28-year-old California woman was the owner of a new $22,000 Jeep, five credit cards, an apartment, and a $3,000 loan. The problem was that she asked for none of it and never saw any of it. Another woman had impersonated her by obtaining personal information without the victim's knowledge. Generally, knowledge of an individual's Social Security number, employer, address, and driver's license number are enough to begin the fraud. It took months of phone calls, court appearances, and legal expenses for the victim to reclaim her identity and escape the bills in her name.[A]

An e-mail message was sent in to America Online subscribers titled, "Important AOL Information." At the end of a letter from the chairman of AOL, subscribers were asked to enter their name, address, phone number, and credit card numbers to "update" AOL's new computers. The message, letter, and request were all fraudulent. They turned out to be part of a scam involving a thief who wanted to commit credit card fraud.[B]

These are examples of how criminals use computer technology to commit frauds that can have a devastating impact on victims. Despite such problems, however, companies and consumers remain anxious to make the Internet a secure forum in which to buy and sell merchandise. In order to offer greater security in credit card transactions via computer, companies are writing more and more sophisticated encryption programs that scramble transactions to make it difficult for hackers and others to eavesdrop or steal consumer information or credit card numbers.

The FBI fears that clever criminals will obtain similar encryption capabilities and use them to hide money laundering, drug distribution schemes, or terrorist plots. It has asked Congress to enact legislation to prohibit the private manufacture of encryption codes that it cannot break, unless law enforcement agencies are given access to the codes for investigative purposes. According to the director of the FBI, "The widespread use of uncrackable encryption will devastate our ability to fight crime and prevent terrorism."[C] Others argue that dissemination of encryption codes without the knowledge of consumers violates the right of privacy and will make electronic transactions even more vulnerable to forgery and fraud.[D]

These views reflect an important debate regarding what controls, if any, should be placed on technological advances in a free marketplace. Should law enforcement officials respond to frauds only after they occur, or should they be granted access to all commercial encryption codes in order to take preventive actions? This debate involves at least two significant issues:

- Should potential threats to government security supersede threats to commercial security?
- How should we balance the government's interest in preventing crime against the privacy of individual citizens and businesses on the Internet?

The way that these issues are resolved may shape the nature of criminal justice in the years to come.

NOTES

[A]T. Trent Gegax, "Stick'Em Up? Not Anymore. Now It's Crime by Keyboard," *Newsweek* (July 21, 1997), p. 14.

[B]"AOL Users Target of Cyberthief's E-Mail Scam," *Richmond Times-Dispatch* (August 26, 1997), p. 1.

[C]Louis J. Freeh, "Let Law Keep Weapons," *USA Today* (September 26, 1997), p. 14.

[D]Steven Levy, "Trying to Find the Key," *Newsweek* (October 14, 1996), p. 91; "Computer Privacy at Risk if FBI Gets the Codes," *USA Today* (September 26, 1997), p. 14.

first century. Automobiles provided opportunities for illegal activity ranging from manufacturing shortcuts to repair frauds, as well as theft. It is likely that computers will have a similar impact as the technology becomes more sophisticated and more popular. Legal codes are being modified to eliminate opportunities for misuse similar to those that emerged when automobiles became commonplace.[30]

TABLE 17.4

Types of Computer Crime

COMPUTER AS INSTRUMENT	COMPUTER AS OBJECT
Theft by computer (using a computer as a tool to steal)	Damage to software/hardware (physical or electronic damage to computers or computer programs)
Harassment/extortion (using a computer as a means for intimidation or threats)	Data alteration (changing information for undue advantage or revenge)

SOURCE: *CRIME IN AMERICA: SOME EXISTING AND EMERGING ISSUES* by ALBANESE, JAY, © 1993. Reprinted by permission of Prentice-Hall, Inc., Upper Saddle River, NJ.

Computers are most often used to steal, but they can be used to commit other crimes as well. There are several different types of computer crimes, which can be grouped into two basic categories: crimes in which computers are used as the *instrument* of the offense and those in which computers are the *object* of the offense. Computers are used as an instrument in crimes of theft such as embezzlement, fraud, or larceny by computer. They can also be instruments of crime when they are used for purposes of extortion or harassment. The recent spread of computer "viruses," hidden programs that threaten or simply bother users, is an example.

Computers can be the object of a crime when the intention is to cause damage to computer hardware (machines) or software (programs). Data destruction and theft or vandalism of computers or programs are examples of such crimes. Likewise, computers can be the object of crime when the intention is to alter data stored in them. Attempts to alter financial statements, credit history, or college grades are examples of this type of computer crime. Table 17.4 illustrates the two categories of computer crime and the two types of crime in each category.

Crimes in Which Computers Are the Instrument

The most common form of computer crime is theft by computer. In 1998, the computer manager at King Soopers stores in Colorado was charged with stealing two million dollars by manipulating computer records at the stores while he was supposed to be fixing "bugs" in the system.[31] A New Jersey woman was sentenced to six to ten years in prison for her role in a scheme in which bogus Blue Cross insurance claims were processed through a special "override" computer terminal designed to rush checks in emergency cases.[32] In these cases computers were used as an instrument to carry out thefts in the form of fraud and embezzlement.

A former executive at Squibb and Sons, Inc., one of the largest pharmaceutical firms in the United States, pleaded guilty to fraud in a scheme to steal more than one million dollars of merchandise from the company. In one instance the executive arranged through a computer order to have $8,000 worth of merchandise shipped from a Massachusetts distribution center. Moments later he arranged to have the computer "kill" the invoice without leaving a trace. The goods were eventually sold to a middleman, who distributed them at a discount to drugstores.[33]

Examples of computer crimes abound. To cite just a few:

- Stanley Mark Rifkin stole $10.2 million from a California bank in less than an hour, using a computer to transfer the money by wire to a New York bank and later to Zurich to buy diamonds.[34]
- Kevin Mitnick was charged with four counts of fraud for using a friend's office computer to break into the computer system at Digital Equipment Corporation and copying software that had cost one million dollars to develop.

He was also charged with electronically entering the Leeds University computer system in England and transferring his telephone charges to a nonexistent MCI long-distance account.[35]

- Three members of the "Legion of Doom" pleaded guilty to fraud and conspiracy for bilking BellSouth and credit firms by invading their computers.[36]
- Computer hackers apparently stole twelve million dollars in telephone charges from NASA over two years, using long-distance credit card numbers.[37]

These are all examples of a trend toward using computers as a "burglar's tool"; that is, computers are the instrument used to conduct a theft.[38]

The second type of instrumental computer crime is use of a computer to harass or extort a victim. Perhaps the most notorious case of this type is that of Donald Burleson, who inserted a "virus" (a program that continuously duplicated itself, interfering with the normal operation of computers) into the computer systems at a brokerage firm from which he had been fired. The virus erased 168,000 sales commission records.[39] Many other viruses have been planted in computer programs. Some are relatively innocuous, flashing "Peace" or other messages on thousands of computer screens, but others can be extremely harmful.[40] The potential for damage has intensified efforts to improve security technology.

Examples of instrumental computer crimes abound. Robert Morris, a 23-year-old graduate student, released a virus program that copied itself over and over again, bringing more than 6,000 university, research, and military computers to a standstill, although no information was taken or lost.[41] A 19-year-old college student in Los Angeles was arrested for using his home computer to break into a Defense Department international communications system.[42] A group of 13- to 17-year-old computer users in Milwaukee unlawfully gained access to the computer at New York City's Memorial Sloan-Kettering Cancer Center and erased a file. They also gained access to unclassified material at the Los Alamos nuclear weapons laboratory in New Mexico.[43] In 1997, nine regional Internet service

Computers can be used as the instrument to commit crimes (such as theft or harassment) or as the object of crime (to alter data or damage hardware or software).

providers were infiltrated by hackers.[44] In each of these cases the computer was used as an instrument to harass, invade privacy, or extort a victim.

Crimes in Which Computers Are the Object

The second type of computer crime includes offenses in which the computer is the object of the criminal act. One crime of this type is causing damage to hardware or software; the damage can be physical or competitive. For example, Microsoft Corporation, working with U.S. marshals, seized more than one million dollars in counterfeit software in Los Angeles that had been produced by ten illicit businesses.[45] Pirated software has been copied and smuggled to Hong Kong and elsewhere, where programs like "Windows 95" are sold for only five dollars.[46]

There have been a number of cases in which companies claim damages for losses due to "stolen," or altered, computers or programs. These cases often allege theft of ideas or "trade secrets." Trade secrets can include inventions, client and inventory lists, pricing and marketing strategies, research and development data, or other nonpublic information.[47]

A case that illustrates these principles occurred in Minnesota. A computer software company filed suit against several employees who had formed a software company of their own. The new company had solicited several of their former employer's clients, attempting to sell them software that was nearly identical to the employer's. The Court of Appeals of Minnesota affirmed that the software was a trade secret and had been wrongfully misappropriated.[48] The court held that reasonable efforts had been made to maintain the secrecy of the program through written warnings of proprietary ownership and copyright protection. Therefore, the company was entitled to monetary damages and an injunction against the employees' activities.

Another type of crime in which the computer is the object is alteration of data for an unlawful purpose. An example is the case of Eddie Lee Alston, a Washington, D.C., car dealer. Alston was involved in a scheme in which he would pay an accomplice to delete unfavorable credit information from computerized files, and add favorable, but false, credit information for people who had difficulty obtaining loans. The altered credit records were then sent to banks for approval, allowing these people to secure car loans.[49] Since this case of data alteration occurred before the passage of a federal computer crime law, Alston was charged with mail fraud for sending the altered credit applications to banks. His conviction was reversed, however, because the mailings occurred *after* each applicant had taken possession of a car and *prior to* the actual fraud taking place (i.e., a bank loan secured on false pretenses). Mail fraud did not apply in this case because the mailings themselves did not obtain the loan, and they did not conceal Alston's fraudulent representations in the loan applications. This case shows why it became necessary to pass laws making it possible to prosecute computer-based schemes regardless of whether or not the offenders achieved their objective.

Computer crimes are often committed by "hackers," individuals with sophisticated technical knowledge who go to great lengths to infiltrate business and government computer systems. TRW Information Services, the largest credit bureau in the United States, has admitted that "hackers" were able to get into its system and view information but were unable to change any of it.[50] A computer systems manager at Lawrence Berkeley Laboratory in California realized that an unauthorized user was looking at his computer files, so he set up a phony "star wars" computer file that the hacker could not resist. The suspect was eventually tracked to Hanover, West Germany, where three people were charged with selling secrets to the Soviet Union.[51] In each of these cases, unauthorized attempts were made to alter data stored in computer files.

Rates of computer crimes of all types are increasing, posing problems for law enforcement. A survey of 250 businesses found that the dollar value of losses from computer crimes totaled $137 million in 1997, up from $100 million in 1996. Thefts of proprietary company information rose from approximately $1 million to $1.7 million between 1996 and 1997.[52] Employees account for nearly two-thirds of suspected cases of computer crime, and some estimates place the number as high as 90 percent.[53] A sample of more than 2,700 ATM incidents resulting in account-holder complaints found that 45 percent involved a potential fraud. A survey for the National Institute of Justice found that losses occurred in 56 percent of reported incidents involving wire transfers among banks and businesses.[54] In sum, as computer ownership increases, together with computing power and access to databases via networks and the Internet, the opportunities for computer crime will increase as well.

The causes of computer crime have not been studied extensively but a survey of six hundred university students found that 34 percent had pirated software and 16 percent had gained illegal access to a computer system. The study found that in many cases these behaviors were learned from others or imitated.[55] A complication in understanding the nature and scope of computer crime is the fact that few businesses want to admit to vulnerability and therefore underreport breaches of computer security. In 1996, the Department of Justice established its Computer Crime and Intellectual Property Section to investigate and prosecute computer-related crimes. Thus far, the biggest challenge has been convincing businesses to report these offenses.[56]

Despite these problems, there have been some notable successes in combating computer crime, many of which have resulted from the work of the FBI's National Computer Crime Squad, which commenced operations in 1992. Undercover "sting" operations and businesses sharing information about suspected computer hacking are the two most common methods of investigation. In 1996, for example, seventy-eight people were convicted for trading child pornography over the Internet in an FBI sting operation.[57] A 37-year-old computer repairman was found to have infiltrated Internet service providers and collected 100,000 credit card numbers. He was ready to sell a CD-ROM with these stolen numbers on it for $260,000 at San Francisco Airport but walked into an FBI sting operation.[58] Two raids on suspected Internet gambling operations in the Northeast found proceeds estimated at $56 million. Thus, it appears that computers are being used to commit both white collar and organized crimes.

Organized Crime

Organized crime has always been a fascinating form of criminal behavior, yet its definition and true scope are often unclear. More than thirty years ago, the President's Crime Commission concluded that "our knowledge of the structure which makes 'organized crime' organized is somewhat comparable to the knowledge of Standard Oil which could be gleaned from interviews with gasoline station attendants."[59] A similar commission, appointed by Ronald Reagan in 1987, also did not offer any clear definition of organized crime. Nevertheless, a definition of organized crime based on the work of researchers in the field reads as follows:

> **Organized crime is a continuing criminal enterprise that rationally works to profit from illicit activities that are often in great public demand. Its continuing existence is maintained through the use of force, threats, monopoly control, and/or the corruption of public officials.[60]**

Even this definition is incomplete, however. For example, how does an otherwise legitimate corporation that collects toxic waste, but dumps some of it illegally, fit into this definition? Is a motorcycle gang that sells drugs as a sideline part of organized crime? What about a licensed massage parlor that offers some customers sex for money?

As many investigators have pointed out, perhaps organized crime should be seen as a "degree" of criminal activity or as a point on the "spectrum of legitimacy."[61] Thus, for example, loansharking can be seen as a matter of degree—the only difference between it and a legitimate loan is the interest rate charged. Further, the real difference between criminal and noncriminal distribution of narcotics lies in whether or not the distributor is licensed by the state (i.e., a doctor or pharmacist). The point here is that organized crime is actually a part of a larger category of behavior that also includes white collar crime.

Crimes committed by corporations during the course of business, or by politicians or government agencies, can also be considered examples of "organized" crime because they fit the above definition. For example, official misconduct by a government official, obstruction of justice as in the Iran–Contra and Watergate scandals, and commercial bribery are all types of organized criminal behavior. As the National Advisory Committee on Criminal Justice Standards and Goals has recognized, there are more similarities than differences between organized and so-called white collar crimes: "The perpetrators of organized crime may include corrupt business executives, members of the professions, public officials, or members of any other occupational group, in addition to the conventional racketeer element."[62]

There are also some important differences between organized and white collar crime. Perhaps the most significant distinction is the fact that white collar crimes generally occur as a *deviation from legitimate business activity.* On the other hand, organized crime takes places through a *continuing criminal enterprise* that exists to profit *primarily* from crime.

It is important to keep in mind the fact that organized crime is not restricted to the activities of criminal syndicates. As Henry Pontell and Kitty Calavita concluded in their study of the savings and loan scandal of the 1980s, if we reserve the term *organized crime* for continuing conspiracies that include the corruption of government officials, "then much of the savings and loan scandal involved organized crime."[63] In interviews with the Federal Bureau of Investigation, Secret Service, and regulatory agencies, they found a "recurring theme" of conspiracies between savings and loan officials ("insiders") and accountants, lawyers, and real

FUTURE ISSUES

Organized Crime and the Shadow Economy

Mikhail owns a woodworking shop in Russia, where ten craftsmen make tables and chairs. Mikhail holds no business license, does not advertise, and does not pay taxes. His customers pay in cash for his products. About half of Russia's gross domestic product is estimated to operate in this way as part of a "shadow economy." According to economist John Tedstrom, "There isn't a Russian who isn't involved or whose family isn't involved one way or another in the informal economy."[A] Thus, even though official unemployment rates are high and salaries low, purchases of cars, computers, and telephones are rising. This is evidence of income not being earned "on the books."

In many countries, including the United States, large numbers of workers (carpenters, waiters, roofers, painters, and so on) perform work for cash that is not declared to the government for the purposes of taxation. The shadow economy allows people to earn untaxed income and improve their quality of life. There also exists a parallel shadow economy that consists of people who make money from illicit activities. Examples include individuals involved in illegal gambling enterprises, drug distribution, loansharking, and prostitution.[B] The size of these shadow economies is difficult to estimate, for obvious reasons, but they are probably large.

Two primary reasons for the size and growth of shadow economies are taxes and the criminal law. Taxes that are perceived to be either unfair or too high promote disobedience to tax laws, as do laws for crimes that are only weakly agreed to be serious. For example, gambling is seen by many people as recreational behavior or as a matter of private consensual conduct rather than criminal behavior. To a lesser extent, the same is true of drug use and prostitution. As countries move toward tightening tax enforcement and controlling the vices, it will be interesting to see whether this expands the shadow economy.

FUTURES QUESTION

If tax enforcement and control of the vices are tightened, what do you believe will be the impact on the shadow economy and on society in general?

NOTES

[A]Christian Caryl, "Only a Fool Pays Taxes in Capitalist Russia," *U.S. News & World Report* (March 30, 1998), p. 38.

[B]U.S. Comptroller General, *Drug Control: U.S. Counternarcotics Efforts in Colombia Face Continuing Challenges* (Washington, D.C.: U.S. General Accounting Office, 1998); Dan McGraw, "The Iowan Connection: Powerful Mexican Drug Cartels Have Hit Rural America," *U.S. News & World Report* (March 2, 1998), pp. 33–4; Matt Bai, "White Storm Warning," *U.S. News & World Report* (March 31, 1997), p. 66.

estate developers ("outsiders"). Comparisons of these kinds of corrupt relationships with more traditional organized crime techniques, such as no-show jobs at construction sites or payoffs for "protection," reveal that they are more similar than different. Examples such as this illustrate that much of the crime committed by corporations, politicians, and government agencies is as serious and harmful as the crimes of criminal enterprises.[64]

A Typology of Organized Crime

For all the mystique that permeates discussions of organized crime, relatively little attention has been given to establishing the precise behaviors that are involved. What types of illegal acts are we referring to when we speak of organized crime?

Organized crime falls into three basic categories: provision of illicit services, provision of illicit goods, and infiltration of legitimate business. Within each of these categories there are more specific crimes that often come to the attention of the criminal justice system.

Provision of illicit services involves attempts to satisfy the public's demand for certain services that are not provided by legitimate society. The specific crimes in this category include loansharking, prostitution, and gambling. Loansharking is the lending of money at an interest rate above that permitted by law. Organized prostitution offers sex for pay on a systematic basis. Numbers gambling is a type of lottery that operates without the approval of the state. Each of these crimes is a continuing enterprise that fulfills needs for money, sex, or gambling that cannot be satisfied in a legitimate way, such as through bank loans, marriage, or state lotteries.

Provision of illicit goods involves offering particular products that a segment of the public desires but cannot obtain through legitimate channels. The sale and distribution of drugs and the fencing and distribution of stolen property are examples of crimes in this category. There is a great demand for drugs, such as marijuana, cocaine, Valium, and heroin, that are either illegal or distributed under very strict regulations imposed by the government. In a similar way, many people desire to buy products at the lowest possible price, regardless of where the seller originally obtained them. In response to this demand, organized criminals "fence" stolen merchandise by buying stolen property and then selling it to customers who are not concerned with its origin.

The third category of organized crime is *infiltration of legitimate business*. Labor racketeering and the takeover of waste disposal companies are examples of this type of crime. Labor racketeering involves the use of force or threats to obtain money in return for labor peace. This often entails the threat to employers or employees that if money is not paid, the business will be subjected to violence, strikes, and/or vandalism. In a similar way, organized crime syndicates have taken over waste disposal companies by coercing the legitimate owners to sell the business or have it operated by an outsider. This infiltration provides a way to launder proceeds from illegal drug or gambling enterprises.

Table 17.5 illustrates this typology of organized crime. Provision of illicit goods and services is distinguished from infiltration of legitimate business by its consensual nature and the lack of inherent violence. Organized crime figures who offer illegal betting, loansharking, or drugs rely on the public's unsatisfied demand for these services. Since they also rely heavily on return business, they want the illicit transaction to go well. It is very unusual for criminal syndicates to *solicit* business. Instead, those interested in illicit goods and services seek out the

TABLE 17.5

A Typology of Organized Crime

TYPE OF ACTIVITY	NATURE OF ACTIVITY	HARM
Provision of illicit goods and services	Gambling, lending, sex, narcotics, stolen property	Consensual activities No inherent violence Economic harm
Infiltration of legitimate business	Coercive use of legal businesses for purposes of exploitation	Nonconsensual activities Threats, violence, extortion Economic harm

SOURCE: Jay Albanese, *Organized Crime in America*, 3rd ed. (Cincinnati: Anderson Publishing, 1996).

provider. Violence plays no inherent role in the activities themselves, although bad debts cannot be collected through the courts, as they can for loans and sales in the legitimate market. Therefore, violence or threats occur when one party to the transaction feels cheated or shortchanged, and there is no legal alternative for resolving the dispute. Violence can also occur when an organization attempts to control or monopolize an illicit market. If a group wishes to corner the market on illicit gambling in a particular area, it may threaten or intimidate its illicit competitors. Once again, these threats are used as an enforcement mechanism rather than as part of the activity of providing illicit goods and services.

The infiltration of legitimate business is more predatory than the provision of illicit goods and services. In this case organized crime groups attempt to *create* demand for their services rather than exploiting an existing market. Demands for "protection" money or no-show jobs in return for avoidance of property damage, work stoppages, or violence illustrate the predatory nature of this type of crime. In legal terms, organized crime uses coercion or extortion in the infiltration of legitimate business. Coercion and extortion are not necessary to provide illicit goods or services because the demand for these goods and services already exists.

Organized Crime and Ethnicity

Some typologies classify crimes in terms of who is involved in the activity rather than in terms of the activity itself. For example, it is common to see discussions of traditional "street" crimes that categorize them by sex, race, or other demographic factors. Organized crime typologies focus more often on ethnicity and the nature of the structure of organized crime groups. Ethnicity is perhaps the most common basis for categorizing organized crime, although it might be misleading. This is true for several reasons:

- Organized crime is committed by a wide variety of ethnic groups, making ethnicity a poor indicator of organized crime activity.
- There is evidence that organized crime activities often are not carried out *within* the boundaries of a specific ethnic group; therefore, it is interethnic.
- Other variables, such as local market conditions and available criminal opportunities, may be much better indicators of organized crime.

There is a growing body of evidence that organized crime is not limited to the activities of a single, or even a few, ethnic groups. The President's Commission on Organized Crime described "organized crime today" as being carried out by eleven different groups:

- La Cosa Nostra (Italian)
- Outlaw motorcycle gangs
- Prison gangs
- Triads and Tongs (Chinese)
- Vietnamese gangs
- Yakuza (Japanese)
- Marielitos (Cuban)
- Colombian cocaine rings
- Irish organized crime

- Russian organized crime
- Canadian organized crime[65]

The President's Commission on Organized Crime included outlaw motorcycle gangs as a type of organized crime group.

This curious mixture includes groups defined by their ethnic or national origin, by the nature of their activity (cocaine rings), by their geographic location (prison gangs), and by their means of transportation (motorcycle gangs). While such attributes may help describe a group, they are not very useful as explanations of behavior. Moreover, there is evidence that these and other organized crime groups sometimes work together.[66]

It should be clear that ethnicity is not a very powerful explanation for the existence of organized crime; in fact, it is probably no more significant than motorcycles as a causal factor. This conclusion is supported by the results of several studies of ethnically based organized crime. These studies show not only that no single ethnic group or combination of groups accounts for most organized crime, but also that ethnicity is secondary to local criminal opportunities in explaining organized crime. A study by historian Alan Block of the illicit cocaine trade in New York City early in the twentieth century identified major players with Jewish backgrounds but also found considerable evidence of interethnic cooperation among New York's criminals.[67] There was evidence of involvement by Italians, Greeks, Irish, and blacks who did not always work within their own ethnic group. Block described these criminals as "criminal justice entrepreneurs" who were not part of a particular organization but were involved in a "web of small but efficient organizations."[68]

A more recent study of the underground drug market in "Southwest County" found the market to be largely competitive. Participants "entered the market, transacted their deals, [and] shifted from one type of activity to another" in response to the demands of the market rather than the dictates of an ethnically based organization.[69]

Similarly, a study of illegal gambling and loansharking in New York by Peter Reuter found that economic considerations dictated entry and exit from the illicit marketplace. Reuter found that these criminal enterprises were "not monopolies in the classic sense or subject to control by some external organization."[70] Instead, local market forces shaped the criminal behavior more than did ethnic ties or other characteristics of the criminal groups.

There is evidence that organized crime groups evolve around specific illicit activities, rather than the reverse. Illicit activities that are attractive because of public demand, conditions in the local market, or other factors appear to dictate how and what type of criminal group will emerge to exploit the opportunity. Less often, a group will attempt to "manufacture" a criminal opportunity through intimidation or extortion. This is probably a reflection of human nature: It is easier, and takes less energy, to exploit an existing market for illegal gambling, drugs, or stolen property than it is to "move in" on a preexisting legal or illegal business for illicit purposes.

In a classic ethnographic study, Francis Ianni became a participant–observer of an organized crime group for two years; he also made observations of two other criminal groups. He found these groups to "have no structure apart from their functioning; nor do they have structure independent of their current 'personnel'."[71] Joseph Albini's pioneering study of criminal groups in the United States and Italy reached a similar conclusion. Rather than belonging to an organization, those involved in organized crime formed relationships based on the particular activity in which they were engaged at any given time. The criminal "syndicate" is, in fact, "a system of loosely structured relationships functioning primarily because each participant is interested in furthering his own welfare."[72] These studies suggest that the structure of organized crime groups is derived from the activities in which they are engaged, rather than from preexisting ethnic ties.

The Extent of Organized Crime

The true extent of organized crime is unknown. Characteristic organized crimes such as conspiracy, racketeering, and extortion are not counted in any systematic way. Other offenses are known only when they result in arrests. The problem with relying on arrests as a measure of criminal activity is apparent: Much crime is undetected, some that is detected is not reported to police, and arrest rates go up or down depending on police activity and do not necessarily reflect levels of criminal activity. However, these are the only available statistics, and they provide some indication of the amount of organized crime committed each year.

The Federal Bureau of Investigation tabulates arrests for several offenses that are characteristic of organized crime. Trends in these arrests over the last twenty-five years are presented in Table 17.6. As can be seen, arrests for three of the four offenses have increased markedly over the last twenty-five years, whereas arrests for gambling have dropped dramatically. These increases and decreases can be attributed to two primary factors: change in law enforcement priorities and change in the overall population and in the numbers of police. Both the population and the number of sworn police officers in the United States have grown significantly during the last three decades. Therefore, one would expect a "natural" increase in numbers of arrests simply because there are more potential offenders and victims in the population, as well as more police looking for them.

At the same time, the public mood has shifted, especially with regard to gambling and drugs. Gambling in many forms has been legalized in a majority of the states in response to a shift from the perception of gambling as a "vice" to its perception as a "form of recreation."[73] Conversely, public concern about drugs in-

TABLE 17.6

Arrests for Offenses Related to Organized Crime

OFFENSE	1970	1980	1990	1995	25-YEAR CHANGE
Drug abuse violations	265,734	351,955	785,536	1,144,228	4 times higher
Gambling	75,325	37,805	13,357	15,676	5 times lower
Prostitution and commercialized vice	45,803	67,920	80,888	81,064	2 times higher
Stolen property (buy, receive, possess)	46,427	76,429	119,102	127,844	3 times higher

SOURCE: Data compiled from Federal Bureau of Investigation, *Uniform Crime Reports* (Washington, D.C.: U.S. Government Printing Office, published annually).

creased over the same period. The large increases in drug arrests (four times higher in 1995 than in 1970) are matched only by the huge decline in gambling arrests (five times lower over the same period). These changes clearly indicate shifting public, and hence law enforcement, views regarding the seriousness of these forms of criminal behavior.

It is possible that the incidence of these offenses has changed over the years, but we cannot determine this from arrest statistics. The fact that prostitution and commercialized vice arrests have doubled in twenty-five years, and arrests for stolen property have tripled from the 1970 level, suggests that more police, greater enforcement efforts, and increases in the numbers of cases have combined to produce these large increases in arrests.

In the future organized crime is likely to pose even greater problems than it has in the past. Technological change and economic globalization are likely to contribute to growth in organized crime. Organized crime groups are making increasing use of stolen and forged credit cards, airline tickets, cell phones, and currency.[74] New Visa check cards and MasterMoney cards require only a signature and no personal identification number to withdraw funds, making it easy for forgers to withdraw large amounts of money quickly.[75] The fall of national barriers in Europe and Asia also have made crossborder commerce and crime easier, as is discussed in Chapter 16. With each advance in technology, new criminal opportunities emerge. Gambling and pornography on the Internet and banking by telephone and by personal computer are examples of new opportunities for both organized and white collar crime to grow in the future.

Critical Thinking EXERCISE

An Antidrug Sales Tax?

In 1989, Jackson County, Missouri, became the first U.S. jurisdiction to approve a sales tax dedicated to reducing drug abuse. Jackson County, which includes Kansas City, is the second largest county in the state. The tax is called COMBAT (Community-Backed Anti-Drug Tax), and it brings in more than fourteen million dollars annually. The funds collected in this way are administered through the county prosecutor's office and are directed to three efforts: jailing dangerous criminals and drug dealers, providing treatment for nonviolent offenders who want to get off drugs, and preventing children from experimenting with drugs.

Programs designed to achieve these goals include community policing in six Kansas City neighborhoods, a prosecution unit that handles drug cases exclusively, a police drug enforcement task force, expansion of county jail facilities, funding of nonprofit drug treatment programs, a separate drug court, and funds for juvenile court support and probation officer counseling and teaching in the public schools.

The COMBAT program has produced thousands of drug investigations, prosecutions, and significant efforts in drug education and treatment. A full evaluation of the program has not been completed, but in 1995 Jackson County voters approved a seven-year renewal of the antidrug tax by a margin of more than two to one.

Critical Thinking Questions

1. What are the advantages and disadvantages of a sales tax directed toward a single issue such as drugs?
2. Would you vote to increase the sales tax in your jurisdiction and dedicate that increase to antidrug efforts? Why or why not?

SOURCE: Gregory Mills, *Community-Backed Anti-Drug Tax: COMBAT in Jackson County, Missouri* (Washington, D.C.: National Institute of Justice, 1996).

Critical Thinking EXERCISE

Is the Internet an Avenue for Terrorists?

The Internet has come under fire for posting information that is inaccurate, inflammatory, or dangerous. A "police brutality" web page on the Internet admits to not verifying the facts posted. The publisher of the web page said, "I don't think twice about badmouthing presidents, newspaper reporters, or other public officials."[A] In June 1997, the Supreme Court struck down a law barring the posting of "indecent" material on the Internet because that term was too vague. Nevertheless, the government retains the right to prosecute individuals who post obscene material or child pornography on the Internet, since these are more clearly defined in law.[B]

At the same time, the FBI has stated that some Internet sources "are repositories for inflammatory rhetoric which can influence extremists. Other databases contain recipes for bombs, hold information on unconventional weapons, or offer computer viruses for download."[C] For those who spend time "surfing" the Internet, it is clear that a wealth of useful information is posted there. Some of that information could easily be used for destructive purposes. The Oklahoma City and World Trade Center bombing incidents have sharpened this debate, as have the attacks on U.S. embassies in six countries during the last ten years.[D]

Critical Thinking Questions

1. Should bomb recipes be barred from publication on the Internet? Why or why not?
2. Should inflammatory rhetoric that incites racial, ethnic, or government hatred be prohibited on the Internet? Why or why not?

Notes

[A]Mark Johnson, "Lawsuits Spur New Rules for Internet," *Richmond Times-Dispatch* (September 9, 1997), p. 12.

[B]*Reno, Attorney General of the United States v. American Civil Liberties Union,* 117 S. Ct. 2329 (1997).

[C]Federal Bureau of Investigation, *Terrorism in the United States* (Washington, D.C.: U.S. Government Printing Office, 1997), p. 14.

[D]Alan Cooperman, "Terror Strikes Again: Attacks on U.S. Embassies Prompt New Fears," *U.S. News & World Report* (August 24, 1998), pp. 8–17.

Summary

CONSPIRACY

- Sophisticated crimes are characterized by planning and organization. The closest the criminal law comes to punishing criminal planning is the crime of conspiracy.
- Conspiracy takes place when two or more persons agree to commit a crime, or to carry out a legal act in an illegal manner.
- For conspiracy to be established, it is necessary that the offenders be aware of the illegal venture and participate in it voluntarily.
- Withdrawal from a conspiracy requires proof of action designed to defeat the conspiracy.

WHITE COLLAR CRIME

- White collar crimes are distinguished by the manner in which they are carried out. Whereas street crimes are characterized by the use of force or stealth, white collar crimes are characterized by planning and deceit.
- White collar thefts include embezzlement (purposeful misappropriation of property entrusted to one's control, to which one is not entitled), extortion (purposely obtaining property from another person with his or her consent, induced through wrongful use of force or official authority), forgery (falsely making or altering an official document with intent to defraud), and fraud (purposely obtaining the property of another person through deception).
- Offenses against public administration include bribery (the voluntary giving or receiving of anything of value with the intent of influencing a public official), obstruction of justice (intentionally preventing a public servant from performing an official function), official misconduct (unauthorized exercise of an official function with intent to benefit or injure another), and perjury (false swearing).
- Regulatory offenses include administrative offenses (failure to comply with court orders or agency requirements), environmental violations (emissions or dumping in violation of legal standards), labor violations, manufacturing violations, and unfair trade practices.
- Arrest trends and demographic factors suggest that white collar crime will increase in the future.

COMPUTER CRIME

- There are several types of crime in which computers are the instrument. The most common of these is theft by computer.
- Other types of instrumental computer crimes include use of a computer to harass or extort a victim.
- Crimes in which computers are the object of the criminal act include causing damage to hardware or software, theft of trade secrets, and alteration of data for an unlawful purpose.
- As computers proliferate and computer literacy increases, rates of computer crime can be expected to increase as well.

ORGANIZED CRIME

- Organized crime is a continuing criminal enterprise that rationally works to profit from illicit activities that are often in great public demand. Its continuing existence is maintained through the use of force, threats, monopoly control, and/or the corruption of public officials.
- In contrast to white collar crimes, which generally occur as a deviation from legitimate business activity, organized crime takes place through a continuing criminal enterprise that exists to profit primarily from crime.
- The main types of organized crime are provision of illicit services (loansharking, prostitution, gambling), provision of illicit goods (drug dealing, fencing of stolen property), and infiltration of legitimate business (demands for "protection" money or no-show jobs).

- Research findings show that organized crime is not limited to the activities of particular ethnic groups; rather, organized crime groups evolve around specific illicit activities.
- The true extent of organized crime is unknown, although there have been large increases in arrests for certain types of crime.

Key Terms

conspiracy	fraud	perjury
embezzlement	bribery	regulatory offense
extortion	obstruction of justice	
forgery	official misconduct	

Questions for Review and Discussion

1. What characteristics are common to all types of sophisticated crimes?
2. What factors must be present for conspiracy to be established?
3. What are the three main types of white collar crime? Give an example of each.
4. Why is there reason to believe that white collar crime will increase in the future?
5. In what kinds of crimes are computers the instrument? In what kinds are computers the object?
6. What is organized crime?
7. Give examples of each of the three basic types of organized crime.
8. What connection, if any, is there between organized crime and ethnicity?

Notes

[1]Andrew Murr, "Living High on the Hog," *Newsweek* (October 27, 1997), p. 48.

[2]Michael McConnell, *Challenger: A Major Malfunction* (Garden City, NY: Doubleday, 1987).

[3]Morton Mintz, *At Any Cost: Corporate Greed, Women, and the Dalkon Shield* (New York: Pantheon Books, 1985).

[4]Jay S. Albanese," *Organized Crime in America,* 3rd ed. (Cincinnati: Anderson Publishing, 1996), pp. 120–6.

[5]Michael Hirsh and Daniel Klaidman, "Bad Practices," *Newsweek* (August 11, 1997), pp. 42–3.

[6]Jay S. Albanese, *White Collar Crime in America* (Englewood Cliffs, NJ: Prentice Hall, 1995), pp. 87–95.

[7]Dennis B. Levine with William Hoffer, *Inside Out* (New York: Berkeley, 1992).

[8]"Lee to Settle with SEC for $25M," *USA Today* (August 3, 1989), p. 1B.

[9]Murr, p. 48.

[10]James D. Calder, "Al Capone and the Internal Revenue Service: State-Sanctioned Criminology of Organized Crime," *Crime, Law and Social Change,* vol. 17 (1992), pp. 1–23; Laurence Bergreen, *Capone: The Man and the Era* (New York: Simon and Schuster, 1994).

[11]*U.S. v. Beech-Nut Nutrition Corp.,* 871 F. 2d 1181 (2nd Cir. 1989).

[12]*U.S. v. Zambrano,* 776 F. 2d 1091 (2nd Cir. 1989) at 1193.

[13]*Proceedings of the Academic Workshop* (Morgantown, WV: National White Collar Crime Center, 1996).

[14]"Ex-Rochester Police Chief is Guilty of Embezzlement," *The Buffalo News* (February 26, 1992), p. 7.

[15]Bethany Kandel, "Top N.Y. Judge Faces Charges," *USA Today* (November 9, 1992), p. 2.
[16]"Counterfeit Arrests," *USA Today* (September 26, 1991), p. 3.
[17]"Mount Pleasant Suit," *USA Today* (February 28, 1992), p. 8.
[18]Joseph Stedino with Dary Matera, *What's in It for Me?* (New York: HarperCollins, 1993); Mark Mayfield, "S. Carolina Bribery Scandal Widens," *USA Today* (March 21, 1991), p. 4.
[19]"Bribery Plea," *USA Today* (February 20, 1991), p. 5.
[20]Albanese, *White Collar Crime in America*, pp. 47–51.
[21]"Albany: Ex-State Trooper," *USA Today* (January 23, 1992), p. 8.
[22]Aaron Epstein, "Poindexter Guilty on All Counts," *The Buffalo News* (April 8, 1990), p. 1.
[23]"Equifax Settlement," *USA Today* (July 1, 1992), p. 1B.
[24]Jana Mazanec, "Rockwell Critics Hail Guilty Plea," *USA Today* (June 30, 1992), p. 3.
[25]"Chicken Plant Executives Charged in Deadly Fire," *USA Today* (March 10, 1992), p. 3.
[26]"Cheese Biz," *USA Today* (April 7, 1989), p. 3.
[27]"Baby Food Companies Fixed Price, Florida Says," *USA Today* (January 4, 1991), p. 3.
[28]Edward Cornish, "92 Ways Our Lives Will Change by the Year 2025," *The Futurist* (January–February 1996), pp. 1–15; David E. Bloom and Adi Brender, "Labor and the Emerging World Economy," *Population Bulletin*, vol. 48 (October 1993), pp. 2–39.
[29]U.S. Bureau of the Census, *Statistical Abstract of the United States*, 115th ed. (Washington, D.C.: U.S. Government Printing Office, 1996), p. 14.
[30]Donn B. Parker, *Fighting Computer Crime* (New York: Charles Scribner's Sons, 1983); Jack Bologna, *Computer Crime: Wave of the Future* (San Francisco: Assets Protection, 1981).
[31]Kim S. Nash, "PC Manager at Center of $2 Million Grocery Scam: Inside Job Spotlights Critical Security Threat," *Computerworld* (March 30, 1998), p. 1.
[32]"Woman Jailed for Computerized Bilk," *The Star-Ledger* (Newark) (October 22, 1977).
[33]Robert Rudolph, "Ex-Drug Firm Computer Exec Admits Million-Dollar Product Bilk," *The Star-Ledger* (Newark) (April 30, 1980), p. 32.
[34]Peter J. Schuyten, "Computers and Criminals," *The New York Times* (September 27, 1979), p. D2.
[35]Kathy Rebello, "'Sensitive Kid' Faces Fraud Trial," *USA Today* (February 28, 1989), p. 1B.
[36]Debbie Howlett, "Computer Fraud: A Big Bite Crime," *USA Today* (July 7, 1990), p. 3; "Hackers Guilty," *USA Today* (July 10, 1990), p. 3.
[37]"Computer Security a Mess, Report Says," *USA Today* (December 6, 1990), p. 3; see also "Arrest in Hacking at NASA," *The New York Times* (March 19, 1998), p. 19.
[38]M. Ball, "To Catch a Thief," *Security Management*, 32, no. 3 (March 1988), p. 72; P. Hyman, "Computer Crime Easy As A-B-C," *Niagara Gazette* (September 4, 1983), p. 5C.
[39]Mark Lewyn, "Computer Verdict Sets 'Precedent'," *USA Today* (September 21, 1988), p. 1.
[40]Philip Elmer-DeWitt, "Invasion of the Data Snatchers!," *Time* (September 26, 1988), pp. 62–7; Mark Lewyn, "First 'Computer Virus' Trial Starts Today," *USA Today* (September 6, 1988), p. 3.
[41]Kathy Rebello and Leslie Werstein, "Brilliance Has Its Roots in Family Life," *USA Today* (November 10, 1988), p. 1B; Ted Eisenberg et al., "The Cornell Commission on Morris and the Worm," *Communications of the ACM*, 32, no. 6 (June 1989), pp. 706–9; William Kates, "Cornell Student Convicted in Computer Case," *Buffalo News* (January 23, 1990), p. 3.
[42]Sam Meddis, "Lawmakers: Pull Plug on Hackers," *USA Today* (November 4, 1983), p. 3.

[43]Patrick O'Driscoll, "At 17, A Pro at Testifying on Computers," *USA Today* (September 26, 1983), p. 2.

[44]Hoag Levins, "Hackers Devastate Texas Newspapers' Servers," *Editor & Publisher* (June 28, 1997), p. 45.

[45]"Bogus Software," *USA Today* (August 30, 1991), p. 1D.

[46]Carroll Bogert, "Windows 95, 5 Bucks," *Newsweek* (May 26, 1997), p. 82.

[47]Jon Friedman and Sam Meddis, "White Collar Crime Cuts Into Companies' Profits," *USA Today* (August 30, 1984), p. 1B.

[48]*Aries Information Systems, Inc. v. Pacific Management Systems Corporation,* 366 N.W. 2d 366 (1985).

[49]*United States v. Alston,* 609 F. 2d 531 (cert. denied 1980).

[50]Richard Benedetto and Timothy Kenny, "Computer Crooks Spy on Our Credit," *USA Today* (June 22, 1984), p. 1.

[51]Clifford Stoll, *The Cuckoo's Egg: Inside the World of Computer Espionage* (New York: Doubleday, 1989).

[52]Laura DiDio, "Computer Crime Costs on the Rise," *Computerworld* (April 20, 1998), p. 55.

[53]Katie Hafner, "Morris Code," *New Republic* (February 19, 1990), pp. 15–16; Joseph O'Donoghue, *Mercy College Report on Computer Crime in the Forbes 500 Corporations* (1986); J. J. Bloombecker, "Short-Circuiting Computer Crime," *Datamation* (October 1, 1989), p. 71.

[54]James M. Tien, Thomas F. Rich, Michael F. Cahn, and Carol G. Kaplan, *Electronic Fund Transfer Fraud* (Washington, D.C.: Bureau of Justice Statistics, 1985).

[55]William F. Skinner and Anne M. Fream, "A Social Learning Analysis of Computer Crime Among College Students," *Journal of Research in Crime & Delinquency,* vol. 34 (November 1997), pp. 495–519.

[56]Wendy R. Leibowitz, "Low-Profile Feds Fashion Laws to Fight Cybercrime," *The National Law Journal* (February 2, 1998), p. 1.

[57]Laura DiDio, "Special FBI Unit Targets Online Fraud, Gambling," *Computerworld* (April 27, 1998), p. 47.

[58]Carol Levin, "Internet Capers," *PC Magazine* (October 21, 1997), p. 29.

[59]President's Commission on Law Enforcement and Administration of Justice, *Task Force Report: Organized Crime* (Washington, D.C.: U.S. Government Printing Office, 1967), p. 33.

[60]Albanese, *Organized Crime in America,* p. 3.

[61]Dwight C. Smith, "Paragons, Pariahs, and Pirates: A Spectrum-Based Theory of Enterprise," *Crime & Delinquency* (July 1980), vol. 26, pp. 358–86; Martin W. Allen, "Toward Specifying a Spectrum-Based Theory of Enterprise," *Criminal Justice Review,* vol. 6 (Spring 1981), pp. 54–7; Jay Albanese, "What Lockheed and La Cosa Nostra Have in Common: The Effect of Ideology on Criminal Justice Policy," *Crime & Delinquency,* vol. 28 (April 1982), pp. 211–32; Frank E. Hagan, "The Organized Crime Continuum," *Criminal Justice Review,* vol. 8 (Spring 1983), pp. 52–7; Vincent F. Sacco, "An Approach to the Study of Organized Crime," in R. A. Silverman and J. J. Teevan, eds., *Crime in Canadian Society,* 3rd ed. (Toronto: Butterworth, 1986).

[62]National Advisory Committee on Criminal Justice Standards and Goals. *Report of the Task Force on Organized Crime* (Washington, D.C.: U.S. Government Printing Office, 1976), p. 213.

[63]Henry N. Pontell and Kitty Calavita, "White-Collar Crime in the Savings and Loan Scandal," *The Annals,* 525 (January 1993), p. 39.

[64]See Albanese, *White Collar Crime in America.*

[65]President's Commission on Organized Crime, *The Impact: Organized Crime Today* (Washington, D.C.: U.S. Government Printing Office, 1987), pp. 33–128.

[66]Alan A. Block, "The Snowman Cometh: Coke in Progressive New York," *Criminology,* vol. 17 (May 1979), pp. 75–99; President's Commission on Organized Crime, pp. 64, 81, 91.

[67]Block, p. 95.
[68]Ibid.
[69]Patricia A. Adler, *Wheeling and Dealing: An Ethnography of an Upper-Level Drug Dealing and Smuggling Community* (New York: Columbia University Press, 1985), p. 80.
[70]Peter Reuter, *Disorganized Crime: The Economics of the Visible Hand* (Cambridge, MA: MIT Press, 1983), pp. 175–6.
[71]Francis A. J. Ianni with Elizabeth Reuss-Ianni, *A Family Business: Kinship and Social Control in Organized Crime* (New York: New American Library, 1973), p. 20.
[72]Joseph L. Albini, *The American Mafia: Genesis of a Legend* (New York: Irvington, 1971), p. 288.
[73]See Jay S. Albanese, "Casino Gambling and Organized Crime: More Than Reshuffling the Deck," in J. Albanese, ed., *Contemporary Issues in Organized Crime* (Monsey, NY: Willow Tree Press, 1995).
[74]Kevin Johnson, "Cell Phone 'Cloners' Pushing the Law's Buttons," *USA Today* (June 21, 1996), p. 3.
[75]Margaret Mannix, "Keeping a Check on Debit Card Liability," *U.S. News & World Report* (September 8, 1997), p. 7.

For Further Reading

Jay Albanese, Dilip Das, and Arvind Verma, eds., *Organized Crime: A World Perspective* (Incline, Nevada: Copperhouse Publishing, 1999).

W. Steve Albrecht, Gerald W. Wernz, and Timothy L. Williams, *Fraud: Bringing Light to the Dark Side of Business* (New York: Irwin, 1994).

Kitty Calavita, Henry N. Pontell, and Robert H. Tillman, *Big Money Crime: Fraud and Politics in the Savings and Loan Crisis* (Berkeley: University of California Press, 1997).

Louis R. Mizell, *Masters of Deception: The White-Collar Crime Crisis and Ways to Protect Yourself* (New York: Wiley, 1996).

chapter eighteen

Juvenile Justice

Even the best of us can serve as horrible examples.

ANONYMOUS

- Over a period of only six months in 1998, five major shooting incidents occurred in public schools in five states, involving young teenagers who killed fellow students, teachers, and parents.[1]
- Three youths in Los Angeles videotaped themselves firing paint gun pellets at passersby and attacking bicyclists with a baseball bat while riding in a car.[2]
- Teenagers in Pennsylvania broke into their high school to steal bomb-making chemicals from a shopping list of ingredients.[3]
- A 12-year-old boy in Texas shot a cab driver in the back of the head for no apparent reason.[4]
- Five teenagers in Florida videotaped each other vandalizing homes, causing hundreds of thousands of dollars in damage.[5]
- Four 13- and 14-year-old boys doused an 8-year-old boy with polish remover and set him on fire.[6]

Events such as these make headlines around the country. Where does such destructive, reckless, and malicious behavior originate? Are these events typical, or are they rare? What should be done with young people who commit crimes like these? The answers to these questions form the basis

CHAPTER OUTLINE

for the juvenile justice system. This chapter examines the nature and extent of delinquency and the workings of juvenile justice in dealing with young offenders.

delinquency
A criminal act committed by a person under the age of majority.

In the eyes of the law, the only difference between a juvenile delinquent and an adult criminal is age. If a criminal act is committed by a person under the age of majority, the act is considered **delinquency.** If the illegal act is committed by someone who has reached the age of majority, that person has committed a crime. Depending on the state, a person becomes an adult in the eyes of the law at some point between age 16 (in three states) or 17 (seven states) and age 19 (in one state). In thirty-nine states a person becomes an adult at age 18. In addition, an individual under a certain age (7 years old in many states) cannot be held legally responsible for an illegal act. This is because small children are not seen as being old enough to fully understand the consequences of their actions. They cannot be adjudicated in either criminal or juvenile court. Juvenile delinquency is generally concerned, therefore, with the misdeeds of young people between the ages of 7 and 18.

status offenses
Undesirable behaviors that are unlawful only for juveniles, including habitual truancy, curfew violations, repeated running away, and ungovernability or incorrigibility in failing to respond to the reasonable requests of parents.

Besides delinquency, there are acts for which juveniles can be forced to appear in juvenile court. These acts are called **status offenses** and do not involve violations of the criminal law. In fact, they are merely undesirable behaviors that are unlawful only for juveniles. They are designed to thwart predelinquent behavior that is not serious in itself but that can lead to juvenile delinquency in the future. Examples of status offenses include habitual truancy, curfew violations, repeated running away, and ungovernability or incorrigibility in failing to respond to the reasonable requests of parents.

The range of behaviors that are considered status offenses varies greatly among the states. Some states view the use of alcohol, tobacco, or marijuana; profanity; or having delinquent associates as status offenses. Also, different states use differing terminology in referring to status offenders. In New York State, for example, they are called PINS (persons in need of supervision); in New Jersey, JINS (juveniles in need of supervision); and in Washington, D.C., CHINS (children in need of supervision). Juveniles can be taken into custody, adjudicated, and incarcerated for the commission of status offenses, as well as for delinquency. Therefore, the juvenile justice system deals with two distinct types of juvenile behaviors: delinquency and status offenses. The system also hears cases involving neglect or abuse of children, but these cases result from adult rather than juvenile misbehavior.

Juvenile Justice versus Criminal Justice

Because of their age, juveniles are treated separately from adults in the justice process. Police departments often have officers who deal exclusively with juveniles. Every state has a separate juvenile court system that deals exclusively with youths. In addition, every state has separate facilities for the incarceration of juvenile offenders. The legal status of juveniles in this justice process also differs significantly from that of adults in the criminal justice system. For example, cases involving motor vehicle theft are handled quite differently depending on the age of the offender. For an adult the official charge would be motor vehicle theft, but in the case of a juvenile the charge would be simply delinquency. In a criminal case the defendant's name, the court proceedings, and the trial transcripts would all be matters of public record. In juvenile court, however, all of this information would be confidential. Finally, upon a finding of guilty the adult would be convicted of motor vehicle theft, whereas the juvenile would be adjudicated a delinquent.

The differences in treatment of juveniles and adults in the justice process are largely a function of historical views of juvenile conduct. At the turn of the century, it was argued that equal treatment of juveniles and adults in the eyes of the law violated American ideals. According to this view, minors who broke the law were actually victims of improper care and treatment at home. When juveniles violated the law, it was a sign that their parents could not or would not take care of them adequately, and it was up to the state to step in and act in the best interests of the child and thus prevent future misbehavior. This view is called **parens patriae** (the state acts as a parent).

parens patriae
(the state acts as a parent) The view that juvenile law violations are a sign that parents cannot or will not take care of their child adequately and that it is up to the state to step in and act in his or her best interests, thus preventing future misbehavior.

The philosophy of parens patriae meant that the state should not punish children for their criminal behavior but instead should try to help them control themselves and prevent future criminality. As a result, it made no sense to convict children of such crimes as motor vehicle theft, burglary, or robbery because they would be labeled as criminals and their chances of reform would be reduced. Instead, the label of delinquency was used to indicate that the child needed the care and treatment of the state. It was on the basis of this notion of parens patriae that the first juvenile court was established in the United States in 1899.

In recent years, however, considerable controversy has arisen over the legal treatment of juveniles. The effectiveness of the state in acting as a surrogate parent has been questioned, as has the adequacy of the legal protections for juveniles in court. The question of whether the philosophy of parens patriae should be abandoned (in favor of the treatment of juveniles as adults) has been considered. A similar controversy has arisen in the handling of status offenders in the juvenile justice process. It is claimed that some status offenders are incarcerated for nonserious behavior and that the definitions of some status offenses are vague. Some question whether status offenders and delinquents should be adjudicated separately, whether juvenile justice processing makes status offenders better or worse, and whether status offenses should be abolished altogether. Each of these arguments makes fundamental assumptions about the philosophy and purpose of juvenile justice. It is important to be aware of these assumptions because they determine whether juveniles are treated like adults in an adversarial process or as children in a treatment process.

As Table 18.1 indicates, the juvenile justice system uses more neutral terminology than does the adult adversarial system, with its formal accusations and convictions. This illustrates the philosophical basis of juvenile justice.

The establishment of juvenile courts corresponded with the rise of a philosophy known as positivism, which saw crimes as the product of external influences rather than free will. The purpose of juvenile justice, therefore, is to correct the way a young person responds to those influences, rather than to punish him or her. However, prevailing views regarding the treatment of juveniles have shifted over the years. Currently there is much disagreement over the proper goals of the juvenile justice system.[7]

TABLE 18.1

Adult and Juvenile Justice System Terminology

PROCEDURE	JUVENILE	ADULT
Act	Delinquency	Crime
Apprehension	Custody	Arrest
	Petition	Indictment
Preadjudication	Detention	Jail
	Agree to finding	Plead guilty
	Deny the petition	Plead not guilty
Adjudication	Adjudicatory Hearing	Trial
	Adjudicated	Convicted
	Delinquent	Criminal
Corrections	Disposition	Sentence
	Commitment	Incarceration

contemporary issues

A Rebirth of Youth Gangs?

Self-report studies confirm that virtually all juveniles engage in criminal behavior at some point in their lives. Many of these acts of delinquency occur in small groups, though not necessarily in gangs. Youth *gangs* are distinguished from simple *groups* by their organization, identifiable leadership, territorial identification, continuous association, and specific purpose.[A] To what extent do youth gangs pose a threat in the future?

In the early decades of the twentieth century, youth gangs were highly visible. Sociologist Frederick Thrasher conducted a landmark study of gangs in 1927. He found that most gangs were small (six to twenty members) and formed "spontaneously" in poor and socially disorganized neighborhoods. Rather than having a criminal purpose, most gangs were formed to fulfill a youthful need for play and adventure that sometimes led to acts of delinquency. Continued conflict with authorities helped solidify gangs, according to Thrasher.[B]

During the 1950s and 1960s, there was renewed interest in gangs and their formation. In 1960, sociologists Richard Cloward and Lloyd Ohlin published an influential study of gangs that concluded that they emerge from "blocked opportunity" for legitimate success, resulting in one of three outcomes: juveniles becoming organized or career criminals, wanton violence in search of status within gangs, or a retreat into drug use and "dropping out." This typology of gangs has been confirmed by a number of studies in recent years.[C]

After the 1960s, concern about gangs virtually disappeared. In fact, in 1976 the National Advisory Committee on Criminal Justice Standards and Goals reported that "youth gang violence is not a major crime problem in the United States." In the late 1980s, however, concern about gangs experienced a rebirth, and it remains high today.[D] Immigration of young foreign-born people into the United States, economic conditions, and increased violence have been identified as contributing to the reemergence of gangs.[E]

Attempts to control youth gangs take two main forms: police sweeps or crackdowns and community reforms. Law enforcement sweeps are essentially mass arrests of gang members on minor charges. They have the effect of taking young people off the streets for a night, but most of these offenders are released by the next day. This has only a temporary effect on gangs, and on gang violence. As the commanding officer of the Gang Crime Section of the Chicago Police Department observed,

A national commission reported in 1976 that youth gang violence was not a problem in the United States. The illicit cocaine market, immigration patterns, economic conditions, and increased violence have all been identified as contributing to the resurgence of gangs in the United States.

> **Today, we are arresting more gang members than ever before; we are getting more convictions than ever before; and we are getting longer sentences than ever before. But ironically, we have more gangs than ever before. Arrest and prosecution are not the deterrent we expected them to be.[F]**

A review of eighteen case studies of police crackdowns in various cities found similar results: The impact "began to decay after a short period, sometimes despite continued dosage of police presence."[G]

An alternate approach is to change the responses of young people to poor social environments, or else to change the social environment itself so as to offer more opportunities for legitimate suc-

The Nature and Extent of Delinquency

Establishing the true extent of delinquency helps citizens assess their actual risk of becoming victims. It also helps public officials determine the degree of urgency that should be attached to delinquency prevention efforts. Unfortunately, the precise level and types of delinquent acts are difficult to establish.

cess. These strategies employ a variety of interventions, including tutoring, job training, and counseling, but have had only limited success thus far.[H]

Something more is needed than police work alone, or neighborhood outreach by itself, to break the cycle of gang delinquency. A continuing roadblock has been the lack of community interest in and support for gang reduction initiatives. In many communities gang violence is tolerated as long as gang members victimize each other and do not bother the rest of society.[I] Without community support, the cycle of youth gang activity will continue.[J] As C. Ronald Huff concludes, "If families, schools, and churches don't socialize children to act responsibly, and if the national and local economies don't provide adequate *legal* opportunity structures, then we as a society are in deep trouble."[K] Community and political institutions, beginning with the family itself, must be better organized and more committed to changing the aspects of the social environment that give rise to gang delinquency.

NOTES

[A]Walter B. Miller, *Violence by Youth Gangs as a Crime Problem in Major Cities* (Washington, D.C.: U.S. Government Printing Office, 1975).

[B]Frederick Thrasher, *The Gang* (Chicago: University of Chicago Press, 1927).

[C]Richard A. Cloward and Lloyd E. Ohlin, *Delinquency and Opportunity: A Theory of Delinquent Gangs* (New York: The Free Press, 1960); Jeffrey A. Fagan, "The Social Organization of Drug Use and Drug Dealing among Urban Gangs," *Criminology*, vol. 27 (1989), pp. 633–69; Ronald C. Huff, "Youth Gangs and Public Policy," *Crime & Delinquency*, vol. 35 (1989), pp. 524–37; Carl S. Taylor, "Gang Imperialism," in C. R. Huff, ed., *Gangs in America* (Newbury Park, CA: Sage Publications, 1990).

[D]Paul A. Perrone and Meda Chesney-Lind, "Representations of Gangs and Delinquency: Wild in the Streets?," *Social Justice*, vol. 24 (Winter 1997), pp. 96–115.

[E]Miller, *Violence by Youth Gangs as a Crime Problem in Major Cities;* G. David Curry, Richard A. Ball, and Scott H. Decker, *Estimating the National Scope of Gang Crime from Law Enforcement Data* (Washington, D.C.: National Institute of Justice, 1996); Malcolm W. Klein and Cheryl L. Maxson, "Street Gang Violence," in N. Weiner and M. E. Wolfgang, eds., *Violent Crime, Violent Criminals* (Newbury Park, CA: Sage Publications, 1989); James Diego Vigil, "Cholos and Gangs: Culture Change and Street Youth in Los Angeles," in C. R. Huff, ed., *Gangs in America.*

[F]Dan Bryant, "Community-Wide Responses Crucial for Dealing with Youth Gangs," *Juvenile Justice Bulletin* (September 1989), p. 1.

[G]Lawrence W. Sherman, "Police Crackdowns: Initial and Residual Deterrence," in M. Tonry and N. Morris, eds., *Crime and Justice: A Review of Research* (Chicago: University of Chicago Press, 1990); Claire Johnson, Barbara Webster, and Edward Connors, *Prosecuting Gangs: A National Assessment* (Washington, D.C.: National Institute of Justice, 1995).

[H]Irving Spergel et al., *Gang Suppression and Intervention: Problem and Response* (Washington, D.C.: Office of Juvenile Justice and Delinquency Prevention, 1994); Irving A. Spergel, *Youth Gangs: Problem and Response* (Washington, D.C.: Office of Juvenile Justice and Delinquency Prevention, 1989).

[I]Ruth Horowitz, "Community Tolerance of Gang Violence," *Social Problems*, vol. 34 (December 1987), pp. 437–50.

[J]Joan W. Moore et al., *Homeboys: Gangs, Drugs, and Prison in the Barrios of Los Angeles* (Philadelphia: Temple University Press, 1978); Kay C. McKinney, "Juvenile Gangs and Drug Trafficking," *Juvenile Justice Bulletin* (September 1988), pp. 1–8.

[K]C. Ronald Huff, "Denial, Overreaction, and Misidentification: A Postscript on Public Policy," in C. R. Huff, ed., *Gangs in America*, p. 316; Pamela Irving Jackson, "Crime, Youth Gangs, and Urban Transition: The Social Dimensions of Postindustrial Economic Development," *Justice Quarterly*, vol. 8 (September 1991), pp. 379–97.

The FBI's annual *Uniform Crime Reports* (UCR) records all crimes known to the police. However, this compilation is of little use in assessing juvenile delinquency because it is impossible to know whether the crimes were committed by juveniles or adults, and victimization surveys reveal that less than 40 percent of all serious crime is actually reported to the police. As a result, one must rely on alternate measures of the extent of delinquency.

Arrest Figures

The most commonly used indicator of delinquency is the rate of juvenile arrests. Arrest figures provide information about the age of suspects, and make it possible to see whether juveniles are engaging in more or less criminal behavior compared to adults. Table 18.2 summarizes the proportion of arrests during the last twenty-five years that involved juveniles. The crimes listed in the table are among the offenses considered in the Federal Bureau of Investigation's annual compilation of arrest data. The first eight offenses, collectively, are called the crime index and are often used as a barometer of serious crime (as described in Chapter 3). Criminal homicide, forcible rape, robbery, and aggravated assault are considered violent crimes (i.e., crimes against persons), whereas burglary, larceny, motor vehicle theft, and arson are treated as property crimes (i.e., property is the victim).

As is indicated in Table 18.2, a total of 11.4 million arrests were made in the United States in 1995. Of these, 18.3 percent involved juveniles (those under age eighteen). Twenty-five years earlier, however, more than 25 percent of all those arrested were under age eighteen. Table 18.2 makes it clear that a drop occurred in the proportion of juveniles arrested from 1970 to 1995. This is a remarkable finding, given the amount of attention devoted to the "delinquency problem" in recent years. If arrests are used as an indicator of criminal involvement, juveniles are arrested significantly less often now than they were more than two decades ago. This has occurred despite the fact that nearly five million more people were arrested in 1995 than in 1970.

Table 18.2 indicates that 20.8 percent of all those arrested for forcible rape in 1970 were juveniles. Twenty-five years later, the proportion of juveniles arrested for this crime had decreased to 15.8 percent. Similarly, 52 percent of those arrested for burglary in 1970 were juveniles. By 1995, this number had dropped to 35.1 percent. The same is true for most of the other offenses listed. Simply stated, the proportion of juvenile arrests has decreased significantly in virtually every crime category during the last two decades.

Juveniles commit many more property crimes than violent crimes. Vandalism remains one of the most common offenses for which juveniles are arrested.

TABLE 18.2

Offenses of Persons under Eighteen Years of Age that Result in Arrests

(Percent of Total Arrests)

OFFENSE	1970	1980	1990	1995
Criminal homicide	10.5	9.3	14.0	15.3
Forcible rape	20.8	14.8	14.9	15.8
Robbery	33.4	30.1	24.2	32.3
Aggravated assault	16.5	14.7	13.6	14.7
Burglary	52.0	44.9	33.0	35.1
Larceny	50.7	37.5	30.0	33.4
Motor vehicle theft	56.1	45.3	43.3	42.0
Arson	59.5	44.2	43.8	52.3
Total violent crime	22.6	19.3	16.2	18.7
Total property crime	51.7	40.2	31.9	34.7
Index crime total	46.1	35.9	28.1	30.2
Simple assault	18.2	17.9	14.9	16.7
Forgery/counterfeiting	10.6	13.0	9.1	7.2
Fraud	4.0	2.8	3.4	5.8
Embezzlement	4.3	11.3	7.2	8.2
Stolen property	30.2	29.9	25.9	25.7
Vandalism	72.2	49.4	40.4	44.9
Weapons offenses	16.6	15.3	18.2	23.1
Prostitution	2.3	3.6	1.4	1.3
Other sex offenses	21.1	17.5	15.9	17.0
Drug offenses	22.4	18.9	7.41	22.9
Gambling	1.9	3.7	5.2	8.3
Offenses against family	1.5	4.1	4.0	4.8
DWI	1.1	2.3	1.1	1.0
Liquor laws	33.8	33.1	22.1	20.2
Drunkenness	2.7	4.1	2.7	2.9
Disorderly conduct	21.0	16.5	16.6	23.2
Vagrancy	12.2	13.7	8.1	13.5
Suspicion	27.5	17.6	17.0	10.9
Other (not traffic)	29.6	21.6	9.7	16.9
Curfew and loitering violations	100	100	100	100
Runaways	100	100	100	100
Total % juvenile arrests	25.3	20.9	15.6	18.3
Total no. of arrests (in millions)	6.6	9.7	11.3	11.4

SOURCE: Federal Bureau of Investigation, *Uniform Crime Reports* (Washington, D.C.: U.S. Government Printing Office, published annually).

There are exceptions to these trends, however. Arrests of juveniles for criminal homicide increased from 10.3 percent of all arrests to 15.3 percent in the period from 1970 to 1995. Likewise, arrests of juveniles for weapons offenses increased from 16.6 percent to 23.1 percent over the same period. These are important trends and imply a connection between increases in juvenile weapons use and the homicide rate. Some have argued that these trends result from the crack cocaine epidemic that increased the level of violence in the drug trade in inner-city neighborhoods. Others see random homicides at schools to be the result of increasing depictions of violence in entertainment and the lack of proper

TABLE 18.3

Offenses for which Juveniles Are Most Often Arrested

(Arrests of Persons Under Eighteen, Percent of Total Arrests)

OFFENSE	1970	1995	CHANGE
Arson	59.5	52.3	-7.2%
Motor vehicle theft	56.1	42.0	-14.1
Vandalism	72.2	44.9	-27.3
Burglary	52.0	35.1	-16.9
Larceny	50.7	33.4	-17.3
Stolen property	30.2	25.7	-4.5
Liquor laws	33.8	20.0	-13.8
Robbery	33.4	32.3	-1.1

SOURCE: Compiled from Federal Bureau of Investigation, *Uniform Crime Reports* (Washington, D.C.: U.S. Government Printing Office, published annually).

supervision from adult role models.[8] Nevertheless, by 1996 juvenile murder arrests had dropped to their lowest level in the 1990s, but still were 50 percent above the level of a decade earlier.[9] Total arrests of juveniles for all index crimes have shown a more consistent decline, dropping from 46.1 percent to 30.2 percent of all arrests between 1970 and 1995.

Given the information in Table 18.2, we can identify the crimes for which juveniles are most often arrested. First, it can be seen that every person arrested for curfew and loitering violations, as well as runaways, was a juvenile. This is because these are status offenses that apply only to juveniles. The eight crimes for which juveniles are most often arrested, other than status offenses, are presented in Table 18.3.

The property crimes of vandalism, arson, motor vehicle theft, burglary, larceny, and stolen property accounted for the highest proportion of juvenile arrests in 1970, a trend that still held true twenty-five years later. As Table 18.3 indicates, however, the proportion of juveniles arrested for these crimes has decreased steadily during the last two decades. Juveniles thus appear to be responsible for a shrinking proportion of the crime problem. In 1970, they accounted for more than half of all arrests for vandalism, arson, burglary, motor vehicle theft, and larceny. By 1995, they did not comprise the majority of arrests in *any* crime category counted by the FBI, except arson.

TABLE 18.4

Total Arrests, by Age

(Percent of Total Arrests)

AGE	1970	1980	1990	1995
10 and under	1.2	0.6	0.4	0.3
11–12	2.0	1.4	1.3	1.4
13–14	6.0	4.2	3.6	4.5
15	4.9	3.9	2.9	3.6
16	5.7	5.1	3.5	4.1
17	5.4	5.7	4.0	4.3
Under age 15	9.2	6.2	5.3	6.2
Under age 18	25.3	20.9	15.6	18.3
Ages 18 and over	74.7	79.1	84.4	81.7

SOURCE: Compiled from Federal Bureau of Investigation, *Uniform Crime Reports* (Washington, D.C.: U.S. Government Printing Office, published annually).

ARRESTS BY AGE It is widely believed that *younger* juveniles are engaging in more criminal acts now than was the case years ago. However, this claim is not supported by the facts. Table 18.4 summarizes total arrests in the United States by age for the last twenty-five years.

It is evident from the data in Table 18.4 that younger juveniles are arrested significantly less often than older juveniles, a fact that was true in 1970 and remains true now. Juveniles under age fifteen accounted for 9.2 percent of all arrests in 1970 and for 6.2 percent of all arrests in 1995.[10] In addition, adults aged eighteen and older account for the overwhelming majority (81.7 percent) of all arrests.

ARRESTS BY SEX Another frequently heard claim is that girls are becoming increasingly involved in criminal activity, especially delinquency. Table 18.5 summarizes total arrests of persons under age eighteen, by sex.

The data in Table 18.5 indicate that far more boys than girls are arrested for delinquency, although their numbers are declining slowly. Seventy-five (75) percent of all juveniles arrested are male, a proportion that has fallen by 4 percent over the years. Correspondingly, arrests of females have risen by 4 percent, to 25 percent of all arrests, over the same period. Eighty-six percent of those arrested for violent crimes (homicide, rape, robbery, and serious assaults) are male. The number of arrests of girls for violent crimes has increased (from 9 to 14 percent) during the last twenty-five years. These figures reveal a slow but steady increase in female involvement in juvenile delinquency.

TABLE 18.5

Arrests of Persons Under Age Eighteen, by Sex

(Percent)

SEX	1970	1980	1990	1995
All crimes				
Male	79	79	77	75
Female	21	21	23	25
Violent crimes only				
Male	91	90	88	86
Female	9	10	12	14

SOURCE: Compiled from Federal Bureau of Investigation, *Uniform Crime Reports* (Washington, D.C.: U.S. Government Printing Office, published annually).

Self-Reports

One problem with these figures is that arrests are not an accurate indicator of actual crime rates. As indicated in earlier chapters, arrests are a better measure of police activity than of criminal activity. Moreover, juveniles are overrepresented in arrest statistics because they often commit less sophisticated crimes (such as vandalism and larceny) and are less mobile than adults. Therefore, they are less likely to escape detection.

Self-reports are an alternative way to measure the extent of delinquency. In self-report studies, a sample of juveniles are asked to indicate the types and numbers of crimes they have committed in the past (whether or not they were caught); the information is kept confidential. Self-reports were first attempted to see if there are differences between juveniles who have been caught and those who have not. As sociologist Albert Cohen recognized more than forty years ago, "The defect of these [official] data, of course, is not that they represent too small a sample but that we cannot tell what sorts of delinquency may be over represented or under represented."[11]

In 1946, Austin Porterfield conducted the first self-report study ever attempted. He asked 200 precollege men, 130 precollege women, and 100 college men to report delinquent acts on a confidential questionnaire. The precollege men admitted to an average of eighteen offenses each, the women admitted to an average of five offenses, and the college men admitted to an average of eleven offenses. Significantly, every respondent admitted having committed at least one criminal act or status offense.[12] Similar findings were reported in subsequent studies of adults, high school students, and inmates in a juvenile correctional facility.[13]

In addition to showing how common delinquency really is, self-report studies provide an indication of what percentage of juvenile offenders are caught. Martin Gold administered a self-report questionnaire to a random sample of teenagers in Flint, Michigan. Of those admitting to crimes, only 16 percent had been caught.[14] Maynard Erickson and LaMar Empey administered a self-report to a group of fifteen- to seventeen-year-old boys. Fifty of the boys had never been to court, thirty had been adjudicated only once, fifty were recidivists (repeat offenders), and fifty were currently incarcerated in a juvenile institution. Nearly every boy admitted to some offenses surveyed and over 95 percent of their delinquent acts were undetected.[15]

Comparisons of self-report surveys and official statistics also provide information about the *types* of juveniles who engage in delinquency. Although official statistics indicate that males engage in delinquency at a rate of four to eight times that of females, self-reports have shown the actual rate of male offenses to be only about twice the female rate (depending on the crime). A national self-report survey found that females engage in petty larceny and use of drugs, and run away from home, as often as males do. Males were found to engage in such offenses as joy-riding, alcohol use, and truancy only twice as often as females.[16]

Official statistics also indicate that delinquency is much more common among poor and working-class juveniles than among middle-class juveniles (by about five to one). Self-report surveys, however, suggest that juvenile offenders from lower-class families are just as common as juvenile offenders from middle-class families. In addition, official statistics indicate that most delinquents are nonwhite, but self-reports show rates of delinquency by white and black youths to be very similar.[17]

Perhaps the most significant contribution of self-reports to our knowledge of delinquency is that they reveal that nearly all juveniles break the law at one time or another. Only a small proportion, however, engage in persistent or serious criminal behavior. Official statistics include a greater proportion of the most serious and frequent delinquents. Finally, in contrast to official statistics, self-reports have shown that delinquents are not limited to a particular sex, race, or social class.

The accuracy of self-reports has been questioned on methodological grounds. Questions have been raised about their validity (was the act really a crime?) and their reliability (are many offenses concealed or exaggerated?). Self-report studies have been administered in different ways to try to reduce these problems and retests have been conducted to check their accuracy.[18] They have been found to provide a generally accurate measure of undetected juvenile crimes. Perhaps the strongest evidence for the validity and reliability of self-reports is the similarity in findings among all studies that have been done. All studies find that delinquency is a nearly universal experience.

Victimization Surveys

As can be seen in Chapter 3, efforts have been made to estimate the true extent of crime victimization through surveys of a representative sample of the U.S. population. A primary advantage of victim surveys is that they record all victimizations, whether or not they were reported to the police. In addition, they provide much more information about criminal incidents than is included in official statistics.

Victimization surveys have not been very useful in the study of juvenile delinquency. This is because most delinquent acts are victimless crimes, as is evident in Table 18.2. Self-report studies have shown that juveniles most often commit crimes that involve voluntary participation by the victim and the offender, such as drug use, fornication, gambling, alcohol use, and prostitution. These crimes are

FUTURE ISSUES

Adolescent Motherhood and Criminal Outcomes

Nearly one million teenagers become pregnant each year in the United States, representing about 10 percent of all female teenagers. One third of these teenagers have abortions, 14 percent miscarry, and 52 percent bear children; 72 percent of the children are born out of wedlock. Of those teenagers who give birth, 25 percent are mothers for the second time. More than 80 percent of these young mothers are poor.[A]

A follow-up study of children of teenage mothers found direct implications for the criminal justice system. It was found that sons of adolescent mothers are 2.7 times more likely to be incarcerated than sons of older mothers. Approximately 5 percent of all young men in the United States are incarcerated, but the rate for those born to adolescent mothers is more than 10 percent. The study concluded that a delay in childbearing until age 20.5 would reduce the national average incarceration rate by 3.5 percent, producing an annual savings of one billion dollars in correctional costs. Delaying childbearing even further into adulthood would result in even larger reductions in the incarceration rate.[B]

In a related study, children of adolescent mothers in Illinois were found to be twice as likely to be victims of abuse or neglect than were children born to 20- and 21-year-old mothers from similar backgrounds. The difference increased as the age of the mother at the time of childbearing increased. Likewise, more children of adolescent mothers are placed in foster care than children of older mothers.[C] It is clear from these studies that children of teenage mothers are at a disadvantage compared to children of older mothers.

FUTURES QUESTIONS

1. Why do you believe that children born to adolescent mothers are more likely to end up in the criminal justice system?
2. What do you see as the best way to reduce teenage pregnancy? Why do you believe it would be effective?

NOTES

[A]Rebecca A. Maynard and Eileen M. Garry, *Kids Having Kids: A Robin Hood Foundation Report on the Costs of Adolescent Childbearing* (New York: Robin Hood Foundation, 1996).

[B]K. Grogger, "Crime: The Influence of Early Childbearing on the Cost of Incarceration," in R. Maynard, ed., *Kids Having Kids: Economic Costs and Social Consequences of Teen Pregnancy* (Washington, D.C.: Urban Institute Press, 1997).

[C]D. George and K. Lee, "Abuse and Neglect: Effects of Early Childbearing on Abuse and Neglect of Children," in R. Maynard, ed., *Kids Having Kids: Economic Costs and Social Consequences of Teen Pregnancy.*

not included in victimization surveys. In the case of property crimes, it is often impossible to determine the age of offenders. Moreover, in the crimes of burglary, larceny, and motor vehicle theft the "victim" is property; therefore, it is not possible to determine through victimization surveys who the offenders are. In the case of violent crimes, few victims can be positive about the age of the offender. Rape, robbery, and assault all involve personal confrontations, yet it is often difficult for victims to know whether the offender was fifteen, eighteen, or twenty-one years old.

One interesting finding of victimization surveys is that young people are ten times more likely than older citizens to be victims of violence. Likewise, young people are six times more likely to be victims of theft than are older persons. These findings contradict the common belief that the elderly are particularly prone to criminal victimization. Studies by the Bureau of Justice Statistics have found that most teenage offenders victimize other teenagers whom they know. Stranger attacks are less common, probably because more than a third of violent crimes against young teenagers occur on school grounds.[19]

Foundations of Juvenile Justice

The way we deal with juveniles in criminal matters reflects the way that we treat juveniles in other areas of life. As was noted earlier, the establishment of the first juvenile court in 1899 corresponded with the rise of positivism, which saw the social environment as an important cause of behavior. The 1800s also witnessed the establishment of "houses of refuge," which were set up to protect wayward youths by reforming them in a family-like atmosphere.[20] Such developments were a manifestation of the philosophy of parens patriae, in which the state took the right of parental control over juveniles from parents who were unwilling or unable to take proper care of the child.[21]

The juvenile court was a significant innovation in that the concept of juvenile justice was altered from adjudication of guilt to diagnosis of a condition. The emphasis of the justice process was changed from deterrence and incapacitation to rehabilitation, in order to assist, rather than punish, the juvenile. Behavior patterns were seen as more important than specific acts because the acts were considered to be symptoms of some underlying problem. Also, juvenile court proceedings were civil rather than criminal proceedings, on the assumption that the interests of the child were best served through informal adjudication involving no stigma of criminality.[22] By 1920, every state in the country had established a juvenile court based on these principles of positivism and rehabilitation.

Although the idea of the juvenile court spread quickly, it was not carried out in a uniform or standardized manner. As the President's Commission on Law Enforcement and Administration of Justice pointed out in 1967,

> **The mere passage of a juvenile court statute does not automatically establish a tribunal of the sort the reformers contemplated. A U.S. Children's Bureau survey in 1920 found that only 16 percent of all so-called juvenile courts in fact had separate hearings for children and an officially authorized probation service and recorded social information on children brought to court. A similar survey conducted . . . in 1966 revealed significant gaps still existing between ideal and actual court structures, practices, and personnel. Indeed, it has been observed that "there is nothing uniform" in the operation of children's courts.[23]**

Although consensus may have been reached about how the juvenile court should operate, the implementation of this model was not consistent.[24] This inconsistency continues today as states strive "to do something" more effective with juveniles in view of public perceptions of escalating violent juvenile crime.[25]

Objections to Parens Patriae

The juvenile court concept, though widely accepted, was also subjected to criticism. One of the leading critics was Paul Tappan, who wrote during the 1940s. Tappan argued that juveniles were deprived of the due process protections afforded to adults; for example youthful offenders lacked legal counsel and were charged with over-broad status offenses.[26] Tappan also charged that the juvenile court must measure up to the promise of scientific and humane treatment.

Tappan's allegations were not far off the mark. Many state institutions that were supposed to look after the best interests of children sometimes did not do so. Juvenile reform schools were often harsh, the treatment cruel, and rehabilitation forgotten as juveniles were warehoused like prison inmates.[27] These abuses added strength to Tappan's claims that the rehabilitative juvenile court denied the legal rights of juveniles in exchange for hypothetical benefits of dubious value.

Tappan's arguments received more and more support during the 1950s, while support for the juvenile court concept waned. Because of abuses and the failure of the state to reform delinquents, emphasis shifted to issues such as legal fairness, unjustified detention, and the inability of the juvenile court to deliver on its promise to protect and reform juveniles.[28] These criticisms ultimately led to changes in the juvenile court structure.

California and New York were the first states to reflect this changing outlook. California, for example, had had a typical juvenile court system since 1915. A juvenile could be taken to court for any one of fourteen violations, including begging, habitually visiting a poolroom or saloon, habitual truancy, refusal to obey parents, being feeble-minded or insane, or being afflicted with syphilis or gonorrhea. There was no clear right to legal counsel, adjudication was based on a preponderance of the evidence (unlike "beyond a reasonable doubt" for adults), and the court's jurisdiction extended up to age twenty-one. In 1957, the governor of California appointed a commission to investigate the operation of the juvenile courts. In its reports the commission confirmed many of Tappan's allegations:

> **While supporting the fundamental protective and rehabilitative ideology of the socialized court, the Commission reported a number of serious deficiencies: (a) an absence of well-defined standards and norms to guide juvenile court work meant that dispositions were more often dependent upon the community where a child got into legal trouble than on the intrinsic merits of the case or the needs of the child; (b) basic legal rights of the child were neither uniformly nor adequately protected; (c) the quality of rehabilitative services was questionable and decisions about treatment plans often seemed based on consideration of expediency and administrative convenience rather than on consideration of the needs of the child; and (d) there was excessive and unwarranted detention of children.[29]**

Modifications of the Juvenile Justice System

The commission made numerous recommendations, which led to major modifications in the California juvenile court system. The juvenile court's jurisdiction was divided into three categories: dependent, neglected, and abused children; status offenses; and delinquency (criminal violations). Legal counsel became mandatory for serious (felony) cases, and a pretrial diversion process (six months of "informal probation") was established to remove nonserious cases from formal adjudication. Finally, a two-stage trial process was established, consisting of an adjudication (fact-finding) hearing and a disposition (sentencing) hearing, similar to the procedure for adults.

New York State followed California's lead in 1962, when it abolished its juvenile court and replaced it with a broader "family court." The revisions in New York's system were similar to those in California's, but the due process protection was extended even further. For example, the use of legal counsel was expanded

The original parens patriae philosophy behind the juvenile court changed to a more legalistic approach that treated juveniles more like adults beginning in the 1960s.

through the establishment of "law guardians," defense lawyers who were paid by the state to represent juveniles exclusively. This innovation rapidly escalated the role of defense counsel in juvenile courts. By 1967, 96 percent of juveniles appearing in family court in New York City were represented by counsel.

The emphasis on due process continued when the U.S. Supreme Court heard its first cases involving juvenile courts in 1966 and 1967. These cases involved the application to juveniles of constitutional protections and procedures that had previously been reserved for adults. They marked a trend toward making adjudication more "adult-like," which carried over into the 1970s. This trend eventually led to still another change in philosophy. From the mid-1970s to the present, further changes in law, policy, and court interpretation have resulted in a virtual abandonment of the parens patriae philosophy in favor of treating juvenile offenders as adults.

The Law and Procedure of Juvenile Justice

As a result of a series of U.S. Supreme Court cases that began during the mid-1960s, the operation of juvenile justice became more uniform and the trend toward due process in juvenile court proceedings solidified. The first of those cases was *Kent v. United States.*[30] Morris Kent, age sixteen, was on probation for several housebreakings and an attempted purse-snatching. Two years into his probation, an intruder entered the apartment of a woman in the District of Columbia, raped her, and took her wallet. The police found latent fingerprints in the apartment that matched Kent's fingerprints. Kent was taken into custody by police. He subsequently was convicted of burglary and robbery and was found not guilty by reason of insanity on the rape charge. He was sentenced to thirty to ninety years in prison.

Kent's conviction was appealed on several alleged violations of due process. Although the Supreme Court agreed that each of these contentions was a matter of substantial concern, it ruled only on the judge's decision to transfer Kent's case to criminal court. This was held to be a violation of due process because no hearing was held, no reasons were given, no findings were made by the juvenile court, and his counsel was denied access to his social-service file. The Court ruled that the juvenile court should have "considerable latitude" to determine whether or not a juvenile's case should be transferred to criminal court. It went on to state that the "special concern" society shows for children does not allow for such treatment.

> **We do not consider whether, on the merits, Kent should have been transferred; but there is no place in our system of law for reaching a result of such tremendous consequences without ceremony—without hearing, without effective assistance of counsel, without a statement of reasons. It is inconceivable that a court of justice dealing with adults, with respect to a similar issue, would proceed in this manner. It would be extraordinary if society's special concern for children, as reflected in the District of Columbia's Juvenile Court Act, permitted this procedure. We hold that it does not.**

In rejecting the way Kent's case was handled by the juvenile court judge, the Supreme Court noted that the judge's decision was "potentially as important to Kent as the difference between five years confinement [the maximum in juvenile court] and a death sentence [the maximum for rape at that time in criminal court]." The Court concluded that

> **. . . as a condition to a valid waiver order, petitioner was entitled to a hearing, including access by his counsel to the social records and probation or similar reports which presumably are considered by the court, and to a statement of reasons for the Juvenile Court's decision. We believe that this result is required by the statute read in the context of constitutional principles relating to due process and the assistance of counsel.**

As a result of this case, in all future referrals of juveniles to criminal court, the juvenile must receive a hearing, effective assistance of counsel, and a statement of reasons for the juvenile court's decision.

The *Kent* case is significant because it was the first time the U.S. Supreme Court examined juvenile court procedure, and it found that the procedure in question (referral to criminal court) must measure up to basic standards of due process and fair treatment. Therefore, it can be seen that the due process trend begun in California and New York was continued. As the Supreme Court suggested in *Kent,* the failure of juvenile courts to live up to their promise of scientific and humane treatment was probably the largest factor in the shift toward due process. It concluded that "there is evidence, in fact, that there may be grounds for concern that the child receives the worst of both worlds: that he gets neither the protections accorded to adults nor the solicitous care and regenerative treatment postulated for children."

Lawyers and Self-Incrimination

The Supreme Court made perhaps its most far-reaching decision involving the juvenile court in 1967 in a case that involved several Fifth and Sixth Amendment guarantees. It was an unusual case in that the Court ruled on several issues at once, rather than following its usual pattern of addressing only one legal issue per case.

On June 8, 1964, Gerald Francis Gault and his friend, Ronald Lewis, were taken into custody by the sheriff of Gila County, Arizona. The action followed a verbal complaint by a neighbor of the boys, Mrs. Cook, about a telephone call to her in which the caller or callers made lewd or indecent remarks. The remarks were of the "irritatingly offensive, adolescent, sex variety." The actual remarks made were in the form of three questions: "Do you give any?" "Are your cherries ripe today?" "Do you have big bombers?"

At the time that Gault was picked up by police, his parents were both at work. No notice that he was taken into custody was left at the home, and no other steps were taken to advise them that their son had, in effect, been arrested. Gault was taken to the Children's Detention Home. When his mother arrived home at 6:00 P.M., Gault was not there. His older brother was sent to look for him at the home of the Lewis family. He apparently learned then that Gault was in custody. He and his mother then went to the detention home. Deputy Probation Officer Flagg, who was also superintendent of the Detention Home, told Mrs. Gault "why Jerry was here" and said that a hearing would be held in juvenile court at 3:00 P.M. the following day.

On the next day Gault, his mother, his older brother, and probation officers Flagg and Henderson appeared before the juvenile court judge. (Gault's father was out of town on business.) Mrs. Cook, the complainant, was not present. No one was sworn in at this hearing, no transcript or recording was made. There were conflicting accounts of what Gault said. His mother recalled that he said only that he had dialed Mrs. Cook's number and then handed the telephone to his friend, Ronald. Officer Flagg recalled that Gault admitted making the lewd remarks. Judge McGhee testified that Gault "admitted making one of these [lewd] statements." At the conclusion of the hearing, the judge said he would "think about it."

Gault was taken back to the detention home rather than being sent to his own home with his parents. After being in detention for three or four days, he was released and driven home. There was no explanation as to why he was kept in the detention home or why he was released.

On the next day the Gaults received an informal note from Officer Flagg telling them that a further hearing on their son's delinquency would be held. Witnesses at this proceeding differed in their recollections of his testimony. Mr. and Mrs. Gault recalled that he again testified that he had only dialed the number and that the other boy had made the remarks. Officer Flagg agreed that at this hearing Gault did not admit making the lewd remarks. Judge McGhee recalled, however, that "there was some admission again of some of the lewd statements. He—he didn't admit any of the more serious lewd statements." Again the complainant, Mrs. Cook, was not present. Mrs. Gault asked that Cook be present "so she could see which boy had done the talking, the dirty talking over the phone." The juvenile court judge said that she was not required to be present. In fact, the judge did not speak to Cook or communicate with her at any time, and Officer Flagg had talked to her only once, by telephone. At the conclusion of the hearing the judge committed Gault to the State Industrial School "for the period of his minority [that is, until age twenty-one], unless sooner discharged by due process of law." The court's order stated that "after full hearing and due deliberation the Court finds that said minor is a delinquent child, and that said minor is of the age of 15 years." Thus, because Gault was fifteen years old and was sentenced to the juvenile institution until he was twenty-one, he effectively received a sentence of six years. The maximum penalty for an adult on the same charge was two months in jail and a fifty-dollar fine.

Gault's case eventually reached the U.S. Supreme Court on seven separate grounds. Gault charged that the juvenile court procedure in Arizona was unconstitutional because it failed to provide adequate notice of the charges against him, he was not advised of his right to counsel, his protection against self-incrimination was not observed, he was denied the right to confront and cross-examine witnesses against him, he had no right to appeal the juvenile court's holding in Arizona, no transcript was made of the proceedings, and the judge gave no reasons for his finding.

In *In re Gault* the Supreme Court examined each of these issues and their application to juvenile court.[31] The Court agreed with Gault's contention that both a juvenile and his or her parents must be notified of the charges early and in writing. The Court reasoned that due process of law does not allow a hearing to take place in which a youth's freedom and his parents' right to custody are at stake without giving them advance notice of the specific charges alleged. The Court also upheld Gault's claim that juveniles must be notified of their right to counsel, or to appointed counsel if they are indigent, in cases in which commitment to an institution could result. Because a delinquency proceeding is comparable to a serious felony prosecution, the Court supported the right to counsel in delinquency cases.

The Supreme Court also held that juveniles, like adults, have the right of protection against self-incrimination and the right to cross-examine witnesses against them:

> **We conclude that the constitutional privilege against self-incrimination is applicable in the case of juveniles as it is with respect to adults. We appreciate that special problems may arise with respect to waiver of the privilege by or on behalf of children, and that there may well be some differences in technique—but not in principle—depending upon the age of the child and the presence and competence of parents. The participation of counsel will, of course, assist the police, Juvenile Courts, and appellate tribunals in administering the privilege. If counsel was not present for some permissible reason when an admission was obtained, the greatest care must be taken to assure that the admission was voluntary, in the sense not only that it was not the product of ignorance of rights or of adolescent fantasy, fright, or despair.**

In order to prevent untrustworthy confessions the Court ruled that there are no grounds for a distinction between adults and juveniles in these areas.

The Supreme Court did not hold that juveniles had a right to appeal, to have transcripts of proceedings, or to learn a judge's reasons for his or her adjudication decision. It did address their desirability, however, in its ruling in *Kent*.

In sum, the Court's decision in *Gault* applied to juveniles many of the due process protections that had previously been reserved for adults. Justice Stewart dissented, however, arguing that the decision was "wholly unsound," given the original purpose of the juvenile court:

> **Juvenile proceedings are not criminal trials. They are not civil trials. They are simply not adversary proceedings. Whether dealing with a delinquent child, neglected child, a defective child, or a dependent child, a juvenile proceeding's whole purpose and mission is the very opposite of the mission and purpose of a prosecution in criminal court. The object of one is the correction of a condition. The object of the other is conviction and punishment for a criminal act. . . .**
>
> **The inflexible restrictions that the Constitution so wisely made applicable to adversary criminal trials have no inevitable place in the proceedings of those public social agencies known as juvenile or family courts. And to impose the Court's long catalog of requirements upon juvenile proceedings in every area of the country is to invite a long step backwards into the nineteenth century.**

Justice Stewart expressed his belief that the Court's ruling in *Gault* would have the effect of replacing the rehabilitative model with an adult, criminal trial. Future Supreme Court decisions would confirm the trend he feared.

The Burden of Proof

For a person to be found guilty of a crime in criminal court, guilt must be proved beyond a reasonable doubt. From its inception, however, the juvenile court has been viewed as a civil proceeding. In civil cases liability is determined by a preponderance of the evidence, which is a somewhat lower standard than beyond a reasonable doubt. This distinction was the central issue in another Supreme Court case dealing with the juvenile court and the Fourteenth Amendment.

Winship was a twelve-year-old boy in New York State who was taken into custody for entering a locker and taking $112 from a woman's pocketbook. In juvenile court the judge acknowledged that the evidence might not constitute proof beyond a reasonable doubt, but he denied Winship's contention that such proof was required by the Fourteenth Amendment to the U.S. Constitution (which guarantees the due process protection of all citizens). The judge claimed that a preponderance of the evidence is all that is required in juvenile court.

Proof beyond a reasonable doubt means that after consideration of all the evidence the judge believes that there is a moral certainty of the truth in the criminal charge against the defendant. Proof by a preponderance of evidence is a lower standard of proof in which a decision of responsibility is made based on the most impressive or convincing evidence offered in court. Traditionally, proof beyond a reasonable doubt is required in criminal cases, whereas proof by a preponderance of the evidence is the standard of proof in civil cases.

Winship was adjudicated delinquent and placed in a training school for boys for an initial period of eighteen months, subject to annual extensions until he reached the age of eighteen. Because he was twelve at the time that the crime was committed, Winship effectively received a six-year sentence.

Winship's appeal reached the U.S. Supreme Court on the grounds that his due process protections had been violated. The question before the Court was whether proof beyond a reasonable doubt was essential to the fair treatment of a juvenile charged with an act that would be a crime if committed by an adult.

The Court agreed with Winship that such a standard of proof is required during the adjudicatory stage of a delinquency proceeding. "Where a 12-year-old

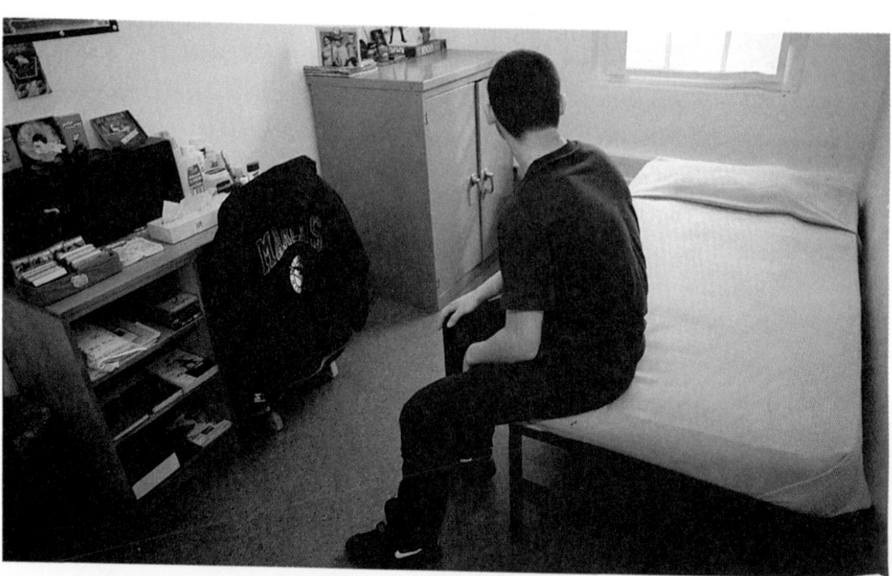

The burden of proof required to convict a person is proof beyond a reasonable doubt. The Supreme Court applied this standard to juveniles in 1970 stating, "it is far worse to convict an innocent man than to let a guilty man go free."

Media and Criminal Justice

BAD BOYS

The 1983 film *Bad Boys* may be dated, but it still serves as an excellent portrayal of typical situations of juvenile delinquency as well as the inner workings of a juvenile detention facility. The story revolves around Mick O'Brien, a Chicago "bad boy" who plans a drug heist of a rival gang headed by Paco Moreno. His robbery backfires, however, and results in the murder of Mick's best friend. Fleeing from police in desperation, Mick wrecks his stolen car and hits a little boy standing on the sidewalk. The slain child turns out to be Paco's little brother.

In sentencing Mick for his crimes, the judge makes a statement that reveals his frustration and cynicism with the juvenile justice system:

> **Mr. O'Brien, you have committed the crimes of an adult. Your previous record of arrest is extensive and indicates a sociopathic personality. However, you are protected by the law. Your status as a juvenile prevents me from imposing the punishment you deserve. Until the criminal codes are revised to incorporate a more realistic definition of juvenile offenders, society will continue to suffer.**

Mick is thus sentenced to Rainford Juvenile Correctional Facility "until such a time as your rehabilitation is complete." It is immediately evident, however, that rehabilitation is not the objective of the facility. As Mick enters the main cell block of the facility, the juvenile detainees form a line and welcome the newcomers with applause and spit, jeering and blowing smoke into their faces in an attempt to exert power and break their spirit. This initiation is just the beginning. Mick's cellmate explains the hierarchy of the dorm: There are large bullies charged by the guards with controlling the others, there are leaders and lieutenants who run contraband, and there are the small and helpless who are regularly molested and beaten by the higher-ups. Mick realizes it will be hard to stay out of trouble in the facility, because trouble will come looking for him.

On the outside, Paco is obsessed with avenging his brother's death, and rapes Mick's girlfriend as a retaliation. He is caught for the offense, and coincidentally sentenced to Rainford's Dorm C—exactly where Mick is struggling to behave and earn an early release. The violence and peer pressure of Dorm C soon pushes Mick and Paco to a showdown, where only one is expected to survive the fight.

It is striking how little has changed since *Bad Boys* was made. Mick and Paco's characters are very realistic; today, juveniles commit the same sorts of crime with little provocation. The real focus of the movie, however, is the issue of juvenile corrections. The gang activity and inmate code in such facilities make rehabilitation unrealistic. It is not until Mick attempts to escape, and his counselor takes him to the adult state penitentiary to glimpse his future, that Mick turns his life around. *Bad Boys* thus remains timely in its message of skepticism about our juvenile justice system. Without reform, juvenile corrections facilities often serve as warehouses for violent offenders, where youths are placed until they outgrow their juvenile status.

MEDIA AND CRIMINAL JUSTICE QUESTION

How would you propose to balance more effectively the objectives of punishment and rehabilitation for juvenile offenders?

child is charged with an act of stealing which renders him liable to confinement for as long as six years, then, as a matter of due process . . . the case against him must be proved beyond a reasonable doubt." The Court stated that the moral force of the criminal law would be diluted if a weaker standard of proof was used "that leaves people in doubt whether innocent men are being condemned." In one of its most famous statements, it held that "it is far worse to convict an innocent man than to let a guilty man go free."[32] As a result of this ruling, proof beyond a reasonable doubt is now required during the adjudicatory stage of any delinquency proceeding.

The Supreme Court's decision in the *In re Winship* case was not unanimous, however, because of differing views regarding the philosophy and purpose of the juvenile court. Justice Harlan, for example, hoped that the higher burden of proof would not impede the rehabilitative functions of the juvenile court. He hoped that procedural constraints in juvenile court hearings would not "(1) interfere with the worthy goal of rehabilitating the juvenile, (2) make any significant difference in the extent to which a youth is stigmatized as a 'criminal' because he has been found to be a delinquent, or (3) burden the juvenile courts with a procedural requirement that will make juvenile adjudications significantly more time consuming, or rigid." He believed that the decision in Winship's case "simply requires a juvenile court judge to be more confident in his belief that the youth did the act with which he has been charged."

On the other hand, Justices Burger and Stewart dissented on grounds that the rehabilitative model had, in effect, been negated in favor of treating juveniles as adult criminals. They hoped that the *Winship* decision "will not spell the end of a generously conceived program of compassionate treatment intended to mitigate the rigors and trauma of exposing youthful offenders to a traditional criminal court." They believed that "each step we take turns the clock back to the pre-juvenile-court era." These justices believed that juvenile court was becoming too much like criminal courts, given the growing similarity in court procedures and due process concerns.

Juries in Juvenile Court

The Supreme Court continued its examination of juvenile court procedures in the 1971 case of *McKeiver v. Pennsylvania.*[33] Joseph McKeiver, who was sixteen years old, was a member of a group of twenty to thirty youths who pursued three other juveniles and took twenty-five cents from them. McKeiver had an attorney present at his adjudication hearing. He also asked for a jury trial but was denied it. He was adjudicated delinquent.

The Supreme Court combined McKeiver's case with three others to consider whether or not juveniles had the right to a trial by jury under the Sixth Amendment. McKeiver argued that the Sixth Amendment is applicable to juveniles because juvenile court proceedings are similar to criminal trials. He also claimed that juvenile detention and incarceration are substantially the same as jail and prison for adults. Moreover, the procedures are the same, and the stigma of delinquency is the same as that of an adult conviction. Finally, it was argued that a jury would not deny any of the supposed benefits of the juvenile justice process, such as wide discretion in sentencing.

The Supreme Court did not agree with this rationale and held that "trial by jury in the juvenile court's adjudicatory stage is not a constitutional requirement." This decision was based on several concerns. First, the Court did not believe that juries are a necessary part of a fair and equitable proceeding. Second, there was concern with the possibility that juries would make juvenile proceedings a fully adversarial process. Third, juries would not add to the fact-finding function of juvenile court. It should be noted, however, that although the Court did not require juries in juvenile proceedings, it did not prohibit them either. State juvenile court systems and individual juvenile court judges were free to experiment with juries. The Court merely said that the use of juries in juvenile court is not a constitutional requirement. The *McKeiver* decision, therefore, temporarily halted the growing trend toward providing juveniles with due process protections that were previously held only by adults.

Double Jeopardy

In a case that eventually reached the Supreme Court, a juvenile court petition was filed against a 17-year-old Los Angeles boy, Allen Breed, alleging that he had committed an armed robbery. A detention hearing took place, and Breed was placed in detention. At the adjudication hearing, the court took testimony from Breed and two witnesses. The judge found that the allegation of armed robbery was supported by the evidence, and he adjudicated the juvenile delinquent. The judge then ordered the youth detained pending a disposition hearing.

At the disposition hearing the judge said that he found the juvenile "not amenable to the care, treatment and training program available through the facilities of the juvenile court." Breed's counsel immediately asked for a continuance "on the ground of surprise." The disposition hearing was rescheduled for the following week.

A week later the judge, after considering the report of the probation officer, declared Breed "unfit for treatment as a juvenile" and ordered that he be prosecuted as an adult. The juvenile was subsequently tried in criminal court and convicted of armed robbery; he was committed to the California Youth Authority.

This case attracted the attention of the Supreme Court when it was alleged that Breed's Fifth Amendment protection against being "twice put in jeopardy of life and limb" for the same offense had been violated. This constitutional provision means that a person cannot be criminally prosecuted twice for the same offense; it is commonly known as protection against **double jeopardy.**

double jeopardy
A constitutional provision that a person cannot be criminally prosecuted twice for the same offense.

In its decision in *Breed v. Jones,*[34] the Court considered the argument that the protection against double jeopardy had not been violated because the procedure in the case was analogous to retrial after reversal of a conviction on appeal. The Supreme Court did not agree with this view.

> **The Court has granted the Government the right to retry a defendant after a mistrial only where "there is a manifest necessity for the act, or the ends of public justice would otherwise be defeated." [Breed] was subjected to the burden of two trials for the same offense; he was twice put to the task of marshaling his resources against those of the State, twice subjected to the "heavy personal strain" which such an experience represents.**

The Court held that adequate constitutional protections for the juvenile were lacking, given the facts in the case. This decision continued the trend toward applying due process protections in juvenile court proceedings that had emerged from the *Kent, Gault,* and *Winship* rulings. As a result of this series of decisions, the distinction between juvenile and adult proceedings rapidly diminished, beginning in the mid-1960s and continuing through the mid-1970s.

Preventive Detention

During the 1980s, the Supreme Court made several rulings that produced a further shift toward the treatment of juveniles as adults. One case involved a challenge to the New York State Family Court Act, which authorized the use of pretrial detention for juveniles who pose a "serious risk" of committing a crime before their court appearance.

Gregory Martin was arrested after he and two companions allegedly hit a youth on the head with a loaded gun and stole his jacket and sneakers. Martin was fourteen years old and had possession of the gun when he was arrested. The incident occurred at 11:30 at night, and Martin lied to the police about where and with whom he lived. He was detained overnight. The day after his arrest Martin appeared in Family Court accompanied by his grandmother. Citing possession of the loaded weapon, the false address given to the police, and the lateness of the hour as evidence of lack of supervision, the judge ordered Martin placed in detention. A probable cause hearing was held five days later, and probable cause was found to exist for all the crimes charged.

At the fact-finding hearing held the following week, Martin was found guilty of robbery and criminal possession of a weapon. He was adjudicated a delinquent and placed on two years' probation. Between the initial appearance and the completion of the fact-finding hearing he had been in detention for a total of fifteen days.

This case of *Schall v. Martin*[35] became a class-action suit involving a large number of juveniles who, like Martin, had been detained for one to two weeks and then either released or placed on probation. The Supreme Court assessed the balance between the needs of the juvenile and the need for protection of the community. It stated that the "legitimate and compelling state interest" in "protecting the community from crime cannot be doubted," nor can the "juvenile's countervailing interest in freedom" from incarceration before trial, "even for the brief time involved here." The Court held, however, that "juveniles, unlike adults, are always in some form of custody." It went on to explain that because children do not take care of themselves, they are subject to the control of their parents, and to the state (via parens patriae), if the parents do not adequately control the child. As a result, the juvenile's liberty may, in appropriate circumstances, be subordinate to the state's interest in controlling the child. Preventive detention "serves the legitimate state objective . . . of protecting both the juvenile and society from the hazards of pretrial crime."

The Court's reasoning in this case went beyond mere due process concerns to those of community protection, in accordance with the crime control model for juvenile justice. By placing the protection of the community above the needs of the child, the Court showed its preference for crime control and community protection over rehabilitation and treatment of the juvenile.

Three justices dissented in this case, recognizing the apparent trend toward treating juveniles as adults. They attempted to show that neither the goal of due process nor crime control is achieved through preventive detention of juveniles:

> **The majority's arguments do not survive scrutiny. Its characterization of preventive detention as merely a transfer of custody from a parent or guardian to the State is difficult to take seriously. Surely there is a qualitative difference between imprisonment and the condition of being subject to the supervision and control of an adult who has one's best interests at heart [under the rehabilitative model].**

The dissenting justices also noted that other courts have concluded that "only occasionally and accidentally does pretrial detention of a juvenile under [New York's law] prevent the commission of a crime." This is because the judges in juvenile court "are incapable of determining which of the juveniles who appear before them would commit offenses before their trials if left at large and which would not." On the basis of its own review, the District Court found that "no diagnostic tools have as yet been devised which enable even the most highly trained criminologists to predict reliably which juveniles will engage in violent crime."

The dissenters also pointed out that preventive detention is not limited to juveniles with prior records. Preventive detention is authorized for juveniles without any prior contacts with the juvenile court, and a finding of probable cause of law violation also is not a prerequisite for preventive detention. Moreover, the vast majority of the cases in this class-action suit involved juveniles who were released either before or immediately after their trials, suggesting that "most detainees, when examined more carefully than at their initial appearances, are deemed insufficiently dangerous to warrant further incarceration." The dissenters concluded by arguing that any vestige of the rehabilitative model of juvenile justice has disappeared.

Similar laws in other states have been challenged on these grounds as well, but this Supreme Court decision ended the litigation. It is clear that the original rehabilitative purpose of the juvenile court has been replaced by an emphasis on due process, beginning in the 1960s with the findings in *Kent* and *Winship*. The *Schall v. Martin* case suggests a further shift toward the crime control model, beginning in the 1980s.

Searches and the Fourth Amendment

Most cases requiring court interpretation of the Fourth Amendment deal with police searches. The only U.S. Supreme Court case of this kind that addressed juvenile justice involved a different type of government agent.

A teacher at Piscataway High School in Middlesex County, New Jersey, discovered two girls smoking in a lavatory in violation of a school rule. One of the girls was T. L. O., a 14-year-old ninth-grader. The teacher took the girls to the principal's office, where they met with the assistant vice principal, Mr. Choplick. T. L. O.'s companion admitted to violating the school rule, but T. L. O. denied smoking in the lavatory and denied that she smoked at all.

Choplick asked T. L. O. to come into his office and demanded to see her purse. In the purse he found a pack of cigarettes and a package of cigarette rolling papers, which are associated with marijuana use. Upon finding these items, the vice principal searched the purse more thoroughly. He found a small amount of marijuana, a pipe, empty plastic bags, a large amount of money in one-dollar bills, an index card that appeared to be a list of students who owed T. L. O. money, and two letters that implicated T. L. O. in marijuana dealing.

Choplick notified T. L. O.'s mother and turned the evidence over to the police. At the police station, T. L. O. confessed that she had been selling marijuana at school. On the basis of the evidence seized by Choplick, delinquency charges were filed against T. L. O. She was adjudicated delinquent and sentenced to one year on probation.

The Supreme Court held in 1985 that "reasonable grounds" of a law or school rule violation is needed to search a student at school. This is a standard lower than the probable cause required by the Fourth Amendment for other searches.

T. L. O. appealed her sentence on the ground that the incriminating evidence (i.e., the contents of her purse) had been seized in violation of the Fourth Amendment's prohibition against unreasonable searches and seizures. That is to say, her purse had been searched without probable cause. The vice principal had no reason to believe that T. L. O. was guilty of marijuana possession or sale *before* his search of the purse. Moreover, nothing he found in the purse could shed light on the original charge against her, smoking in the lavatory. Therefore, T. L. O. argued, Choplick's search of the purse was both unnecessary and in violation of the Fourth Amendment.

In *New Jersey v. T. L. O.* the U.S. Supreme Court affirmed T. L. O.'s delinquency adjudication on three grounds.[36] First, the Court agreed with T. L. O. that the Fourth Amendment is designed to protect citizens from agents of the government. It further agreed that the Fourth Amendment applies to public school teachers as representatives of the state (in addition to the police). Second, the Court held that students have a legitimate expectation of privacy that must be balanced against "the school's equally legitimate need to maintain a [learning] environment." As a result, the school setting was found to require "some easing of restrictions" on searches by public officials. Third, the Court found that the probable cause standard need not be followed for school searches. Rather, "the legality of a search of a student should depend simply on the reasonableness, under all the circumstances, of the search." Therefore, searches of students in public schools are justified when there are "reasonable grounds" that evidence will be found of violations of law *or* school rules. Probable cause is not needed.

Three Justices dissented in this case, arguing that this new "reasonableness" standard, unlike the probable cause standard stated in the Fourth Amendment, is "unclear, unprecedented, and unnecessary" and "carves out a broad exception" to existing standards of permissible searches and seizures. The new "reasonableness" standard, they declared, "will likely spawn increased litigation and greater uncertainty among teachers and administrators." The dissenters also expressed concern that the new "reasonableness" standard "will permit teachers and school administrators to search students when they suspect that the search will reveal evidence of even the most trivial school regulation." They added that the Court's decision makes no distinction between searches for haircurlers or sunglasses and searches for drugs or weapons. To allow school officials to search for mere violation of school rules (rather than only for law violations), they argued "displays a shocking lack of all sense of proportion."

It is clear from this decision that protection of the community (the school in this case) was given priority over either the rights or the possible needs of the student. As a result, this case follows the philosophy in *Schall v. Martin*, applying the crime control model to juvenile justice.

Punishment and the Eighth Amendment

Most forms of punishment other than torture have been found to be constitutional, and in 1976 the U.S. Supreme Court stated specifically that the death penalty does not constitute cruel and unusual punishment.[37] Current death penalty cases heard by the Court challenge only the *manner in which they are carried out.*

The U.S. Supreme Court did not rule on the possibility of the death penalty for juveniles until 1988, in the case of *Thompson v. Oklahoma.*[38] William Thompson was fifteen years old when he participated with three older men in the murder of his former brother-in-law. Thompson believed that his brother-in-law had physically abused his sister. The brother-in-law was shot twice; his throat, chest, and abdomen were cut; and the body was chained to a concrete block and thrown into a river, where it was recovered four weeks later. After a hearing, Thompson was sent to criminal court and tried and convicted as an adult. At the sentencing hearing it was found that aggravating factors were present in that "the murder was especially heinous, atrocious, [and] cruel." Thompson was sentenced to death.

Thompson appealed his sentence, arguing that the execution of a person for a murder committed at age fifteen violated the Eighth Amendment prohibition against "cruel and unusual punishment." In a six to three decision, the U.S. Supreme Court overruled Thompson's death sentence. The Court argued that the applicability of the Eighth Amendment depends on "evolving standards of decency that mark the progress of a maturing society." Indicators of these standards included the facts that half the states with the death penalty bar execution of offenders under age sixteen, and few people under sixteen have ever been sentenced to death in the history of the United States. Only 5 of the nearly 1,400 people sentenced to death between 1982 and 1986 were under sixteen years of age at the time of the offense, and no execution of a young person has taken place since 1948. Also, the views of professional organizations, and the practices of many other countries, lead to the "unambiguous conclusion that the imposition of the death penalty on a 15-year-old offender is now generally abhorrent to the conscience of the community."

The three dissenting justices were not convinced. In their opinion, the statistics suggest only that executions of fifteen-year-olds should be rare. In addition, they observed that there is a trend among the states to *lower* the age at which a juvenile may be punished as an adult. In 1989, this dissenting view became the majority view in two cases that upheld the imposition of capital punishment on individuals who commit crimes at age sixteen or seventeen. These cases, *Stanford v. Kentucky* and *Wilkins v. Missouri,*[39] were decided by a five to four margin, indicating a sharp division on this subject. Despite this division, the Supreme Court ruled that it is unconstitutional to execute a fifteen-year-old offender, but a sixteen- or seventeen-year-old offender may be executed.

Juveniles in the System: Police, Courts, Corrections

Police Disposition of Juveniles Taken into Custody

Once police take a juvenile into custody, they have several options in deciding how to handle the case. Most small police departments make one officer responsible for handling juvenile matters for the entire department. When an officer on patrol encounters a juvenile crime suspect, he or she will often refer the case to the juvenile officer, or to a juvenile unit or division in larger departments. The National Advisory Committee on Criminal Justice's Task Force on Juvenile Justice and Delinquency Prevention recommended that every police department with more than seventy-five sworn officers establish a separate juvenile unit or division.[40] Today, nearly every department has either juvenile officers or a formal juvenile division. These officers are usually able to use their own discretion in dealing with juveniles, using five alternatives: (1) warn and release, (2) refer to juvenile court, (3) refer to a social welfare agency, (4) refer to another police department (often juveniles are sent back to the town where they live if the offense was committed elsewhere), or (5) refer to criminal court for prosecution as an adult.

Table 18.6 indicates how police utilize these five alternatives once a juvenile is taken into custody. It can be seen that in 1970 a total of 1.27 million juveniles were taken into custody. This number rose during the 1970s but decreased to 1.37 million by 1995, reflecting the general decrease in the proportion of juveniles being arrested.

Despite the overall decline in the number of juveniles taken into custody, an increasing proportion of juvenile suspects are being handled more severely. In 1970, 50 percent of juveniles were sent to juvenile court, while 45 percent were warned and released. Twenty-five years later, nearly 66 percent were sent to juvenile court, while only 28 percent were released. It is clear that fewer juveniles are released and more are being sent to court. Table 18.6 also makes clear that in 1970 fewer than 1 percent of all juveniles were referred to criminal court to be tried as adults, but that twenty-five years later the proportion was more than 3 percent. In 1996, the percentage sent to criminal court jumped to 6 percent.[41] This is occurring despite the fact that juveniles account for fewer arrests than ever before, and despite the fact that the most common offenses for which juveniles are arrested have remained virtually unchanged. The increasing numbers of referrals to juvenile court and criminal court (now accounting for nearly 70 percent of all police dispositions

TABLE 18.6

Police Disposition of Juveniles Taken into Custody
(Percent)

DECISION MADE	1970	1980	1990	1995
Released	45.1	33.8	28.3	28.4
Sent to welfare agency	1.6	1.6	1.6	0.7
Sent to other police department	2.2	1.7	1.6	1.7
Sent to juvenile court	50.3	58.1	64.5	65.7
Sent to criminal court	0.8	4.8	4.5	3.3
Total juvenile encounters (in millions)	1.27	1.47	1.11	1.37

SOURCE: Compiled from Federal Bureau of Investigation, *Uniform Crime Reports* (Washington, D.C.: U.S. Government Printing Office, published annually).

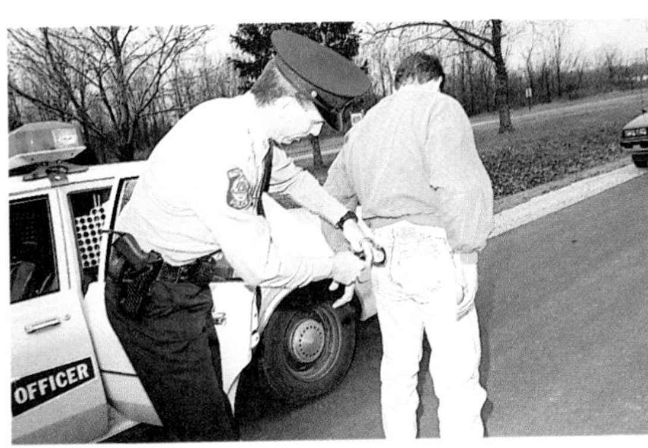

There has been a nationwide decline in the number of juveniles taken into police custody, but fewer of those taken into custody are being released and more are sent to court for adjudication.

of juveniles) indicate greater willingness to adjudicate juveniles as delinquents or criminals. This trend among police agencies corresponds with the more punitive philosophy of the U.S. Supreme Court regarding juvenile justice in recent years.

Juvenile Court Outcomes

The adjudication process for juveniles is a bit more complicated than it is for adults because a juvenile can be dealt with in many more ways than can an adult. Figure 18.1 indicates that in 1995 1.7 million cases were processed in juvenile court. Fifty-five percent of these were referred on a petition requesting that the court hold a formal hearing. The others were handled informally without a petition or formal hearing. A juvenile court judge or a probation officer makes the decision on how to handle a particular case. This screening or "intake" decision can

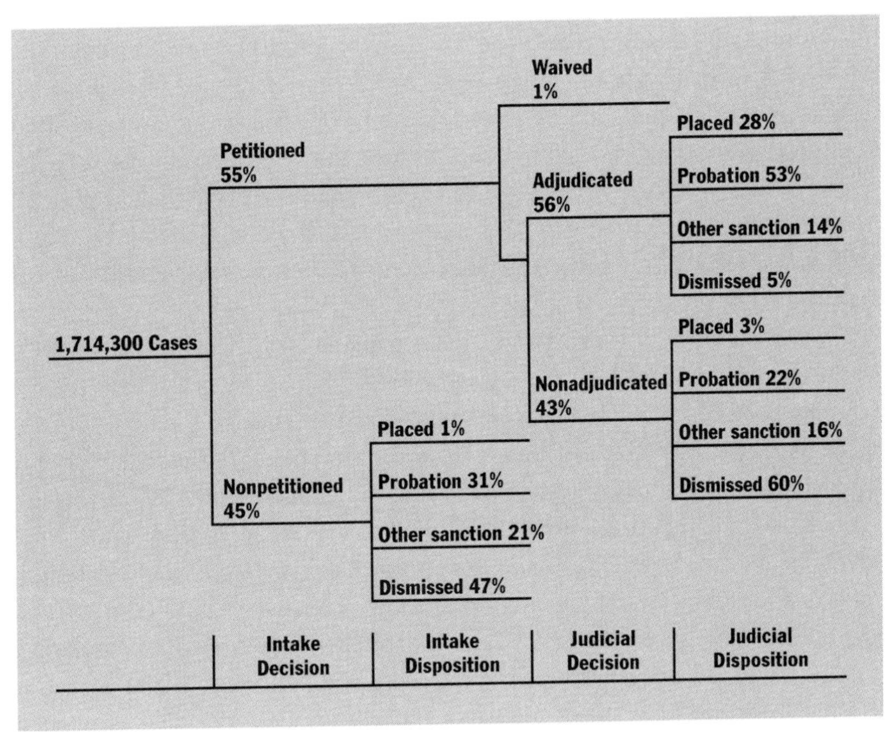

FIGURE 18.1

Juvenile court processing of delinquency cases, 1995

SOURCE: Melissa Sickmund, *Offenders in Juvenile Court, 1995* (Washington, D.C.: Office of Juvenile Justice and Delinquency Prevention, 1997).

result in one of several outcomes. For cases handled informally, the charge is not usually serious. If the juvenile admits to committing the offense, the case can be closed without further action or the juvenile can be required to make restitution, undergo psychological counseling, or obtain social assistance. No further official action is taken as long as the juvenile fulfills these conditions and stays out of further legal trouble for a certain period of time. If the juvenile denies the charge alleged, there is an automatic referral to juvenile court for adjudication. In some jurisdictions, a case can be referred to a juvenile conference committee (JCC). The JCC is a group of citizens appointed by the juvenile court to recommend a disposition for the juvenile in nonserious cases. Its purpose is to involve the community in the justice process. Normally, only first-time and minor offenders are referred to the juvenile conference committee.

If the case is handled formally, it is sent to juvenile court, where the judge can choose to handle it through an adjudication hearing, or without such a hearing if the juvenile admits to committing the offense. The adjudication hearing in juvenile court is the equivalent of an adult trial, involving a hearing on the petition against the juvenile where the facts of the case are established. If it is shown that the juvenile did not commit the acts alleged, the petition will be dismissed, as an indictment would be for an adult. If it is found that the juvenile committed the delinquent act, he or she will be adjudicated either a delinquent or a status offender, depending on the precise behavior alleged. Once a juvenile is adjudicated a delinquent or a status offender, the juvenile court judge usually adjourns the case and sets a date for a disposition hearing. In the meantime, a probation officer completes a background investigation of the juvenile to help the judge in deciding on a disposition.

The disposition hearing in juvenile court is analogous to a sentencing hearing in criminal court. It is here that the judge determines the best way to resolve the case. As the figure indicates, the juvenile court judge has a number of options in choosing a disposition. The judge can dismiss the case on the condition that the juvenile does not get into further legal trouble within the next year. Other conditions may be added such as requiring the juvenile to undergo diagnostic or therapeutic services or else to make restitution to the victim, observe a curfew, or perform community service. The completion of these obligations would have to take place within a certain period of time (usually one to six months) in order for the case to be terminated. The judge may resentence the juvenile if the conditions are not met.

A juvenile court judge can also choose to place a juvenile on probation. The juvenile normally would be supervised by a probation officer on a weekly or monthly basis for one, two, or three years, similar to the adult system. In 1995, more than 600,000 juveniles were placed on probation. The third option for a disposition is placement in a juvenile facility or institution. Juveniles involved in serious delinquent behavior may be committed to a secure facility, which would be analogous to an adult prison. Nonsecure facilities would include training schools and camps for delinquent children. Community-based programs include youth development centers, foster care, and independent living arrangements. In 1995, 166,000 juveniles were placed in secure and nonsecure facilities.

Juvenile court judges have a great deal of discretion in deciding upon an appropriate disposition for a juvenile. From outright dismissal to commitment to an institution, a juvenile may be sentenced in any number of ways that can involve many different conditions.[42]

Juvenile Dispositions

Until the 1800s, juveniles were confined together with adult offenders in prisons. Neglected and abused children, as well as delinquents, were incarcerated. The horrible conditions in prisons led to the development of houses of refuge and reform schools specifically for juveniles, culminating in the invention of the juvenile court in 1899 and the development of a separate juvenile justice system.[43] Since then, juveniles and adults have been adjudicated separately for the most part. Today juveniles are held in six different types of facilities:

1. **Detention center:** A short-term secure facility that holds juveniles awaiting adjudication, disposition, or placement in an institution.
2. **Shelter:** A short-term nonsecure facility that operates like a detention center but within a physically unrestricted environment.
3. **Reception/diagnostic center:** A short-term facility that screens sentenced juveniles for assignment to an appropriate level of custody.
4. **Training school:** A long-term secure facility for adjudicated juveniles.
5. **Ranch, forestry camp, or farm:** A long-term nonsecure setting for adjudicated juveniles.
6. **Halfway house or group home:** A long-term nonsecure facility that permits juveniles to participate in schools, employment, and other community agencies.

It can be seen that there are two basic levels of custody. Secure facilities are characterized by locks, bars, and fences, and the movement of juveniles within the institution is monitored closely. Nonsecure facilities are not restricted by "hardware restraints" and permit greater freedom of movement within, and sometimes outside, the facility.[44]

Juvenile corrections is also characterized by the widespread use of private facilities in addition to public institutions. Private facilities are operated by nongovernmental agencies under contract with the government. They are often smaller than public institutions and hold fewer juveniles, and only 12 percent of them are secure facilities. Public facilities are operated directly by a state or local government agency and staffed by government employees. About 70 percent of public institutions for juveniles are secure facilities.

Another way to gauge trends in juvenile justice philosophy is to examine the handling of juvenile delinquency cases by the juvenile court. As Table 18.7 indicates, a total of 93,400 delinquents were sent to out-of-home placements in 1985. This number increased by 51 percent to 141,300 in 1994. Out-of-home placements include commitment to an institution or other residential facility for juveniles. The table also illustrates an increase in the number of juveniles who were transferred to criminal court to be tried as adults.[45] A total of 7,200 cases were transferred in 1970. This number rose to 12,300 in 1994, an increase of 71 percent. These trends provide additional evidence of greater severity and punitiveness in dealing with juveniles.

detention center
A short-term secure facility that holds juveniles awaiting adjudication, disposition, or placement in an institution.

shelter
A short-term nonsecure facility that operates like a detention center but within a physically unrestricted environment.

reception/diagnostic center
A short-term facility that screens sentenced juveniles for assignment to an appropriate level of custody.

training school
A long-term secure facility for adjudicated juveniles.

ranch, forestry camp, or farm
A long-term nonsecure setting for adjudicated juveniles.

halfway house or group home
Long-term nonsecure facilities that allow juveniles to attend school and employment in the community.

TABLE 18.7

Trends in Juvenile Court Outcomes

YEAR	DELINQUENCY CASES RESULTING IN OUT-OF-HOME PLACEMENTS	DELINQUENCY CASES TRANSFERRED TO CRIMINAL COURT
1985	93,500	7,200
1990	122,400	8,700
1994	141,300	12,300
Percent change	+51%	+71%

SOURCE: Compiled from Jeffrey A. Butts et al., *Juvenile Court Statistics* (Washington, D.C.: Office of Juvenile Justice and Delinquency Prevention, 1996).

Trends in Legislation

A national assessment of legislative changes regarding jurisdiction, sentencing, corrections programming, information sharing, and the role of victims found that forty-seven states and the District of Columbia made "substantive changes" between 1992 and 1996. Changes of this nature and extent have occurred only three times before: at the turn of the century, when the juvenile court was established; after the U.S. Supreme Court decision in *Gault;* and after the enactment of the Juvenile Justice and Delinquency Prevention Act of 1974.[46] These changes reflect a "fundamental shift in juvenile justice philosophy. Traditional notions of individualized dispositions based on the interests of juveniles are being diminished by interests in punishing criminal behavior."[47] Since 1992, forty states have made it easier to try juveniles as adults, for more types of offenses, and at younger ages in most cases. Thirteen states have enacted mandatory minimum sentences for juveniles convicted of certain serious crimes. These legislative trends reflect the national trend toward punitive treatment of juveniles in a manner similar to the treatment of adults. In fact, we may be closer to treating juveniles as adults under law than at any time since the establishment of the juvenile court.[48]

The Outlook for Juvenile Justice

A look at the backgrounds of juveniles serving time in state facilities provides clues to future prevention strategies. Public facilities hold more serious delinquents: 80 percent of the juveniles held in public facilities are in secure institutions, whereas only 15 percent of those held in private facilities are in secure settings.[49]

As Table 18.8 shows, the typical juvenile delinquent is a male serving time for a property crime, has been arrested at least three times in the past, and has been on probation and in an institution before. He is a regular user of drugs and alcohol and began using major drugs (cocaine, heroin, PCP, LSD) at age fourteen. He has not finished the ninth grade, and comes from a single-parent home. A family member has been incarcerated in the past.

In order to reduce the number of serious delinquents such as these (most of whom end up in secure institutions), action must be taken to address the conditions in which they live. These juveniles have problems that began long before their delinquency that involved bad family situations, and school and drug problems. Most juvenile delinquents are at high risk for committing crimes for years before the crimes actually occur.[50] Relatives, neighbors, teachers, churches, and social service agencies are aware of which juveniles and which families are not acting properly, but action often is not taken until the juvenile commits a serious crime. By then it is often too late. Continued inattention to these problems helps to perpetuate the problem of juvenile delinquency. The outlook for juvenile delinquency in the future will depend on the amount of attention given to these underlying problems associated with delinquency.

TABLE 18.8

Background of Youths in Custody

Offense	
Violent crime	39 %
Property crime	46 %
Drug offenses	6 %
Public order	7 %
Status offenses	2 %
Prior record	
3 or more arrests	72 %
Prior probation	82 %
Prior incarceration	58 %
Substance use	
Regular drug use	63 %
Under drug influence at time of offense	39 %
Age at onset of major drug use	14 years
Regular alcohol use	57 %
Under alcohol influence at time of offense	32 %
Education level	
Median education	8 years
Home situation	
Single parent	70 %
Family member ever incarcerated?	52 %
Friends involved in crime?	31 %
In company of others at time of crime?	62 %

SOURCE: Howard N. Snyder and Melissa Sickmund, *Juvenile Offenders and Victims: A National Report* (Washington, D.C.: Office of Juvenile Justice and Delinquecy Prevention, 1995); Allen Beck, Susan Kline, and Lawrence Greenfield, *Survey of Youth in Custody* (Washington, D.C.: Bureau of Justice Statistics, 1988).

Critical Thinking EXERCISE

Abolish the Age of Majority?

A problem arises when juveniles commit "adult" crimes. That is, sometimes juveniles commit extremely serious crimes with little reflection, remorse, or fear. The brutal nature of some of these crimes results in demands for punishment as an adult, despite the age of the juvenile. "Treatment" as a juvenile simply is not an adequate punishment for the act and is not a sufficient deterrent to the juvenile or to others. Although rehabilitation is hoped for, it is clearly secondary to the desire for punishment.

In recent years many states have passed laws that make it easier to hold violent juvenile offenders responsible as adults. In these states, juveniles who are charged with certain serious crimes, such as murder, rape, and aggravated assault, are *presumed* to be responsible as adults. These defendants are tried and punished as adults in criminal court unless it can be shown that the juvenile deserves treatment according to the philosophy of rehabilitative juvenile justice.

"Waivers" from juvenile to adult court are often based entirely on the nature of the crime charged. If the crime is serious enough, juveniles are very likely to be tried and punished as adults. The juvenile's actual age or background matters relatively little in these decisions.

The underlying issue is that the age of majority is arbitrary. There is no magic that occurs at age eighteen that makes one a responsible adult. In fact, everyone knows some young people who are mature and responsible at age fifteen, and some who are still immature at age twenty-one. Perhaps arbitrary age distinctions should be eliminated so as to avoid the problem of adjudicating young people as adults or juveniles solely on the basis of their age or the nature of the charges they face. Neither of these factors is a reliable indicator of whether punishment or treatment is most appropriate.

An alternative is to abolish the age of majority, whether it be sixteen, eighteen, or nineteen. Instead, all crime suspects, regardless of age, would be tried at a fact-finding hearing, the sole purpose of which would be to determine whether the suspect did indeed commit the crime alleged. If evidence beyond a reasonable doubt is established, the offender would face a dispositional hearing at which a judge would impose some combination of punishment or treatment, or both, after a complete investigation had been made of the suspect's background. This punishment and/or treatment would be based on the offender's needs, maturity, and skill level and the safety of the community, not on the offender's age.

The juvenile court system is based on an unrealistic assumption: that age is an appropriate indicator of adult behavior. Instead, investigations by the court should replace the current practice of deciding whether to try juveniles as adults before the charges have been proven. This would have a significant impact on outcomes. In the present system, once a juvenile has been waived to criminal court he or she is unlikely to be viewed as a candidate for treatment (versus punishment), regardless of which alternative would best protect the community in the short term and result in responsible behavior by the offender in the long term. Under the proposed system, a broader and more meaningful range of outcomes would be possible.

Critical Thinking Questions

1. What is your opinion regarding the proposal to abolish the age of majority? How do you defend it?
2. Explain how you would change the sentencing system, given your answer to the preceding question?

Critical Thinking EXERCISE

Juries for Juveniles?

Why did the U.S. Supreme Court change its position on due process in *McKeiver v. Pennsylvania*? Beginning with *Kent, Gault,* and *Winship,* and continuing in *Breed,* the Court supported due process protections for juveniles in all its cases from 1966 through 1975. *McKeiver* is the only case during this period in which the Court believed such protection was not a "necessary component of accurate fact finding."

In explaining its decision the Court argued that juries in juvenile court could make these proceedings a fully adversarial process, like criminal court for adults, and that the rehabilitative goals of juvenile justice would not be met. It might be argued, instead, that the Court was afraid of how juries in juvenile court might work as a practical matter and that in this decision the Court actually made it more difficult to achieve rehabilitation.

If juries were available in juvenile court, could a juvenile demand to have his or her case heard by a jury of juveniles, since they are the true peers of a juvenile charged with a crime? If so, how would juvenile jurors be obtained? Would a school release program be necessary for jurors? How could one ensure that juvenile jurors would take their task seriously? All these questions were effectively avoided through the Supreme Court's denial of the right to a jury for juveniles, even though it is guaranteed in the Sixth Amendment as a right of the accused.

If one reads the Court's decision in *McKeiver v. Pennsylvania* carefully, it can be seen that the Court took pains to avoid making juries available to juveniles. The Court found it "of more than passing interest" that twenty-eight states denied the right to a trial by jury in similar cases. Of course, ten states specifically *permitted* juries in juvenile court. Rather than look for ways to make juries available, the Court actively sought reasons to deny this Sixth Amendment right to juveniles. It quoted the President's Crime Commission, the Uniform Juvenile Court Act, and the Standard Juvenile Court Act, which all stopped short of recommending jury trials in juvenile court. The Court believed that such juries would bring to the juvenile justice system "the traditional delay, the formality, and the clamor of the adversary system and, possibly, the public trial."

The three Justices who dissented in the *McKeiver* case went back to the Magna Carta to demonstrate that the right to a trial by jury has historically been seen as fundamental to due process. They noted that in states where juvenile court juries are available, few jury trials are ever requested by the accused. Interestingly, they also observed that the phrase "judgment of his peers" is taken from the Magna Carta and that the only restriction on juries is that there be "no systematic exclusion" of eligible potential jurors. "Thus, it is quite possible that we will have teenage jurors sitting in judgment of their so-called 'peers,'" they concluded.

The use of advisory juries was not prohibited in *McKeiver.* Therefore, individual states and juvenile court judges are free to use juries if they wish. In Duluth, Minnesota, for example, juvenile juries made up of volunteers from junior and senior high schools have sat in judgment of accused first offenders in their peer group. According to a court administrator there, "The main advantage of the program is that it helps keep administrative costs down and helps keep the time for processing down to under ten days."[A] The presiding judge believed that the primary value of the youth jury is "the education it gives to the jurors and their peers." This education includes a better understanding of how the system works, experience in making difficult decisions that affect the lives of others, and the recognition of the consequences of violation of the law. Experimentation with "teen," "youth," or "peer" courts has grown dramatically in recent years, and there are now 250 teen court programs in thirty states.[B] The guiding principles of these teen court programs are accountability for behavior, knowledge about the law, and assistance in resolving the problems of peers. Inculcation of these principles on a national level would go a long way toward integrating young people into society and its institutions as *participants,* rather than only as defendants.

Critical Thinking Questions

1. **What are potential disadvantages of peer juries in juvenile court?**
2. **What is preventing the establishment of a peer jury in the juvenile court in your own jurisdiction? If one exists, what was the primary force behind its establishment?**

Notes

[A]Nathaniel Sheppard, "For Teenagers in Duluth, Teenage Juries," *The New York Times* (March 31, 1980), p. 6.

[B]Tracy M. Godwin, *Peer Justice and Youth Empowerment* (Washington, D.C.: Office of Juvenile Justice and Delinquency Prevention, 1996).

Summary

JUVENILE JUSTICE VERSUS CRIMINAL JUSTICE

- The philosophy that the state should act in the best interests of children who receive improper care and treatment at home is known as parens patriae.
- In recent years controversy has arisen over the legal treatment of juveniles, and there is much disagreement over the proper goals of the juvenile justice system.

THE NATURE AND EXTENT OF DELINQUENCY

- The most commonly used indicator of delinquency is the rate of juvenile arrests. Most of these arrests are for property crimes, although the proportion of juveniles arrested for those crimes has decreased in the last two decades.
- Younger juveniles are arrested significantly less often than older juveniles, and the majority of those arrested are male.
- Self-reports show that delinquency is extremely common and that relatively few delinquents are caught. They also reveal that offense rates do not differ greatly by race or social class.

FOUNDATIONS OF JUVENILE JUSTICE

- When the first juvenile court was established in 1899, the emphasis of the juvenile justice process changed from deterrence and incapacitation to rehabilitation.

- Objections to the parens patriae philosophy centered on the lack of legal counsel and basic due process protections, as well as the failure of the state to reform delinquents.
- In the 1960s, these concerns were addressed through various modifications of the juvenile justice system.

THE LAW AND PROCEDURE OF JUVENILE JUSTICE

- In *Kent v. United States,* the Supreme Court ruled that a juvenile must receive a hearing before being referred to criminal court for trial as an adult.
- The Supreme Court has ruled that a juvenile offender and his or her parent must be notified of the charges early and in writing and that juveniles have a right to counsel and the right of protection against self-incrimination.
- During the adjudicatory stage of a delinquency proceeding the charges must be proved beyond a reasonable doubt.
- The Supreme Court has ruled that juveniles have the same protection against double jeopardy as adults.
- In ruling on preventive detention, the Court has placed the protection of the community above the needs of the child.
- Searches of students in public schools are justified when there are "reasonable grounds" that evidence will be found of violations of law or school rules.
- Offenders over the age of sixteen who commit capital crimes are subject to the death penalty.

JUVENILES IN THE SYSTEM: POLICE, COURTS, CORRECTIONS

- Police generally have five alternatives in deciding how to handle a juvenile: (1) warn and release, (2) refer to juvenile court, (3) refer to a social welfare agency, (4) refer to another police department, or (5) refer to criminal court for prosecution as an adult.
- Recent statistics show that fewer juveniles are released and more are being sent to court; an increasing number are being tried as adults.
- An increasing number of delinquents are being placed in institutions or other residential facilities for juveniles.
- Recent legislation reflects the national trend toward punitive treatment of juveniles in a manner similar to the treatment of adults.

THE OUTLOOK FOR JUVENILE JUSTICE

- The typical juvenile delinquent is a male serving time for a property crime, is a regular user of drugs and alcohol, has not finished the ninth grade, and comes from a single-parent home.
- To reduce the number of serious delinquents, action must be taken to address the conditions in which they live.

Key Terms

delinquency
status offenses
parens patriae
double jeopardy
detention center
shelter
reception/diagnostic center
training school
ranch/forestry camp/farm
halfway house or group home

Questions for Review and Discussion

1. What is meant by parens patriae?
2. What information sources are used to establish the nature and extent of delinquency?

3. What do arrest statistics reveal about the age and gender of juvenile delinquents?
4. How do the findings of self-report studies differ from official statistics on the types of juveniles who engage in delinquency?
5. How has the juvenile justice system evolved over the course of the twentieth century?
6. What is the significance of the Supreme Court's decision in *Kent v. United States*?
7. What principles have been established by the Supreme Court with respect to the right to counsel for juveniles?
8. What standard has the Supreme Court established with respect to the burden of proof in juvenile proceedings?
9. Are juries required in juvenile proceedings?
10. How has the Supreme Court ruled with respect to preventive detention of juveniles?
11. How has the Supreme Court ruled with respect to searches of juveniles?
12. Are juveniles subject to capital punishment?
13. What trends can be seen in police disposition of juveniles taken into custody, juvenile court dispositions, and legislation related to juvenile justice?

Notes

[1]Gordon Witkin et al., "Again," *U.S. News & World Report* (June 1, 1998), pp. 16–21.

[2]Adam Weintraub, "Paint Gun Attacks," *USA Today* (July 9, 1996), p. 3.

[3]Paul Leavitt, "Teen Bomb Makers," *USA Today* (July 23, 1996), p. 5.

[4]"Young Killer," *USA Today* (February 2, 1992), p. 3.

[5]Paul Leavitt, "Taped in the Act," *USA Today* (March 10, 1995), p. 3.

[6]Paul Leavitt, "Burned Boy," *USA Today* (March 21, 1995), p. 3.

[7]Patricia Torbet et al., *State Responses to Serious and Violent Juvenile Crime* (Washington, D.C.: Office of Juvenile Justice and Delinquency Prevention, 1996); Douglas C. Dodge, *Due Process Advocacy* (Washington, D.C.: Office of Juvenile Justice and Delinquency Prevention, 1997); Fox Butterfield, "Few Options or Safeguards in a City's Juvenile Courts," *The New York Times* (July 27, 1997), p. 1; Christine Todd Whitman, "Bringing Balance to the Criminal Justice System," *Crime & Delinquency*, vol. 44 (January 1998), pp. 70–5.

[8]Jonathan Alter, "Harnessing the Hysteria," *Newsweek* (April 6, 1998), p. 27; Richard Lacayo, "Toward the Root of the Evil: Schoolboy Massacres May Be an Aberration, But the Question Remains: Why Do Kids Kill?," *Time* (April 6, 1998), pp. 38–40; Anthony N. Doob and Jane B. Sprott, "Is the 'Quality' of Youth Violence Becoming More Serious?," *Canadian Journal of Criminology*, vol. 40 (April 1998), pp. 185–94.

[9]Howard N. Snyder, *Juvenile Arrests 1996* (Washington, D.C.: Office of Juvenile Justice and Delinquency Prevention, 1997).

[10]See Jeffrey A. Butts and Howard N. Snyder, *The Youngest Delinquents: Offenders Under Age 15* (Washington, D.C.: Office of Juvenile Justice and Delinquency Prevention, 1997).

[11]Albert K. Cohen, *Delinquent Boys: The Culture of the Gang* (1955 reprint) (New York: The Free Press, 1971), p. 170.

[12]Austin L. Porterfield, *Youth in Trouble* (Fort Worth: Texas Christian University Press, 1946).

[13]J. S. Wallerstein and C. L. Wylie, "Our Law-Abiding Lawbreakers," *National Probation* (March–April 1947), pp. 107–12; James F. Short and Ivan F. Nye, "Extent of Unrecorded Juvenile Delinquency," *Journal of Criminal Law, Criminology, and Police Science*, vol. 49 (1958), pp. 296–302; Jerald Bachman, Lloyd Johnston, and Patrick O'Malley, *Monitoring the Future: Questionnaire Responses from the Nation's High School Seniors* (Ann Arbor, MI: Institute for Social Research, 1987).

[14]Martin Gold, "Undetected Delinquent Behavior," *Journal of Research in Crime & Delinquency*, vol. 3 (1966), pp. 27–46.

[15]Maynard L. Erickson and LaMar T. Empey, "Court Records, Undetected Delinquency and Decision Making," *Journal of Criminal Law, Criminology, and Police Science*, vol. 54 (1963), pp. 465–9; see also Franklyn Dunford and Delbert Elliott, "Identifying Career Offenders Using Self-Reported Data," *Journal of Research in Crime & Delinquency*, vol. 21 (1984), pp. 57–86.

[16]Suzanne S. Ageton and Delbert S. Elliott, *The Incidence of Delinquent Behavior in a National Probability Sample* (Boulder, CO: Behavioral Research Institute, 1978).

[17]Delbert S. Elliott and Suzanne S. Ageton, "Reconciling Race and Class Differences in Self Reported and Official Estimates of Delinquency," *American Sociological Review*, vol. 45 (February 1980), pp. 95–100; Michael J. Hindelang, Travis Hirschi, and Joseph G. Weis, *Measuring Delinquency* (Beverly Hills, CA: Sage Publications, 1981); David Huizinga and Delbert S. Elliott, "Juvenile Offenders: Prevalence, Offender Incidence, and Arrests by Race," *Crime & Delinquency*, vol. 33 (April 1987), pp. 206–23.

[18]John P. Clark and Larry L. Tift, "Polygraph and Interview Validation of Self-Reported Deviant Behavior," *Journal of Criminal Law, Criminology, and Police Science*, vol. 58 (1967), pp. 80–6; Gold, pp. 27–46.

[19]Catherine Whitaker, *Teenage Victims* (Washington, D.C.: Bureau of Justice Statistics, 1986); Tina Dorsey and Jayne Robinson, *Criminal Victimization in the United States, 1994* (Washington, D.C.: Bureau of Justice Statistics, 1997).

[20]Jane Addams, *Twenty Years at Hull House* (New York: Signet Classic, 1961).

[21]Ira M. Schwartz, *(In)justice for Juveniles: Rethinking the Best Interests of the Child* (Lexington, MA: Lexington Books, 1989), p. 150; Benjamin Fine, *1,000,000 Delinquents* (New York: Signet, 1957), p. 207.

[22]Julian W. Mack, "The Juvenile Court," *Harvard Law Review*, vol. 23 (1909), p. 104.

[23]President's Commission on Law Enforcement and Administration of Justice, *Task Force Report: Juvenile Delinquency and Youth Crime* (Washington, D.C.: U.S. Government Printing Office, 1967).

[24]Steven L. Schlossman, *Love and the American Delinquent: The Theory and Practice of "Progressive" Juvenile Justice, 1825–1920* (Chicago: University of Chicago Press, 1977).

[25]Torbet et al., p. 61.

[26]Paul W. Tappan, "Treatment without Trial," *Social Forces*, vol. 24 (1946), p. 306.

[27]Alexander W. Pisciotta, "Saving the Children: The Promise and Practice of Parens Patriae, 1838–89," *Crime & Delinquency*, vol. 28 (July 1982), p. 425.

[28]Patrick T. Murphy, *Our Kindly Parent—the State* (New York: Penguin Books, 1977).

[29]Paul J. Brantingham, "Juvenile Justice Reform in California and New York in the Early 1960s," in F. L. Faust and P. J. Brantingham, eds., *Juvenile Justice Philosophy*, 2nd ed. (St. Paul: West Publishing, 1979), p. 263.

[30]383 U.S. 451 (1966).

[31]387 U.S. 1 (1967).

[32]*In re Winship*, 397 U.S. 358 (1970).

[33]403 U.S. 528 (1971).

[34]421 U.S. 519 (1975).

[35]104 S. Ct. 2403 (1984).

[36]105 S. Ct. 733 (1985).

[37]*Gregg v. Georgia*, 96 S. Ct. 2909 (1976).

[38]108 S. Ct. 2687 (1988).

[39]*Stanford v. Kentucky* and *Wilkins v. Missouri*, 109 S. Ct. 2969 (1989).

[40]National Advisory Committee on Criminal Justice Standards and Goals, *Report of the Task Force on Juvenile Justice and Delinquency Prevention* (Washington, D.C.: U.S. Government Printing Office, 1976).

[41]Howard N. Snyder, *Juvenile Arrests 1996*.

[42]Joseph B. Sanborn, Jr., "Factors Perceived to Affect Delinquent Dispositions in Juvenile Court: Putting the Sentencing Decision into Context," *Crime & Delinquency,* vol. 42 (January 1996), pp. 99–113.

[43]J. Hawes, *Children in Urban Society: Juvenile Delinquency in Nineteenth Century America* (New York: Oxford University Press, 1971).

[44]Sue Kline, *Children in Custody* (Washington, D.C.: Bureau of Justice Statistics, 1989).

[45]Dale Parent, Terence Dunworth, Douglas McDonald, and William Rhodes, *Transferring Serious Juvenile Offenders to Adult Courts* (Washington, D.C.: National Institute of Justice, 1997).

[46]Torbet et al., p. 59.

[47]Ibid., p. xi; see Stephen W. Baron and Timothy F. Hartnagel, "Lock' em Up: Attitudes Toward Punishing Juvenile Offenders," *Canadian Journal of Criminology,* vol. 38 (April 1996), pp. 191–212.

[48]Ibid., p. 59.

[49]Howard N. Snyder and Melissa Sickmund, *Juvenile Offenders and Victims: A National Report* (Washington, D.C.: Office of Juvenile Justice and Delinquency Prevention, 1995), p. 165.

[50]Rolf Loeber and David P. Farrington, eds., *Serious and Violent Juvenile Offenders: Risk Factors and Successful Interventions* (Thousand Oaks, CA: Sage Publications, 1998).

For Further Reading

William Ayers, *A Kind and Just Parent: The Children of Juvenile Court* (Boston: Beacon Press, 1997).

Geoffrey Canada, *Fist, Stick, Knife, Gun: A Personal History of Violence in America* (Boston: Beacon Press, 1995).

Peter Greenwood et al., *Diverting Children from a Life of Crime* (Santa Monica, CA: Rand Corporation, 1996).

Edward Humes, *No Matter How Loud I Shout: A Year in the Life of Juvenile Court* (New York: Simon and Schuster, 1996).

Appendix I

The Constitution of the United States of America

We the People of the United States, in Order to form a more perfect Union, establish Justice, insure domestic Tranquility, provide for the common defence, promote the general Welfare, and secure the Blessings of Liberty to ourselves and our Posterity, do ordain and establish this Constitution for the United States of America.

ARTICLE I

SECTION 1. All legislative Powers herein granted shall be vested in a Congress of the United States, which shall consist of a Senate and House of Representatives.

SECTION 2. The House of Representatives shall be composed of Members chosen every second Year by the People of the several States, and the Electors in each State shall have the Qualifications requisite for Electors of the most numerous Branch of the State Legislature.

No person shall be a Representative who shall not have attained to the Age of twenty five Years, and been seven Years a Citizen of the United States, and who shall not, when elected, be an Inhabitant of that State in which he shall be chosen.

Representatives and direct Taxes shall be apportioned among the several States which may be included within this Union, according to their respective Numbers which shall be determined by adding to the whole Number of free Persons, including those bound to Service for a Term of Years, and excluding Indians not taxed, three fifths of all other Persons. The actual Enumeration shall be made within three Years after the first Meeting of the Congress of the United States, and within every subsequent Term ten Years, in such Manner as they shall by Law direct. The Number of Representatives shall not exceed one for every thirty Thousand, but each State shall have at Least one Representative; and until such enumeration shall be made, the State of New Hampshire shall be entitled to chuse three, Massachusetts eight, Rhode-Island and Providence Plantations one, Connecticut five, New-York six, New Jersey four, Pennsylvania eight, Delaware one, Maryland six, Virginia ten, North Carolina five, South Carolina five, and Georgia three.

When vacancies happen in the Representation from any State, the Executive Authority thereof shall issue Writs of Election to fill such Vacancies.

The House of Representatives shall chuse their speaker and other Officers; and shall have the sole Power of Impeachment.

SECTION 3. The Senate of the United States shall be composed of two Senators from each State chosen by the Legislature thereof, for six Years; and each Senator shall have one Vote.

Immediately after they shall be assembled in Consequence of the first Election, they shall be divided as equally as may be into three Classes. The Seats of the Senators of the first Class shall be vacated at the Expiration of the second year, of the second Class at the Expiration of the fourth Year, and of the third Class at the Expiration of the sixth Year, so that one third may be chosen every second Year and if Vacancies happen by Resignation, or otherwise, during the Recess of the Legislature of any State, the Executive thereof may make temporary Appointments until the next Meeting of the Legislature, which shall then fill such Vacancies.

No Person shall be a Senator who shall not have attained to the Age of thirty Years, and been nine Years a Citizen of the United States, and who shall not, when elected, be an Inhabitant of that State for which he shall be chosen.

The Vice President of the United States shall be President of the Senate, but shall have no Vote, unless they be equally divided.

The Senate shall chuse their other Officers, and also a President pro tempore, in the Absence of the Vice President, or when he shall exercise the Office of President of the United States.

The Senate shall have the sole Power to try all Impeachments. When sitting for that Purpose, they shall be on Oath or Affirmation. When the President of the United States is tried, the Chief Justice shall preside: And no Person shall be convicted without the Concurrence of two thirds of the Members present.

Judgment in Cases of Impeachment shall not extend further than to removal from Office, and disqualification to hold and enjoy any Office of honor, Trust or Profit under the United States; but the Party convicted shall nevertheless be liable and subject to Indictment, Trial, Judgment and Punishment, according to Law.

SECTION 4. The Times, Places and Manner of holding Elections for Senators and Representatives, shall be prescribed in each State by the Legislature thereof; but the Congress may at any time by law make or alter such Regulations, except as to the Places of chusing Senators.

The Congress shall assemble at least once in every Year, and such Meeting shall be on the first Monday in December, unless they shall by Law appoint a different Day.

SECTION 5. Each House shall be the Judge of the Elections, Returns and Qualifications of its own Members, and a Majority of each shall constitute a Quorum to do Business; but a smaller Number may adjourn from day to day, and may be authorized to compel the Attendance of absent Members, in such Manner, and under such Penalties as each House may provide.

Each House may determine the Rules of its Proceedings, punish its Members for disorderly Behaviour, and with the Concurrence of two thirds, expel a Member.

Each House shall keep a journal of its Proceedings, and from time to time publish the same, excepting such Parts as may in their judgment require Secrecy; and the Yeas and Nays of the Members of either House on any question shall, at the Desire of one fifth of those present, be entered on the Journal.

Neither House, during the Session of Congress, shall, without the Consent of the other, adjourn for more than three days, nor to any other Place than that in which the two Houses shall be sitting.

SECTION 6. The Senators and Representatives shall receive a Compensation for their Services, to be ascertained by Law, and paid out of the Treasury of the United States. They shall in all Cases, except Treason, Felony and Breach of the Peace, be privileged from Arrest during their Attendance at the Session of their respective Houses, and in going to and returning from the same; and for any Speech or Debate in either House, they shall not be questioned in any other Place.

No Senator or Representative shall, during the Time for which he was elected, be appointed to any civil Office under the Authority of the United States, which shall have been created, or the Emoluments whereof shall have been encreased during such time; and no Person holding any Office under the United States, shall be a Member of either House during his Continuance in Office.

SECTION 7. All Bills for raising Revenue shall originate in the House of Representatives; but the Senate may propose or concur with Amendments as on other Bills.

Every Bill which shall have passed the House of Representatives and the Senate, shall, before it become a Law, be presented to the President of the United States; If he approves he shall sign it, but if not he shall return it, with his Objections to that House in which it shall have originated, who shall enter the Objections at large on their journal, and proceed to reconsider it. If after such Reconsideration two thirds of that House shall agree to pass the Bill, it shall be sent, together with the Objections, to the other House, by which it shall likewise be reconsidered, and if approved by two thirds of that House, it shall become a Law. But in all such Cases the Votes of both Houses shall be determined by Yeas and Nays, and the Names of the Persons voting for and against the Bill shall be entered on the Journal of each House respectively. If any Bill shall not be returned by the President within ten Days (Sundays excepted) after it shall have been presented to him, the Same shall be a Law, in like Manner as if he had signed it, unless the Congress by their Adjournment prevent its Return, in which Case it shall not be a Law.

Every Order, Resolution, or Vote to which the Concurrence of the Senate and House of Representatives may be necessary (except on a question of Adjournment) shall be presented to the President of the United States; and before the Same shall take Effect, shall be approved by him, or being disapproved by him, shall be repassed by two thirds of the Senate and House of Representatives, according to the Rules and Limitations prescribed in the Case of a Bill.

SECTION 8. The Congress shall have Power To lay and collect Taxes, Duties, Imposts and Excises, to pay the Debts and provide for the common Defence and general Welfare of the United States; but all Duties, Imposts and Excises shall be uniform throughout the United States;

To borrow Money on the credit of the United States;

To regulate Commerce with foreign Nations, and among the several States, and with the Indian Tribes;

To establish a uniform Rule of Naturalization, and uniform Laws on the subject of Bankruptcies throughout the United States;

To coin Money, regulate the Value thereof, and of foreign Coin, and fix the Standard of Weights and Measures;

To provide for the Punishment of counterfeiting the Securities and current Coin of the United States;

To establish Post Offices and post Roads;

To promote the Progress of Science and useful Arts, by securing for limited Times to Authors and Inventors the exclusive Right to their respective Writings and Discoveries;

To constitute Tribunals inferior to the supreme Court;

To define and punish Piracies and Felonies committed on the high Seas, and Offences against the Law of Nations;

To declare War, grant Letters of Marque and Reprisal, and make Rules concerning Captures on Land and Water;

To raise and support Armies, but no Appropriation of Money to that Use shall be for a longer Term than two Years;

To provide and maintain a Navy;

To make Rules for the Government and Regulation of the land and naval Forces;

To provide for calling forth the Militia to execute the Laws of the Union, suppress Insurrections and repel Invasions;

To provide for organizing, arming, and disciplining, the Militia, and for governing such Part of them as may be employed in the Service of the United States, reserving to the States respectively, the Appointment of the Officers, and the Authority of training the Militia according to the discipline prescribed by Congress;

To exercise exclusive Legislation in all Cases whatsoever, over such District (not exceeding ten Miles square) as may, by Cession of particular States, and the Acceptance of Congress, become the Seat of the Government of the United States, and to exercise like Authority over all Places purchased by the Consent of the Legislature of the State in which the Same shall be for the Erection of Forts, Magazines, Arsenals, dock-Yards, and other needful Buildings;—And

To make all Laws which shall be necessary and proper for carrying into Execution the foregoing Powers, and all other Powers vested by this Constitution in the Government of the United States, or in any Department or Officer thereof.

SECTION 9. The Migration or Importation of such Persons as any of the States now existing shall think proper to admit, shall not be prohibited by the Congress prior to the Year one thousand eight hundred and eight, but a Tax or duty may be imposed on such Importation, not exceeding ten dollars for each Person.

The Privilege of the Writ of Habeas Corpus shall not be suspended, unless when in Cases of Rebellion or Invasion the public Safety may require it.

No Bill of Attainder or ex post facto Law shall be passed.

No Capitation, or other direct, Tax shall be laid, unless in Proportion to the Census or Enumeration herein before directed to be taken.

No Tax or Duty shall be laid on Articles exported from any State.

No Preference shall be given by any Regulation of Commerce or Revenue to the Ports of one State over those of another; nor shall Vessels bound to, or from, one State, be obliged to enter, clear, or pay Duties in another.

No Money shall be drawn from the Treasury, but in Consequence of Appropriations made by Law; and a regular Statement and Account of the Receipts and Expenditures of all public Money shall be published from time to time.

No Title of Nobility shall be granted by the United States: And no Person holding any Office of Profit or Trust under them, shall, without the Consent of the Congress, accept of any present, Emolument, Office, or Title, of any kind whatever, from any King, Prince, or foreign State.

SECTION 10. No state shall enter into any Treaty, Alliance, or Confederation; grant Letters of Marque and Reprisal; coin Money; emit Bills of Credit; make any Thing but gold and silver Coin a Tender in Payment of Debts; pass any Bill of Attainder, ex post facto Law, or Law impairing the Obligation of Contracts, or grant any Title of Nobility.

No State shall, without the Consent of the Congress, lay any Imposts or Duties on Imports or Exports, except what may be absolutely necessary for executing its inspection Laws: and the net Produce of all Duties and Imposts, laid by any State on Imports or Exports, shall be for the Use of the Treasury of the United States, and all such Laws shall be subject to the Revision and Controul of the Congress.

No State shall, without the Consent of Congress, lay any Duty of Tonnage, keep Troops, or Ships of War in time of Peace, enter into any Agreement or Compact with another State, or with a foreign Power, or engage in War, unless actually invaded, or in such imminent Danger as will not admit of delay.

ARTICLE II

SECTION 1. The executive Power shall be vested in a President of the United States of America. He shall hold his Office during the Term of four Years, and, together with the Vice President, chosen for the same Term, be elected as follows.

Each State shall appoint, in such Manner as the Legislature thereof may direct, a Number of Electors, equal to the whole Number of Senators and Representatives to which the State may be entitled in the Congress; but no Senator or Representative, or Person holding an Office of Trust of Profit under the United States, shall be appointed an Elector.

The Electors shall meet in their respective States, and vote by Ballot for two Persons, of whom one at least shall not be an Inhabitant of the same State with themselves. And they shall make a List of all the Persons voted for, and, of the Number of Votes for each; which List they shall sign and certify, and transmit sealed to the Seat of the Government of the United States, directed to the President of the Senate. The President of the Senate shall, in the Presence of the Senate and House of Representatives, open all the Certificates, and the Votes shall then be counted. The Person having the greatest Number of Votes shall be the President, if such Number be a Majority of the whole Number of Electors appointed; and if there be more than one who have such Majority, and have an equal Number of Votes, then the House of Representatives shall immediately chuse by Ballot one of them for President; and if no Person have a Majority, then from the five highest on the List the said House shall in like Manner chuse the President. But in chusing the President, the Votes shall be taken by States, the Representation from each State having one Vote; A quorum for this Purpose shall consist of a Member or Members from two thirds of the States, and a Majority of all the States shall be necessary to a Choice. In every Case, after the Choice of the President, the Person having the greatest Number of Votes of the Electors shall be the Vice President. But if there should remain two or more who have equal Votes, the Senate shall chuse from them by Ballot the Vice President.

The Congress may determine the Time of chusing the Electors, and the Day on which they shall give their Votes; which Day shall be the same throughout the United States.

No Person except a natural born Citizen, or a Citizen of the United States, at the time of the Adoption of this Constitution, shall be eligible to the Office of President; neither shall any Person be eligible to that Office who shall not have attained to the Age of thirty five Years, and been fourteen Years a Resident within the United States.

In Case of the Removal of the President from Office, or of his Death, Resignation, or Inability to discharge the Powers and Duties of the said Office, the Same shall devolve on the Vice President, and the Congress may by Law provide for the Case of Removal, Death, Resignation or Inability, both of the President and Vice President, declaring what Officer shall then act as President, and such Officer shall act accordingly, until the Disability be removed, or a President shall be elected.

The President shall, at stated Times, receive for his Services, a Compensation, which shall neither be encreased nor diminished during the Period for which he shall have been elected, and he shall not receive within that Period any other Emolument from the United States, or any of them.

Before he enter on the Execution of his Office, he shall take the following Oath or Affirmation—"I do solemnly swear (or affirm) that I will faithfully execute the Office of President of the United States, and will to the best of my Ability, preserve, protect and defend the Constitution of the United States."

SECTION 2. The President shall be Commander in Chief of the Army, and Navy of the United States, and of the Militia of the several States, when called into the actual Service of the United States; he may require the Opinion, in writing, of the principal Officer in each of the executive Departments, upon any Subject relating to the Duties of their respective Offices, and he shall have Power to grant Reprieves and Pardons for Offences against the United States, except in Cases of Impeachment.

He shall have Power, by and with the Advice and Consent of the Senate, to make Treaties, provided two thirds of the Senators present concur; and he shall nominate, and by and with the Advice and Consent of the Senate, shall appoint Ambassadors, other public Ministers and Consuls, Judges of the supreme Court, and all other Officers of the United States, whose Appointments are not herein otherwise provided for, and which shall be established by Law: but the Congress may by Law vest the Appointment of such inferior Officers, as they think proper, in the President alone, in the Courts of Law, or in the Heads of Departments.

The President shall have Power to fill up all Vacancies that may happen during the Recess of the Senate, by granting Commissions which shall expire at the end of their next Session.

SECTION 3. He shall from time to time give to the Congress Information of the State of the Union, and recommend to their Consideration such Measures as he shall judge necessary and expedient; he may, on extraordinary Occasions, convene both Houses, or either of them, and in Case of Disagreement between them, with Respect to the Time of Adjournment, he may adjourn them to such Time as he shall think proper; he shall receive Ambassadors and other public Ministers; he shall take Care that the Laws be faithfully executed, and shall Commission all the Officers of the United States.

SECTION 4. The President, Vice President and all civil Officers of the United States, shall be removed from Office on Impeachment for, and Conviction of, Treason, Bribery, or other high Crimes and Misdemeanors.

ARTICLE III

SECTION 1. The judicial Power of the United States, shall be vested in one supreme Court, and in such inferior Courts as the Congress may from time to time ordain and establish. The Judges, both of the supreme and inferior Courts, shall hold their Offices during good Behaviour, and shall, at stated Times, receive for their Services, a Compensation, which shall not be diminished during their Continuance in Office.

SECTION 2. The judicial Power shall extend to all Cases, in Law and Equity, arising under this Constitution, the Laws of the United States, and Treaties made, or which shall be made, under their Authority;—to all Cases affecting Ambassadors, other public Ministers and Consuls;—to all Cases of admiralty and maritime Jurisdiction;—to Controversies to which the United States shall be a Party;—to Controversies between two or more States;—between a State and Citizens of another State;—between Citizens of different States,—between Citizens of the same State claiming Lands under Grants of different States,—and between a State, or the Citizens thereof, and foreign States, Citizens of Subjects.

In all Cases affecting Ambassadors, other public Ministers and Consuls, and those in which a State shall be Party, the supreme Court shall have original Jurisdiction. In all the other Cases before mentioned, the supreme Court shall have appellate Jurisdiction, both as to Law and Fact, with such Exceptions, and under such Regulations as the Congress shall make.

The Trial of all Crimes, except in Cases of Impeachment, shall be by Jury; and such Trial shall be held in the State where the said Crimes shall have been committed; but when not committed within any State, the Trial shall be at such Place or Places as the Congress may by Law have directed.

SECTION 3. Treason against the United States, shall consist only in levying War against them, or in adhering to their Enemies, giving them Aid and Comfort. No Person shall be convicted of Treason unless on the Testimony of two Witnesses to the same overt Act, or on Confession in open Court.

The Congress shall have Power to declare the Punishment of Treason, but no Attainder of Treason shall work Corruption of Blood, or Forfeiture except during the Life of the Person attainted.

ARTICLE IV

SECTION 1. Full Faith and Credit shall be given in each State to the public Acts, Records, and judicial Proceedings of every other State. And the Congress may by general Laws prescribe the Manner in which such Acts, Records and Proceedings shall be proved, and the Effect thereof.

SECTION 2. The Citizens of each State shall be entitled to all Privileges and Immunities of Citizens in the several States.

A Person charged in any State with Treason, Felony, or other Crime, who shall flee from Justice, and be found in another State, shall on Demand of the executive Authority of the State from which he fled, be delivered up, to be removed to the State having Jurisdiction of the Crime.

No Person held to Service or Labour in one State under the Laws thereof, escaping into another, shall, in Consequence of any Law or Regulation therein, be discharged from such Service or Labour, but shall be delivered up on Claim of the Party to whom such Service or Labour may be due.

SECTION 3. New States may be admitted by the Congress into this Union; but no new State shall be formed or erected within the Jurisdiction of any other State; nor any State be formed by the Junction of two or more States, or Parts of States, without the Consent of the Legislatures of the States concerned as well as of the Congress.

The Congress shall have Power to dispose of and make all needful Rules and Regulations respecting the Territory or other Property belonging to the United States; and nothing in this Constitution shall be so construed as to Prejudice any Claims of the United States, or of any particular State.

SECTION 4. The United States shall guarantee to every State in this Union a Republican Form of Government, and shall protect each of them against Invasion, and on Application of the Legislature, or of the Executive (when the Legislature cannot be convened) against domestic Violence.

ARTICLE V

The Congress, whenever two thirds of both Houses shall deem it necessary, shall propose Amendments to this Constitution, or, on the Application of the Legislatures of two thirds of the several States, shall call a Convention for proposing Amendments, which, in either Case, shall be valid to all Intents and Purposes, as Part of this Constitution, when ratified by the Legislatures of three fourths of the several States, or by Conventions in three fourths thereof, as the one or the other Mode of Ratification may be proposed by the Congress; Provided that no Amendment which may be made prior to the Year One thousand eight hundred and eight shall in any Manner affect the first and fourth Clauses in the Ninth Section of the first Article; and that no State, without its Consent, shall be deprived of its equal Suffrage in the Senate.

ARTICLE VI

All Debts contracted and Engagements entered into, before the Adoption of this Constitution, shall be as valid against the United States under this Constitution, as under the Confederation.

This Constitution, and the laws of the United States which shall be made in Pursuance thereof; and all Treaties made, or which shall be made, under the Authority of the United States, shall be the supreme Law of the Land; and the Judges in every State shall be bound thereby, any Thing in the Constitution or Laws of any State to the Contrary notwithstanding.

The Senators and Representatives before mentioned, and the Members of the several State Legislatures, and all executive and judicial Officers, both of the United States and of the several States, shall be bound by Oath or Affirmation, to support this Constitution; but no religious Test shall ever be required as a Qualification to any Office or public Trust under the United States.

ARTICLE VII

The Ratification of the Conventions of nine States, shall be sufficient for the Establishment of this Constitution between the States so ratifying the Same.

Done in Convention by the Unanimous Consent of the States present the Seventeenth Day of September in the Year of our Lord one thousand seven hundred and Eighty seven and of the Independence of the United States of America the Twelfth. IN WITNESS whereof we have hereunto subscribed our Names,

Go. WASHINGTON
Presid't. and deputy from Virginia

Attest
WILLIAM JACKSON
Secretary

DELAWARE
Geo. Read
Gunning Bedford jun
John Dickinson
Richard Basset
Jaco. Broom

MASSACHUSETTS
Nathaniel Gorham
Rufus King

CONNECTICUT
Wm. Saml. Johnson
Roger Sherman

NEW YORK
Alexander Hamilton

NEW JERSEY
Wh. Livingston
David Brearley
Wm. Paterson
Jona. Dayton

PENNSYLVANIA
B. Franklin
Thomas Mifflin
Robt. Morris
Geo. Clymer
Thos. FitzSimons
Jared Ingersoll
James Wilson
Gouv. Morris

NEW HAMPSHIRE
John Langdon
Nicholas Gilman

MARYLAND
James McHenry
Dan of St. Thos. Jenifer
Danl. Carroll

VIRGINIA
John Blair
James Madison, Jr.

NORTH CAROLINA
Wm. Blount
Richd. Dobbs Spaight
Hu. Williamson

SOUTH CAROLINA
J. Rutledge
Charles Cotesworth Pinckney
Charles Pinckney
Pierce Butler

GEORGIA
William Few
Abr. Baldwin

Articles in addition to, and amendment of the Constitution of the United States of America, proposed by Congress and ratified by the Legislatures of the several states, pursuant to the Fifth Article of the original Constitution.

(The first ten amendments were passed by Congress on September 25, 1789, and were ratified on December 15, 1791.)

Amendment I

Congress shall make no law respecting an establishment of religion, or prohibiting the free exercise thereof; or abridging the freedom of speech, or of the press; or the right of the people peaceably to assemble, and to petition the Government for a redress of grievances.

Amendment II

A well regulated Militia, being necessary to the security of a free State, the right of the people to keep and bear Arms, shall not be infringed.

Amendment III

No Soldier shall, in time of peace be quartered in any house, without the consent of the Owner, nor in time of war, but in a manner to be prescribed by law.

Amendment IV

The right of the people to be secure in their persons, houses, papers, and effects, against unreasonable searches and seizures, shall not be violated, and no warrants shall issue, but upon probable cause, supported by Oath or affirmation, and particularly describing the place to be searched, and the persons or things to be seized.

Amendment V

No person shall be held to answer for a capital, or otherwise infamous crime, unless on a presentment or indictment of a Grand Jury, except in cases arising in the land or naval forces, or in the Militia, when in actual service in time of War or public danger; nor shall any person be subject for the same offence to be twice put in jeopardy of life or limb; nor shall be compelled in any criminal case to be a witness against himself, nor be deprived of life, liberty, or property, without due process of law; nor shall private property be taken for public use, without just compensation.

Amendment VI

In all criminal prosecutions, the accused shall enjoy the right to a speedy and public trial, by an impartial jury of the State and district wherein the crime shall have been committed, which district shall have been previously ascertained by law, and to be informed of the nature and cause of the accusation; to be confronted with the witnesses against him; to have compulsory process for obtaining witnesses in his favor, and to have the assistance of counsel for his defence.

Amendment VII

In Suits at common law, where the value in controversy shall exceed twenty dollars, the right of trial by jury shall be preserved, and no fact tried by a jury, shall be otherwise re-examined in any Court of the United States, than according to the rules of the common law.

Amendment VIII

Excessive bail shall not be required, nor excessive fines imposed, nor cruel and unusual punishments inflicted.

Amendment IX

The enumeration in the Constitution, of certain rights, shall not be construed to deny or disparage others retained by the people.

Amendment X

The powers not delegated to the United States by the Constitution, nor prohibited by it to the States, are reserved to the States respectively, or to the people.

Amendment XI *(Ratified on February 7, 1795)*

The Judicial power of the United States shall not be construed to extend to any suit in law or equity, commenced or prosecuted against one of the United States by Citizens of another State, or by Citizens or Subjects of any Foreign State.

Amendment XII *(Ratified on June 15, 1804)*

The Electors shall meet in their respective states, and vote by ballot for President and Vice-President, one of whom, at least, shall not be an inhabitant of the same state with themselves; they shall name in their ballots the person voted for as President, and in distinct ballots the person voted for as Vice-President, and they shall make distinct lists of all persons voted for as President, and of all persons voted for as Vice-President, and of the number of votes for each, which lists they shall sign and certify, and transmit sealed to the seat of the government of the United States, directed to the President of the Senate;—The President of the Senate shall, in the presence of the Senate and House of Representatives, open all the certificates and the votes shall then be counted;—The person having the greatest number of votes for President, shall be the President, if such number be a majority of the whole number of Electors appointed; and if no person have such majority; then from the persons having the highest numbers not exceeding three on the list of those voted for as President, the House of Representatives shall choose immediately, by ballot, the President. But in choosing the President, the votes shall be taken by states, the representation from each state having one vote; a quorum for this purpose shall consist of a member or members from two-thirds of the states, and a majority of all the states shall be necessary to a choice. And if the House of Representatives shall not choose a President whenever the right of choice shall devolve upon them, before the fourth day of March next following, then the Vice-President shall act as President, as in the case of the death or other constitutional disability of the President.—The person having the greatest number of votes as Vice-President, shall be the Vice-President, if such number be a majority of the whole number of Electors appointed, and if no person have a majority, then from the two highest numbers on the list, the Senate shall choose the Vice-President; a quorum for the purpose shall consist of two-thirds of the whole number of Senators, and a majority of the whole number shall be necessary to a choice. But no person constitutionally ineligible to the office of President shall be eligible to that of Vice-President of the United States.

Amendment XIII *(Ratified on December 6, 1865)*

SECTION 1. Neither slavery nor involuntary servitude, except as a punishment for crime whereof the party shall have been duly convicted, shall exist within the United States, or any place subject to their jurisdiction.

SECTION 2. Congress shall have power to enforce this article by appropriate legislation.

Amendment XIV *(Ratified on July 9, 1868)*

SECTION 1. All persons born or naturalized in the United States, and subject to the jurisdiction thereof, are citizens of the United States and of the State wherein they reside. No State shall make or enforce any law which shall abridge the privileges or immunities of citizens of the United States; nor shall any State deprive any person of life, liberty, or property, without due process of law; nor deny to any person within its jurisdiction the equal protection of the laws.

SECTION 2. Representatives shall be apportioned among the several States according to their respective numbers, counting the whole number of persons in each State, excluding Indians not taxed. But when the right to vote at any election for the choice of electors for President and Vice President of the United States, Representatives in Congress, the Executive and Judicial officers of a State, or the members of the Legislature thereof, is denied to any of the male inhabitants of such State, being twenty-one years of age, and citizens of the United States, or in any way abridged, except for participation in rebellion, or other crime, the basis of representation therein shall be reduced in the proportion which the number of such male citizens shall bear to the whole number of male citizens twenty-one years of age in such State.

SECTION 3. No person shall be a Senator or Representative in Congress, or elector of President and Vice President, or hold any office, civil or military, under the United States, or under any State, who, having previously taken an oath, as a member of Congress, or as an officer of the United States, or as a member of any State legislature, or as an executive or judicial officer of any State, to support the Constitution of the United States, shall have engaged in insurrection or rebellion against the same, or given aid or comfort to the enemies thereof. But Congress may by a vote of two-thirds of each House, remove such diability.

SECTION 4. The validity of the public debt of the United States, authorized by law, including debts incurred for payment of pensions and bounties for services in suppressing insurrection or rebellion, shall not be questioned. But neither the United States nor any State shall assume or pay any debt or obligation incurred in aid of insurrection or rebellion against the United States, or any claim for the loss or emancipation of any slave, but all such debts, obligations and claims shall be held illegal and void.

SECTION 5. The Congress shall have power to enforce, by appropriate legislation, the provisions of this article.

Amendment XV *(Ratified on February 3, 1870)*

SECTION 1. The right of citizens of the United States to vote shall not be denied or abridged by the United States or by any State on account of race, color, or previous condition of servitude.

SECTION 2. The Congress shall have power to enforce this article by appropriate legislation.

Amendment XVI *(Ratified on February 3, 1913)*

The Congress shall have power to lay and collect taxes on incomes, from whatever source derived, without apportionment among the several States, and without regard to any census or enumeration.

Amendment XVII *(Ratified on April 8, 1913)*

The Senate of the United States shall be composed of two Senators from each State, elected by the people thereof, for six years; and each Senator shall have one vote. The electors in each State shall have the qualifications requisite for electors of the most numerous branch of the State legislatures.

When vacancies happen in the representation of any State in the Senate, the executive authority of such State shall issue writs of election to fill such vacancies: Provided, That the legislature of any State may empower the executive thereof to make temporary appointments until the people fill the vacancies by election as the legislature may direct.

This amendment shall not be so construed as to affect the election or term of any Senator chosen before it becomes valid as part of the Constitution.

Amendment XVIII *(Ratified on January 16, 1919)*

SECTION 1. After one year from the ratification of this article the manufacture, sale, or transportation of intoxicating liquors within, the importation thereof into, or the exportation thereof from the United States and all territory subject to the jurisdiction thereof for beverage purposes is hereby prohibited.

SECTION 2. The Congress and the several States shall have concurrent power to enforce this article by appropriate legislation.

SECTION 3. This article shall be inoperative unless it shall have been ratified as an amendment to the Constitution by the legislatures of the several States, as provided in the Constitution, within seven years from the date of the submission hereof to the States by the Congress.

Amendment XIX *(Ratified on August 18, 1920)*

The right of citizens of the United States to vote shall not be denied or abridged by the United States or by any State on account of sex.

Congress shall have power to enforce this article by appropriate legislation.

Amendment XX *(Ratified on February 6, 1933)*

SECTION 1. The terms of the President and Vice President shall end at noon on the 20th day of January, and the terms of Senators and Representatives at noon on the 3d day of January, of the years in which such terms would have ended if this article had not been ratified; and the terms of their successors shall then begin.

SECTION 2. The Congress shall assemble at least once in every year, and such meeting shall begin at noon on the 3d day of January, unless they shall by law appoint a different day.

SECTION 3. If, at the time fixed for the beginning of the term of the President, the President elect shall have died, the Vice President elect shall become President. If a President shall not have been chosen before the time fixed for the beginning of his term, or if the President elect shall have failed to qualify, then the Vice President elect shall act as President until a President shall have qualified; and the Congress may by law provide for the case wherein neither a President elect nor a Vice President elect shall have qualified, declaring who shall then act as President, or the manner in which one who is to act shall be selected, and such person shall act accordingly until a President or Vice President shall have qualified.

SECTION 4. The Congress may by law provide for the case of the death of any of the persons from whom the House of Representatives may choose a President whenever the rights of choice shall have devolved upon them, and for the case of the death of any of the persons from whom the Senate may choose a Vice President whenever the right of choice shall have devolved upon them.

SECTION 5. Sections 1 and 2 shall take effect on the 15th day of October following the ratification of this article.

SECTION 6. This article shall be inoperative unless it shall have been ratified as an amendment to the Constitution by the legislatures of three-fourths of the several States within seven years from the date of its submission.

Amendment XXI *(Ratified on December 5, 1933)*

SECTION 1. The eighteenth article of amendment to the Constitution of the United States is hereby repealed.

SECTION 2. The transportation or importation into any State, Territory, or possession of the United States for delivery or use therein of intoxicating liquors, in violation of the laws thereof, is hereby prohibited.

SECTION 3. This article shall be inoperative unless it shall have been ratified as an amendment to the Constitution by conventions in the several States, as provided in the Constitution, within seven years from the date of the submission hereof to the States by the Congress.

Amendment XXII *(Ratified on February 27, 1951)*

No person shall be elected to the office of the President more than twice, and no person who has held the office of President, or acted as President, for more than two years of a term to which some other person was elected President shall be elected to the office of the President more than once. But this Article shall not apply to any person holding the office of President when this Article was proposed by the Congress, and shall not prevent any person who may be holding the office of President, or acting as President, during the term within which this Article becomes operative from holding the office of President or acting as President during the remainder of such term.

Amendment XXIII *(Ratified on March 29, 1961)*

SECTION 1. The District constituting the seat of Government of the United States shall appoint in such manner as the Congress may direct:

A number of electors of President and Vice President equal to the whole number of Senators and Representatives in Congress to which the District would be entitled if it were a State, but in no event more than the least populous State; they shall be in addition to those appointed by the States, but they shall be considered, for the purposes of the election of President and Vice President, to be electors appointed by a State; and they shall meet in the District and perform such duties as provided by the twelfth article of amendment.

SECTION 2. The Congress shall have power to enforce this article by appropriate legislation.

Amendment XXIV *(Ratified on January 23 1964)*

SECTION 1. The right of citizens of the United States to vote in any primary or other election for President or Vice President, for electors for President or Vice President, or for Senator or Representative in Congress, shall not be denied or abridged by the United States or any State by reason of failure to pay any poll tax or other tax.

SECTION 2. The Congress shall have power to enforce this article by appropriate legislation.

Amendment XXV *(Ratified on February 10, 1967)*

SECTION 1. In case of the removal of the President from office or of his death or resignation, the Vice President shall become President.

SECTION 2. Whenever there is a vacancy in the office of the Vice President, the President shall nominate a Vice President who shall take office upon confirmation by a majority vote of both Houses of Congress.

SECTION 3. Whenever the President transmits to the President pro tempore of the Senate and the Speaker of the House of Representatives his written declaration that he is unable to discharge the powers and duties of his office, and until he transmits to them a written declaration to the contrary, such powers and duties shall be discharged by the Vice President as Acting President.

SECTION 4. Whenever the Vice President and a majority of either the principal officers of the executive departments or of such other body as Congress may by law provide, transmit to the President pro tempore of the Senate and the Speaker of the House of Representatives their written declaration that the President is unable to discharge the powers and duties of his office, the Vice President shall immediately assume the powers and duties of the office as Acting President.

Thereafter, when the President transmits to the President pro tempore of the Senate and the Speaker of the House of Representatives his written declaration that no inability exists, he shall resume the powers and duties of his office unless the Vice President and a majority of either the principal officers of the executive department or of such other body as Congress may by law provide, transmit within four days to the President pro tempore of the Senate and the Speaker of the House of Representatives their written declaration that the President is unable to discharge the powers and duties of his office. Thereupon Congress shall decide the issue, assembling within forty-eight hours for that purpose if not in session. If the Congress, within twenty-one days after receipt of the latter written declaration, or, if Congress is not in session, within twenty-one days after Congress is required to assemble, determines by two-thirds vote of both Houses that the President is unable to discharge the powers and duties of his office, the Vice President shall continue to discharge the same as Acting President; otherwise, the President shall resume the powers and duties of his office.

Amendment XXVI *(Ratified on July 1, 1971)*

SECTION 1. The right of citizens of the United States, who are eighteen years of age or older, to vote shall not be denied or abridged by the United States or by any State on account of age.

SECTION 2. The Congress shall have power to enforce this article by appropriate legislation.

Amendment XXVII *(Ratified on May 7, 1992)*

No law varying the compensation for the services of Senators and Representatives shall take effect until an election of Representatives shall have intervened.

Appendix II

Career Opportunities in Criminal Justice

The opportunities for employment and further education in the field of criminal justice are numerous and diverse. Concern about crime, the treatment of offenders, the intricacies of criminal procedure, and the management of the criminal justice system have created many interesting and important employment opportunities to serve society. Employment opportunities include positions in law enforcement, adjudication, corrections, offender counseling, and forensic science. Options for advanced education include graduate school, law school, and paralegal certification.

Law Enforcement

Federal law enforcement consists of jobs that most often are in the executive branch of the federal government. These jobs are very competitive, pay well, and often involve shift work and overtime.

Federal Bureau of Investigation

The largest federal law enforcement agency is the FBI, which is responsible for enforcing all federal laws not specifically assigned to other agencies. The FBI requires a minimum of a Bachelor's degree and recruits those possessing skills in police work, teaching, foreign language, engineering, accounting, computer sciences, chemistry, or law.

Drug Enforcement Administration

The Drug Enforcement Administration enforces all federal narcotics laws. Like the FBI, their background requirements are stringent, requiring a Bachelor's degree. The agency is especially interested in lawyers, accountants, pilots, and those who are fluent in a foreign language.

U.S. Marshals Service

The Marshals Service provides security in U.S. Courtrooms, transports federal prisoners across the country, and operates the federal witness protection program. A Bachelor's degree and work experience is required for appointment.

Secret Service

The U.S. Secret Service enforces all federal laws relating to forgery and counterfeiting U.S. currency. The agency protects the President, candidates for the Presidency, and other governmental officials. A Bachelor's degree is required and a graduate degree is desirable. The Secret Service is also interested in those who are proficient in a foreign language.

U.S. Customs Service

The Customs Service is involved primarily with narcotics interdiction and illegal currency violations at the nation's borders. It also investigates fraud and imported and exported merchandise. A Bachelor's degree is required and prior law enforcement experience is desirable.

Immigration and Naturalization Service

The Immigration and Naturalization Service investigates illegal immigration and handles deportations from the United States. A college degree is required, and prior experience desirable.

Border Patrol

The Border Patrol is responsible for the areas between points of entry into the United States. The agency is primarily concerned with illegal immigration. A Bachelor's degree or work experience is required and competency in Spanish.

State Police

Every state has a state police force, which is responsible for the enforcement of laws on state roads, and for investigation of crimes that cross county lines or that are beyond the ability of local police to handle. Many state police agencies require a minimum of 2 years of college education but a Bachelor's degree makes the candidate more competitive for employment and promotion.

County and Municipal Police

Local police comprise the vast majority of all police in the United States. They consist of big city to small town departments. Competitive entrance examinations are announced periodically by the village, town, city, or county. Many local police agencies now seek those with Bachelor's degrees or provide incentives to attract candidates who possess the degree.

Regulatory Enforcement

Specialized law enforcement functions are performed by government regulatory agencies. These agencies have police powers in defined areas such as environmental protection, alcoholic beverage control, casino gambling, postal regulations, forests, parks, and wildlife protection. Qualifications vary by agency, but a Bachelor's degree is usually a requirement.

Private Security

Many insurance companies, banks, and other businesses utilize private security to protect private property not easily safeguarded by the police. Many corporations and virtually all banks use private security to investigate crimes by employees and customers. Independent private security companies also hire investigators for work on a contract basis.

Adjudication

There are numerous careers in the adjudication process in both adult and juvenile courts. These involve the prosecution and defense of persons accused of crimes, and services to victims and witnesses.

Prosecution

Prosecutors, District, or Commonwealth Attorneys exist in most counties and large cities in the United States. They represent their jurisdiction in bringing charges against accused persons arrested by the police. To become an assistant prosecutor, it is necessary to be a law school graduate and to pass the bar examination. Once accomplished, these positions are available through application to the Commonwealth or District Attorney.

Legal Assistants

Legal assistants, also called paralegals, are employed by prosecutors, defense counsel, and law firms to assist in the preparation of civil and criminal cases. Paralegal certification requires completion of approximately 10 college-level courses offered at a certified school.

Defense

Defense attorneys represent accused persons in court proceedings. Graduation from law school and passing the bar exam are prerequisites to becoming a defense attorney. Public Defenders are salaried attorneys who work for indigent defendants exclusively. Attorneys in private practice also represent clients accused of crimes.

Victim & Witness Assistance

Many counties and states have victim-witness assistance programs that coordinate and provide services to those who become involved in the criminal justice process who are not accused of crimes. This assistance consists of information, counseling, and other support services.

Corrections

Probation officers work for the courts of a particular county or city. They are responsible for conducting presentence investigations to assist the judge in selecting an appropriate sentence. They also supervise both juvenile and adult offenders in the community. Increasingly, the work involves the use of electronic monitoring equipment.

Parole officers are most often state employees, responsible for the community supervision of offenders *after* they have been released from prison. In many states, parole officers have police powers, and it is a requirement that parole officer candidates possess an earned Bachelor's degree and relevant experience.

Corrections officers are responsible for enforcing the law in jails and prisons and for the transportation of prisoners. In some states, corrections officers have police powers. A competitive examination is required to qualify, and some states provide financial incentives for candidates with Bachelor's degrees. The salary of corrections officers is competitive with other criminal justice professionals.

Delinquency and Adult Counseling

There are a large number of positions available in treatment programs for juvenile, adult and family offenders. These include diversion programs for juveniles, halfway houses, community treatment centers, and other programs designed to reintegrate the offenders back into the community. These positions usually require a Bachelor's degree, and many require a Master's degree in Criminal Justice, Social Work, or Psychology.

Forensic Science

Forensic science is the study of criminal evidence from the perspectives of chemistry and biology. There is growing reliance on DNA, drug, blood testing, as well as physical evidence in criminal cases (e.g., fingerprints, hair, fibers, questioned documents, gun shot and explosives residue). Students wishing to pursue careers as forensic scientists must acquire a strong background in chemistry and biology lab courses. A Master's degree is often required for these positions.

For further career information, please refer to *Careers in Criminal Justice,* by W. Richard Stephens, Jr., published by Allyn and Bacon. Using a series of real-life case studies, this brief book explores careers in criminology and criminal justice, including how people enter the field, and how a degree in criminal justice can be a preparation for careers in a wide variety of areas.

Glossary

acquittal: A finding of not guilty after trial.

actual possession: A condition in which a person has exclusive control over an object.

actus reus: The behavior that must be committed to meet the definition of a crime.

administrative regulations: Rules applied to organizations that are designed to protect public health, safety, and welfare in the marketplace.

aggravated assault: A thrust against another person with the intention to cause serious bodily harm or death.

anomie: A "normlessness" or lack of attachment felt by some people to conventional social goals or means for attaining them.

appeal: A review of a criminal conviction by a higher court on grounds of law or procedure.

appellate courts: A court that hears appeals from lower courts.

appellate jurisdiction: The jurisdiction of a court that reviews specific legal issues raised in trial courts.

arraignment: An appearance before a judge at which the accused is given legal rights and enters a plea.

arrest: Taking a suspect into custody for the purpose of prosecution.

arson: Burning property of another without the lawful consent of the owner.

assigned counsel: Private attorney who is appointed by the court on a case-by-case basis from a list of available attorneys.

Auburn system: A philosophy of imprisonment that emphasized labor and meditation. Offenders worked every day, but they did so in complete silence.

authentic justice: Sanctions should be more closely related to the crime and offenders should be punished in ways that neutralize their gain.

authoritarian: A person who favors blind obedience to authority.

bail: An insurance policy designed to ensure that an accused person will appear at trial.

battered woman syndrome: An ongoing pattern of severe physical abuse that constitutes a continual threat of harm.

bench trial: A trial in which a judge determines guilt or innocence.

biological determinism: The view that crime is the product of biological attributes that produce criminal behavior.

booking: An official administrative record of an arrest.

bribery: Voluntarily giving or receiving anything of value with the intent of influencing the action of a public official.

burglary: Unlawful entry into a building in order to commit a crime while inside.

case law: Judicial application and interpretation of laws as they apply in a given case.

citation (summons): A written notice to appear in court.

civil law: Formal rules that regulate disputes between private parties.

classical school: The view that crime is the product of the rational exercise of free will guided by the pursuit of pleasure and minimizing pain.

community corrections: Sanctions that are *alternatives to incarceration* in jail or prison (such as monetary penalties, probation, intensive supervision, and home confinement and electronic monitoring), or supervision in the community *after a sentence of incarceration* has been served (such as parole, work release, furloughs, and halfway houses).

community policing: A service-oriented style of law enforcement that focuses on disorder in the community, crime prevention, and fear reduction.

commutation: A modification or reduction of a sentence imposed on an offender.

computer crime: Unauthorized use of a computer to damage its hardware or software, or as an instrument of theft, harassment, or extortion.

conflict view: The view that an act becomes a crime only when it serves the interests of those in positions of power.

consensus view: The view that law reflects society's consensus regarding behavior that is harmful enough to warrant government intervention.

conspiracy: Agreement of two or more persons to commit a crime or carry out a legal act in an illegal manner.

constable: A citizen in charge of weapons and equipment for one hundred families in his geographical area. In England constables were appointed by a local nobleman beginning around the year 900.

constitution: The fundamental principles of a society that guide the enactment of specific laws and the application of those laws by courts.

constructive possession: A condition in which a person has the opportunity to exercise control over an object.

continuance: A court-authorized postponement of a case to allow the prosecution or defense more time to prepare its case.

contract attorney: Private attorney, firm, or local bar association that provides legal representation to indigents for a specific period contracted with the county.

conviction: A finding of guilt by a judge, jury, or plea.

corporal punishment: Physical punishment for a commission of a crime.

correctional institutions: Medium security federal correctional institutions.

court administrator: A person who manages court case loads with reference to the availability of judges, courtrooms, jurors, clerks, stenographers, courtroom security, and court budgeting.

courtroom work group: The group of prosecutors, defense counsel, judges, and other courtroom personnel who represent distinct interests but share the goal of shepherding large numbers of cases through the adjudication process.

crime control model: A perspective that views repression of criminal conduct as the most important function to be performed by the criminal justice system, through speed, efficiency, and finality in criminal justice processing.

crime rates: The number of crimes committed divided by the population at risk. This provides an indication of the risk of victimization per capita.

crime: Conduct that threatens the social order as defined by legislatures.

criminal (penal) code: A compilation of all the criminal laws of a jurisdiction.

criminal homicide: Murder or manslaughter.

criminal justice: The management of the criminal justice system, including the study of police, courts, and corrections in addition to criminology.

criminal law: Formal rules designed to maintain social control. The legal definitions of all crimes taken together.

criminal liability: Establishing the presence of the elements of a crime in a given case, thereby subjecting the accused person to criminal penalties.

criminology: The study of the causes of crime and the treatment of offenders.

cultural transmission: The process through which criminal values or traditions are passed among generations in socially disorganized neighborhoods.

cynicism: A belief that human conduct is motivated entirely by self-interest. A cynical person attributes all actions to selfish motives and has a pessimistic outlook on human behavior.

defense attorney: An attorney who represents the legal rights of the accused in criminal or civil proceedings.

defense mechanism: A psychological adjustment that an individual makes in order to relieve anxiety or guilt.

delinquency: A criminal act committed by a person under the age of majority.

detention center: A short-term secure facility that holds juveniles awaiting adjudication, disposition, or placement in an institution.

determinate sentencing: A sentencing system that permits judges to impose fixed sentences that cannot be altered by a parole board.

deterrence: Prevention of crime through the example of offenders being punished.

differential association: The view that crime is learned when one disproportionately associates with those who condone law violation.

discovery: A process that entitles a suspect to review certain information gathered by the prosecutor.

displacement: A defense mechanism in which one substitutes a target that unconsciously means the same thing as the actual target.

diversion programs: Alternatives to the formal criminal justice process that occur after charging but before adjudication; they attempt to achieve a noncriminal disposition of the case.

dogmatism: An attitude characterized by tenacious adherence to one's opinions even though they may be unwarranted and based on insufficiently examined premises.

double jeopardy: A constitutional provision that a person cannot be criminally prosecuted twice for the same offense.

Drug Use Forecasting: A government program consisting of urinanalysis and self-report information on drug use taken from a sample of arrestees in selected cities across the United States.

due process model: A perspective that considers preservation of individual liberties to be the most important function of the criminal justice system, through accuracy, fairness, and reliability in criminal procedure.

duress: A defense in which a person claims to have engaged in criminal conduct because of a threat of immediate and serious bodily harm by another person.

ego: According to Freud, personality construct that mediates between the desires of the id and the values of the superego.

embezzlement: The purposeful misappropriation of property entrusted to one's care, custody, or control, to which one is not entitled.

entrapment: A defense designed to prevent the government from manufacturing crime by setting traps for unwary citizens.

ethical view: The view that crime results when criminal acts bring pleasure, rather than guilt, owing to failure to learn how to prioritize values in difficult situations.

exclusionary rule: A legal principle holding that illegally seized evidence must be excluded from use in trials.

excuse defense: Defense that claims that criminal conduct should be excused because the defendant cannot be held responsible for it. Insanity and duress are examples.

extortion: Purposely obtaining property from another person with his or her consent, induced through wrongful use of force or fear or under the guise of official authority.

felony: A serious crime punishable by more than one year in prison.

forgery: Falsely making or altering an official document with the intent to defraud.

fraud: Purposely obtaining the property of another person through deception.

frisk: A patting-down of the outer clothing of a suspect based on reasonable suspicion, designed to protect a police officer from attack with a weapon while an inquiry is being made.

furlough: Unsupervised leave from prison that is granted for only a few hours to permit an eligible inmate to attend a relative's funeral, visit loved ones, attend a job interview in preparation for release, or otherwise attend to personal or family matters.

general defenses: Justifications or excuses for criminal conduct that are applicable to all criminal offenses.

general jurisdiction: The jurisdiction of courts where most trials for felonies occur, as well as trials in major civil cases.

"good faith" exception: A rule stating that illegally seized evidence may be introduced at trial even if police conducted a search based on a search warrant that later turned out to be invalid owing to a judge's error.

grand jury: A group of citizens who hear evidence from a prosecutor to determine whether probable cause exists to formally charge a person with a crime.

habitual offender laws: Subjecting of multiple offenders to periods of incarceration ranging up to life imprisonment on the ground that they must be physically separated from society in order to protect fellow citizens from their criminal conduct.

halfway house or group home: Long-term nonsecure facilities that allow juveniles to attend school and employment in the community. halfway house: Residential center for ex-offenders in the community. Most halfway house residents are parolees or similar inmates near the end of their sentence.

hate crimes: Criminal acts motivated by racial, religious, or sexual bias.

house arrest: A condition of probation or parole in which an offender is not permitted to leave his or her residence for purposes other than work, school, treatment, or other approved reasons.

id: According to Freud, the innate primitive, instinctual drives of aggression and sex.

incapacitation: Prevention of further criminal behavior by physically restraining the offender from engaging in future misconduct (usually through incarceration).

incarceration: Segregation of offenders from society in a correctional institution.

necessarily (or "lesser") included offenses: Crimes that are included as part of another, more serious, offense.

indeterminate sentencing: A system of sentencing that empowers the judge to set a maximum sentence (up to the limit set by the legislature), and sometimes a minimum sentence, for the offender to serve in prison.

indictment: A "true bill" of a grand jury that formally charges a person with a crime.

informal collective security: When neighborhood residents believe that neighbors will take steps to protect them when necessary.

information: A formal accusation of a crime filed by a prosecutor on the basis of a preliminary hearing.

insanity defense: A claim that the defendant was not sane under law at the time of the act.

intensive supervision: Maintaining small case loads, frequent contact with offenders under supervision, and special conditions such as random drug tests, curfews, restitution to victims, electronic monitoring, or house arrest.

intention: Conduct that is carried out knowingly or purposely.

intermediate sanctions: A sentence designed to provide more rigorous supervision than normal probation, yet something less expensive than incarceration.

judge: A person who objectively assesses the strength of a case and rules on issues of law and procedure, and in many instances determines the disposition of a case.

judicial review: The U.S. Supreme Court's authority to review the constitutionality of acts of Congress.

jury nullification: Acquittal of a defendant despite facts that show guilt.

jury trial: A trial in which a jury determines guilt or innocence.

justice of the peace: An office established by Edward II in 1326 to assist the sheriff in enforcing the law. Eventually the role of the justice of the peace shifted to adjudication, while the sheriffs retained their local peacekeeping function.

justification defenses: Defenses that admit that criminal conduct occurred but claim that it was justified by overwhelming circumstances, such as self-defense.

labeling theory: The view that when a person is labeled criminal through the adjudication process, further criminality is produced through negative public image and self-image.

larceny: Taking property of another person with the intent of depriving the owner.

limited jurisdiction: The jurisdiction of courts that have narrow legal authority over specific types of matters (e.g., surrogate court, tax court).

mala in se: Acts evil in themselves.

mala prohibita: Acts prohibited by law that are not necessarily evil in themselves.

malfeasance: A form of police corruption involving commission of an illegal act.

mandatory sentence: Fixed sentence for offenders convicted of certain types of crimes such as gun-related crimes, drug offenses, and drunk-driving offenses.

manslaughter: A mitigated murder: causing a death recklessly, or intentionally under extenuating circumstances.

mass murder: Homicides in which a number of people are killed in the same criminal incident.

maximum security: Prisons with a wall surrounding the entire facility that house dangerous felons (about 26 percent of all inmates are incarcerated in such institutions).

medium security: Prisons that have some facilities outside the main enclosure surrounded by two rows of chain-link fence, topped with barbed wire (half of all inmates are serving time in these institutions).

mens rea: The guilty mind or conscious decision to commit a criminal act.

merit selection plan: A method for selecting judges that involves a combination of appointment and election.

metropolitan correctional centers (detention centers): Federal jail facilities for pretrial detention and for those serving short sentences.

Metropolitan Police of London: The first organized police department in London, established in 1829. The popular English name for police officers, "bobbies," comes from Sir Robert Peel, a founder of the Metropolitan Police.

minimum security: Prison facilities that usually have no fences but have locking outside doors and electronic surveillance devices around the perimeter of the institution (about 23 percent of all inmates are in these institutions).

Miranda warning: A five-point warning derived from the case of *Miranda v. Arizona.* Its purpose is to provide fair notice to crime suspects of their basic constitutional rights.

misdemeanor: A less serious crime punishable by one year or less in jail.

misfeasance: A form of police corruption involving failure to perform a legal duty in a proper manner.

mistrial: A trial outcome that is legally invalid owing to errors of law or procedure.

multijurisdictional task forces: Multiagency efforts designed to combat multijurisdictional crimes, allowing for pooling of evidence, personnel, and expertise while reducing unnecessary duplication of effort.

murder: All intentional killings, as well as deaths that occur in the course of dangerous felonies.

mutual pledge system: A system of community self-responsibility that existed in Britain during the Middle Ages in which residents were held responsible for the conduct of their neighbors.

net-widening: The process by which more offenders are placed under supervision of the criminal justice system even though the intent of the intervention was to divert offenders out of the system.

nolle prosequi (or nol. pros.): A decision by a prosecutor not to press charges.

nonfeasance: A form of police corruption involving failure to perform a legal duty.

obstruction of justice: Intentionally preventing a public servant from lawfully performing an official function.

official misconduct: The unauthorized exercise of an official function by a public official with intent to benefit or injure another.

organized crime: A generic term that encompasses the provision of illicit goods and services and the infiltration of legitimate business.

overcriminalization: Conduct that is criminalized even though it does not cause great social harm and is not uniformly regarded as criminal conduct by many.

pardon: A reprieve from a governor or the President that excuses a convicted offender and allows him or her to be released from prison without any supervision.

parens patriae (the state acts as a parent): The view that juvenile law violations are a sign that parents cannot or will not take care of their child adequately and that it is up to the state to step in and act in his or her best interests, thus preventing future misbehavior.

parole: A conditional release from incarceration to serve the remainder of the sentence under supervision in the community.

penitentiaries: Maximum security federal correctional institutions.

Pennsylvania system: A philosophy of imprisonment that promoted repentance through solitary confinement and prevented offenders from being corrupted by mixing with other offenders.

perjury: Making a false statement under oath in an official proceeding.

personal risk: The purpose of measuring crime is to assess personal risk. This can be determined only through knowledge of crime rates.

plea-bargaining: An arrangement in which a prosecutor agrees to press a less serious charge, drop some charges, or recommend a less severe sentence if the defendant agrees to plead guilty.

plea: A defendant's formal answer to a charge against him or her.

police brutality: Use of excessive physical force by police in carrying out their duties.

police corruption: Illegal acts or omissions of acts by police officers who, by virtue of their official position, receive (or intend to receive) any gain for themselves or others.

positivism: The view that crime is determined by internal and external influences on a person.

precedent: Previous court decisions that are followed in current cases to ensure consistency in the application of the law.

probable cause: The legal threshold required to arrest and search an individual; a reasonable link between a specific person and a particular crime.

probation: A criminal sentence of community supervision of the offender that is conducted by a probation officer.

procedural law: The rules for adjudication of individuals suspected of violating the law.

progressive era for policing: A period of reform that began during the early twentieth century and emphasized efficiency, professionalism, and improved technology as ways to improve the quality of policing.

prosecutor: An elected or appointed official who represents the community in bringing charges against an accused person.

public defender: Salaried attorney who is paid by the government to represent indigents charged with crimes.

public safety exception: A rule stating that police do not have to provide the *Miranda* warning to suspects when circumstances indicate public safety would be jeopardized.

ranch, forestry camp, or farm: A long-term nonsecure setting for adjudicated juveniles.

rape: Sexual intercourse without effective consent.

reaction formation: A defense mechanism in which one denies an unacceptable part of one's personality by engaging in behavior that suggests the opposite.

reasonable suspicion: A situation in which a police officer has good reason to believe that criminal activity may be occurring; this permits a brief investigative inquiry of the suspect.

reasonableness standard: A standard under which persons are culpable for their actions if they understand the consequences of those actions. Young children and the mentally ill are generally not held culpable owing to their inability to reason effectively.

reception/diagnostic center: A short-term facility that screens sentenced juveniles for assignment to an appropriate level of custody.

recklessness: Conscious disregard for a substantial and unjustifiable risk.

regulatory offenses: Five categories of offenses designed to ensure fairness and safety in the conduct of business, including administrative, environmental, labor, and manufacturing violations, as well as unfair trade practices.

rehabilitation: The view that sees criminal behavior as stemming from social or psychological shortcomings; the purpose of sentencing is to correct or treat these shortcomings in order to prevent future crimes.

restorative justice: Sanctions should be directed primarily at repairing the injury to the victim rather than focusing on the adversarial relationship between the government and the offender.

retribution: Punishment is applied simply in proportion to the seriousness of the offense.

robbery: A theft from a person using threats or force.

search: An exploratory inspection of a person or property based on probable cause of law violation.

selective enforcement: An unwritten policy in which police are not required to fully enforce all laws as written.

selective incapacitation: Identification of potential high-rate offenders for incarceration for longer periods as a means of reducing crime.

serial murder: Homicides in which three or more people are killed over a period of more than 30 days.

shelter: A short-term nonsecure facility that operates like a detention center but within a physically unrestricted environment.

shire reeve: An official appointed by the British Crown who was responsible for overseeing the constables and several hundred families in a given area (called a "shire"). The modern word *sheriff* is derived from this term.

shock incarceration: Short-term military-style "boot camps" designed primarily for nonviolent young offenders and featuring a military atmosphere and strict discipline.

simple assault: A thrust against another person with the intention of injuring that person.

social bond: A person's attachment to others, commitment to conventional activities, involvement in those activities, and belief in widely shared moral values.

status offenses: Undesirable behaviors that are unlawful only for juveniles, including habitual truancy, curfew violations, repeated running away, and ungovernability or incorrigibility in failing to respond to the reasonable requests of parents.

statute: Specific laws passed by legislatures that prohibit or mandate certain acts.

statutory rape: Nonforcible sexual intercourse with a minor.

structural/conflict view: The view that there is lack of consensus on basic values, so that crime is defined in such a way as to protect the interests of the powerful.

study release: A program similar to work release where an inmate attends school by day and returns to the jail or prison at night.

substantive criminal law: The specific behaviors prohibited under the criminal law.

sudden infant death syndrome (SIDS): Infants die from prolonged sleep apnea in which breathing stops for fifteen seconds or more.

superego: According to Freud, a personality construct that reflects the values learned early in life, acting as a conscience.

surety: The posting of bail by someone other than the accused (usually a bondsman).

suspended sentence: A delayed imposition of a prison sentence that requires the offender to fulfill special conditions such as alcohol, drug, or gambling treatment or payment of restitution.

synnomie: The sharing of values to the point of harmonious accommodation of divergent views.

terrorism: Offenses designed to intimidate or coerce a government or civilians in furtherance of political or social objectives.

terrorism: The use of violence for political purposes.

training school: A long-term secure facility for adjudicated juveniles.

trial jury: A group of citizens (usually twelve) who decide on the guilt or innocence of a defendant.

truth-in-sentencing: A sentencing provision that requires offenders to serve the bulk of their sentence (usually 85 percent) before they can be released.

U.S. courts of appeals: Intermediate federal appellate courts.

U.S. district courts: Federal trial courts of general jurisdiction.

U.S. magistrate judge: An official appointed by U.S. district court judges to conduct pretrial hearings and trials for minor civil and criminal offenses in federal court.

U.S. Supreme Court: The highest court in the United States, which hears final appeals in cases that involve federal law, suits between states, and interpretations of the U.S. Constitution.

Uniform Crime Reports: A compilation by the FBI of all crimes reported to the police in the United States.

victimization: An incident in which a crime occurred against a victim. A representative sample of the U.S. population is surveyed annually to determine the extent of victimization and the extent to which these incidents were reported to police.

warrant: A sworn statement by police that attests to the existence of probable cause in a given case; it is signed by a judge who agrees with the officer's assessment of the facts.

watch and ward system: A system established in 1285 to aid constables in their law enforcement efforts. Men from each town were required to take turns standing watch at night. Crime suspects were turned over to the constable.

white collar crimes: A generic term that encompasses crimes of fraud, crimes against public administration, and regulatory offenses.

work release: A program that permits eligible inmates to work during the day at regular jobs outside the jail or prison, returning to the prison at night.

writ of certiorari: A legal order from the U.S. Supreme Court stating that a lower court must forward the record of a particular case for review.

Name Index

Subject Index

Photo Credits

p. 37, Liaison International/Stan Godlewski; p. 39, The Picture Cube, Rick Berkowitz; p. 40, Corbis-Bettmann; p. 47, AP Photo/NBC News Today; p. 51, Liaison International/Benali; p. 52, Liaison International/Steve Liss; p. 61, Impact Visuals/David Rae; p. 66, Image Works/Lichtenstein; p. 71, AP/Richard Drew; p. 79, AP/Nick Ut; p. 82, Liaison International/Mark Gubin; p. 89, The Image Works/Bob Daemmrich; p. 95, Liaison International/Paul Howell; p. 97, Liaison International/Gilles Mingasson; p. 99, AP/Ron Edmonds; p. 107, The Image Works/Bob Daemmrich; p. 111, The Image Works/Steven Rubin; p. 112, The Image Works/Bob Daemmrich; p. 113, The Image Works, H. Dratch; p. 114, Liaison International/Craig Filipacchi; p. 120, Impact Visuals/Ansell Horn; p. 122, Paramount Pictures/Shooting Star; p. 133, Impact Visuals/Jim West; p. 136, Corbis-Bettmann; p. 142, The Image Works/Bob Daemmrich; p. 145, The Picture Cube/MacDonald Photography; p. 151, Impact Visuals/Michael Kaufman; p. 159, Image Works/M. Reinstein; p. 167, The Image Works, S. Agricola; p. 172, Liaison International/James H. Pickerell; p. 176, The Image Works/Cameramann; p. 178, Impact Visuals/Gabe Kirchheimer; p. 185, Liaison International; p. 189, The Image Works/Steven Rubin; p. 191, The Image Works/Alan Carey; p. 196, Impact Visuals/Andrew Lichtenstein; p. 198, Impact Visuals/T. L. Litt; p. 202, Liaison International/Craig Filipacchi; p. 219, The Image Works/Bob Strong; p. 222, Impact Visuals/Carolina Kroon; p. 224, The Image Works/Li-Hua Lan; p. 227, Impact Visuals/Mike Kamber; p. 241, The Image Works/Bob Daemmrich; p. 251, Liaison International/Bill Swersey; p. 261, Agence France Presse/Vince Bucci; p. 263, S.S. Archives/Shooting Star. All rights reserved; p. 266, Liaison International/Sandra Baker; p. 272, Impact Visuals/Martha Tabor; p. 273, Impact Visuals/Evan Johnson; p. 276, AP/Paul Sakuma; p. 280, The Picture Cube/Frank Siteman; p. 289, AP/Reed Saxon; p. 291, The Picture Cube/Frank Siteman; p. 295, AP/Khue Buit; p. 302, Liaison International/Photo Rotolo; p. 315, AP/Mark Foley; p. 318, UPI/Corbis-Bettmann; p. 324, AP Photo/Bruce Shields, The Times-News; p. 325, Tony Stone Images/David Young-Wolff; p. 326, The Image Works/Bob Daemmrich; p. 329, AP Photo/fls; p. 330, AP/Ed Andrieski; p. 339, Barry Chin/The Boston Globe; p. 343, The Picture Cube/John Boykin; p. 346, Tony Stone Images/Bruce Ayres; p. 359, AP/Pat Sullivan; p. 361, AP/George Widman; p. 373, Liaison International/Frank White; p. 377, Impact Visuals/Piet van Lier; p. 382, The Picture Cube/Don B. Stevenson; p. 383, The Image Works/Okonewski; p. 386, Liaison International/Bill Swersey; p.389, Liaison International, J. Peter Mortimer; p. 405, Liaison International/J. Peter Mortimer; p. 413, Liaison International/Jon Levy; p. 414, The Image Works/J. Nubile; p. 424, The Image Works/J. Nubile; p. 428, Liaison International/Lester Sloan; p. 433, Corbis-Bettmann; p. 451, AP/Peter Dejong; p. 452, Liaison International/Stennett; p. 457, Tony Stone Images/Sylvain Grandadam; p. 459, Liaison International/Jeff Christensen; p. 463, Liaison International/Bob Linder; p. 470, AP/Marcela Aguilo/EFE; p. 479, The Image Works/Lee Snider; p. 482, The Picture Cube/Frank Siteman; p. 490, The Picture Cube/Len Rubenstein; p. 497, The Image Works/C. Gatewood; p. 507, AP Photo/The Paducah Sun/Steve Nagy; p. 510, Liaison International/Douglas Burrows; p. 512, The Image Works/Joe Sohm; p. 520, Impact Visuals/Jack Kurtz; p. 524, Impact Visuals/Jack Kurtz; p. 530, The Image Works/Bob Daemmrich; p. 533, The Picture Cube/D & I MacDonald

Photo Credits

p. 37, Liaison International/Stan Godlewski; p. 39, The Picture Cube, Rick Berkowitz; p. 40, Corbis-Bettmann; p. 47, AP Photo/NBC News Today; p. 51, Liaison International/Benali; p. 52, Liaison International/Steve Liss; p. 61, Impact Visuals/David Rae; p. 66, Image Works/Lichtenstein; p. 71, AP/Richard Drew; p. 79, AP/Nick Ut; p. 82, Liaison International/Mark Gubin; p. 89, The Image Works/Bob Daemmrich; p. 95, Liaison International/Paul Howell; p. 97, Liaison International/Gilles Mingasson; p. 99, AP/Ron Edmonds; p. 107, The Image Works/Bob Daemmrich; p. 111, The Image Works/Steven Rubin; p. 112, The Image Works/Bob Daemmrich; p. 113, The Image Works, H. Dratch; p. 114, Liaison International/Craig Filipacchi; p. 120, Impact Visuals/ Ansell Horn; p. 122, Paramount Pictures/Shooting Star; p. 133, Impact Visuals/Jim West; p. 136, Corbis-Bettmann; p. 142, The Image Works/Bob Daemmrich; p. 145, The Picture Cube/MacDonald Photography; p. 151, Impact Visuals/Michael Kaufman; p. 159, Image Works/M. Reinstein; p. 167, The Image Works, S. Agricola; p. 172, Liaison International/James H. Pickerell; p. 176, The Image Works/Cameramann; p. 178, Impact Visuals/Gabe Kirchheimer; p. 185, Liaison International; p. 189, The Image Works/Steven Rubin; p. 191, The Image Works/Alan Carey; p. 196, Impact Visuals/Andrew Lichtenstein; p. 198, Impact Visuals/T. L. Litt; p. 202, Liaison International/Craig Filipacchi; p. 219, The Image Works/Bob Strong; p. 222, Impact Visuals/Carolina Kroon; p. 224, The Image Works/Li-Hua Lan; p. 227, Impact Visuals/Mike Kamber; p. 241, The Image Works/ Bob Daemmrich; p. 251, Liaison International/Bill Swersey; p. 261, Agence France Presse/Vince Bucci; p. 263, S.S. Archives/Shooting Star. All rights reserved; p. 266, Liaison International/Sandra Baker; p. 272, Impact Visuals/Martha Tabor; p. 273, Impact Visuals/Evan Johnson; p. 276, AP/Paul Sakuma; p. 280, The Picture Cube/Frank Siteman; p. 289, AP/Reed Saxon; p. 291, The Picture Cube/Frank Siteman; p. 295, AP/Khue Buit; p. 302, Liaison International/Photo Rotolo; p. 315, AP/Mark Foley; p. 318, UPI/Corbis-Bettmann; p. 324, AP Photo/Bruce Shields, The Times-News; p. 325, Tony Stone Images/ David Young-Wolff; p. 326, The Image Works/Bob Daemmrich; p. 329, AP Photo/fls; p. 330, AP/Ed Andrieski; p. 339, Barry Chin/The Boston Globe; p. 343, The Picture Cube/John Boykin; p. 346, Tony Stone Images/Bruce Ayres; p. 359, AP/Pat Sullivan; p. 361, AP/George Widman; p. 373, Liaison International/Frank White; p. 377, Impact Visuals/Piet van Lier; p. 382, The Picture Cube/Don B. Stevenson; p. 383, The Image Works/Okonewski; p. 386, Liaison International/Bill Swersey; p.389, Liaison International, J. Peter Mortimer; p. 405, Liaison International/J. Peter Mortimer; p. 413, Liaison International/Jon Levy; p. 414, The Image Works/J. Nubile; p. 424, The Image Works/ J. Nubile; p. 428, Liaison International/Lester Sloan; p. 433, Corbis-Bettmann; p. 451, AP/Peter Dejong; p. 452, Liaison International/Stennett; p. 457, Tony Stone Images/ Sylvain Grandadam; p. 459, Liaison International/Jeff Christensen; p. 463, Liaison International/Bob Linder; p. 470, AP/Marcela Aguilo/EFE; p. 479, The Image Works/ Lee Snider; p. 482, The Picture Cube/Frank Siteman; p. 490, The Picture Cube/Len Rubenstein; p. 497, The Image Works/C. Gatewood; p. 507, AP Photo/The Paducah Sun/Steve Nagy; p. 510, Liaison International/Douglas Burrows; p. 512, The Image Works/Joe Sohm; p. 520, Impact Visuals/Jack Kurtz; p. 524, Impact Visuals/Jack Kurtz; p. 530, The Image Works/Bob Daemmrich; p. 533, The Picture Cube/D & I MacDonald